The Papers of Dwight David Eisenhower

THE PAPERS OF DWIGHT DAVID EISENHOWER

THE PRESIDENCY: KEEPING THE PEACE
XX

EDITORS

LOUIS GALAMBOS   DAUN VAN EE

EXECUTIVE EDITOR
ELIZABETH S. HUGHES

ASSOCIATE EDITORS
JANET R. BRUGGER   ROBIN D. COBLENTZ
JILL A. FRIEDMAN

ASSISTANT EDITOR
NANCY KAY BERLAGE

THE JOHNS HOPKINS UNIVERSITY PRESS
BALTIMORE AND LONDON

This book has been brought to publication with the generous assistance of the National Endowment for the Humanities, the National Historical Publications and Records Commission, the Eisenhower World Affairs Institute, and the France-Merrick Foundation.

The Johns Hopkins University Press, 2715 North Charles Street,
Baltimore Maryland 21218-4363
www.press.jhu.edu

All illustrations in this volume are from the
Dwight D. Eisenhower Library, Abilene,
Kansas, unless indicated otherwise.

Library of Congress Cataloging-in-Publication Data

Eisenhower, Dwight D. (Dwight David), 1890–1969.
The papers of Dwight D. Eisenhower.

Vol. 6 edited by A. D. Chandler and L Galambos;
v. 7–   , by L. Galambos.
Includes bibliographies and index.
Contents: v. 1–5. The war years.—[etc.]—
v. 10–11. Columbia University.—v. 12–13. NATO and the
Campaign of 1952.
1. World War, 1939–1945—United States.   2. World War,
1939–1945—Campaigns.   3. United States—Politics and
government—1953–1961.   4. Presidents—United States—
Election—1952.   5. Eisenhower, Dwight D. (Dwight David),
1890–1969.   6. Presidents—United States—Archives.
I. Chandler, Alfred Dupont, ed.   II. Galambos, Louis, ed.
III. United States. President (1953–1961 : Eisenhower)
IV. Title.
E742.5.E37   1970   973.921′092′4[B]   65-027672
ISBN 0-8018-1078-7 (v. 1–5)
ISBN 0-8018-2061-8 (v. 6–9)
ISBN 0-8018-2720-5 (v. 10–11)
ISBN 0-8018-3726-x (v. 12–13)
ISBN 0-8018-4752-4 (v. 14–17)
ISBN 0-8018-6638-3 (v. 18)
ISBN 0-8018-6684-7 (v. 19)
ISBN 0-8018-6699-5 (v. 20)
ISBN 0-8018-6718-5 (v. 21)

Published in cooperation with
The Center for the Study of Recent American History
at The Johns Hopkins University

We dedicate these four concluding volumes of *The Papers of Dwight David Eisenhower* to the Board of Advisors of the Eisenhower Papers and to the Board of Trustees of the Johns Hopkins University, who together made it possible for us to complete this grand project.

Contents

The Papers of Dwight David Eisenhower

The Presidency: Keeping the Peace

VII

Berlin and the
Chance for a Summit

MARCH 1959 TO AUGUST 1959

16

A "staunch bulwark resigns"

To Harold Macmillan   *March 2, 1959*
Cable. Secret

Dear Harold: Following your return to London, I hasten to felicitate
you on the firmness of your presentation respecting Western rights
in the Berlin situation.[1] At the very least you demonstrated to the
world that strength does not depend upon discourtesy, a great contrast to the provocative attitude and statements of Khrushchev during your visit there. Thank you very much for the care you took to
inform us on a day by day basis of your Russian experience.

I assume that you are now going to visit both Bonn and Paris. I
assure you once again that you will be most welcome if you find it
desirable to come to Washington. We could have a most informal
meeting, without any social engagements, and should have a day or
two of good talks while you are here. I am quite sure that nothing
is so important as to have our ideas and plans concerted among the
four of us and, so far as possible, with the complete NATO group.
Certain elements of the situation constantly change so it is extremely
important that our agreements and our plans are in accord therewith.[2]

Do let me know as soon as convenient whether you can come and
approximate timing.

With warm regard, *As ever*

P.S. Just as I was finished dictating this note, I had yours that was
written apparently the first thing Monday morning. I was delighted
to note the change in Khrushchev's tone and assure you that I will
pay very great attention to the final paragraph of your message.[3]

[1] For background on Macmillan's trip and Khrushchev's provocative statements see
nos. 1074 and 1076; see also Macmillan, *Riding the Storm*, pp. 594–634.

[2] Macmillan would leave for France on March 9 and for Germany on March 12. He
would arrive in the United States on March 19 (see *ibid.*, pp. 636–50; and no. 1091).

[3] In his March 2 message Macmillan had told Eisenhower that the Russians had been
showing "a fairer face" since Khrushchev's inflammatory speech and were trying "to
restore a cordial atmosphere." He had received a reply from Soviet officials to the
February 16 call for a foreign ministers' meeting (see no. 1074), and the response
he said, indicated a change in the Soviet attitude. In his final paragraph Macmillan
suggested that Eisenhower's advisers should study the reply "carefully" and that the
President should "ensure that they refrain from any hasty or too hostile reaction"
(Macmillan to Eisenhower, Mar. 2, 1959, State Department Files, Presidential Correspondence, and PREM 11/2690; see also Telephone conversations, Eisenhower
and Herter, Mar. 2, 1959, Herter Papers, Telephone Conversations). On the Soviet
note see no. 1116; for developments on the Berlin situation see no. 1106.

To Christian Archibald Herter   *March 2, 1959*

Memorandum for the Acting Secretary of State:
Subject: Limited release of information on letter from
Prince Sihanouk
I have studied your memorandum of February 28, 1959 in which
you recommend that we orally inform the governments of Thailand
and Viet-Nam of the substance of Prince Sihanouk's letter to me of
February 23, 1959. I think that in view of the circumstances this must
be done.[1]

However, in view of the unusual nature of such an action, I think
some explanation is called for. Therefore, please instruct the officials who inform the governments of Thailand and Viet-Nam to
stress (1) that we habitually treat such communications between
heads of government as strictly confidential, and (2) that it is only
the circumstance of Sihanouk's release of his letter to the Australian,
British, and French mission chiefs that prompts us to pass its substance on to the other governments concerned.[2]

[1] For background on U.S.-Cambodian relations see Galambos and van Ee, *The Middle Way*, no. 882. On recent relations between the two governments and on tensions
between Cambodia and the neighboring countries of South Vietnam and Thailand
see State, *Foreign Relations, 1958–1960*, vol. XVI, *East Asia–Pacific Region; Cambodia;
Laos*, pp. 228–33, 246–47, 252–64, 267–82, 285–88; see also Norodom Sihanouk,
My War with the CIA: The Memoirs of Prince Norodom Sihanouk, as related to Wilfred
Burchett (New York, 1973), pp. 104–9.
    Prime Minister Norodom Sihanouk had written Eisenhower regarding threats
along Cambodia's borders by forces intent on overthrowing the government. The
threatening countries were strong, Sihanouk maintained, because of economic and
military aid supplied to them by the United States. He asked that Eisenhower ensure that U.S. assistance to South Vietnam and Thailand was "not used improperly
to foster political or territorial ambitions against non-Communist neighbors." If this
could not be done, he asked that Eisenhower "at least supply us with the means to
defend ourselves" (Sihanouk to Eisenhower, Feb. 23, 1959, AWF/I: Cambodia).
    On February 25 Acting Secretary Herter had suggested that Eisenhower send an
interim reply to the Cambodian leader as quickly as possible to let him know that
his appeal was receiving Eisenhower's attention (Herter to Eisenhower, Feb. 25, 1959;
and Eisenhower to Sihanouk, Feb. 26, 1959, both in *ibid.*).
    Herter had subsequently told Eisenhower that Sihanouk had given copies of the
letter to Western diplomats in Phnom Penh and had mentioned it in an oral presentation to all diplomatic and consular mission chiefs, including representatives
from Communist countries. "Prince Sihanouk appears to view the letter as he would
a diplomatic note, and therefore has not perceived the need to keep it in strict confidence" (Herter to Eisenhower, Feb. 28, 1959, AWF/D-H; see also Telephone conversation, Eisenhower and Herter, Mar. 2, 1959, Herter Papers, Telephone Conversations).
[2] For developments see no. 1123.

To Arthur Ellsworth Summerfield, Sr.   *March 2, 1959*

Dear Arthur: I have no disagreement with the basic objectives of your talk—a thriving, free economy, with its necessary features of a sound dollar and a carefully designed tax structure that will both produce the necessary revenue and strengthen incentive.[1]

In the margin of the text I see some pencilled notations; I do not know who made them and I do not, of course, have the time to discuss any editorial changes.

With warm regard, *As ever*

[1] A copy of Postmaster General Summerfield's speech, "How Deeply Do You Believe in America?" which would be delivered to the New York Sales Executives Club on March 10, 1959, is in AWF/A. He would urge support for a balanced national budget and a bold anti-inflation program, a fairer tax system and legislation to crush "union monopolists" (*New York Times,* Mar. 11, 1959). Summerfield would also take note of the economic competition with the Soviet Union and the need in the United States to offer high incentives for outstanding individual performance.

1087   *EM, AWF, Name Series*

To William Edward Robinson   *March 2, 1959*

Dear Bill: I'm sorry you could not be here this weekend, but of course I understand that—after all—Coca Cola Board meetings have priority number one![1]

Once more let me merely say how much I appreciate all you are doing on behalf of the balanced budget. I hope I am not unduly optimistic but from the material you have sent me and from reports I have gotten from other sources I do think we are making at least a dent in public and editorial thinking.[2]

With warm regard, *As ever*

[1] On March 6 Robinson, chairman of the board of the Coca-Cola Company, would reply that he was deeply disappointed "at having to forego the privilege and pleasure" of spending the weekend with the President at the White House (AWF/N).
[2] For background on Robinson's efforts to help keep federal expenditures down see no. 1042. On February 25 (AWF/N) Robinson had reported that he had been talking to newspaper friends, magazine writers, editors and commentators about the fight for fiscal integrity. He had concluded that the President had general public support for a balanced budget and that the subject of inflation was being covered by the media. Robinson also said he had been asking people to contact their senators and representatives. From all accounts, he wrote, "this has borne some fruit."

This morning the two Democratic Senators from West Virginia, Randolph and Byrd came in to see me.[1] They were quite decent about their presentation, arguing the plight of the coal industry in competition with residual oil, and therefore arguing there must be some restrictions. I am afraid myself that restricting importation of residuals will merely mean the replacement of that much oil fuel by American oil supplies, rather than giving the coal industry an opportunity to take up some of the slack. This was brought about, I think, by the rising costs of the past twenty years in coal production.[2]

Also this morning I had a message from George Love, another coal producer which made some of the arguments represented by the two Senators. (A copy of Mr. Love's message is attached).[3]

Other individuals, particularly the Eastern seaboard consumers, are very much on the other side of the argument.

Another factor that neither side mentions is that any time we restrict imports we make it more difficult for us to export the products from our industry because we deny other people to earn the dollars they need with which to purchase our goods. This makes for an unhappy, lowered, level of mutual trade and, eventually, a general decline in economic activity, including our own. It likewise has the result of driving more of our friends into other channels of trade, an increased percentage of which will be with the Communistic bloc.[4]

All this is bad. Yet there seems to be no possibility of giving to the oil and coal producers of our own country some kind of assurance that they are not to be eliminated as productive industries. This we cannot afford to do if for no other reason than in the event of emergency we shall need their facilities operating at an increasing tempo.[5]

[1] Eisenhower's morning meeting with Democratic Senators Jennings Randolph (A.B. Salem College 1924) and Robert Carlyle Byrd was not listed on the daily calendar. Randolph had been a member of Congress since 1933, and Byrd, since 1953.

[2] The importation of residual oil, an industrial fuel used primarily for heating and the generation of electric power, had been seen as a threat by the coal industry since the early 1950s. A report prepared in 1950 for the Secretary of the Interior by the National Bituminous Coal Advisory Council had alleged that imported residual was being sold at artificially low prices in the United States. Concerned over possible reactions from both overseas and domestic oil producers, the Administration had declined to impose tariffs or formal restrictions and had instead instituted voluntary import quotas (see nos. 596, 608, and 706; see also Galambos and van Ee, *The Middle Way*, nos. 1392, 1748, and 1763).

The problems for coal producers had, however, continued. By 1956 production had declined 39 percent from its peak in 1947. The industry had also been beset by problems arising from competition with the natural gas industry, adverse government energy policies, and structural fragmentation (see Vietor, *Energy Policy in America Since 1945*, pp. 100–31, 163–67).

[3] George Hutchinson Love, chairman of the board of the Pittsburgh Consolidation Coal Company, had sent a telegram to the President on March 2 (AWF/AWD). Educated at Princeton and the Harvard Business School, Love had served as chief negotiator for the coal industry in talks with John L. Lewis and the United Mine Workers in 1949 and 1950. He would head the Chrysler Corporation from 1961 until 1966. Love—emphasizing the dependence of the eastern seaboard states on residual oil and the possibility of disruption of supply in case of hostilities—noted that the uncontrolled importation of residual oil was "contributing substantially to the reduction in coal production, capacity, manpower and transportation facilities needed to meet foreseeable national defense requirements and inhibits the investment, exploration and development necessary to maintain a healthy industry." Love compared the problems in the coal industry to those of crude oil and concluded that "the reasons advanced for limiting imports of residual oil are identical in every way to the reasons advanced for restricting imports of crude oil except that coal is in a much weaker economic position to withstand the impact of these market encroachments." He urged the Administration to act to protect the "scores of thousands of highly skilled unemployed workers in the defense vital coal and railroad industries."

[4] For more on Eisenhower's position on mutual trade see nos. 674 and 753.

[5] For developments see nos. 1098 and 1144.

1089   *EM, AWF, Ann Whitman Diary Series*

DIARY   *March 3, 1959*

Bob Cox, President of the Junior Chamber of Commerce, was in to see me. I told him that I would look over the possibility of addressing the Junior Chamber of Commerce on June sixteenth at Buffalo.[1] In some ways I look upon the invitation as an opportunity because these young men are normally possessed of a real sense of civic responsibility as well as enthusiasm.

However, June is going to be a busy month for me, with many engagements already made.[2] I promised Cox to give him a final answer no later than April tenth. I do this because I want to find out whether I could get some very rough draft quickly so that I could look it over and see whether or not it would be useful as a vehicle for me to produce a talk that I would consider worth while.[3]

The general theme of the convention is to be "The Dignity of Man," but these young men are hopeful that each speaker will develop his own views on this theme from the standpoint of his own current responsibility and interests. For example, they would like me to talk on the relationship between sound fiscal measures, frugality in government and so on, in the relationship of these values to man's freedom.[4]

[1] Robert Vinsant Cox (A.B. University of North Carolina 1948; M.A. University of North Carolina 1949), a former football player and assistant coach at the University of North Carolina, had been a member of the President's Citizens Youth Fitness Advisory Committee since 1958. Cox had become a member of the U.S. Junior Chamber of Commerce in 1952. He would become director at large of the U.S. Chamber of Commerce in June. On April 27 the President would deliver an informal speech to members of the U.S. Chamber of Commerce attending its 47th annual meeting (*New York Times*, Apr. 28, 1959).

[2] In June Eisenhower would entertain the White House staff at his Gettysburg home, address members of the American Medical Association, dedicate the St. Lawrence Seaway, and preview a Soviet exhibit in New York City (*New York Times*, June 7, 17, 20, 27, 29, 1959; on the Soviet exposition see no. 1228).

[3] According to Ann Whitman, the President asked a White House speechwriter to prepare a draft (Ann Whitman memorandum, Mar. 3, 1959, AWF/AWD).

[4] As it turned out, the President would not attend the U.S. Junior Chamber of Commerce meeting. On the convention see *New York Times*, June 17, 1959.

1090   *EM, AWF, DDE Diaries Series*

To CHRISTIAN ARCHIBALD HERTER,   *March 3, 1959*
ROBERT BERNERD ANDERSON,
THOMAS SOVEREIGN GATES, JR.,
WILLIAM PIERCE ROGERS,
LEWIS LICHTENSTEIN STRAUSS,
JAMES PAUL MITCHELL,
AND LEO ARTHUR HOEGH

Memorandum for the Acting Secretary of State, the Secretary of the Treasury, the Secretary of Defense, the Attorney General, the Secretary of Commerce, the Secretary of Labor, and the Director of the Office of Civil and Defense Mobilization: Herewith a copy of a letter I have just received from Mr. Benjamin F. Fairless.[1] I should like for each of the addressees to study this matter insofar as it concerns his Department.

Further, I should like for anyone who has any suggestions to make to send them to me, through the Secretary of Commerce. He is being requested to make a consensus of views and, if possible, to compose any differences to the end that the Administration may have a common position, unless our position must necessarily be one of "hands off." I do not know how urgent the matter is from the standpoint of timing, but I should like to have your answers as soon as convenient.[2]

[1] Former U.S. Steel President Benjamin Franklin Fairless was coordinator of the President's Citizens Advisors on the Mutual Security Program (see no. 76). He had written Eisenhower on March 2 (AWF/D) regarding the controversy between the Amer-

ican maritime unions and American shipowners engaged in international commerce under foreign flags. The American labor unions had claimed the right to organize and represent labor employed in any foreign enterprise financed by American capital (see *New York Times*, Jan. 4, 18, and 23, 1959). Fairless was concerned that the conflict between labor and the ship owners might lead to the "establishment of an international labor principle or international commerce restriction, either of which would seriously affect the Mutual Security Program and other relationships between the United States and other nations of the free world."

[2] In a memorandum to the President (Mar. 31, 1959, AWF/AWD), Special Counsel to the President David Walbridge Kendall would discuss the problem of American-owned vessels sailing under foreign flags. The issue was complicated by defense requirements of getting the ships back immediately to the American flag in the event of a national emergency; the maritime union campaign to recruit the seamen involved; and certain treaty obligations with the nations that permitted "flags of convenience." The Secretaries of State, Labor, Commerce and Defense were giving the matter "constant thought which involves steering a close line between bringing about a serious labor boycott and keeping the ships moving." Kendall suggested that a letter to Fairless along these lines would "keep him down to date."

There is no further correspondence in AWF regarding this issue. The struggle between the maritime unions and the shipowners would continue for the remainder of the Eisenhower Administration; see, for example, *New York Times*, June 9, August 3, November 26, 1959; January 21, June 12, and October 28, 1960. In October 1960 Eisenhower would direct the State Department to try to stop unionization of foreign-flag vessels. In November the State, Justice, and Defense Departments would tell the National Labor Relations Board that it should not exercise jurisdiction in such labor disputes (J. S. D. Eisenhower, Memorandum of Conference, Oct. 5, 1960; *New York Times*, Nov. 19, 1960).

1091   *EM, AWF, International Series:*
                                          Macmillan

To Harold Macmillan   *March 4, 1959*
Cable. Secret

Dear Harold:[1] I am a bit embarrassed because of the fact that I shall have the President of Ireland here in Washington from the 17th through the 19th, and King Hussein on the 24th.[2] I suspect you would not want your visit to overlap with either of these. Would it suit your convenience to arrive here the afternoon of the 19th and start our talks on Friday afternoon, continuing on Saturday, with perhaps a carryover to Sunday. Of course if your schedule is so rigid that you feel you should follow the plan you suggest, we shall of course go ahead on that basis. While my other visitor might feel it a discourtesy, I think the matter could be explained if necessary.[3]

With warm regard, *As ever*

¹ On March 2 the President had invited Macmillan to Washington for informal meetings (see no. 1084; on the Berlin and German question see nos. 1062 and 1063). Macmillan had replied that he would enjoy the opportunity of private and informal discussions. He proposed arriving in Washington on March 18 and meeting with the President the following day (Mar. 4, 1959, AWF/I: Macmillan).

² Sean Thomas O'Kelly had been President of Ireland since 1945. He had served as Ireland's Minister of Finance (1939–1945) and the Irish envoy to the United States (1924–1926). On March 17 Eisenhower would accompany O'Kelly to two St. Patrick's Day dinners, before hosting a dinner in O'Kelly's honor at the White House (Ann Whitman memorandum, Mar. 3, 17, 1959, AWF/AWD; Eisenhower to O'Kelly, Mar. 19, 1959, AWF/I: Ireland; and *New York Times*, Mar. 21, 22, 1959).

At White House meetings on March 24 and 25 Jordan's King Hussein would ask for U.S. aid on a continuing basis. Following his visit to Washington, Hussein would visit several U.S. cities (see *New York Times*, Mar. 23, 24, 27, 28, 1959). For developments on U.S. relations with Jordan see no. 1621.

³ For developments see no. 1093.

1092   *EM, AWF, Administration Series*

TO ALLEN WELSH DULLES   *March 5, 1959*
Top secret

Dear Allen: Please study the attached TOP SECRET document from Prime Minister Macmillan, and confer with the appropriate members of the scientific community, particularly the specialists in atomic weapons and missiles.¹

As you can see from the attached communication, we shall be discussing these matters with the British during the Prime Minister's visit here, and I shall expect you to be ready to participate in the discussion. I assume that you will want to have one associate present from each of the scientific fields that is under discussion.

Should you like to see me about this before Mr. Macmillan arrives, please come to my office at your convenience.² *As ever*

¹ After his return from the Soviet Union (see no. 1071), Macmillan had written Eisenhower about his informal talks with Premier Khrushchev and Deputy Chairman Mikoyan. Khrushchev had told Macmillan "with apparent sincerity" that the Soviet Union was more interested in making the larger megaton weapons than the smaller types. The smaller weapons were too expensive, Khrushchev had said, and he did not believe in the concept of limited nuclear wars in which only tactical weapons would be used. He had also said that his atomic stockpile "had now reached a point where they might already have 'more than enough.'" According to Khrushchev, the Soviet Union could already fire intermediate range ballistic missiles at targets in Europe, North Africa, and Asia from mobile platforms and were close to possessing that capability with intercontinental ballistic missiles. Macmillan had sent the comments of British experts to Ambassador Caccia for delivery with his letter. "You will see that what Khrushchev said," Macmillan wrote, "is not inconsistent with the evidence al-

ready available to us." He asked Eisenhower to show the comments to U.S. technical experts (Macmillan to Eisenhower, Mar. 5, 1959, AWF/I: Macmillan; see also Caccia to Macmillan, Mar. 5, 1959, PREM 11/2860; and Telephone conversation, Eisenhower and Herter, Mar. 5, 1959, Herter Papers, Telephone Conversations).

[2] Scientific advisers and other government officials would meet with Eisenhower and Prime Minister Macmillan on March 21 and 22. Allen Dulles would tell the group that the intelligence communities of both the United States and the United Kingdom believed that the Soviets were still very much interested in smaller nuclear weapons for air defense. His British counterpart added that the intelligence communities did not believe that the Soviets were cutting down on the production of fissile material (State, *Foreign Relations, 1958–1960*, vol. III, *National Security Policy; Arms Control and Disarmament*, pp. 725–27). For more on Eisenhower's meetings with Macmillan see no. 1116.

1093   *EM, AWF, International Series:*
Macmillan

To Harold Macmillan   *March 5, 1959*
Cable. Confidential

Dear Harold: About forty-five or fifty miles outside of Washington I have a recreational spot called Camp David. It is an ideal retreat, and while it has no recreational facilities in winter weather (except for a movie room), it is very comfortable, with all the conveniences.[1] If the idea appeals to you at all, I would suggest that you, Selwyn, your Ambassador, your secretary or other individual or individuals you would like, and we go up there about Friday noon, coming back at our leisure some time on Sunday.[2] Incidentally, there would be no difficulty about bringing up other individuals—technical experts, etc., if we needed them.[3] The helicopter trip is only thirty minutes.

The advantage of such a plan would be that we would lose no time in going or coming, or in any kind of social engagement. We would be free to talk and to rest.

All the above is a suggestion only. We will go along with whatever you feel would be most convenient to yourself.[4]

With warm regard, *As ever*

[1] The British Prime Minister had accepted the President's invitation to Washington for informal discussions on the Berlin crisis and Germany (see no. 1091; see also Macmillan to Eisenhower, Mar. 5, 1959, in AWF/I: Macmillan; Eisenhower to Macmillan, Mar. 5, 1959, AWF/D-H; and Ann Whitman memorandum, Mar. 5, 1959, AWF/AWD). Macmillan would agree to the President's proposed schedule (Mar. 5, 1959, AWF/I: Macmillan).

[2] These were Foreign Secretary Selwyn Lloyd and Ambassador Harold Caccia.

[3] For a list of the "other individuals" in Macmillan's party see Ann Whitman memorandum, n.d., AWF/AWD.

[4] The American and British leaders would spend the weekend of March 20–22 at Camp David (see Ann Whitman memorandum, Mar. 21, 22, 1959, AWF/AWD, and *New York Times*, Mar. 6, 13, 20–25, 1959). On the discussions see, for example, nos. 1095 and 1116. Macmillan would thank Eisenhower on March 23 and again on March 25 for his hospitality and a "most successful" conference (both in AWF/I: Macmillan). For developments see no. 1122.

1094   *EM, WHCF,*
                                                                 Official File 149-B-2 Cotton

TO MILTON STOVER EISENHOWER   *March 6, 1959*

Dear Milton: Thanks for your note, with enclosure of Lamar Fleming's letter to you of February twenty-first. Fleming wrote a separate but similar letter to me.[1]

I am replying to Fleming as indicated by the enclosed carbon.[2] I also sent him a statement prepared in the Department of Agriculture and concurred in by the State Department, which recognizes the mandatory nature of the legislation under which we operate. A copy of this is enclosed also.[3]

The Administration opposed this section of law vigorously. It was passed as part of the over-all Agricultural Act of 1956, which we felt we had to have. I protested the section at the time I signed the Act, and subsequent events have shown this concern was justified.

We hope that discussing these matters in the International Cotton Advisory Committee will be a helpful step.[4]

With warm regard, *As ever*

[1] Milton Eisenhower had written his brother on February 25, 1959, indicating that the letter from Fleming, who was chairman of the board of the food processing firm of Anderson, Clayton and Company, was "worth reading" (all three letters are in same file as document).

[2] Eisenhower's letter of March 6, as well as Fleming's two letters to the President (Jan. 31, Feb. 23, 1959) voicing his concern over the Department of Agriculture's decision to lower cotton export prices and increase subsidy levels (see no. 1062), are in the same file as the document. Fleming had warned of the grave effects these actions would have on the fragile economies of cotton exporting countries in Latin America, the Middle East and the Mediterranean. The cotton export pricing programs, he said, were doing more "fundamental harm" to U.S. foreign relations than "Russian intrigue" (Fleming to Benson, Jan. 31, 1959; see also Benson to Eisenhower, Feb. 17, 1959, and other correspondence in same file as document).

In the letters sent to the President and to Milton Eisenhower (Feb. 21, 1959, same file as document), Fleming had questioned the Department of Agriculture's interpretation of the Agricultural Act of 1956. Section 203 directed the Commodity Credit Corporation to encourage the export of cotton by making it available at prices no greater than those being offered by other exporting countries. The act also provided that such quantities should be sold as would reestablish and maintain a fair historical share of the world market for United States cotton, with the volume to be determined by the Secretary of Agriculture (*U.S. Statutes at Large*, vol. 70, p. 199). Fleming contended that the language of section 203 did not prescribe the actual formulas for determining the pricing, sales, and subsidy levels of cotton exports, as the Department of Agriculture had maintained, but that the numbers were subject to administrative discretion. He had also criticized the methods used by the Department in calculating "fair historical share."

The country most affected by the new cotton subsidies was Mexico, which Eisenhower had visited in February (see no. 1063 and State, *Foreign Relations, 1958–1960*, vol. V, *American Republics*, p. 864; see also Paarlberg to Whitman, Feb. 16, 1959, and Eisenhower to Fleming, Feb. 18, 1959, both in same file as document). During Eisenhower's visit, President Adolfo López Mateos and other Mexican officials complained that the United States had failed to consult with them before announcing the pricing changes. When he returned, the President had met with General Persons and White House aide Don Paarlberg to express his displeasure over the lack of coordination between the Departments of State and Agriculture. They had also discussed Fleming's letter of February 23 (Paarlberg to Whitman, Feb. 26, 1959, AWF/D). Cotton exports would continue to be a subject of discussion between the two countries (for developments see nos. 1163, 1166, and 1170; see also Memorandum of Conversation on Commodity Problems, Oct. 10, 1959, AWF/I: Mexico-Miscellaneous-1).
[3] The statement is in the same file as the document.
[4] Eisenhower had written Fleming that the Administration planned to use the committee, which had been organized in 1939, to monitor cotton export and pricing policies on a continuing basis (*ibid.*; see also Paarlberg to Eisenhower, Feb. 27, 1959, AWF/D). For developments on cotton export policy see State, *Foreign Relations, 1958–1960*, vol. IV, *Foreign Economic Policy*, pp. 202–3, 216, 241–42, 266.

1095   *EM, AWF, International Series*

To Harold Macmillan   *March 9, 1959*
Cable. Secret

Dear Harold:[1] I look forward to meeting with you on March 20 to hear first-hand your impressions from your trip to the Soviet Union and to discuss what we must do on important issues in the coming months.[2]

On one matter I want to give you our views immediately since postponement of decision, even until your arrival here, will increase our difficulties. This matter is the Geneva test suspension negotiations.[3]

We are convinced that the present phase of these negotiations should be recessed at an early date. If we do so, we will be in a position to state openly to the world at large the principle which is essential to a sound and acceptable agreement, an effective international control system not subject to veto or obstruction. If we do not recess, soon we will almost certainly be drawn into prolonged inconclusive discussions which will confuse and obscure the basic issues without making real progress. It has, of course, been indispensable to test, as we have done, the possibilities of shift in the Soviet position. However, the Soviet reception of your informal suggestions to Khrushchev, as indicated by their negotiating line on the veto in Geneva in the past few days, appears to be that they interpret your ideas as signs of Western readiness to compromise on the veto rather than as you intended them.[4]

Our purpose in these negotiations is to reach an agreement on sound principles which will be a good precedent for further disarmament agreements in the establishment of effective international control. Stopping nuclear tests is of secondary importance—these tests, indeed, are already temporarily suspended and Foster has discussed with you our tentative thought that this reciprocal forbearance might (at least for atmospheric tests) be continued indefinitely if a test ban agreement proves unobtainable.[5] If we go on, without a pause to highlight the principles involved, we will be faced with widespread expectation that there will be compromises on these principles of international control for the sake of stopping tests, and the increasing complexity of the debate will make it increasingly difficult to stand on principle.

I should add frankly that we would welcome such a pause also in order to enable us to clarify our thinking on some aspects of the control system itself. We have had our best experts working on the problems of identifying underground explosions and high altitude explosions and their studies are being brought to completion this week. Their conclusions will require careful assessment as to their implications for the control system agreed upon last summer by the experts from both sides.[6]

I feel that a recess well before the end of this month will not interfere with progress toward negotiations with the Soviets on other outstanding issues. I also hope that you will agree that a recess will actually assist in our objective of reaching a sound agreement. We do not want a sharp or complete break and it would be important to handle a recess in such manner as to make this clear. We have in mind a recess, by agreement if possible, to enable delegates to report back to their governments. We would, of course, make clear our intention to continue to withhold nuclear testing under the terms announced in my statements of August 22 and November 7.[7] I would envisage letters from each of us to Khrushchev explaining our approach to the negotiations and our continuing desire to devise an effective international control system. We would be disposed to welcome discussion of the status of the negotiations in the United Nations Disarmament Commission since we believe that even if there were no formal resolutions the principles which we have insisted on would receive general endorsement by the members of the United Nations.[8]

With warm personal regard, *As ever*

[1] State Department officials drafted this message to the British Prime Minister (see Telephone conversations, Herter and Goodpaster, Mar. 7, 9, 1959, Herter Papers, Telephone Conversations). It was delivered to Macmillan through the U.S. embassy in London.

[2] On Macmillan's visit see no. 1093; see also Telephone conversation, Eisenhower and Herter, March 9, 1959, Herter Papers, Telephone Conversations.

[3] For background on the Geneva negotiations, which had begun on October 31, 1958, see no. 1076.

[4] James J. Wadsworth, U.S. representative at the Geneva negotiations, had recommended a recess in the proceedings. Since the differences between the United States and the Soviet Union on the key issues of the veto, staffing, and inspection were clearly defined, Wadsworth said, continued discussion would only provide the Soviets with the opportunity to blur the differences and weaken the U.S. position. After reviewing Wadsworth's recommendations, Eisenhower had told Acting Secretary Herter that breaking off negotiations would be difficult to explain and that any call for a recess should be justified on the grounds of Soviet stubbornness and their demands for a veto in every phase of inspection: "We must make clear that the one thing on which there cannot be retreat is insistence on an effective inspection system" (State, *Foreign Relations, 1958–1960,* vol. III, *National Security Policy; Arms Control and Disarmament,* pp. 706–8; see also Hewlett and Holl, *Atoms for Peace and War,* p. 553).

For Macmillan's suggestions to Khrushchev see no. 1071.

[5] For Secretary Dulles's meetings with Macmillan in London see Dulles to Eisenhower, February 4, 1959; and Eisenhower to Dulles, February 6, 1959, both in AWF/D-H; and State, *Foreign Relations, 1958–1960,* vol. III, *National Security Policy; Arms Control and Disarmament,* pp. 699–700).

[6] On the Geneva technical conference held the previous July see no. 822; on the "Geneva system" of monitoring nuclear explosions and the recommendations for control posts see no. 824, and Hewlett and Holl, *Atoms for Peace and War,* pp. 541–42.

Analysis of the data from recent U.S. atomic tests had indicated that seismic signals produced by nuclear explosions were smaller than previously thought, making the detection of low-level underground tests more difficult. Eisenhower's scientific adviser James Killian had assembled a group of seismologists to evaluate the data in relation to the system of controls agreed to at Geneva. They had concluded that the system would have to be revised. Subsequent studies would indicate the need for a large-scale seismic research program (State, *Foreign Relations, 1958–1960,* vol. III, *National Security Policy; Arms Control and Disarmament,* pp. 682–89, 692–99, 710–12; Hewlett and Holl, *Atoms for Peace and War,* pp. 549–51; Killian, *Sputnik, Scientists, and Eisenhower,* pp. 163–65; Eisenhower, *Waging Peace,* pp. 478–79; see also State, *American Foreign Policy; Current Documents, 1958,* pp. 1313–17; and State, *Documents on Disarmament, 1945–1959,* vol. II, *1957–1959,* pp. 1378–92).

[7] On Eisenhower's two statements on the temporary suspension of nuclear tests and the continued testing by the Soviet Union see no. 824, and State, *Documents on Disarmament, 1945–1959,* vol. II, *1957–1959,* p. 1221.

[8] Although Macmillan wanted the conference to continue, he would agree to a recess. "I entirely support your view that it must not be a sharp or complete break," he said, "and in arranging for any recess I feel we must take great care to ensure that it is not misinterpreted by the public (and is incapable of being misinterpreted

by the Russians) as revealing a desire on the part of our two Governments to break off negotiations." Macmillan would suggest a three-week suspension beginning on March 20, a date close to Easter and before his return from consultations with Eisenhower in the United States.

Macmillan did not agree, however, with Eisenhower's suggestion that the status of the negotiations be discussed in the United Nations Disarmament Commission. The neutral nations might not be convinced by the Anglo-American stand, he said, and such a discussion might "make the Russians more difficult and obstinate." Macmillan also did not believe that the tentative suggestions he had made to Khrushchev had led the Russians to think that Great Britain and the United States were weakening in the disputes over vetoes and controls. "I made it clear that we could not accept a veto on the despatch of inspection teams, and that my ideas were designed to do away with the veto on inspection" (Macmillan to Eisenhower, Mar. 13, 1959, AWF/I: Macmillan and PREM 11/2860; on Macmillan's discussions with Khrushchev see no. 1071). At the bottom of Macmillan's letter Eisenhower would note his approval of the March 20 date. For developments see no. 1103.

1096   *EM, AWF, DDE Diaries Series*

To Oveta Culp Hobby   *March 9, 1959*
Personal

Dear Oveta: Your letter came as a bright contrast to the tenor of some of the messages I received today.[1] During the last few weeks Washington has seemed to be unusually full of people whose requests for help are more insistent, cries of alarm more intemperate and predictions of disaster more strident than even in the days when you were often the target of this drumfire.[2] Knowledge, logic and courage seem unable to hold their own with ignorance, demagogy and panic.

Fortunately, however, there seems to be a growing number of those, many of them inarticulate but still numerous and devoted, who like yourself look to the good of America rather than to the opportunity for selfish advantage as a guide for their own conduct and efforts.

What I am trying to say is that your letter, though delayed, is more than welcome. I am delighted to know that you are throwing your influence into the fight for an expanding economy on the basis of fiscal responsibility and a sound dollar.[3]

With gratitude—and warm regard to you and Governor Hobby,[4]
As ever

[1] Former HEW Secretary Hobby had written on March 6, 1959 (WHCF/OF 107-B) in response to Eisenhower's February appeal for support in behalf of the balanced budget (see no. 1042). She shared the President's concern "over the failure of Democratic leaders in the Congress to give proper recognition to the great dangers which

are inherent in the numerous spending proposals which they are espousing and to support you in your endeavor to prevent future inflation."

[2] See Galambos and van Ee, *The Middle Way*, no. 393.

[3] Hobby had pledged to do everything she could "to help in getting the facts before members of the Congress and the American people." See also no. 1121.

[4] Mrs. Hobby's husband, William Pettus Hobby, had served as governor of Texas from 1917 until 1921.

1097   *EM, AWF, Name Series,*
Edgar Eisenhower Corr.

To Wilton Burton Persons   *[March 9, 1959]*

Jerry—I'll personally not say a word about this. I have heard good things about Bantz—but when political issues are urged by my brother—I can't react.[1]

[1] Edgar Eisenhower had previously brought up the issue of appointing William Bantz, a Spokane lawyer, to a judicial vacancy in Washington state (see no. 978). Once again urging the appointment, Edgar had sent the President a copy of his letter to Attorney General William Rogers asking for quick action. He viewed nomination as a necessary reward for Bantz, who had resigned as district attorney in order to wage an ultimately unsuccessful campaign for the Senate. "It takes the heart out of me when I find that the Party doesn't support a man who is willing to make sacrifices on his own part." He also thought the nomination would present an opportunity to rally the party even if Bantz were to be rejected by the Senate. The issue would "give the Republicans in this state something to get mad about" (Edgar Eisenhower to Rogers, Mar. 9, 1959, AWF/N). The President wrote this note at the top of Edgar's letter to Rogers. As it turned out, Bantz would not be nominated for the position.

1098   *EM, AWF, International Series:*
Canada

To John George Diefenbaker   *March 10, 1959*

Dear John:[1] I am today signing a Proclamation adjusting and regulating imports of crude oil and its principal products into the United States. The basis for this new program is a certification by the Office of Civil and Defense Mobilization that such action is required in the interests of our national defense.[2]

I wish to assure you that in the formulation of this program, every effort was made to insure that its practical effect upon imports from Canada would be minimized, and it is my understanding that there will be no appreciable change in the level of such imports as a result of the new program.[3]

In view of the joint interest in hemispheric defense that we share with Canada and with the other American Republics, it is my sincere hope that in the near future the informal conversations that have already begun will result in an agreed hemispheric approach to this problem.[4]

With warm regard, *Sincerely*

[1] At Eisenhower's request State Department officials had drafted this letter to the Canadian prime minister. After the President approved the text, it was sent by telegram to the U.S. ambassador in Ottawa for delivery to Diefenbaker (see Herter to Eisenhower, Mar. 10, 1959, AWF/I: Canada; Telephone conversation, Herter and Dillon, Mar. 9, 1959, Herter Papers, Telephone Conversations; [Whitman to Eisenhower], n.d., AWF/I: Canada).

[2] For Eisenhower's proclamation see *Public Papers of the Presidents: Eisenhower, 1959*, pp. 240–41. The Administration thought that mandatory controls were necessary because the Voluntary Oil Import Program, in effect since 1957, had failed due to a lack of compliance and to reduced consumption resulting from depressed economic conditions (see nos. 596, 608, 706, and 1088). The Proclamation directed the Secretary of the Interior to form an Oil Imports Appeals Board, consisting of representatives from the departments of Interior, Defense, and Commerce, to adjust quotas and administer the revocation or suspension of allocations and licenses (Douglas R. Bohi and Milton Russell, *Limiting Oil Imports: An Economic History and Analysis* [Baltimore, 1978], pp. 20–98; Daniel Yergin, *The Prize: The Epic Quest for Oil, Money and Power* [New York, 1991], pp. 535–38; and Vietor, *Energy Policy in America Since 1945*, pp. 108–28).

[3] In May Eisenhower would announce a modification of the mandatory program, allowing for "hemispheric preference" for overland imports of oil (for developments see no. 1144. See also Edward H. Shaffer, *Canada's Oil and the American Empire* [Edmonton, Alberta, 1983], pp. 140–67).

[4] As a result of the talks between Eisenhower and Diefenbaker the preceding July, officials of both governments had established the Canada-United States Ministerial Committee on Joint Defense. Discussions with the Canadian and Venezuelan embassies, in progress since January, had been suspended pending the installation of the new Venezuelan government (see State, *Foreign Relations, 1958–1960*, vol. VII, pt. 1, *Western European Integration and Security; Canada*, pp. 688, 710, 754; and State, *American Foreign Policy, Current Documents, 1958*, pp. 471–73; see also no. 206). For developments see no. 1302.

1099

EM, WHCF, Confidential File:
Name Series, Schweitzer Corr.

To ROBERT FRANCIS GOHEEN
Confidential

March 10, 1959

Dear Dr. Goheen:[1] Thank you for your recent letter informing me of Princeton's plans to invite Dr. Schweitzer to receive an honorary degree at your Commencement this June. Such recognition from a distinguished American university will, I am sure, mean much to him.[2]

Although I would, instinctively, like to endorse your invitation to Dr. Schweitzer, I have felt impelled to decide against it. This decision I have reached in spite of the fact that Dr. Schweitzer has come to epitomize in the public mind the unpublicized efforts of many missionaries from America and abroad who are performing such devoted, self-sacrificing services in Africa.[3]

I believe that any participation on my part in urging Dr. Schweitzer to accept would not be wise. In the past I have, once or twice, as with Prime Minister Macmillan, urged a foreign dignitary to accept an honorary degree in this country.[4] However, other requests of this nature have been such that I have had to adopt a policy of avoiding the practice. I am sure that you will understand this position.

I agree with you that if Dr. Schweitzer is able to attend your Commencement at Princeton and to extend his visit to other parts of the country, it will afford him a splendid opportunity to become better acquainted with the people of America, and we with him.[5]

With best wishes and assurance of personal esteem, *Sincerely*

[1] Goheen (Ph.D. Princeton 1947), a former classics professor at Princeton and a former U.S. Army colonel, had become president of the university in 1957.

[2] The Board of Trustees was "tremendously eager" to bestow this honor, Goheen had written, and he hoped that the President would encourage Schweitzer to accept the invitation "to bring to us all a message out of his life and experience and particularly, perhaps, in the cause of world peace" (Goheen to Eisenhower, Feb. 17, 1959; see also Coffey to Percy, Feb. 5, 1959, both in the same file as this document; for more on Schweitzer see no. 29).

[3] Dr. Goheen's parents had been missionaries in India. State Department officials had informed the White House that because of Schweitzer's "dubious political attitudes," they did not recommend that Eisenhower join Goheen in the invitation. Schweitzer had criticized U.S. atomic testing and contended that statements by Secretary Dulles had misled public opinion regarding the dangers of thermonuclear weapons (Calhoun to Goodpaster, Feb. 27, 1959; Calhoun to Goodpaster, Mar. 4, 1959; Views of Albert Schweitzer on the Thermonuclear Bomb, June 19, 1958; Schweitzer, "Peace or Atomic War?" Mar. 13, 1958, all in the same file as this document).

[4] On Macmillan's receipt of an honorary degree at the Johns Hopkins University see no. 652.

[5] Eisenhower would later tell Goheen that if Schweitzer agreed to accept the invitation, he would be delighted to meet him in Washington: "Actually I was under the impression that this thought was implicit in the last paragraph of the letter I sent you on March 10, but in a re-reading I see that I was remiss in failing to make the point clear." Goheen would inform the President, however, that "because of the heavy demands of his many-sided activities," Schweitzer would not be able to accept the invitation (Eisenhower to Goheen, Apr. 4, 1959; Goheen to Eisenhower, Apr. 10, 1959; see also [Whitman to Eisenhower, Apr. 4, 1959], all in the same file as this document).

In August the president of the board of directors of the Albert Schweitzer Education Foundation would suggest that Eisenhower include a meeting with Schweitzer in his upcoming goodwill trip to Europe. State Department officials, citing the President's "tight and inflexible schedule," would recommend against such a meeting (Phillips to Eisenhower, Aug. 6, 1959; Stephens to John Eisenhower, Aug. 11, 1959; McElhiney to Goodpaster, Aug. 12, 1959; White to John Eisenhower, Aug. 12, 1959; White to Phillips, Aug. 20, 1959; and McElhiney to Goodpaster, Aug. 26, 1959; all in the same file as this document). For more on Eisenhower's trip see no. 1186.

1100   *EM, AWF, DDE Diaries Series*

To Malcolm Charles Moos   *March 11, 1959*
Memorandum

Re: Television talk[1]
1. The title should be: "The General Security Situation of the United States and the Free World and Some Details of the Berlin Situation."
In general the discussion on Berlin seems to me to be okay. I am dictating my own suggestions and corrections into it.
2. The discussion of our security is presented in too much detail as long as we are putting the emphasis on the philosophy of defense. I would not mind a few illustrations. Suppose we wanted to give a feeling of our progress in missile production by naming them in order from the shortest range to the longest range, and including air to air, ground to ground, and air to ground.
3. It seems to me important to show that our safety lies not merely in American guns and tanks and planes, but in the strength of free world spirit, its confidence in ourselves and in our allies and their ability to sustain with reasonable help from us the forces in their sectors that are adequate to maintain internal order and freedom in their own countries and to do their own part in maintaining themselves against aggression.
4. And finally, we must talk about the permanence, or rather the indefiniteness of the period of tension through which we must live. Steadiness and adherence to our own clearly thought out defense plans, both domestic and international in character, plans that we can carry forward confidently over the years—these are the things we must stress rather than fall prey to the hysteria of any particular moment.[2]

[1] According to Ann Whitman's diary, the impetus for this speech came from Presidential Assistant Wilton Persons, Press Secretary James Hagerty, and White House speechwriter Malcolm Moos, who wanted the President to explain the Berlin situation to the American people before British Prime Minister Macmillan arrived on

March 19. Eisenhower "tentatively agreed, providing a good talk was presented to him" (Ann Whitman memorandum, Mar. 9, 1959, AWF/AWD; see also Telephone conversation, Herter and Moos, Mar. 13, 1959, Herter Papers, Telephone Conversations). For background on Berlin see no. 1084; on Macmillan's visit, no. 1091.

State Department officials had drafted portions of a speech, which were then combined with Moos's own draft (see Telephone conversations, Herter and Merchant and Herter and Moos, Mar. 10, 1959, Herter Papers, Telephone Conversations).

[2] After editing the revised draft, Eisenhower would deliver the televised talk on March 16. Using maps, he first explained the agreements (signed by the Allied Powers) that had provided for the occupation of Germany. He then outlined the choices available to the Western democracies and emphasized the need for meaningful negotiations. Using a chart, the President showed forty-one different types of missiles either currently available to the United States or in the research and development stage. He concluded by expressing the confidence he had in the courage and capacity of the American people to face the realities of the present and the future. "Our security shield," he said, "is the productivity of our free economy, the power of our military forces, and the enduring might of a great community of nations determined to defend their freedom" (*Public Papers of the Presidents: Eisenhower, 1959*, pp. 273–82; see also Ann Whitman memorandums, Mar. 14 and 16, 1959, AWF/AWD).

Secretary Dulles would later tell Eisenhower that too many people had been involved in preparing the speech. Indeed, Eisenhower himself would respond that he "was not happy about it" (see Ann Whitman memorandum, Mar. 16, 1959, AWF/ AWD; Telephone conversation, Eisenhower and Dulles, Dulles Papers, Telephone Conversations; and Eisenhower, *Waging Peace*, pp. 349–50). For developments on the Berlin situation see no. 1106.

1101   *EM, AWF, Administration Series*

To Arthur Frank Burns   *March 11, 1959*
Personal

Dear Arthur: I have no disagreement whatsoever with the first three observations you make in your letter.[1] Also I agree with the objectives stated in your item five.[2]

I do begin to have some difficulty in following your reasoning when you, in item four, put the burden for setting up a national unemployment insurance system on the Federal government and the entire cost on the states. I agree with the second part of this statement, most emphatically. My trouble is a doubt amounting almost to a negative conviction that the Congress, once having put its hands to the business of "laying down the law" to the states, could refrain from getting into financing on a grant basis.[3]

More and more I tend to discount the desire of either state governments or of the Congress to put appropriate responsibilities, the execution of which involves money, on the states where they belong rather than on the Federal government to which they tend to gravitate.

Through centralization of the appropriations function in the Federal government, the Congressman feels that he gains a political advantage over a governor. He is in the position of a rich man giving something away and he thinks his constituents increasingly lean toward him rather than toward the governor. On the other hand the governor does not want to undertake the unpopular role of asking for more local taxes to perform additional functions. Under this dual influence we, as citizens, tend to fall prey to the old belief that we can get something for nothing—in other words—get it from the Federal government.

In spite of the fact that your letter is marked "Personal and Confidential," I should like to have it studied by Jim Mitchell, who has just walked into the office. I shall tell him to keep it on an "Eyes Only" basis.

Thanks for writing; possibly one of these days we can get a chance to talk this subject over a little more exhaustively.[4]

With warm regard, *As ever*

---

[1] Burns had written on March 10, 1959 (AWF/A) to comment on pending legislation to extend the temporary unemployment insurance (see no. 1081). Burns believed that while the 1958 act was flawed, an extension of the law was "bound to appeal to many citizens on humanitarian grounds, whether or not they are aware of its shortcomings." He feared, however, that if the law were to be extended for another year, there would be "a danger that once the year runs out another extension will be attempted, and so on."

[2] Burns had said permanent unemployment legislation should cover practically all wage-earners and raise the amount of benefits to the level that Eisenhower had recommended in the past. He also thought that permanent legislation should increase the maximum duration of benefits, and "put the entire financial burden on the states—where it has historically been."

[3] Burns had written that since reform of unemployment insurance was inevitable, it would be wise to take preemptive measures lest during the next recession the Congress "saddle the Federal Treasury permanently with the costs."

[4] Congress would vote on March 25, 1959, to extend the limit for receiving unemployment insurance benefits an additional three months (see *Congressional Quarterly Almanac*, vol. XV, *1959*, pp. 219–21).

1102　　　　　　　　　　　　　　　　　*EM, AWF, International Series:*
　　　　　　　　　　　　　　　　　　　　　　　　　　　　　Macmillan

To Harold Macmillan　　　　　　　　　　　　　　*March 11, 1959*
Cable. Secret

Dear Harold: Thank you very much for your informative note after your Paris meeting. The only disagreement that I would have with your description as Eighteenth Century is that I place the period in the "Early Nineteenth."[1]

From what you said I feel there must be some hope of getting a little better expression of intention with respect to De Gaulle's participation in NATO and the use of his Fleet.

I am eagerly looking forward to your arrival, and I only wish that I could take you to a sunny climate rather than to ask you to endure some more of the winter weather that you have encountered during your many travels.[2]

With warm regard, *As ever*

---

[1] Macmillan had spent several days visiting Germany and France after his trip to the Soviet Union (see no. 1084). He had told Eisenhower that he had spoken firmly to French President de Gaulle, whom he found "quite mellow and friendly," about NATO and the French fleet and hoped that it had had some effect. "I fear that he does not really understand the modern concepts of integration and interdependence," Macmillan wrote. "He is fundamentally an Eighteenth Century figure, and therefore the problem of dealing with him is largely a psychological one—as you and I know well" (Macmillan to Eisenhower, Mar. 11, 1959, AWF/I: Macmillan, and PREM 11/2860; see also Macmillan, *Riding the Storm*, pp. 637–38; on de Gaulle and his plans to remove the French fleet from NATO see no. 1029).

[2] Macmillan would arrive in the United States on March 19. For developments see no. 1106.

1103

EM, AWF, *International Series: Macmillan*

To Harold Macmillan
Cable. Secret

March 14, 1959

Dear Harold: I agree with the date of March 20 which you suggest in your message of March 13 for a temporary recess in the Geneva nuclear test negotiations.[1] I would suggest that we try to set a date of April 13 for reconvening. We will send immediate instructions to our delegation to work out with your people a joint approach to the Russians.

Your visit to Washington and the subsequent breathing spell will give us an opportunity to work out our plans for the future of the negotiations.[2]

With warm personal regard, *As ever*

---

[1] For Macmillan's March 13 response to Eisenhower's original suggestion for a recess in the negotiations see no. 1095; see also Staff Notes, March 14, 1959, AWF/D; and Telephone conversation, Eisenhower and Herter, March 13, 1959, Herter Papers, Telephone Conversations.

² Macmillan would arrive in the United States on March 19. For developments see no. 1116.

1104 EM, AWF, Name Series

To Harry Cecil Butcher March 14, 1959
Personal

Dear Butch: Thank you for your letter which, incidentally, Mrs. Whitman did not find an opportunity to give to me until about ten minutes before seven, after a long, hard day at the office. Even so I had her try to find you on the telephone, with the hope that I could see you personally concerning the 1946 letter of mine that Montgomery used in his book. Unfortunately you had already left the city, so I am taking a few minutes early this morning to reply.[1]

First of all, it would be rather futile, after all these years, to offer any apology for the writing of the letter itself. I had completely forgotten it until Mrs. Whitman brought it to my attention last evening. However, I must say one word in my own defense.

As you recall, I had agreed for you to use the diary for writing a book if you so chose, but it was my understanding that we also agreed, at least originally, that you would not touch upon matters of operational orders, decisions and planning. In other words, the book, as I understood it, was to be a personal one, giving your own experiences and reactions rather than conclusions and opinions about plans and operations.[2]

The letter shows that I was irritated, but I simply had no business in writing it. I have made it a firm policy for many years to avoid public criticism of others—I have no excuse for having done so privately. So you can imagine my chagrin when I learned last evening that this twelve year old letter had been published—needless to say, without my permission or without notification to me, by Montgomery.

Incidentally, one reason why this incident had not earlier come to my knowledge is that I had never even opened Montgomery's book. I saw some of the excerpts in the newspapers and they convinced me that it was a waste of time to read it if I was looking for anything constructive. I am naturally not interested in anything destructive.[3]

I found intriguing your information that Murrow and Montgomery are to immortalize Montgomery in film.[4] Some gullible people will probably take him at his own evaluation—to that extent his effort will undoubtedly be a great success.

Again I assure you of my regret over something that I did twelve years ago and which I certainly would not do today, and I express the hope that you will forget the matter as quickly as possible.

To return for a moment to the reason for your trip East. I first met Arthur Pew when I was at Columbia, and while I have seen him only two or three times since then, I like him. So I think it appropriate to send him a note expressing my sympathy over the death of his son.[5]

The next time you are in Washington I shall hope that my schedule is not as crowded as it has been these last two or three days. When you call my office, please tell either Tom Stephens or, if he is not there, Mrs. Whitman, that I personally asked you to let me know immediately upon your arrival. In this way I hope I shall have more flexibility in trying to set up a date.[6]

With warm regard, *As ever*

[1] On March 13 (AWF/N) the President's wartime naval aide had written that he had not had sufficient time to meet with Eisenhower during his brief trip to Washington (see also Telephone Calls, Mar. 13, 1959, AWF/D). In February 1946 Eisenhower had written to Field Marshal Montgomery regarding the serial publication of Butcher's *My Three Years With Eisenhower* (the letter appears in Galambos, *Chief of Staff*, as no. 696). For background on the 1958 publication of Field Marshal Montgomery's memoir, in which the 1946 letter to Butcher had been published, see, for example, nos. 933 and 948).

[2] Embarrassed by Butcher's passing "judgments with an air of the greatest authority," Eisenhower had apologized to Montgomery after Butcher's diary had appeared. The President said he deplored Butcher's use of his confidential position to form his own conclusions on several matters, "including personalities and operations." "My real error," he wrote, "was in selecting as his confidential aide a man who "wanted to be a 'writer' after the war."

[3] For Eisenhower's reaction to Montgomery's publication see nos. 970 and 1012.

[4] Butcher recently had visited television and radio news analyst Edward R. Murrow. Murrow had been with Columbia Broadcasting Systems since 1935 and had worked on the popular television programs *Person to Person*, *See It Now*, and *CBS Reports*. According to Butcher, Murrow was planning to produce two one-hour segments on Montgomery: the first would be aired in the near future and the second in the event of Montgomery's death.

[5] Arthur E. Pew, Jr., grandson of the Sun Oil founder, had been a director of Sun Oil Company since 1927. Pew had helped develop processes used in the manufacture of lubricating oils and in the production of gasoline through the catalytic refining of crude oil. Pew's twenty-eight-year-old stepson, Jimmy, had died from the effects of hepatitis, which he apparently had contracted in the Navy.

[6] Butcher would thank Eisenhower for this letter on April 6 (WHCF/PPF 522). Eisenhower and Butcher would next meet on May 22, 1960, at the President's Gettysburg farm.

EM, AWF,
Administration Series

To Nelson Aldrich Rockefeller   *March 14, 1959*

Dear Nelson: Thanks for your note and for the clipping. I need not add that Albany has no monopoly on confusion, as well you know.

You had a tough job and you proved, early in your Administration, that you do not shirk from a fight.[1] I am still hoping that I can keep Federal expenditures below receipts.[2]

With warm regard, *As ever*

[1] New York Governor Rockefeller had sent Eisenhower a news story about an attempted revolt in Iraq. The headline had mistakenly incorporated a headline from another story about Rockefeller's recent political difficulties regarding the New York State budget: "REBEL CHIEF CONCEDES DEFEAT: Budget Row Ends; GOP Leaders Wary." In a handwritten note Rockefeller said, "This clipping will give you some idea of the confusion that exists here!" (Mar. 12, 1959, AWF/A; see also *New York Times,* Mar. 12, 1959). For background on the fiscal problems Rockefeller inherited upon his inauguration as governor see nos. 1047 and 1061. For developments see no. 1124.

[2] On Eisenhower's fight against inflation and battle for a balanced budget see no. 1042. For developments see, for example, no. 1121.

1106   *EM, AWF, International Series:*
de Gaulle

To Charles André Joseph Marie de Gaulle   *March 14, 1959*
Cable. Secret

Dear General de Gaulle:[1] I have received and read with great care your letter of March 12 and wish to reply immediately to express my gratification at having this expression of your views.[2]

Your analysis of the artificial crisis precipitated by the announced intentions of the Soviets to change the status of Berlin, and the existing arrangements for our access to Berlin seems to me to sum up the situation admirably. More than two million people in West Berlin look to us for the protection of their continued safety and welfare. We could not think of risking our honor by accepting, under the threat of force, conditions which would undermine our ability to fulfill our commitment to the people of Berlin. Our rights are clear. I share your view that if force is used to oppose our exercise of these rights, the world will know precisely who in this controversy first resorted to force to settle a dispute. The more we and you and our

NATO allies are firm and united, the less chance it seems to me that we shall run the risk of dangerous Soviet counteraction.

As you say, there is every reason to convoke a conference of Foreign Ministers, and to let such a conference run on while both sides exhaustively canvass possibilities for solution. We should not commit ourselves to go to a "summit" conference until there was some promise that such a conference could, in fact, yield satisfying results. I am communicating these same considerations, which appear of major political importance to me, to Prime Minister Macmillan.[3]

The reunification of Germany would effectively remove from Central Europe the main cause of tension there. Other important political consequences, which we would all welcome, would undoubtedly follow in its train. This happy event, as you suggest, is not likely to occur very soon, and I agree entirely that in the interim contacts between the two parts of Germany should be encouraged. I would here only enter a note of caution, with which I am sure you would agree, that, for many reasons, contacts which risk enhancing the position and prestige of the Soviet puppet government should be minimized.

In discussing the Berlin crisis and the difficult situation in Germany, the vital importance of the continued strength and unity of our NATO alliance inevitably also comes to my mind. I am sure you will of course agree that our common defenses must be maintained at maximum effectiveness if we are to deal with the Soviets with the firmness which both you and I desire. I believe we should proceed on this score calmly and purposefully. We should not take hasty measures designed superficially to build up our defenses which would only be interpreted as a sign of fear on our part, nor should we do anything to weaken our defenses, or make moves which could be interpreted as weakness or lack of determination. In addition to maintaining our military strength, we must also maintain a spirit of common political purpose among all members of the Alliance. Otherwise we will increase our vulnerability to Soviet efforts to divide us. Everything possible should be done to ensure that the military strength and political unity of the Alliance are maintained.[4]

With reference to another portion of your letter, I am gratified to note that your views on the subject of "disengagement" are very close to my own.[5] We have, as you know, felt that a technical approach to the problem of surprise attack, with measures not confined to a narrow or limited area, would be a worthwhile next step in the disarmament field. Unfortunately the conference with the Soviets on this matter at Geneva last fall made it clear that their approach to the problem was completely unacceptable.[6] The Soviet proposals would have led to the creation of a narrow demilitarized zone in Central Europe without any real assurance that the danger of surprise attack would be reduced. I continue to hope, of course, that it will be possible to make progress in the disarmament field, but I fully agree with you that we cannot accept measures which would jeopardize our basic security interests.

I also wished to refer briefly to our previous correspondence regarding a closer tripartite relationship among France, Great Britain and ourselves.[7] I believe, as you expressed last month to Secretary Dulles in Paris, that these talks have already begun to serve a useful purpose.[8] We, for our part, are disposed to continue these talks, and I am gratified that a date has been set early next month for the next meetings in this series.[9]

I will be discussing these vital subjects, particularly those concerning Germany, with Prime Minister Macmillan next week and will, of course, keep in mind during these talks your cogently expressed ideas. In the light of these talks I will write to you again to give you my appreciation of the situation and actions which we might wish to take. It is essential that we seek common accord and that our mutual strengths be concerted. These private exchanges of views can contribute importantly to that end.[10]

Please accept, Mr. President, the expression of my highest consideration and sincere friendship.

---

[1] The State Department drafted this message for Eisenhower (see State, *Foreign Relations, 1958–1960*, vol. VIII, *Berlin Crisis 1958–1959*, p. 488).

[2] French President de Gaulle had agreed that the Western powers must not give in to the Soviet ultimatum over Berlin access rights. Hindrance to passage into the city would constitute an act of force, which, he said, would have to be met with a similar act of force. He supported a meeting of foreign ministers before any summit conference could be considered—a meeting which should "remain in session for some time." The reunification of Germany, although not possible at that time, was the ultimate goal, and he called for the creation of opportunities to establish relations between the two halves of the nation. West Berlin was a Western city and wanted to remain so, de Gaulle wrote. "Our presence is a right which we do not have to debate, even if the Russians pretend to waive that right for themselves" (de Gaulle to Eisenhower, Mar. 12, 1959, AWF/I: de Gaulle).

[3] Eisenhower was probably referring to a message from Acting Secretary Herter to British Ambassador Harold Caccia, written at Eisenhower's request, that expressed the President's views (State, *Foreign Relations, 1958–1960*, vol. VIII, *Berlin Crisis 1958–1959*, pp. 484–86).

[4] On March 3 French Ambassador Hervé Alphand had told State Department officials that because of the Algerian situation and the need for national control over its navy, France was withdrawing its Mediterranean fleet from NATO control. The fleet would continue to participate in NATO maneuvers during peacetime and would cooperate—to an extent consistent with French national interests—with the alliance during wartime. France had officially notified the North Atlantic Council of its intentions on March 6 (State, *Foreign Relations, 1958–1960*, vol. VII, pt. 1, *Western European Integration and Security; Canada*, pp. 415–21; see also no. 1029).

[5] For background on the policy of disengagement—the removal of both NATO and Soviet forces from a central zone in the middle of Europe—see no. 508. De Gaulle

had said that disengagement proposals depended on whether the question was one of controlled limitation of armaments of all kinds over a widespread area or demilitarization of East and West Germany, Poland, and Czechoslovakia. "In the first case, we should have no reason to refuse to engage in discussions. In the second case, we should do it only if the States that are to become buffer States are first returned to their own people through free elections giving rise to the formation of free governments, without which their neutralization would only be a means of tricking us."
[6] For background on the surprise attack conference see no. 943.
[7] See no. 901. For Eisenhower's most recent correspondence with the French president, in which he had notified de Gaulle of Henry Cabot Lodge's trip to Europe, see Eisenhower to de Gaulle, February 16, 1959, AWF/I: de Gaulle.
[8] For the meetings between Secretary Dulles, de Gaulle, and Foreign Minister Couve de Murville on February 6 and 7, see State, *Foreign Relations, 1958–1960*, vol. VIII, *Berlin Crisis 1958–1959*, pp. 325–34; see also Eisenhower to Dulles, February 6, 1959, AWF/D-H. On the tripartite meetings see State, *Foreign Relations, 1958–1960*, vol. VII, pt. 2, *Western Europe*, pp. 181–82.
[9] Tripartite talks focusing on Africa would begin on April 16 (*ibid.*, pp. 192–94).
[10] Macmillan would arrive in Washington on March 19. For developments see nos. 1112 and 1116.

1107   *EM, WHCF, Official File 107-B*

To Newell Windom Ellison   *March 16, 1959*

Dear Mr. Ellison: Thank you very much for your letter of Saturday. The idea that I would let a balanced budget take priority over what I consider adequate security for our country is, of course, fantastic.[1] I tried to knock it down in the press conference last week, as you know, and I shall speak again of the matter tonight.[2]

My great difficulty is in realizing that anyone in this country, even for partisan reasons, would entertain for a moment the thought that I would let our defense structure be undermined to a danger point. What I am trying to do is to keep a clearly adequate security and our economy sound, preserving the integrity of our dollar both at home and abroad.[3] At the same time we must not drain off from our economy so much money in taxes that we diminish too markedly the private funds needed for expansion. If we are to meet Mr. Khrushchev's often repeated challenge on the economic front, our own economy must be equal to the demands that will be made in it.[4]

As I say, I think my philosophy is so fundamental that it is hard for me to believe that in this respect my opponents can possibly mean what they say—or that what they say can be taken seriously by any thinking person in America.

Again my thanks for your letter.[5]

With best wishes, *Sincerely*

[1] A partner in Washington's Covington and Burling law firm, Ellison (LL.B. George Washington University 1921) had written on March 14 regarding the "defense-budget controversy with Congress." Eisenhower's critics, Ellison wrote, wanted people to believe that the President was "against an adequate defense because of a paramount desire on your part to balance the budget, while they stand for an adequate defense even if it means an unbalanced budget." Ellison had grown "irritated and concerned with the Democrats (including my partner Dean Acheson) framing what I consider a false issue and making political capital out of it." It was imperative that Eisenhower make clear that American defenses were "fully adequate to protect us and to enable us to carry out our obligations to others."

[2] At his March 11 news conference the President had said: "I'm just tired even of talking about the idea of a balanced budget against national security; I don't see where this thing ever comes into it. I say that a balanced budget in the long run is a vital part of national security" (*Public Papers of the Presidents: Eisenhower, 1959*, pp. 250–51). In his March 16 radio and television address on "Security in the Free World," Eisenhower would reassure the American people: "I believe that the American people want, are entitled to, can indefinitely pay for, and now have and will continue to have a modern, effective and adequate military establishment. In this overall conviction, I am supported by the mass of the best military opinion I can mobilize, and by scientific and every other kind of talent that is giving its attention to a problem to which I personally have devoted a lifetime" (*ibid.*, pp. 279–81).

[3] See nos. 637, 753, and 784.

[4] At an embassy reception in November 1956 Khrushchev had remarked in a speech that although the West might find the prospect disagreeable, "history is on our side. We will bury you." Although the remark was sometimes interpreted as a military threat, Khrushchev later stated that he had been referring to the inevitable victory of socialism in peaceful economic competition with capitalism (William J. Tompson, *Khrushchev: A Political Life* [Oxford, 1995], pp. 171–72).

[5] Ellison would respond on March 20 (same file as document). Thanking the President for his letter, he complemented Eisenhower on his March 16 speech, which delivered "a clear, forceful message." "What you said will fortify the country and should at least reduce the mouthiness of the Simple Symingtons, and to the extent it does not stop them the American people will now hear them for what they really are."

1108

EM, AWF,
Administration Series

To Lewis Lichtenstein Strauss

March 16, 1959

Dear Lewis: I am delighted that the American Telephone and Telegraph Company has joined the "anti-inflation" movement.[1] If you think it would be advisable, I would be glad to send a personal letter to the President of the Company.[2]

Incidentally, I have just seen an enclosure sent to the stockholders of Armstrong Cork Company. And, in case you did not know, the Manufacturers Trust Company has prepared a clear and attractive little brochure for their employees, and plan also to include it with their next dividend payment.[3]

With warm regard, *As ever*

[1] Since February Strauss had been sending the President reports on the results of his letter writing campaign on behalf of the balanced budget (see, for example, Strauss to Eisenhower, Feb. 12, 1959, and Strauss to Whitman, Feb. 16, 1959, AWF/A). A.T.& T. had promised to send out a statement to its shareholders. For background see no. 1042.

[2] There is no correspondence between Eisenhower and Frederick Russell Kappel, who then headed A.T.& T., in AWF.

[3] See no. 1121.

1109

EM, WHCF, Official File 114

To Lewis Lichtenstein Strauss
Personal

March 16, 1959

Dear Lewis: I am appalled by the contents of your letter of March thirteenth. Are our communications, after all, as "free" as we like to think?[1]

Thanks for keeping me informed.

With warm regard, *As ever*

[1] On March 13 Strauss had sent Eisenhower a report on CBS President Frank Stanton's plan to have four hour-long programs on the dangers of inflation and the devalued dollar (for background see no. 1073). The first show had aired on Sunday, March 8, but Stanton had told Strauss that "the Washington affiliate of CBS—the *Washington Post*—refused to carry it either on television or on radio. As little as I think of that paper," Strauss wrote, "it nevertheless surprises me that they would exercise what amounts to censorship since they regularly carry the CBS program."

Displeased with the first show, Stanton had complained that the "AFL-CIO representative walked all over the management man (Ford) and the economist-journalist panel members did not ask good questions." The public response to the program had, according to Strauss, been favorable, and CBS was hoping to improve the remaining programs. Strauss's letter is in the same file as the document.

1110

EM, WHCF, Official File 107-B

To Percy Poe Bishop

March 17, 1959

Dear Percy:[1] How nice to hear from you again! Quite naturally, I am glad that you approve of my efforts in these days of tension and crises.[2]

My television talk last night was designed to give the public a clearer understanding of the causes of the Berlin situation and the possible choices that face the Western world. At the same time I wanted again to try to point out that we are doing everything possible to provide for our country adequate security and, at the same time, maintain a sound dollar and not drain off from our economy so much money in taxes that we diminish too markedly the private funds needed for expansion.[3]

I doubt if I should put in any letter, even one to an old friend, some of the bitter lessons I have learned about "politicians." However, I completely agree with your statement that what we need are politicians who put the interest of the government and of all the people first.[4]

With warm personal regard, *As ever*

---

[1] For background on retired Major General Bishop, an old friend of Eisenhower, see Galambos, *Columbia University*, no. 647.

[2] Bishop had applauded Eisenhower's leadership and told the President that the people he knew in New England and in the South were totally supportive of the President's support for fiscal responsibility and opposition to Communist aggression. He also criticized "liberals who press for extravagance in Government" and were "eroding the moral bases of our system of free government and . . . brain-washing too many of our good citizens" (Bishop to Eisenhower, Mar. 13, 1959, same file as document).

[3] On Eisenhower's speech see no. 1100.

[4] For another correspondent's comments regarding politicians see no. 1083.

1111

EM, WHCF,
President's Personal File 1241

TO WRIGHT FRANCIS MORROW   *March 17, 1959*

Dear Mr. Morrow: Thank you very much for your message regarding the convictions I outlined in my television talk of last evening. I worked over the manuscript long and hard hours in an effort precisely to outline the Berlin situation as I see it, and the choices that we have before us.[1]

I am gratified by the response I have received from you and other good friends indicating that the American people are united in support of our firmness of purpose.[2]

With warm regard, *Sincerely*

P.S. I probably failed to tell you that on at least two occasions I tried to bring your name to the attention of President Lopez Mateos, as well as your interest in the execution of certain orders of the courts involving a law suit in Mexico. Since there seemed to be no reaction of any kind, I did not think it good manners to go further than this.[3]

[1] In his radio and television broadcast entitled "Security in the Free World," the President had discussed the nation's mutual security policies and defense capacity in the context of continuing Soviet efforts to modify the agreements prescribing the postwar occupation of Berlin and Germany. Although he had stated that the United States and its allies must "stand firm," Eisenhower had also expressed a willingness to "talk with Soviet representatives at any time" (*Public Papers of the Presidents: Eisenhower, 1959*, pp. 273–82. For background on the Berlin crisis see nos. 983, 1079, and 1106). Eisenhower would later write that after his March 11 news conference, when he had tried to explain the "fundamentals" about the relationship "between the Berlin crisis and the numerical strength of our Armed Forces," he had decided to expand the answer into a short television talk (Eisenhower, *Waging Peace*, p. 349; see also *Public Papers of the Presidents: Eisenhower, 1959*, pp. 242–52; Ann Whitman memorandum, Mar. 16, 1959, AWF/AWD; no. 1100; and the following document).

[2] Texas attorney Morrow had written in the first of two congratulatory telegrams that he sent to Eisenhower: "I cannot help but believe the decision to remain steadfast against any giving in to threats of Khrushchev is right and has the support of the American people. . . . I hope you stand firm–willing to negotiate but not to retreat and allow continuing and further demands and threats to get worldwide publicity and be effective propaganda" (Mar. 16 and 17, 1959, same file as document). Ann Whitman calculated that the speech was "On all accounts . . . superb. The count I see now is 758 pro, 58 against. All the friends have been unusually enthusiastic. I think it was a triumph, both from the standpoint of clarifying the situation and from the standpoint of the President getting on record before the Prime Minister came over" (Ann Whitman memorandum, Mar. 16, 1959, AWF/AWD).

[3] Morrow was serving as arbitrator in a disputed Mexican court decision. In anticipation of the President's February visit to Mexico's President López Mateos, Morrow had asked Eisenhower to mention him and vouch for his "integrity and veracity." Eisenhower had responded: "If . . . I find the opportunity, I shall be glad to tell him of my high regard for you and my confidence that your presentation in any argumentative matter would represent only the truth as you might see it" (see Morrow to Eisenhower, Feb. 10, 1959, and Feb. 17, 1959, and Eisenhower to Morrow, Feb. 12, 1959, all in same file as document).

1112   *EM, AWF, International Series: De Gaulle*

To Charles André Joseph Marie de Gaulle   *March 19, 1959*
Cable. Secret

Dear General de Gaulle:[1]As I said in my letter to you of March fourteenth, I continue to attach the greatest importance to maintaining the strength of our military posture through the fullest and closest cooperation in NATO.[2] As you are aware, I have long had a deep and natural interest in this common effort, because of my conviction that the fate of France and of Free Europe is of incalculable importance to my own country. Since assuming the office of the

Presidency, I have earnestly supported the concept of the NATO "shield" as an indispensable element of Western security. Because of your long association with Western military cooperation and planning, I know that you too have a particular interest in these subjects.

I believe that in NATO we have the best guarantee of mutual defense. Through it, additionally, the Federal Republic of Germany has been brought into close political and military union with the West.[3] NATO has become a flexible instrument, as is well illustrated by the growth of political consultation within its framework in recent years.

In light of these views, I believe I would be remiss if I did not inform you of the concern caused us by the letter from the French Government regarding the withdrawal of its Mediterranean fleet from its earmark for assignment to NATO in time of war.[4] I do not consider the NATO structure as unalterable; it is an organism which must grow to survive. We have long sought to improve and perfect it. It was in this spirit that I asked Secretary Dulles to talk to you on this subject when he was in Paris in February and to tell you that the United States would view sympathetically a French request to NATO for greater status within NATO for the French naval forces in the Mediterranean.[5]

I cannot hide from an old friend my fears that the action of your Government has had unfortunate psychological and political repercussions. As you said in your letter of March twelfth, Western solidarity in the critical Berlin and German issue is of paramount importance.[6] I fear that the unilateral action of the French Government may give the impression of divisions within our alliance, divisions which I am convinced do not exist on fundamental issues.

It is my hope that the military command structure of NATO will always be such as to deserve support of all the member nations. Specifically, I believe that in this respect the Mediterranean fleets of the United States, United Kingdom and France should be on equal footing. For the present, the most logical status for all three would appear to be that held at present by the fleets of the United States and the United Kingdom, that is, under national control during peacetime, earmarked for NATO in the event of war. I further hope that, as we have said before, France will impart to NATO her thoughts on such arrangements. I am sure NATO would view such action with sympathy and would give the most careful consideration to France's views. The result of such consultation in NATO would, I am sure, contribute to the strong and united posture which we all desire in this crucial period.[7]

Please accept, Mr. President, the expression of my highest consideration and sincere friendship.

[1] State Department officials drafted this letter to the French president (see Herter to Eisenhower, Mar. 16, 1959, AWF/I: de Gaulle). A notation on the cable indicated that Eisenhower had asked that the message be shown to General Norstad, Supreme Allied Commander in Europe, "to be sure it does not create great difficulties for him."

[2] See no. 1106.

[3] For West Germany's acceptance into the NATO alliance in 1955 see Galambos and van Ee, *The Middle Way*, no. 1340.

[4] For background see no. 1106. The French government had informed the North Atlantic Council that France's African interests and the assurance of communication between both shores of the Mediterranean necessitated the action. The decision would have no consequences in peacetime, the government asserted, because the fleet was already under French control (State, *Foreign Relations, 1958–1960*, vol. VII, pt. 1, *Western European Integration and Security; Canada*, pp. 415–21; see also State, *Foreign Relations, 1958–1960*, vol. VII, pt. 2, *Western Europe*, pp. 183–87).

[5] For Dulles's talk with de Gaulle regarding the French fleet see *ibid.*, pp. 181–82.

[6] For de Gaulle's letter see no. 1106.

[7] In his memorandum accompanying the draft of this letter, Acting Secretary Herter had told Eisenhower that the State Department was not proposing that de Gaulle withdraw the message to the NAC. "Our letter may serve, however, to cause him to reflect on this decision and perhaps to change its emphasis so as to make it a declaration of intent rather than an ultimatum." Herter added that some French officials supported such a modification (Herter to Eisenhower, Mar. 16, 1959, AWF/I: de Gaulle).

For developments see nos. 1116 and 1192.

1113   *EM, AWF, Administration Series*

To Neil Hosler McElroy   *March 19, 1959*

Dear Neil: Meyer Kestnbaum has given me an encouraging report— of which I attach a copy—on the progress you are making in reviewing proficiency flying. Needless to say, I am delighted. This kind of study, it seems to me, represents a fine effort in the direction of economy and good management.[1]

With warm regard, *Sincerely*

[1] Special Assistant to the President Kestnbaum's memorandum dated March 19, 1959, is in AWF/A, McElroy Corr. In the latter half of 1958 the Department of Defense had begun a critical study of the system of incentive pay for military flying, with particular reference to arrangements for "proficiency" flying. Under current regulations military personnel not actually assigned to flying units were entitled to flight pay provided they were rated as having flying status and engaged in at least 100 hours a year of "proficiency" flying. Criticism had been leveled at the program both because of its cost in terms of salary and flight operations, and because officers who earned flight pay on missions involving substantial hazards resented the fact that those without regular flying assignments could qualify for comparable flight pay by undertak-

ing only a minimum of routine flights. The Defense Department had called for changes in the program, including reduced total flying activity and personnel screening to remove from active flying status those lacking potential as rated officers. The Defense Department also planned to develop a revised system of flight pay in the future. Kestnbaum had written that the reforms would result in savings of $46.5 million annually.

1114

EM, WHCF, Official File 107-B

To Henry Junior Taylor
Personal

March 20, 1959

Dear Harry: Many thanks for your letter. Of course I think I am right in my efforts to keep the budget balanced and to prevent a rash of spending that would encourage inflation and lead us precisely toward that "economic hara-kiri" about which you wrote in 1948.[1] I detect, or hope I detect, a ground swell of support that promises more support than I could possibly have expected two months ago. For example, just yesterday the House voted on a bill cutting the amount for airport facilities from $297 million to $200 million. The motion lost, but we picked up a surprising number of Democratic votes, and the Republican side stood—almost to a man—firm. That augurs well that any veto on such a bill will be sustained.[2]

At any rate, I keep on doing the best I can. Certainly Mr. Khrushchev himself has been perfectly plain about his aims; incidently, I find the same thing in a document by Joseph Stalin written about 1906 or 1907: he says, "Our main task is to help abolish capitalist property and to establish socialist property."[3]

Give my best to Fay,[4] and, of course, warm regard to yourself, *As ever*

[1] Taylor, a foreign correspondent for the Scripps-Howard newspaper chain during World War II and a widely published commentator on economic and social issues, had served as U.S. Ambassador to Switzerland since 1957. For further background see Galambos, *Chief of Staff*, no. 692. Taylor had written on March 17 (same file as document) regarding criticism of Eisenhower's balanced budget plan (see nos. 1042 and 1107). He had quoted from an article he had published in the February 1948 *Reader's Digest*: "Russia intends to have us commit economic hara-kiri. She intends to force us into economic suicide long before the chips are down. She expects us to knock ourselves out in our own gymnasium. And our task is to be warned that *this is Russia's fundamental plan*—pursued every hour of every day."

[2] On March 19 the House passed legislation authorizing federal grants to help communities build and improve airport facilities during fiscal 1960–1963. The bill also provided $45 million in funds for airport modernization for jet traffic, but limited the use of federal funds in the construction of airport buildings to that portion of a project intended to provide space for use by federal agencies. The House defeated

an amendment that would have reduced grant authorization by $32.3 million in 1961 and 1962, and by $32.4 million in 1963 (*Congressional Quarterly Almanac*, vol. XV, *1959*, pp. 225–28). The House and Senate would reach a compromise on the two versions of the legislation, and would adopt instead a two-year extension of the $63 million-a-year program in effect since 1955. Eisenhower would sign the bill on June 29, 1959.

[3] We have been unable to identify the quote to which Eisenhower refers. See J. V. Stalin, *Works*, 13 vols. (Moscow, 1952–1955), vol. 1, *1901–1907* (1952); see also Adam B. Ulam, *Stalin: The Man and His Era* (Boston, 1989), pp. 47–113. On Khrushchev see no. 1107.

[4] Taylor's wife, the former Olivia Fay Kimbro.

1115

To Charles Douglas Jackson   *March 21, 1959*

Dear C.D.: Many thanks for your two recent letters. Certainly there was no harm done by the incident and, judging from the reactions I have heard, the article itself—despite a few inaccuracies—has been on the plus side.[1] (That statement admits an appalling lack of modesty, I must admit!)

At any rate the matter is closed, and the only bitterness is on the part of Ann, who says you might at least have found a decent photograph to plaster over two pages![2]

With warm regard, *As ever*

[1] Former presidential aide Jackson had apologized to the President on March 12 (AWF/A) for releasing some of Eisenhower's private letters to him for publication by *Life* magazine (see "The Private Letters of the President," *Life*, Mar. 16, 1959, pp. 104–22). Jackson explained that he had been assured by the magazine editor that the White House had approved the project and that Press Secretary James Hagerty, "who for obvious reasons wished to remain the invisible man," had gone over the draft article carefully. Later Jackson had learned that the President had had no knowledge of the forthcoming article (Marie McCrum to Whitman, Mar. 10, 1959, Mar. 12 [two letters], 1959, AWF/A, Jackson Corr.; Ann Whitman memorandum, Mar. 12, 1959, AWF/AWD; and *New York Times*, Mar. 11, 1959).

Jackson had written again on March 19 (AWF/A) to thank the President for the "very generous humor" in his message, which had relieved the tension. Eisenhower's letter to Jackson had read: "Dear C.D.: Don't tell anyone, but I do wish you a 'Happy Birthday'" (Mar. 13, 1959, WHCF/PPF 423). The President's letter was marked "PERSONAL," "CONFIDENTIAL," "SECRET," "TOP SECRET," and "EYES ONLY."

[2] On the first two pages of the article the editors had pictured Ann Whitman leaning over her stenographer's pad while taking dictation from Eisenhower.

To Charles André Joseph Marie De Gaulle
Cable. Secret   *March 24, 1959*

Dear General de Gaulle: As promised in my letter of March 14 I want
to give you a report of my conversations with Prime Minister Macmillan.[1] We have had an extremely close and useful exchange of views
and were successful in achieving our aim of a common appreciation
of the dangers we face and a determination to stand firm in the face
of threat.

We discussed at length the matter of meetings with the Soviets.
The Prime Minister gave me his impressions of the Soviets, particularly Khrushchev, and informed me of his discussions with you.
From this we went into a general study of the reply we should make
to the Soviet note of March 2.[2] This reply, of which you have by now
received the text, takes into account the preoccupations which we
both expressed in our recent exchange of letters.[3] Without going
into the details I believe that we are adopting the best possible posture, one of firmness and determination accompanied by a willingness to talk and negotiate.

We agreed that considerable further work is required to perfect
a comprehensive Western proposal and we suggest that the Working Group reconvene shortly after the NATO Ministerial Meeting.[4]
We hope that the Working Group will be able to give agreed recommendations to our governments no later than April 20. In the meantime our Foreign Ministers will have reviewed the Working Group's
present report and will have had the opportunity to discuss these
matters fully at their meetings here in Washington on March 31 and
April 1.[5]

The Prime Minister and I also confirmed our approval of the general principles underlying our plans to deal with possible contin-
gencies relating to Berlin and access to that city.[6] These studies are
those which have been discussed tripartitely here in Washington and
on which, I am sure, Ambassador Alphand has reported to you fully.[7]
We agreed that we can assume that in view of the possibility of negotiations beginning with the Soviets in May it is unlikely that the
Soviets would take unilateral action with regard to West Berlin in
the intervening period.[8]

We covered a number of other subjects in our talks including ap-
preciations of the situations in the Middle East and the Far East. I
do not believe your appreciation of these situations would differ ma-
terially from ours. We also gave serious consideration to the implications to the Free World of the Soviet economic offensive.[9]

In my letter of March 14 I mentioned the tripartite talks we have had here in Washington arising out of your letter to me of last September.[10] I discussed the general subject with the Prime Minister and we both agreed that these talks are mutually profitable and that the discussion of Africa scheduled to begin on April 9 can serve an important purpose.[11]

I am sure that unity among the three of us is, as you have expressed, essential to the Free World. It remains a leading objective of mine.[12]

Please accept, Mr. President, the expression of my highest consideration and sincere friendship.

[1] For background see no. 1106. Macmillan had arrived in the United States on March 19. On the following day he and Eisenhower had met with Secretary Dulles at Walter Reed Hospital before traveling to Camp David for three days of talks (see Dulles, Memorandum of Conversation, Mar. 20, 1959, Dulles Papers, White House Memoranda Series; see also Eisenhower, *Waging Peace*, pp. 350–55; and Macmillan, *Riding the Storm*, pp. 642–50; John S. D. Eisenhower, *Strictly Personal*, pp. 228–31; Ann Whitman memorandums, Mar. 21, 22, 1959, AWF/AWD; and Telephone conversations, Eisenhower and Herter, Mar. 18, 1959, Herter Papers, Telephone Conversations).

[2] Macmillan had told Eisenhower that Khrushchev, whom he described as "the undisputed boss," wanted to maintain the status quo and had emphasized the importance of negotiations in order to settle disputes peacefully. He had told Macmillan that the May 27 deadline regarding the Berlin situation was not meant to be an ultimatum.

The French appeared to agree with the British "on everything," Macmillan had reported. De Gaulle "seemed obsessed with the atom bomb" as the ultimate weapon "which left nations not possessing it in a secondary role." He also appeared to believe that mobilization or other defensive measures were of little use in preparing for a possible attack (State, *Foreign Relations, 1958–1960*, vol. VII, pt. 2, *Western Europe*, pp. 837–42; see also State, *Foreign Relations, 1958–1960*, vol. VIII, *Berlin Crisis 1958–1959*, pp. 459–61; and nos. 1074 and 1102).

The Soviet note of March 2 had proposed a summit meeting to consider a German peace treaty, the future of Berlin, European security, and disarmament. Alternatively, they had suggested that the foreign ministers of the United States, the United Kingdom, France, the Soviet Union, Poland, and Czechoslovakia meet in April to negotiate a German peace treaty and a solution to the Berlin question. Representatives from the United States, Great Britain, France, and West Germany (the Four-Power Working Group) had begun meetings in Paris on March 9 to draft a reply. At British insistence, however, work had been suspended until after Macmillan's Washington visit (State, *Foreign Relations, 1958–1960*, vol. VIII, *Berlin Crisis 1958–1959*, pp. 482–84, 529, 532; and State, *American Foreign Policy; Current Documents, 1959*, pp. 618–20).

Eisenhower and Macmillan had argued about the importance of the foreign ministers' meeting. Although he had agreed to the preliminary discussions, Macmillan wanted to include a date for a summit meeting in the Western reply. He had told Eisenhower that he was "an old man," who "owed a duty to his people." Eisenhower replied that he would not "be dragooned to a Summit meeting." He would attend if there were even the slightest progress at preliminary meetings, but he "absolutely refused to promise unconditionally at this point to go to a Summit meeting 'come hell or high water.'" The two men eventually agreed on compromise language that called for a foreign ministers' meeting to begin on May 11, with a summit meeting to follow "as soon as developments justify" (State, *Foreign Relations, 1958–1960*, vol. VII, pt. 2, *Western Europe*, pp. 845–47; State, *Foreign Relations, 1958–1960*, vol. VIII, *Berlin Crisis 1958–1959*, pp. 522–23, 532; and Eisenhower, *Waging Peace*, p. 355; see also Telephone

conversations, Herter and Goodpaster, Mar. 12, 1959, Herter Papers, Telephone Conversations). The final text of the reply, which would be sent to the Soviet Union on March 26, is in *U.S. Department of State Bulletin* 40, no. 1033 [April 13, 1959], 507–11.
[3] See nos. 1106 and 1112.
[4] The Ministerial Meeting of the North Atlantic Council, held in Washington April 2–4, included the foreign ministers and permanent NATO representatives of the fifteen member nations, except Greece and Iceland (State, *Foreign Relations, 1958–1960,* vol. VII, pt. 1, *Western European Integration and Security; Canada,* pp. 447–54; and State, *Foreign Relations, 1958–1960,* vol. VIII, *Berlin Crisis 1958–1959,* pp. 576–84).
[5] The report of the Four-Power Working Group included a review of Soviet and Allied objectives regarding Berlin, security measures in Europe, methods of reunifying Germany, and the future status of a reunified Germany and Berlin. For the discussions among the foreign ministers of the United States, Great Britain, France, and the Federal Republic of Germany see *ibid.,* pp. 553–73; see also pp. 482–83, 529.
[6] For background on contingency planning see no. 1079; and Telephone conversation, Herter and Goodpaster, Mar. 13, 1959, Herter Papers, Telephone Conversations. On the meetings of the Berlin Contingency Planning Group see State, *Foreign Relations, 1958–1960,* vol. VIII, *Berlin Crisis 1958–1959,* pp. 441–44, 456–59, 471–78; see also *ibid.,* pp. 495–99; and Burr, "Avoiding the Slippery Slope," pp. 201–3. The plans Acting Secretary Herter and Defense Secretary McElroy had presented to Eisenhower included provisions for test flights above 10,000 feet in and out of Berlin, details of the composition of the first units to enter the Berlin corridors after the announced takeover by East German officials, and alternative uses of force to maintain access to Berlin (*ibid.,* pp. 500–501; see also Telephone conversation, Herter and Goodpaster, Mar. 13, 1959, Herter Papers, Telephone Conversations). Macmillan had told Eisenhower that the British had not prepared a contingency plan, and the two men discussed the issue of interference or obstruction, ways to develop a tripartite plan, and the desirability of taking the issue to the United Nations (*ibid.,* pp. 527–29).
[7] On the tripartite meetings see *ibid.,* pp. 240–44, 249–53, 311–14, 398–400.
[8] The foreign ministers would begin meetings in Geneva on May 11.
[9] For background on the Soviet economic initiatives see Galambos and van Ee, *The Middle Way,* nos. 1653 and 1870; and no. 603 in these volumes.
[10] See no. 1106.
[11] The tripartite talks would begin on April 16 (see State, *Foreign Relations, 1958–1960,* vol. XIV, *Africa,* pp. 44–53).
[12] In his response de Gaulle would tell Eisenhower that he was pleased that the President and Prime Minister Macmillan had agreed with him on the need to be firm with the Soviets on the Berlin issue (State, *Foreign Relations, 1958–1960,* vol. VIII, *Berlin Crisis 1958–1959,* p. 191; see also Calhoun to Goodpaster, Apr. 1, 1959, AWF/I: de Gaulle). For developments see nos. 1132 and 1169.

1117

EM, AWF,
Dulles-Herter Series

TO CHRISTIAN ARCHIBALD HERTER
Secret

March 24, 1959

Memorandum for the Acting Secretary of State: I have already sent you a copy of the Prime Minister's note to me dated March twenty-third.

I think the Economic Division of the State Department should study thoroughly the latter half of his note.[1]

Even though the matter may not necessarily be one to be taken up by the Security Council, I think that a presentation of State's view as to the damage caused by additional trade restrictions should be presented at an early meeting of the Council.

It seems to me important that when OCDM is required to make a judgment as to the effect on our nation's security of certain imports, that there should be taken into consideration the effects on that same security of particular restrictions.[2]

In advance of any presentation at the NSC of State's view on this matter, I believe you should arrange to discuss the matter with OCDM, Defense, Commerce and the Chairman of the Council of Economic Advisers.[3]

[1] During Macmillan's five-day visit to Washington he and Eisenhower had discussed the restrictions placed upon British exports by the U.S. government (see State, *Foreign Relations, 1958–1960*, vol. IV, *Foreign Economic Policy*, pp. 42–43, 199–201; see also *Public Papers of the Presidents: Eisenhower, 1959*, pp. 295–96). Macmillan's letter had referred to the importation of woolen textiles and heavy electrical equipment, especially turbines and large generating equipment. Excluding the latter class of imports "would be a serious blow" to U.S.-British relations, Macmillan said, and no one in Britain would understand the national security argument. "Protectionism is very good at finding all kinds of cloaks to disguise itself, but it remains the same underneath" (PREM 11/2684 and AWF/I: Macmillan; see also Macmillan, *Riding the Storm*, pp. 648–49, 650; on the selection of U.S. turbines over British imports for the Greer's Ferry Dam see no. 1033).

[2] For other actions of the Office of Civil and Defense Mobilization (the Office of Defense Mobilization until July 1958) regarding imports and national security see no. 261.

[3] Herter would tell Eisenhower that the State Department was "very conscious" of the problem and that he would meet with representatives from the departments Eisenhower had listed as well as with Special Presidential Assistants Don Paarlberg and Clarence Randall (Herter to Eisenhower, Mar. 25, 1959, AWF/D-H; see also Telephone conversations, Herter and Paarlberg, Mar. 27, 1959; and Herter and Saulnier, Mar. 30, 1959, Herter Papers, Telephone Conversations).

On May 11 representatives from all of the interested government departments had unanimously disagreed with OCDM Director Leo Hoegh's determination that national security was adversely affected by the importation of hydraulic turbines (State, *Foreign Relations, 1958–1960*, vol. IV, *Foreign Economic Policy*, pp. 206–9). After meeting with Hoegh on May 29, Eisenhower would tell the National Security Council that the U.S. decision against the importation of British electrical equipment had caused "near hysteria" in Britain. Such trade restrictions, he said, would do much more harm in the long run to U.S. security than forcing an American industry to respond to British competition (NSC meeting minutes, June 4, 1959, AWF/NSC).

Later this year, Eisenhower and Macmillan would emphasize the importance of international trade during the President's visit to Great Britain (see State, *American Foreign Policy, Current Documents, 1959*, p. 909; see also no. 1282).

To Clifford Roberts   *March 24, 1959*

Dear Cliff: The impact of the Macmillan talks was as nothing compared to the shattering news of your 75, especially to that 35 on the
second nine.[1]

In searching my mind for the secret of your success, I have decided only that marriage is a wonderfully steadying institution.[2] Just
think what your regular score might now be if you had adopted it
earlier in life!

With warm regard, *As ever*

P.S. It's still on the lap of the Gods about April sixth.[3]

[1] British Prime Minister Macmillan had met with the President at Camp David March
20–22. On the discussions see nos. 1095 and 1116.

[2] Roberts had attended the Jamboree at Augusta National Golf Club and planned to
return for the Masters Tournament the week of April 1 (see Ann Whitman memorandum, [Mar. 11, 1959], AWF/N, Roberts Corr.). On Roberts's recent marriage see
no. 984.

[3] Eisenhower was referring to his traditional holiday in Augusta, Georgia, the week
following the Masters Tournament (for background see Galambos and van Ee, *The
Middle Way*, no. 535). As it turned out, the Eisenhowers would leave for Augusta on
April 7. The President would return briefly to Washington April 13–14, and would
remain in Augusta until April 21 (see Telephone Calls, Eisenhower and Mrs. Eisenhower, Apr. 6, 1959, AWF/D; and Eisenhower to Roberts, Mar. 12, 1959, AWF/N).

1119   *EM, WHCF, Official File 107-B*

To Deane Emmett Ackers   *March 26, 1959*
Personal

Dear Deane: Your letter of the twenty-fourth followed me up here to
Gettysburg, where Mamie and I are for the Easter holiday. I was delighted to hear from you.[1]

Your first paragraph troubles me and I do want to correct the misapprehension you had with regard to Sherman Adams' role in the
White House.[2] He was one of the most valuable and dedicated staff
officers I have ever known, but never did he attempt to interfere
with communications from my personal friends or, for that matter,
keep anything unfavorable from me. He presented to the public, at
times, a gruff and forbidding exterior simply because he was always
harassed and pressed for time. Contrary to that exterior, he is a perfectly delightful personality, and I feel badly that friends such as you
would believe otherwise.

As to the budget—today I had a letter from an informed friend in banking circles in New York.[3] He believes the tide has turned. Certain votes in the Congress have likewise been mildly encouraging.

In answer to your question as to what more you can do to help, I believe that in your conversations you are probably starting a chain reaction that is more important than you realize.[4] Some companies are distributing pamphlets to stockholders and to employees pointing out the dangers of inflation to the individual family; these seem to be highly effective.[5] Everyone should, at all times, suggest letters to the Congressional delegations; the members of the Congress pay close attention to the mail they get from home. If you have any influence with any magazines or newspapers, you might also suggest an article or a series of articles on the subject. In certain parts of the country radio and television facilities have effectively been used.[6]

I did not mean this to be quite so much of a "lecture"; I started out merely to thank you most deeply for your support on this important issue.

With warm regard, *As ever*

[1] A high-school classmate of Eisenhower, Ackers was president of the Kansas Power and Light Company. His March 24 letter is in the same file as the document.
[2] Concerned about inflation, Ackers had written to say that he had never before "bothered" Eisenhower with his opinions because he felt that "as long as Adams was sitting at the outer door, my comments would probably never get by him."
[3] See no. 1121.
[4] Ackers had written that he was "100% behind your position in attempting to counteract and offset the political whims of the spendthrifts. I only wish that there were some contributions that I could make other than talking with my friends and acquaintances in a comparatively limited circle."
[5] See no. 1108.
[6] See no. 1073.

1120   *EM, Official File 101-Y*

TO STANLEY HOFLUND HIGH   *March 26, 1959*
Personal

Dear Stanley: Ann tells me that you have had another bout with illness and, indeed, that you were hospitalized for a time. I am sorry and I do hope that you will keep in good order that clean bill of health that the doctors now give you.

I wouldn't want to be quoted, but can't you sell Mr. Wallace on doing a constructive piece on the accomplishments of the Administration? Despite our critics, I think the record is a good one. I feel, further, that we have fallen down somewhere along the line in "selling" that record. If you did decide to do the story (and I can think of no one better equipped to do it), I can assure you that we would be helpful in every possible way.[1]

But the main purpose of this note is simply to say "take care of yourself."

With warm regard to you and Mrs. High, *Sincerely*

[1] *Reader's Digest* senior editor High would initially respond with enthusiasm: "How I'd love the assignment!" (High to Eisenhower, [Mar. 31, 1959], and High to Merriam, Apr. 6, 1959, both in same file as document). He would later decide, however, to postpone writing such an article. Deputy Assistant to the President Robert E. Merriam would report that High and *Digest* publisher DeWitt Wallace (for background see Galambos, *NATO and the Campaign of 1952*, no. 277) wanted to hold off because there were numerous other articles concerning the Administration in the works; they did not want to be known as "The Republican Digest" (Merriam to Persons, Apr. 9, 1959, same file as document; for developments see no. 1296).

1121   *EM, AWF, Administration Series*

To Gabriel Hauge   *March 27, 1959*

Dear Gabe: Your interesting letter of the twenty-third followed me up here to Gettysburg, where Mamie and I are trying to get a little much-needed rest.[1] A few of the early flowers are out, but in general the countryside is still gray and dull.

I cannot quarrel with any of your observations, particularly with regard to the imperfections in the television speech last week.[2] But if the net result was, to use your own term, "effective" I am content. When I get approval in the same mail from such diverse personalities as my brother Edgar and C. D. Jackson, for instance, I judge that the effort was at least not in vain![3]

As far as the budget goes, there are evidences that more and more people are taking up the cudgels for our position. I understand the A.T. and T. sent out a statement to its large number of stockholders;[4] the Chamber of Commerce is distributing to some one hundred thousand an exchange between Mr. McDonnell and myself.[5] Some of the votes in Congress have been encouraging by virtue mainly of the number of Southern Democrats who have joined with the majority of the Republicans. The legislation that worries me the most at the moment is the mutual security appropriations; you know how vital I consider that part of our whole defense effort.[6]

Just before I left Washington, Nelson telephoned the office. He is greatly relieved by the closing of his first legislative session. From all I can judge, he seems to have come through it remarkably well.[7]

Do send me frequent reports from that other end of the telescope. I am always glad to have your suggestions and, as I have told you so many times, I value highly your opinions.

Give my affectionate regard to all the members of your nice family and, of course, the best to yourself. *As ever*

[1] Hauge's letter is in AWF/A. Eisenhower would vacation in Gettysburg from March 26–30.

[2] On March 16 the President had delivered a radio and television address on "Security in a Free World." Eisenhower had discussed the situation in Berlin and the state of American military preparedness (see no. 1107; see also *Public Papers of the Presidents: Eisenhower, 1959*, pp. 273–82). Hauge had commented that he thought the speech was "effective." "The structure was a little unusual but the points about the connection of a sensible defense establishment and a mutual security program with the Berlin crisis was clearly made." Hauge felt that the charts on missiles had not been as clear as necessary, and he noted that Eisenhower's glasses kept sliding down his nose. "Basically, however,—and this is what ninety percent of the people look for—you came through as Mr. No. 1, vigorous in health, calm and confident in spirit, and determined to [do] what was necessary to represent them in the maze of foreign affairs."

[3] Jackson's letter is not in AWF. Edgar Eisenhower had forwarded a letter from a Seattle lawyer who had approved of the President's March 16 speech (Edgar Eisenhower to Eisenhower, Mar. 23, 1959, and Whitman to Edgar Eisenhower, Mar. 27, 1959, AWF/N, Edgar Eisenhower Corr.).

[4] See no. 1108.

[5] William Archie McDonnell (LL.B. Vanderbilt University 1917) was chairman of the board of the First National Bank, St. Louis, and brother of James Smith McDonnell, Jr., the president and founder of McDonnell Aircraft Corporation, St. Louis. He was also chairman of the board of directors of the U.S. Chamber of Commerce. Eisenhower had written McDonnell that he hoped Chamber of Commerce members would "seize the opportunity" of the Easter recess to encourage representatives and senators to vote against legislation that would unbalance the budget. Eisenhower's letter had been published in the Chamber's newsletter, *Washington Report* (see *New York Times*, Apr. 2, 1959; Eisenhower's correspondence with McDonnell is not in AWF).

[6] See *Public Papers of the Presidents: Eisenhower, 1959*, pp. 255–72; see also *Congressional Quarterly Almanac*, vol. XV, *1959*, pp. 178–94.

[7] For background see nos. 1047 and 1061. For developments see no. 1124.

1122
EM, AWF, International Series:
Macmillan

TO HAROLD MACMILLAN
March 27, 1959
Cable. Secret

Dear Harold: Thank you for the note that was delivered to me within a half hour after you left on your return flight to London. I am glad that you and the members of your party liked—despite the cold weather—the informal Camp David atmosphere; for my part I too felt that the absence of protocol and social "appearances" enabled us to discuss our problems more frankly and more thoroughly than would have been possible in Washington.[1]

Those of us in our government who are charged with the responsibility for international relations have not been insensible to the problem you pose in your final substantive paragraph. Acting on my request, priority is now being given to a thorough study of the entire matter. I understand your position thoroughly, as I hope you do the pressures that the advocates of trade restrictions are able to assert in this country.[2]

This note is necessarily brief, since I am in Gettysburg for a little rest over this Easter holiday.[3] I shall write to you later at length.[4]

Again let me tell you what a real pleasure it was to have you as my guest.

With warm regard, *As ever*

[1] For background on Macmillan's visit to Camp David see no. 1093. On March 23 Macmillan had thanked the President for the "happy and friendly surroundings" in which they had discussed international questions (AWF/I: Macmillan).

[2] Macmillan had referred to U.S. restrictions on the importation of British woolen textiles and such major electrical products as turbines and large generating equipment. Exclusion of these items would be a "serious blow to our relations," Macmillan said, because the British would not understand the U.S. plea that national security called for protection. For developments see no. 1117.

[3] The Eisenhowers had arrived in Gettysburg on March 26. They would celebrate the Easter holiday with their son John and his family, and would return to the White House on Monday, March 30.

[4] See no. 1127.

1123   *EM, AWF,*
                                              International Series: Cambodia

To Samdech Preah Norodom Sihanouk Upayvareach
Cable. Secret   *March 28, 1959*

Dear Prince Sihanouk: I have given most serious thought to your letter of February 23, 1959, which I acknowledged on February 26.[1] Your expression of friendly regard and confidence recalled to my mind the mutual understanding we affirmed on the occasion of your visit to my country last year.[2] Therefore, I have received your letter in this spirit of amity and frankness, and wish to respond to it in the same vein.

I gather from your letter that the difficulties you describe stem essentially from misunderstandings in the relationships between your country and some of its neighbors. The resolution of such underlying problems depends primarily, I believe, on the actions and attitudes of the countries directly concerned. Nevertheless, the existence of amicable relations among all free nations, and particularly among those with which the United States shares close bonds of friendship, is of vital interest to me. Therefore, I was glad to request the Department of State to consult the Governments of Thailand and of the Republic of Viet-Nam in the context of our friendly relations with these countries.[3]

In the course of those consultations, the Government of Thailand affirmed its respect for the sovereignty and integrity of the Royal Cambodian Government. It expressed the opinion that internal disorder and instability in Cambodia would be harmful to the interests of the Free World and serve only the designs of international communism whose expanding activities in the area are of grave concern to Thailand. Furthermore, it indicated its willingness to cooperate with the Royal Cambodian Government in strengthening friendly relations on the basis of mutual respect and consistent good will. Finally, the Government of Thailand as a member of the Southeast Asia Treaty Organization reaffirmed its respect for the sovereign right of the Royal Cambodian Government as well as that of any other government to decide whether or not it wishes to adhere to Free World collective security arrangements.

In discussions with Government of the Republic of Viet-Nam, that Government expressed its disapproval of any actions against the independence and liberty of Cambodia. It reaffirmed its desire to maintain friendly relations on a reciprocal basis with the Royal Cambodian Government as well as other Free World countries. The Government of the Republic of Viet-Nam also proposed in these discussions specific means of jointly controlling illegal activities in the Cambodian-Vietnamese frontier zone. The Government of the Republic of Viet-Nam expressed the convictions that agreement with the Royal Cambodian Government on such proposals would promote the maintenance of the best relations.

I trust that these views of the Governments of Thailand and of the Republic of Viet-Nam, if combined with an attitude of conciliation and good will on the part of the Royal Cambodian Government, will provide the basis for an improvement in mutual understanding and confidence between your country and its neighbors, which in turn will permit the three nations to develop sound, direct relations through normal diplomatic channels. I have discussed the substance of your letter with The Honorable William C. Trimble, whom His Majesty The King has agreed to accept as our new Ambassador at Phnom

Penh, and expect to forward through him additional thoughts on this subject.[4]

My impression that the difficulties you describe stem essentially from inter-relationships between your country and its neighbors, does not ignore certain obligations which the United States incurs in the extension of American military assistance. You correctly perceive that the purpose of this assistance is to help free nations defend their independence. Just as we sought in Cambodia to insure certain safeguards on the use of this aid, we have sought and will continue to seek to insure that other governments use our assistance only for the purposes intended. The United States attaches the utmost importance to these international obligations.

Your proposal for supervised elections in Cambodia appears to involve a purely internal Cambodian matter on which I believe I cannot appropriately comment.[5] At the same time, the United States Government has no reservation whatsoever in reaffirming its continued recognition of your full attributes and prerogatives as the President of the Council of Ministers of the Kingdom of Cambodia.

I was distressed to hear of the illness of His Majesty King Norodom Suramarit and I take this opportunity to express my personal best wishes for your father's rapid and complete recovery.[6]

With warm regard. *Sincerely*

[1] For Sihanouk's letter and Eisenhower's interim response see no. 1085. Sihanouk had complained that South Vietnam and Thailand were plotting, possibly with American assistance, to overthrow Cambodia's government. Colonel John S. D. Eisenhower had kept his father informed of these developments; see J. S. D. Eisenhower, Synopsis of State and Intelligence Material Reported to the President, January 2–3, March 6–7, 24, 1959, AWF/D. State Department officials had drafted this message after consultations with the governments of Thailand and South Vietnam (see Herter to Eisenhower, Mar. 27, AWF/I: Cambodia; see also State, *Foreign Relations, 1958–1960*, vol. XVI, *East Asia–Pacific Region; Cambodia; Laos*, pp. 300–301).

[2] The Cambodian prime minister had met with Eisenhower, Secretary Dulles, and other State Department officials on September 30. They had discussed the Communist threat in Southeast Asia and the neutrality of the Cambodian state (see *ibid.*, pp. 253–56).

[3] Two weeks of consultations between the U.S. embassies in Bangkok and Saigon and the host governments had begun on March 10 (*ibid.*, p. 300; see also Herter to Eisenhower, Mar. 27, 1959, AWF/I: Cambodia).

[4] William Cattell Trimble (Princeton 1930), former minister and deputy chief of mission in Rio de Janeiro and Bonn, had become U.S. Ambassador to Cambodia on February 16. Because of Sihanouk's departure for medical treatment in France, Trimble would deliver the oral message, drafted by the State Department, to the Cambodian minister of foreign affairs (Suggested Statement from the President to Prince Sihanouk to be Delivered Orally by Ambassador Trimble, AWF/I: Cambodia; see also Herter to Eisenhower, Mar. 14, 1959, *ibid.*; and State, *Foreign Relations, 1958–1960*, vol. XVI, *East Asia–Pacific Region; Cambodia; Laos*, p. 305).

[5] Sihanouk had told Eisenhower that in order to assure his neighbors that the Cambodian government was not a dictatorship, he was willing to resign, dissolve the na-

tional assembly, and call for new elections in which all parties could freely participate (Sihanouk to Eisenhower, Feb. 23, 1959, AWF/I: Cambodia).
[6] We have been unable to document the nature of King Suramarit's illness.

The U.S. Chargé would tell State Department officials that both Sihanouk and the
Cambodian foreign minister were disappointed with Eisenhower's letter (State, *For-
eign Relations, 1958–1960*, vol. XVI, *East Asia–Pacific Region; Cambodia; Laos*, p. 302).
For developments see no. 1152.

1124   *EM, AWF,*
                                                         Administration Series

To Nelson Aldrich Rockefeller   *March 30, 1959*
Personal

Dear Nelson: Thank you for your two letters. I was interested both in
your summary of the budget situation and in the resume of the more
important legislative measures passed.[1]

No one who knows you could ever accuse you of "soaking the
poor", but statements like that are the delight of the press and the
opposition, as well you know.[2]

Now that your difficult first three months are over, I hope you can
relax a bit.[3] Incidentally, that business of having a legislative session
of only three months strikes me as a very wise procedure, something
I would not mind at all seeing adopted here on the national scene!

Congratulations—and warm regard, *As ever*

[1] Rockefeller's letters of March 25 and 27 (AWF/A) dealt with the final results of
the New York legislative session. For background see nos. 1047 and 1061. Rockefeller
had reported that his objective for the New York State budget was to apply a "pay-
as-you-go" philosophy in order to close a $424 million gap between expenditures and
revenue. He had therefore cut requested budget increases by fifty percent and increased taxes by $277 million. The state increased gasoline taxes by two cents a gal-
lon and cigarette taxes by two cents a pack. Rockefeller had also increased the number of days of horse racing at New York's racetracks, raised estate taxes, and instituted
a state tax withholding system.
[2] On January 31, 1958, the New York State Democratic party chairman had labeled
Rockefeller's tax program a "soak the poor fiscal package" that would weigh the heav-
iest upon the two-thirds of the taxpayers who earned less than $6,000 a year. Much
criticism had been directed at Rockefeller's plan to raise gasoline and cigarette taxes
(*New York Times*, Feb. 1, 1959). The legislature had passed the budget on March 11
(*New York Times*, Mar. 12, 1959).
[3] The New York State legislature had ended its session on March 27, 1959 (for a summary of its legislative actions see *New York Times*, Mar. 27, 28, 1959).

To Hugh Meade Alcorn, Jr.   *April 1, 1959*

Dear Meade: Your decision to resign as Chairman of the Republican National Committee causes me great regret, as I know it will the vast number of Republicans with whom you have worked closely during the twenty-six months of your stewardship. The zeal with which you have devoted yourself to the work of the Party has been an inspiration to all those who are fostering Republican ideals at every level of government.[1]

You have been an outstanding spokesman for our Party, and have represented it forthrightly and with honor throughout the length and breadth of the land. The program which you have recently initiated to build for the future will, I confidently expect, be a major milestone in Republican history.[2]

Particularly heartening to me has been your constant emphasis upon the role of youth. On the vision and the vigor that they bring to the councils of our Party depends significantly the ability of Republicans, as a political entity, to contribute through future decades to the shaping of sound and effective governmental policies. I am confident that in their achievements to come, you will see frequent and satisfying reflections of your own dedicated efforts.[3]

Although you will soon be relinquishing your official responsibilities as Chairman, I know there will be many calls on you for further assistance, and I hope to see you often as you visit here.

With gratitude for your fine services, and warm personal regard, *Sincerely*

P.S. Not long ago I saw a copy of the Resolution of thanks for your services adopted by the National Committee at its meeting in Des Moines. I agree with every word the Committee had to say; the Resolution expresses the affection, admiration and respect in which the rank and file of the Republican Party hold you.

[1] Alcorn, who had served as Republican National Committee chairman since February 1, 1958 (see no. 20), had written Eisenhower on April 1, 1959 (AWF/A), of his intention to submit his resignation on April 10. He intended to return to his law practice in Connecticut (see *New York Times*, Apr. 1, 2, 1959).

[2] Following the November 1958 election defeats (see nos. 926 and 935), Eisenhower had been pressured to fire Alcorn (see no. 962). Eisenhower had refused. The President would later write that Alcorn's "intelligence, energy, imagination, and dedication had been exemplary. Indeed, he had worked so hard during the campaign that at times I feared he might be risking his health" (Eisenhower, *Waging Peace*, p. 382).

On the Republican Committee on Programs and Progress see no. 963; see also no. 1025.

[3] See no. 590; for background on the President's interest in bringing young people into the Republican party see Galambos and van Ee, *The Middle Way*, nos. 1782 and 1852.

To John Foster Dulles   *April 2, 1959*

Dear Foster: I hope the Florida weather is being kinder to you than the Washington variety has been today to the NATO visitors. It has rained steadily almost the entire day.[1]

The meeting this morning seemed to go well; I thought the arrangements made by State were efficiently handled. Before I gave my brief talk of welcome, I listened to the remarks by Herter, President Luns and Spaak. Luns was, as you could have expected, interminable.[2]

The luncheon seemed to go fairly well and I found myself giving another little talk stressing the fact that the whole destiny of Western civilization is bound up in NATO, and that we were, for our part, proud to be associates with these countries.[3]

I didn't pick up much information that would be new to you. The Germans are showing, I think, some signs of uncertainty as to their best position. Blankenhorn is being replaced, as I am sure you know, over a "scrap of paper."[4]

Saturday I give my lecture on mutual security at Gettysburg College and then, I hope, I shall have a breather for at least a week in Augusta.[5]

The newspapers report that you have been swimming, which ought to be helpful in getting your strength back. Everyone I talked with today asked about you, and sent their very best wishes. You are greatly missed.

With warm regard, *As ever*

[1] After receiving treatment for cancer at Walter Reed Hospital, Secretary Dulles had left on March 30 for the Palm Beach home of Under Secretary of State C. Douglas Dillon. The North Atlantic Council Ministerial Meeting, which would last for three days, had begun in Washington on this same day.

[2] The opening ceremony celebrated the tenth anniversary of the North Atlantic Treaty Organization. Eisenhower's remarks as well as those of Acting Secretary of State Herter, Honorary President of the Council and Foreign Minister of the Netherlands Joseph Marie Antoine Hubert Luns, and Secretary General Paul-Henri Spaak are in *U.S. Department of State Bulletin* 40, no. 1034 [April 20, 1959], 543–53. On the conference proceedings see State, *Foreign Relations, 1958–1960*, vol. VII, pt. 1, *Western European Integration and Security; Canada,* pp. 447–54.

[3] Eisenhower had hosted a luncheon for the delegates and the ambassadors of the NATO countries (see Ann Whitman memorandum, Apr. 2, 1959, AWF/AWD).

[4] Herbert A. von Blankenhorn, former West German Permanent Representative to NATO, had recently been appointed Ambassador to France. On March 2 he had gone on trial for falsely accusing a civil service colleague of accepting bribes. He would receive a four-month suspended sentence after his conviction on April 23 and an indefinite leave of absence from his diplomatic post (*New York Times,* Mar. 3, Apr. 23, 24, 1959).

[5] The speech, on which, according to Ann Whitman, the President had spent "an in-

1127

EM, AWF, International Series:
Macmillan

To Harold Macmillan
Cable. Secret

April 4, 1959

Dear Harold: One of the most heartening aspects of our talks here was the accord we found in our strong convictions as to the importance of the negotiations in Geneva for the controlled suspension of nuclear weapons tests.[1] These talks offer the one early possibility for a first step toward enforceable disarmament and toward control over the future development and spread of modern means of destruction.

I have been giving further thought to what we might do to revitalize these negotiations. I believe it is important to give a note of hope to the talks. We cannot achieve this merely by resuming interminable wranglings over the veto and the composition of inspection teams. If that is what faces our negotiators then I think there will be increasing discouragement in our own countries and throughout the world.

What we might do is make clear immediately that these important differences in approach need not be a bar to putting into effect promptly the elements of a control system which are not in dispute—control posts and agreed aircraft flights, together with the banning of the atmospheric tests which these elements can adequately monitor. As fast as the political and technical problems of monitoring underground and outer space tests are worked out, an initial agreement would, of course, be broadened to include these also.

What I propose is the very opposite of an ultimatum. We would make clear by our statements and actions that we are prepared and determined to continue negotiating a comprehensive test suspension agreement. We would simply be offering a way to get started promptly in a limited area of agreement, if the Soviets remain adamant on the veto. Indeed, between us, I think that advancing such a reasonable alternative course of action may be the only effective way to test the real Soviet position on the veto.

The Soviets are no doubt considering their own moves. We should act when talks resume on April 13, if we are to retain leadership and to take action to restore a sense of purpose and hope in the negotiations. Our representatives might make carefully prepared statements at the opening session in Geneva on April 13, recapitulating the progress and difficulties in the negotiations, and pointing out the possibility of action to capitalize immediately on the areas of agreement already reached or in prospect.

Simultaneously letters from you and me to Premier Khrushchev, perhaps along the lines of the enclosed draft, might be delivered in Moscow endorsing the approach. In order that our suggestion might not seem to be advanced as a propagandistic gesture, it might be made privately and released publicly only after sufficient time for a Soviet response—unless, of course, a premature leak forces our hand.[2]

These thoughts are being discussed here with Selwyn and your Embassy. Because I believe we have an opportunity to give a new and sounder impulse to these negotiations, I wanted to bring them to your attention directly and to hear your views.[3]

With warm regard, *As ever*

[1] For background on the Geneva negotiations, which had adjourned until April 13, and the Camp David discussions regarding the issue see nos. 1093 and 1116; see also State, *Foreign Relations, 1958–1960,* vol. III, *National Security Policy; Arms Control and Disarmament,* pp. 720–29. State Department officials drafted this letter to the British Prime Minister (see Herter to Eisenhower, Apr. 3, 1959, AWF/D-H).
[2] Eisenhower's message to Khrushchev is no. 1135.
[3] For developments see no. 1129.

1128   *EM, AWF, Name Series*

To George Edward Allen   *April 8, 1959*
Personal

Dear George: On looking over the number of different standards that I am supposed to achieve, per the argument between you and Mrs. Whitman, I see that you have set one much too low to be fair to yourself.[1] By and large I should not *normally* have more than three or four double bogeys.[2] Consequently, I am sending you this note to say that I shall from now on play, as far as bogeys are concerned, on the following program:

> I will give you 6 bogeys without taking credit. So far as bogeys are concerned, we will play only on the remaining twelve (except, of course, if I don't even make six bogeys you will get paid—and deserve to).

Now for yesterday's score: I double bogeyed holes #1 and #5; I had four pars and one birdie; the rest were bogeys.[3]

I will try to get this message to you as soon as possible so that you will know the new conditions.[4] *As ever*

[1] The President was vacationing in Augusta, Georgia (see no. 1118). Presidential Secretary Ann Whitman and Allen had spoken on the telephone several times on April 2 (see Telephone conversations, AWF/D). For background on Eisenhower's golf wagers with Allen see, for example, Galambos and van Ee, *The Middle Way*, no. 1988 (see also Whitman to Allen, May 31, 1958, AWF/A, and The President's Scores, Augusta, Nov. 20–Dec. 2, 1958, AWF/A, Allen Corr.).

[2] A bogey is one stroke over par; a double bogey is two strokes over par.

[3] A birdie is one stroke under par. If par was 72, then Eisenhower would have scored 86.

[4] On April 18 Allen would join the President at Augusta. They would return to Washington on April 21.

1129
EM, AWF, International Series:
Macmillan

To Harold Macmillan
April 9, 1959
Cable. Secret

Dear Harold: I have just received your comments on my message to you concerning the Geneva Nuclear Test Conference.[1]

As you will have recognized, my message was mainly an attempt to reduce to writing the tentative agreements that you and I reached during our personal talks at the time of the meeting at Camp David. In accordance with my understanding of what we agreed during our talks, I suggested in my message (A) that we should reopen the Geneva Conference with a restatement of the nuclear test problem and our hopes to secure some kind of an agreement that would not be encumbered by the possibility of veto; and (B) that if the Soviets could not at this time agree to an effective comprehensive control system we should seek an agreement to cease atmospheric tests with only limited control posts. In addition you and I agreed that if we encountered failure even in this limited effort we would nevertheless continue for an unstated period our voluntary abstention from any testing that would further pollute the atmosphere.

In your reply you put forward as an additional proposal the idea that all three nations should informally bind themselves to abstain from every kind of test for a given period without any agreed control system for the underground and high altitude tests, and, should the Soviets refuse to be a party to such a tripartite statement, we would on our side nevertheless announce our readiness to abstain for one or two years.

While time does not permit an exhaustive study and final conclusion on your new suggestion, frankly, Harold, I think that for us to announce such an intention would weaken our position seriously.

While such a moratorium would have a considerable propaganda impact, I fear that, once we committed ourselves to do this, the pressure would be on us to continue to withhold testing even if there was no progress in negotiations for extension of the quite limited controls applicable to an atmospheric test suspension. What we want of course is to put pressure on the Soviets to agree to extend controls in order to get tests brought to a halt; I believe this can best be done if we do not reduce our bargaining power in this voluntary way.

It seems to me that, since we have suspended tests for the time being (and the Soviet Union has never felt it necessary to make a similar explicit renunciation), our public posture is not vulnerable. If we are challenged as to our long-range plans we can simply point out that we are not now testing and that it is up to the Soviet Union to demonstrate its intentions in serious negotiation for an atmospheric test ban rather than for us, without any quid pro quo, to answer for the indefinite future. We will not of course want to assert any specific intention to resume underground or high altitude testing.

Incidentally I shall have to ask the State Department to give you the figure our experts use in measuring the upper limit of the earth's atmosphere.[2]

I hope that you will agree to go ahead with the proposal I have sent you, when the talks resume on April 13, without committing ourselves at that time on our long-range testing plans. I think that we will miss a unique opportunity to take a new lead in these negotiations if we are not ready to act then.[3]

With warm personal regard, *As ever*

[1] For background see no. 1127. Two drafts of this message, prepared by State Department officials, include Eisenhower's handwritten emendations (see AWF/I: Macmillan). Macmillan had written Eisenhower that "at first sight" the proposals constituted "a constructive approach" to the problem (Macmillan to Eisenhower, Apr. 6, 1959, AWF/I: Macmillan). In a more detailed message Macmillan told the President that he thought that Eisenhower's offer was reasonable, in accord with current scientific possibilities, and would allay the "public disappointment and criticism" that abandonment of their original, more ambitious objectives would undoubtedly produce. Fearing that the Soviets would not accept any agreement that fell short of a complete ban on all tests, he suggested that the United States and Great Britain propose a moratorium on all tests underground and above 50 kilometers as long as the Soviet Union agreed to do the same. "This moratorium," Macmillan said, "would be a voluntary arrangement outside any formal agreement—thus preserving the important principle that the agreement itself should only commit us to steps which we know can be controlled." Macmillan hoped that during such a moratorium scientific

advances would allow for a more comprehensive ban (Macmillan to Eisenhower, Apr. 8, 1959, PREM 11/2860).

[2] Eisenhower added this paragraph to the State Department draft. In the telegram transmitting this message Acting Secretary Herter had informed the American embassy in London that the figure was 50 kilometers.

[3] For developments see no. 1132.

1130

EM, AWF, International Series: Venezuela

To Rómulo Betancourt
Cable

April 9, 1959

Dear Mr. President:[1] I am most grateful to you for your personal initiative in bringing directly to my attention your proposal to establish the Inter-American Development Bank in Caracas.[2]

Your views and the forthright manner in which you expressed them made a deep impression on me. I truly regret that your telegram did not reach me until after the working group made its decision on Washington as the site for the new institution.[3]

Although this circumstance precluded my consideration of your message before the decision was taken, your Govt's views were well known to our representatives, and I assure you that those views were given most careful consideration.[4]

But after study of all factors, the United States Govt felt obliged to conclude that the technical and practical advantages of having the institution located in Washington, at least in its initial stages, would greatly facilitate the successful establishment of this important venture in hemispheric cooperation. In reaching that conclusion, we had in mind the desirability of selecting a site that would be near the New York money market and existing banking and financial institutions, including the International Bank for Reconstruction and Development, the International Monetary Fund, and the Export-Import Bank of Washington.

I know that you share my deep personal interest in supporting measures which contribute to the general welfare of all the people of this hemisphere. I look forward to the continued association of our two nations in such important projects as the Inter-American Development Bank as a means of achieving the objectives we consider essential to the peace and prosperity of the Americas.

Thank you for making your views known to me in such a friendly fashion; I hope that you will not hesitate to communicate with me in a similar manner in the future.[5] *Sincerely*

¹ Following the overthrow of Venezuelan dictator Marcos Pérez Jiménez (see Galambos and van Ee, *The Middle Way*, no. 1385), Betancourt had become president of his country in December 1958. After World War II he had briefly served as provisional president, but a military coup in 1948 had forced him into exile for almost a decade.
² Betancourt had urged the Eisenhower Administration to support a proposal to locate the new Inter-American Development Bank in Caracas, Venezuela, rather than in Washington. Noting that the committee responsible for the decision was almost evenly divided, Betancourt had hoped to tip the balance in favor of Caracas by swaying Eisenhower. The Organization of American States could bolster its prestige, he had contended, by locating the bank in a Latin American country such as Venezuela, which was a "solvent state" that would not "press the Bank with repeated requests for credit." The United States would "win friends" by demonstrating its commitment to the policy of regional development. He had also implied that the gesture would alleviate "a certain amount of resentment" over the fact that, although the Organization of American States was a partnership of twenty-one governments, its headquarters and agencies functioned "exclusively in the United States" (Telegram, Betancourt to Eisenhower, Apr. 1, 1959, AWF/I: Venezuela).
³ The Inter-American Development Bank had been chartered the day before, on April 8, seventy years after it had first been proposed at the First International Conference on American States. The United States had resisted the idea. Following Milton Eisenhower's fact-finding tour of Central America in 1958, however, he had called for the establishment of the bank (see nos. 947 and 968), and in August of that year Under Secretary of State for Economic Affairs C. Douglas Dillon had announced that the United States would consider establishing such an institution (*U.S. Department of State Bulletin* 39, no. 1001 [September 1, 1958], pp. 347–48). The creation of the bank, which Eisenhower would call in his memoirs a precedent-shattering innovation, would provide direct assistance for increasing economic development and the flow of public capital and would support regional rather than bilateral control of aid funds (Eisenhower, *Waging Peace*, p. 516; for varying assessments see also Kaufman, *Trade and Aid*, pp. 161–75, and Rabe, *Eisenhower and Latin America*, pp. 84–116; see also U.S. Department of State, *Foreign Relations of the United States, 1959–1960*, vol. V, *American Republics*, p. 114; and William Diamond, *Development Banks* [Baltimore, 1957]). Although the Organization of American States had initiated negotiations on its structure, the new institution would function independently, with the United States supplying a significant proportion of the $1 billion initial capitalization funding designated to finance loans in both hard and soft (local) currencies (*ibid.*, pp. 41–42, 219–21; O. Carlos Stoetzer, *The Organization of American States*, 2d ed. [Westport, Conn., 1969], pp. 128–33). For developments see nos. 1170, 1532, 1580, and 1729.
⁴ The State Department, which had drafted this reply, had recommended that the exchange of messages not be made public because Betancourt's cable had "arrived too late for adequate consideration" (Herter to Eisenhower, Apr. 8, 1959; the draft and the President's handwritten changes are all in AWF/I: Venezuela). At this point in the message Eisenhower had deleted this sentence from the draft: "I sincerely regret that this Government was not able to support your proposal." Although the White House had received the cable (in Spanish) on April 2, the day of the vote, the President had not seen an English translation until April 4.
⁵ Betancourt had written that he had taken "the liberty" of sending the cable directly to Eisenhower, he said, because he believed in the "efficacy of direct communication between chiefs of state" (Telegram, Apr. 1, 1959, AWF/I: Venezuela).

To HARRY CECIL BUTCHER   *April 10, 1959*

Dear Butch: If it is any comfort to you, you are not the only one who has suffered, if that is the correct word, by virtue of association with me.[1] I know that my son John feels, at least at times, very much the same.[2] And so do a half dozen people who have at one time or other been closely identified with me. What remedy there is for such a situation I do not possibly know.

With warm regard, *As ever*

---

[1] Butcher had written on April 6 (same file as document) to thank the President for his recent letter (see no. 1104). Butcher also reported that during a recent broadcasters' convention he had learned that members of the FCC had voted against his interests because of his association with Eisenhower. In another instance, a Pentagon official had told Butcher that he was "too closely identified with the President" to be appointed to an advisory committee.

[2] In July 1957 the press had reported that John Eisenhower had considered separating from the Army (see no. 227). On this association, to which John referred as "the long arm of the White House," see his memoir, *Strictly Personal,* pp. 169–202.

To HAROLD MACMILLAN   *April 11, 1959*
Cable. Secret

Dear Harold: Thank you for your prompt reply to my message. You are quite right in your assumption that I did not fully understand your added suggestion.[1]

In view of the shortness of time, I think it would be wisest for us now to proceed with the original plan. I shall send on Monday a message to Khrushchev along the lines of the one I sent you on April 4th.[2] If, on reconsideration, you wish to send a similar detailed message, I will be delighted. If not, I appreciate your offer to send a briefer message and to give the full support of your Delegation at Geneva.[3]

While my hesitancy respecting your proposal arose in part from a misunderstanding, I was also reluctant to enter, even for a short period, into a mutual undertaking with the Soviet Union to abandon underground and high altitude tests without defined or agreed monitoring arrangements. I feared that such a temporary undertaking would not increase prospects of subsequent achievement of a safeguarded agreement banning all tests but rather would have the reverse effect.

Nevertheless should the Soviets turn down the inspected atmospheric ban which we are now proposing, I would of course be delighted to consider again with you the addendum which you have suggested. We are studying the whole thing urgently to be ready to talk to you about it.[4]

With warm regard, *As ever*

[1] For background see no. 1129. State Department officials drafted this message to Macmillan and sent it to Eisenhower in Augusta, Georgia, for his approval. Macmillan had told Eisenhower that he had misunderstood his proposal. The United States and Great Britain would refrain from underground and high altitude tests only if the Soviets agreed to so the same, Macmillan said; their agreement would be an essential part of the arrangement. The formal agreement would ban "altogether and for all time" atmospheric tests up to 50 kilometers—a ban that could be effectively policed. The short-term ban, agreed to by all three powers, would prohibit underground and high-altitude tests. Although this ban could not be policed at first, effective methods of control could be devised later. "I hope this is clear to you," Macmillan wrote, "and I still hope you will consider this a useful adjunct to your first proposal" (Macmillan to Eisenhower, Apr. 10, 1959, PREM 11/2860).

[2] See no. 1127. Eisenhower's letter to Khrushchev is no. 1135.

[3] Macmillan had told Eisenhower that he would not press the issue further, but if the President decided to proceed with the original plan, Macmillan would not send a detailed message to Khrushchev. "I should be perfectly ready to send a brief message saying that you have told me of your plan and that I support it; and of course our delegation at Geneva would give it full support at the conference" (Macmillan to Eisenhower, Apr. 10, 1959, PREM 11/2860).

[4] "I do appreciate the force of the arguments you still bring forward against my proposal," Macmillan would answer. "But I am glad to hear you will be ready to consider it again if the Russians turn down the proposal you originally made." He enclosed a draft message to Khrushchev indicating his support (Macmillan to Eisenhower, Apr. 11, 1959, *ibid.*; see also Eisenhower to Macmillan, Apr. 11, 1959, AWF/I: Macmillan).

Eisenhower would tell Acting Secretary Herter that in announcing a ban on testing for another year, the United States "would really be giving up nothing that we intend to do." Herter would discuss Macmillan's proposal with Presidential Advisor Killian and AEC Chairman McCone on April 13 (Goodpaster, Memorandum of Conference, Apr. 14, 1959, AWF/D; see also State, *Foreign Relations, 1958–1960*, vol. III, *National Security Policy; Arms Control and Disarmament*, pp. 733–34). For developments see no. 1141.

1133   *EM, WHCF, Official File 195*

To Dillon Anderson   *April 11, 1959*

Dear Dillon: Thank you for your letter of the seventh. I am certain that Doug Dillon has been thinking along the lines of what aid we can give in fostering the development of trade between Japan and her neighbors.[1]

Incidentally, one of my friends here tells me that a new air freight system is being set up which will insure Japan's goods being delivered anywhere in the world within a couple of days at a cost, when all things are considered, not appreciably higher than freight shipments. That presents another problem to the economists, but should stimulate Japan's industrial talents considerably!

It was nice to see you.[2]

With warm regard, *As ever*

[1] The President had sent Anderson, Consultant on National Security Affairs, a copy of the convocation address that he had given on April 4, 1959, at Gettysburg College. Anderson had replied that the United States should use its influence to foster trade between Japan and underdeveloped countries in Southeast Asia, a theme that Eisenhower had addressed at Gettysburg (see Galambos and van Ee, *The Middle Way*, no. 816). Anderson thought that a healthy Japanese economy could be an asset in the cold war: "Japan alone in the area is in a position to compete with China and, indeed, due to the great distance of the area from the United States, Japan is in a better position than we are to engage in this competitive struggle over the long pull" (Apr. 7, 1959, same file as document; see also *Public Papers of the Presidents: Eisenhower, 1959*, pp. 310–15). For trade developments see no. 1193.

[2] On the day before the speech, Anderson had discussed his recent trip to Southeast Asia with the President (Ann Whitman memorandum, Apr. 3, 1959, AWF/AWD; President's daily appointments, Apr. 2, 1959).

1134

EM, AWF,
Administration Series

To LEWIS LICHTENSTEIN STRAUSS
Personal

April 11, 1959

Dear Lewis: Personally I have never had the slightest misgiving about your nomination as Secretary of Commerce.[1]

I am concerned lest the delay in your confirmation bother you unduly. And I most certainly am dismayed that some of our so-called "statesmen" could behave in such a childish fashion.

Just remember that any man in political life has to endure things of this kind. At the very least, the editorial comment ought to be a source of satisfaction.[2]

With warm regard, *As ever*

[1] For background on the nomination see no. 725. Strauss had written Eisenhower, "There must come to a President who has made an appointment that is under at-

tack, moments of misgiving as to his selectee and as to the extent that he is supported" (Apr. 10, 1959, AWF/A).

[2] The Senate Interstate and Foreign Commerce Committee had already delayed the
Strauss nomination hearings that were to have begun February 25, 1959. Senator
Estes Kefauver had initially requested a postponement pending a reply from the Jus-
tice Department to his inquiry on Strauss's role in the Dixon-Yates contract. Strauss
had given two days of testimony on March 17 and 18, but on April 8 Committee
Chairman Warren Grant Magnuson had announced another indefinite delay (*Con-
gressional Quarterly Almanac*, vol. X, *1959*, pp. 665–66). For developments see no. 1215;
Eisenhower, *Waging Peace*, pp. 392–96, and Strauss, *Men and Decisions*, pp. 375–403.

With the same letter the nominee had included "a sampling" of (apparently favorable) "editorials from across the country in Republican, Democratic and Independent newspapers."

1135

*EM, AWF,
International Series:
Khrushchev*

To Nikita Sergeyevich Khrushchev

April 13, 1959

Dear Mr. Chairman: Today the Geneva negotiations for the discontinuance of nuclear weapons tests are resuming.[1] During the recess
I have considered where we stand in these negotiations and what
the prospects are for the successful conclusion which I earnestly desire. I have also talked with Prime Minister Macmillan, who reported
to me of his frank discussions on this matter with you.[2]

The United States strongly seeks a lasting agreement for the discontinuance of nuclear weapons tests. We believe that this would be
an important step toward reduction of international tensions and
would open the way to further agreement on substantial measures
of disarmament.

Such an agreement must, however, be subject to fully effective
safeguards to insure the security interests of all parties, and we believe that present proposals of the Soviet Union fall short of providing assurance of the type of effective control in which all parties
can have confidence: therefore, no basis for agreement is now in
sight.

In my view, these negotiations must not be permitted completely
to fail. If indeed the Soviet Union insists on the veto on the fact finding activities of the control system with regard to possible underground detonations, I believe that there is a way in which we can
hold fast to the progress already made in these negotiations and no
longer delay in putting into effect the initial agreements which are
within our grasp. Could we not, Mr. Chairman, put the agreement

into effect in phases beginning with a prohibition of nuclear weapons tests in the atmosphere? A simplified control system for atmospheric tests up to fifty kilometers could be readily derived from the Geneva experts' report, and would not require the automatic on-site inspection which has created the major stumbling block in the negotiations so far.[3]

My representative is putting forward this suggestion in Geneva today.[4] I urge your serious consideration of this possible course of action. If you are prepared to change your present position on the veto, on procedures for on-site inspection, and on early discussion of concrete measures for high altitude detection, we can of course proceed promptly in the hope of concluding the negotiation of a comprehensive agreement for suspension of nuclear weapons tests. If you are not yet ready to go this far, then I propose that we take the first and readily attainable step of an agreed suspension of nuclear weapons tests in the atmosphere up to fifty kilometers while the political and technical problems associated with control of underground and outer space tests are being resolved. If we could agree to such initial implementation of the first—and I might add the most important—phase of a test suspension agreement, our negotiators could continue to explore with new hope the political and technical problems involved in extending the agreement as quickly as possible to cover all nuclear weapons tests. Meanwhile, fears of unrestricted resumption of nuclear weapons testing with attendant additions to levels of radioactivity would be allayed, and we would be gaining practical experience and confidence in the operation of an international control system.

I trust that one of these paths to agreement will commend itself to you and permit the resuming negotiations to make a far-reaching response to the hopes of mankind.[5] *Sincerely*

[1] This letter was drafted by State Department officials and sent to the U.S. embassy in Moscow for delivery to Khrushchev as early as possible on this date. An earlier draft with Eisenhower's handwritten emendations is in AWF/D-H. For background on the negotiations, which had recessed on March 20, see nos. 1132 and 1103.

[2] See State, *Foreign Relations, 1958–1960*, vol. III, *National Security Policy; Arms Control and Disarmament*, pp. 720–27.

[3] This sentence was added to the original draft after consultation with British Prime Minister Macmillan (see no. 1129).

[4] U.S. Ambassador James J. Wadsworth's statement is in the *New York Times*, April 14, 1959.

[5] For Khrushchev's response see no. 1147; for other developments see no. 1141.

To Lewis Lichtenstein Strauss   *April 13, 1959*
Personal and confidential

Dear Lewis: I have read a copy of Ralph Cordiner's letter to you on
the subject of imports of heavy electrical machinery.[1] I am skeptical
about findings that see danger to our national security in the practice of our theory that expanding trade among the free nations is
one of the best possible ways to strengthen our security arrangements. In other words, immediate technical and commercial problems must be weighed quite carefully against the value of sturdy allies.[2]

A statement in the Cordiner letter is to the effect that private utility companies have stuck pretty close to American products in their
procurement systems. It appears that it is only the Federal government that has made any extensive purchases of foreign equipment.[3]

Would it be helpful if we should notify the Executive Departments
that the Federal government would purchase only domestic equipment and therefore we would not ask for open bids on the world
market?

The above observations are for your information only. I particularly do not want to be expressing any opinions about these things
before OCDM has made a finding.[4]

If you should so like, you can easily get me on the phone at Augusta from tomorrow afternoon on.[5] *As ever*

[1] General Electric President Cordiner had written Strauss on March 13, 1959 (AWF/
A, Strauss Corr.) regarding his concern about "the very real threat to our national
security that results from the growing concentration of foreign-built heavy electric
power equipment at a number of strategic points and areas in this country. Unless
limited and regulated, continuing imports will further aggravate the problem and
the danger." Cordiner's letter to Strauss followed General Electric's March 7 petition
to the Office of Civil and Defense Mobilization for a finding that imports of four
types of heavy power equipment endangered the national security.

[2] See nos. 753 and 810; see also Kaufman, *Trade and Aid*, pp. 113–32.

[3] Cordiner had written that "A continuous and adequate supply of electric energy is
the foundation stone of this country's capacity to produce either for war or for
peace." Foreign-built equipment that was damaged or destroyed could not be put
back into service as rapidly as could U.S.-made equipment. He also claimed that the
United States was the only highly industrialized country that bought heavy electrical
power equipment from foreign manufacturers.

[4] On June 12, 1959, the Office of Civil and Defense Mobilization would rule that imports of heavy electrical equipment did not endanger national security. Leo Hoegh,
director of the OCDM, would find that between mid-1951 and mid-1958, 284 pieces
of foreign equipment were delivered, as compared to domestic sales of more than
30,000 pieces. Moreover, of the 102 power stations that used foreign equipment only
thirty-five were rated "essential" to defense. Hoegh would state that equipment repair

was not a significant problem, but the OCDM would continue to conduct reviews to ensure that there was no "pre-emption of U.S. requirements by foreign hydraulic turbines" as this could raise a question of national security. Hoegh would also emphasize the principle that American decisions to restrict imports could adversely affect U.S. security "in the sense that they can impair our relations with and the strength of, important allies." The OCDM decision would be hailed by representatives of the United Kingdom as removing "a potential threat to continued trade in this field between Britain and the United States." See *New York Times,* June 13, 18, 1959.

[5] Eisenhower had vacationed in Augusta from April 7 to April 13. Although this letter had been drafted around April 1, Presidential Secretary Ann Whitman had delayed sending it pending answers to questions over its content. Whitman had noted that while the first and second paragraphs expressed the President's opinion that "other countries should be allowed to bid on heavy machinery," the third paragraph seemed "to indicate otherwise" (see Ann Whitman memorandum, [c. 4/1/59], AWF/A).

1137   *EM, WHCF, Official File 8*

To John Foster Dulles   *April 16, 1959*

Dear Foster: I accept, with deepest personal regret and only because I have no alternative, your resignation as Secretary of State, effective upon the qualification of your successor.[1]

In so doing, I can but repeat what the vast outpouring of affection and admiration from the entire free world has told you. You have, with the talents you so abundantly possess and with your exemplary integrity of character, employed your rich heritage as well as your unique experience in handling our relations with other countries. You have been a staunch bulwark of our nation against the machinations of Imperialistic Communism. You have won to the side of the free world countless peoples, and inspired in them renewed courage and determination to fight for freedom and principle. As a statesman of world stature you have set a record in the stewardship of our foreign relations that stands clear and strong for all to see.

By this letter I request you to serve in the future, to whatever extent your health will permit, as a consultant to me and the State Department in international affairs.[2] I know that all Americans join me in the fervent hope that you will thus be able to continue the important contributions that only you can make toward a just peace in the world.

With affectionate regard, *As ever*

[1] Secretary of State Dulles had tendered his resignation on April 15. In February he had been diagnosed with abdominal cancer (see no. 1057). His condition had wors-

ened and he had been readmitted to Walter Reed Army Hospital for further tests. On April 13 the President had interrupted his vacation in Augusta, Georgia, to return to Washington to visit Dulles, who had offered to resign. Eisenhower had decided to wait for additional information, however, before making a decision. The following day Dulles's doctors had reported that the cancer probably had spread (Dulles, Memorandum of Conversation with the President, Apr. 13, 1959, Dulles Papers, White House Memoranda Series and *New York Times*, Apr. 14, 15, 16, 1959; see also Hagerty memorandum, Apr. 11, 1959, AWF/D-H).

On April 15 at 8:50 A.M. the President had telephoned Dulles to say he would accept his resignation. That morning Eisenhower had announced the decision at his news conference (see *Public Papers of the Presidents: Eisenhower, 1959*, pp. 327–28). Dulles would telephone the President later that evening (Telephone Conversations, Eisenhower and Dulles, Apr. 15, 1959, AWF/D). Dulles's resignation letter (Apr. 15, same file as document) and Eisenhower's reply would be released to the press immediately (see Telephone Conversations, Eisenhower and Dulles, Apr. 16, 1959, AWF/D; see also Eisenhower, *Mandate for Change*, pp. 357–58, and *Public Papers of the Presidents: Eisenhower, 1959*, pp. 329–30). Dulles had told the President that he had been "brought up in the belief that this nation of ours was not merely a self-serving society but was founded with a mission to help build a world where liberty and justice would prevail." He praised Eisenhower's "inspiring leadership in this essential task" and told him that it had given him "deep satisfaction" to have been "intimately associated" with the President. On Dulles's successor see no. 1139.

[2] Dulles had offered to serve "in a more limited capacity." On April 22 while at Walter Reed he would be sworn in as a special consultant to the President with Cabinet rank (Eisenhower, *Mandate for Change*, p. 359, and Dulles, *The Last Year*, p. 229). For developments see no. 1167.

1138

EM, AWF,
Administration Series

To Lewis Lichtenstein Strauss   *April 16, 1959*

Dear Lewis: Thank you for your note. Of course it is gratifying that your weekly business report continues to be encouraging. But in the face of the news of the last few days, that satisfaction is tinged with the ironic.[1]

With warm regard, *As ever*

[1] Eisenhower had been dealt serious blows in quick succession: that same day, he had formally accepted John Foster Dulles's resignation as Secretary of State. Readmitted to Walter Reed Army Hospital, Dulles had just learned that his cancer had spread (see the preceding document; *New York Times*, Apr. 13–17, 1959; Ann Whitman memorandum, Apr. 13 and 16; and Press Release, Apr. 15, 1959, AWF/AWD; for the President's discussion of these developments see Eisenhower, *Waging Peace*, pp. 357–60). Strauss had sent an expression of sympathy along with a positive report on increases in U.S. Gross National Product, corporate profits and personal income, all of which indicated that the economy was continuing to recover (Strauss to Eisenhower, Apr. 13 and 15, 1959, both in AWF/A).

To Charles W. Wainwright   *April 17, 1959*
Personal

Dear Dr. Wainwright: Thank you for the confidential report you submitted to me regarding the findings of your examination of Christian A. Herter.[1]

I was glad to have the professional opinion of an objective expert
on his physical condition, and am deeply appreciative of your cooperation in the entire matter. As you will know long before this letter reaches you, I am today announcing that I am sending his nomination to be Secretary of State to the Senate.[2]

With best wishes, *Sincerely*

[1] Wainwright (A.B. Western Maryland College 1914; M.D. Johns Hopkins School
of Medicine 1922), a Johns Hopkins professor of internal medicine who specialized in arthritis, had written the President on April 15 and 17 (both in AWF/D-
H). Wainwright had pronounced Under Secretary of State Herter, who suffered
from osteoarthritis of the hip joints, fit to perform the duties of Secretary of
State. "The progress of his disease has been slow," Dr. Wainwright wrote, "and I
feel that his activities will not be further limited by the osteoarthritis in the near
future." Eisenhower considered Herter a logical successor to Secretary of State
Dulles. (On Dulles's resignation see no. 1137; on Herter see Telephone Calls,
Eisenhower and Dulles, Apr. 15, 16, 17, 1959, AWF/D, and Eisenhower, *Waging
Peace*, p. 357).
[2] On April 18 Eisenhower would announce Herter's nomination. The Senate would
confirm the appointment on April 21 and Herter would be sworn in as Secretary of
State on April 22 (Note for Files, Apr. 18, 21, 22, 1959, AWF/D-H, and *Congressional
Quarterly Almanac*, vol. XV, *1959*, pp. 73, 664, 671).

1140   *EM, WHCF, Official File 8*

To George Magoffin Humphrey   *April 20, 1959*
Personal

Dear George: Thank you for your note. It is, as well you know, a great
blow that Foster is unable to continue with his job.[1]

I was interested in your comments about the Advertising Council.
Probably it is too much to expect any group—even one such as
this—to undertake a project that they may believe might work
against their immediate self-interest. But it is incomprehensible to
me why they do not take the long-range view.[2]

Augusta has been almost perfect, weather-wise. George and Al have spent the last few days with me and we have had some good bridge sessions.[3] I would rather not talk about the golf I have played! Give my love to Pam and all the best to yourself. *As ever*

[1] Secretary of State Dulles had resigned on April 15 (see no. 1137). Upon hearing the announcement former Budget Director Humphrey had written that it was a "terrific blow" for the President. He added: "It just seems as though everything is piling on your shoulders all at the same time!" (Apr. 15, 1959, WHCF/OF 8).

[2] On April 13 Eisenhower had interrupted his vacation in Augusta, Georgia, to return to Washington to address 275 executives attending the annual meeting of the Advertising Council (on the vacation see no. 1118). In his remarks the President stressed the importance of the stable dollar and a sound fiscal policy (see *Public Papers of the Presidents: Eisenhower, 1959*, pp. 322–25; and *New York Times*, Apr. 14, 1959). Humphrey said he was "a little disgusted" with the council members because they had been "wishy-washy" about fighting inflation and making "the protection of your balanced budget their main objective in life." On Eisenhower's efforts to maintain public confidence while seeking economic stability see, for example, nos. 1042 and 1114.

[3] George E. Allen and General Alfred M. Gruenther were among the friends who had joined Eisenhower at Augusta.

1141

EM, AWF, International Series:
Macmillan

To Harold Macmillan
Cable. Top Secret

April 22, 1959

Dear Harold: I just received your recent cable with its attachment. I appreciate the sentiments you express about Foster and his illness, and I hope you will agree with me that Herter was the only logical appointment to be made to fill the vacancy created by Foster's necessary resignation. He will fit in admirably.[1]

I am grateful for your thoughtfulness in acquainting me promptly as to the contents of Khrushchev's long message to you. I shall carefully observe your caution as to its confidential character.[2]

Respecting your personal note, I agree with what you have to say about atmosphere being sometimes possibly more important than practical results.[3] However, atmosphere achieves true importance only if it seeps down to populations under conditions where there is confidence in its permanence. Some four years ago the world talked a great deal about the "Spirit of Geneva."[4] This expression reflected the hope that because of Geneva the international atmosphere had become less tense and that some progress could be realized in solving outstanding problems between the West and the

East. At that time both Foster and I pointed out in nation-wide broadcasts that the value of the conference would be measured only by our later ability to make effective and enforceable agreements. As you know, that hope disappeared within a matter of sixty days. Disappointment was widespread.

A good atmosphere is much to be desired but it can be sustained only by solid accomplishment.

Turning to the "Summary of Message," I can accept Khrushchev's suggestion that we should set aside, at any Summit meeting, considerable time for frank and informal discussions among participants. Further, provided there becomes evident on the Soviet side a sincere purpose of conciliation and fruitful negotiation, I share his view that Summit meetings could become somewhat less formal and more periodically scheduled.

I am rather skeptical about his remark that "If, on the other hand, progress at the Foreign Ministers' Conference is unsatisfactory, a meeting of Heads of Government will be all the more necessary." In this statement he apparently rejects every Allied conclusion that if the Foreign Ministers can make no progress whatsoever, then it becomes futile and rather ridiculous to consider a Summit meeting. I hope that he does not believe that either you as the representative of Britain or I as the representative of America can be bulldozed into coming to meet him with our hats in hand. I am sure that others would feel the same.

I note also his assertion that certain American officials are trying to prepare our people psychologically for war. He slyly hints to our Allies that we in the United States are engaged in an attempt to engender a war in which European countries would be engaged, while America stood aside. This is the kind of statement that, to my mind, evidences his lack of sincerity and presages an intention to use a Summit meeting for propaganda purposes only.

Regarding the statement that he says President Truman made at the beginning of the war, I should point out that Mr. Truman was at that time a little known Senator.[5] Moreover I seriously doubt that he ever made any such statement.

As to Khrushchev's accusation that Mr. McElroy and Admiral Burke are guilty of military boastfulness and the twisting of facts, I think there is no need to make any reply.[6]

In American thought, both governmental and popular, there is no feeling that our country could ever be spared any of the suffering that would come to other countries with which we were allied, in the event that we were all plunged into the tragedy of war. In fact, Khrushchev knows that his statement on this point is completely false and is patently another of his "wedge-driving" attempts.

Finally, may I observe that non-aggression pacts were signed by all members of the United Nations when they agreed to adhere to the Charter. A new pact, whether bi-lateral or multi-lateral, would seem to be redundant as far as substance is concerned. It could have no value except possibly in the psychological field or in propaganda.[7]

I thank you again for the cooperative spirit in which your message was sent. I am certain we must do everything in our power to concert our positions in advance of any meeting with the Soviets, whether it be technical, at the Foreign Ministers level, or at the Summit.

No doubt Herter will be communicating to Selwyn Lloyd in some greater detail—particularly on such matters as possible participation by other countries and so on.

To conclude, I want to assure you that I have no rigidly fixed conclusion that Khrushchev is devoid of sincerity in his talk about readiness to negotiate and in his professed fear of Allied intentions, particularly those of the United States. To the contrary, no one is more anxious than I to make an agreement with the USSR in which each side can be assured of compliance by the other. Even if such an agreement were one of only minor or technical significance, it might still be valuable as a stepping stone.

I am glad that you find in the Khrushchev memorandum some ground for believing that he may be partially sincere. If he proves himself to be so, then the world will be the gainer.[8]

With warm regard, *As ever*

---

[1] Illness had forced Secretary Dulles to resign his position on April 15 (see no. 1137). The President had appointed Acting Secretary Herter as Dulles's successor three days later. Macmillan had told Eisenhower that Dulles's resignation must have been "at once a great loss and a great grief" (Macmillan to Eisenhower, Apr. 20, 1959, AWF/I: Macmillan).

[2] Macmillan had sent Eisenhower a summary of Khrushchev's April 14 letter, which, he said, was designed in part to drive a wedge between Britain and her allies. He did think, however, that there was also "some element of genuineness in it" (see *ibid.*; and Macmillan, *Riding the Storm*, p. 652).

[3] In response to a question asked him by the Soviet Ambassador as to whether progress at the foreign ministers' level was a condition of a summit meeting, Macmillan had said "that in these matters atmosphere was perhaps even more important than practical results."

[4] For background on the 1955 Geneva Summit Conference see Galambos and van Ee, *The Middle Way*, no. 1523.

[5] Khrushchev had compared the alleged attempt to produce an intra-European war with a statement attributed to the former president "to the effect that in the conflict between Nazi Germany and Russia the United States should back the weaker side to ensure maximum casualties."

[6] Neil H. McElroy, Secretary of Defense, and Admiral Arleigh A. Burke, Chief of Naval Operations. Both, according to Khrushchev, had said that the Soviet Union held no lead in missile development over the United States and had exaggerated America's military capacity—all to indicate that in a future war the United States would not suffer as much as other countries.

[7] Khrushchev had recommended a bi-lateral agreement between Great Britain and the Soviet Union "in order to prevent the violation of peace by adventurists."
[8] For more on the correspondence between Macmillan and Khrushchev see no. 1151.

1142   *EM, AWF, Dulles-Herter Series*

NOTE   *[April 23, 1959]*

File. We will check in a year!![1]

[1] Eisenhower had penned this notation at the top of a State Department memorandum dealing with the "Unofficial Visit of Prime Minister Castro of Cuba to Washington—A Tentative Evaluation" (Apr. 23, 1959, AWF/D-H; for background on Castro see Galambos and van Ee, *The Middle Way*, no. 1290). Revolutionary leader Fidel Castro Ruz's 26th of July Movement had forced the ouster of former President Fulgéncio Batista on January 1, and the United States had officially recognized a provisional government on January 7. Castro had arrived in Washington on April 15 at the invitation of the American Society of Newspaper Editors and had appeared before the ASNE, the National Press Club, and on the television program "Meet the Press" (see Herter to Eisenhower, Apr. 23, 1959, AWF/D-H; for background on the Cuban situation see Galambos and van Ee, *The Middle Way*, no. 2167; NSC meeting minutes, Sept. 25, Oct. 20, Dec. 8, Dec. 23, 1958, Jan. 22, Mar. 26, 1959, AWF/NSC; Memorandum, Feb. 4, 1959, AWF/D-H; and State, *Foreign Relations, 1958–1960*, vol. VI, *Cuba* [1991]; see also Eisenhower, *Waging Peace*, pp. 520–23; Earl E. T. Smith, *The Fourth Floor: An Account of the Castro Communist Revolution* [New York, 1962]; and Philip Bonsal, *Cuba, Castro, and the United States* [Pittsburgh, 1971], pp. 10–61; on the Castro visit see State, *Foreign Relations, 1958–1960*, vol. VI, *Cuba*, pp. 394–95, 428–31, 432–33, 452–83; and Robert E. Quirk, *Fidel Castro* [New York, 1993], pp. 236–43).

According to State's memorandum, Castro was "a man on his best behavior" who was under the direction of his ministers and an American public relations expert. Although his favorable reception by the public and the media was "contrived," department officials said that "the effect on Castro of the friendliness and openness of the American people and officials in their willingness to hear his plea for understanding of the Cuban revolution" should not be underestimated. Castro had allayed much of the criticism directed against him and had "cautiously indicated that Cuba would remain in the Western camp." Although he had said that he would allow the United States to remain at the naval base at Guantánamo Bay, his land reform program could adversely affect American properties in Cuba. "It would be a serious mistake to underestimate this man," the memorandum concluded. "With all his appearance of naiveté, unsophistication and ignorance on many matters, he is clearly a strong personality and a born leader of great personal courage and conviction." The establishment of a constructive relationship with Castro's government should be determined, the State Department concluded, by his decisions on specific matters he would face in the future. For developments see no. 1370.

EM, WHCF, Official File 8

To Edgar Newton Eisenhower

April 27, 1959

Dear Ed: Thanks for your note about Foster Dulles. It is more than ironic that it took his grave illness to awaken the American people to a true appreciation of his strength and wisdom, particularly in the struggle against Imperialistic Communism.[1]

Your friend Mr. Hoy also invited me to stay at his hotel in case I go to Chicago at the time of the Republican National Convention next year.[2] I thanked him but said that if I should attend the Convention, I would undoubtedly stay at the Blackstone as in former years.[3]

Give my love to Lucy and all the best to yourself. *As ever*

[1] Edgar had written on April 23 that Dulles's resignation made him "particularly sorry" for the President and "equally sorry" for Americans (on the Secretary of State's April 15 announcement see no. 1137). Edgar admitted that although "he could never warm up to Mr. Dulles," he admired his "determination and iron will" in "blocking the Russians in every move they have made."

[2] Patrick Henry Hoy of Chicago was president of the Hotel Sherman, Inc. Hoy had begun his career as executive assistant to the president of Hotel Sherman in 1946. Edgar had received Hoy's invitation to stay at the hotel in Chicago during the 1960 Republican National Convention.

[3] As it turned out the President would stay at the Blackstone Hotel while attending the convention (see no. 1592, and *New York Times*, July 27, 1960). The Blackstone had been Eisenhower's campaign headquarters during the 1952 Republican National Convention (see no. 942).

EM, AWF, International Series: Venezuela

To Rómulo Betancourt

April 28, 1959

Dear Mr. President: Because of the special importance of petroleum reserves to hemisphere security, officials of our two governments have, as you know, been discussing ways to assure, without prejudice to other oil-producing nations and without disruption of established trade patterns, the continued health and vigor of all hemisphere oil industries.[1]

I sincerely believe that the measures adopted by the United States on March tenth serve this objective and also tend to encourage stability in the United States market. I hope you will agree that such stability is in Venezuela's interests.[2]

By this personal note, I want to tell you in advance that these import regulations will shortly be amended in the manner already discussed with your distinguished Ambassador.[3] This amendment will improve the operation of the program and serve the interests of the Western Hemisphere. While the relatively small amount of Canadian oil sold in the north central and northwestern part of the United States does not compete with Venezuelan oil, this amendment will, we hope, reduce the serious risk of a permanent loss to Venezuela of its Montreal market. At the same time, I hope you will agree that our governments should continue their discussions looking toward broader hemisphere arrangements. The United States has been Venezuela's largest market and I am confident that it will continue to be so on an expanding scale.[4]

Your distinguished Ambassador has stressed the special significance to Venezuela of the level of imports of residual fuel oil for burning. I have asked the Administrator of the program to keep this aspect particularly in mind, and I assure you that it will receive careful attention.[5]

In conclusion, Mr. President, permit me to extend to you again my warmest personal greetings and my best wishes for the happiness and prosperity of the Venezuelan people. *Sincerely*

[1] This text was sent for delivery by telegram to the American embassy in Caracas, Venezuela, with instructions that it was not to be made public without authorization.
[2] On March 10 Eisenhower had announced that a mandatory oil import quota program would replace the voluntary one then in effect (see no. 1098). He had also stated that informal conversations were being held with Canada and Venezuela regarding a coordinated approach to oil in recognition of their "joint interest in hemispheric defense" (*Public Papers of the Presidents: Eisenhower, 1959*, pp. 240–41, 296). The United States had first discussed its quota policies with the Venezuelan government when it was controlled by dictator General Marcos Pérez Jiménez, who had protested United States actions and threatened retaliation; later, discussions had continued with the new and democratically installed administration of Betancourt.

Although he had not protested the new program, Betancourt had expressed concern that Venezuelan oil prices would decline, giving rise to public hostility and harming his administration. He would continue to press for preferential treatment (State, *Foreign Relations, 1958–1960*, vol. V, *American Republics*, Microfiche Supplement, VE-28, and for background see VE-5–7, 10–15; Franklin Tugwell, *The Politics of Oil in Venezuela* [Stanford, 1975], pp. 72–74; *New York Times*, Mar. 27, 1959; Chester, *United States Oil Policy and Diplomacy*, pp. 151–55; Cabinet meeting minutes, Mar. 6, 1959, AWF/D).
[3] Marcos Falcón Briceño.
[4] On April 30 Eisenhower would announce modifications to the quota program in ways that benefitted Canada exclusively. Oil imported into the United States through "overland transportation" was now to be exempted from the quotas. Venezuela had protested against these modifications but to no avail. Canada had threatened to restrict its own oil imports and to build a pipeline from the Alberta fields to Montreal, the nation's largest refining center, if the curbs against Canadian imports were not lifted. Responding to pressure from the international companies that controlled Montreal's refineries, the Administration had acquiesced in the adoption of the overland rule (*New York Times*, May 1, 1959; for background see State, *Foreign Relations*,

1958–1960, vol. V, *American Republics*, p. 918, and Microfiche Supplement, ETA-4, VE-21–22, 25–26, 28, 34; Edward H. Shaffer, *The Oil Import Program of the United States* [London, 1968], pp. 109–38; Nash, *United States Oil Policy, 1890–1964*, pp. 205–8; Shaffer, *Canada's Oil and the American Empire*, pp. 146–60).

Eisenhower had approved the proposal to liberalize restrictions on Canadian imports at a meeting on April 27. Eisenhower had also requested that an earlier draft of this text be rewritten because it seemed to "promise more to the Venezuelans than might be forthcoming." The President had addressed potential modifications then under discussion with Venezuelan officials, but no decisions would be immediately forthcoming (Memorandum for Mrs. Whitman, Apr. 27, 1959, AWF/D).

[5] In December 1959 Eisenhower would authorize the Department of Interior to raise the quotas, an action that would favor Venezuela. This modification had been proposed by the Department of State over the objections of the Department of Interior (Proclamation 3328, *First Federal Register*, vol. 24 (no. 244), pp. 10133–34). The State Department would justify the move as a concession equaling that given Canada and one that might prevent Venezuela from shifting toward "nationalistic" oil policies that could adversely affect U.S. oil interests in Venezuela as well as consumers at home (State, *Foreign Relations, 1958–1960*, vol. V, *American Republics*, Microfiche Supplement, VE-35). Venezuelan residual oil—an industrial fuel used extensively to generate electric power—was in direct competition with the lagging U.S. coal industry, an issue its spokespersons would vigorously pursue (State, *Foreign Relations, 1958–1960*, vol. V, *American Republics*, p. 918; *New York Times*, Sept. 20, 1959; Vietor, *Energy Policy in America Since 1945*, pp. 130–33; Shaffer, *Canada's Oil and the American Empire*, pp. 134–36).

1145   *EM, WHCF, Official File 144-B-1-A*

To Henry Robinson Luce   *April 30, 1959*

Dear Harry: In the midst of other preoccupations (some of which admittedly have concerned the Luce family),[1] I do not want to neglect to congratulate you on your success in obtaining such a wonderful piece of ground for the National Presbyterian Church. The site seems to be ideal in every respect. I must say, however, that my sense of satisfaction cannot wholly eliminate the shock of learning that over two million dollars was required to purchase fourteen acres of ground.[2] During my early years in Washington that sum would probably have bought half of the entire District area northwest of Wisconsin Avenue!

With warm regard, *As ever*

[1] On the recent resignation of Secretary of State Dulles and the appointment of his successor see nos. 1137 and 1139, respectively. Eisenhower had nominated Luce's wife, Clare Boothe Luce, to be U.S. Ambassador to Brazil. Although the Senate would confirm her appointment on April 28, Luce had asked his wife to withdraw her name due to the controversy that her nomination had engendered. Shortly after the Senate had voted to confirm her, she had criticized her principal opponent, Oregon

Senator Wayne Morse (see Galambos and van Ee, *The Middle Way*, no. 222), and had attributed his opposition to the fact that he had once been "kicked in the head by a horse." She would resign the post on May 2 (see no. 406, and *New York Times*, Apr. 29, May 2, 1959).

[2] Luce, who was leading the fund-raising campaign for the National Presbyterian Church, had written on April 27 that the site was near Ward Circle in Washington and had considerable frontage on Massachusetts Avenue (for background see no. 1016). Luce had also reported that half the money had been raised and that he hoped that the balance would be obtained by the end of May. Luce thanked Eisenhower for his continued interest in the project (see no. 12; see also Elson to Eisenhower, May 4, 1959). All correspondence is in the same file as the document. For developments see no. 1209.

17

"Sources of division" among allies

To Harold Macmillan   *May 1, 1959*
Personal

Dear Harold: Thank you very much for your note deploring the conduct of your publicity-seeking traveler to Moscow.[1] I can assure you
that, so far as I am concerned, neither you and I, nor our two countries, are going to be divided and troubled by the chatterings of a
very small magpie. As I remarked at a recent press conference, the
British press has already taken care of his "diplomatic" mission to
Moscow.[2]

With warm regard, *As ever*

[1] Macmillan had written regarding statements made by Eisenhower's wartime colleague Field Marshal Bernard Law Montgomery in a CBS television interview, filmed
a month earlier but released in order to coincide with Montgomery's arrival in
Moscow. American leadership, Montgomery had said, had been "rather suspect" in
recent years and the United States was run by "people who are not very well." He
had also criticized Eisenhower's reluctance to participate in a summit meeting and
said that soldiers should stay out of politics. Turning to the recent withdrawal of the
French fleet from NATO (see no. 1112), Montgomery had stated: "I imagine that
General de Gaulle has been having a look at the command set-up in the Mediterranean and he can't make head or tail of it. Neither can I. It's a complete dog's
breakfast, if you ask me."

Montgomery's words were in "bad taste," Macmillan had written, and "they could
do nothing but harm in both our countries" (Macmillan to Eisenhower, Apr. 29,
1959, AWF/I: Macmillan; *London Times*, Apr. 29, 1959; and *New York Times*, Apr. 29,
1959).

[2] On April 29 a reporter had asked Eisenhower about Montgomery's comments.
Avoiding any substantial remarks, the President had referred him to the critical opin-
ions that had been expressed in the British press (see *Public Papers of the Presidents:
Eisenhower, 1959*, pp. 349–50; see also *London Times*, Apr. 30, 1959).

To Nikita Sergeyvich Khrushchev   *May 5, 1959*

Dear Mr. Chairman:[1] I have your reply to my communication of April
thirteenth in which I suggested ways in which we might move more
rapidly toward the achievement of a lasting agreement for the discontinuance of nuclear weapons tests under adequately safeguarded
conditions.[2]

I do not disagree with your statement of the need to conclude a treaty which would provide for the cessation of all types of nuclear weapons tests in the air, underground, under water, and at high altitudes. This is the objective I proposed last August, which my representatives at Geneva have sought since the beginning of negotiations there, and which in my most recent letter I reaffirmed as the goal of the United States. I sincerely hope that your affirmation of this objective will prove to mean that you would now be willing to accept the essential elements of controls which would make this possible.

You refer to the possibility mentioned by Prime Minister Macmillan for carrying out each year a certain previously determined number of inspections.[3] I have also been informed that your representative at the Geneva Conference has formally proposed that agreement be reached on the carrying out annually of a predetermined number of inspections, both on the territory of the Soviet Union and on the territories of the United States, the United Kingdom and their possessions.[4] In keeping with our desire to consider all possible approaches which could lead to agreement for discontinuance of nuclear weapons tests with effective control, the United States is prepared to explore this proposal through our representatives in the negotiations at Geneva. In particular it will be necessary to explore the views of the Soviet Government on the voting arrangements under which this and other essential elements of control will be carried out, the criteria which will afford the basis for inspection, and the arrangements which you would be prepared to accept to assure timely access to the site of unidentified events that could be suspected of being nuclear explosions. It will be necessary to know, also, the scientific basis upon which any such number of inspections would be determined and how it would be related to the detection capabilities of the control system. I have noted your understanding that these inspections would not be numerous. The United States has not envisaged an unlimited number of inspections, but adheres to the concept that the number should be in appropriate relationship to scientific facts and detection capabilities.

As I stated in my last communication, if you are prepared to change your present position on the veto, on procedures for on-site inspection, and on early discussion of concrete measures for high altitude detection, we can proceed promptly in the hope of concluding the negotiation of a comprehensive agreement for suspension of nuclear weapons tests. I hope that your position on these basic issues will change sufficiently to make this possible.

There are reports that your representative in Geneva has given some reason for thinking the Soviet Government may be prepared to modify its approach regarding these questions.[5] If this should prove not to be the case, however, I could not accept a situation in which we would do nothing. In that event I would wish to urge your renewed consideration of my alternative proposal. It is that starting now we register and put into effect agreements looking toward the permanent discontinuance of all nuclear weapons tests in phases, expanding the agreement as rapidly as corresponding measures of control can be incorporated in the treaty. I would again propose that toward this end we take now the first and readily attainable step of an agreed suspension of nuclear weapons tests in the atmosphere up to the greatest height to which effective controls can under present circumstances be extended.[6]

In my communication of April thirteenth, I suggested that the first phase of such an agreement should extend to the altitude for which controls were agreed upon by the Geneva Conference of Experts last summer. We would welcome discussions of the feasibility at the present time of extending the first phase atmospheric agreement to higher altitudes and our representatives in the present negotiations at Geneva are prepared to discuss the technical means for controlling such an agreement.

It is precisely because of my deep desire for a complete discontinuance of nuclear weapons tests that I urge again that you either accept the measures of control that will make such agreement possible now or, as a minimum, that you join now in the first step toward this end which is within our reach. Such a step would assure that no time will be lost in setting up the elements of the system already substantially agreed and in stopping all tests that can be brought under control. While this is being done our negotiators would continue to explore the problems involved in extending the agreement to other weapon tests as quickly as adequate controls can be devised and agreed upon.[7] *Sincerely*

[1] This message, drafted by the State Department, was cabled to the American embassy in Moscow with instructions for delivery to Premier Khrushchev on the afternoon of May 6. Embassy officials were to coordinate the time with British embassy officials, who would be delivering a message from Prime Minister Macmillan on the same day. A copy was also sent to the U.S. permanent representative to NATO to be circulated to the North Atlantic Council, again after coordination with the British (see Goodpaster, Memorandum of Conference, Apr. 28, 1959, AWF/D; see also State, *Foreign Relations, 1958–1960*, vol. III, *National Security Policy; Arms Control and Disarmament*, pp. 737–40).

[2] For background see no. 1135. Khrushchev's April 23 reply is in AWF/I: Khrushchev.

[3] For Macmillan's proposal to limit inspections see no. 1071.

[4] Semen K. Tsarapkin was the Soviet representative to the conference.

[5] The Soviets had said that if a quota of inspections were adopted, they would drop their demand for a veto on the dispatch of inspection teams. They also had indicated that defining the events that would qualify for inspection would not present a problem, and they had agreed to the concept of permanent inspection teams. However, they maintained their insistence on veto power over other areas of the inspec-

tion process (State, *Foreign Relations, 1958–1960,* vol. III, *National Security Policy; Arms Control and Disarmament,* Microfiche Supplement, nos. 462, 463, 464; see also *ibid.,* pp. 741–42).

[6] Eisenhower had told Acting Secretary Herter that he thought it "unwise to use a precise figure like fifty kilometers to define the limit of atmospheric testing" and preferred the general language used in this sentence (Goodpaster, Memorandum of Conference, Apr. 28, 1959, AWF/D). In his April 23 letter Khrushchev had argued that nuclear explosions higher than fifty kilometers would still "poison the atmosphere and the earth, contaminating with radioactive fallout the vegetation which finds its way into the food of animals and into the human organism, just as is occurring at the present time."

[7] For developments see no. 1149.

1148

EM, AWF, International Series:
Macmillan

To Harold Macmillan
Top secret

May 5, 1959

[*Dear Harold:*] In my letter of April twenty-second I did not respond to your kind suggestion that Dick Nixon stop over in London on his return from his proposed trip to Moscow next July.[1]

In planning for his trip to Moscow we have been attracted by the idea of using one of our new jet transport airplanes in order to make the trip as rapidly as possible. We think that this might have a very good psychological effect, in the minds of not only the Soviet leaders and people but also the world public in general. It may be possible to make this trip non-stop in each direction, although a fuel stop might be required.[2]

Given this and the many activities which are in prospect in international affairs in the next few months, together with the possibility that Congress will still be in session at the end of July, I am afraid that it is not really feasible at this time to plan for him to visit London.

I shall, however, keep your suggestion in mind. Should the situation change, we shall let you know.[3]

With warm regard, *As ever*

[1] Eisenhower had approved a United States Information Agency recommendation that Vice-President Nixon represent the United States at the opening of the American National Exhibition in Moscow in July (Herter to Eisenhower, Apr. 9, 1959; Herter to Thompson, Apr. 8, 1959; and Thompson to Herter, Apr. 9, 1959, all in AWF/D-H; see also Nixon, *Memoirs,* vol. 1, pp. 250–52; see also Khrushchev, *Khrushchev Remembers,* pp. 364–67). Macmillan had written that Nixon's visit would be as interesting as his own trip to the Soviet Union had been and that his impressions

would be very useful. Macmillan had added that Nixon would be welcome if it were possible to add a stop in Great Britain to his trip (Macmillan to Eisenhower, Apr. 21, 1959, AWF/I: Macmillan; on Macmillan's trip to the Soviet Union see no. 1074).
[2] Nixon would leave on July 22 on a Military Air Transport Service four-engine jet, the military equivalent of a Boeing 707 passenger aircraft. The plane would refuel in Keflavik, Iceland (*New York Times*, July 23, 1959).
[3] For more on Nixon's trip see no. 1253.

1149

EM, AWF, International Series:
Macmillan

TO HAROLD MACMILLAN   *May 5, 1959*
Cable. Secret

Dear Harold: I have your cable taking up again the question of limiting the number of on-site inspections to be made in the systems for preventing nuclear explosions.[1] In a press conference April 29 I pointed out that the United States has by no means taken a rigid position in the matter of limiting the number of on-site inspections, noting that your original proposal in this line was based on the assumption that the Russians would agree to modify their intransigent attitude on the veto, both as it affects the composition of inspectional teams and the opportunity for inspection itself.[2] This of course is the meat in the coconut. I understand that the Soviet delegation in Geneva has now indicated readiness to drop the veto in the Control Commission on dispatch of inspection teams. It is not clear, however, how far they are prepared to go along with the other essential requirements, both political and technical, to permit really effective inspection.[3]

I cannot find anything in Khrushchev's several messages that clearly indicates his readiness to modify sufficiently his position on these critical veto questions to provide the basis for any immediate move on our part. Moreover, in his April twenty-third letter to me he said that there would be only a "few" of such inspections.[4] This word "few" is very flexible. However, should the veto points be settled to our satisfaction, I agree that we should have to study this particular problem with the utmost seriousness, and attempt to concert a position in the matter. While we would have to take account of the difficulties in practice of mounting inspection teams in establishing a number, I believe the most important consideration will be the point you make well in your draft message to Khrushchev—i.e., "the scientific basis which must underly our determination of the number of inspections adequate to deter any party to the agreement from seeking to carry out a clandestine test."

A lot of scientific and technical work and conclusions would be involved by our experts but assuming these can be solved, we could ourselves argue about the exact numbers.

How are we going to get a definite commitment from Khrushchev that he will abandon the veto throughout operation of the control system? There is the rub.[5]

With warm regard, *As ever*

---

[1] For background see no. 1071. Macmillan had told Eisenhower that he still believed that his tentative proposal for a limited number of inspections "may well prove to be the best way out." If the Russians accepted a reasonable solution on the veto question, the Prime Minister said, the issue could be narrowed down to the number of spot checks in any given year. Macmillan also noted: "Of course, we have the ultimate fall-back position that you and I discussed—that our two countries should simply state our decision no longer to pollute the earth by fall-out. We clearly cannot go on indefinitely with the risks to human health" (Macmillan to Eisenhower, Apr. 29, 1959, PREM 11/2861).

[2] See *Public Papers of the Presidents: Eisenhower, 1959*, p. 351.

[3] See no. 1147.

[4] See *ibid.*

[5] For developments see no. 1151.

1150

EM, AWF, International Series: Macmillan

To Harold Macmillan   *May 5, 1959*
Cable. Secret

Dear Harold: You are, I am sure, fully aware of the current discussions in NATO of requests by the Soviet Union for credits to finance the purchase of plants and equipment. I should, however, like to emphasize my personal concern with this problem. I have been particularly disturbed to hear about the differences between our representatives concerning the extension of credits to the Soviet Union at this time.[1] I realize, of course, the vital importance of foreign trade to the United Kingdom and I realize that we have not always seen eye to eye on economic counter measures with respect to the Soviet Union.[2] On the other hand, at this time, just before we enter into crucial negotiations, I believe strongly that we should attempt to resolve all significant differences which could act as sources of division between us.[3]

My understanding is that the Soviet request to the United Kingdom includes the extension of credit on the order of 50 million pounds per year for a period of five years. This, because of its magnitude and its duration, really involves a net transfer of resources, and bears no relationship to short term, self-liquidating credits which are essential to normal trade relations, and which we support. The Soviets have approached a number of NATO countries, including the U.S., and the aggregate of plants and equipment which they could purchase with these medium and long term credits, if granted, would seem to be quite substantial. These resources the Soviets need for the furtherance of their Seven Year Plan which is, as we well know, a vital element in the long range strategy of the Soviet leaders. Khrushchev is deeply committed to the success of this Seven Year Plan, but the magnitude of the undertaking is placing inexorable pressure on Soviet resources which of themselves are inadequate to insure its success, particularly in certain key sectors. In the Soviet economy, military requirements are currently in strong competition with the prosecution of the Plan. Since Western credits would to some extent relieve this pressure, it seems to me that the granting of them would weaken any Soviet incentive to divert resources from military to economic industry. This easing of Soviet economic pressure internally would, of course, permit the Soviets to step up their economic activities in underdeveloped countries. At the same time, the capabilities of the West to advance resources to these same areas whose political and economic orientation is a major issue of our time, could likewise be adversely affected.

Another important consequence of large scale credits to the Soviet Union would be a strengthening of the Soviet ability to disrupt world markets for basic commodities. It is difficult to see how the Soviet Union would repay any substantial credits except by the sale of basic products—agricultural, forestry and mineral—which many underdeveloped and Commonwealth countries must export. This could put great strains on our goal of liberalizing free world trade, which I know is so close to your heart.

Certain political factors with regard to this matter also concern me, particularly at this time: As I have mentioned, these credits will tend to lessen the pressures resulting from the conflict between military/atomic requirements on the one hand and requirements of the Seven Year Plan on the other. If the Soviets have achieved agreements for long-term and extensive credits while negotiations on other vital matters are in progress, it would seem to me that the Soviet incentive to reach agreement on these other kinds of negotiations would be reduced. Moreover, the possibility cannot be overlooked that any unilateral action by one of us in this direction might well give the Soviets the impression that the West is not united in its determination to be firm in the face of threats to its vital security interests in Central Europe.

Finally, I am concerned over the probability of increased difficulty in this country of obtaining public and Congressional support for our Mutual Security Program and related policies if an extension of long-term credit to the USSR were paralleled by an expansion of Soviet economic penetration of less developed countries.

I realize that these credits might bring some additional profits to Western producers from Soviet purchases to be financed by credits; furthermore, I understand the hope that this increased trade might lead to an easing of political tensions. However, I feel that this hope is largely illusory and that any increase of East-West trade should be on a legitimate quid pro quo basis. As you know, the policies of the United States preclude the extension to the Soviets of any governmental credits whatsoever, or of private credits exceeding a six months period.

To me these reasons seem compelling, but I attach great importance to your views. I earnestly hope that our two Governments and other members of the NATO can agree on a common policy which will recognize the principle that substantial financial support of this nature for the designs of the Soviet rulers would be inimical to our common purpose. It should be made clear at the same time that agreement on this principle will not modify in any way the policies on which we have previously reached accord with respect to the desirability of legitimate two-way trade of peaceful commodities with the Soviet Bloc. If, on the other hand, it is not possible to have a complete meeting of minds at this time, it would seem advantageous to defer any final decision on this matter until after the Foreign Ministers' Conference and a Summit Conference, should the latter take place.

In view of the urgency of this matter, I would welcome your comments and I would hope that it might have your immediate attention.[4]

With warm regard, *As ever*

---

[1] The British government was concerned that the division among the countries in the NATO Economic Advisers Committee regarding extension of credits to the Soviet Union could result in a major split in the alliance. The British believed that the U.S. position against such credits was "clearly designed to operate against the general economic welfare and progress of the USSR." The U.K. was willing to limit credits to five years but would not go beyond that (John S. D. Eisenhower, Synopsis of Intelligence Material Reported to the President, May 4, 1959, AWF/D).

[2] For background see Galambos and van Ee, *The Middle Way*, no. 1854; and no. 161 in these volumes.

[3] The Geneva Conference of Foreign Ministers would begin meetings on May 11 (see no. 1156).

[4] For developments see no. 1161.

To Harold Macmillan

Top secret and personal

Dear Harold: Thank you very much for your Top Secret and Personal letter of May fifth. I am handling it exactly as you suggested; I have made no copy of any kind and I am sending back the two attachments through the British Embassy in a sealed envelope.[1]

Your recent summarization of the Khrushchev message had already given me a quite clear understanding of the entire document; but of course I do appreciate your anxiety to make sure that you and I personally remain as close on these matters as we possibly can.

I should like to say also that I am in complete agreement with your answer. It is courteous but firm.[2]

Winston has just concluded a visit to me which, in spite of the obvious difficulties he has because of his age, was most satisfying. He has gone to the Embassy for today and will return to Britain on Saturday.[3]

With warm regard,

---

[1] Macmillan had sent Eisenhower a copy of the April 14 letter he had received from Soviet Premier Khrushchev, together with his own response. He had previously discussed the general content of Khrushchev's communication with the President, but because of their close relationship, Macmillan wanted Eisenhower to see the actual letters (see no. 1141). He had asked Ambassador Caccia to hand-deliver a sealed packet containing the letters to Eisenhower and to ask that the President keep the exchange "a complete secret." Khrushchev's letter revealed "the strange mixture which these people are—clever, naive, inexperienced, sensitive, suspicious of everybody else, and yet cynical themselves," Macmillan had said. "All the same I think this is a line which it might be useful for me to keep open" (Macmillan to Eisenhower, May 5, 1959, AWF/I; Macmillan; see also Lloyd to Macmillan, May 1, 1959, PREM 11/[2861]; Macmillan to Caccia, May 5, 1959, *ibid.*; Eisenhower to Caccia, May 7, 1959, AWF/D; and Macmillan, *Riding the Storm*, pp. 652–56).

Caccia would report to Macmillan that Eisenhower had assured him no one had seen the contents of the letters and that the President "'had had the hell of a time fixing the scaling wax'" (Caccia to Macmillan, May 8, 1959, PREM 11/[2861]; see also Ann Whitman Note, May 7, 1959, AWF/M: G).

[2] See no. 1141.

[3] On Churchill's visit see no. 1023.

To Samdech Preah Norodom Sihanouk Upayvareach
May 7, 1959

Dear Prince Sihanouk:[1] I appreciate very much the friendly sentiments
which you expressed in your letter of April 13, 1959, from Paris and
I read with interest your further explanation of several points raised
in your earlier letter of February twenty-third.[2]

With respect to your observation that Cambodian rebels are
openly claiming United States support, I wish to assure you most
emphatically that the Government of the United States is in no way
supporting any efforts to overthrow the Monarchy or the duly constituted Government of Cambodia. Any claims to the contrary, whatever the source, are without the slightest foundation. I shall request
the United States Ambassador at Phnom Penh to discuss with the
appropriate officials of your Government the nature of such claims
and the means to counter them should this be deemed necessary.[3]

Your comments on the marked improvement in relations between
Cambodia and Thailand are most reassuring. I trust that the reiteration by you and President Diem of the desire for friendly relations
foreshadows a similar, mutually profitable understanding between
Cambodia and Viet-Nam. You may be sure that the United States
will follow the development of amicable relations among the countries of Southeast Asia with active and sympathetic interest. In particular, I hope that it may soon be possible for positive steps to be
taken toward the resolution of the outstanding differences between
your country and its neighbors. American Ambassadors in the area
stand ready to encourage the development of mutual confidence,
and, wherever possible, to lend friendly assistance to specific endeavors toward this end.[4]

I have taken serious note of the comment toward the end of your
letter indicating your desire to enlist the interest of the United States
in the future of a small country such as Cambodia, and I wish to reassure you on this score. As a matter of principle, the disparity in
size and material resources of our two countries in no way affects
the genuine concern of the United States in Cambodia's welfare. It
is also part of American tradition that we feel a keen sympathy and
understanding for the aspirations of other countries, whether large
or small, to achieve and maintain their freedom.[5] Finally, as a matter of purely personal association, I recall that my inauguration as
President occurred in the same year that Cambodia, largely through
your efforts, finally gained the full measure of national independence.[6]

I believe you will agree that active American interest in Cambodia has been demonstrated not only in words but also in tangible assistance intended to help your country maintain its independence and further develop its material resources.[7] This assistance has been provided in complete conformity with the respect of the United States for Cambodia's sovereignty, which includes respect for Cambodia's sovereign right to choose its own means of protecting Cambodian independence and contributing to the common goal of world peace. As long as Cambodia subscribes to these aims, you may confidently rely on American friendship and understanding.

Since last communicating with you I have heard of your operation in Paris. I take this opportunity to convey my best wishes for your speedy and complete recovery.

With warm regard, *Sincerely*

[1] The text of Eisenhower's letter was transmitted by confidential telegram to the American embassy in Phnom Penh and then forwarded to Prince Sihanouk in Paris, where he was undergoing medical treatment. The Department of State had drafted this message (Herter to Eisenhower, May 6, 1959, AWF/I: Cambodia).

[2] See nos. 1085 and 1123. The Cambodian Ambassador had delivered Sihanouk's second letter to the Department of State (McElhiney to Goodpaster, Apr. 23, 1959; both of Sihanouk's letters to Eisenhower are in AWF/I: Cambodia.

[3] Sihanouk had written that Khmer rebels based in nearby countries were claiming "openly—but wrongly, I am sure—" that the United States was backing them. He had asked the President to "find the means possible to make such a claim impossible or more difficult." He had also written that a Cambodian general, who in February had led a failed coup supported by both Thailand and South Vietnam, had been killed. At the time Eisenhower sent this letter U.S. diplomats were attempting to convince Cambodian officials, who feared that the United States was attempting to overthrow Sihanouk's neutralist government, that the Administration had not had any detailed prior knowledge of or involvement with the planned coup (State, *Foreign Relations, 1958–1960*, vol. XVI, *East Asia–Pacific Region; Cambodia; Laos*, pp. 269–314; and Roger M. Smith, *Cambodia's Foreign Policy* [Ithaca, N.Y., 1969], pp. 140–66).

[4] See no. 1123. Sihanouk had described Cambodia's desire to reach an understanding with Thailand and South Vietnam. Relations with Thailand were so improved due to Eisenhower's "good offices" that Sihanouk had invited the Thai Prime Minister to make an official visit to Phnom Penh. Relations with South Vietnam, he had concluded, were not as good: the Vietnamese continued to encroach upon Cambodian territory and lend support to the Khmer rebels (Sihanouk to Eisenhower, Apr. 13, 1959, AWF/I: Cambodia).

[5] The Prince had written Eisenhower that his victimized "small and weak" country wanted only peace, and he hoped that the United States could convince "its allies and friends" to stop their provocations. "Millions" of Asians "living outside the blocs" were watching this situation, which could end by benefitting "only communism" (*ibid.*).

[6] Sihanouk, then King, had helped negotiate Cambodia's official independence from France in 1953. In 1955 he had abdicated in favor of his father and organized a political party which swept elections held that year. Sihanouk would remain the country's political head until he was deposed in 1970 (Smith, *Cambodia's Foreign Policy*, pp. 49–50, 77–78; and D. R. SarDesai, *Southeast Asia Past & Present*, 4th ed. [Boulder, Col., 1997], pp. 200–201).

[7] The United States was the principal donor of economic and military aid to Cambodia and had used the largest portion—about $34 million—to help construct a 130-mile paved highway connecting Phnom Penh with Sihanoukville, the new French-built seaport on the Gulf of Siam. The roadway would decrease Cambodia's dependence on Vietnamese and Thai ports, but it also had strategic importance as a potential military access route (Smith, *Cambodia's Foreign Policy*, pp. 123–27; Dillon to Eisenhower, May 13, 1959, AWF/I: Cambodia; see also Dillon to Eisenhower, July 11, 1959; Eisenhower to Suramarit, May 15, 1959; and Suramarit to Eisenhower, June 16 and July 25, 1959, all in *ibid.*; and *New York Times*, July 27, 1959). For developments see no. 1268.

1153   *EM, AWF, DDE Diaries Series*

To W. Walter Williams   *May 7, 1959*

Dear Walter: After you left this morning, Ann told me the doctors' findings about your bride. While you said at breakfast that she had been ill, I understood that she was on her way to quick and complete recovery.[1]

This note is simply to tell you how deeply distressed I am. Fate seemingly has no sense of justice or reluctance to strike again and again. My heart and prayers will be with you.

With warm regard, *As ever*

P.S. I shall of course not mention Mrs. Williams' illness to anyone (and no carbons are being made of this letter).

[1] Williams, Under Secretary of Commerce since 1953, had resigned on September 17, 1958. He had spoken with the President about politics and about his efforts on behalf of the budget (see Williams to Eisenhower, July 13, 1958, AWF/A; *New York Times*, Sept. 18, 1958; and Ann Whitman memorandum, May 7, 1959, AWF/D). On Eisenhower's battle for a balanced budget and against inflation see no. 1140. "Ann" was Presidential Secretary Ann Whitman.

On July 7, 1958, Williams had married Mrs. Ruth Garrison Meisnest (Williams to Eisenhower, July 13, 1958, AWF/A, and *New York Times*, July 8, 1958). There is no further record in AWF regarding her illness.

1154   *EM, AWF, International Series: Viet Nam*

To Ngo Dinh Diem   *May 8, 1959*

Dear Mr. President: I recall with pleasure my meeting with you two years ago today on the occasion of your visit to the United States of America.[1] In the intervening years our common effort to further our ideals of freedom and respect for the individual has continued and the understanding between our two countries has grown correspondingly.

It is with this thought in mind, Mr. President, that I take very great pleasure in offering to you as a gift for the people of Viet-Nam the Steuben vase that represents the outstanding contribution of a noted artist from the Republic of Viet-Nam reproduced on crystal by some of America's leading craftsmen. It is a work of art which represents a fusion of the artistry of Viet-Nam and the craftsmanship of the United States.[2]

May this vase serve as symbol of our common ideals. Although heirs to two distinct and diverse civilizations, our peoples are united by an indissoluble bond of friendship based upon a common faith in the dignity of man.

With warm regard, *Sincerely*

[1] See no. 710.
[2] Acting on behalf of the President, U.S. Ambassador Elbridge Durbrow had presented the vase along with this message to President Diem in Saigon. The Department of State, which had initially proposed the presentation, drafted this letter for Eisenhower. A Vietnamese artist had created the vase, "The Floating Village," which formed part of the "Asian Artists in Crystal" exhibit and had been shown throughout Asia and elsewhere under the auspices of the United States Information Agency (Memorandum for the President, Herter to Eisenhower, Apr. 21, 1959, AWF/I: Vietnam). Diem had responded that he could not "conceive of a better symbol of our joint struggle to preserve the independence of free nations than the American-Vietnamese artistry embodied in your gift" (Diem to Eisenhower, May 11, 1959, AWF/I: Vietnam).

1155   *EM, AWF, DDE Diaries Series*

TO ROSINA COTTON QUARLES   *May 8, 1959*

Dear Mrs. Quarles: My feelings of shock and grief this early morning cannot possibly be expressed.[1] My first thought is to tell you that my prayers are with you as you encounter this burden of sorrow.

Don's untimely and sudden death is a tremendous loss to me personally, to the Defense Department and to the Nation. He was a brilliant and dedicated public servant, quiet, able, devoted and loyal. He took his share, perhaps more than his share, of the slings and arrows that come to anyone in public life, and quietly went about his business with courage in his convictions and efficiency in his operations.

You are possibly aware of the fact that I have counted heavily upon his assumption in the future of even heavier duties, in the performance of which I know he would have demonstrated even more fully to America his capabilities and talents.[2]

Mrs. Eisenhower and I join in deepest sympathy to you and the members of your family; you are all in our hearts and thoughts. *Sincerely*

[1] Deputy Secretary of Defense Quarles had suffered an apparent heart attack and had died in his sleep during the night of May 7–8. The sixty-four-year-old Quarles had been appointed May 1, 1957 (see no. 229). He had attended a stag dinner at the White House on May 6 and a National Security Council meeting the morning of May 7 (Goodpaster, Memorandum of Conference with the President, May 8, 1959, AWF/D, and *New York Times*, May 9, 10, 1959).
[2] Eisenhower had been considering Quarles as the successor to Secretary of Defense Neil McElroy, who had planned to retire in the fall (see no. 369, and Diary, May 8, 13, 1959, AWF/D). For developments on filling the position of Deputy Secretary see no. 1158.

1156   *EM, AWF, DDE Diaries Series*

To CHRISTIAN ARCHIBALD HERTER   *May 11, 1959*
Secret

Dear Chris: Thank you very much for the cabled report on your meeting with the Chancellor.[1] I see no disagreement with his thought that we must not allow our thinking about a package to become so rigid as to preclude progress in any of its parts.[2]

I shall be looking forward to an account of your impressions after your first Geneva meeting.[3]

With warm regard,

[1] Secretary Herter had arrived in Bonn on May 9 for a meeting with West German Chancellor Konrad Adenauer. The two men had reviewed Soviet policy, the upcoming Geneva negotiations, and European security. Following the meeting, Herter had left for Geneva and the foreign ministers' meeting. A cabled summary of the conversation is in State, *Foreign Relations, 1958–1960*, vol. VIII, *Berlin Crisis 1958–1959*, pp. 678–81. For background on the Geneva talks see no. 1116.
[2] Adenauer had stressed the necessity of "untying" the package of proposals the West was making to the Soviets. The Chancellor feared that the issue of Berlin might be "left behind and lost" in the effort to reach agreement on other matters (State, *Foreign Relations, 1958–1960*, vol. VIII, *Berlin Crisis 1958–1959*, pp. 679, 681).
[3] Herter would report that the first session had opened nearly three hours late "because of continuous unresolved wrangling . . . over seating arrangements for German delegates and their right to speak during conference deliberations." The conflict had "assumed ridiculous proportions" when, after agreeing to separate tables for the German delegation, the Soviets insisted that the tables "should be not more than six pencil widths apart from [the] main table. In securing this exact measure, many pencils of many sizes were laid out" before the measurements were accepted

and the conference began. If that haggling was indicative of the rest of the conference, Herter wrote, "patience and then some will be a very necessary requisite"
(Herter to Eisenhower, May 11, 1959, AWF/D-H; see also State, *Foreign Relations,
1958–1960*, vol. VIII, *Berlin Crisis 1958–1959*, pp. 682–86). For developments see no.
1169.

1157 *EM, AWF, DDE Diaries Series*

To Billy G. Byars *May 12, 1959*

Dear Billy: Yesterday I inscribed to you, one of my paintings. On two
points I experienced a feeling of astonishment.

The first of these was that apparently you have had no picture of
me—and I am rather surprised at myself for having failed, long before this, virtually to force one upon you.[1] The other point is that
the request for the picture came from Gordon Moore.[2] In view of
the length and warmth of our friendship, I assure you that you need
never go through any intermediary in making any request of this
kind upon me.

After signing the picture, I sent it to Gordon Moore for trans-
mittal to you. If anything happens to it during its journey, please let
me know. I will send you two or three more!

With warm regard, *As ever*

[1] The President had known Texas oil tycoon Byars since 1954. The two had become
acquainted through their mutual interest in Black Angus cattle (see Galambos and
van Ee, *The Middle Way*, no. 1101, and no. 475 in these volumes). Eisenhower was frequently asked for photographs (see, for example, no. 145).
[2] George Gordon Moore, Jr., was the First Lady's brother-in-law. The Eisenhowers
would visit with the Moores on June 7.

1158 *EM, AWF, DDE Diaries Series*

Memorandum *May 13, 1959*

I had a final talk with Mr. McElroy about filling the vacancy created
by the death of Deputy Secretary of Defense, Don Quarles.[1]

The problem was a little more complicated than is usual in such
cases because of the fact that Mr. McElroy's commitment to me of
two years' service in the Defense Department was for a period ter-
minating next October.[2] I have felt that unless Mr. McElroy could
see his way clear to remaining for a longer period, my choice for

the Deputy Secretary would almost necessarily have to settle upon an individual who would be able within a few months to take over the top spot in the Department of Defense.

Today Mr. McElroy informed me of the several reasons that had compelled him to place a limit upon his tour of service in Washington. All but one had been removed or had become of such lesser importance that he thought they should not be weighed in his own personal decision as to his tenure of office.

The one remaining consideration in this particular question is the health of his wife. She is much more nearly an invalid than I had suspected; he is quite worried about her lack of progress in throwing off an apparently tricky case of arthritis.

Under the situation created by Mr. Quarles' death, Neil has decided as follows:

(*a*). He commits himself now to staying until the end of the year, or at least late in December, after the '61 Defense budget has been crystallized.

(*b*). Having been given some hope by the doctors that his wife's health might be expected to improve, he will determine some time later in the year whether it will be possible for him to continue until the end of my term as President.

(*c*). In this situation his first choice for his Deputy is Tom Gates, who is just resigning as Secretary of the Navy.[3] While he knew that if a man was to be taken from the Defense Department organization, my own choice would fall on Mr. Finuncane of the Army, he felt that all in all he would feel better in asking Tom to serve in this post.[4] He has not yet mentioned the matter and does not know what the reply will be, but if it is negative then he will approach Mr. Finucane.

One man he interviewed at my request—Dillon Anderson. I personally think he is the ablest of all the men we have been talking about for appointment here and one who has, through his experience as the President's special assistant in charge of the Planning Board, an experience that would be valuable in the post.[5] However, Mr. McElroy got the impression that Dillon Anderson would consider acceptance only in the event that he were promised appointment to Secretary of Defense at any time thereafter that Mr. McElroy might have to leave the post. Such a commitment I think I should not make at this moment.

Other people considered by Mr. McElroy were Walker Cisler of the Detroit Edison Company,[6] and a younger man named Gray, Chairman of the Board of the Whirlpool Corporation.[7]

[1] For background see no. 1155.
[2] See no. 369.

[3] Thomas Sovereign Gates, Jr. (A.B. University of Pennsylvania 1928), had been appointed Under Secretary of the Navy in 1953, and Secretary in 1957. In January 1959 Gates had announced his intention to resign his position at the end of May to return to his partnership in Drexel & Company, a Philadelphia investment banking house. Eisenhower would nominate Gates to succeed Quarles on May 18 (see *New York Times*, May 19, 1959). Gates would be appointed Secretary of Defense in December (see *New York Times*, Dec. 2, 1959).

[4] Charles Cecil Finucane (B.S. Yale 1928), former Under Secretary of the Army, had served as Assistant Secretary of Defense for Manpower, Personnel and Reserves since July 1958. Prior to government service he had been president of the Sweeny Investment Company in Spokane.

[5] On Anderson's service as Eisenhower's National Security Advisor see no. 261. In a meeting with the President on that day McElroy would express his concern about Anderson's "lack of executive and managerial experience." Anderson's capacity for the top job could be assessed only after seeing how he performed as Under Secretary, if he were to take that position (Goodpaster memorandum, May 14, 1959, AWF/D).

[6] President of Detroit Edison since 1951, Walker Lee Cisler (M.E. Cornell University 1922) had been with that company since 1945.

[7] Elisha Gray II (B.S. Massachusetts Institute of Technology 1928) had joined the Whirlpool Corporation in 1928 and had served successively as vice-president and executive vice-president before becoming president in 1955.

1159   *EM, AWF, Name Series*

To Milton Stover Eisenhower   *May 13, 1959*

Dear Milton: Herewith a photograph of the completed project at the graves of our parents.[1] The pictures were sent to me by Charlie Case.[2]

The actual work was carried out by Harry Darby, one of my warm personal friends. I have already written to Harry to express my thanks and have asked him for a bill. So far he has been silent on this point. I suspect that further prodding will not be any more fruitful but I shall try once again.[3]

I enclose also a copy of a letter from Florence Etherington, who provides a description of the completed work.[4]

With warm regard, *As ever*

[1] While visiting his boyhood home in October the President had visited his parents' gravesite and discussed the idea of constructing a fence around it (see nos. 898 and 911). See also Eisenhower to Earl Eisenhower, May 13, 1959, AWF/N.

[2] Case, vice-president of the Eisenhower Foundation, was one of Eisenhower's childhood friends from Abilene, Kansas (see no. 906).

[3] Eisenhower's letter to former U.S. Senator Darby is not in AWF. For background on Darby's generosity see no. 899.

[4] Florence Musser Etherington was Eisenhower's first cousin (see no. 911). Her letter is not in AWF.

To William Pierce Rogers   *May 14, 1959*

Dear Bill: I am bothered about these rulings involving the theory of "pre-emption" in those cases where both the Federal government and the state government have enacted legislation on the same subject. I would very much like to see legislation that could cure the matter. I realize that you are doubtful that anything can be done except by enacting specific legislation in each case.[1]

Would it not be possible to enact general legislation provided there was no retroactive feature in it? If this would not seem to be feasible, is there any other practical way that we could eliminate this difficulty?[2] *As ever*

---

[1] For background see nos. 689 and 731. Legislation introduced in the House of Representatives in 1959 attempted to bar courts from invalidating state laws on the grounds that the federal government had preempted the field unless Congress had stated specifically its intention to do so, or unless the federal and state laws were in irreconcilable conflict. The bill, H.R. 3, also allowed the states to pass and enforce sedition laws punishing subversive activities against the federal government (see *Congressional Quarterly Almanac*, vol. XV, *1959*, pp. 205–9). These provisions marked a congressional effort to overturn the case of *Pennsylvania* v. *Steve Nelson* (350 US 497), in which the Supreme Court had upheld the Pennsylvania high court decision overturning a conviction for violating the state's Sedition Act. The Court had held that the federal Smith Act (prohibiting the knowing advocacy of the overthrow of the government of the United States by force and violence) superseded the Pennsylvania Sedition Act, under which the defendant had been convicted. The House would pass H.R. 3 on June 24 by a vote of 225–192. The legislation would not, however, reach the Senate floor.

[2] Rogers would respond on May 20, 1959 (AWF/D) emphasizing his opposition to the preemption legislation: "There is only one thing that is clear; that H.R. 3, if enacted into law, would cause great and unnecessary confusion." He was also concerned that the legislation, which applied to all previous acts of Congress, raised a serious constitutional problem: "It is an attempt by this Congress to express the intention of all previous Congresses on all previous legislation in this field of federal-state relations. Congress may, of course, amend any particular statute by expressing its specific intention. There is considerable doubt about its constitutional authority to affect all previous acts of Congress, without regard to any specific statute, by attempting to restate what all other Congresses intended to do in all the laws they enacted in this field." Rogers also noted that the sponsor of the bill was determined to keep the retroactive features in it.

To HAROLD MACMILLAN   *May 15, 1959*
Cable. Secret

Dear Harold: I have spoken both to our State and Defense Departments about your cable suggesting renewal of staff planning in accordance with the continuing agreement that we reached at Bermuda some few years back.[1] They assure me that they will take the necessary steps so that this planning can go forward.

Concerning your letter about your Trade Mission, it is clear that your proposed program is far less ambitious than perhaps we had thought and does not constitute a menace to the solidarity of the NATO Alliance. I shall be interested to learn about the results obtained by the Mission.[2]

I have given a copy of your letter on this subject to the State Department.

Thank you very much for the completeness of your exposition.

With warm regard, *As ever*

[1] Macmillan had written Eisenhower regarding threats to Kuwait from both the United Arab Republic and the purportedly communist-dominated government of Iraq. The two men had discussed the situation at their Camp David talks in March, and the British, who received one-half of their oil from Kuwait, had since been planning their strategy in the event that Iraq invaded Kuwait. Although U.S. and British planners had worked in London on a general study of the problem, Macmillan believed that the Iraqi threat to Kuwait was serious enough to warrant joint planning along the lines of the 1958 troop deployments to Lebanon (Macmillan to Eisenhower, May 14, 1959, PREM 11/2753; see also Goodpaster, Memorandum of Conference, May 15, 1959, AWF/D). For background on the Anglo-American agreements regarding the Middle East, formulated in Bermuda, see no. 78; see also State, *Foreign Relations, 1958–1960*, vol. XII, *Near East Region; Iraq; Iran; Arabian Peninsula*, pp. 216–18, 781–87. For background on the political situation in Iraq see no. 784; see also NSC meeting minutes, February 12, March 26, April 23, May 8, 1959, AWF/NSC; and J. S. D. Eisenhower, Synopsis of Intelligence Material Reported to the President, May 8 and 9, 12, 14, 15, 1959, AWF/D. On the Lebanon deployments see no. 776; on the Camp David talks see no. 1116.

According to a State Department memorandum, British and American officials were actively involved in contingency planning in the event of a Communist takeover in Iraq. A State Department committee would recommend a further study of the circumstances that would require military action, a U.S.-U.K. survey of the requirements to insure peaceful access to Middle Eastern oil, and continued joint military planning to counteract an expansion of Soviet influence in the area (State, *Foreign Relations, 1958–1960*, vol. XII, *Near East Region; Iraq; Iran; Arabian Peninsula*, pp. 786–89).

[2] For background see no. 1150. Macmillan had told Eisenhower that the British had no intention of giving the Russians long-term credit or loans on a government-to-government basis but wanted to increase trade with the Soviet Union "on an ordinary commercial basis." He explained that business firms could accept contracts

from the Russians and give them credit provided that the items were not on the strategic embargo list. If the Russians asked for a large loan, he said, the British would refuse "and the negotiations would not amount to very much." Macmillan was not certain how much additional trade would result from the negotiations of the Trade Mission. He hoped, however, that the two countries could increase trade "on the normal basis" (Macmillan to Eisenhower, May 12, 1959, AWF/I: Macmillan).

1162   *EM, AWF, Administration Series*

To Clarence Douglas Dillon   *May 15, 1959*

Memorandum for the Acting Secretary of State: Would you please have a study made to determine what executive agreements, laws, executive orders, etc., intended to restrict or curtail our trade with the Soviet Union there might be that are in existence on the books at the present time, but are of little or no effectiveness.[1] My idea is to determine what there might be, the rescission of which would remove an irritant without substantially affecting what we are now actually doing in the field of trade.[2]

[1] Eisenhower was undoubtedly referring to ongoing correspondence and discussions with Soviet Premier Khrushchev to improve U.S.–U.S.S.R. trade relations. The Soviets had asked the United States to liberalize its trade policies and loosen restrictions on imports (see nos. 521 and 768). The President was particularly concerned about related Soviet requests for long-term credit extensions (see nos. 1150 and 1161). Eisenhower and Khrushchev would address trade restrictions during talks in September at Camp David (see no. 1328 and President's Trip to Europe: East-West Trade, Aug. 22, 1959, WHCF/CF). For background see State, *Foreign Relations, 1958–1960,* vol. IV, *Foreign Economic Policy,* pp. 714–18; *ibid.,* vol. X, *Eastern Europe Region; Soviet Union, Cyprus,* pt. 1, pp. 237–39, 241–52, 257, 470–76, 501–6.
[2] Dillon's report to the President (May 20, 1959, AWF/A) listed three categories of U.S.–Soviet trade restrictions. Among those that might well be lifted without harmful consequences were bans on the importation of furs and crabmeat. A second category included provisions, such as the most-favored nation tariff treatment, that could be liberalized if the Soviets were to make a corresponding and substantial concession. Removal of restrictions in the third category "would constitute so sharp a change in basic U.S. policy that no action on these restrictions would be justified unless the Soviet Union were to undertake a basic shift in its policy towards the West." One measure in this category was the ban on extending public credits to the Soviet Union.

To Clarence Douglas Dillon   *May 15, 1959*
Confidential

Memorandum for the Acting Secretary of State: At my meeting with the President of Mexico in Acapulco last February, a proposal was considered by the two of us that we set up a sort of informal and continuing joint study group.[1] It was felt that this would be a very small group, initially possibly comprising only one man from each nation. The purpose of this group would be to examine together both short term and long term problems confronting our two countries, with no formal agenda, no official title and preferably working practically anonymously.

President Mateos thought that for the American representative my brother would be a natural, and he remarked that before naming his own representative he would seek a later opportunity to talk to my brother himself.[2]

For my part I believe that if we could keep two such men in fairly good contact with each other, we might do something to forestall problems or at least to ameliorate their effects.[3]

Later developments along this line are indicated in the attached letter which I have just received from my brother. If any action is indicated on the part of the State Department, I know you will take care of the matter.

You might like to discuss this with me later but I assume that first you would prefer to talk to Milton.

[1] See nos. 1062 and 1063.

[2] The two presidents would set up the informal study group, with Milton Eisenhower as the U.S. representative.

[3] Milton had written his brother about the invitation to visit Mexico that López Mateos had previously extended, explaining that he had just spoken with the Mexican President and had suggested July or August for the visit. He had also told Eisenhower about proposals for dealing with the problem of access to the U.S. cotton market that the Mexican and American agriculture secretaries and the American Under Secretary of State of Economic Affairs, C. Douglas Dillon, would discuss at their upcoming meetings (May 13, 1959, AWF/N).

Milton Eisenhower would make a low-key, two-week visit to Mexico in August (12–27). Upon his arrival, he would announce that he would "discuss anything anybody wants to talk about," including "lead and zinc or fish or cotton"—export commodities that had been of particular concern in multilateral and bilateral trade discussions of the past year (*New York Times*, May 18, Aug. 13, 14, 26; Memorandums of Conversation, Feb. 19 and May 18; Dillon to Eisenhower, May 20; Eisenhower to López Mateos, May 23, and López Mateos to Eisenhower, June 18, 1959, all in AWF/I: Mateos; for background on these trade issues see nos. 774, 859, 959, 1062, 1094, and 1170.

Meeting briefly with López Mateos on August 12, Milton would discuss several subjects, including territorial waters, cotton, the Soviet Union and Poland, and the President's visit to the United States. He would also invite Mexican scientists and universities to participate in Project Mercury, the U.S. program to launch a manned capsule into space, and ask for cooperation in locating a space observation station in Guaymas, Mexico (State, *Foreign Relations, 1958–1960*, vol. V, *American Republics*, pp. 875–78). The President would later note in his memoirs that the relationship cultivated between Milton and López Mateos had indeed proved fruitful in gaining approval to construct the Guaymas station (*Waging Peace*, p. 344).

1164
EM, AWF,
Administration Series

To Lewis Lichtenstein Strauss
May 15, 1959
Personal

Dear Lewis: Thank you for your note of yesterday.[1] Of course my faith in you is so great that automatically I consign, in my own mind, any and all of your attackers to a classification so low I do not care to give it a name!
  With warm regard, As ever

[1] Strauss's personal and political opponents had launched an intense assault on his integrity, dragging out various AEC issues during the Senate committee hearings on his confirmation as Commerce Secretary. A few days earlier, Eisenhower had defended the Admiral's character during a news conference (*Public Papers of the Presidents: Eisenhower, 1959*, pp. 382–84, and *New York Times*, May 14, 1959; for background and developments see nos. 1134 and 1215). Strauss had responded by thanking the President for his "confidence and support" (Strauss to Eisenhower, May 14, 1959, AWF/A).

1165
EM, AWF, International Series: Belgium

To Baudouin I
May 15, 1959

Your Majesty: This is the first opportunity I have had since the delightful evening at the Belgian Embassy to thank you formally for the lovely gift that you brought to Mrs. Eisenhower and me. The candelabra and crystal bowl are beautiful.[1] My wife has asserted in emphatic terms her right of possession, a right I am sure she intends to exercise until finally relinquished to the grandchildren.
  It was a distinct pleasure to welcome you on your return trip to this country: I trust that you will enjoy and find interesting the tour that has been arranged for you.[2]

Just this morning General Schweizer delivered to my office the photograph that you inscribed to Mrs. Eisenhower and me.[3] It is something that we shall treasure.

When you return to Belgium, you will take with you the expressions of affection and high esteem of millions of Americans, among whom Mrs. Eisenhower and I are included, both for you personally and for the sturdy people of Belgium whom we are proud to call our allies.[4]

With warm regard and best wishes, *Sincerely*

[1] The twenty-eight-year-old Baudouin had become King of the Belgians in 1951. He had arrived in Washington, D.C., on May 11. Eisenhower had attended the dinner at the Belgian embassy on May 13 (Eisenhower to Baudouin, Mar. 20, 1959, AWF/ I: Belgium; Ann Whitman memorandums, May 11, 13, 15, 1959, AWF/D; and *New York Times*, May 10, 12, 1959).

The Belgian cut crystal bowl, which sat on a gold-trimmed mirror base, had been crafted at the King's request (Colle to Whitman, May 14, 1959, and undated memorandum, both in AWF/I: Belgium).

[2] Baudouin had traveled to the United States in 1948 (*New York Times*, Feb. 27, 1948; May 10, 12, 1959). While in Washington in 1959 as the guest of the President, he would address a joint session of Congress. Baudouin later would make a goodwill tour of several U.S. cities (*New York Times*, May 10, 12–15, June 1, 1959).

[3] Brigadier General John M. Schweizer, Jr., had attended the President's dinner for King Baudouin on May 11. He was Director of Estimates for the Assistant Chief of Staff, Intelligence, United States Air Force.

[4] Upon his departure on May 31 King Baudouin would say that his visit had left him with "warmth and affection" for the United States (*New York Times*, June 1, 1959).

1166   *EM, AWF, Administration Series*

To CLARENCE DOUGLAS DILLON   *May 18, 1959*

Memorandum for the Acting Secretary of State: I understand that you have had for some time a copy of a letter sent to me on the twenty-seventh of April by the President of Mexico.[1] I trust that a draft reply can be completed soon because I think I should send an answer as promptly as possible.[2]

[1] On this same day Eisenhower had received López Mateos's April 27 letter (AWF/ I: Mateos), which was hand-delivered by the Mexican Ambassador Antonio Carillo Flores (President's daily appointments and Ann Whitman memorandum, AWF/D; Memorandum of Conversation, AWF/I:Mateos, all May 18, 1959; State, *Foreign Relations, 1958–1960*, vol. V, *American Republics*, p. 332). Several days earlier, the Mexican embassy had sent a copy of the letter to the State Department asking that it be circulated in anticipation of a meeting of the International Cotton Advisory Council on May 13. The State Department had subsequently notified the White House

and the embassy that it could take no action until the original letter had been delivered to the President and then referred back to the Department for action, but that those officials concerned with the cotton question had been informed (McElhiney to Goodpaster, May 12, 1959; Dillon to Eisenhower, May 20, 1959, both in AWF/I: Mateos). López Mateos had written to the President to continue the "friendly" talk on difficult economic issues broached during Eisenhower's visit to Acapulco, Mexico, the previous February (for background see no. 1062). López Mateos had been particularly concerned about U.S. participation in international negotiations on cotton production (see no. 1094). He had also briefly discussed lead and zinc exports; private and public investment; long-term measures to alleviate poverty; international monetary loans and the liberalization of credit and interest rates; equitable international trade relations; and Milton Eisenhower's proposed visit to Mexico (see no. 1163).

[2] Dillon would provide the President with a draft reply on May 20 (Memorandum, AWF/I: Mateos). For Eisenhower's response see no. 1170.

1167   *EM, AWF, Administration Series*

To Christian Archibald Herter   *May 18, 1959*
Secret

Dear Chris: There is, as you have been told, a progressive weakening of Foster's condition.[1] The doctors seem to believe that our worst fears may possibly be soon sorrowfully realized, but there can be no prediction as to exact timing. I believe that unless your associates at the Conference should voluntarily and unanimously suggest a recess for you of something like 48 to 72 hours, you should remain at your post of duty.[2] There can be no question in the minds of any American as to the sincerity of your desire to pay your last respects in person, should the occasion for this arise during the Geneva Conference. But I think that there would be an equally clear realization that your continued presence at the negotiations would be vital to our nation's interest.

Should anything arise to convince you that your absence for two or three days would be largely immaterial, I suggest that you cable or telephone to me.[3]

With warm regard, *As ever*

[1] On Dulles's illness and resignation see no. 1141.

[2] Herter had been attending the Geneva Conference of Foreign Ministers since May 11 (see no. 1156). Presidential Secretary Ann Whitman sent the text of this message to Acting Secretary of State C. Douglas Dillon for transmission to Herter.

[3] For developments see no. 1171.

To Aksel Nielsen   *May 20, 1959*

Dear Aks: Your note about the log house reminds me that I have been negligent in not writing you before this to tell you how delightful it was to see you in Denver.[1] I was certainly pleased to find Helen looking so well and glad that she could come along with you to the plane when we left so that at least I had a chance to speak to her.[2]

Both John and I were highly impressed with the progress in your several development projects.[3] Every time I come to Denver I am amazed at the city's capacity to expand. I am not, however, amazed at *your* capacity to grow along with the city. You are doing a wonderful job, and I only hope that you will find the time now and then to relax and take it easy.[4]

With affectionate regard to Helen and, as always, the best to yourself. *As ever*

[1] The President and his son had joined the First Lady in Denver May 16 and 17 (Telephone conversations, May 15, 1959, AWF/D). On May 19 Nielsen had written about the origins and ownership of a log house near Denver (AWF/N).

[2] Mrs. Nielsen had suffered a heart attack in November (see no. 954).

[3] Nielsen had been overseeing the Eisenhowers' real estate investments near Denver (see, for example, no. 1070).

[4] For background on Nielsen's health see no. 1002.

To Clarence Douglas Dillon   *[May 22, 1959]*
Secret

Dillon: I think there would be considerable risk in asking Russkys to assure no unilateral action *until* completion of summit meeting.[1] To make such a request would seem to be acknowledgment of their *right.* I think we should merely assume their preservation of status quo and if later they do act then our hands are not tied.[2]

[1] Dillon was Acting Secretary of State while Secretary Herter was in Geneva attending the foreign ministers' conference (see no. 1167). Eisenhower had originally written "Herter" but later crossed out the name and wrote in Dillon's.

The President had penned this message at the bottom of a cable from Herter, received on this same day, reporting on a meeting he had just had with the other Western ministers. He and his colleagues had concluded that the presentations of the Western peace plan and the Soviet treaty proposal, followed by rebuttals and counter-rebuttals, had brought the first phase of the conference as far as it could go. The ministers assumed that the conference would have no conclusive outcome, but they knew that some progress was necessary to meet the conditions established to warrant a summit meeting. One area of possible agreement would be an improvement in the Berlin situation without the impairment of Western rights.

Herter had reported that West German Foreign Minister von Brentano had "expressed extreme uneasiness" concerning any attempt to seek from the Soviets an agreement to take no unilateral action on Berlin until after the conclusion of a summit meeting. He argued that this kind of agreement would give the Soviets "a free hand at [the] conclusion [of] any summit meeting and in a sense placed Western participants under pressure." He preferred that the Allies insist on an acknowledgment from the Soviets of Western rights of presence in and access to Berlin as a condition for a summit meeting (Herter to Dillon, May 22, 1959, AWF/D-H); see also Herter to Eisenhower, May 22, 1959, *ibid.*; and State, *Foreign Relations, 1958–1960*, vol. VIII, *Berlin Crisis 1958–1959*, pp. 747–51. For Eisenhower's position on a summit meeting see no. 1116; for a detailed account of the conference proceedings see Conference of Foreign Ministers, *Foreign Ministers Meeting, May–August, 1959, Geneva*, [Washington, D.C., 1959]).

[2] For developments see no. 1171.

1170 *EM, AWF, International Series: Mateos*

To Adolfo López Mateos *May 23, 1959*

Dear Mr. President: I have read with interest and appreciation the frank and friendly expression of your views on Western Hemisphere economic problems in your letter of April 27, 1959, which was delivered to me by your distinguished Ambassador, Antonio Carillo Flores, on May 18, 1959.[1]

Your personal interest in these problems is of the greatest importance, not only because of the stature of Mexico and its President in the inter-American family, but because the extraordinary economic progress of your country in the past several years provides an example of the significant role of sound fiscal and monetary policies in promoting economic growth.[2] The cultural, economic and political ties between our two countries make your views especially meaningful to us who are next-door neighbors.

I share your opinion that a continuing exchange of views so auspiciously initiated at Acapulco is most desirable, and I appreciate your friendly references to my brother, Milton, who tells me that he will be able to accept your kind invitation for this summer.[3] I shall ask him to consult with your Embassy here on a time convenient to you.

Meanwhile, I am pleased to know that significant progress has been made in the last week in consultation with your Minister of Agriculture toward agreement on a procedure for continuing consultation on the problem of cotton which is so important to the economies of both our countries. I am confident that with your help ways can be found, consistent with our laws, better to coordinate international efforts to achieve a greater degree of market stability.[4]

Your Ambassador mentioned to me his satisfaction with the progress made in the recent United Nations meetings on lead and zinc.[5] We may both hope that, as Governments gain experience in the search for economically sound ways to cope with difficult and complex commodity problems, we shall be able to make significant advances. Certainly we can view with satisfaction the gains which have already been made in international cooperation in coffee.[6]

Similarly, there is reason to view with satisfaction results of the recent conference in Buenos Aires on economic problems. I was gratified to learn that your delegation made a significant contribution to that conference.[7] It has been my view that the value of meetings of this kind is to be measured, not only by the content of the resolutions agreed upon, but by the better appreciation on the part of each participating Government of the views and the problems of all the others. This improved understanding facilitates constructive solutions to problems as they arise day by day.

I, too, am gratified at the speed with which the Charter of the Inter-American Development Bank was negotiated and at the vista which it opens for making available additional capital resources for sound development projects within this hemisphere. I have asked Congress to authorize payment of the United States subscription to the capital of this bank in the hope that it can begin functioning to supplement the activities of the International Bank for Reconstruction and Development and the Export-Import Bank in the near future.[8] As you may know, during 1958 the Export-Import Bank made available medium- and long-term credits in Latin America totaling $497 million, the largest volume of loans authorized for Latin America in any one year and appreciably larger than the amount made available to any other area of the world. The Export-Import Bank's interest rates are, as you know, necessarily related to the rates at which the United States Government itself borrows money in the private capital market.[9]

While the points of view which I have expressed are necessarily general, they will serve, I hope, to indicate my desire that the United States make the most effective contribution possible to our common task of accelerating the rate of economic growth.[10]

I keenly anticipate your visit next autumn when we shall have an opportunity for further discussion of ways in which the American States can best pursue our common goal of a united, peaceful, and prosperous America.[11]

With warm regard, *Your friend*

¹ See no. 1166.
² The term "inter-American" referred to the pattern of treaties and conferences that had developed among cooperating American nations. This system of foreign relations had crystallized with the Organization of the American States in 1948 (Stoetzer, *The Organization of American States*).
³ On Eisenhower's February visit to Mexico see nos. 1062 and 1063, and on Milton's proposed trip see no. 1163. The Mexican President had complimented Milton for his "superior intelligence, interest in Latin America, and familiarity with its problems" (López Mateos to Eisenhower, Apr. 27, 1959, AWF/I: Mateos).
⁴ López Mateos had discussed the cooperative actions taken not only by Mexico, but also by other Latin American nations, to deal with the cotton crisis (see nos. 1062, 1063, and 1094). He had described how the Ministers of Agriculture from several countries had signed a "Hemispheric Producer's Agreement" at the first Inter-American Cotton Conference held March 20, 1959, in San Salvador, El Salvador. While the United States had sent "only an observer to this meeting," López Mateos hoped that the American government would support the agreement or a similar solution at upcoming international discussions (López Mateos to Eisenhower, Apr. 27, 1959, AWF/I: Mateos; *New York Times*, Mar. 24, 1959).
⁵ For the substance of the Ambassador's meeting with Eisenhower (n. 2) see State, *Foreign Relations, 1958–1960*, vol. V, *American Republics*, pp. 871–73, and for background on the zinc and lead trade problems see nos. 764, 859, and 959. Mexico had objected to the quotas that the United States had unilaterally imposed on lead and zinc imports and had continued to press for joint international regulation of commodity problems (Calhoun to Goodpaster, Feb. 16, 1959, WHCF/CF: Mexico Trip). To that end, the United Nations Lead and Zinc Committee had met in New York City on May 2, and Mexico, along with two other exporting countries, had volunteered to reduce their production of these metals. At the same time, the United States had expressed a willingness to consider dropping its quotas when an agreement to limit supplies had been reached by all participants (*New York Times*, Apr. 8 and May 2, 1959). López Mateos had suggested that "in exchange for the sacrifice that the exporting countries might make" by reducing production, the United States might "adopt certain internal measures" since it would "benefit indirectly" and because it seemed "fair that all the countries involved should contribute" (López Mateos to Eisenhower, Apr. 27, 1959, AWF/I: Mateos).
⁶ The Administration had begun to explore multinational solutions to commodity problems, to participate in international commodity study groups, and to consider international trade agreements. Eisenhower had publicly endorsed international "cooperation on the problems of basic commodities" in connection with the Economic Conference of American States held in Buenos Aries the previous year (for Eisenhower's statement see State, *Foreign Relations, 1958–1960*, vol. IV, *Foreign Economic Policy*, p. 564). Eisenhower would later describe in his memoirs the "reversal of policy" demonstrated by the Administration in its support for those "commodity stabilization agreements," such as the coffee agreement that the government would sanction in 1959 (Eisenhower, *Waging Peace*, pp. 516–17; Milton Eisenhower, *The Wine is Bitter*, pp. 57–63, 91–110, and 252–53; State, *Foreign Relations, 1958–1960*, vol. V, *American Republics*, pp. 29, 219, 233, 562–70; see also Rabe, *Eisenhower and Latin America*, pp. 100–16).
⁷ López Mateos had referred to the Committee of Twenty-One—a special study group that had been created to consider new ways to promote economic growth in Latin America—and its upcoming meeting (April 27–May 9). The Mexican President feared that the participants would reiterate old and unsuccessful approaches to problems. He thought the solution lay with increased public, rather than private, investment. While agreeing that the economy of Mexico—and the other Latin American countries—should depend "fundamentally on private enterprise," he had maintained that only the State could solve such dire problems as illiteracy, poverty, and inade-

quate sanitation and housing (López Mateos to Eisenhower, Apr. 27, 1959, AWF/I: Mateos; *New York Times*, Mar. 22, 27, Apr. 27, and May 9, 1959).

[8] The bank charter had recently been approved in Washington (see no. 1130), and López Mateos had promised that Mexico would do all it could "to make its results beneficial to the people of our Hemisphere" (López Mateos to Eisenhower, Apr. 27, 1959, AWF/I: Mateos). On May 11 Eisenhower had asked Congress to approve legislation enabling the United States to participate in and fund the bank which, he had stated, should "complement" rather "than substitute for private investment" (*Public Papers of the Presidents: Eisenhower, 1959*, pp. 373–76). Congress would subsequently approve an initial sum of 450 million dollars (*Congressional Quarterly Almanac*, vol. XV, *1959*, p. 217). For developments regarding the banks and Latin America see nos. 1580, 1640, and 1644.

[9] López Mateos had urged the United States to add its voice to the chorus calling for the Export-Import Bank and the World Bank to "act imaginatively, even boldly," liberalize credit policy, and lower interest rates (López Mateos to Eisenhower, Apr. 27, 1959, AWF/I: Mateos). For general background on the banks see nos. 674 and 831, and Galambos and Van Ee, *The Middle Way*, nos. 1324 and 1883.

[10] López Mateos had argued that while the bank loans were a "first step in the right direction," the most promising long-range solution to difficult development problems would be the establishment of equitable international trade relations. The United States could "head a great crusade" for that purpose (López Mateos to Eisenhower, Apr. 27, 1959, AWF/I: Mateos).

[11] See also López Mateos to Eisenhower, June 18, 1959; Herter to Eisenhower, July 7, and Eisenhower to López Mateos, July 6, 1959, all in AWF/I: Mateos. The Mexican President would visit the United States October 9–19 (State, *Foreign Relations, 1958–1960*, vol. V, *American Republics*, pp. 884–85).

1171   *EM, AWF,*
                                              Administration Series

To Christian Archibald Herter   *May 25, 1959*
Secret

Dear Chris: I appreciate very much the action of your colleagues making it possible for you to come back to be present for Foster's funeral.[1] I am sure that Foster's family will be extremely gratified by the presence of Chancellor Adenauer, Selwyn Lloyd and Couve de Murville.

Please do not concern yourself unduly about the possibility of finding an alternative to Geneva as the site for a Summit meeting. I am perfectly ready to go there if Geneva seems to command the support of the majority in your conference.[2] *As ever*

[1] For background see no. 1167. After a long illness Secretary of State John Foster Dulles had died on May 24. Herter's colleagues had agreed to a two-day recess in the Geneva Conference of Foreign Ministers to allow participants to attend the funeral scheduled for May 27 (State, *Foreign Relations, 1958–1960*, vol. VIII, *Berlin Cri-*

sis 1958–1959, pp. 761, 766; and Herter to Eisenhower, May 23, 1959, AWF/D-H).
² Herter had informed Eisenhower there were questions regarding the site for a possible summit conference. The British disliked Geneva, but the French were insistent that Geneva was the best place for the meeting. Herter had told the Western foreign ministers that the United States did not consider the location very important and had cabled Eisenhower that his could be "the determining voice" in the selection (Herter to Eisenhower, May 19, 1959, *ibid.*; see also Herter to Eisenhower, May 23, 1959, *ibid.*). For developments see no. 1178.

1172   *EM, AWF, Name Series*

To Milton Stover Eisenhower   *May 25, 1959*

Dear Milton: Again this morning I read over the memorandum that records the thinking of the group that gathered at your house on the twenty-second.¹

I think that the next thing to do is to have a committee of my staff agree tentatively on such details as location, length, and stage management. Such a committee would, of course, have to obtain advice, in particular instances, of representatives from the various departments.² For example, I note that five or six of the talks suggested lean heavily toward the foreign field; obviously, a trusted State Department representative should be heard.

Number 7 deals with the subject of the American economy.³ This is a vast subject; indeed, I have the feeling that the subject of the American economy, like that of foreign affairs, should flavor every single talk that is delivered formally or informally by one in my position. These two subjects cannot be separated from each other and certainly they cannot be ignored in considering any matter of vital importance to our people, no matter what the composition of a particular audience. In addition to #7, I think another talk on the whole economy may have to be scheduled.

As to #4, I am impressed, as I told you last evening, with the importance of getting our people to understand that local affairs have a definite relationship to foreign affairs. Local papers in our country normally show no interest in the important incidents in Iran, in Moscow, or in Japan—even though these clearly affect the interest of the locality in which the paper is published.

Under the general subject of education, I think this talk might be dedicated to the need for understanding the simple relationships I have just mentioned.⁴ When foreign news becomes local news, then our public will be much better equipped to deal with the critical issues of our time.

As to #13, I have, as yet, no fixed idea that I should deliver a so-called "farewell" talk to the Congress, even if that body should invite me to do so. The reason I have been toying with this idea is because of my experience—which by that time will have extended to a full six years—in working with a Congress controlled by the opposite political party.[5]

Needless to say, there would be no profit in expressing, in such a setting, anything that was partisan in character. Rather I think the purpose would be to emphasize a few homely truths that apply to the responsibilities and duties of a government that must be responsive to the will of majorities, even when the decisions of those majorities create apparent paradoxes. A collateral purpose would be, of course, merely to say an official "goodbye."

Finally, I am somewhat disturbed by the number of talks that the committee considered a bare minimum.[6] I hasten to say that I do not disagree with its conclusion: I mean rather that the burdens implied are not inconsiderable. For example, the mere going to and returning from a place like Brown, Harvard, Kansas City and so on, normally involves motorcades, a meeting with dignitaries, and similar activities. The actual delivery of a talk is the least tiring of all the chores involved. On top of this, of course, is the matter of preparation of talks. I have a feeling, in order to get some variety in approach and expression, that each of these might be farmed out to some particular section of the government. It seems to me that this might be done by first deciding, with my immediate staff, on the specific part of the general subject that is to be developed and emphasized.

Thereafter, the basic directive could be sent to the appropriate section for production of raw material—fact, argument and conclusion—and thereafter Malcolm, assisted by other staff officers, should begin the process of coordination and polishing. At a fairly early stage each talk should be brought to me both for study and decision. I may be temperamental about these matters, but I can never be happy with a talk that in the long run is not developed according to my ideas and not put in my own words.

All the above remarks reflect my immediate reaction. I shall call Malcolm in to talk over these matters and if possible get the ball to rolling. If this system should work out fairly well, I shall be seeing you from time to time for conferences in which we could either talk together, alone, or have with us others that we trust.

With warm regard, *As ever*

[1] On May 24 presidential speech writer Malcolm Moos had prepared a memorandum (AWF/N, Milton Eisenhower Corr.) regarding the major presidential addresses and speech commitments between June 1959 and January 1961. The President and his brother Milton had discussed the subject with James Hagerty, Thomas Stephens and Malcolm Moos at a meeting at Milton Eisenhower's home on May 22, 1959.

[2] There is no indication that such a committee was formed.

[3] A speech on "The American Economy: Its Strength and Its Weaknesses" was tentatively scheduled for winter 1960. The plan was to highlight, among other subjects, deficiencies in the U.S. transportation system and the need to meet the urgent problems involved with the growth of urban areas.

[4] A speech on one of the problems of education was scheduled to be delivered at Brown University on October 21, 1959. For developments see no. 1198.

[5] This address tentatively planned to stress "the need for common sense to accommodate the broad range of belief in the political spectrum of America," especially when the nation might have a President and a Congress from two different parties.

[6] The proposed talks also included a speech to the Lions International in New York in June on restating America's purposes in the world; a late July or mid-August report to the American people on a possible summit conference; a speech in late September, at the dedication of the Harvard University International Law School, on foreign economic policy and its relevance to world trade and world peace (see no. 1290); an address on Latin America to the Council on Foreign Relations; the State of the Union message in January 1960; a talk on Lincoln and the Republican party to be delivered in Kansas; a talk on juvenile delinquency for the White House Conference on Youth in April 1960; an address to the National War College in June 1960 on the nation's defense; one major presidential campaign address; and miscellaneous foreign policy speeches on disarmament and the Soviet Union. Other possible topics for major speeches included an address on national goals and a discussion of administrative problems in the management of the nation's affairs.

1173   *EM, AWF, DDE Diaries Series*

To Clifford Roberts   *May 25, 1959*

Dear Cliff: I think that the figure quoted in your first paragraph is incorrect to the extent that the decimal point should have preceded it instead of following the final zero. Even at that price any buyer would have been stung![1]

With warm regard, *As ever*

[1] On May 22 Roberts had sent the President a copy of a picture of a woodcarving entitled "Ike the Golfer," which had appeared in the *Chicago Daily News* on March 17, 1956. In a cover letter Roberts had explained that the owner of the original woodcarving had offered to sell it to him for $10,000. Roberts "rather clearly" believed that over the years he had repeatedly expressed his loyalty to Eisenhower as well as his interest in perpetuating the President's image. Therefore, he trusted, his "failure to lay out Ten Grand" would not suggest a lack of "admiration and respect" (both in AWF/N).

To WINSTON SPENCER CHURCHILL   *May 26, 1959*

Dear Winston: Thank you so much for inscribing for me one of the photographs taken on our memorable trip to Gettysburg earlier this month.[1] I can't tell you how delighted I am to have it.

Stories are still appearing in some of our magazines about your visit to this country.[2] America of course claims at least half of you as her very own, and just to have you here once again did us all good. I most sincerely trust that you have completely recovered from the exhaustion that the journey must have provoked.

Just as I was dictating this note, your telegram about Foster came to my desk.[3] I am grateful for your sympathy. At the same time, may I mention how touched I was by the statement you issued Sunday?[4] His death, inevitable though it had seemingly been for some time, nonetheless came as a blow both personally and officially.

Incidentally, for the time being I have put the "Valley of the Ourika and Atlas Mountains" in my office, so that I may display it proudly to each and every visitor there.[5]

With affectionate regard, *As ever*

[1] Churchill had been the President's guest May 4–7. On May 6 they had flown to Gettysburg in a helicopter to tour Eisenhower's farm. Although the copy of the photograph from Churchill is not in AWF, it was probably one of those that appeared in the newspapers. According to Presidential Secretary Ann Whitman, the press featured "Sir Winston hanging on for dear life as the President took him across the bumpy terrain in a golf cart" (Ann Whitman memorandum, May 4–7, 1959, AWF/D; *London Times*, May 7, 1959; and *New York Times*, May 5–9, 11, 12, 1959). See also *Public Papers of the Presidents: Eisenhower, 1959*, pp. 370–73, and Eisenhower to Churchill, May 8, 1959, AWF/D. Churchill's May 8 and May 11 thank-you notes to the President are in AWF/I: Churchill.

[2] On this same day Eisenhower would send the former Prime Minister an excerpt from an editorial that appeared in the *Montreal Gazette* on April 30. Churchill would thank the President for the quote on June 13 (both in AWF/I: Churchill).

[3] Secretary of State John Foster Dulles had died on May 24 (see no. 1178). On May 25 Churchill had expressed his sympathy to Eisenhower over the "sad loss" of a "faithful friend" (AWF/I: Churchill).

[4] Churchill had described Dulles as "a man of principle and integrity" whose courage had "commanded the admiration of the whole world" (*London Times*, May 25, 1959).

[5] For background see no. 909. The President had thanked him for the gift of the painting on May 8 (AWF/D).

DIARY *May 27, 1959*
Secret

Conversation with Chancellor Adenauer:[1] Chancellor Adenauer, as usual, laid out his general thinking toward the Communist menace. In this he shows no great change—indeed, if he did I would be greatly disappointed.

He seems to have developed almost a psychopathic fear of what he considers to be "British weakness."[2] I went over with him some of my conversations with Mr. Macmillan and also described in rough fashion some of the British problems in the world. I told him that I am certain that in basic conviction and belief, Harold Macmillan and the Conservative Party leadership stand squarely with the rest of us. On the other hand, Britain has some economic and political problems that are almost unique, at least they are delicate and never ending. Since there is a very sharply divided opinion in that nation affecting such matters, Macmillan has had to tread a very careful path. In spite of this I told the Chancellor that in my opinion in any show-down Macmillan would stand firmly on principle.

The Chancellor discussed the continuing objective of re-uniting Germany. He stated, or implied, that the practicalities of the situation were such that the end would have to be achieved in a step-by-step process in which the two sides of Germany would themselves have to exhibit a clear readiness to be conciliatory and reasonable.[3]

[1] West German Chancellor Adenauer was in Washington to attend the funeral of John Foster Dulles, who had died on May 24. Adenauer had met with Eisenhower alone for approximately one-half hour at the Chancellor's request. They were joined for a short period at the end of the meeting by German Secretary of State and Foreign Minister Heinrich von Brentano. For more on the meeting see Eisenhower, *Waging Peace*, pp. 397–98; see also Ann Whitman memorandum, May 27, 1959, AWF/D.
[2] Adenauer had previously told Secretary Herter that he had noted "a basic change" in British policy after Prime Minister Macmillan's trip to Moscow (State, *Foreign Relations, 1958–1960*, vol. VIII, *Berlin Crisis 1958–1959*, pp. 678–79; see also no. 1156).
[3] For developments see no. 1178.

1176 *EM, WHCF, Official File 156-D-1*

To FRED G. GURLEY *May 27, 1959*

Dear Fred: Thank you for your letter about the bill to amend the railroad retirement and unemployment insurance laws.[1]

My decision on this bill was one of the most difficult I have had to make.

Of the bill's features which on first impression appeared questionable, nearly all of them, after study and reflection, proved less durable as objections than had been supposed. The most unyieldingly objectionable feature was the provision to exclude railroad retirement pensions and annuities from future determinations of veterans' eligibility for non-service-connected disability pensions.[2]

The bill's principal provisions—those relating to retirement and unemployment benefits and to their financing by employer and employee contributions—were not, in the last analysis, greatly at variance with what the Administration itself has recommended in the railroad field and in other areas. In other words, the differences, such as they were, reduced themselves ultimately to matters almost entirely of degree.

My task, as you know, was to resolve these conflicting considerations. After weighing the bill until the final day, I concluded that it should be signed.[3]

Finally, I was of course aware of the varied political judgments that had been offered regarding the bill. I can assure you, however, that I made my decision solely on the merits as I saw them.[4]

It was a pleasure to see you on your recent visit.[5]

With warm regard, *Sincerely*

---

[1] On May 19 the President had signed Public Law 86-28, a measure that increased both railroad retirement benefits as well as the employer-employee taxes used to finance them. Gurley, a former chairman of the board of the Atchison, Topeka and Santa Fe Railway System, had written to complain about the additional financial costs that the already beleaguered railroad industry would incur as a result (May 22, 1959, same file as document).

[2] Section 4 of the Act excluded retirement pensions and annuities payments from veterans' income limitations set by section 522 of Public Law 85-857 (see *U.S. Statutes at Large*, vol. 72 [1958], pt. 1, p. 1136, and vol. 73 [1959], p. 28).

[3] Although Congress had increased retirement benefits in 1956, it had not provided for additional funding. After having unsuccessfully urged Congress to make the necessary appropriation in 1957 and 1958, Eisenhower had asked in his 1959 budget message that railroad retirement taxes be increased in order to place the program on a sound "actuarial basis." He had also requested that the wage base for taxes be raised to be in line with other social security programs and that the law governing federal payments to the railroad retirement accounts of veterans be revised (*Public Papers of the Presidents: Eisenhower, 1959*, pp. 104–5). The President was particularly concerned about the bill's proviso authorizing individuals to draw both veterans and railroad pensions and the "very liberal" provision for unemployment benefits (Legislative Leadership meeting notes, AWF/D, May 12, 1959). The 1959 Act increased pensions, annuities, and survivor benefits for workers; daily unemployment insurance benefits; and the number of weeks that certain employees could receive unemployment benefits. It raised both the monthly wage base on which taxes were levied and the employer and employee railroad retirement taxes (*Congressional Quarterly Almanac*, vol. XV, *1959*, p. 311).

[4] Gurley had referred to speculation that Eisenhower, fearing that Congress might override his veto, had caved in to political pressure to sign the bill. Gurley believed that the House would have "gone along" with a presidential veto. He had also written that the Republican attempt to court the labor vote would fail because the labor leaders were not going to support the party (Gurley to Eisenhower, May 22, 1959, same file as document; see also Legislative Leadership meeting notes, May 6 and 12, 1959, AWF/D, and *New York Times*, May 20, 21, and June 4, 1959).

[5] Eisenhower had met with Gurley on May 11 to discuss the bill, then awaiting a presidential signature (Ann Whitman memorandum, AWF/D). Like Gurley, the President had been concerned for some time about the precarious financial situation of many of the nation's railroad companies (see nos. 377, 610, and 633).

1177   *EM, AWF, DDE Diaries Series*

DIARY   *May 27, 1959*

In April 1946, President Truman sent for me to come to the Presidential yacht, then tied up at the dock at Quantico, Virginia. The purpose of the visit was to talk to me about an impending vacancy in the office of Secretary of State. He said that Secretary Byrnes, then occupying the office, had suffered a deterioration of health and wanted to resign by the middle of the year. He said that there were only two men he would even consider for the appointment, one of whom was General George C. Marshall, then in China. I told him that I was just starting on a trip through the Orient and would be happy to carry a message to General Marshall. He directed, of course, that the utmost secrecy should be observed in making known his wishes to General Marshall.

At the meeting in Chunking, General Marshall indicated his readiness to accept the offer, requesting me to keep him informed of developments. In order that we might keep our correspondence confidential, General Marshall made out, in his own handwriting, a simple code for the key words that might be used in our cabled interchanges. For some years I carried this little paper in a coin purse. This explains its dilapidated appearance.

Incidentally, the arrangement for appointing General Marshall was considerably postponed, the President informing me later that Mr. Byrnes wished to put off his resignation date for some months. Some time later General Marshall did become Secretary of State.[1]

The code:

PINEHURST - Secretary of State   COURIER - President

AGENT - Byrnes   AGREEMENT - Confirmation

[1] General Eisenhower, then Chief of Staff, had boarded the U.S.S. *Williamsburg* on April 26, 1946, for an off-the-record meeting with Truman. Secretary of State James Francis Byrnes did not announce his resignation until January 8, 1947, and Marshall was sworn in on January 21 of that same year (for background see no. 1017; Galambos, *Chief of Staff*, nos. 844, 909, and 921; Eisenhower, *Mandate for Change*, p. 81, and Dean Acheson, *Present at the Creation: My Years in the State Department* [New York, 1969], pp. 192–93).

1178 *EM, AWF, DDE Diaries Series*

DIARY *May 28, 1959*

Secret

I had an official visit with the four Ministers who had been in Geneva and later held a luncheon for all of the foreign dignitaries present for Secretary Dulles' funeral.[1]

My purpose was to thank both groups for their courtesy in paying their respects to a man that we, here, thought to be one of our greatest and, of course, in both cases, I wanted to try to help improve the atmosphere both in general and in the specific sense. I say specific because I am referring here to the atmosphere in which negotiations are being conducted in Geneva.[2]

Gromyko was personally agreeable, laughing frequently, and expressing the hope that real progress could be made. I told the group that I was personally anxious that such progress be accomplished, because only in this way could America agree to go to a Summit meeting. To go without such progress would be not only an exercise in futility, but would have an adverse effect upon world thinking when it was understood that the meeting was condemned in advance to sterility.[3]

Surprisingly Gromyko did not disagree with this in our office conversation, even though we know that the attitude of Khrushchev has been that any progress at the Foreign Ministers' level was of little concern or meaning. This comes about of course, at least in part, because of the relatively minor position held by Gromyko in the Soviet system. In that system there is only one boss and Gromyko is nothing but an errand boy.

Respecting the luncheon, each of the individuals present took the occasion, during the coffee period, to assure me of his nation's respect for Mr. Dulles and for the policies that Mr. Dulles and I have advocated and carried out. I asked each to convey to his respective head of government or state my personal thanks for the courtesy, and all in all, I think the meeting was worth while.[4]

[1] Meeting with Eisenhower were British Foreign Secretary Selwyn Lloyd, French Foreign Minister Maurice Couve de Murville, and Soviet Foreign Minister Andrei Gromyko. In planning the meeting, Eisenhower had told Secretary Herter and Under Secretary Dillon that he simply wanted to tell them that it was "ridiculous" that the world was divided "into segments facing each other in unending hostility. He felt that decent men should be able to make progress toward a better state of things" (Goodpaster, Memorandums of Conference, May 28, 1959, AWF/D; see also Eisenhower, *Waging Peace*, p. 398. For background on the Geneva Conference see no. 1169).

[2] For Eisenhower's tribute to Dulles see Eisenhower, *Waging Peace*, pp. 361–73.

[3] After the conversation Secretary Herter reported that Eisenhower had told the foreign ministers that although he was "willing to go anywhere at any time to talk with anyone" to advance the cause of peace, a summit meeting without some hope of progress "would be a hoax on the hopes of mankind" (State, *Foreign Relations, 1958–1960*, vol. VIII, *Berlin Crisis 1958–1959*, pp. 771–72).

[4] For developments see no. 1187.

1179   *EM, WHCF, President's Personal File 1872*

To Earl Lee Hering   *May 29, 1959*
Personal

Dear Ig: Arising very early this morning, I was suddenly struck with a desire, which translated itself into determination, to write to you and Lucy immediately. Frequently a similar thought has crossed my mind, but far too often it happens when I am much too busy or, what is more likely, toward the end of the day when I am just weary enough to want to postpone even those things which I would like to do. So this morning I propose to give myself no such excuses.

Where to begin and exactly what to say would be real problems for me if I should turn my thoughts only to incidents or developments that might interest you both. However, since the purpose of this letter is primarily to tell you that Mamie and I often find that your names come up during our personal reminiscences, and to inquire about the health and happiness of you and yours, I think it matters very little if my mind skips around a bit both as to subject and as to time.

Strangely enough, one of the things I think about so often is the time we used to put in, on Sunday mornings, in repairing, polishing, and tidying up our respective Model T's. In those days they were a real pride and joy to the four of us.[1]

—FOUR DAYS LATER—

I remember also that another Sunday morning habit was to go over to your dental office where we (my own capacity that of a spectator) made up a number of fishing appliances such as sinkers, steel leaders and the like.

Strangely enough, the incidents of that particular period seemed to stand out more clearly in my mind than do some of those that we enjoyed together when you were at Fitzsimons General Hospital.[2] Of course this may come about from the general belief that the older one grows, the more acute his memory becomes for incidents of the long ago, as he tends to forget what he had for breakfast today.

In any event our friendship with you has been very dear to us and our association one we wish we could more closely pursue.

I doubt that you would be interested in any recitation of my current problems; most of these are reported—but far too frequently with a dismaying inaccuracy—in the daily press. As you know, my beliefs are simple but strongly held because of my conviction that they are based upon the logic of the times and the need for being true to the institutions that have made this country great.

I believe that we must pay as we go and that, more than this, we must begin in these times of prosperity to reduce our huge and well-nigh unmanageable national debt, or we will pay a great price for our neglect. I believe we should keep the Federal government less, rather than more, in the business that traditionally belongs to the individual, the locality and the state.[3]

Unnecessary centralization of power in the Federal government is, in my opinion, evil. One reason that this is true is because the reckless piling up of debt upon debt in the Federal government leads finally to printing money, depreciating its value rapidly. A state or city can issue public bonds only as the investing public will buy them. In the political sub-division the market tends to compel frugality, thrift and efficiency, while in the Federal scene the demagogue has the opportunity for a field day.

Of course we realize that the central fact of today's problem is to prevent Communist imperialism from achieving its announced purpose of world revolution and the Kremlin's control of the entire earth. The struggle is not merely a military one; in fact I believe that today its other phases—economic, social and political—are far more threatening than the military.

If the free world is to make itself secure against this threat and still be true to its own tradition of settling international quarrels by negotiation rather than war, we must individually and as a nation be ready to sacrifice. Moreover, we must provide leadership so as to bring about true and effective cooperation among the free nations. The economic, military and spiritual strength of our allies is well nigh as important as is America's strength in these same fields.[4]

It suddenly occurs to me that after saying that I would not bore you with a statement of my own problems, I am doing just that.

Give my love to Lucy and, of course, all the best to yourself.
Devotedly

[1] Colonel Hering (Dental Corps) had retired from the Regular Army in January 1949 due to a disability. Eisenhower and Hering had met and had become good friends while stationed in Panama in the early 1920s. Lucy was Hering's wife (for background see Galambos, *Chief of Staff*, no. 537; Eisenhower to Peterson, Apr. 23, 1942, and Hering to Eisenhower, Nov. 21, 1945, both in EM).

[2] The President probably is referring to the fall of 1955, when he spent seven weeks at Fitzsimons Army Hospital in Denver, Colorado, while recovering from his heart attack (see Galambos and van Ee, *The Middle Way*, nos. 1595 and 1624).

[3] On Eisenhower's efforts to maintain public confidence while seeking economic stability see, for example, nos. 1042 and 1114.

[4] For background on the President's long-held belief that personal sacrifice was necessary for mutual security see no. 1083; see also nos. 1123, 1137, and 1190.

1180   *EM, WHCF, Official File 135*

To Arthur Krock   *May 29, 1959*
Personal

Dear Arthur: Yours is one of three newspaper columns that I read with such frequency as my personal habits seem to allow.[1] Often I feel like sending to you a word of admiring approval; that I do not more frequently write messages of that kind is because of my certainty that you already understand my confidence in your knowledge, integrity and professional skill.

The above is merely to introduce an expression of my approval of your column of today. Not only did you write something that will, I am sure, please Dr. Killian and will, moreover, give to the public a better understanding of the dedication and accomplishments of this remarkable man,[2] but may I add that your article lost nothing for me in its succinct final paragraph about Lewis Strauss.[3] I would that we had a hundred more writers doing the same thing.[4]

With warm regard, *As ever*

P.S. I hope you will look upon the cancellation of the Menzies luncheon as automatically providing, in your case, a rain check for use the next time we have some kind of "State" affair at the White House.[5]

[1] Journalist Arthur Krock's column, "In the Nation," appeared in the *New York Times*. The two others were syndicated columnists Roscoe Drummond and David Lawrence (for background see no. 808).

[2] Desiring to return to his position as president of the Massachusetts Institute of Technology, Special Assistant to the President for Science and Technology James R. Killian had submitted his resignation on May 27. On the following day Eisenhower had agreed to Killian's request with "sincere regret" (both in AWF/A; see also *New York Times*, May 29, 1959). For background on Killian's appointment see no. 396.

Krock had credited Killian with establishing the civilian agency for space exploration that had become the National Aeronautics and Space Administration. His actions, wrote Krock, had enabled the U.S. government to meet the challenges of the space age.

[3] Strauss had been serving as Acting Secretary of Commerce since his November 13, 1958, recess appointment. Eisenhower had sent his nomination to the Senate in January, and the Senate Interstate and Foreign Commerce Committee had held hearings intermittently between March 17 and May 14. Contrasting Killian's experience with the Senate's acrimonious debates over Strauss's integrity, Krock had noted that Killian had been able to function without the hindrances and unjustified assaults that "had caused many officials to regret they ever exposed themselves" by agreeing to hold public office. The nation owed Strauss a debt of gratitude, Krock wrote, for his vital contribution to its security. For background on Eisenhower's views of the hearings see no. 1164. For developments see no. 1215.

[4] Krock would thank Eisenhower on June 1 (same file as document). He had written the article, he said, "out of a sense of the duty" to "publicize such public service."

[5] Prime Minister Robert Gordon Menzies of Australia had met with the President at the White House the morning of May 27. The scheduled luncheon had been canceled due to Secretary of State Dulles's funeral services (Eisenhower to Menzies, [May 27, 1959], AWF/I: Australia; Ann Whitman memorandum, May 27, 1959, AWF/D; see also *New York Times*, May 29, 1959). On Dulles's death see no. 1183.

1181   *EM, WHCF,*
                                           President's Personal File 1490

To E. Frederic Morrow   *May 29, 1959*

Dear Fred: The letter you sent to Ann is one that I shall cherish knowing, as I do, that it was written with the heart. Thank you for all the things you say.[1]

I look forward to meeting your brother; I trust that the Senate will be in a mellow mood when his name comes up and that he will not have to endure too hard a time in the committee hearing.[2]

With warm regard, *Sincerely*

[1] White House aide for Special Projects Morrow (for background see Galambos and van Ee, *The Middle Way*, no. 1809) had thanked Eisenhower for nominating his brother John Howard Morrow (A.B. Rutgers 1931) for an ambassadorship. John, who was chair of the French Department of historically black North Carolina College at Durham, had served as a former member of the President's Committee on Government Security. He would become the first American ambassador to the new Republic of Guinea (1959–1961). Frederic had written that Eisenhower had made a great impact on his life, and that he was the first to have given him opportunity to "aspire beyond the formerly fixed boundaries of race and class." He added that "perhaps the greatest significance of this whole thing is the fact that ninety years ago, my grandparents were slaves." Comparing Eisenhower's action to Lincoln's Emancipation Proclamation, Morrow claimed that his "noble friend" had "done as great a deed not only for my family, but for my entire race" (Morrow to Whitman, May 28, 1959, same file as document; see also Morrow, *Black Man in the White House*, pp. 285 ff).

² Eisenhower was undoubtedly referring to the difficulties several of his nominees to major appointments had encountered that year during confirmation hearings; see, for example, no. 1164.

1182   *EM, Official File 101-JJ*

To Norman Cousins   *May 30, 1959*
Personal

Dear Mr. Cousins: As you know, I have had the "Rule of Law" concept on my mind for many years.[1] Perhaps now is the time to devote an entire talk to the subject, although I am not precisely certain what kind of a forum would be best.[2] I am most appreciative of your offer to send me the draft that you have prepared, and I gladly accept.[3] Perhaps at some future time we might have an opportunity to discuss the matter but since it is agreeable to you to let me see the draft first, I would prefer that arrangement.[4]

Of one thing I must warn you. I am an incorrigible editor (and the despair of my staff who always insist that they can't relax until five minutes before the delivery of any given talk). But to make any speech effective I simply must arrange the presentation in what I think is the proper order, and the text must be in my own words. I mention all this simply to prepare you for the shock that some of my speech writers in the past have felt when a totally unrecognizable script is returned to them.[5]

Needless to say, I am truly appreciative of your suggestion. *Sincerely*

[1] For background on Eisenhower's interest in the concept of world peace through law and his relationship with Cousins see nos. 458 and 900; see also Eisenhower's memoir, *Crusade in Europe*, pp. 475–78.

[2] Cousins had written (May 22) that Eisenhower's concept of the need for world law could "serve as the great theme and rallying call for the creation of peace with justice on earth." On May 22 the President had met with advisers to discuss the subjects and schedules of the speeches he would deliver throughout the remainder of his Administration; the subject of international law may have been discussed at that time (see no. 1172, and Moos to Whitman, May 27, 1959).

[3] Cousins had used Eisenhower's writings, speeches and statements "as the thematic framework for a general draft" of a speech on the subjects of world law and the need to build a durable peace (see also Cousins to Whitman, May 22, 1959). On June 9 Cousins would send the speech to the White House (see Eisenhower to Cousins, June 10, 1959). The draft speech is not in EM.

[4] Eisenhower and Cousins would meet on August 6. As it turned out the President would not make the speech.

[5] See, for example, no. 1290.

     All correspondence is in the same file as the document.

To John Hay Whitney   *May 30, 1959*
Personal

Dear Jock: Because you shared my affection and admiration for Foster, you understand completely the void that is left by his death.[1] Quite apart from the loss to the world of a distinguished statesman, I feel, and I know you do too, a shock every time I realize that never again will he come through the door of my office and that never again will I experience the warmth of his unusual, gay and at times almost puckish, personality.

I, too, am gratified by the phenomenon in the change of European public opinion toward him; at the same time I resent in a peculiar way the fact that his critical illness was the basis for the change.[2]

Some time I shall tell you in full all the details of my visit with Winston.[3] As you know, it is terribly difficult to communicate with him these days, but nonetheless his very presence in a room is a gratifying and reassuring experience.

Give my love to Betsey and, of course, all the best to yourself. *As ever*

[1] On May 27 (AWF/A) Whitney had expressed his condolences on the passing of Eisenhower's "great friend," Secretary of State Dulles. Whitney said he had shared with the President the effects of Dulles's "strength" and "grace." Dulles had died on May 24 (see no. 1178).
[2] Whitney had called the swing in European public opinion of Dulles an "astounding phenomenon." He added that he was glad that Dulles "could have the little satisfaction" derived from the "tributes of his harshest critics." In sympathy letters to the President, many foreign dignitaries had praised Dulles for his accomplishments in public life (see, for example, no. 1174; Macmillan to Eisenhower, May 25, 1959, AWF/I: Macmillan; Eisenhower to Menzies, [May 27, 1959], AWF/I: Australia; Segni to Eisenhower, May 29, 1959, AWF/I: Italy; and de Gaulle to Eisenhower, May 29, 1959, AWF/I: de Gaulle).
[3] Sir Winston Churchill had been Eisenhower's guest at the White House May 4–7 (see no. 1174).

To Nathan M. Pusey   *June 1, 1959*

Dear Dr. Pusey:[1] I support the statement made by the Secretary of Health, Education and Welfare as to the desirability of amending the National Defense Education Act so as to eliminate the oath and affidavit required of recipients of Federal aid.[2] I shall seek an opportunity personally to voice this conviction.[3]

You and I can well understand the resentful feelings of a citizen who believes himself singled out to make a special affirmation of his loyalty to his country. I am sure the Congress had no intention of creating such resentment. Each individual who enters into the service of the Federal government, including every member of the Civil Service from top to bottom, and all appointees whether or not confirmed by the Senate, is required to take an oath to defend the Constitution and to perform his duties loyally. Unquestionably the Congressional feeling in this instance was that since any individual who works for his government for pay should be required to take a loyalty oath, then anyone who receives Federal aid should be ready to do the same.

I think most of us would be quite willing to repeat every morning, with the school children, the pledge of "allegiance to flag and to the nation for which it stands," yet any of us, if singled out to do something over and above that expected from the ordinary citizen, would feel a resentment.[4]

All I am saying here is that I think we can well understand the instinctive reactions of the Congress in this case, at the same time that we try to use persuasion in bringing about that necessary sober second thought which would eliminate the requirement.

Incidentally, I assure you of the Federal government's concern about the requirements of higher education. At the same time I believe that one of the gravest mistakes we could make would be to permit this kind of education to become too much dependent upon Federal decision and appropriation.[5]

With personal regard, *Sincerely*

---

[1] Pusey (B.A. Harvard 1928), president of Harvard University since 1953, had served as president of Lawrence College from 1944–1953. After receiving his Ph.D. from Harvard University in 1937 he had taught liberal arts and the classics at Scripps College and Wesleyan University.

[2] The President had signed the National Defense Education Act of 1958 (P.L. 864) on September 2, 1958 (for background see nos. 767 and 784). The law prohibited payments or loans to individuals unless they executed an affidavit that they did not believe in or belong to any organization that advocated the illegal overthrow of the government. After the act had gone into effect, nine educational institutions declined to participate because of the required affidavits. Harvard, which had originally participated, also withdrew (*Congressional Quarterly Almanac*, vol. XVI, *1960*, p. 238, and Clowse, *Brainpower for the Cold War*, pp. 131, 154).

On May 4 HEW Secretary Flemming had reported to the chairman of the committee on labor and public welfare that he believed the provision requiring an individual to sign the affidavit should be repealed (Flemming to Hill, May 4, 1959; see also *New York Times*, Mar. 24, May 13, June 10, 1959).

On May 7 Pusey had written that Health, Education and Welfare Secretary Flemming had "already signified his hope that this portion of the Act may be done away with, and his position has been applauded by numerous college and university presidents and faculties throughout the country. Harvard and several other universities have taken the moderate position on this matter" (see also Pusey to Kennedy, Apr. 28).

[3] Pusey had asked Eisenhower, "as a former university president," to comment publicly on the loyalty affidavit in order to "remove some of the hate from a needlessly inflamed situation." Eisenhower would recommend repeal of the provision in his annual Budget address on January 18, 1960 (*Public Papers of the Presidents: Eisenhower, 1960–61*, p. 89).

[4] The non-Communist disclaimer, Pusey said, discriminated against a particular group (see also Pusey to Kennedy, Apr. 28).

[5] In 1960 Congress would consider legislation to eliminate the loyalty oath requirement from the National Defense Education Act. Testifying for the Association of American Universities on June 22, 1960, Pusey would say that the affidavit was "futile, ineffective and unnecessary" and threatened "some of the basic elements" in the American democratic tradition (*Congressional Quarterly Almanac*, vol. XVI, *1960*, pp. 238–39). The non-Communist disclaimer affidavit would not be repealed until October 1962, however (*New York Times*, Oct. 18, 1962, and Clowse, *Brainpower for the Cold War*, p. 154).

Drafts of this letter containing Eisenhower's handwritten emendations and all other correspondence are in the same file as the document.

1185

EM, AWF,
DDE Diaries Series

To Alfred Maximilian Gruenther

June 1, 1959

Dear Al: Regarding the National Goals Committee:[1] Contrary to the expectations of some of the staff, the matter of financial support looks like it may become sticky. All further progress is dependent upon success in this item.[2]

I have talked to Arthur Burns and Frank Pace about your feeling that current demands upon your time and effort would greatly diminish your usefulness as a member of the Committee. I gave them the gist of your convictions.[3]

Their first feeling is that the demands upon the time of the top Committee members will be very slight during the early months; moreover, that even when the time comes for the crystallization of views and findings, it would be far preferable to have you on a part-time basis than to choose someone that they respect less. They think your name, as a top Committee member, would be very good.[4]

Next time I see you we will talk about the matter.[5] *As ever*

[1] For background see nos. 999 and 1059.

[2] Fundraising for the Goals Committee would remain difficult. On July 8 the President would tell staff members that he could not understand why American corpo-

rations and large foundations would not give money for the kind of planning that was done by India or the Soviet Union, but instead "went around in circles on things that they said produced concrete results" (Ann Whitman memorandum, July 8, 1959, AWF/AWD). See also *Public Papers of the Presidents: Eisenhower, 1959*, pp. 514–15.

[3] On June 15 the President would name former Chairman of the Council of Economic Advisers Arthur Burns and General Dynamics President Frank Pace, Jr. as cochairmen of the National Goals Committee (*New York Times*, June 16, 1959).

[4] Gruenther would ultimately accept appointment to the Committee (see *New York Times*, Feb. 7, 1960).

[5] For developments see no. 1364.

1186   *EM, AWF, DDE Diaries Series*

To Harold Rupert Leofric George Alexander

June 1, 1959

Dear Alex: Thank you so much for your note of sympathy in the death of Foster Dulles. Your tribute to him gratifies me greatly, as I know it will both Mrs. Dulles and Allen.[1]

And I cannot fail to tell you how deeply I am touched by your assurance that you recall with real satisfaction our personal association in wartime; on my part I have always in the past and shall continue in the future to feel a tremendous admiration, respect and affection inspired by your selfless and unexcelled performance of duty and leadership of the Allied armies.[2]

I am grateful also for the evidence that your letter presents that you are once again feeling stronger.[3] I trust that you are—or soon will be—enjoying life as much as ever.

As for the suggestion in your last paragraph, at present, of course, I have no idea where, or if, a Summit Conference will take place. But I do assure you that nothing would give me greater pleasure than to see you again; one of these days you and your Lady might find it possible to pay us a visit here. A warm welcome would await you.[4]

With personal regard, *As ever*

[1] Secretary of State John Foster Dulles had died on May 24 (see no. 1178). In his May 25 letter of condolence Alexander had expressed empathy at Eisenhower's loss because he knew of the President's friendship with and his admiration for Dulles. In addition to his "outstanding service to peace," Alexander said, Dulles had set "a magnificent example" of courage and fortitude during his illness. Alexander added that he had known and respected Allen Dulles since 1945 (AWF/D).

[2] Alexander said he was "proud and happy to have served" under Eisenhower during World War II.

[3] On Alexander's health see no. 989.

[4] As it turned out, in the late summer the President would make a goodwill trip to Europe. While in London he would host a stag dinner for his wartime associates, including Alexander (see no. 1294, and *New York Times*, Sept. 2, 1959).

1187   *EM, AWF, DDE Diaries Series*

To CHRISTIAN ARCHIBALD HERTER   *June 2, 1959*
Secret

Dear Chris: Thank you for your periodic reports.[1] I saw the press stories out of London concerning Selwyn Lloyd, as well as Macmillan's denial of their authenticity.[2] It is my impression that Selwyn has grown very much in maturity and ability in his job. Personally I would hate to see him transferred. Such things are barred from public comment by us, but I am hopeful that the reports are erroneous. It was unfortunate that such gossip should be published at this particular time.

I think that your rebuttal of Gromyko's charge that West Berlin propaganda and subversive activities create danger for the East Germans and the Soviets was both necessary and effective.[3] Regarding Gromyko's typewritten draft protocol for West Germany, it is a typical Soviet trick to advance a proposal that is completely unacceptable.[4] They cannot conceive of a conference that must first of all be a test of patience and endurance. I do hope that Gromyko took my words seriously when I warned him that no Summit meeting was possible except as some progress at the Foreign Secretary level would warrant it.[5]

With warm regard, *As ever*

[1] Herter's first report concerned the meeting the four foreign ministers had held on the flight back to Geneva after Secretary Dulles's funeral (see no. 1178). Soviet Foreign Minister Gromyko had made three concessions regarding Berlin during the airborne conference: any arrangement regarding Berlin would be temporary pending German reunification; the Russians, or the East Germans, would guarantee the political and economic freedom of Berlin and free access to the city; and a small and symbolic detachment of allied troops, together with a Russian contingent, would remain in West Berlin as a token presence. Although the relinquishing of occupational rights to Berlin was a "completely unacceptable concept," Herter said, after agreement on these issues, this one point could be settled at a summit conference. In a subsequent message, however, Herter had told the President that Gromyko had "hardened his line" after arriving in Geneva (Herter to Eisenhower, May 29, 30, 1959, AWF/D-H; see also State, *Foreign Relations, 1958–1960*, vol. VIII, *Berlin Crisis 1958–1959*, pp. 773–81).

Presidential Secretary Ann Whitman sent the text of this letter to Acting Secretary of State Robert Murphy for transmission to Secretary Herter, as the President had instructed. She wrote: "As I am sure you know, he always wants me to send such messages through the Acting Secretary."

[2] On the preceding day the *London Times* had reported that Prime Minister Macmillan was planning to replace Lloyd as foreign minister and shift him to another government position. Macmillan had sent a personal message of confidence to Lloyd in Geneva, expressing his astonishment at the report and assuring him that the Foreign Office had played no part in the story (*New York Times*, June 2, 1959; see Harold Macmillan, *Pointing the Way, 1959–1961* [London, 1972], p. 65). Herter had told the President that the article had caused much speculation among the delegates and had placed Lloyd "in a most uncomfortable position" (Herter to Eisenhower, June 1, 1959, AWF/D-H).

[3] Herter had pointed out to Gromyko that subversive activities carried out from East Berlin made any such activities from the West "look puny." He cited excerpts from East German radio broadcasts alleging that he and West German Foreign Minister von Brentano had "engaged jointly in homosexual activities"—a revelation that had, according to Herter, shaken Gromyko up a bit (*ibid.*; see also State, *Foreign Relations, 1958–1960*, vol. VIII, *Berlin Crisis 1958–1959*, pp. 803–5).

[4] Gromyko had told the conference members that the Soviet delegation, after full consultation with representatives of the German Democratic Republic, had developed a free-city proposal for Berlin. The protocol authorized the stationing of small military contingents of the four major powers in Berlin or, if agreed to by those powers, military contingents maintained by neutral states. A permanent commission composed of the four major powers and the German Democratic Republic would supervise the status of the city and ensure its independence (*ibid.*, pp. 810–11).

[5] On this same day Herter would tell Eisenhower that Gromyko had given no indication that he would accept any of the Western proposals or any modification of his own proposals that would justify a summit meeting. Herter also criticized Khrushchev's "threatening noises," which had been "far from helpful." He had asked the President to emphasize during his news conference the following day that developments in Geneva did not encourage Eisenhower to believe that a summit conference was justified. "This would," Herter said, "give a real impetus to the possibility of our securing some progress on the Berlin situation which, in turn, might justify such a conference." Eisenhower would agree that the time had come to "stir up a little action" (Herter to Eisenhower, and Eisenhower to Herter, June 2, 1959, *ibid.*; for the President's remarks see *Public Papers of the Presidents: Eisenhower, 1959*, pp. 425–27, 430, 432). For developments see the following document.

1188   *EM, AWF, International Series: Macmillan*

To Harold Macmillan   *June 3, 1959*
Cable. Secret

Dear Harold: I am glad that you have given Selwyn such firm support. Before your cable arrived I had sent to Herter a message telling him that I thought Selwyn had developed well in his post and that in my opinion he was doing a fine job. I think your statement should neutralize any damage done to his prestige by the *Times* article of June first.[1]

This morning I shall be in a press conference and I shall undoubtedly be questioned closely about any discernable progress at Geneva and therefore the possibility of a Summit Conference.[2]

As you know, I adhere to my position that a Summit meeting based on nothing more than wishful thinking would be a disaster. The world would interpret such a move as being a virtual surrender, while Soviet prestige would be enhanced.

On the other hand, we agreed in our conversations at Camp David that we could afford to make a rather liberal definition of progress.[3] While I agree that a document formulating our two positions would be a useful document, I do think we must also have something recognizable as a specific accomplishment.[4] For example there might be included a prerequisite in your formula something of this sort: "Since the Geneva Conference is partially a result of the crisis of Berlin, created by the Soviet Union, there must be an agreement confirming the continuing status of Berlin pending the reunification of Germany." I do not see how any of us can with self-respect go to a Summit meeting unless such a statement has been issued by the Soviets or an agreement to this effect has been consummated.

While I shall not try to give at my press conference a full list of the things that would spell additional real progress at the Foreign Ministers' meeting, we might hope for a widening of contacts between the two sides of the Iron Curtain, particularly in the fields of press exchanges, books and travel by private citizens. Other ways in which progress might be achieved would be by some firm agreement for initial steps in banning of particular tests and control thereof.

I repeat that the production by the Foreign Ministers of a reasonable paper for us to work on at a Summit Conference, together with the assurance that there will be no further attempts to restrict our rights and privileges with respect to Berlin, constitute the very minimum that would justify a Summit meeting.

These are not new ideas; so far as I know, all of us are agreed on them.[5]

With warm regard, *As ever*

---

[1] For background see the preceding document. Macmillan had written Eisenhower that the story regarding Lloyd's replacement "was a complete fabrication." He was doing very well and had increased his stature, Macmillan said. "It is annoying that The Times should have printed this rumour, but at least their article assumed five more years of Conservative government here" (Macmillan to Eisenhower, June 2, 1959, PREM 11/ 2685).

[2] See the preceding document. Eisenhower would tell his questioner that there had not been "any detectable progress" that would justify holding a summit meeting, al-

though he had expressed his "readiness to . . . define satisfactory progress rather liberally" (*Public Papers of the Presidents: Eisenhower, 1959*, pp. 425–26).
3 On the Camp David talks see no. 1116.
4 Macmillan had told Eisenhower that he thought that only a minimal amount of progress was required in order to agree to a summit "with a clear conscience." He suggested that all that was necessary was "an agreed formulation of our two positions," plus a statement regarding any points that could be reconciled.
5 For developments see no. 1196.

1189   *EM, AWF, DDE Diaries Series*

To Neil Hosler McElroy   *June 3, 1959*
Secret

Memorandum for the Secretary of Defense: I have noted press reports about the Soviet objection to our deploying IRBMs into Greece.[1] In December, 1957, when you, Foster and I went to the NATO meeting, we made our position absolutely clear that we would not try to induce any NATO nation to accept IRBMs for deployment in its territory. We made it clear also that we would be ready to make these available to any nation that voluntarily requested them and where we believed their deployment would be useful as a deterrent and for defense.[2]

In connection with the foregoing, I should like to have the following questions answered:

(*a*). Do we in fact have a firm plan for stationing IRBMs in Greece?[3]

(*b*). Did the Greek government initiate a firm request for these weapons?[4]

(*c*). Assuming the answer to be "yes," did the appropriate NATO authority concur?[5]

(*d*). What additional numbers from the uniformed services would be stationed in Greece?[6]

(*e*). What would be the total number of such American strength in that country?[7]

(*f*). What particular advantage do we expect to gain from putting these weapons into Greece in view of the fact that that country is both small and exposed?[8]

(*g*). Does the State Department see any great advantage in stationing these weapons in this particular country?[9]

(*h*). Finally, what additional sums for defense support and economic assistance will be requested of the Congress as a result of any such action?[10]

I do not want this memorandum widely circulated or worked on by junior staffs. Except for a few statistics that I desire, these matters involve high policy and so I should like to have this paper handled by the fewest possible people.[11]

[1] The Soviet Union had charged that the United States "was taking dangerous uni lateral action" in establishing missile bases in Greece and other NATO countries. They had also warned Greece that accepting these bases would constitute "hostile action" and had urged the Greeks to withdraw from NATO (*New York Times*, Apr. 23, May 14, 27, 29, 1959).

[2] On the 1957 NATO meeting see no. 501.

[3] The United States hoped to begin deployment of missile squadrons in Greece in the latter part of 1960, McElroy would answer (McElroy to Eisenhower, June 12, 1959, AWF/A). The Greek government, however, had not yet agreed in principle to accept the missiles.

[4] Greece had not initiated such a request but had indicated that they would "give favorable consideration" to such a recommendation.

[5] "State and Defense agree that a recommendation by SACEUR to the U.S. and the proposed host government for deployment of IRBM's is the only formal NATO action required to proceed," McElroy would tell the President. "Following U.S.-Greek agreement to proceed with IRBM negotiations, SACEUR will request the NATO Standing Group to inform the Military Committee and the North Atlantic Council that such negotiations are underway in accordance with his recommendations."

[6] Between 1,100 to 1,500 would be needed, depending on the exact location in Greece.

[7] The total number would be 2,650 to 3,050, depending on the site selected.

[8] Missiles fired from Greece would be able to hit many targets unreachable by missiles located in Great Britain and would aid in completing the system "with which we hope to ring the Soviet Bloc," McElroy would answer. Greek bases would be no more exposed than those being planned in Great Britain, Italy, and Turkey. Moreover, Greece seemed to be the only NATO country that would agree to a third squadron to meet SACEUR's requirements.

[9] McElroy would state that although the State Department did not see any great advantage to these deployments, it did believe the action was necessary to meet NATO requirements.

[10] Overall costs for a one-squadron deployment was estimated to be $11 million in FY 1960, $34.6 million in FY 1961, $33 million in FY 1962, and $33 million in FY 1963.

[11] The Joint Chiefs of Staff considered the missile program in Greece "high priority," McElroy would tell Eisenhower, and he promised to arrange a complete briefing at the President's request.

On the following day Greek government officials would inform the Soviet Union that "the matter of defense was Greece's own business" and that withdrawal from NATO would isolate the country and was therefore unacceptable (*New York Times*, June 5, 1959).

On June 17 Eisenhower would tell McElroy and Acting Secretary C. Douglas Dillon that the placement of IRBM bases in "flank" areas such as Greece seemed to him "very questionable." "If Cuba or Mexico were to become Communist inclined, and the Soviets were to send arms and equipment," he said, ". . . we would feel that we would have to intervene, militarily if necessary." Dillon and McElroy, however, remained unwilling to treat Greece and Turkey differently from other NATO countries and urged the President to go forward with the deployments. Eisenhower asked that action be delayed as long as advisable (Goodpaster, Memorandum of Conference, June 17, 1959, AWF/D).

To Syngman Rhee   *June 4, 1959*
Cable. Confidential

Dear Mr. President:[1] I appreciate your recent message reaffirming Korea's role as an ally in the defense of the Free World.[2] I am glad that you were pleased with the statement concerning military aid which I made at my press conference on May 5 and note that you have expressed your confidence that my statements will carry influence with the American people and the Congress. You will, of course, recognize that the Congress and the American people are influenced largely by their own good judgment of the attachment of Korea to those fundamental democratic principles which are in fact the primary target of Communist subversion.[3]

You may be sure that the American people look upon Korea as an important, steadfast and valued friend of the United States and the Free World in the global struggle against the forces of totalitarian Communism and are cognizant of the special needs of Korea, exposed as it is to the ever-present threat of renewed Communist aggression.[4]

Please accept, Mr. President, my best wishes for your continued good health. *Sincerely*

[1] The text of this letter, drafted by the Department of State, was to be sent to the American embassy in Seoul for delivery to President Rhee (Murphy to Eisenhower, June 2, 1959, and the draft with the President's changes are in AWF/I: Rhee).
[2] See nos. 244, 404, 985, and 1536. President Rhee had sent a message thanking Eisenhower for his statement at a news conference on May 5 in response to a question on mutual security and military aid costs (Yang to Eisenhower, May 13, 1959, AWF/I: Rhee). Eisenhower had said that the United States needed to give "a large portion of military aid" to Korea in order to hold and protect the area (*Public Papers of the Presidents: Eisenhower, 1959*, p. 362). The Department of State had suggested to Eisenhower that sending a response to Rhee would offer him opportunity to reaffirm U.S. support for its "ally" (Murphy to Eisenhower, June 2, 1959, AWF/I: Rhee).
[3] The State Department had recommended that Eisenhower make this point because the U.S. press and Congress were criticizing the Korean government for its "undemocratic practices," including the suppression of the nation's second largest newspaper. The Department had also advised that no publicity be given to this letter (*ibid.*).
[4] President Rhee had also written that continued military assistance meant "survival itself in the struggle against communism" and that Korea would do its full part defending itself and the Free World (Yang to Eisenhower, May 13, 1959, AWF/I: Rhee).

TO WILTON BURTON PERSONS   *June 4, 1959*

Memorandum for General Persons: Attached is the second Interim Report from the Draper Committee, which I believe Bob Merriam received this morning.[1]

I want it studied on an urgent basis so that I can comment further to the Committee on their manifestly searching analysis.

I am not certain whether or not we sent a copy of the first report to the Congress; if we did so, did we transmit it before or after we had attached our own comments?[2]

[1] On the recommendation of the Secretaries of State and Defense, Eisenhower had created the President's Committee to Study the Military Assistance Program in November 1958. Under the chairmanship of William Henry Draper, Jr., board chairman of Mexican Light and Power Company and former U.S. Special Representative in Europe and Under Secretary of the Army, the committee was to undertake "a completely independent, objective, and non-partisan analysis" of the military assistance component of the Mutual Security Program. Eisenhower had told Draper that he hoped the committee would "take a good hard look" at the program, particularly the overextension of defense forces in underdeveloped countries (Eisenhower to Draper, Nov. 24, 1958, AWF/D; see also State, *Foreign Relations, 1958–1960*, vol. IV, *Foreign Economic Policy*, pp. 431–33). For background on Draper see Galambos and van Ee, *The Middle Way*, no. 5. Robert Edward Merriam, former Assistant Director of the Bureau of the Budget, had become Deputy Assistant to the President for Interdepartmental Affairs in September 1958.

The first interim report, submitted on March 17, 1959, had stated that the program lacked administrative continuity. Since the methods used to provide assistance were not compatible with the plans and resources of the recipient countries, deliveries had been delayed and costs had increased. The United States must recognize the long-term nature of the program, the report stated, by replacing obsolete equipment with modern weapons. An additional $400 million was needed in FY 1960 to modernize current forces in the NATO countries and in other parts of the world. Draper had told Eisenhower that criticisms of the program were justified but were incidental compared to its value (Goodpaster, Memorandum of Conference, Mar. 20, 1959, AWF/D; see also *U.S. Department of State Bulletin* 40, no. 1040 [June 1, 1959], pp. 796–804).

The second report dealt with the organization and administration of the program. Recommendations included the programming of military assistance on a long-term basis, continued authorization of military assistance appropriations with funds from the Defense Department, and participation of the State Department and the ambassadors in the early stages of the operations. Draper had told Eisenhower that success in these areas required an effective working relationship between the State and Defense departments. The State Department should not become involved in the details of the operation, Draper advised, and the Defense Department should willingly accept competent and timely foreign policy guidance (Draper to Eisenhower, June 3, 1959, AWF/A, Draper Committee; see also Eisenhower to Draper, June 4, 1959, *ibid.*; and *U.S. Department of State Bulletin* 40, no. 1046 [July 13, 1959], pp. 46–49).

[2] The first report had been sent, with comments, to Congress on April 29. It did not include a request for additional funds (Legislative Leadership meeting notes, Apr. 22, 1959, AWF/D; Goodpaster, Memorandum of Conference, Apr. 23, 1959, *ibid.*; and White House staff memorandum, June 4, 1959, AWF/A, Draper Committee).

On June 24 Eisenhower would transmit the second interim report to Congress, together with his endorsement of the proposals that required legislative action. In a letter to Draper on that same day the President would "fully concur" with the recommendations for continued reappraisal and evaluation to assure that the military assistance programs did "not tend to continue simply through their own existing momentum beyond the period of their real need" (Eisenhower to Draper, and Eisenhower to Nixon and Rayburn, June 24, 1959, *ibid.*).

Persons would tell Eisenhower on June 30 that implementation of the recommendations of the detailed report would be coordinated by the Director of the Bureau of the Budget (Persons to Eisenhower, June 30, 1959; see also Dillon to Eisenhower, June 8, 1959; both in *ibid.*).

The final report, sent to Eisenhower on August 17 and to Congress three days later, would reiterate the committee's previous recommendations for funding and improvements in the administration of the program (Eisenhower to Nixon and Rayburn, June 24, July 23, Aug. 20, 1959, AWF/A, Draper Committee). For action in Congress on the Mutual Security Appropriations Act, which Eisenhower would sign on September 28, see State, *Foreign Relations, 1958–1960,* vol. IV, *Foreign Economic Policy,* pp. 463–67; and *Congressional Quarterly Almanac,* vol. XV, *1959,* pp. 178–94.

On October 31, 1960, Under Secretary of State C. Douglas Dillon would tell the National Security Council that a Five Year Military Assistance Plan had been effected as a result of the recommendations of the Draper Committee (NSC meeting minutes, Nov. 2, 1960, AWF/NSC).

1192   *EM, AWF, International Series:*
                                                                            De Gaulle

To Charles André Joseph Marie De Gaulle   *June 5, 1959*

Dear Mr. President: I am very appreciative of your letter of May twenty-fifth and of the careful thought that you have put into it. It raises subjects of the highest importance to which we must both direct our thoughts in order to achieve the harmony of purpose so essential to the free world.[1]

I have given a great deal of thought to your letter and have come to the conclusion that we can deal with these problems best through a personal exchange of views. It had been my hope that you could come to the United States. I realize, however, that you have had tremendous tasks to perform in France and the Community which have prevented you from making such a journey. An opportunity for our meeting together may present itself, however, should the present Foreign Ministers' meeting in Geneva reach a point where a Summit Meeting might be justified and desirable.[2] Such a meeting would probably be held in Europe. Should this be the case, I would be delighted to accept your invitation and would be glad to come to Paris in advance of that meeting in order to see you alone. We could then discuss frankly and fully the problems which confront us and the means by which we can best concert our strengths.

Once we have a clearer indication whether or not a Summit Meeting should indeed take place, I shall write you again to see if we can get a mutually agreeable date.

While realizing the complexity of some of the problems which confront our nations, I place special significance on our basic solidarity of purpose. Particularly, I refer to your statement that in the present situation the alliance of the free nations is absolutely necessary. With our agreement on this as a starting point, I am certain that we can bring all of our difficulties into line.[3]

Please accept, Mr. President, the expression of my highest consideration and sincere friendship.[4]

With warm personal regard, *Sincerely*

[1] De Gaulle had told Eisenhower that although France was "taking certain measures in her own behalf" his country did not wish to change its alliance with NATO (for background see no. 1112). Since the alliance was concerned only with the security of Western Europe, de Gaulle stated, the United States, Britain, and France had different attitudes and undertook different actions in other areas of the world. France would establish its own command of the Mediterranean and North African areas in cooperation with its allies.

De Gaulle also expressed concerns about atomic weapons and the conditions under which they might be used. France was required "to take certain precautions," he said, that would not be necessary if the United States were willing to share its atomic secrets. The Franco-American alliance meant that an atomic war involving the United States "would automatically expose France to total and immediate destruction." Therefore, he said, France would no longer agree to the storage of atomic weapons on her soil "without complete and permanent control over them" (AWF/I: de Gaulle).

[2] For background on the foreign ministers' conference see no. 1188.

[3] For developments regarding the foreign ministers' meeting see no. 1196; on Eisenhower's trip to Europe see no. 1276.

[4] At the end of this message Eisenhower had handwritten the following postscript in answer to de Gaulle's message of sympathy on Secretary Dulles's death: "Thank you very much for your generous tribute to Foster Dulles. He was a wise and courageous man and a valued friend whose fortitude and determination to maintain the peace and security of the world will be missed by all of us."

1193   *EM, WHCF, Confidential File:*
State Department

To Robert Rodolf Mullen   *June 8, 1959*
Personal and confidential

Dear Bob: For your information I send along to you some of the comments given to me by our experts on the proposal you made at Waseda University in Tokyo last April.[1]

1. To underwrite the Japanese Export-Import Bank as a substitute for United States-controlled bilateral assistance could, in effect, deny us a major instrument for our aid programs.
2. To make Japan the chosen instrument of United States development assistance would be resented by other Asian countries, such as India, which tend to view Japanese prominence and power without enthusiasm.
3. Japan could not administer development assistance more effectively than the United States or existing multilateral institutions such as the International Bank for Reconstruction and Development.
4. The proposal involves a direct United States subsidy for Japanese exports. This is to the detriment of exports from other countries, including the United States, in a period when our exports already face increasing competition in world markets.
5. A program of the proposed magnitude would be inconsistent with our attempts to encourage greater European participation in Asian economic development and with our attempts to stimulate the greater use of private foreign capital in economic development abroad.

   "Certainly Japan has the skills and industrial resources to make an important contribution to the economic development of other Asian countries. Japan has already supplied many millions of dollars in goods and services to Asian countries under our direct aid programs. She has also benefitted from our offshore procurement and, indirectly, from our assistance to other countries in the area.

   "We are now exploring ways to coordinate Japanese skills and resources with our own efforts on a project-by-project basis. As one recent example, the United States and Japan are jointly financing the expansion of Indian iron ore facilities to permit annual shipments of some two million tons from India to Japan.

   "The benefits of further cooperation with Japan are recognized by many other Asian countries. Such cooperation can expand in the future as the lingering fears of Japanese power and control are overcome."[2]

With some of these arguments I have no doubt you will disagree. However, it is a fact that almost any broad proposal affecting our relationship with other nations is bound to have repercussions in other areas that must be carefully examined and evaluated.

In any event I am more than delighted that you are interesting yourself in this kind of project.[3]

With warm regard, *Sincerely*

[1] For background see no. 1133. Mullen, a public relations executive and a former Eisenhower campaign director (see Galambos and van Ee, *The Middle Way*, no. 891), had sent a copy of his April 27 speech, in which he had suggested that the United States underwrite the Japanese Import-Export Bank as an "investment loan." The United States, instead of giving direct aid to poor Southeast Asian countries, could let Japan finance industrial expansion there. This strategy would both open up a market for Japanese capital formerly constrained by anti-Japanese sentiment and also provide Southeast Asia with much-needed resources. Mullen had warned that without a strong economy Japan could turn Communist (May 21, 1959). Eisenhower had asked White House aide Don Paarlberg to have the proposal evaluated by the relevant agencies and in the interim had thanked Mullen for quoting his own statements on the "natural economic affinity between Japan and Southeast Asia" (May 25, 1959).
[2] Up to this point in the letter, Paarlberg's draft (Paarlberg to Eisenhower, June 5, 1959) had used quotations culled from the agency reports, including those submitted by the Departments of State and Commerce (May 29, 1959). Eisenhower did not address Mullen's point that the American people were "weary" of providing foreign aid.
[3] Thanking the President for his comments, Mullen would state his intention of "stirring up wider and deeper interest" in U.S. problems with Asia. All correspondence is in the same file as the document.

1194 *EM, AWF, Name Series*

TO FRANCIS WILFRED DE GUINGAND *June 9, 1959*

Dear Freddie: I haven't had time these last few days to go over the list of names I promised you,[1] but I do not want to delay sending you estimates as to our aluminum consumption.[2] I find that predictions are that the United States will need from all sources about 10% more each succeeding year. Our consumption is estimated at 2,600,000 tons in 1960. I am further told that if our growth figures are realized, additional capacity or resources will be required from 1963 onward.

It was wonderful to see you the other day. I hope that you made your connections easily and that the trip to London was uneventful.[3]

I shall be in touch with you further shortly.[4]

With warm regard, *As ever*

[1] At an off-the-record luncheon on June 4 the President and Major General de Guingand had discussed Eisenhower's plan to have a reunion of wartime colleagues in 1960 (for background see no. 991; see also Whitman to de Guingand, June 11 and 13, 1959, AWF/N, de Guingand Corr.).
[2] De Guingand, who served on the board of directors of Britol Aluminum, Ltd., and Canadian Aluminum, Ltd., probably had spoken with Eisenhower about U.S. aluminum consumption at the June 4 luncheon (see Ann Whitman memorandums, June 4, 8, 1959, AWF/AWD; *New York Times*, June 7, 1959; Telephone conversation, Eisenhower and Mitchell, July 28, 1959, AWF/D). De Guingand would thank the President for the information on June 14 (AWF/N).

On the upcoming strike in the aluminum industry see no. 1249.

[3] Following the luncheon de Guingand had traveled to New York in order to meet his flight to London (*ibid.*).
[4] For developments see no. 1197.

1195   *EM, AWF,*
                                  Administration Series

TO ARTHUR ELLSWORTH SUMMERFIELD   *June 9, 1959*

Dear Art: Of course I am delighted to have the first piece of "Official Missile Mail." I shall see that your letter and the envelope are sent to Abilene for display and safekeeping.[1]

At the same time, I want to congratulate you again on thus dramatizing the use to which guided missiles can be put for communication between peoples. I am delighted to know, also, that the project resulted from the close cooperation of the Department of Defense and the Post Office Department.[2]

With warm regard, *As ever*

[1] Postmaster General Summerfield had written undated letters to several government officials, including the President, and had placed them in a Regulus I Training Guided Missile aboard the guided missile submarine U.S.S. *Barbero.* On June 8, while the submarine was one hundred miles out to sea on a training mission it fired the Regulus, a pilotless bomber guided by remote control, at the Naval Auxiliary Air Station at Mayport, Florida. When the Regulus was recovered, Summerfield's letter to Eisenhower was then canceled and forwarded to the White House as "a significant philatelic souvenir." The envelope bore a four-cent stamp and a picture of the Regulus with the words: "first official missile mail" (AWF/A and *New York Times,* June 9, 1959). The Eisenhower Museum, containing memorabilia bestowed upon Eisenhower over the course of his career, had been dedicated in Abilene, Kansas, in November 1954 (Galambos and van Ee, *The Middle Way,* no. 760).
[2] Summerfield had said that the Post Office Department would continue to cooperate with the Defense Department in order to use technology in the delivery of the mail.

1196   *EM, AWF, Dulles-Herter Series*

TO CHRISTIAN ARCHIBALD HERTER   *June 10, 1959*
Cable. Secret

Dear Chris: Yesterday was one of my busiest days, starting at seven and, without respite, ending at 11:30 as I arrived back at the White House from Atlantic City.[1] Because of my preoccupations I could not personally answer your cable asking for certain decisions, and I suggested to Dillon, after a personal conference with him, that he do so on my behalf. I am sure that he reflected my views accurately.[2]

Of course we stand firm on the conclusion that I cannot attend any so-called Summit meeting unless there is sufficient progress in your present meeting to give some hope of accomplishment at the projected later meeting. I continue to believe that it would be not only a mistake but a great disservice to the world to go to a Summit meeting that would be barren of promise.

In this connection I suggested to Dillon that you might find it useful to remind your colleagues at the Conference that the United States does not send her Secretary of State to an international conference to act as an errand boy. Consequently, from our viewpoint, there is no validity to any argument that a Summit meeting would be certain to bring about some beneficial results, while a Foreign Ministers meeting would be certain to show complete failure.[3] Within the limits of policy approved by the President, the Secretary of State has considerable latitude as to tactics and substantive detail. Incidentally, this demand for so-called Summit talks is a rather modern development. The history of the meetings that have been held does not impress me as presenting a record of brilliant accomplishments.

With respect to the matter of assurances on our rights and responsibilities in Berlin, I have little concern as to the manner of its accomplishment so long as there can be no possible mistake of our common understanding, including the understanding of all other governments.

I rather concur in the thought that a recess might be a better tactical move than complete cessation of the meeting. If, of course, there were some unexpected break and some clear and definite progress should be accomplished, then the entire situation would be changed. The present outlook for such accomplishment seems to be indeed dim.

I cannot tell you how pleased I am with the obvious skill with which you have conducted these difficult negotiations on the part of our government. Your combination of firmness and correct deportment and conciliatory attitude is commanding the respect of all thoughtful readers.[4]

With warm regard, *Sincerely*

---

[1] After meeting with various staff members early in the morning, Eisenhower had met for over two hours with the legislative leaders. He then addressed the delegates of the National Conference on Civil Rights at the Statler Hotel, after which he returned to the White House for additional appointments. At 5:00 P.M. he left for Atlantic City, where he addressed the annual convention of the American Medical Association (see the Chronology; and *Public Papers of the Presidents: Eisenhower, 1959*, pp. 447–56).

[2] In his cable from Geneva Secretary Herter had told Eisenhower that the foreign

ministers' conference, entering its fifth week, had "reached a crossroads" and required an American initiative to break the deadlock. He noted that Soviet Foreign Minister Gromyko, who had acknowledged Western rights in Berlin, had consistently refused to include any reference to those rights in a political settlement or a future peace treaty with the German Democratic Republic.

Herter suggested telling Gromyko privately that "the conference was getting nowhere" and repeating the points in the allied position that were "immovable and not open to negotiation": Any agreement must include Western rights of presence in and access to Berlin; the West might consider a modest reduction in the strength of its forces, but it would not agree to the inclusion of a Soviet detachment; the Western allies would not recognize East Germany, and although they could accept the turnover of functions regarding military traffic into Berlin to the East Germans, all complaints would be directed to the Soviet Union. If agreement could be reached on those points, then Eisenhower would meet with the heads of government in a summit conference. He advocated a brief recess to allow the Soviet officials to study the proposal (Herter to Eisenhower, CAHTO 91, 92, June 9, 1959, AWF/D-H; see also State, *Foreign Relations, 1958–1960*, vol. VIII, *Berlin Crisis 1958–1959*, pp. 856–58; and Eisenhower, *Waging Peace*, p. 399).

In their meeting on the preceding day Acting Secretary Dillon had told Eisenhower that Gromyko had just presented the Western allies with a new proposal: the Soviet Union would agree to a one-year recognition of Western occupation rights under the conditions that the West would reduce their forces and armaments to a symbolic level; would end all hostile propaganda and all espionage activities originating in West Berlin; and would agree not to station atomic or rocket facilities in the area. If Berlin became a free, demilitarized city in conformity with these proposals, access commitments would be honored until the reunification of Germany. Eisenhower thought the proposal "was very bad" because the Soviets had not acknowledged Western rights in Berlin (Goodpaster, Memorandum of Conference, June 10, 1959, WHO/OSS Subject [State], State Dept.; see also State, *Foreign Relations, 1958–1960*, vol. VIII, *Berlin Crisis 1958–1959*, pp. 865–67, 869–73).

Dillon had cabled Herter that Eisenhower endorsed his plan to meet with Gromyko and that he would accept any means to guarantee Western rights that Herter found satisfactory, including a unilateral declaration of Western rights "not objected to by the Soviets" (Dillon to Herter, June 9, 1959, AWF/D-H).

[3] Dillon had shown Eisenhower excerpts from Soviet Premier Khrushchev's speech, implying that foreign ministers lacked authority to reach agreement and that only heads of government could make meaningful decisions. The Soviet Union, Khrushchev emphasized, could not accept an agreement on Berlin that perpetuated the occupation of Germany (*ibid.*; see also State, *Foreign Relations, 1958–1960*, vol. VIII, *Berlin Crisis 1958–1959*, p. 859).

[4] Eisenhower would tell Dillon that one purpose of his message to Herter was to "'buck him up' a little since the President well knew how he might be feeling a little 'down' and rather 'alone' as the conference approaches an end which is unsatisfactory from our standpoint" (Goodpaster, Memorandum of Conference, June 11, 1959, AWF/D).

Herter would cable Eisenhower on the following day that he planned to meet privately with Gromyko that afternoon. The Soviets were trying to correct the Western interpretation of the latest Soviet proposal as a threat, Herter said, "but without too great success." He also told the President that he would suggest to Gromyko a three-week to one month recess in the talks (Herter to Eisenhower, June 11, 1959, *ibid.*; see also Herter to Dillon, June 10, 1959, *ibid.*).

After his two-hour meeting with Gromyko, Herter would cable Dillon that little of any significance had emerged from the talk (see State, *Foreign Relations, 1958–1960*, vol. VIII, *Berlin Crisis 1958–1959*, pp. 879–84). For developments see no. 1200.

To Francis Wilfred de Guingand   *June 10, 1959*
Personal

Dear Freddie: Herewith the list of the British officers whose presence I believe would add a great deal to our reunion and to the project that we have in mind.[1] Since it would be difficult for me to find out the state of health and other conditions that would influence the decisions of these individuals, I give you the names that you and I agreed upon at the luncheon. All that I shall need to know in the near future are the names of those who feel, with a reasonable degree of assurance, that they could probably come.

If a sufficient number of replies should be favorable as to indicate the desirability of going ahead with the project, I would propose to invite also General Pierre Joseph Koenig to represent French participation.[2] (I shall probably also ask General Crerar).[3]

As a third list, I send you the names of the Americans that I would hope could attend, although some of them might have to come on a part-time or intermittent basis. Our total of permanent guests could not exceed about twenty-two.

I feel that if we could get from nine to twelve agreements from the British officers, we would have the basis for effective planning.

If we should do the thing in 1960, I rather believe that some time in the middle of May or early October might be the most convenient dates.[4]

With warm regard, *As ever*

[1] On June 4 Eisenhower and de Guingand had discussed having a reunion of wartime colleagues in order to renew valued friendships and to compose an agreed-upon document regarding events during the European phase of World War II. For background on the reunion and the guest list see nos. 989, and 991. The lists and a draft of this letter showing Eisenhower's extensive handwritten emendations are in AWF/N: War Reunion.

[2] Koenig had commanded the French Forces of the Interior during World War II.

[3] Crerar had commanded the Canadian First Army.

[4] For developments see nos. 1205 and 1220.

To Barnaby Conrad Keeney   *June 10, 1959*

Dear Dr. Keeney: Thank you very much for reaffirming, by letter, your cordial invitation to address the convocation to be held at Brown

University in October.[1] I have placed the date of the twenty-first on my calendar. While, of course, this acceptance is subject to the hazards of unforeseen circumstances that might necessitate an abrupt cancellation, I assure you that I shall do my best to fulfill the engagement.

As to details of my visit, I think you should, at an appropriate time, communicate with my Appointment Secretary, Thomas E. Stephens. Such details would include time of day or evening, the program for the convocation, and any activities expected of me other than attendance at the single convocation.

Although it had slipped my memory that Brown had voted me an honorary degree in 1948, I assure you that I would be complimented by its presentation on October twenty-first.[2]

With personal regard, *Sincerely*

[1] Eisenhower and Keeney had met in New York on May 14.
[2] In March 1948, while President of Columbia University, Eisenhower had declined an invitation to receive an honorary degree from Brown University (Galambos, *Columbia University*, no. 19). For developments see no. 1290.

1199   *EM, AWF, Administration Series*

To WILLIAM PIERCE ROGERS   *June 11, 1959*

Dear Bill: Many thanks for sending me a copy of your excellent talk at the graduation exercises of St. Lawrence University. I like the way you worked into it our thought about the necessity for self-discipline, and I hope you will find the opportunity you seek for an entire speech on the subject.[1] I, too, shall try to emphasize the same idea whenever it seems appropriate.

With warm regard, *As ever*

[1] On June 8 Attorney General Rogers had sent the speech, delivered on June 7, to the President (AWF/A; see also *New York Times*, June 8, 1959). In his cover letter Rogers had said he tried "to some small extent" to fulfill Eisenhower's request to emphasize the "necessity for self-discipline" (see nos. 798 and 994). Rogers had told the graduates that by exercising various aspects of self-discipline they could prevent racketeering, labor disputes, rising crime rates, and, especially, racial discrimination. Rogers had added that he hoped to make an entire speech on the subject in the future.

To Nikita Sergeyevich Khrushchev   *June 15, 1959*
Cable. Secret

Dear Mr. Chairman: The point seems to have been reached in the discussions among the four Foreign Ministers in Geneva at which I feel impelled to address to you this personal and private note.[1] I shall give it no publicity whatsoever unless you should desire otherwise.

It has been my sincere hope that the progress at the Foreign Ministers' meeting would be such as to justify a summit meeting at which final settlements of some of our problems could be reached. This note is a personal effort to explain to you why I feel that recent developments at Geneva imperil the achievement of this objective.

The Soviet Delegation, while unwilling to discuss in a serious way the broad peace plan which we put forward, has now, after some weeks of both private and plenary sessions, put forward proposals with respect to Berlin which are from our viewpoint a clearly unacceptable challenge to our position in that city.[2] At the same time Mr. Gromyko has stated that "in the opinion of the Soviet Government there is no foundation for any link between the results of this conference and the convening of a summit meeting."[3] Because of your original acceptance on March 30 of my March 26 proposal with respect to the current negotiations between us, I had come to believe that we were coming closer together in this important matter.[4] You will probably recall that in part of my March 26 proposal I said, "The purpose of the Foreign Ministers meeting should be to reach positive agreements over as wide a field as possible and in any case to narrow the differences between the respective points of view and to prepare constructive proposals for consideration by a conference of Heads of Government later in the summer. On this understanding and as soon as developments in the Foreign Ministers Meeting justify holding a summit conference, the US Government would be ready to participate in such a conference. The date, place, and agenda for such a conference would be proposed by the meeting of Foreign Ministers."

You in your March 30 reply then stated: "The Soviet Government expresses the hope that all participants of the conference of the Ministers of Foreign Affairs will make their positive contribution to the work of this conference and that it will be an important step in the cause of creating a firm peace in Europe. The Soviet Government, on its part, will do everything possible to assist in the attainment of this goal."

I sincerely hope that both you and I continue to hold to the spirit of this understanding and will do what we can in assuring that the Foreign Ministers talks will produce satisfactory results.

It seems to me, unfortunately, that the latest Soviet position at Geneva as presented by Mr. Gromyko creates an impossible situation for the United States in that it implies the convocation of a Summit Meeting without prior progress of any kind.

I am quite prepared to recognize that final agreements on the critical questions affecting world peace could probably be best concluded at a meeting of the Heads of Government. However, I want to say very earnestly that our Secretary of State has gone to Geneva with full authority from me and from the US Government to engage in serious negotiations of the type contemplated in the exchange of communications between us which led to the holding of the Foreign Ministers conference. I have no way of knowing, of course, Mr. Chairman, to what extent your own Foreign Minister is empowered by you to negotiate with this same degree of flexibility within the framework of what I thought was a firm understanding between you and me. But I do assure you that our purpose in the Foreign Ministers meeting has been to clear the way for a fruitful or at least hopeful meeting of Heads of Government.

I hope you will urgently consider the situation as it now stands. I write to you in no sense of attempting to bargain or to establish conditions. It is my thought only to see whether we will be able to achieve some greater measure of understanding between ourselves and eventually to reach settlements in some of the issues that divide us. Only thus, I think, can we bring about a real relaxation of the present tensions in the world. It would give me great satisfaction if we could meet later this year for that purpose.

I add only that if such a meeting were to offer hope of success it would certainly have to take place in an atmosphere in which neither side was posing a threat to the other and on the basis of such preparatory work by our Foreign Ministers as could give us reason to believe that the Heads of Government would be able to reach agreement on significant subjects. Anything less, it seems to me, would be a betrayal of the hopes of men everywhere.[5] *Sincerely yours*

---

[1] For background see no. 1196. Continued Soviet pressure for a summit meeting had prompted Eisenhower to consider the idea of a conciliatory message to Khrushchev. Eisenhower believed that an impossible situation was created when the Soviets acted as though the foreign ministers were incapable of concluding any substantive agreements. He had later told Acting Secretary Dillon: "Our trouble is that we have taken a position in the conference and they have taken a position. We say they are inflexible and they say we are inflexible." Eisenhower added, "There are a few essentials on which we stand which are not negotiable, and these seem to be the very things that the Soviets are interested in." He had "racked his head" to think of new sub-

jects on which to negotiate but was at his "wits end" (Goodpaster, Memorandum of Conference, June 17, 1959, AWF/D).

A draft of this message was sent to Secretary Herter in Geneva, who suggested various changes. After Eisenhower's approval, the final draft was sent to the American embassy in Moscow for delivery to the Soviet leader (see State, *Foreign Relations, 1958–1960*, vol. VIII, *Berlin Crisis 1958–1959*, pp. 894–901; see also Dillon to Herter, June 13, 1959, AWF/D-II).

[2] On the Soviet proposals see no. 1187; see also Conference of Foreign Ministers, *Foreign Ministers Meeting, May–August, 1959, Geneva*, pp. 260–66.

[3] During a two-hour private meeting on June 12, Gromyko had told Herter that a summit conference "was too important to be made the object of bargaining" and that no relationship existed between it and the foreign ministers' meeting. The Western attitude was like an ultimatum, Gromyko said, and the Soviets would not "pay concessions" to obtain a summit meeting (State, *Foreign Relations, 1958–1960*, vol. VIII, *Berlin Crisis 1958–1959*, pp. 881, 882, 886).

[4] The March 26 proposal was in the form of a note from the American embassy in Moscow to the Soviet Ministry of Foreign Affairs (see State, *American Foreign Policy; Current Documents, 1959*, pp. 638–39; see also no. 1116; on the Soviet reply see Royal Institute of International Affairs, *Documents on International Affairs 1959*, edited by Gillian King [London, 1963], pp. 33–34; see also *U.S. Department of State Bulletin* 40, no. 1034 [April 20, 1959], 554).

[5] For developments see the following document.

1201   *EM, AWF, International Series:*
                                                       Macmillan

To HAROLD MACMILLAN   *June 16, 1959*
Cable. Secret

Dear Harold: I shall probably want to write you further as soon as we know Khrushchev's reaction to my letter of June 15.[1] As you probably know, it was a most urgent suggestion to him to reconsider the Soviet position at Geneva, which has in fact retrogressed in recent days, and to live up to his own pledge to us last March that the Soviet Government would do everything possible to make a positive contribution to the work of the Foreign Ministers Conference. As to his reaction to my message I am not particularly sanguine but I also do not believe that we have yet necessarily reached an impasse.

As respects the question of a Summit meeting, I reiterated to Khrushchev the formula that we agreed to at Camp David last spring and made it clear that such a meeting "would certainly have to take place in an atmosphere in which neither side was posing a threat to the other, and on the basis of such preparatory work by our Foreign Ministers as could give us reason to believe that the Heads of Government would be able to reach agreement on significant subjects."[2]

From this statement I could not and, in my opinion, should not retreat. One reason for this conviction is that if I should agree, in the absence of the stated prerequisites, to go to a summit meeting, such a reversal on my part at this time would seriously impair any influence that I might hope to exercise with Khrushchev. Moreover it would be interpreted here as a dangerous exhibition of weakness, as indeed I would interpret it myself.

Frankly, it seems to me that any encounter of the three Western Heads of Government with Khrushchev would, in fact, be a Summit meeting. I think the public would see no difference between an informal and a more formal gathering and I can't see what advantage there would be in the "informal" formula for us. As you say, we would certainly want our Foreign Ministers. They would want at least a few selected advisers. Adding the clerical housekeeping and security personnel, we would willy-nilly have a full-fledged Summit conference on our hands with world attention focused on it. The presence of a thousand representatives of the press would be the frosting on the cake.[3]

I fully agree that public opinion is a factor of greatest importance and realize that you have some particular difficulties in this respect.[4]

However, I do believe that should Khrushchev face us with a call for a Summit meeting, we are not necessarily limited to a yes or no answer. I think, for example, that we would be in good posture to demand that the Foreign Ministers Conference be resumed after a few weeks recess. Possibly in some way or another we might find an opportunity to impress upon him personally the seriousness with which we regard failure to bring about a resumption of that conference. For instance, if Khrushchev should decide to replace Koslov in visiting the Soviet Exhibit in New York later this month, I would be ready, assuming no objection on the part of our allies, to meet with him in an effort to get the Foreign Ministers Meeting back on the tracks.[5] While such an occurrence would seem most unlikely, yet it is the kind of thing that could be done without presenting the picture of a "summit" meeting. It would indeed represent only a fortuitous circumstance of which advantage could be taken.

The essential element is of course the continued unity of the West. Above all this applies with special force to our two governments. I am therefore letting Chris Herter know that I believe the Western Foreign Ministers should take no initiative to break up the conference finally but, if necessary, should seek a recess of a few weeks during which we could develop an agreed allied position as to our next moves. I hope you might make similar suggestions to Selwyn.

As I said in the beginning of this letter, I shall want to write you further as soon as we hear from Khrushchev. Meanwhile, I should be glad to have your reactions to the foregoing.[6]

With warm regard, *As ever*

[1] For background on the Geneva foreign ministers' meeting see no. 1196. Eisenhower's letter to Khrushchev is the preceding document.
[2] On the Camp David meetings with Macmillan see no. 1116.
[3] Seeking to forestall a public request by Khrushchev for an immediate summit meeting, Macmillan had suggested that the heads of the four governments meet informally to discuss the situation either in the United States or in London. "We must be ready to make a fresh move," Macmillan had said, "and without delay" (Macmillan to Eisenhower, June 16, 1959, PREM 11/2685). Eisenhower thought that the proposal, which originally had been Secretary Herter's idea, was "unacceptable;" everyone would regard such a meeting as a summit. Before sending this message, which had been drafted by State Department officials and later edited by Eisenhower, the President had told British Ambassador Harold Caccia that he was trying to understand just what was in Macmillan's mind. "The picture of going hat in hand to see the Russians at a summit meeting" did not appeal to him or to the American people. Although he gave "some weight" to Macmillan's argument that a summit was necessary because "in a dictatorship no one but the dictator has power to commit the government," Eisenhower did not believe that this was a good reason to agree to Soviet demands (State, *Foreign Relations, 1958–1960*, vol. VIII, *Berlin Crisis 1958–1959*, pp. 892–95; Goodpaster, Memorandum of Conference, June 19, 1959, WHO/OSS, Subject [State], State Dept.; and Herter to Eisenhower, June 12, 1959, AWF/D-H; see also Eisenhower, *Waging Peace*, pp. 400–403; and Macmillan, *Pointing the Way*, pp. 66–70).
[4] Herter had told Eisenhower that he believed Macmillan had made a commitment during his trip to Moscow to press for a summit regardless of the outcome of the foreign ministers' meetings. Macmillan had, in fact, done so. He knew that Eisenhower would not agree to a summit without reasonable progress at the preliminary meeting. He was, however, facing elections in the fall and thought he was under constant pressure from the British people to produce results (Herter to Eisenhower, June 12, 1959, AWF/D-H; and Macmillan, *Riding the Storm*, p. 636).
[5] Eisenhower had told Ambassador Caccia that he would examine the possibility of a bilateral meeting with Khrushchev "if the others wanted him to do so" (Goodpaster, Memorandum of Conference, June 17, 1959, WHO/OSS, Subject [State], State Dept.). Soviet Deputy Premier Frol R. Kozlov would arrive in the United States on June 28 and would officially open the Soviet Exhibition of Science, Technology, and Culture in New York on the following day. Eisenhower would meet Kozlov for a short preview of the fair and would later spend over an hour with the Soviet official in Washington (see no. 1228; State, *Foreign Relations, 1958–1960*, vol. X, pt. 1, *Eastern Europe Region; Soviet Union; Cyprus*, pp. 287–325; and *New York Times*, June 29, 30, 1959; see also Ann Whitman memorandums, July 1, 1959, AWF/AWD; and Eisenhower, *Waging Peace*, pp. 404–5).
[6] For developments see the following document.

1202   *EM, AWF, Dulles-Herter Series*

To Christian Archibald Herter   *June 17, 1959*
Secret

Dear Chris: My thoughts have been with you often as you go through the trying routine that must frequently seem both futile and frustrating. I think, however, that from your messages we here have been able to appreciate your problems and have also been able to achieve what seems to me at least a most practical meeting of minds on the major questions raised.[1]

Of course Dillon communicates with you far more often than I do, but he invariably makes certain that I am acquainted with your messages.[2]

Just this minute I saw your recommendation that we make available to our Ambassadors in London, Paris and Bonn a copy of my message to Khrushchev. I approved, with the caution that the message should be sent to the Ambassadors on an eyes only basis.[3]

Incidentally, I had at my press conference this morning a question seeking to get an answer from me on the possibility that I had sent to Khrushchev a special message. I replied that I never affirm or deny the existence of any message that may or may not have been sent by me as a head of one government to another, unless publication is by mutual consent or by the initiative of the other party.[4]

If and when Khrushchev gives me an answer, we shall of course be in prompt communications with you.[5]

With the hope that you are not losing patience and with warm personal regard, *As ever*

---

[1] For background see nos. 1196 and 1201. In his most recent cables from Geneva, Herter had reported on discussions held with the British and French to revise the five-point proposal presented to Gromyko on June 8 so that it would more closely represent the Western position and have a better "effect on public opinion." Herter and Gromyko had then met privately and went "back and forth over the old harrowed field." If the Western proposals were still unacceptable, Herter told Gromyko, they should recognize that no agreement was possible and should end the conference after setting a date to meet in the future (State, *Foreign Relations, 1958–1960,* vol. VIII, *Berlin Crisis 1958–1959,* pp. 856–58, 904–6; see also Conference of Foreign Ministers, *Foreign Ministers Meeting, May–August, 1959, Geneva,* pp. 312–13).

[2] Eisenhower had told Acting Secretary Dillon that if an impasse developed on Berlin, the solidarity of the Western position should be assured at the highest level. Dillon then suggested a Western summit to settle minor disagreements and solidify the Western position. Eisenhower said he would be glad to go to London and then to Paris for a short visit to President de Gaulle if Herter thought such a meeting would be helpful (State, *Foreign Relations, 1958–1960,* vol. VIII, *Berlin Crisis 1958–1959,* pp. 910–11).

[3] For Eisenhower's message to Khrushchev see no. 1200; see also Dillon to Ambassadors, June 17, 1959, AWF/D-H.

[4] See *Public Papers of the Presidents: Eisenhower, 1959,* pp. 461–62.

[5] Herter would cable Eisenhower on the following day that Gromyko had postponed the informal meeting to discuss the Western proposals. "This must mean your correspondence with Khrushchev has had results," he said. "While we have predicted daily that the next session would be decisive . . . the patience is holding out and we may find ourselves engaged in a new negotiation" (Herter to Eisenhower, June 18, 1959, AWF/D-H). For developments see no. 1206.

1203   *EM, AWF, International Series:*
                                                      Macmillan

To Harold Macmillan   *June 17, 1959*
Secret

Dear Harold: I think that for the moment at least we are doing all
that humans can do—and must hope for the best.[1] *As ever*

<hr>

[1] For background see no. 1201. This message was sent through Acting Secretary of
State C. Douglas Dillon in response to Eisenhower's latest letter from Prime Minister Macmillan. The President's message to Khrushchev (no. 1200) might produce
some conciliatory moves, Macmillan said. If not, a short adjournment of the foreign
ministers' meeting was the best procedure to follow (Macmillan to Eisenhower, June
17, 1959, AWF/I: Macmillan). For developments see no. 1206.

1204   *EM, AWF,*
                                            Administration Series

To Lewis Lichtenstein Strauss   *June 17, 1959*

Dear Lewis: Many thanks for your note of yesterday. The projected
figures as to gross national product and personal income for the second quarter of this year are most encouraging.[1]

I must say that I welcome an occasional item of good news among
the papers that come to my desk!

With warm regard, *As ever*

<hr>

[1] Interim Secretary of Commerce Strauss had sent Eisenhower the projections for
the second quarter of 1959. He had reported that GNP was up by two and one half
percent over the previous quarter, and personal income had also increased (June
16, 1959, AWF/A).

1205   *EM, AWF, Name Series*

To Lionel Hastings Ismay   *June 17, 1959*
Personal

[Dear Pug:] It was wonderful to have news of you.[1] I shall not bother
you with a long message at the moment; I have only one thought I
want to communicate to you.

For some time I have been wondering whether I could not

arrange at some period during the year 1960 for a small reunion of certain of my best wartime friends. The purpose of the reunion would be first of all, a renewal of valued comradeships; secondly, it would give us an opportunity to review our own memories and records of our war experiences to see whether we could not produce a document that would have a unique character in the military history of the war, even if not any great value.[2]

Not long ago Freddie de Guingand was here and I charged him with inquiring from a number of my British friends as to the possibility of their coming. I have a recreation camp in the hills not far from here, where the reunion could well be held, and it would be a great honor for me to be the personal host of a group of British and Americans (with possibly one Canadian and one Frenchman) numbering something on the order of twenty to twenty-four.[3]

Freddie has the details of what I have in mind and possibly he will find some opportunity to talk to you about it. By no means do I mean to push you or to ask anything that might be inconvenient for you. But if you should feel like making such a trip, no one could possibly add more to the get-together. I have been thinking of the middle of May next year or the middle of October as possibly the best times, from my viewpoint.

This requires no answer but if you do have any thoughts you should like to communicate to me on this, I would, of course, welcome them.[4]

With warm regard, *As ever*

---

[1] Ismay had written on June 8 that his health continued to improve (for background see nos. 1012 and 1018; see also Ismay to Eisenhower, May 24, 1959 and Eisenhower to Ismay, June 1). In a reference to Field Marshal Bernard Law Montgomery, whose criticism of Eisenhower had recently attracted attention (see no. 1146), Ismay added, "If only someone would muzzle, or better still chloroform Monty, I should be spared the constant danger of blood pressure. I have come to the conclusion that his love of publicity is a disease, like alcoholism or taking drugs, and that it sends him equally mad." See no. 1220.

[2] For further background on the reunion see nos. 989 and 991.

[3] Eisenhower was referring to Camp David, the presidential retreat in the Catoctin Mountains in Maryland. On de Guingand's visit and Eisenhower's subsequent letters to him see nos. 1194 and 1197.

[4] Ismay would reply on June 25 that the President's idea was "perfectly splendid." He said he would want nothing more than to accept the invitation extended to a "fortunate few." He was afraid, however, that his health would have to improve a great deal before his physicians would allow him to undertake the trip. He added that he "might easily be rejuvenated" as May of next year is a "long way off." For developments see nos. 1697 and 1722.

All correspondence is in AWF/N.

1532

To Harold Macmillan   June 19, 1959
Cable. Secret

Dear Harold: As you will see, Khrushchev's reply was not responsive
to the points made in my letter. Worse still, it was an artfully de-
ceptive effort to reduce the fundamental differences which have
been exposed at Geneva to one or two fictitious issues.[1] Moreover,
Khrushchev has now come out publicly with pretty much the same
line in his speech today before the East German communist leaders in Moscow.[2]

Now that we have a recess we will have to see where we stand and
consult together as respects our next moves.[3] I am of course anxious to talk with Chris Herter about this and shall do so as soon as
he returns. I assume you will be doing the same with Selwyn after
which we will be in touch again.

I must say that my current feeling is that I can be just as firm and
just as patient and just as persistent as Khrushchev and this, I am
sure, is true of all of us.[4]

With warm regards, *As ever*

[1] For background see no. 1200. The foreign ministers' meetings had "a certain positive significance," Khrushchev had stated in his June 17 letter, insofar as they clarified positions and drew the different viewpoints closer together. The Western powers, however, had refused to discuss the latest Soviet proposals and had persistently
continued "to foist on the Soviet Union" an agreement that would preserve the occupation of West Berlin and further delay the conclusion of a peace treaty with Germany. If the ministers could not reach an understanding, Khrushchev said, then a
summit meeting would "become even more urgently necessary" (State, *Foreign Relations, 1958–1960*, vol. VIII, *Berlin Crisis 1958–1959*, pp. 914–17; see also Eisenhower,
Waging Peace, p. 403).

[2] For Khrushchev's speech see Conference of Foreign Ministers, *Foreign Ministers Meeting, May–August, 1959, Geneva,* pp. 316–28.

[3] On this day, after repeating their positions and acknowledging a stalemate, Foreign
Minister Gromyko and the Western foreign ministers had agreed to recess the conference until July 13 (State, *Foreign Relations, 1958–1960,* vol. VIII, *Berlin Crisis 1958–
1959,* pp. 918–29; see also Goodpaster, Memorandum of Conference, June 19, 1959,
AWF/D).

[4] Macmillan would write Eisenhower that "although Khrushchev was unwilling to admit it," Macmillan thought the President's message had had "a considerable effect
on him" (Macmillan to Eisenhower, June 22, 1959, AWF/I: Macmillan). For developments see no. 1212.

In June of 1953 President Hoover came to my office, for the first time, to pay a courtesy call.[1] He fell to discussing the character of the problems facing me, particularly those in the field of the nation's economy.

He pointed out that for twenty years the conservatives and middle-of-the-roaders, had discerned a drift toward greater governmental controls—or at least interference—in the nation's economy. People who belonged to the extreme right became very worried about this and became very critical in their condemnation of the whole thing as "socialism" and so on and so on. On the other hand, there were many people who listened to the oratory of the 1953 campaign who thought that I was not sufficiently "liberal" to meet the requirements of a modern democracy. He pointed out therefore that I was strictly in the "middle"—the most difficult position that a political leader can take up.

I interrupted long enough to tell him that on September 3, 1949, at a time when I was certain that any thought of a political career for me was now eliminated from the public mind, I made a speech before the American Bar Association in St. Louis, in which I had voiced the same convictions about the middle-of-the-road position that he had expressed to me.[2]

He went on to say that this whole matter gave to me a problem greater, in the domestic field, than any other President had ever encountered and been called upon to solve. He said that the rightists expected that on the day after inauguration there would be an immediate return to the "good old days"; some of them, he felt, would argue for a much lesser application of the anti-trust laws and greater control of unions and, indeed, some even would insist that there should be no unions except on a company level. He carried these examples into taxes and regulatory commissions and so on.

In the same way he said that I would be beseeched by the so-called liberals to enlarge and increase every welfare program in the country, and that I would be bitterly accused of being the tool of Wall Street unless I acceded to such demands. Then he said that it is quite true that the curve representing the interference of government into private life, private business, and into the responsibilities of states and cities, had risen rapidly and steadily over the past twenty years. He pointed out that we have to take as a starting point in such matters, the position at which we now stand. He stated flatly that it was impossible to take this curve and bend it sharply downward, as the rightists would have me do, and certainly a man who took the middle-of-the-road course could not be happy with the degree to which it was now rising. He stated, in other words, that all I could do—the very maximum any Administration could bring about—would be a flattening of the curve in this particular trend. He pointed out, of course, that there had to be constant expansion of the economy to meet our increased obligations in the world and at home, but that if I should be successful after my years in office, in stopping future encroachment of the Federal government into the field of regulation, control and direction of the economy, that this would indeed be a brilliant victory. He again repeated that no more could possibly be done, and to get this much done would be an achievement that would be long remembered.

[1] For an earlier reference to this meeting see, Galambos and van Ee, *The Middle Way*, no. 1861. Although former President Herbert C. Hoover had attended one of Eisenhower's stag dinners on June 8, 1953, and a luncheon with the President on July 21, he had not visited him in the Oval Office until July 23.

[2] For background on his speech, "The Middle Way," see *ibid.*, no. 118, and no. 1381 in these volumes. Historians have associated this concept—a constant theme in Eisenhower's views on political economy (see Introduction, *ibid.*)—with Herbert Hoover; see, for example, Robert W. Griffith, "Dwight D. Eisenhower and the Corporate Commonwealth," *American Historical Review* 87, no. 1 (1982), pp. 87–122; for background on this comparison see Ellis W. Hawley, *Herbert Hoover and the Historians* (West Branch, Iowa, 1989).

1208
EM, AWF,
International Series:
Churchill

To Winston Spencer Churchill   *June 23, 1959*

Dear Winston: Thank you for your letter of the thirteenth. By no means do I feel that your May visit, about which Mamie and I are still talking, was the last one you will make to America; I assure you that a warm welcome awaits you at any time.[1]

Last Tuesday Dr. Franklin Murphy stopped briefly at the White House to convey to me your personal greetings.[2] He and Joyce Hall thoroughly enjoyed their afternoon with you and Clemmie, and I was glad to hear from Dr. Murphy that things go well with you.[3]

Among other things, Dr. Murphy told me of the project which he and Mr. Hall discussed with you concerning the microfilming of your papers and the distribution of copies of the microfilm to the Library of Congress, presidential libraries and certain major university libraries in this country. I share with them an enthusiasm for this project, if it is possible and appropriate, for it would be a tremendous boon to scholarly research and teaching of history and political science in the United States. For the scholars of the present and the future, an intimate knowledge of your role in world affairs during your lifetime is obviously crucial and central.

I mean of course by this note to put no personal pressure on you to accede to the project Dr. Murphy and Mr. Hall have in mind; I simply want you to know that if you decide to go ahead with it, I shall most heartily approve.[4]

With warm regard, *As ever*

[1] Churchill had thanked the President for making his visit to the United States "most memorable" and had said he hoped that the visit would not be his last. On the former Prime Minister's stay at the White House see no. 1174.

[2] University of Kansas Chancellor Murphy had visited the White House on June 16 (see also Ann Whitman memorandum, June 16, 1959, AWF/AWD).

[3] Greeting card manufacturer Hall also had organized an exhibition of Churchill's paintings (for background see no. 86).

[4] Churchill would reply on July 14 (AWF/I: Churchill) that most of his papers did not belong to him, but to the Chartwell Trust. He was flattered by the offer to have his archives in America, he wrote, and he assured the President that when the papers were made available in Great Britain something could be arranged. There is no further correspondence on this subject in AWF, however, and the project was never undertaken.

1209   *EM, AWF, DDE Diaries Series*

To EDWARD L. R. ELSON   *June 23, 1959*
Personal

Dear Dr. Elson: I have today authorized 100 shares Carter Products, Inc., to be placed in the National Presbyterian Church Building Fund account.[1] These shares have a current market value of $5,556.25.

This account is with Johnston, Lemon and Company, investment bankers, of Washington, D.C., attention Mr. James M. Lemon.[2] They will await your instruction as to the disposition of this stock.

With best wishes, *Sincerely*

[1] For background on the fund-raising campaign to build the National Presbyterian Church see no. 1145. Eisenhower had telephoned Elson to ask that no publicity be given to the gift (Telephone conversation, Eisenhower and Elson, June 23, 1959, AWF/D).

[2] James *H.* Lemon, an investment banker and director of the Washington Mutual Investors Fund, frequently played golf with Eisenhower. The President had talked to

Lemon earlier this day (Telephone conversation, Eisenhower and Lemon, June 23, 1959, AWF/D).

1210   *EM, AWF, DDE Diaries Series*

To Henry Merritt Wriston   *June 24, 1959*
Personal

Dear Henry: Your letter is most interesting.[1] While I think I have never seen your 1941 book, it is clear that you were more foresighted than a good many people in the government.[2] It is possible, of course, that former Secretaries of State have recommended the establishment of the kind of school you had in mind, but even yet we cannot be certain that Congress will support the school on a necessary and reasonable basis.

Respecting your suggestion about Ambassadors, I personally would favor the provision of representation allowances, of appropriate size, in the different embassies so that any individual, regardless of financial circumstances, could be appointed to any post.[3] As you know, Foster and I have greatly increased the ratio of career to political appointments in the diplomatic service.[4] Moreover, we tried—and I think succeeded except in one case—in obtaining people of ability as well as means. Nevertheless the implementation of your suggestion could provide a great deal more flexibility.

I shall have the State Department study your letter.[5]

With warm regard, *As ever*

[1] Wriston, President Emeritus of Brown University, had written (AWF/D) to congratulate Eisenhower on the speech he gave at the commencement exercises of the Foreign Service Institute on June 12 (Wriston's letter was erroneously dated May 15; it was postmarked June 15). The President had referred to the nineteen graduates as "soldiers of peace for all men" and called for diplomats who were "capable of thinking—thinking objectively on the problem that is before them—who can give the best information with the best interpretation and the best advice they can provide to the State Department" (see *Public Papers of the Presidents: Eisenhower, 1959*, pp. 457–59, and *New York Times,* June 13, 1959).

In 1958 Eisenhower had considered establishing an Undergraduate Foreign Service Academy to train officers for the foreign service, but the State Department, which already provided advanced training in the Foreign Service Institute, had resisted the idea (see no. 828).

[2] Wriston had proposed a course for foreign officers in *Prepare for Peace!* (New York, 1941). The purpose of the training, he wrote, would be "to encourage foreign service officers . . . to sort out the significance of what they already know. Its function would be to make thought more orderly, more effective—and to give rein to imaginative and critical analysis of meanings." Wriston said it was "wonderful, eighteen years later," to have Eisenhower's "warm endorsement and powerful influence."

[3] Wriston also had suggested ending patronage appointments to diplomatic posts. "Diplomacy, like war," he said, "had become technical and complicated," and appointees should not be considered because of party and campaign contributions. Nor should diplomats be required to pay their own way; as long as they did so they would "be said to have 'bought' the job." Such accusations were unfair to the President and "a serious handicap to the ambassador."

[4] Former Secretary of State John Foster Dulles had died on May 24 (see no. 1171).

[5] As signed into law on September 8, 1960, PL 86-723, the Foreign Service Act Amendments of 1960, would increase language requirements for Foreign Service personnel and provide facilities and incentives for language training; require Foreign Service officers to have a thorough knowledge of the country in which they served; give the Secretary of State more flexibility in hiring and promoting personnel; revise and expand the services' retirement and disability program; and authorize a $10 million increase for buildings (*Congressional Quarterly Almanac*, vol. XV, *1959*, p. 218, and *ibid.*, vol. XVI, *1960*, p. 345).

1211   *EM, WHCF, Official File 72-F*

To Lyndon Baines Johnson   *June 25, 1959*

Dear Senator Johnson: I have, as President, sought consistently to refrain from interjecting my views in respect to such Congressional matters as Senate or House Resolutions which in our system do not contemplate Presidential participation. Senate Resolution 115, however, raises considerations so significant to our country that I feel I must call it to your attention in the hope that it can be withdrawn or further action withheld.[1]

Although I realize its declared purpose is to inquire only into national security procedures, this Resolution would inescapably thrust Congressional investigative activities deeply into the Nation's highest national security and foreign policy deliberative processes which traditionally as well as Constitutionally have remained within the province of the Chief Executive. Such an undertaking at a time of delicacy and danger in international relations could not avoid harmful consequences, for it would thrust the Executive and Legislative Branches into needless controversy over jurisdictional issues which have been argued throughout our history and cannot now be resolved without either Congressional or Executive concessions which over the years neither has been willing to make. An embroilment of this kind in our government in the present state of world affairs would be poorly timed to say the least; it would surely trouble our own people and sorely perplex our allies throughout the world.

Aside from such general considerations as these, I should remind you that the National Security Council, though a statutory body, has only an advisory function. It convenes and deliberates as the President may direct on such national security matters as he may specify. More than 300 meetings of this body have been held these past six and half years—a much greater use of it, I am informed, than was previously the practice, a fact which I cite only to highlight my conviction that this machinery has great value in assisting a President in reaching decisions on the Nation's security policies. I would regret very much to see any arm of the Congress so impinge upon this process as to incline me or any of my successors to avoid its use or incline the Council's members to withhold, in these weekly meetings, frank and vigorous expressions of their convictions on our critical security concerns. I do not doubt that a Congressional probing into this advisory process—an effort not heretofore undertaken by the Congress—would dispose future Presidents to avoid its use entirely, or would inhibit and constrict the Council's deliberations. Either result would be injurious to our security and, indeed, directly contrary to the ends which I am advised the Resolution itself is designed to serve.[2]

I would additionally point out that through the great volume of testimony steadily taken in the open and executive sessions of the Foreign Relations, Armed Services, Atomic Energy, and Appropriations Committees of the Senate and House, all relevant information on the nation's security problems is provided unhesitatingly to the Congress by the top security officials of the Executive Branch. I believe this system has functioned satisfactorily over the years in keeping the Congress adequately advised of our security plans and programs. May I add also that I have highly valued the cooperation in these fields that Congressional leaders have accorded to the Executive during these past six years and more.

For such reasons, sensitive though I am to Congressional prerogatives in such a matter as this, I feel compelled, in the interest of our national security, to suggest that further action on Senate Resolution 115 be indefinitely withheld.[3] *Sincerely*

---

[1] See also no. 585. Eisenhower was opposed to the resolution introduced by Senator Henry Martin Jackson (LL.B. University of Washington Law School 1935), the junior Democrat from Washington State. The resolution called for a congressional investigation into the government's ability to develop and execute "national policy for survival in the contest with world communism" (U.S., Congress, Senate, *S. Res. 115*, 86th Cong., 1st sess., Report No. 302, May 5 and 20, 1959). The President had met with Senate Majority Leader Lyndon Johnson, as well as other Democratic leaders, and Presidential Assistants Bryce N. Harlow and Gordon Gray, to discuss the proposal (Memorandum for the Record, Bryce Harlow, June 29, 1959, AWF/D).

[2] Eisenhower had expressed similar concerns about the effects an investigation would have on the National Security Council at the previous day's meeting with Johnson (*ibid.*). In April Jackson had criticized the NSC for its inability to produce a coherent national program (John Prados, *Keepers of the Keys: A History of the National Security Council from Truman to Bush* [New York, 1991], pp. 57–80, 92–95; Grenville Gar-

side, "The Jackson Subcommittee on National Security," in *Staying the Course: Henry M. Jackson and National Security*, Dorothy Fosdick, ed. [Seattle, 1987], pp. 45–60).
[3] Despite the President's opposition, the Senate Government Operations Committee had formed a Subcommittee on National Policy Machinery chaired by Jackson, which would hold hearings and gather testimony into the next year. The White House, however, would negotiate a set of guidelines redefining the subcommittee's "investigation" as a "study" and limiting its probe into the National Security Council (*ibid.*; see also *Congressional Quarterly Almanac*, vol. XVI, *1960*, pp. 721–27). Jackson would send a copy of the guidelines to the President, asking him to confirm their "understanding" (Jackson to Eisenhower, July 9, 1959, and Harlow to Eisenhower, July 10, 1959, both in same file as document). Eisenhower would respond that he was satisfied with the rules and would cooperate as long as the study was directed toward "procedures and machinery and not to substance" (Eisenhower to Jackson, July 10, 1959; see also McCabe to Jackson, Aug. 26 and Dec. 11, 1959, all in *ibid.*).

1212   *EM, AWF, DDE Diaries Series*

To Christian Archibald Herter   *June 27, 1959*
Secret

Memorandum for the Secretary of the State: I think that your outline of suggestions, contained in a theoretical communique, for use in concerting the Western Position among the three governments provides a good basis for prompt decision.[1]

It is my understanding that, on July 13th, there would be no intention of tabling a "complete" Western Position. Rather our purpose now would be to obtain a thorough understanding (assuming Von Brentano's general agreement) of all the things the West would be ready to suggest, piece by piece, in return for a moratorium of considerable length on Soviet threats against our position in Berlin, with agreement as to a "standing group" of negotiators (with German advisers on both sides) to attempt solution of some of the more obvious differences between us.[2]

Your paper would yield nothing in principle but does suggest a number of items that might possibly be acceptable to the Soviets. If so, the "Commission" might make some significant progress.

I am attaching a draft of a message to Harold Macmillan; if you think it is all right, please send it off.[3]

[1] For background see no. 1206; and State, *Foreign Relations, 1958–1960*, vol. VIII, *Berlin Crisis 1958–1959*, pp. 919–43; see also Conference of Foreign Ministers, *Foreign Ministers Meeting, May–August, Geneva*, pp. 335–60. On July 25 Secretary Herter had shown Eisenhower the draft of a communique outlining the position that the Western powers might take at the resumption of the Geneva Conference of Foreign Ministers on July 13. The draft provided for the establishment of a four-power commission to study the reunification of Germany and the preparation of a peace treaty;

an agreement by the Western powers to a ceiling on the combined total of their armed forces; an agreement by the Soviet Union to maintain Western access to Berlin; and provisions for the strict monitoring of all disruptive activities within or directed at Berlin. Eisenhower told Herter that if the four foreign ministers could agree on the issues as presented, a summit meeting would be warranted, even though such details as the number of troops to be stationed in Berlin and the number of years that the arrangement might last were not specified (State, *Foreign Relations, 1958–1960*, vol. VIII, *Berlin Crisis 1958–1959*, pp. 943–47).

[2] Heinrich von Brentano was foreign minister of the German Federal Republic.

[3] See the following document.

1213   *EM, AWF, International Series: Macmillan*

To Harold Macmillan   *June 27, 1959*
Secret

Dear Harold: I was glad to have your letter assessing the situation at the close of the present phase of the Foreign Ministers Conference and suggesting a line which we might take when the Conference resumes on July 13.[1]

We too have been considering where we go from here. We are working very hard on the issues which the Conference has developed. Chris will be in touch with Selwyn on the thoughts which the latter has conveyed to him. I hope that we may be able to work out a concerted position in time to consult with the French and Germans before July 13th. The issues are so large and the time so short that this may not be possible. However, we shall do our best.[2]

I agree with you, of course, that our tactical position in Berlin is indeed weak in that the Russians have many physical and geographical advantages. Their opportunity to exert economic pressure against the Western part of the city is obvious.[3]

Because Chris is, as I say, communicating to Selwyn our current thinking for an ad interim arrangement, I think it would be futile for me to try to get into details at this point. I can say only that I have studied his paper and agree generally with it.

Yesterday Mamie and I spent the day with The Queen and Prince Philip. The Prime Minister of Canada was of course present.[4] I noted with some interest that he repeated what I believe has been an earlier suggestion of his—that Quebec might be a nice place to hold a summit meeting if one should ever become practical. I merely replied that the place would be most convenient from my viewpoint, but the location and time made very little difference to me.[5]

With warm regard, *As ever*

¹ Macmillan had suggested an "interim settlement" which would be easier for the Russians to accept and to honor. Any such agreement, however, had to lead to new negotiations and should not leave the West in a worse position than they were at the beginning. "We must maintain a public posture in which we can rally our people to resist a Russian attempt to impose their will by force. All the same," he said, "it would not be easy to persuade the British people that it was their duty to go to war in defense of West Berlin. After all, in my lifetime we have been dealt two nearly mortal blows by the Germans. People in this country will think it paradoxical, to use a mild term, to have to prepare for an even more horrible war in order to defend the liberties of people who have tried to destroy us twice in this century" (Macmillan to Eisenhower, June 23, 1959, AWF/I: Macmillan).

² For Secretary Herter's proposals for the reopening of the conference see the preceding document. The State Department draft of this letter to Macmillan ended with this paragraph; Eisenhower had added the following three paragraphs (a draft of this message is in AWF/D; see also State, *Foreign Relations, 1958–1960*, vol. VIII, *Berlin Crisis 1958–1959*, pp. 943–45). For Herter's conversations and later correspondence with British Foreign Secretary Lloyd see *ibid.*, pp. 930–32, 935–38.

³ Macmillan had warned that Soviet pressure on the economy of West Berlin could result in massive unemployment and a loss of morale. He also did not believe that any settlement of the Berlin question would last until the reunification of Germany. "I do not think myself that there is any chance of the Soviet Government actually underwriting our occupation rights," Macmillan had written.

⁴ For background on the opening of the St. Lawrence Seaway see no. 877; see also Ann Whitman memorandum, June 26, 1959, AWF/AWD; and the Chronology. John G. Diefenbaker was the Canadian Prime Minister.

⁵ On this same day the State Department sent the text of this letter to London for delivery to the Prime Minister. Macmillan would later write that he was "naturally very worried," because the time was so short and the decisions to be made were so grave. "History will never forgive us if we do it wrong" (Macmillan to Eisenhower, June 29, 1959, PREM 11/2686). For developments see no. 1243.

1214   *EM, AWF, International Series: Haiti*

To Francois Duvalier   *June 27, 1959*
Cable.

Dear Mr. President: I have received through the good offices of the Embassy of Haiti at Washington the text of your recent telegram requesting my assistance with regard to the proposed barter of Haitian bauxite for United States wheat.¹

Although barter contracts are a matter of agreement between the Commodity Credit Corporation and private United States firms, the possible effects of such contracts on the economies of other countries are naturally factors to be taken into consideration.² With regard to the specific proposal in which you are interested, the Reynolds Metals Company has had several discussions with United

States Government officials, including officials of the Barter Division in the Department of Agriculture.[3]

I understand that over-all U.S. policy considerations will probably prevent full compliance with your proposal at this time. However, the officials who are studying this matter are fully familiar with Haiti's current economic problems. I have instructed them to make every effort, within the limits imposed by these policy considerations, to work out a barter program acceptable to both parties to the contract and beneficial to the economy of Haiti.[4] *Sincerely*

[1] On June 9 Eisenhower had received a translation of the original French telegram in which the Haitian President had asked him to help secure a five-year contract with the U.S. Commodity Corporation to exchange Haitian bauxite (the clay-like ore from which aluminum is obtained) for wheat (June 4, 1959, AWF/I: Haiti).

[2] Duvalier had written that the benefits of a long-term contract would be "vital" to Haiti's economy, doubling employment and tripling government revenue from royalties and income tax (*ibid.*); for background see nos. 811 and 1353, and State, *Foreign Relations, 1958–1960*, vol. V, *American Republics*, pp. 817–19.

[3] In a memorandum providing the background for the President's response to Duvalier, C. Douglas Dillon, who had become Under Secretary of State on June 12, explained that the Reynolds Metals Company had offered to barter $5 million worth of bauxite for wheat annually for five years. Under the current barter program, however, contracts for Haitian bauxite were limited to one year because the need for strategic stockpiles had been met. He had also advised that it was against policy to allow one firm to supply a country's total requirement for an agricultural commodity. Nevertheless, officials had recommended a one-year contract, with the option to renew, to alleviate Haiti's economic difficulties (June 19, 1959, AWF/I: Haiti).

[4] The Commodity Credit Corporation and the Reynolds Metal Company would reach agreement on September 30, 1959, on a one-year barter exchange (McElhiney to Goodpaster, Oct. 29, 1959, AWF/I: Haiti).

1215   *EM, AWF, Administration Series*

To Lewis Lichtenstein Strauss   *June 27, 1959*
Personal

Dear Lewis: I have just signed the official letter accepting your resignation as Secretary of Commerce.[1] In so doing I could not escape a conviction that the nation will share with me a profound distress because one of my most valuable associates has been needlessly lost to the service of the public.[2] Beyond this, I believe that all those members of the Senate who voted against your confirmation will eventually come to reflect with deep regret upon the day they decided to refuse confirmation to one whose reputation for courage, integrity and good judgment makes him one of our distinguished Americans.[3]

But what is done is done. Words are quite inadequate to describe the depth of my admiration for the major contributions you have made to our country under four Presidents. I am especially proud of the services you have performed in the present Administration and the selfless cooperation you have given to me and to your associates in government. I salute you for the calm and even generous attitude in which you have accepted what will surely go down in history as one of the most erroneous and unfortunate verdicts of our time.

I assure you that for me there will be no end to the friendship I have shared with you and which I value so highly.[4] Moreover, I am gratified by your promise that whenever I may feel the need of it, your counsel, in many of the critically important problems of government, will be at my disposal.[5]

To you and Alice I send, as always, my affectionate regard. *As ever*

[1] Rejected by the Senate for confirmation as Secretary of Commerce, Strauss had tendered his resignation on June 23 (for background see nos. 1134 and 1164). Both his letter and the President's official acceptance (dated June 27) would be released to the public on June 30, the day the resignation was to take effect (Strauss to Eisenhower, AWF/A; Eisenhower's acceptance and drafts with his numerous handwritten emendations are all in AWF/A and WHCF/OF 2; see also *Public Papers of the Presidents: Eisenhower, 1959*, pp. 487–88).

Sharp personality conflicts, party divisions, and policy differences had shaped the outcome of the confirmation hearings. After months of delays and acrimonious debate, the full Senate had voted against the nomination despite the fact that the Senate Interstate and Foreign Commerce Committee had recommended confirmation. Throughout the hearings, opponents had assailed Strauss's professional and personal character, leveling charges about various improprieties, including dishonesty, misconduct, and the withholding of information. The critiques centered on issues that had developed during Strauss's service on the Atomic Energy Commission, including the J. Robert Oppenheimer security problem, atomic testing, and the Dixon-Yates power contract (on Oppenheimer, see Galambos and van Ee, *The Middle Way*, nos. 929 and 1206; on nuclear fallout testing, see *ibid.*, no. 1968; in these volumes, no. 223, and Hewlett and Holl, *Atoms for Peace and War*, pp. 346–48; on Dixon-Yates see Galambos and van Ee, *The Middle Way*, nos. 979, 985, 1017, and 1206; and in these volumes, no. 1248. See also Strauss, *Men and Decisions*, pp. 375–403; Eisenhower, *Waging Peace*, pp. 392–96; Richard Pfau, *No Sacrifice Too Great: The Life of Lewis L. Strauss* [Charlottesville, 1984], pp. 221–41; and *Congressional Quarterly Almanac*, vol. XV, *1959*, pp. 665–69).

[2] The President had already publicly stressed the themes of loss and regret in a statement released on the day of the vote (see *Public Papers of the Presidents: Eisenhower, 1959*, p. 472; see also no. 1248).

[3] On June 25 Strauss had sent the President a collection of editorials from newspapers throughout the country criticizing the Senate rejection. Eisenhower had responded that it was "cold comfort but at least the newspapers are displaying more statesmanship than many of our distinguished Senators did" (Strauss to Eisenhower, June 24, 1959; Eisenhower to Strauss, June 25, 1959; and editorials, all in AWF/A).

[4] Strauss had handwritten a note expressing his feelings of friendship as well as his gratitude for the President's support while he was "under attack," adding that "the past six and a half years of service under your leadership were the most challenging and the most satisfying" (June 22, 1959, AWF/A).

[5] Although Strauss's government career ended, the two men would continue to share

their avid interest in cattle and would communicate occasionally over official matters; see nos. 1312 and 1487.

1216   *EM, AWF, Name Series*

To Frederick Andrew Seaton   *June 27, 1959*

Dear Fred: Thank you for sending me a copy of your memorandum to the Assistant Secretaries of the Department of the Interior requesting that each individual take another look at the budget requests for fiscal year 1961.[1] I am gratified by your approach to the problem that concerns all of us so much.

Incidentally, I like particularly your last paragraph.[2] It is plain common sense—and it hits squarely at the "bureaucracy" that has threatened to destroy the usefulness of some of our most needed Agencies.

With warm regard, *As ever*

[1] Secretary of the Interior Seaton had wanted the President to know that Interior officials were "still trying" to bring their budget proposals for FY 1961 "down to the absolute bare minimum" (Seaton to Eisenhower, June 25, 1959, AWF/A). Recognizing that some increases were necessary, Seaton had asked his department's various bureau offices to reexamine their estimates for possible reductions because the total exceeded the 1960 budget by about fifteen percent. He had suggested that they might shift funds away from older programs to cover new, more important commitments or could eliminate some activities altogether (Seaton to Assistant Secretaries for Fish and Wildlife; Mineral Resources; Public Land Management; and Water and Power, June 25, 1959, AWF/A).

[2] Seaton had commented that the government could not "go on year-after-year adding new programs and never discontinuing any of the old" (*ibid.*). On the President's strong commitment to limited government spending, balanced budgets, and efficient bureaucratic organizations see, for example, no. 1114; Eisenhower, *Waging Peace*, pp. 385–88; Saulnier, *Constructive Years*, pp. 19–24; Charles E. Neu, "The Rise of the National Security Bureaucracy," in *The New American State*, Louis Galambos, ed. (Baltimore, 1987), pp. 85–108; Greenstein, *The Hidden-Hand Presidency*, pp. 100–151. On the 1961 budget see Morgan, *Eisenhower versus 'The Spenders,'* pp. 152–60.

1217   *EM, WHCF,*
                                                       President's Personal File 430

To Charles Vincent McAdam   *June 27, 1959*
Personal

Dear Charlie: Thank you for sending me the two columns by Holmes Alexander. I am, of course, highly gratified by his comments.[1]

Sometime when you and I have an opportunity for a little chat, I would like to take up the whole subject. It seems to me a curious phenomenon that reporters profess to have discovered in me a "new" Eisenhower.[2] I may have—I hope I have—gained a little experience in this job, but fundamentally I seriously question whether a man of my age ever changes his habits of thinking and expression.[3] But, be that as it may, I cannot fail to be pleased by the tenor of the two columns.

I don't know how frequently you come to Washington, but I suggest that if you are here some not too hot day you give my Secretary, Mrs. Whitman, a ring. She will know if I am planning to golf. The games I have are always arranged at the last minute and I would, of course, like nothing better than a round with you.[4]

With warm regard, *Sincerely*

[1] On June 24 McAdam, president of McNaught Syndicate, Inc., had sent Eisenhower the articles ("Ike in the Homestretch") written by McNaught's Washington correspondent Holmes Moss Alexander (for background see Galambos and van Ee, *The Middle Way*, no. 1642 and 1283, respectively; see also Alexander to Hagerty, Apr. 29, 1959, same file as document). The columns would appear in newspapers throughout the United States on June 29 and 30.

[2] Alexander had said that Eisenhower had "started rather shakily as a campaigner and as President," but had "become the unsung master of his trade. . . ." Citing examples of the President's recent news conferences, Alexander said that at the end of his tenure Eisenhower was reaching "a high and unexpected plateau of performance"—a conviction few reporters "could have mustered a year or two ago." He added that intelligent questions drew "the sort of responses which read very well the next morning and which will make sense this time next year." Alexander concluded that the "real change in the White House" had been "its rise from a school room to something like a highly charged executive suite."

[3] In a note dated June 27 (AWF/D) Ann Whitman, who had drafted this letter, said that it originally had read "habits of thinking and of speech." The President had changed the word "speech" to "expression" because, he said, "he had conscientiously tried to change his habits of speech" by speaking more deliberately "to outsiders."

[4] McAdam had added that he hoped to play golf at some time convenient to Eisenhower. On July 27 McAdam would thank Eisenhower for his reply and add that he would be in Washington early in August. On August 3 McAdam would be included in the President's foursome at the Burning Tree Country Club.

1218   *EM, WHCF, Official File 2*

To W. WALTER WILLIAMS   *June 27, 1959*
Straight Telegram

Dear Walter: My only prescription is to ignore houseflies.[1] Don't take your time to become angry at them.[2]

¹ Williams had written Eisenhower about journalist Drew Pearson's column in the *Washington Post.* Pearson had asserted that Williams had resigned as Under Secretary of Commerce because the President had reneged on a pledge to give him the position of Secretary when it became vacant. If he had "carried out his promise," Pearson said, the President "could have saved himself a lot of headaches over Admiral Strauss" (Williams to Eisenhower, June 25, 1959, same file as document, and *Washington Post and Times Herald,* June 25, 1959; for background see no. 1215). Pearson had been a vocal opponent of Strauss's candidacy. Declaring himself "really agitated," Williams had reaffirmed his loyalty to the President and had avowed, "*I have never said nor implied anything of the sort dished out in this Pearson article*" (June 25, 1959). Williams had resigned as Under Secretary of Commerce in September 1959 to return to his career as a mortgage banker (*New York Times,* Sept. 18, 1958).
² Williams had written to Ann Whitman that Pearson's "crack at the President's integrity has had me sizzling all day" (June 25, 1959, same file as document).

1219 *EM, AWF, Name Series*

To Edgar Newton Eisenhower *June 27, 1959*

Dear Ed: I understand your feeling about cost of the cemetery fence, but frankly I do not have any hopes of getting Harry Darby to accept payment for the construction cost.¹ He has steadfastly refused to answer my queries on the subject; he is a very good friend of mine and I believe that to press him further would embarrass and perhaps offend him.²

You have no obligation to write Harry, of course. I have adequately expressed the thanks of all the brothers.

With warm regard, *As ever*

¹ Edgar had written on June 23 that he was pleased with the fence constructed around the gravesite of their parents (for background see nos. 898 and 911). He did not know, however, how to get in touch with former U.S. Senator Darby, who had paid for the project.
² On the President's attempt to reimburse Darby see no. 1159; see also no. 899.

1220 *EM, AWF, Name Series*

To Francis Wilfred de Guingand *June 29, 1959*
Personal and confidential

[Dear Freddie:] Your letter is truly interesting. I am sorry that so many people seem to get a little wisdom only with hindsight.¹

As you know, I have said not a word publicly in criticism of any officer of World War II, including Monty. Following the policy of ignoring such criticism publicly, I have also, except in such circumstances as when you and I met, avoided conversations of this type, even in private.[2] In other words, I have never allowed such matters to disturb me more than momentarily.

But this does not mean that many others—especially my old military friends and associates—have failed to voice considerable resentment, possibly out of a feeling of loyalty to me.[3]

The telecasting of an interview (which many of my friends saw but which I did not) has seemed to many people here as a deliberate affront. A number of people, including editorial writers and military friends, have expressed the thought that no matter what might be the advantage now of pondering the military "might-have-beens", the fact remains that the war in Western Europe was conducted under the program that I personally laid out in broad outline and victory was achieved much more rapidly than "official" prophets had foreseen.[4]

All this you know. I merely make the point that, because of the resentment on the part of some of my old friends, it would likely be bad judgment, at this particular time, for Monty to make any attempt to visit me.[5]

I assure you that my feeling is merely one of disappointment, not of rancor. Even Winston, when he was here, remarked that obviously I felt little personal resentment toward Monty's publicity endeavors because he (Winston) had noted that, in our living quarters on the second floor of the White House, Monty's picture occupied the same place as in former years.[6]

My feelings about any visit apply also to any explanatory statement Monty might conceivably make about the affair. He obviously cannot retreat from a public position that he has already made clear; consequently there would be no hope of such a statement making for better "allied" feeling. Likewise, I think any correspondence between us could not be very helpful because of the reason that Monty, both by publications and broadcasts, has made the whole matter a public affair, not a private one.

All this is, of course, negative. But I feel that if the matter is to be healed in any way, that time will have to be relied on as the healer.

I hope you are getting along with making inquiries of our British friends about the possibility of the "reunion" next year.[7] I did not include Winston in the list because obviously he is far from strong and I think we should not ask him to waste any of his energy. Similarly I hope you will not urge anyone else to make a trip that would impose any kind of health risk.

I cannot tell you what a great privilege I felt it was to me to have Winston here. The same goes for your visit. I thoroughly enjoyed it.

Write to me when you can.

P.S. If you personally have any different opinions about any of this, of course I will be glad to hear them.

[1] De Guingand had written June 14 (AWF/N) that he had met with Field Marshal Montgomery, who "admitted that he had gone too far and had 'overstated the case'" in his *Memoirs* and in a recent televised interview (see also de Guingand to Eisenhower, May 8, 1959, AWF/N). In his *Memoirs* Montgomery had found fault with Eisenhower's wartime military leadership as Supreme Allied Commander in Europe (for background on the controversy surrounding the volume, and the President's reaction to the publication see, for example, nos. 989 and 1012). In an interview aired on April 28 Montgomery had criticized U.S. leadership since World War II and repeated his criticism of Eisenhower's role during the war (see no. 1146 and *New York Times*, Apr. 29, 1959).

[2] The President had had lunch with de Guingand on June 4 (see no. 1194).

[3] For examples of the correspondence Eisenhower had received see nos. 933 and 970.

[4] Montgomery had maintained that a direct thrust toward Berlin would have shortened the war. On January 14 Eisenhower had said that at the outset of operation OVERLORD (June 6, 1944), the "most optimistic prediction" of German surrender was two years. In fact the war in Europe ended eleven months following the Normandy invasion (*Public Papers of the Presidents: Eisenhower, 1959*, p. 31; also see nos. 948, 1018, 1381, and 1722).

[5] Montgomery had considered writing to the President or making a short visit to the United States in an effort to restore Anglo-American relations, de Guingand had written.

[6] On Churchill's visit to the White House see no. 1174.

[7] On Eisenhower's plans to have a reunion of wartime friends see no. 1197. For developments see no. 1229.

1221   *EM, AWF, Administration Series*

To LEWIS LICHTENSTEIN STRAUSS   *June 30, 1959*

Dear Lewis: I am assuming a great deal in venturing to send you one of my so-called "paintings," but I could think of no other way in which to express to you personally my admiration and affection.[1] Perhaps you can find an obscure corner for it somewhere.

At the same time I am sending you a medallion to officially record my appreciation of your services in this Administration.[2]

With warm regard, *As ever*

P.S. I send you this painting since I don't think it is quite as bad as the one I gave you a few years ago—and only if you will promise to hide the first!

[1] Secretary of Commerce Strauss had resigned on June 22 (see no. 1215). On June 29 the Eisenhowers had given a dinner party in honor of Admiral and Mrs. Strauss

(Ann Whitman memorandum, June 29, 1959, AWF/AWD). The painting was probably the "Mountain Fall Scene" (see Kenneth S. Davis, *The Eisenhower College Collection: The Paintings of Dwight D. Eisenhower* [Los Angeles, 1972], plate 33). Strauss would thank Eisenhower for the painting on July 10 (AWF/A).

[2] Strauss would say that he was "more proud" of the medallion than anything he possessed, other than Eisenhower's "wonderful letters" (July 10, 1959, AWF/A; see also Eisenhower to Strauss, July 8 and 11, 1959, both in AWF/A, and Eisenhower to Hartley, July 11, 1959, AWF/A, Strauss Corr.).

18

"These extremist approaches"

EM, WHCF,
President's Personal File 264

To Deane Emmett Ackers
Personal
July 1, 1959

Dear Deane: Thank you for your note of the twenty-ninth. I, too, am gratified by the support the people of the country are evidencing in the fight to promote an expanding economy on the basis of fiscal integrity and a sound dollar.[1]

As to your comments about one of the two men believed to be prominent as candidates for the Republican nomination in 1960, I can only say that Nelson Rockefeller is not only my friend; he is also a dedicated, hard-working and conscientious public official.[2] I can say, with equal truthfulness, exactly the same thing about the Vice President.

With best wishes, *Sincerely*

[1] See nos. 1042 and 1119 for background. Ackers, president of the Kansas Power and Light Company, had written that he and other Kansans were encouraged by the progress Eisenhower was making in the struggle with the "spendthrift" Congress. "The people," he had stated, were now willing to do something about "the destruction and loss of their savings," and the Republicans could win the 1960 election if they continued the fight against inflation (June 29, 1959, same file as document).
[2] Ackers had criticized Rockefeller, writing that it was "very easy to be liberal with some other party's money when you are a multi-millionaire." He hoped that Eisenhower could "avoid being pushed into Rockefeller's corner" (*ibid.*). Richard M. Nixon was the other potential candidate.

EM, AWF, DDE Diaries Series

To Edward H. Teller
July 1, 1959

Dear Dr. Teller: Thank you for your letter. I personally and deeply appreciated your testimony before the Senate Committee on behalf of Admiral Strauss and, as you know, I share your feeling of shock and resentment concerning his ultimate rejection by the Senate itself.[1] He has been an invaluable public servant whom I shall greatly miss, both personally and in the conduct of the business of government.

Personally, I agree with you and Admiral Strauss as to the desirability of replacing the English system of measurements by the metric.[2] A program for doing so will have many critics and the way will be rough.

With best wishes, *Sincerely*

[1] Atomic physicist Teller had enclosed his letter to the President in a note he had sent after the Senate had voted to deny Lewis Strauss the position of Secretary of Commerce (Teller to Eisenhower, June 22, 1959; Strauss to Goodpaster, June 24, 1959, both in WHCF/OF 2). Teller, who in May had testified at the Strauss confirmation hearings, had written that he was "deeply shocked" by the Senate's rejection (see *New York Times*, May 7, 1959).

[2] Teller had urged Eisenhower to continue with Strauss's plans to adopt the metric system in order to eliminate the disadvantage in world trade the United States suffered in competition with the Soviet Union (June 22, 1959, WHCF/OF).

1224   *EM, WHCF, Official File 120*

To Owen Robertson Cheatham   *July 1, 1959*
Personal

Dear Owen: Thank you for your message. When the housing bill comes to the White House, I assure you that it will be studied very earnestly and very seriously.[1]

The problem is how, while sustaining prosperity, to prevent inflation. With this thief and robber stalking across the country, we can easily have an *apparent* prosperity for a time, but not for long. Inflation must be avoided, and this means that the Federal government must not only live within its means but must, in times of prosperity, begin reducing the nation's debt.

So, I repeat, every money bill that comes before me must be examined with the most painstaking concern.[2]

With personal regard,[3] *Sincerely*

[1] See no. 1042 for background. Georgia-Pacific Corporation chairman Cheatham had cabled the President asking him to sign the housing bill before Congress "in order to assure prosperity" and prevent the recession which, he noted, a "majority" of business people and economists thought would otherwise occur (Cheatham to Eisenhower, June 26, 1959, same file as document).

[2] In his effort to balance the budget Eisenhower would deadlock with Congress over the proposed housing act. He would veto S. 57, the first housing bill, on July 7, citing among other reasons that it was inflationary. He would veto a second housing bill but sign a third into law on September 23 (*Congressional Quarterly Almanac*, vol. XV, *1959*, p. 253; see also Press Release, Sept. 4, 1959, AWF/AWD).

[3] Cheatham would write again later and suggest that housing construction, described by a *Wall Street Journal* editorial (Sept. 25, 1959) as America's biggest growth industry, was as important to the economy as fiscal policy. In a brief reply, Eisenhower would thank him for calling his attention to the matter (Cheatham to Eisenhower, Sept. 25, 1959; Eisenhower to Cheatham, Sept. 29, 1959, same file as document).

To PHILIP YOUNG *July 2, 1959*

Dear Phil: Thanks for your candid appraisal of the new Embassy in The Hague.[1] I have the utmost confidence that you and Faith will somehow produce the furniture necessary properly to impress your guests at the time of the public opening. But I will admit that, whenever I hear of them, some of the peculiarities of operation of the State Department puzzle me.[2]

As always, I enjoyed this latest chapter in the saga of Philip Young, diplomat.

With warm regard, *As ever*

P.S. I, too, will want to be guided by Chris Herter's recommendation as to whether or not I should see Luns with you when you are here; of course, I like him personally and am always glad of an opportunity to talk to him.[3]

[1] The new embassy building, which was to open to the public on July 4, was "a most controversial building of extreme modern design," Young had written, "set down plunk in the middle of the oldest, most traditional part of The Hague." Although the Dutch did not object to modern architecture, he told Eisenhower, they were concerned about the building's proximity to older buildings in the area. "I must say I have great sympathy with the Dutch point of view on this, and it is a very difficult thing to explain" (Young to Eisenhower, June 26, 1959, AWF/N).

[2] Young had told Eisenhower that although the building had been under construction for two years, the State Department had only recently awarded the contract for its furniture. He hoped to have enough furniture by July 4 to "show off some of the rooms." He also told the President that the State Department had "refused to make any funds available to cover the expense of dedicating, opening, or christening [the] new building."

[3] Luns was the Dutch Foreign Minister. Young had suggested that he bring Luns in "for a few minutes' chat" during the foreign minister's upcoming visit to Washington. Eisenhower, however, would meet with Luns in Paris in September and in Washington in October 1960 (see State, *Foreign Relations, 1958–1960*, vol. VII, pt. 1, *Western European Integration and Security; Canada*, pp. 480–84; see also no. 1126; and Chronology).

To FREDERICK ANDREW SEATON *July 6, 1959*

Memorandum for the Secretary of the Interior: Attached is a letter from the Chairman of the Board of the Standard Oil Company of California, Mr. R. G. Follis.[1]

Please have a study made of Mr. Follis' complaints, and send him a direct reply.[2] I should like to see a copy of that reply.[3]

Incidentally, I have heard comments similar to those of Mr. Follis from other individuals. It is possible that we have to have some change in policy. If that is true, I assume that the original Oil Imports Board would have to be reconvened.

[1] Ralph Gwin Follis (B.S. Princeton 1924) had written to criticize the replacement of voluntary oil import quotas by the new mandatory program (see no. 1098 for background). Follis, whose company had unsuccessfully appealed rulings made by the Oil Import Control Board, agreed that there was a need for restrictions but argued that the present system failed to encourage American overseas investment or to contribute to national security. Many new import companies and domestic refiners had received larger quotas than the older and larger companies. Administrators had also given domestic refiners exclusive license to import foreign crude even though, he maintained, they were physically incapable of processing it. These refiners traded the cheaper foreign oil for more expensive domestic oil, thus gaining a "windfall subsidy." Instead of protecting threatened companies, the program was redistributing income and economic advantage within the industry (Follis to Eisenhower, July 2, 1959, AWF/D).

[2] On this same day Eisenhower wrote Follis that he would have the matter "studied exhaustively by appropriate government officials" (AWF/D). Responding to the President's request, Seaton would explain that one of the reasons the mandatory program had been imposed was to allow new importers to come into the foreign crude oil market more easily (Seaton to Follis, July 10, 1959, AWF/A). He would also point out that the new method for determining allocations gave Standard Oil and other long-established importers protection by ensuring that their allocations were proportionate to those of newcomers. As a result, Standard Oil was benefitting from the new program; its allocation was higher than under the voluntary one. Seaton would further note that program administrators had decided to confine allocations of imports of crude oil to domestic refiners because that was the most accurate way to measure oil requirements for national defense. This policy had not, however, given the refiners a competitive advantage, as Follis suggested, since long-established importers with foreign production were also free to profit by selling foreign oil to newcomers and exchanging domestic crude with them.

[3] Seaton would send Eisenhower a copy of the report and a note saying that he would be happy to discuss the matter further (July 10, 1959, AWF/A). Follis would thank both the President and Seaton (July 27, 1959, WHCF/OF 149-B-2).

1227   *EM, AWF, Administration Series*

TO ALLEN WELSH DULLES   *July 6, 1959*
Personal

Dear Allen: Thank you very much for your note of June twentieth, enclosing the copy of the often-quoted letter written by Macaulay in 1857.[1] Macaulay was of course a very shrewd observer. Nevertheless he could not have foreseen the great changes that would have come about in any democratic government, particularly our own, as a result of the achievement of higher educational levels than obtained a hundred years ago. On top of that we have developed numerous programs calculated to retard the progress of recessions and to lessen the danger than any such recession could speed rapidly into a catastrophic depression. Finally, I think it is fair to say that he thought of capitalistic nations as comprising mainly a few rich people with a great horde of exploited working men and women, with the relatively weak middle class helplessly caught between. Actually what Macaulay then wrote of as the "working class" is now the middle class.[2]

Nevertheless free government will always have to be watchful and alert lest at times it fall prey to pressure groups. As each of these tries to better its own economic situation through political means, the cumulative effects could be most unfortunate and damaging.[3] *As ever*

[1] Central Intelligence Agency Director Dulles had observed (AWF/A) that a recent National Security Council discussion about the future of democracy in developing countries had prompted him to send the letter to the President. First Baron Thomas Babington Macaulay (1800–1859), an English historian, author and statesman, had written the letter to an American friend (AWF/A, Allen Dulles Corr.). The U.S. Constitution "is all sail and no anchor," Macaulay wrote. Sooner or later, he said, "institutions purely democratic . . . destroy liberty, or civilisation, or both." Surely, he argued, the poor would destroy civilization by plundering the wealthy, or a military government would restore order and property and liberty would perish.
[2] Economic distress, Macaulay explained, brought about mutinous and discontented laborers who were inclined to eagerly listen to "agitators" preaching the "monstrous iniquity that one man should have a million while another cannot get a full meal." The day would come, he warned, "when a multitude of people, none of whom has had more than half a breakfast, or expects to have more than half a dinner, will choose a Legislature. Is it possible to doubt what sort of a Legislature will be chosen?"
[3] Dulles had noted that Macaulay's dire predictions about the future of the United States had been proven wrong. Dulles added, however, that Macaulay's theory would "raise its ugly head in many parts of Asia and Africa and even Latin America."

1228   *EM, AWF, DDE Diaries Series*

To Andre de Saint-Phalle   *July 6, 1959*
Personal

Dear Mr. de Saint-Phalle: I appreciated having your thoughtful letter about our art exhibit at the American Exhibition in Moscow. While I personally do not believe that the pictures and sculpture that we have sent over there are broadly representative of America or what America likes in art, I do believe that it would be unwise, by Administrative action, to censor the work of the selecting Commission by withdrawing what the jury chose.[1]

Whether it would be possible at this late date to augment what has already been chosen with pictures that will give to the Soviets a wider understanding of American life, I do not know. This is being explored.[2]

In any event, I hope your daughter will be able to ignore the things she dislikes in this small portion of the American Exhibition, and find real pride in the important work she will do as a guide.[3]

Again, many thanks for your letter.

With best wishes, *Sincerely*

[1] De Saint-Phalle, who had immigrated to New York from Paris in 1925, was a New York investment banker and securities analyst. In 1957 he had founded Saint-Phalle, Spalding & Company. On June 29 he had written that he disapproved of some of the modern and abstract art chosen for the American National Exposition in Sokolniki Park outside Moscow (de Saint-Phalle to Morgan, WHCF/OF 139-B-5). The exhibition, part of a program designed to inform Americans and the people of Russia about each other, would open on July 25 and would feature displays on science, research, education, labor productivity, health, social services, fashion, the latest in home and entertainment technology, agriculture, photography, art, and architecture. The President had viewed the U.S.S.R. exhibition in New York on June 29 (Ann Whitman memorandum, June 29, 1959, AWF/AWD).

Some of the U.S. art had caused considerable controversy, and at his July 1 news conference the President had said that he refused to become a censor. A four-man jury of non-government art experts had selected the paintings, he explained (see *Public Papers of the Presidents: Eisenhower, 1959*, pp. 490–91; Montgomery to Eisenhower, July 2, and Eisenhower to Montgomery, July 7, 1959, WHCF/OF 139-B-5; and *New York Times*, Jan. 24, June 14, July 3, 12, 25, 27, 1959; and Hans N. Tuch and G. Lewis Schmidt, eds., *Ike and USIA: A Commemorative Symposium* [Washington, D.C., 1991], pp. 37–38. See also Eisenhower, *Waging Peace*, pp. 408–11).

[2] As it turned out, Eisenhower would increase the size of the exhibition by including nineteenth-century American art works (Hans and Tuch, *Ike and USIA*, pp. 37–39; Morgan to de Saint-Phalle, July 23, 1959, WHCF/OF 139-B-5; and *New York Times*, July 22, 1959). For developments see no. 1262.

[3] The de Saint-Phalles' daughter had been among seventy-five Russian-speaking young Americans chosen to serve as guides at the exposition. The President had met with the group on June 15 (Telephone conversation, Hudson and de Saint-Phalle, June 25, 1959, WHCF/OF 139-B-5; *New York Times*, July 8, 1959; and The President's Extemporaneous Remarks, June 15, AWF/D).

1229   *EM, AWF, Name Series*

TO FRANCIS WILFRED DE GUINGAND   *July 6, 1959*
Personal

Dear Freddie: I can well understand that Alanbrooke, Alexander and Dempsey, because of reasons of health, could not consider the plan of a trip to the United States next year.[1] Moreover, in view of what you say about Koenig possibly it would not be helpful to ask him.[2]

Respecting the three men who were on your staff, I would think it well worth while to find out whether at least two of them could not find it possible to come. I feel this would be important because only a very few of the people named in my former list accompanied you all the way from Cairo to the Elbe. I think it would be most helpful to you and to all the rest of us if at least, as I say, two of the three could make the trip.[3]

The matter of the cost of transportation can, I realize, be quite important to some of the individuals about whom we have been thinking. As I told you, I would plan to have the entire party as my personal guests during the period that we would all be together at Camp David. Moreover, should the different individuals come to this country as a group, I could unquestionably arrange for their transportation from New York to the point of meeting and return. However, the overseas costs are another matter.[4]

I shall ponder this particular problem a bit, but at the moment I cannot think of a worthwhile suggestion.

Nevertheless I think if you could, in the meantime, get together a list of the people that you think would be ready to participate, we could at least decide whether the project can be considered to have any feasibility whatsoever and, assuming that the answer to this one is yes, we might find some way of overcoming the financial difficulties.[5]

With warm regard,

[1] For background on Eisenhower's plans to host a reunion of wartime colleagues see nos. 989 and 991. On June 10 Eisenhower had sent de Guingand a list of those he planned to invite (see no. 1197). De Guingand had studied the list and had sent his comments to the President on July 3 (AWF/N).
[2] Koenig, commander of the French Forces of the Interior during World War II, had "lost considerable prestige" among the French, de Guingand had replied.
[3] As Field Marshal Montgomery's Chief of Staff for Intelligence and Operations, de Guingand had participated in all phases of the operations in Sicily and Northwest Europe (for background see Chandler, War Years, nos. 948 and 1473). De Guingand had suggested inviting his chief operations officer, Major General Ronald Frederick King Belchem; the director of covert operations, First Baron Oliver Brian Sanderson Poole; and the 21st Army Group intelligence officer, Edgar Trevor ("Bill") Williams.
[4] The only "snag" de Guingand had foreseen was whether some of the men could afford the cost of transportation.
[5] As it turned out, the President would abandon his plans for a reunion on American soil (see no. 1436). In September Eisenhower would travel to London and while there he would host a stag dinner for his British wartime friends (see nos. 1282 and 1294).

TO THOMAS JEFFERSON DAVIS   *July 7, 1959*

Dear T. J.: I have delayed much too long an acknowledgment of your telegram of June eighteenth. Nonetheless, I assure you that I greatly appreciated your message and that I did read the cited editorial.[1]

This retired pay problem has troubled me a great deal these past several months and I have had it reconsidered from various standpoints a number of times.[2] How it reached its present state you probably know; it is, simply, the result of a transformation of active duty incentive pay into a general pay increase.

At the outset, the intention, two years ago, was exclusively to supplement the pay of certain military *specialists.* This, of course, would not have affected retired pay. But when this effort was shifted to a complete pay revision, we generated the retired pay questions you and others have brought to my attention.

Initially I felt that the 6 percent cost of living increase for the retired was an equitable adjustment; the act as passed so provided, and the Budget for FY 60 that I sent to the Congress early this year was prepared on that basis. Since then, however, I have concluded that the history of the relationship between active duty pay and retired pay has been such as to dictate the maintenance of the traditional formula, not only in the interest of equity among those retired but also because the active duty pay level has been governed at least in part by the anticipated level of retired pay.[3]

This is to say that I am now convinced that the adjustment you call for ought to be made. In recent weeks the possibility of making this adjustment by having the Department of Defense absorb the approximately $25 million a year added cost has been carefully studied. The Department is insistent that this additional cost cannot be absorbed within its personnel budget. I am not yet persuaded that this position is fully tenable, but for the moment I am thereby confronted with the decision whether to urge a supplemental appropriation to remedy this flaw, or to defer corrective action until next year's program which will be submitted to Congress six months hence.

I have determined upon the latter course inasmuch as I am confronted by an exceedingly difficult struggle with special interest groups of various types and, indeed, with persistent pressures throughout the government to expand heavily all areas of public spending, with no comparable enthusiasm for providing additional revenues. My own breaching of my 1960 budget, at this juncture, by the submission of a supplemental appropriation request, would be a grave disservice to everyone by releasing the restraints that continued insistence upon budget balance imposes upon inflationary pressures. I would add that the loss of this struggle against the continuing depreciation of our currency would inflict hardships falling most severely upon our retired citizens, including the military.

This reasoning leads me to the conclusion that we should ask for the authorization next January and in the meantime determine whether the Defense Department could absorb the cost from January first onward. If this is found impossible, then my next budget will include the appropriation item, as well as the authorizing legislation.[4]

Mamie joins me in warmest greetings to you and Nina. We look eagerly to the time when we can all gather once again for a good visit.[5]

With warm regard, *As ever*

[1] Brigadier General Davis had urged the President to read an editorial in the June 13 issue of the *Army, Navy and Air Force Journal.* The editorial entreated Eisenhower to mobilize support for the military retirement pay proposals stalled in Congress (June 18, 1959; see also Boye to Eisenhower, Apr. 24, 1959, both in same file as document).

[2] See nos. 564, 721, and 969.

[3] Military retirement pay had traditionally been based on a percentage of the basic salary of active personnel. Pay increases for those retired before the 1958 act would have been greater if they had been computed by this formula (see the debate in *Congressional Record*, 86th Cong., 2d sess., 1960, 106, pt. 8:10192–98).

[4] In his budget message for FY 1962 Eisenhower would request legislation returning retirement pay to the traditional formula (*Public Papers of the Presidents: Eisenhower, 1960–1961*, p. 956; see also Memorandum of Conference, May 19, 1959, AWF/D). Congress would, however, take no action on repeated proposals to equalize pay until May 1960, when the House would pass H.R. 11318 and refer it to the Senate. Still, Congress would pass no bill during that session (*Congressional Record*, 86th Cong., 2d sess., 1960, 106, pt. 8:10192–98). For developments see no. 1570.

[5] On July 10 Davis would thank the President for taking time to acknowledge his telegram (same file as document; see also Eisenhower to Boyce, July 4, 9, 1959, *ibid.*).

1231   *EM, AWF, Administration Series*

To Harold Edward Stassen   *July 7, 1959*

Dear Harold: I have your letter outlining the steps that you believe should be taken in the financial and economic field.[1] Since I cannot, at the moment, undertake to answer you personally, I shall refer your communication to Steve Saulnier for a detailed reply.[2]

With warm regard, *Sincerely*

[1] Stassen had written on July 6 (AWF/A) regarding his concerns about inflation. Recent newspaper reports had indicated that consumer credit had increased to an all time high. Stassen viewed this as "a significant inflationary pressure" and suggested "placing modest restraints on consumer credit as one of the new precise tools for restraining inflation." Stassen was also concerned about reports of widespread inventory buildups and urged "moderate restraint" on inventory credit. Raising interest rates was a blunt weapon against inflation, one which caused the federal budget, small business, and the home buyer to suffer the most. He urged the Administration to establish "a multiple set of precise tools to curb inflation without relying so heavily upon high interest and tight money."

[2] Stassen would reply on July 8 (AWF/A). He had not expected any reply "in substance," he said, and was thus pleased that Eisenhower had referred his letter to Dr. Saulnier, whom he felt was under no obligation to reply. Saulnier would, however, write Stassen on July 17 (AWF/A, Stassen Corr.). Although he was skeptical about using "selective credit controls rather than a general control over the lending power of banks," Saulnier said he would not hesitate to call for credit restriction measures if he thought they were appropriate. He did not advocate such action at the present time, he wrote, because the increase in consumer credit was due to a rise in automobile sales. Tougher lending restrictions would fail to check inflation and would serve only to prevent the automobile industry, which was operating far below capacity, from achieving full recovery. Saulnier explained further that selective credit controls presented "very great administrative difficulties." If accompanied by the general easing of credit that Stassen desired, they would produce "a very large inflationary force" which would defeat the program.

1232

To Frances L. Zeluff *July 8, 1959*

Dear Mrs. Zeluff: I have your letter, brought to me by Congressmen Utt and Wilson, who visited me this morning to discuss the general problems besetting the American tuna industry.[1] I am directing immediate action on the part of government to explore possibilities that might be helpful. I shall ask the State Department to keep your two Congressmen informed of developments.[2]

Problems such as this are always difficult—they are never wholly one-sided. But I assure you that I am completely sympathetic with the situation as you have outlined it in your letter, and I am hopeful that some reasonably satisfactory solution can be found.[3]

I appreciate your attitude in making certain that I would have a personal opportunity to look into the matter.[4]

With best wishes, *Sincerely*

[1] Mrs. Zeluff, of San Diego, California, was chair of the Tuna Fishermen's Wives Emergency Committee. James Boyd Utt (LL.B. University of Southern California 1946) represented California's Twenty-eighth District; Robert Carleton Wilson represented

California's Thirtieth District. Both had been Republican members of the House of Representatives since 1953.

² The American tuna industry had been facing stiff competition from Japanese fishermen, who were selling frozen tuna to American canneries below the domestic prices. The number of American fishing vessels had decreased from 214 in 1952 to 125, and employment on tuna boats had decreased from 2,730 in 1952 to 1,550. The commodity did not come under the Reciprocal Trade Agreements Act, and neither the State Department nor Congress supported tariff or quota legislation. The industry was "pinning its hopes on government-to-government discussions" in an effort to persuade the Japanese to place voluntary restrictions on tuna exports (Memorandum for the President, [July 8, 1959], AWF/D).

In June the American Tunaboat Association had announced that tunaboat owners in San Diego were considering operations with foreign crews and permanent berths in foreign waters in order to compete with the Japanese (*New York Times*, June 6, 1959).

After the meeting with Utt and Wilson the President had telephoned the Secretary of State to say he thought there might be some basis for negotiation and that the Japanese might be reasonable. On this same day the President would send a copy of this reply and Mrs. Zeluff's letter to the State Department (Eisenhower to Herter, July 8, 1959, and Telephone Conversation, Eisenhower and Herter, July 8, 1959, both in AWF/D; see also Ann Whitman memorandum, July 8, 1959, AWF/AWD).

³ Mrs. Zeluff had asked Eisenhower to initiate a conference between the United States and Japanese governments (with advisors from the tuna industry from each country) to discuss the problem and arrive at a mutually beneficial understanding.

⁴ In September Japan would be among eight nations investigated by a committee of the thirty-six-nation General Agreement on Tariffs and Trade (GATT) in Tokyo. The questioning would precede a month-long GATT ministerial meeting beginning October 26. On October 12 following a thirteen-day conference between the United States and Japan, Japanese tuna fishermen would pledge to supply the United States market only when the American industry could not meet its demands (*New York Times*, Oct. 13, 1959). On the GATT conference see *U.S. Department of State Bulletin* 41, no. 1062 (November 2, 1959), 633, 680, and State, *Foreign Relations, 1958–1960*, vol. IV, *Foreign Economic Policy*, pp. 235–36.

1233 *EM, AWF, Administrative Series*

To Sherman Adams   *July 8, 1959*

Dear Sherm: This note has no purpose other than to make inquiry as to the health and happiness of you and Rachel. I have had no direct news about you for a long time—the only thing I know is that you cannot possibly be out on the ski courses this time of year.¹

Needless to say I—as well as many others—continue to miss you. Among these others is Mamie, who frequently speculates as to your preoccupations and state of well-being.

I assume that you shared my enthusiasm for Lewis Strauss—his character, his dedication and high abilities. Therefore I am sure that you must have shared my amazement upon finding that so many people were ready to make him a victim of personal animus and partisanship.[2] With the loss of Foster Dulles,[3] Don Quarles[4] and Lewis Strauss from the intimate circle, I have been deeply disturbed and upset.

Do let me have a word from you when convenient, and in the meantime convey my warm greetings to Rachel.[5]

With personal regard to yourself, *As ever*

[1] The former Assistant to the President had resigned under pressure in October 1958 (see no. 862). Adams, who had returned to New Hampshire, would reply in a terse note of July 11 (AWF/A) that the snow had finally melted and he had taken up "agricultural and literary" pursuits.

[2] Acting Secretary of Commerce Strauss had resigned on June 22 following acrimonious congressional debate over his record as chairman of the Atomic Energy Commission (see no. 1215). Adams would tell the President that he shared his respect and fondness for Strauss.

[3] Secretary of State Dulles had died on May 24 (see no. 1167).

[4] Deputy Secretary of Defense Quarles had died unexpectedly the night of May 7 (see no. 1155).

[5] Adams would note that although the President had reservations about the value of free advice, he would recommend that Eisenhower go fishing more often. "It seems to straighten out a lot of things."

1234   *EM, WHCF, Official File 188*

To Ward Murphy Canaday   *July 9, 1959*
Personal

Dear Ward: I have read with great interest the excerpt from your correspondent that was attached to your note to me of the third of July. It is most informative—and I must confess that I was not aware of the astonishing industrial progress made by Hungary.[1]

Readily admitting that your correspondent shows capacity for keen observation and reporting, I am yet constrained to comment on an allusion he makes toward our State Department. He says that the "State Department would soon have to change its stony attitude toward Hungarian trade," and in the next paragraph, "For years American State Department officials and propagandists have been belittling the industrial developments of Hungary."[2]

I am certain that the State Department has no misconceptions as to the capacity of Communist dictatorships to produce goods of high quality and in large quantity. However, the attitude of this government is based on other considerations. It flows from our revulsion over the brutal and murderous suppression of freedoms in Hungary.[3]

We like the Hungarian people, as we have proved by our concern for the refugees from Communist tyranny, and because of a long history of friendly association with them. We would of course like to trade with them, but we do not seek to encourage our contacts and relations with oppressors.

What I have written is not meant as a criticism of your correspondent. I merely mean that he has overlooked a very important point in his anxiety to set our thinking straight on the purely material aspects of Hungarian development.[4]

Again my thanks for your thoughtfulness in sending me the paper.

With warm regard, *Sincerely*

[1] Canaday, president of the Overland Corporation, had sent the President a copy of a report (dated May 23) by an anonymous author who, he said, was in very close touch with Eastern European countries dominated by the Soviets. Canaday's original letter was dated June 30 but was stamped "received" at the White House on July 3, 1959 (same file as document). The report had praised the high quality of various Hungarian capital and consumer goods, particularly machine tools, water turbines, electric generators and harbor equipment. The author had also stated that Hungarians, eager to increase trade with the United States, were attempting to "get under the high tariff wall" into North American and South American markets by setting up trans-shipping corporations in Germany (*ibid.*).

[2] The correspondent had written that Western industrialists attending a recent industrial fair in Budapest were "intent on doing business," and had predicted that there would be too much pressure from businessmen for the State Department to continue its trade policies. Although American State Department officials were skeptical of Hungary's industrial capabilities, the report went on, many American industrialists at the 1958 World's Fair in Brussels had been impressed with the number of prizes the Hungarians had taken (*ibid.*). For background on the Brussels World's Fair see nos. 405 and 756.

[3] This paragraph was revised at the suggestion of the State Department. Eisenhower deleted two sentences from his original draft: "The attitude of our State Department has been the same that it has adopted toward all countries dominated by the international communist conspiracy.... The 'stony' attitude of this government is that we do not like murderers and tyrants and we will not deal with them except to the extent that is compelled by international necessity." The change was made in order to indicate that Hungary was a "special case," unlike such countries as Poland, where the United States was trying to increase trade and contacts (Dillon to Whitman, July 8, 1959, same file as document).

[4] For background on American relations with Hungary see Galambos and van Ee, *The Middle Way*, nos. 2044 and 2067, and in these volumes see nos. 832 and 1485; see also *Foreign Relations, 1958–1960*, vol. X, *Eastern European Region; Soviet Union, Cyprus*, pt. 1, pp. 24–29, 95–98, 65–66, 74–75, 110–13; and, for a contemporary Hungarian analysis, see Egon Kemenes, "The Hungarian Economy, 1945–1969," in *Modern Hungary: Readings from The New Hungarian Quarterly*, edited by Denis Sinor (Bloomington, Ind., 1977), pp. 128–44.

To William Alton Jones   *July 10, 1959*

Dear Pete: Like most grandfathers, I have always been rich in excuses as to why I have failed to tell my grandchildren bedtime stories. Distance, evening movies, television, social engagements, a book to read—all provide what seem, at the moment, to be valid reasons for neglecting a practice that could conceivably, have an influence—possibly a good one—on a youngster's thinking throughout all the years during which he or she may live.

There is one story that I am sure every grandfather, indeed, every father, should tell to those who are still young enough to enjoy or, at least, endure stories that are told to them by their elders.

The particular one which I propose for telling and re-telling is entitled, "How you are supporting me!"

The words and phrases of story-telling are all individualistic, but the bare-bone facts of this particular story are quite clear and easily understood. They are:

(1). I am one of the people who has lived for many years under the American government. I and my fellow citizens want and often get a number of things from the Federal government.

(2). All of these cost something—some a great deal.

(3). While we want and will insist on getting these things, we are not willing to pay for all of them. So we borrow money.

(4). We have borrowed so long and so much that we have piled up huge debts—a mortgage on the future.

(5). When you were born, your first present was a notice from the Federal government that your part of this mortgage was more than $1,600.

(6). The mortgage grows larger and since we will not pay it, we are bequeathing it to you.

(7). Some day you must start gradually to pay it off. If you don't, it will continue to grow and eventually our American system of free, competitive enterprise will not work. This means that you will not know the great value of free competition and individual liberty.

(8). Until you begin to pay for what I and my generation have bought you will not be a truly free man or woman.

(9). Since I don't want you to look back at your grandfather as self-indulgent, improvident and dishonest individual who, in effect, stole from his own grandchildren, I have resolved to pay for everything I get through the Federal government, and to reduce regularly and by a little bit, the mortgage you are inheriting from me.

(10). If the story finally ends this way, it will be one on which you can go to sleep happily.

*　　*　　*　　*　　*

Possibly grandchildren will not always understand or be interested in such a prosaic bedtime story. But the retelling of it may at the very least remind ourselves of our own duty. And if fathers and grandfathers would tell and retell the story, this country would be a stronger, happier and more prosperous one.[1]

With warm regard, *As ever*

---

[1] This letter may have been prompted by a conversation with Eisenhower's friend and political supporter Jones. See also nos. 334, 497, and 958. On Eisenhower's efforts to achieve a balanced budget see nos. 976 and 1042; on concerns over the growth of the national debt see Morgan, *Eisenhower versus 'The Spenders,'* pp. 127–51. For developments see no. 1474.

1236
EM, AWF,
International Series:
Khrushchev

To Nikita Sergeyevich Khrushchev　　　*July 11, 1959*

Dear Mr. Chairman: For some time past, it has seemed to me that it would be mutually profitable for us to have an informal exchange of views about problems which interest both of us. This thought has been reinforced by a suggestion attributed to you at the time of the recent visit of the American Governors to the Soviet Union.[1]

Accordingly, I have asked Mr. Robert Murphy to communicate to First Deputy Prime Minister Frol R. Kozlov, who is departing from the United States this Sunday evening, some ideas for your consideration.[2] Perhaps when you have had time to consider my suggestions, you would be kind enough to communicate your reaction via your Ambassador to Washington, Mr. Menshikov. I am sure that you will agree with me regarding the importance of keeping this matter confidential for the present.[3]

Hoping that this method of communication may be satisfactory to you, believe me *Yours sincerely*

---

[1] Nine U.S. governors had visited the Soviet Union in early July and had met with Khrushchev on July 7. After he had been questioned about the possibility of a Khrushchev visit at a news conference on July 8, Eisenhower had told Secretary Herter that it might be a good move if they were "ever going to break the log jam." He also told Herter that if, after careful consideration, "we don't reach any answer we have

got to have a good excuse for not doing it" (Telephone conversation, Herter and Eisenhower, July 8, 1959, Herter Papers, Telephone Conversations and AWF/D; see also Goodpaster, Memorandum of Conference, July 13, 1959, AWF/D; State, *Foreign Relations, 1958–1960*, vol. X, pt. 1, *Eastern Europe Region; Soviet Union; Cyprus*, pp. 294, 309–11; *Public Papers of the Presidents: Eisenhower, 1959*, pp. 506–8; and Eisenhower, *Waging Peace*, pp. 405–6).

[2] On the preceding day Eisenhower, Herter, Deputy Under Secretary Murphy, and other State Department officials had agreed that a meeting was worthwhile. If the results of the foreign ministers' meeting warranted, Murphy was to tell Kozlov, a summit conference could be held in Quebec, making it possible for Khrushchev to come to the United States a few days early for meetings at Camp David. Eisenhower would then visit Moscow in October. The President suggested changes in the draft of this letter "to make it clear that this is not a pressure tactic on Khrushchev." He added that a meeting with the Soviet leader would be useful in that if "Khrushchev were to threaten war or use of force," Eisenhower would "immediately call his bluff and ask him to agree on a date to start" hostilities (Goodpaster, Memorandum of Conference, July 13, 1959, AWF/D; see also Murphy, *Diplomat Among Warriors*, p. 438). On Kozlov's visit to the United States see no. 1213; see also State, *Foreign Relations, 1958–1960*, vol. VIII, *Berlin Crisis 1958–1959*, p. 977).

[3] Herter would cable Eisenhower that he had made his observations based on "French and German expectations that it would be possible to work out interim Berlin arrangements without sacrifice of principles." He was certain that "the French feel strongly, as you and I do, that no . . . agreement on a summit should be reached unless substantial progress with respect to such an interim settlement has been achieved" (Herter to Eisenhower, July 16, 1959, AWF/D-H).

Murphy would report that both the oral and written messages had had "quite an impact" on Koslov, who promised there would be no publicity (Ann Whitman memorandum, July 13, 1959, AWF/AWD). For developments see no. 1253.

1237   *EM, AWF, Administration Series*

TO CHARLES DOUGLAS JACKSON   *July 13, 1959*
Personal

Dear C. D.: Whenever you get steamed up on any subject which you make the topic of a letter to me, your communication is bound to be interesting, even provocative.[1] So far as my first hasty reading of your letter gives me an opportunity to understand your purpose, I assure you that I have no disagreement with what you say. Further, I would be delighted to have the kind of meeting that you suggest; I think a small stag dinner would provide the best possible opportunity for the kind of conversation you envision. Moreover, I believe that we should have present, in addition to those you name, George V. Allen and probably young Mr. Harr, who is quite a student in this field.[2] Beyond this, I would like one or two of my own staff present to make an informal record of the conversation.

I assure you also that neither I nor any of the State Department officials you mentioned have ever for a moment forgotten the cold war. We are spending a great deal in its waging.

As I understand your letter, your concern is to get our targets more specifically outlined and the methods we use greatly improved.

If Herter is to be with us, we cannot have the meeting for some time, but I shall not allow Ann to let me forget the matter.[3] Indeed, if you think we could proceed without Chris, I would be quite ready to set up the dinner within the next couple weeks. Should you think that desirable, just give Ann a ring.[4]

With warm regard, *As ever*

[1] Jackson had urged Administration officials to make a conscious decision to commit to the practice of "political warfare"; if so, he had written, then the ambassadors to the Iron Curtain countries and the United Nations needed to learn "the basic difference between diplomacy and political warfare." Even before taking office, he said, Eisenhower had understood that "skillfully conducted political warfare, while ostensibly 'making trouble' for diplomacy, actually *sets up* the situations for diplomacy to score its points." Jackson thought that although there seemed to be a great deal of misunderstanding regarding the practice, political warfare could still play a major role as a "catalyst assistant and helper" for American diplomacy (Jackson to Eisenhower, July 10, 1959, AWF/A).

[2] Jackson had recommended (*ibid.*) a quiet, off-the-record meeting to address the issue. The group should include, in addition to the President, Secretary of State Christian Herter, and other State Department leaders, Secretary of Defense Neil McElroy, CIA Director Allen W. Dulles, and Special Assistant to the President for National Security Affairs Gordon Gray. Karl G. Harr, Jr., (A.B. Princeton, 1943), Special Assistant to the President (for security operations coordination), since March 1958, had been a trial lawyer with the New York law firm of Sullivan and Cromwell. In 1954 he was appointed Special Assistant to the Under Secretary of State, and two years later had become Deputy Assistant Secretary of Defense for International Security Affairs. George V. Allen was Director of the United States Information Agency.

[3] Herter had returned to Geneva for the meeting of foreign ministers (see no. 1243).

[4] See no. 1273 for developments.

1238

EM, AWF, Name Series:
DDE Personal

To Elivera Carlson Doud

July 13, 1959

Dear Min: I think I mentioned something in my last letter that you probably already knew from Mamie—namely, that John and Barbara and the children had moved permanently to Gettysburg.[1] They seem to like it very much, and last weekend most of the family came down to Washington to stay with us. John and Barbie had a number of social engagements (very late ones, to John's disgust); Anne stayed with a girl friend somewhere nearby;[2] and the two younger girls were at the White House.[3] It was great fun.

John and Barbie seem to feel that the move to Gettysburg was a good one. Susie loves the horses and spends every moment she is allowed with them. I had worried somewhat that John might feel the commuting too much of a strain (as a general rule he goes up one evening during the middle of each week), but outside of the common complaint that all Washingtonians have about the traffic, he seems to enjoy his new routine.

We had a nice note from David last week, saying that he was hunting and fishing—and climbing mountains.[4] I don't believe Mamie feels the latter was any too healthy an experience for a growing boy, but I am sure such expeditions are thoroughly supervised. I understand he will be coming back through Denver in a couple of weeks or so, and I know he wants to come in to see you again.

Outside of my constant problems, everything is going reasonably well. We have no "vacation" plans, and await signs from Congress as to when they will decide to adjourn.[5] To date the amount of worthwhile legislation that has been passed is disappointing, but as usual they will, I imagine, put on a big spurt when the end is in sight.[6]

Needless to say, Mamie and I think and speak of you constantly, and only wish we could be closer to Denver so that we could see you frequently.[7]

With affectionate regard, *Devotedly*

[1] On June 18 the President had written to his mother-in-law, who had been ill since 1957 (WHCF/PPF 31-E; on Mrs. Doud's health see no. 612 and Ann Whitman memorandum, July 13, 1959, AWF/AWD). John and Barbara Eisenhower had moved into a house on the northwest corner of the President's farm in late June (see John S. D. Eisenhower, *Strictly Personal*, p. 281, and *New York Times*, June 22, 1959).

[2] Barbara Anne had celebrated her tenth birthday on May 30.

[3] Susan Elaine would turn eight on December 31, and Mary Jean would turn four on December 21.

[4] Eisenhower's eleven-year-old grandson was spending five weeks on a ranch in northern Colorado. David had visited his great-grandmother on June 22 (*New York Times*, June 23, 1959).

[5] The Eisenhowers would vacation in La Quinta, California (*New York Times*, Sept. 29, 30, Oct. 1–6, 12, 14, 15, 1959). The first session of the Eighty-sixth Congress would adjourn on September 15 (*Congressional Quarterly Almanac*, vol. XV, *1959*, p. 24; see also no. 1278).

[6] On the last-minute legislation see, for example, nos. 1250 and 1317.

[7] For developments see no. 1297.

To Earl Dewey Eisenhower   *July 13, 1959*

Dear Earl: You will remember that our brother, Paul, who died in infancy, is buried in the Belle Springs Cemetery (some eight or ten miles south of Abilene).[1] In this same cemetery are also buried our great-grandfather and grandfather.[2]

I understand that the church in Belle Springs has been abandoned, although the cemetery is cared for by someone. It has been suggested to me that we have Paul's remains removed from Belle Springs and brought to Abilene, to be buried in the family lot behind the graves of our parents.[3] I have no convictions about this proposition one way or the other, but I rather think it might be nice to have him buried in Abilene because we would be certain that the grave would have perpetual care. If you think the idea is a good one, I imagine the Cemetery Association in Abilene could make the necessary arrangements. I would appreciate having your reaction to this matter.[4]

With warm regard, *As ever*

[1] Paul A. Eisenhower was born May 12, 1894. He died of diphtheria March 16, 1895.
[2] The President's great-grandfather Frederick Eisenhower (1794–1884) and grandfather Jacob Frederick Eisenhower (1826–1906), members of an offshoot sect of the Mennonites known as the River Brethren, had owned farms in Dauphin County, Pennsylvania. In 1878 they had migrated west to Dickinson County, Kansas, with a colony of River Brethren from Pennsylvania and neighboring states.
[3] The President and his brothers recently had a fence constructed around the gravesite of their parents at Abilene Cemetery (see nos. 898 and 911).
[4] On this same date Eisenhower would send identical letters to brothers Milton and Edgar. Milton and Edgar would reply (July 16 and 17, respectively) that they wished to abide by what they thought had been their parents' decision to leave Paul's remains at Belle Springs. Both brothers expressed a desire to cooperate with the others on the matter.

On July 21 the President would reply to Edgar and Earl that in light of Milton's and Edgar's opinions he had abandoned the idea. He would later receive Earl's reply (July 21) which had crossed his in the mail. He had not known Paul, Earl would write, and was "completely disinterested." Although he would suggest leaving the remains at Belle Springs Cemetery and establishing a perpetual care fund to care for the family members buried there, he was willing to do whatever the others agreed upon. Paul's grave is still at the Belle Springs site. All correspondence is in AWF/N.

To David Lawrence   *July 14, 1959*
Personal

Dear David: Thank you for sending me a copy of the article from the
Saturday Evening Post that you wrote more than forty years ago.[1] I am
struck by the fact that now, as then, the real problem in this country is to make certain that there is an informed public opinion. The
techniques of mass communication have been vastly improved; nevertheless it often becomes painfully clear that the public is not as
fully informed concerning basic problems as it should be.[2]

Regardless of the need for observing secrecy in those areas where
to reveal information would give a great advantage to potential enemies, I believe that—except for this single restriction—government should not obstruct the flow of news and information. Indeed,
it has a positive duty of communicating the facts, concerning vital
issues, to as much of our population as can be reached.[3]

With personal regard,[4] *As ever*

[1] The article, "America Must Advertise," had appeared April 1918. Lawrence had criticized the government for the regulations that prevented newspapers and magazines
from bringing the news of World War I "home to the American people." Americans
had not been sold on the war, Lawrence wrote, and that is why they appeared to lack
enthusiasm and patriotism (WHCF/OF 139-D).

[2] In his cover letter (July 13, 1959, *ibid.*) Lawrence had said that he had written the
article at a time when similar "problems of propaganda" were facing the United
States. He added that the experience in World War I had been helpful during the
second World War.

[3] In his conclusion Lawrence had asked the government to cooperate with the press
in an appeal to Americans. "Publicity can not only unite us but it can disunite our
foes," Lawrence wrote.

[4] In August Lawrence would send the President a copy of another article he wrote
during World War I; see no. 1281.

1241   *EM, WHCF, Official File 101-J*

To Albert Collins Burrows   *July 14, 1959*

Dear Admiral Burrows:[1] Thank you for your note of the tenth. I am
delighted that you believe my casual, but nonetheless deeply felt, remark at the last press conference was effective. I don't want to sound
unduly prejudiced, but I doubt that any man, trained as you and I
were in the service of our country, could act with any motivation
other than that of the "public good."[2]

With best wishes, *Sincerely*

[1] Burrows (USN, ret.) was president of the Profit Sharing Research Foundation in Chicago. During World War II he had commanded submarines and submarine divisions 12 and 13 in the Atlantic Submarine Force.

[2] During Eisenhower's July 8 news conference a reporter had asked if the frequent use of the President's veto power would boomerang and result in a negative public image of the presidency. Eisenhower had replied that he was "not thinking so much of public image" as he was "the public good" (see *Public Papers of the Presidents: Eisenhower, 1959*, pp. 506–16). Burrows had written (same file as document) that the remark had filled him with "great and very real pride." The answer had "at once struck down the puffery of how would it look? And how will it sound?" and was "the very essence of honest dedication to the good of all."

1242   *EM, AWF, Name Series:*
                                      Gettysburg College Office

To WILLARD STEWART PAUL   *July 14, 1959*
Personal

Dear Stewart: There seems to be some misunderstanding—at least on my part—about your more than generous offer to provide, in the Gettysburg College, an office suite for me after 1961.[1]

A suggestion—which was by no means an expression of a definite intent—was brought to me by General Nevins who, I understood, was speaking with the authority of the Chairman of your Board.[2] The suggestion was to the effect that Gettysburg College would like to provide for me a suite of offices after I had left the Presidency.

I told Nevins that I was most grateful for the offer. At the same time I informed him that my future activities and preoccupations were so uncertain that I would not feel it fair to the College to ask them to reserve or to design any space for my use.[3]

As of this date I am not sure what I will be doing after January, 1961. I do not know whether I shall be able to keep my principal office in Gettysburg, nor what amount of space I may need, regardless of its location. I simply do not have the facts nor even the probabilities on which I could now make a decision. For this reason I hope that you will again assure the Board of my very great appreciation of their kind offer, together with the conclusion I reached, as above recorded. I may say, also, that after I have been relieved of the responsibilities of my present office, I hope to show a lively interest in the affairs and progress of Gettysburg College.[4]

With many thanks and best wishes. *Sincerely*

[1] In January 1958 Gettysburg College President Paul first had offered to install a suite of rooms for Eisenhower for use after June 1959 (see no. 544). On July 9 Paul had

again written to White House aide Tom Stephens and had enclosed a copy of a blue-print of the project. Paul told Stephens that Eisenhower had given "the green light" and needed to see the plans so that the college could incorporate the President's ideas into the design of the suite. Paul suggested that Eisenhower authorize a representative to meet with the college's architect (AWF/N: Gettysburg College Office). See also Ann Whitman memorandum, July 14, 1959, AWF/AWD, and Whitman to Nevins, July 15, 1959, *ibid.*

[2] The President had spent the July 4 weekend at his Gettysburg farm and probably had spoken with Nevins then. John Stanley Rice (B.S. Gettysburg College 1921) was chairman of the board of trustees of Gettysburg College. Rice had served as a Pennsylvania state senator 1932–1940 and as a colonel in the United States Army Air Force during World War II.

[3] On July 15 Eisenhower would send Nevins, who had been hospitalized at Walter Reed Army Medical Center on July 7, the correspondence with Paul (Whitman to Nevins, AWF/N: Gettysburg College Office and Eisenhower to Whitney, July 7, AWF/Gettysburg). On July 16 Nevins would reply that he thought Paul had "taken for granted" the President's acceptance (Nevins to Whitman, AWF/Gettysburg: College Office).

[4] For developments see no. 1437.

1243   *EM, AWF, DDE Diaries Series*

To Christian Archibald Herter   *July 15, 1959*
Cable. Secret

Dear Chris:[1] I am interested in your observation about the general feeling at Geneva, to the effect that a Summit Conference some time this fall is inevitable.[2] The existence of such a feeling must mean that our Allies are convinced that there will be sufficient progress at Geneva to justify such a meeting on the part of the Western Powers. Unless they do have this confidence in some progress, then they must be assuming that the West will surrender to pressure from the other side.

You and I have long ago agreed that we have no idea of being either belligerent or unnecessarily rigid. But we have stood and intend to stand on principle. Moreover, we have made it abundantly clear that we are ready to interpret progress at Geneva in a liberal manner. It would be most unfortunate if our associates should assume that regardless of the absence of progress, this government will consent to attend a Summit Conference. For us this would be such an unacceptable retreat that it would virtually spell surrender. This we will not do.

*   *   *   *   *

NEW SUBJECT. As a result of my press conference this morning, there was an assertion on the part of some press representatives that you and I were giving different answers to the same question, that of the possibility of bringing Bohlen to Washington. I had not previously read the transcript of your most recent press conference and so I answered a query put to me on the basis of the two discussions you and I had in my office during the past ten days or two weeks. Twice I brought up the subject and you said that there were no plans of any kind to bring Bohlen to Washington and that the matter was not now under discussion. It was in this sense that I answered.[3]

A reporter then called attention to your press conference. I have since read the applicable excerpts. A careful reading shows that while you discussed this matter, you were not talking about any current plans or negotiations looking toward such a move, but on the contrary pointed out that Bohlen was so busy that we could not even consider his transfer now. However, since I did not know about the conversations that you said started some months ago, my answer was completely negative, and it was because of these different answers that the interest of the press was aroused.[4]

I have had Mr. Hagerty explain the matter to the reporter who asked the question, and I doubt that any great damage has resulted. But I do regret that I had no inkling of the complete situation as described in your press conference.[5]

*   *   *   *   *

I know that your Geneva task is wearisome but, as you say, there seems to be nothing to do but keep on plugging. All of us admire your performance.[6]

With warm regard, *As ever*

[1] Acting Secretary of State Dillon had cabled this message to Secretary Herter, who had returned to Geneva on July 12 for the resumption of the foreign ministers' conference (for background see no. 1212).

[2] Herter had told Eisenhower that the meetings were "off to a very slow start" and that the Western ministers were beginning to believe in the inevitability of a summit conference. "I wish I could be as optimistic that we will have achieved sufficient progress to allow such a meeting to be held in reasonable atmosphere," Herter said. "I will keep right on plugging" (State, *Foreign Relations, 1958–1960*, vol. VIII, *Berlin Crisis 1958–1959*, p. 987).

[3] After having served for four years as Ambassador to the Soviet Union, Charles E. ("Chip") Bohlen had been appointed U.S. Ambassador to the Philippines in 1957 (see Galambos and van Ee, *The Middle Way*, no. 118; no. 537 in these volumes; and Bohlen, *Witness to History*). On this same day *New York Times* reporter William H. Lawrence had asked Eisenhower if Herter had discussed bringing Bohlen back to Washington as an advisor on Soviet affairs. Bohlen had told Eisenhower in February that the Manila post would be his last for family and financial reasons, and in April he had told Under Secretary of State Dillon that he would defer his resignation if he thought he could aid the department in negotiations with the Soviet Union (Bohlen to Eisenhower, July 29, 1959, AWF/A; see also Bohlen, *Witness to History*, p. 457; and for stories about the transfer, *New York Times*, June 24, 27, 1959). In prepa-

ration for the President's news conference on July 1, Herter had advised White House staff members that if Eisenhower were asked about the news stories, he should say that he knew "nothing about it" (Telephone conversation, Herter and Wheaton and Kendall, July 1, 1959, Herter Papers, Telephone Conversations; see also Eisenhower to Herter, July 7, 1959, AWF/D-H).

According to Ann Whitman, Eisenhower had "erupted" during a pre-press briefing on this same day. He had called Deputy Under Secretary Robert Murphy, demanding "to know why Herter had told him that he was not considering bringing Bohlen back—and yet the State briefing book said it was under discussion" (Ann Whitman memorandum, July 15, 1959, AWF/AWD; Telephone conversation, Eisenhower and Murphy, July 15, 1959, AWF/D. Eisenhower's news conference is in *Public Papers of the Presidents: Eisenhower, 1959*, pp. 527–28).

[4] For Herter's news conference on July 9 see *U.S. Department of State Bulletin* 41, no. 1048 [July 27, 1959], 113.

[5] On the following day Eisenhower would tell Acting Secretary Dillon that "he was very disturbed about the whole handling of the Bohlen affair. He now found that, despite the regard he holds for Mr. Bohlen—having appointed him Ambassador to Russia and to the Philippines—he is being represented as lacking confidence in Bohlen and opposing his reassignment." He said that he had understood from Herter "that this was not a live issue" and that he had advised senators "that there was nothing in the story" (Goodpaster, Memorandum of Conference, July 20, 1959, AWF/D).

Herter would cable his apologies to Eisenhower on the following day. He thought what he had said in his press conference was in accordance with their conversation, and that he had explained that Bohlen's financial situation would lead to his retirement unless he could be appointed to "some advisory job on Russian affairs." The matter stood where Eisenhower had indicated, Herter said, and nothing would be done until his return (Herter to Eisenhower, July 16, 1959, AWF/D-H). For developments see no. 1245.

[6] In his July 16 cable Herter would tell Eisenhower that he had made his observations on the summit conference on the basis of "French and German expectations that it would be possible to work out interim Berlin arrangements without sacrifice of principles." He was certain that the French also thought "that no agreement on a summit should be reached unless substantial progress with respect to such an interim settlement has been achieved" (Herter to Eisenhower, July 16, 1959, AWF/D-H). For developments see no. 1253.

1244   *EM, WHCF, Official File 182*

To George Meany   *July 15, 1959*

Dear Mr. Meany: Thank you very much for your letter of yesterday. For a long time I have been keenly aware and appreciative of the firm stand taken by the AFL-CIO in support of the government's refusal to abandon either the free people of West Berlin or our rights and responsibilities respecting that city.[1]

Your present letter should convince everyone, including the Soviets, that in the United States labor is free—and because it is free, it is part of the decision-making process in our country. When free citizens form their conclusions and convictions on matters that affect America's international position, they cannot be divided on the basis of vocation, creed or partisan politics. The efforts of any outsider to divide America are bound to fail when the basic beliefs and the vital interests of this nation are at stake.

I am grateful for your letter because even though I have had no doubt in my own heart or mind of AFL-CIO solidarity in this matter, I salute your entire membership for reaffirming this solidarity before the entire world.[2]

With warm regard, *Sincerely*

[1] AFL-CIO President Meany had written to deny Khrushchev's claims, reportedly made to Averell Harriman during his recent six-week visit to the Soviet Union, that American workers did not support Eisenhower on the Berlin crisis. Meany had quoted part of a resolution the AFL-CIO leadership had passed on February 20, 1959, commending NATO's actions (Meany to Eisenhower, July 14, 1959, same file as document). Meany's letter and the President's response would be released to the press the next day (*New York Times*, June 24, 26, and July 16, 1959).

[2] Meany had also refuted Khrushchev's reported assertion that the American working class had no voice in political affairs. The Soviet Premier knew, Meany had written, that workers influenced social, economic, and foreign policy issues through "independent" political activities: indeed, "American labor" had prompted the United Nations' condemnation of forced labor behind the Iron Curtain and Soviet aggression in Hungary.

1245   *EM, AWF, Dulles-Herter Series*

To Charles Eustis Bohlen   *July 16, 1959*
Personal. Eyes only

Dear Chip: Rarely have I seen the Washington press in such a state of confusion and misunderstanding, and indulging in so much misinterpretation amounting to some distortion, as they have over the question of your possible return to Washington for duty in the State Department.[1] Because you are an old hand in government, you expect some of this all the time—and normally I know most of us shrug off this kind of thing with a chuckle, even though at times it may be a rueful one.

A headline on a little story in the *Star* last evening annoyed me enough that I felt the urge to set the record partly straight, at least, as between you and me. The headline said: "Eisenhower Cool to Idea of High Job for Bohlen."

I do not have to go through the history of our relationship ever since the time I met you in Algiers to assure you again of the admiration and respect with which I have always regarded your qualifications and capabilities. So far as I know, I have never missed an opportunity to give appropriate public expression to these views and, after all, I have twice nominated you—and you have been confirmed—for the post of Ambassador.

All this merely is a preliminary to saying that I still hold these convictions. I am anxious that you remain in the Foreign Service and I am quite ready to approve any recommendation of Herter's that might possibly make it more feasible for you to continue in the Service and still make it easier for you to discharge obligations toward your own family.

To some extent there was reason for misunderstanding on the part of the press corps. I had not been aware of certain conversations, some weeks or months ago, between you and Chris Herter, regarding the possibility of your coming to Washington. Because Herter had decided that at least for the present you could not be spared from Manila because of the complexity of certain negotiations in which you are now engaged, he had said to me in reply to my query something to the effect that "there were no discussions *now* going on touching on this possibility."[2] Consequently when I, in a later press conference, said that there was nothing whatsoever to this story—and I had been so informed by Herter—the press representatives made their own interpretation of the matter since they were of course aware of the fact that these conversations had taken place. This is all there is to the story.

Of course as usual some Senators injected themselves into the matter with expressions of opinion—favorable or unfavorable.[3] This is something that is none of their business. They are aware of the fact that foreign relations are the responsibility of the President and his Secretary of State, and except when confirmation of an appointment is involved, you might suppose that they would avoid comment. In any event, to these comments I have paid no attention at all—in fact, in one case I let the man personally know how I felt about such interference.

This unusually long letter is prompted only by the feeling that I myself may have contributed a little bit to the misunderstanding that has arisen. I hope only that it has caused you no embarrassment.[4]

With warm regard, *Sincerely*

[1] For background see no. 1243.

[2] Bohlen had discussed his return to Washington with Under Secretary of State Dillon in April. Secretary Herter had written Bohlen before leaving for the resumption of the foreign ministers' meeting in Geneva that he hoped to arrange for the new assignment but a final decision could not be made until his return (Bohlen to Eisenhower, July 29, 1959, AWF/A). For negotiations with Philippine government officials regarding the revision of the 1947 Military Bases Agreement see State, *Foreign Rela-*

tions, 1958–1960, vol. XV, *South and Southeast Asia,* pp. 917–19, 928–29, 946–57; see also Galambos and van Ee, *The Middle Way,* nos. 319 and 1859.

[3] Republican Senators Bourke B. Hickenlooper of Iowa, H. Styles Bridges of New Hampshire, and Everett McKinley Dirksen of Illinois had indicated that they would oppose any move to bring Bohlen into the State Department (see Telephone conversations, Herter and Harlow, Dirksen, and Smith, July 9, 10, 1959, Herter Papers, Telephone Conversations). On August 24 Herter would tell Eisenhower that he had spoken "to the 'recalcitrant' senators" who said that they would accept the proposal but asked Herter to wait until Congress had adjourned (Goodpaster, Memorandum of Conference, Aug. 25, 1959, WHO/OSS: Subject [State], State Dept.).

[4] On the following day Eisenhower would tell Dillon that "he was very much troubled" to see in the press that he had sent this message to Bohlen. Such a leak made him "very 'jumpy,'" he said, when he realized "that his own correspondence may be improperly disclosed" (Goodpaster, Memorandum of Conference, July 20, 1959, AWF/D; see also Dillon to Bohlen, July 16, 1959, WHO/OSS: Subject [State], State Dept.).

On September 21 State Department officials would announce that Bohlen would return to the United States to serve as an advisor on Soviet affairs. He would leave Manila on October 15 (see *New York Times,* Oct. 15, 1959; and Bohlen, *Witness to History,* p. 458).

1246   *EM, AWF, Administration Series*

To James Rhine Killian, Jr.   *July 16, 1959*

Dear Jim: Your note of yesterday reminds me that, although I sent you some two months ago a formal letter telling of my appreciation of your work as Special Assistant for Science and Technology—and regretfully accepting your resignation—I have never told you personally, in a letter at least, how I value our association and friendship.[1]

At the time, almost two years ago, when millions, startled by sputniks, wanted to plunge headfirst and almost blindly into the space age, you assumed the complex responsibilities of trying to coordinate, for me, the governmental activities in this field and to help develop programs that, while adapted to requirements, were not dictated or designed in an atmosphere of panic. No one did more than you, in those early days, to bring reason, fact and logic into our plans for space research and adventure. I shall never cease to be grateful for the patience with which you initiated me into the rudiments of this new science and the part the government should play in its development, and for the skill with which you assembled a capable scientific group of people to take over the many resulting responsibilities.[2]

More than all this, every contact with you has been, for me, interesting, informative and often inspiring. I shall forever be in your debt for your willingness to interrupt your important work at M.I.T. long enough to assume the difficult post you have so successfully filled.[3]

With the hope that Mrs. Eisenhower and I will see you often in the future, even if you are moving the base of your operations, and warm personal regard to both you and Mrs. Killian,[4] *As ever*

[1] For background on Killian's resignation see no. 1180. On July 14 Eisenhower had presented to Killian an inscribed medallion containing a relief of the President mounted in wood from the White House. The following day Killian had thanked Eisenhower for the gift and expressed his "sense of deep privilege in having had the opportunity to work" on the President's team (AWF/A). On June 29 Eisenhower had given Killian a small White House farewell dinner party (*New York Times*, June 30, 1959).

[2] On the American reaction to the launch of the Soviet earth satellites, the Sputniks, in the fall of 1957, see nos. 389, 394, and 434. On Killian's appointment and accomplishments see nos. 396, 522, and 1180.

[3] Killian had resigned in order to return to his position as president of the Massachusetts Institute of Technology.

[4] Killian would continue to serve on the President's Science Advisory Committee (*New York Times*, Mar. 14, May 29, 1959). They would meet on July 20, October 19, 1959, and October 11, 1960. Mrs. Killian was the former Elizabeth Parks.

1247   *EM, WHCF,*
Official File 144-B-1-A

To Sidney Williams Richardson   *July 16, 1959*

Dear Sid: As you know from my letter in which I invited you to a stag dinner some time ago, I am quite interested in the development of a National Presbyterian Church Center here in Washington.[1] One of the trustees is Tom Clark, a Justice of the Supreme Court.[2] I am quite sure you know him well.

Justice Clark is to be in Texas in the near future and he hopes to talk to you about the project—I am sure you would like to hear about it in more detail than I could possibly send in a letter.[3]

It has been far too long since I have seen you. I trust that your health and your convenience will both permit you to make us a visit one of these days.[4]

With warm regard, *As ever*

[1] Eisenhower's May 11 letter to Richardson and Richardson's May 14 reply are in the same file as the document. On the President's active interest in the plans for building in Washington a National Presbyterian Church Center see nos. 12 and 281; Woodruff to Whitman, July 9, 1959, AWF/N, Woodruff Corr.; Eisenhower to Wood-

ruff, July 13, 1959, AWF/N; Eisenhower to McCabe, March 11, 1960, AWF/D; and the related correspondence in the same file as the document.

[2] Texas native Thomas Campbell Clark (A.B. University of Texas 1921; LL.B. University of Texas 1922) had been Associate Justice of the U.S. Supreme Court since 1949. He had served in various positions in the Justice Department since 1932, including that of Attorney General of the United States (1945–1949).

[3] Clark would meet with Richardson, and Richardson would agree to make a donation to the building project (Telephone Conversation, Elson and Whitman, Sept. 12, 1959, same file as document).

On the occasion of his seventy-seventh birthday (October 14, 1967), Eisenhower would unveil the cornerstone of the National Presbyterian Church. Formal dedication would take place on May 10, 1970 (Telephone conversation, Elizabeth Stone, Librarian and archivist, National Presbyterian Church, July 27, 1999, and *New York Times*, Oct. 15, 1967, May 11, 1970).

[4] In his May 14 letter Richardson said he had suffered the flu in April and was unable to travel to Washington until he could get his "chin up a little higher."

1248 *EM, AWF, Administration Series*

To LEWIS LICHTENSTEIN STRAUSS *July 17, 1959*
Personal

Dear Lewis: Thanks for your letter of yesterday.[1] I would hope we could get one of our columnist friends to point up the Court of Claims' negation of Senator Anderson's biased charge. It can't help now, but I am all for setting the record straight as much as possible. I don't suppose at this date I shall get another press conference question on the subject, but how I would love to have one that would permit me a statement on the Court's decision![2]

Ann[3] says she is surprised that the *women* weren't 99% favorable in the Trendex poll. Anyhow the feminine reaction is one aspect of the situation in which you can take real comfort.[4]

With warm regard, *As ever*

[1] Strauss had suggested that Eisenhower "might draw some satisfaction" from the recent Court of Claims decision on the controversial Dixon-Yates contract (AWF/A). In 1954 the federal government had contracted with a privately-owned corporation to construct a power plant in the Tennessee Valley region. After Eisenhower canceled the contract, the corporation filed suit for termination costs. In its July 15 finding, the court ruled against Justice Department claims that the contract was invalid because a Budget Bureau consultant had violated conflict-of-interest statutes (see Galambos and van Ee, *The Middle Way*, nos. 1017, 1026, and 1515; see also *Congressional Quarterly Almanac*, vol. XV, *1959*, pp. 665–69; Aaron Wildavsky, *Dixon-Yates: A Study in Power Politics* [New Haven, 1962], pp. 278–88; and *New York Times*, July 16, 1959).

[2] Strauss claimed that the ruling "explodes one of the main charges" made by his senatorial opponents, who had alleged that Strauss had been involved in a conflict

of interest while he had been chairman of the AEC (Strauss to Eisenhower, July 16, 1959, AWF/A). The issue had been raised during the Senate hearings on Strauss's nomination as Secretary of Commerce; see no. 1215.

[3] Ann C. Whitman, the President's personal secretary.

[4] A Trendex Public Opinion Poll quoted by Strauss had reported that seventy percent of those who had followed the Senate confirmation hearings in the press had disapproved of the decision to reject his nomination. "Amusingly," he wrote, "in light of Margaret Chase Smith's vote, the answers from *women* were 83.3% in disapproval of the Senate's action." Smith was one of two Republican senators who had voted against his confirmation (Strauss to Eisenhower, July 16, 1959, AWF/A).

1249   *EM, WHCF, President's Personal File 350*

To Charles R. Yates   *July 17, 1959*

Dear Charlie: I wish I could join you in the statement that "there is nothing on my agenda."[1] Today, for instance, I have had the steel strike,[2] the Geneva negotiations,[3] a Cabinet meeting dealing with possibly ten domestic matters,[4] the new head of the Navy League,[5] and other sundry problems (none capable of solution—at least easily). So I, too, long for November and, hopefully, a comparatively free ten days or so in Augusta.[6]

At any rate, many thanks for your letter. And warm personal regard, *As ever*

[1] Yates had reminded the President of the time when he attended an Augusta National Golf Club board meeting during which Yates had told Cliff Roberts that there was nothing on the agenda (July 14, 1959, same file as document).

[2] The United Steelworkers of America had called a strike on July 15. On the strike's effect on the nation's economy and security see, for example, no. 1367; see also Eisenhower, *Waging Peace*, pp. 453–59.

[3] On the frustrations surrounding the Geneva meetings see nos. 1243 and 1253.

[4] Among the matters discussed at the Cabinet meeting were the Dixon-Yates contract (see the preceding document); verbatim transcripts of committee meetings; removal of papers by retiring department and agency heads; and the upcoming Agriculture Fair in New Delhi. At the conclusion of the meeting the President asked: "Anybody else want to take some time for belly-aching?" (Cabinet meeting minutes, July 17, 1959, AWF/D).

[5] At noon Eisenhower had met with Frank Gard Jameson (B.S. Stanford 1947), the newly-elected president of the Navy League of the United States (see Memorandum for the Record, July 20, 1959, AWF/D, and *New York Times*, May 9, 1959). Jameson was founder and chairman of the board of Pacific Automation Products, Inc., in Glendale, California. During the meeting the President stressed the need to avoid emphasis on the single-service concept in order to meet over-all defense requirements. Eisenhower said that the Navy League should avoid consideration of corporate profits when it assessed the requirements for national security.

[6] Yates said that he had "happy prospects" of seeing the President in November at

Augusta. The Eisenhowers would take their traditional Thanksgiving vacation in Augusta November 12–23.

1250   *EM, AWF, Name Series*

TO ROBERT WINSHIP WOODRUFF   *July 20, 1959*

Dear Bob: Jerry Persons told me about his telephone conversation with you on the T.V.A. bill. I shall study the final bill closely.[1]

Frankly, there are many kinds of "pressure groups." When one begins to function in the legislative procedure, it strives to develop a bill that is all in its favor. Even if a particular bill contains features which would have adverse effects upon the whole country, but also contains clauses favoring the special group, the pressure is still applied in order to get the bill enacted.

No one has worked harder than I to stop the expansion of the area of the T.V.A. But at the same time no one has worked harder than I to make certain that through the medium of a law Congress does not, in fact, ignore the responsibilities of the Chief Executive and reduce him to a state of impotency in his power to act in the interest of the whole country.[2]

When the bill comes to my desk, I shall study it both respecting the features I like and those I dislike.[3]

With warm regard, *As ever*

[1] For background see Galambos and van Ee, *The Middle Way*, no. 1515. Eisenhower was referring to H.R. 3460, pending legislation to authorize the TVA to finance expansion of its power facilities by issuing revenue bonds. The expansion was necessitated by an anticipated power shortage of 600,000 kilowatts during 1961–1962, and of 1,000,000 watts in 1963.
[2] In 1955 the TVA had announced that, in response to a request by the President, it had developed a plan to issue revenue bonds to finance its expansion without recourse to governmental appropriation. In 1956, 1957, and 1958, however, Congress had refused to authorize the TVA bond issues, citing insufficient executive and legislative review, failure in the legislation to make provisions for repayment of the money already invested in the TVA, and lack of limitation on the amount of the bond issue. In May 1959, the House had passed legislation authorizing the TVA to issue up to $750 million worth of bonds to finance the construction or replacement of facilities needed for the generation or transmission of electric power. The bill also limited TVA's service area to the boundaries in existence in July 1957, and required that the TVA return to the Treasury at least $10 million a year until it had repaid $1.2 billion previously appropriated by Congress for the Agency. The Senate had passed the legislation on July 9 and returned it to the House (*Congressional Quarterly Almanac*, vol. XV, *1959*, pp. 261–65). At his July 15 news conference the President had expressed his displeasure with the bill's failure to provide for executive review of the legislation, and its failure to include "a proper

restriction on the expansion" of the TVA (*Public Papers of the Presidents: Eisenhower, 1959*, p. 523).
³ For developments see no. 1270.

1251 *EM, AWF, DDE Diaries Series*

TO CLIFFORD ROBERTS *July 20, 1959*

Dear Cliff: I am properly impressed (though I suspect your bride's influence) to receive the program of an exhibition at the Royal Academy. When you return I shall expect a complete listing of all the Museums you have visited, and more importantly, a short concise, informative talk on the various schools of art and which one appeals to you most.¹

With warm regard, *As ever*

¹ The program is not in AWF. Roberts and his new wife had been traveling throughout Europe since June 18 (see Roberts to Eisenhower, June 2, 1959, and Eisenhower to Roberts, June 4, 1959, both in AWF/N). On Roberts's recent marriage see no. 984. For developments see no. 1257.

1252 *EM, AWF, DDE Diaries Series*

TO RUTH EAKIN EISENHOWER *July 20, 1959*

Dear Ruth: Your pre-anniversary party was a great success. Your Aunt Mamie and I had a wonderful time.¹

Now that you are completely emancipated from the disadvantages of childhood, I think you ought to buy something womanly—that is, something that will be completely useless. Among such things I can list perfume, lipstick, nail polish, bath oil and spiked heel pumps.²

Once again, happy birthday! *Devotedly*

¹ Eisenhower's niece Ruth would turn twenty-one-years-old on July 21. On July 19 the President and First Lady had motored to Baltimore to dine with Ruth and her father Milton at his home on the campus of the Johns Hopkins University (Ann Whitman memorandum, July 18, 19, 1959, AWF/AWD).
² Enclosed with this letter was a fifty-dollar bill. Milton Eisenhower would report that Ruth was "thrilled" with the gift and planned to purchase a white cashmere sweater (Telephone conversation, Milton Eisenhower and Eisenhower, July 22, 1959, AWF/D).

To Christian Archibald Herter   *July 21, 1959*
Cable. Secret

Dear Chris: Thank you for your report.[1] You certainly are having
an unproductive and difficult time with Gromyko. I quite agree
that this cannot continue for long. However, I do feel that if we
take any action to terminate things this week it would inescapably
transfer the burden of negotiation to the Vice President during
his meeting with the Soviets over the coming weekend.[2] I see no
reason on the other hand why you should not tell Gromyko privately, as I gather you have already intimated to him, that unless
the negotiations begin to show more progress in the near future
it will not be possible to continue. A two or three days' recess might
possibly serve to indicate publicly that we are considering termi-
nating the farce.[3] I have just been informed that Menshikov has
been in touch with Murphy and apparently has some information to convey.[4] Maybe this will have some bearing on our decision. In any event we should see things more clearly in about a
week.

I thought your statement yesterday was excellent.[5]

P.S. I have just seen Ambassador Menshikov who has verbally
given me a rough translation of Khrushchev's reply to my letter
which was carried to him by Koslov.[6] The greater part of the letter
is an expression of readiness and even a keen desire to exchange
visits. He indicated he would prefer that his visit here should take
place after the termination of the hottest part of our weather. However, when he discussed the condition I laid down—namely that
there should be some degree of progress at Geneva which would
justify a Summit meeting, he simply played the same old record. He
thinks there is no virtue in our arguing that without such progress,
meetings at the highest level would have no reason and no beneficial result.

Tomorrow the State Department will make a careful translation
of the letter and we will start drafting a reply which will, of course,
be sent to you for comment before dispatching. We will send it
through Menshikov, but Thompson will be provided a copy.[7]

Incidentally, in discussing a possible visit here, he mentioned a
period of some ten to fifteen days and observed that it would make
little difference to him whether the visit was formal or informal.

As of this moment no real progress is observable.

I think it is important that this whole matter be kept confidential
for the time being.[8] *With best regard*

¹ For background see no. 1243. Before the recess in the Geneva foreign ministers' meetings Soviet Foreign Minister Gromyko had proposed that a committee comprising members from both East and West Germany should work out the problems of reunification and negotiate the principles of a peace treaty. Gromyko insisted that some form of all-German negotiations take place before there could be an interim settlement of the Berlin problem. On July 17 Secretary Herter had cabled Eisenhower that since the recess the Soviet position had "hardened" on the subject of an all-German committee, and the conference had "taken a serious turn for the worse" (Herter to Eisenhower, July 17, 1959, AWF/D-H; see also State, *Foreign Relations, 1958–1960*, vol. VIII, *Berlin Crisis 1958–1959*, pp. 865–66, 874, 988, 1005).

On this day Herter had cabled Eisenhower that neither the Western ministers nor the West Germans could accept the Soviet proposal according the German Democratic Republic *de facto* recognition. Their counter-proposal was to continue the conference with designated deputies carrying on the negotiations; German advisors would be included. If Gromyko continued to insist on establishing an all-German committee then Herter thought that the United States faced a "complete impasse." He wanted permission to ask Gromyko privately how they could bring the meetings to a close without increasing the inevitable tensions. Herter feared that if the conference continued for more than a few days, the Soviets would "interpret our inexhaustible patience as evidence of weakness and anxiety" (Herter to Eisenhower, July 21, 1959, AWF/D-H; see also State, *Foreign Relations, 1958–1960*, vol. VIII, *Berlin Crisis 1958–1959*, pp. 1019–20).

² Vice-President Nixon would leave Washington on July 22 to open the American National Exhibition in Moscow (see no. 1148). State Department officials had told Eisenhower that a decision to terminate the conference was premature and would "throw the Vice President into the middle of negotiations when he sees Khrushchev." A short recess, Eisenhower believed, would provide Nixon an opportunity to tell Khrushchev that it appeared the conference could not be saved. The President insisted that "the Vice President must not get into any negotiating activity" (Goodpaster, Memorandum of Conference, July 21, 1959, AWF/D).

Eisenhower inserted the word "inescapably" for "merely" in an earlier draft of this letter (see AWF/D-H).

³ Eisenhower added this sentence to the paragraph.

⁴ Ambassador Menshikov would convey the substance of Khrushchev's reply before Eisenhower finished this letter; see n. 6.

⁵ For Herter's statement to the twenty-second plenary session, presenting the new Western proposals for continuing the conference, see *U.S. Department of State Bulletin* 41, no. 1050 [August 10, 1959], 191–94.

⁶ Eisenhower's letter to Khrushchev is no. 1236. The President had thanked Menshikov for Khrushchev's "prompt and courteous response." The United States, he said, had never defined the requirements for a summit meeting. "The important thing was to be able to point to progress as men of good will and to the maintenance of U.S. rights in Berlin" (State, *Foreign Relations, 1958–1960*, vol. X, pt. 1, *Eastern Europe Region; Soviet Union; Cyprus*, p. 324). Khrushchev's reply is in *ibid.*, pp. 324–25.

⁷ In a handwritten notation at the top of Khrushchev's letter Eisenhower had indicated that a draft would be cabled first to Herter (*ibid.*, p. 324). Llewellyn E. Thompson was the U.S. Ambassador to the Soviet Union.

⁸ For developments see no. 1258.

To Harold Macmillan   *July 22, 1959*
Cable. Secret

Dear Harold: Thank you so much for sending me, for the benefit of
the Vice President, some of your impressions concerning Mr. Khrushchev.[1] Dick came in to pay a farewell call on me a little while ago,
before departing for Moscow, and he read your memorandum. I am
certain he will express his personal appreciation to you at the first
opportunity.[2]

From the tone of your message, I would conclude that you are
much more hopeful than I am of any worthwhile result at Geneva.[3]
Unless there is an abrupt reversal in the Soviet attitude, it would appear to me that the accomplishment will be zero, or even a minus.
I think that the only bright spot in the exercise has been the solidarity of the West on basic issues.

As you know, I have been quite ready to interpret progress in a
most liberal fashion. So long as we could have the assurance of complete respect of our rights in Berlin and there could be agreed any
kind of program that could be presented by the Foreign Ministers
to Heads of Government for study and discussion, our own minimum criteria for the holding of such a meeting would be realized.
Unless there is at least this much justification for a Summit, it is still
my conviction that such a meeting would be a fraud on our peoples
and a great diplomatic blunder.

I know that there has been some argument that the less the
progress at the Foreign Ministers level, the more necessary a Summit meeting becomes. I am quite clear in my mind that such a feeling is not shared by the bulk of our people.

This may sound to you overly pessimistic. But you know that I have
very much wanted to participate in a meeting in which there was
even the slightest promise of a successful outcome. No one would
be more thankful than I if my evaluation of the final Geneva outcome should be demonstrated wrong. But I am trying to be realistic, based on what we know of Khrushchev and his henchmen.[4]

With warm regard, As ever

[1] Prime Minister Macmillan had visited the Soviet premier in February (see nos. 1065
and 1074). Macmillan had told Eisenhower that because of the development of modern weapons, the Soviet leaders probably "would like to move into an era of 'competitive co-existence.'" Khrushchev, who appeared to believe in normal international
relations, could possibly be persuaded to concentrate his energies in building up the
country's economy. He wanted to be "respectable," Macmillan said, and to be recognized as an equal by Eisenhower and the United States. And yet, Khrushchev was

"intensely suspicious of the West, very quick to take offense and extremely naive about the world." He resented plain speaking which could sound threatening, Macmillan added, and the only way to make a point was either by heavy-handed bantering "or by serious and conciliatory conversation on a high philosophical note" (Macmillan to Eisenhower, July 21, 1959, State Department Files, Presidential Correspondence; see also Eisenhower to Whitney, July 20, 1959, AWF/A). Nixon would leave on this day for Moscow to open the American National Exhibition (see no. 1148).

[2] For Eisenhower's meeting with Nixon see Goodpaster, Memorandum of Conference, July 22, 1959, AWF/D.

[3] Macmillan had said that he thought the Geneva negotiations seemed "to be going ahead fairly steadily, if rather slowly," and he was still optimistic that the negotiations would succeed.

[4] In his July 24 response Macmillan would tell Eisenhower that he thought the news from Geneva was "extremely complicated and confusing" and he felt "a deepening anxiety" as time slipped by. "It does seem to me vital to keep the initiative" (PREM 11/2686). For developments see no. 1258.

1255   *EM, AWF, Administration Series*

To CHARLES DOUGLAS JACKSON   *July 22, 1959*
Personal

Dear C.D.: Thanks for your letter—and for the book on our friend.[1] You may just possibly have gotten hold of a brilliant idea. Being considerably slower than you are, I shall have to churn it around in my mind for a few days.[2]

I am grateful to you, as always.

With warm regard, *As ever*

[1] Jackson had sent Eisenhower what he called "a remarkable new book" on Charles de Gaulle, covering the years 1943 and 1944. The author had given Eisenhower credit "for having sized up the De Gaulle problem and the De Gaulle potential as neither Roosevelt nor Churchill seemed to have been able to do." Jackson had sent the book because he believed that previous misunderstandings regarding the French leader were about to be repeated and that once again Eisenhower was "the key to the problem." A day's conversation with de Gaulle in Paris "would relax and resolve nine tenths of the problem," Jackson said, and the fifteenth anniversary of the liberation of Paris on August 25 would provide the perfect opportunity to make the trip (Jackson to Eisenhower, July 22, 1959, AWF/A; see also Arthur L. Funk, *Charles de Gaulle: The Crucial Years* [Norman, Oklahoma, 1959]).

[2] For developments see no. 1276.

To Robert Winship Woodruff

July 23, 1959

Dear Bob: As you know, I finally decided to nominate Under Secretary Mueller to fill the vacancy as Secretary of Commerce.[1] I was very anxious to find a highly qualified man and sought information from a variety of sources.

My action, of course, reflects my own confidence in Mr. Mueller, a confidence that I trust you share. I have no doubt as to his character, intelligence, dedication, and his breadth of experience in government. He is, of course, what is called a "small" businessman, but I am sure that this fact will not be a handicap.[2]

Naturally I am anxious that he should get off on the right foot in the BAC, and if there is anything that you can do to be helpful in this particular aspect of his work, I would be grateful.[3]

With warm regard, *As ever*

[1] On July 21 Eisenhower had appointed Frederick Henry Mueller (B.S. Michigan State University 1914) to succeed interim Secretary Lewis Strauss. Mueller had served as Assistant Secretary for Domestic Affairs from 1956 until November 1958, when he became Under Secretary of Commerce. He had been serving as Acting Secretary of Commerce since June 30 (*New York Times*, June 3, 20, July 22, 1959). For background on the controversy over Mueller's predecessor see nos. 1134 and 1215.

On August 5 the Senate Commerce Committee would unanimously approve Eisenhower's nomination, and the following day the Senate would confirm it. Mueller would be sworn in as Secretary of Commerce on August 10 (*New York Times*, Aug. 6, 7, 11, 1959).

[2] Mueller was a furniture manufacturer in Grand Rapids, Michigan. He was founder and president of the Grand Rapids Furniture Guild and president of Grand Rapids Industries, a group of woodworking companies that had pooled efforts to make military gliders during World War II.

[3] Woodruff was a member of the Commerce Department's Business Advisory Council (BAC) (see also Eisenhower to Nielsen, July 22, 1959, AWF/N).

On July 28 Woodruff would reply that he had no doubt that Secretary Mueller would receive "the full cooperation of the BAC" because he was "favorably known" by its members.

To Clifford Roberts

July 23, 1959

Dear Cliff: In something over eleven years of spasmodic telephonic, telegraphic and letter correspondence with you, I have just received the longest and best report you have ever sent to me. It covered friends, miscellaneous acquaintances, golf, cemeteries, jackasses, favorite hotels and eating places, perfume, and jet airplanes.[1] On top of this, it was intriguing; but in view of your new status and interests I am just a bit astonished that your stationery was neither perfumed, embossed nor colored.[2] Moreover, I am looking forward to your promised supplementary submission on the Trade Mart in Rome.[3]

I was a little surprised to learn from your letter that Mamie had never met Laura Houghton.[4] This is something that must be corrected as soon as possible. I endorse your opinion that she is a "grand gal."

To go back to the jets: most travelers have reported to me favorably about the operation of the jets, and I assumed that refueling was no more of a problem than it is on the conventional type of airplane.[5] For example, Dick Nixon left here last evening at 9:05, and landed in Moscow at 8:05 in the morning—our time.[6] I think that eleven hours for the entire trip would be considered very fine time. In any event, I am quite certain that if passengers are unhappy about the jets, the manufacturers will get busy to make the necessary modifications. So far as noise and vibration are concerned, everyone I have talked to reports a vast improvement over our old planes.[7]

It has turned off very hot here, but I am going to start out for Burning Tree now and begin a round of golf about four o'clock—unless I feel it is just too darn uncomfortable. Tomorrow I think we shall go to the farm.[8]

Give my love to Letitia and, of course, all the best to yourself. *As ever*

P.S. Thank you for remembering my liking for French bread. I must tell you that when it got here it was so hard that when I insisted on having some for luncheon the major domo reported that he had to use an axe. However, I cannot give up this easily. Tonight I shall have them wrap it up in a damp towel and see whether I can't use my aging teeth to make a dent on it. Of course I could just let it stay as it is and use it for a club!

---

[1] Roberts had written en route to New York City after an extended visit to London, Paris, and Rome (July 21, 1959, AWF/N; for background see no. 1251). While in Paris Roberts had visited some of the friends, hotels and restaurants he and General Eisenhower had seen during the summer of 1951 (see Galambos, *NATO and the Campaign of 1952*, nos. 177 and 217).

[2] Roberts had recently married (see no. 984).

[3] Roberts had described the permanent Trade Mart in Europe. He considered the buildings, which had been constructed by the Italian Fascist dictator Benito Mussolini, "finer than could ever be done except by a Dictator." Swiss capitalists currently financed the project, Roberts reported, but he had not been able to obtain information on how sound the investment was.

[4] The former Laura DeKay Richardson was the wife of U.S. Ambassador to France Amory Houghton.

[5] In a postscript dated January 22 Roberts had complained that until jets could fly "non-stop to Europe—and back—they are no damn good."

6 Nixon had traveled to Moscow as the President's representative at the opening of the American National Exposition (see no. 1228; and Eisenhower to Khrushchev, July 25, 1959, and Khrushchev to Eisenhower, Aug. 1959, both in AWF/I: USSR).

7 Roberts would explain that it had taken twelve hours to jet to Europe and sixteen hours to return (July 28, AWF/N). In spite of his disappointment in American jets, he added, he would go if invited for a ride in the President's jet, whenever the President obtained one.

8 Later this same day the President would play eighteen holes of golf at Burning Tree Country Club. On July 24 the Eisenhowers would motor to their Gettysburg farm. They would return to the White House the morning of July 27.

1258   *EM, AWF, Dulles-Herter Series*

To Christian Archibald Herter   *July 27, 1959*
Top secret

Dear Chris: It appears to me that Dillon's recent telegram to you has cleared up whatever confusion there was in your mind concerning any possible difference between the expression I used concerning the "rights in Berlin" and the June 16th statement, "The Ministers agree that unless subsequently modified by 4-power agreement, these arrangements will continue until the reunification of Germany."[1]

NEW SUBJECT. I have received Harold Macmillan's message urging me to "call a Summit meeting" at an early date. Harold's entire message starts off with the statement, "If the formula of the Western proposal of June 16th is taken as a basis that should be good enough for us." I have not been informed that the Soviets have unequivocally agreed to the proposals of the June 16th statement. Consequently the further proposals made by Harold seem to me to be largely hypothetical.[2]

I am somewhat puzzled by his impatience to get a Summit meeting started, unless he has more assurances than I have that real results will be achieved from such an exercise.[3] However, I have always made it clear that I would participate in such a meeting when and if real progress was in prospect as indicated by the results of the Foreign Ministers meeting.

Respecting the timing and location of such a meeting, if one is thus authorized, I have already announced my position that these details might be agreed upon by the Foreign Ministers Conference. Of course I suppose there would be consultation with the respective governments. In the absence of such assurance, I cannot see how I could in accordance with my previously stated position and my own initiative, as suggested by Harold, "invite" Heads of Government to such a conference.

Respecting timing, another complication may be found in Mr. Khrushchev's reluctance to come to the United States during our hot weather period.[4] Harold would like to see a Summit meeting held beginning by the end of August. Should Mr. Khrushchev desire to visit this country prior to a Quebec Summit meeting, he would therefore obviously prefer a later date. Moreover, I have heard from Moscow that he is planning a period of rest and relaxation for the near future.[5]

As I understand it, you have now seen the details of Harold's message and you will note that he expresses also a readiness to participate in a Summit meeting in November, but I am quite sure that if Khrushchev and I are to meet, he, Khrushchev, would not want to agree that the personal meeting should be delayed until that late date.

All of this poses something of a dilemma, but one that I think need not become an impossible one. Dillon will be cabling you later. In the meantime, I think that everything hinges on the reasonable assurance that we may actually achieve some progress at the Foreign Ministers meeting.[6]

With warm regard, *As ever*

[1] Eisenhower is referring to his July 22 message to Prime Minister Macmillan about a possible summit (see no. 1254). Secretary Herter had asked Acting Secretary Dillon for clarification of Eisenhower's statement that if the Soviets gave assurances of their "complete respect of our rights in Berlin" and the foreign ministers agreed upon a program for their chiefs to study and discuss, then the U.S. minimum criteria for holding a summit meeting would have been satisfied. Herter reminded Dillon that the American proposal of June 16 had made no reference to rights. Western rights did not need to be "explicitly reaffirmed," Herter said, since they had derived from postwar agreements which the Soviets had ratified. "The only thing that is contemplated at this time is the modification of the agreements spelling out how these rights are to be exercised" (State, *Foreign Relations, 1958–1960*, vol. VIII, *Berlin Crisis 1958–1959*, pp. 1044–45; on the June 16 Western proposal see no. 1202; and Conference of Foreign Ministers, *Foreign Ministers Meeting, May–August, 1959, Geneva*, pp. 312–13). Dillon's telegram to Herter is not in AWF.
[2] On July 24 British Foreign Secretary Lloyd had showed a draft of Macmillan's letter to Herter, who had described the message to Eisenhower as "an almost hysterical plea that you yourself call a summit meeting at once." Although Herter had temporarily persuaded Lloyd to discourage Macmillan from sending the letter at that time, the Prime Minister had cabled the text of his message for delivery to Eisenhower on that same day (State, *Foreign Relations, 1958–1960*, vol. VIII, *Berlin Crisis 1958–1959*, pp. 1051–52, 1069–71; see also Macmillan, *Pointing the Way*, pp. 71–80).

Believing that the Soviets would observe a moratorium during which they would maintain Western rights in Berlin, Macmillan had proposed in his cable that the heads of government work out agreements on the Berlin force levels and the composition of the group that would attempt a resolution of the whole German problem. With the possibility of a Khrushchev visit to the United States in mind, Macmillan had advocated a summit meeting before September 1, a date that would necessitate bringing the foreign ministers' meetings to a rapid conclusion (Macmillan to Eisenhower, July 27, 1959, PREM 11/2686). Eisenhower had told Acting Secretary Dillon that he had the feeling that the British were "trying to manipulate his activities with respect to an exchange of visits with Khrushchev, and a summit meeting, much too closely" (Goodpaster, Memorandum of Conference, July 27, 1959, WHO/OSS: Subject [State], State Dept.).

[3] Macmillan's letter may have been prompted by a message from Foreign Secretary Lloyd stating that Eisenhower had decided that a summit should be held regardless of progress at Geneva (Macmillan, *Pointing the Way*, p. 76).

[4] For background on Khrushchev's proposed visit to the United States see no. 1236.

[5] Vice-President Nixon had sent this information to Eisenhower by telegram on the preceding day (see State, *Foreign Relations, 1958–1960*, vol. X, pt. 1, *Eastern Europe Region; Soviet Union; Cyprus*, p. 372).

[6] For developments see no. 1265.

1259   *EM, AWF, Dulles-Herter Series*

To Clarence Douglas Dillon   *July 27, 1959*
Top secret

Memorandum to the Acting Secretary of State: The possible solution to the timing dilemma (assuming that within two or three days we get sufficient assurances from Geneva that we could begin the arranging of a Summit) might be as follows:[1]

(*a*). Receipt of assurances from Herter.[2]

(*b*). The fixing of a time and place by the Foreign Ministers in coordination with their several governments.

(*c*). The announcing of the date of such meeting as any time between August 25th and September 1st, or at the beginning of November.

(*d*). Immediately authorizing our Ambassador in Moscow to arrange details of personal visits after receipt of the information in (*a*) above, so that announcement could be made simultaneously or nearly simultaneously with the announcement on the Summit meeting.[3]

What do you think?[4]

[1] This memorandum was probably written after a meeting with Acting Secretary Dillon on this same day. Eisenhower and Dillon had discussed Prime Minister Macmillan's request for a summit meeting, messages from Vice-President Nixon (then in Moscow), and dispatches from Secretary Herter from Geneva (see the preceding document; Goodpaster, Memorandum of Conference, July 28, 1959, WHO/OSS: Subject [State], State Dept.; Ann Whitman memorandum, July 27, 1959, AWF/AWD; and State, *Foreign Relations, 1958–1960*, vol. VIII, *Berlin Crisis 1958–1959*, pp. 1057–71).

[2] Eisenhower was referring to assurances that the Soviets would accept the most recent Western proposals regarding Berlin and the reunification of Germany (see no. 1202; and Conference of Foreign Ministers, *Foreign Ministers Meeting, May–August, 1959, Geneva*, pp. 312–13).

³ On the exchange of visits see no. 1236.

⁴ Herter would cable Dillon his suggestions for a timetable, which would include meetings of the Western heads of state, an exchange of visits by Eisenhower and Khrusuchev, and subsequent meetings of the foreign ministers to prepare for a summit in late November or early December (State, *Foreign Relations, 1958–1960*, vol. VIII, *Berlin Crisis 1958–1959*, p. 1080; see also Ann Whitman memorandum, July 28, 1959, AWF/AWD).

1260   *EM, AWF, DDE Diaries Series*

To Richard Milhous Nixon   *July 27, 1959*

Dear Dick: From all the reports I have received about your journey to the USSR, it is clear that you have so conducted yourself as to gain the respect and admiration of almost all Americans.¹ I recognize many of the difficulties which you have to meet and I am grateful to you for the manner in which you are doing it.

It is my understanding that the State Department has been providing you with current information and so I have no additional suggestions to make.²

Please give my warm greetings to Pat, Milton and to the rest of the party, and, of course, all the best to yourself,³ *As ever*

¹ Vice-President Nixon had left Washington on July 22 to open the American National Exhibition in Moscow (see no. 1148). His reports on his widely publicized and spirited debates with Khrushchev and other Soviet officials are in State, *Foreign Relations, 1958–1960*, vol. X, pt. 1, *Eastern Europe Region; Soviet Union; Cyprus*, pp. 333–73; and State, *ibid.*, vol. VIII, *Berlin Crisis 1958–1959*, pp. 1057–69; see also Nixon, *Six Crises*, pp. 235–81; Milton S. Eisenhower, *The President Is Calling* (New York, 1974), pp. 327–34; and Khrushchev, *Khrushchev Remembers*, pp. 364–67.
² For background on events at the Geneva foreign ministers' meeting see no. 1258.
³ In addition to his wife and Milton Eisenhower, the Vice-President's party included Vice-Admiral Hyman G. Rickover, Deputy Assistant Secretary of State for European Affairs Foy D. Kohler, USIA Director George V. Allen, and Herbert G. Klein, Nixon's press secretary.

1261   *EM, AWF, DDE Diaries Series*

To Melvin Robert Laird   *July 27, 1959*

*Dear Mel:*¹ On reading your July 21 letter, my first thought is that every American is of course deeply concerned with adequate investment in the improvement of health. This concern is clearly reflected in the record of steady progress in the health field during the Administration.[2]

On the other hand, some seem to have the attitude that wherever a prudent investment of the taxpayers' dollars is found to be in the public interest, greater and greater spending for the same purpose will be even more in the public interest. This unsound thinking seems to be particularly applicable to appropriations for the Department of Health, Education, and Welfare.

It would be no less reasonable to contend that because the people favor frugal government, all public spending should at once be cut in half.

I cannot subscribe to either of these extremist approaches to the problems confronting our country today. I believe the overwhelming majority of the people feel the same way. Continued indefinitely, that kind of government would collapse the Nation from within and in the process destroy individual freedom and responsibility.

Moreover, the actions on certain of the HEW appropriations seem to me to rest upon a fallacy with implications almost as serious. This fallacy is that a cascade of taxpayers' dollars will guarantee progress in research. The assumption that dollars alone can produce discoveries seems to underlie the disproportionate increase of 63% in a single year for the National Institutes of Health.[3]

The trouble with this is not only that the end being sought would not thereby be assured, but that we would also risk lowering present research quality, reducing research support from non-Federal sources, and impairing our already hard-pressed teaching and medical care efforts throughout America.

Projecting present trends in the expenditures per professional research worker, the Public Health Service estimates that about 5,000 more M.D.'s and Ph.D.'s would be needed in order to make full use of the medical research funds provided in the Senate allowance. This is nearly twice as many as normally become available for medical research each year. The additional number required could, therefore, be obtained only at the expense of teaching and medical care. Moreover, if private supporters of medical research attempt to keep pace with the explosive expansion proposed for the National Institutes of Health, still more physicians and teachers would have to be diverted from medical practice and from training others for research and practice. If, on the other hand, these private supporters of medical research are discouraged from competing with the Federal Government, the inescapable result would be over-Federalization of medical research.

So it seems to me that these increases are so massive as to work against the very goals being sought—improved health for all the American people. I say this without regard to the serious fiscal implications of the increases.

You correctly point out that the proposed appropriations for the Department of Health, Education and Welfare go beyond my budget by $390 million.[4] Obviously there can never be a commonly-agreed yardstick by which to measure the comparative importance of Federal expenditures in widely different fields, so it is possible to obscure the budgetary impact of increases in health, education and welfare appropriations by making reductions in other areas. My budget request this year for the Department of Health, Education and Welfare exceeds my request of only six years ago by more than one and one-quarter billion dollars—indeed a tremendous growth. For medical research alone, the amount requested is four times as much as the Congress appropriated six years ago.[5] In other areas of high priority, the increases I have requested above last year's budget would assure continuance of significant and well-ordered progress in meeting our people's needs in the Department's areas of responsibility.

Just as I regard the appropriations requested for health, education and welfare as both necessary and sufficient when viewed in relation to other national demands, so I regard the amounts requested for other governmental activities as both necessary and sufficient. I cannot persuade myself that it is good government to slash other essential programs, as, for instance, our mutual defense efforts with the free world, to clear the way for exorbitant spending in particularly appealing areas. That kind of approach will, in my opinion, be harmful to America.[6]

With warm regard, *Sincerely*

[1] Laird (B.A. Carlton College 1942) had served in the House of Representatives representing Wisconsin's Seventh District since 1952. He had been a member of the House Appropriations Committee since 1958. Following service in the U.S. Navy during World War II, he had served as Wisconsin State Senator from 1946–1952.

[2] Laird had asked the President to comment on the proposed budget increase for the Department of Health, Education, and Welfare (HEW) (WHCF/GF 169). The fiscal 1960 appropriations bill for HEW and the Labor Department had been in conference for several weeks because the House and Senate conferees had disagreed over the amount of the increase. Both bills had exceeded Eisenhower's recommended amounts. The Senate bill, the larger of the two, had appropriated an extra $306 million for medical research and construction of medical facilities (*Congressional Quarterly Almanac*, vol. XV, *1959*, pp. 328–30). A desire to raise health care standards had been a factor in Eisenhower's establishment of HEW in 1953 (see Galambos and van Ee, *The Middle Way*, nos. 64, 1212, and 1218, and nos. 396 and 1345 in these volumes).

[3] The House had increased the National Institutes of Health budget by $50 million; the Senate increased it by $186 million. The fiscal 1958 budget for NIH had been $294,383,000—$53.2 million over the Administration's request (*Congressional Quarterly Almanac*, vol. XIV, *1958*, p. 341, and *ibid.*, vol. XV, *1959*, pp. 329–30).

[4] The exact figure for the Senate bill was $365,369,500 (see n. 1 above).

[5] For background on the first HEW budget see Galambos and van Ee, *The Middle Way*, no. 393.

[6] Eisenhower would discuss the increases in appropriations and his letter to Laird at a Legislative Leadership Meeting on July 28. The President would decide to hold the letter until the conference report was out (Staff Notes, July 28, 1959, AWF/D). A handwritten note on the file copy of this letter indicates that it was retained as a "record of Pres' thinking" (AWF/D).

On July 29 the Senate and House conferees would report a version of H.R. 6769 (H. Rept. 734) that represented compromise between the lower House allotments and higher Senate allotments. The total appropriation (P.L. 86-158) was $3,950,938,981 (*Congressional Quarterly Almanac*, vol. XV, *1959*, p. 330).

Signing the bill into law on August 14, Eisenhower would say that the increase could lower the quality of medical research projects, divert resources away from teaching and practice, and discourage private support for such projects. He further directed the Secretary of HEW and the Surgeon General to "satisfy themselves" that new projects would not produce these results. Eisenhower also said that the construction grants in the bill seemed "entirely too high in relation to other essential Government programs." The bill would appropriate $400 million to the National Institutes of Health (*Public Papers of the Presidents: Eisenhower, 1959*, pp. 584–85; *New York Times*, July 24, 30, Aug. 15, 1959; and *Congressional Quarterly Almanac*, vol. XV, *1959*, p. 330).

1262   *EM, AWF, Administration Series*

To Clarence Douglas Dillon   *July 27, 1959*
Cable. Secret

Memorandum for the Acting Secretary of State: Please send the following message—or a similar message containing the sense of the below— to our Ambassador in Moscow, in reply to incoming cable EUR 310 addressed to you, for attention of Washburn:[1]

"Some weeks back the President gave Mr. McClellan on a personal loan basis a painting of his production for use in McClellan's office during the period of the Sokolniki Fair.[2] Sometime thereafter there developed a public argument in this country concerning the character of the American Art Exhibit at the Fair.[3] The President immediately ordered Mr. Washburn to direct the return of this particular piece at the earliest possible date in order that there could be no possible involvement of this personal matter in an exhibit that was arranged by recognized artists and art critics.

"From the telegram received today, it appears that nothing has been done to comply with this directive and the situation has become further complicated by the fact that unwarranted leaks have generated a number of requests for viewing the picture.[4] To prevent further confusion and misunderstanding in the matter, the President again directs that the picture be properly and promptly packed up and, as soon as convenient, returned to this office for delivery to him."

The message should of course be signed by you.[5]

[1] EUR 310 is not in AWF. Abbott M. Washburn directed the U.S. Information Agency, which had designed, planned and coordinated the American National Exposition in Sokolniki Park outside Moscow (see no. 1228 and Tuch and Schmidt, *Ike and USIA*, pp. 37–39).

[2] Assistant Secretary of Commerce Harold Chadick McClellan was director general of the Moscow exhibition. The painting was a portrait of the President's grandson David.

[3] On the controversy over the art selected see no. 1228.

[4] Eisenhower had attempted to have the painting returned on July 2 and again on July 11. Recent publicity had generated two or three hundred Soviet requests to view the painting (see Ann Whitman memorandums, July 2, 11, 27, 1959, AWF/AWD, and Washburn to Whitman, July 10, 1959, AWF/A, George V. Allen Corr.).

[5] On this same day Dillon would send this telegram to Moscow for U.S. Ambassador Llewellyn Thompson, who would reply (July 28) that McClellan had never unpacked the painting, that no one in Moscow had seen it, and that McClellan was arranging for its return (Dillon to Thompson and Thompson to Herter, both in AWF/A, George V. Allen Corr.).

1263   *EM, AWF, Administration Series*

To Ezra Taft Benson   *July 28, 1959*
Personal and confidential

Dear Ezra: This morning I took up at the Legislative meeting your suggestion that I should once more send a letter to the Senate and to the House, restating the Administration recommendations affecting agriculture.[1]

Charlie Hoeven said that this would be a completely futile gesture.[2] He called it "shadow boxing." Others present seemed to agree with him. He further stated that the Committee was now trying to work out some kind of acceptable compromise. He definitely felt that a letter from me, at this moment, would serve to muddy the water rather than to clear it.

Nevertheless I shall have one of the liaison officers discuss the details of your letter with such people as Charlie Halleck, Charlie Hoeven and Les Arends,[3] to see whether or not they can discern any advantage in following your suggestion.[4] *Sincerely*

[1] Benson had written the President (July 24, 1959, AWF/D) criticizing members of both political parties, especially the Democrats, for not passing legislation to allevi-

ate the surplus wheat crisis. He advised Eisenhower to write congressional leaders about the situation, and, if necessary, he urged the President to appear on television to castigate their failure to take action "courageously." Benson argued that this would work to the President's advantage by placing Congress in the "unenviable position" of either submitting another unworkable bill and facing a veto, or doing what the President requested. This strategy, he said, would make it difficult for either presidential nominee to dodge the issue in the next election. Otherwise he feared it would "fuzz" in the mind of the public, making the Administration vulnerable to criticism. For background on this issue see no. 931.

On June 25 Eisenhower had vetoed the wheat bill passed by Congress. Concerned about the rising costs of subsidies and the failure of the current program to curtail surpluses, he had recommended lower, more flexible price supports or, alternatively, stricter production controls. Congress had instead offered growers a choice—to be determined by referendum—between an increase in price supports accompanied by a modest reduction in acreage allotments, or lower subsidies with unlimited production (*Congressional Quarterly Almanac*, vol. XV, *1959*, pp. 238–42). On July 23 wheat producers had voted to retain current federal production controls on the 1960 crop (*New York Times*, July 23 and 24, 1959).

[2] The minutes of the Legislative Leadership Meeting on July 28, 1959, do not include Eisenhower's conversation with Hoeven (Legislative Leadership meeting notes, AWF/LM). Deputy minority whip Charles Bernard Hoeven was a lawyer from Iowa. Benson would later recall that Hoeven had also said that a letter from the President would only "muddy the water rather than clear it" (Benson, *Crossfire*, pp. 459–66).
[3] Minority whip Leslie C. Arends was a farmer from Illinois; Charles A. Halleck, the House minority leader, was from Indiana.
[4] Commenting that he owed it to Benson, the President asked his administrative assistant to have the legislative leaders consider the Agriculture Secretary's suggestions (Eisenhower to Harlow, July 28, 1959, AWF/A: Benson Corr.). Benson would send a copy of a newspaper article describing a meeting between government representatives and "wrathful" Central Plains farmers and businessmen who called for more realistic price supports and the abolition of acreage controls. These proposals, Benson would write, gave further evidence that "the farmers of this country are far ahead of many of their representatives in the Congress on the matter of farm policy." In a handwritten notation in the margin, Eisenhower would ask to have copies of the article distributed at the next legislative meeting (Benson to Eisenhower, July 30, 1959, AWF/A).

As it turned out, Eisenhower would not act on Benson's recommendations. He would, however, again appeal to Congress for a more effective program during its next session (*Public Papers of the Presidents: Eisenhower, 1960–61*, pp. 162–63; see also *New York Times*, Aug. 20, 1959). For developments see no. 1498.

1264   *EM, AWF, International Series:*
Macmillan

To Harold Macmillan   *July 28, 1959*
Cable. Confidential

Dear Harold: As you know, the British Overseas Airways Corporation's application to fly between Hong Kong and San Francisco via Tokyo is now before me. Although I suppose I will have to approve this application, I believe you should know personally of my concerns in the matter.[1]

In 1946 the United States, without objection from the United Kingdom, unilaterally added Tokyo to its San Francisco-Hong Kong route across the Pacific. In 1957 the United Kingdom took similar action, describing it as "merely a balancing up process."

All of my experts are agreed, however, that a balance did not result and that, in fact, the economic value to the United Kingdom of the Tokyo addition is many times the value of its counterpart to the United States. But because a subordinate of this government assumed much more authority than he had, the United Kingdom's notification of its addition of Tokyo was not considered at the policy level and, as a consequence, the Bermuda Agreement procedures for questioning that addition were not invoked by the United States.[2]

It appears that, in all probability, the excess of authority I have referred to was assumed because the United Kingdom's required notice of the proposed addition was conveyed to the United States in a personal and highly informal letter, addressed to the individual I have mentioned and signed by one equally subordinate in your government.

This unfortunate history has probably tied my hands in a practical sense, but I am frank to confess that the prospect of placing my stamp of approval on so unequal a result makes me most uncomfortable.

My other principal concern is that, mindful of the imbalance I have described, I find it difficult to understand why the United Kingdom has so strongly resisted arrangements regarding route changes which the United States has earnestly requested. Admittedly, these changes could result in some diversion of traffic from British carriers but BOAC service between Tokyo and San Francisco would have a similar effect on United States carriers.

Although I am concerned by these matters, I am also certain that they can be resolved to the satisfaction of both countries. Surely it is possible for our two governments to consider these problems and to reach a true balance of our common interests.[3]

With warm regard, *As ever*

---

[1] In October 1958 the British airline had applied to the Civil Aeronautics Board for permission to fly between San Francisco and Tokyo as part of its round-the-world passenger service from London to Hong Kong. The CAB had delayed its decision, to the consternation of British officials, because Northwest Airlines had objected that the new route would divert profits from American carriers.

[2] The Anglo-American "Bermuda Agreement," signed in February 1946, had established the basic air routes assigned to each nation's carriers. Subsequent route exchanges within the United States were subject to CAB consideration (for background

on the CAB see Galambos and van Ee, *The Middle Way*, nos. 1217 and 1080; see also Mahlon R. Straszheim, *The International Airline Industry* [Washington, D.C., 1969], pp. 31–35; and *London Times*, Mar. 1, June 19, 29, July 2, 1957). The CAB had eventually recommended approval, but the ultimate decision lay with the President, who had reportedly waited several weeks before signing the application. (Questions about the extent of CAB authority over an international agreement would linger afterwards (*New York Times*, Apr. 1, 4, 5, 14, 18, 19, July 29, Aug. 8, 15, 27, 1959; *London Times*, May 7, June 24, 27, 1959; see also Ann Whitman memorandum, July 28, 1959).

[3] Macmillan would thank Eisenhower for approving the application and would comment that this was the first time since the Bermuda Agreement that the British had added a significant foreign route, whereas the United States had added several. He would add that he and the President should not have to deal with one another "on a matter of this sort on the basis of argument and counter argument. We are both anxious that the Bermuda Agreement should work smoothly" (Aug. 1, 1959, PREM 11/2614).

1265

EM, AWF, International Series:
Macmillan

To Harold Macmillan

July 29, 1959

Top secret

Dear Harold:[1] Thank you for your letters of July twenty-seventh to which I have given careful thought.[2] In the first place, I am inclined to agree with you that we may have reached the point where little good can come from continuing the talks at Geneva much longer. I would propose that we aim at bringing them to a conclusion about the middle of next week. In any event, Chris will have to leave about then to prepare for the meeting of the Foreign Ministers of the Organization of American States which convenes at Santiago, Chile, on August twelfth to consider the explosive situation in the Caribbean.[3]

The problem then is what next? The answer seems to me to depend on whether or not Gromyko will accept our position of June sixteenth on our rights in Berlin with provision for a reasonable moratorium period of at least two and one-half years.[4] If he does so, I would agree that the minimal requirement for progress had been met and that the way would be open for the Foreign Ministers to agree on arrangements for a Summit. Indeed, they could even pass the final decision on the length of the moratorium to the Heads of Government.

Unfortunately, my interpretation of what has happened so far at Geneva is that there has been no agreement by Gromyko on our rights formula but only a certain clarification of positions and a sharpening of the issues. This view, I may say, is fully shared by Chris, and he informs me that he has made this very clear to Selwyn. There-

1601

fore, barring a last-minute shift by Gromyko, which I do not entirely exclude, we are faced with an awkward situation where our minimum hope for progress has not been met. To go immediately to a Summit under these conditions would run the grave risk of spectacular failure or unthinkable capitulation.

It was with this in mind that I have been in communication with Khrushchev about a visit to the United States.[5] It seems to me that this would be a logical next step. A ten-day tour by Khrushchev through the United States might be most helpful in giving him a better picture of our strength and of our way of life, and would certainly take the crisis edge off the Berlin situation. If, as I expect would be the case, I were to follow this up with a much briefer visit to Moscow, the stage might be set for further progress at the Foreign Ministers' level which could then lead to a Summit.

As you remember, one of the tasks assigned the Foreign Ministers was to arrange the date and place for a Summit Meeting once they had made adequate progress on substantive issues. I think we must stick to this arrangement. A sudden announcement of an "invitation" by me to a Summit would inevitably lend an additional air of crisis to the Meeting, the very thing we must strive to avoid if we are to achieve any worthwhile results at such a gathering.[6]

Khrushchev has expressed the desire to rest during August so I would envision his visit here taking place in mid-September with my return visit to Moscow to be later arranged. That would open the way toward a Summit some time in November or early December. I recognize of course that Adenauer and to a lesser extent de Gaulle might have some concern about such an exchange of visits. Therefore, I would propose to come to London or Paris for a Western Summit some time before Khrushchev's arrival here. This would also give me a long overdue opportunity to talk out some of our problems with de Gaulle. I would think that such a schedule would fully meet your preoccupations for the next three months. It would take the edge off the crisis and enhance the prospect of useful talks at the Summit.

I realize of course that there is a chance that Gromyko may suddenly give us what we want at Geneva. I had hoped that my exchanges with Khrushchev would lead to just this result. He must realize that his reception here would be far better if there had been at least a minimum of progress at Geneva. If we do have this helpful development, I would still think it desirable to adhere to my proposal to hold the Summit Meeting in November preferably in Quebec. This would enable me to talk with Khrushchev in the meantime and to do whatever I can to assure that his attitude during a Summit Meeting is based on maximum understanding of our Western attitudes, power, and resources. I don't want to overestimate the value of my conversations with and the impact on him of an exposure to the people and facts of life in this country. Nevertheless, I cannot help but believe that the effect might be considerable and it might promote the very result at the Summit which you and I are so eager to achieve. This would be in line with your thinking, as I remember it, incident to your own visit to Moscow.[7]

Apart from the substantive considerations, there remains the risk of leakage. I would hope that this matter could be held most securely for a few days to permit determination of the Russian attitude at Geneva.[8]

With warm regard, *As ever*

---

[1] On the preceding day Acting Secretary of State Dillon had suggested to Secretary Herter that this letter be sent to Ambassador Whitney for delivery to Macmillan. Dillon told Herter that if Whitney were "to deliver it to Macmillan personally we might get an interesting first hand reaction which would not otherwise be available to us" (July 28, 1959, AWF/D-H).

[2] For Macmillan's first letter of July 27 see no. 1258. In his second letter Macmillan had called for a summit meeting beginning on September 1 (Macmillan to Eisenhower, July 27, 1959, PREM 11/2686).

[3] For background on Fidel Castro Ruz's rise to power in Cuba see no. 1142. Castro had stated his opposition to dictatorial governments throughout the Caribbean area and was believed to have assisted revolutionary groups in exile, particularly in Nicaragua and the Dominican Republic. A series of invasions and invasion attempts, reportedly assisted by Cuban forces and arms, had taken place in Panama, Nicaragua, and the Dominican Republic between April and June; these attempts had been thwarted by lack of support within the countries themselves. Haiti had also been threatened by revolutionaries who sought a base of operations for an attack against the Dominican Republic. The United States had begun consultations on June 18 with all the Latin American governments and together with Brazil, Chile, and Peru had proposed a meeting of the OAS foreign ministers to deal with the situation (State, *Foreign Relations, 1958–1960*, vol. V, *American Republics*, pp. 322–33, 558–60; see also NSC meeting minutes, June 25, July 9, 1959, AWF/NSC; see also Bonsal, *Cuba, Castro, and the United States*, pp. 76–77).

[4] For background on the Western position regarding Berlin see no. 1258.

[5] For Eisenhower's correspondence with the Soviet leader see the following document.

[6] In a draft of this message sent to Secretary Herter on July 28 (AWF/D-H), this paragraph had appeared in an altered form at the end of the letter.

[7] Macmillan had visited Moscow in February (see no. 1065).

[8] Macmillan would cite signs of Soviet accommodations, which, he told Eisenhower, might produce "a conclusion at Geneva which you could regard as progress." He did not believe that they should proceed immediately to a summit meeting, however, and agreed with Eisenhower's timetable (Macmillan to Eisenhower, July 30, 1959, PREM/11 2686; see also Macmillan to Lloyd, July 30, 1959, *ibid.*).

For developments at Geneva and a change in the Soviet position see no. 1269; on the Caribbean situation, no. 1370; and on the exchange of visits, no. 1276.

To Nikita Sergeyevich Khrushchev   *July 29, 1959*

Dear Mr. Chairman: As I informed Ambassador Menshikov, I am grateful for your courteous and thoughtful reply that you so promptly made to my letter carried to you by your First Deputy Premier Mr. Kozlov.[1]

I am glad that the exchange of visits which I suggested appeals to you and I hope that this exchange will in fact lead to a much better understanding between us on our many problems. I can understand that you might prefer to come to the United States in the cooler weather and suggest that we mutually consider some date in September which would permit us informally to exchange views in or near Washington for a period of two or three days and also enable you to spend ten days or so traveling in our country. For my part, if it were convenient for you I would plan to return the visit later in fall. If you concur, Mr. Robert Murphy will be available to discuss with Ambassador Menshikov the matter of dates and more detailed planning, including that of public announcement.

I believe you will agree that your visit to the United States as well as my later visit to the Soviet Union should take place in an atmosphere conducive to fruitful results and improved relations between our two countries.

I can assure you that as far as the American people are concerned I cannot emphasize too strongly how great an improvement there would be in public opinion if our meeting could take place in an improved environment resulting from progress at Geneva.

As I have repeatedly said, and I earnestly hope you understand, I have no other purpose than to help bring about agreements, in which we can have mutual confidence, designed to promote better understandings, greater tolerance, and peaceful development among the world's peoples including the USSR and the US. There is no greater achievement to which the world's leaders can aspire.

You will correctly deduce from what I have just said that progress at Geneva so far has been disappointing to me and not sufficient to justify holding a Summit conference of the four powers engaged in that conference. From such a Summit conference I believe great good could come and I by no means despair of achieving the progress which would justify it. My suggestion specifically would be that the Foreign Ministers in Geneva make as rapid progress as may be possible in the next few days and if they do not reach agreement they plan to come together again with a view to accomplishing such interim and preparatory work as would justify us in holding a Summit meeting of the four Heads of Government this autumn.[2]

With best wishes for your continued good health, *Sincerely*

[1] Under Secretary of State Robert Murphy delivered this letter by hand to Ambassador Menshikov on this same day (see State, *Foreign Relations, 1958–1960*, vol. X, pt. 1, *Eastern Europe Region; Soviet Union; Cyprus*, p. 374; see also Murphy, *Diplomat Among Warriors*, p. 438). For Eisenhower's letter to Khrushchev suggesting an exchange of visits see no. 1236. On the apparent misunderstanding between Eisenhower and State Department officials regarding the linkage between a visit by the Soviet leader and progress in the Geneva negotiations see Goodpaster, Memorandum of Conference, July 22, 1959, AWF/D; and Ann Whitman memorandum, July 23, 1959, AWF/AWD.

Menshikov had given Eisenhower an oral translation of Khrushchev's message and had left the written message with the President (see Staff Notes, July 21, 1959, AWF/D). Although Khrushchev had readily accepted the invitation delivered by Frol Kozlov, he had expressed a preference for a September visit to the United States in order to avoid the hot summer weather. Khrushchev had reaffirmed the Soviet position that failure in Geneva would make a summit meeting even more necessary. "We . . . must not halt when confronted with difficulties," he said (State, *Foreign Relations, 1958–1960*, vol. X, pt. 1, *Eastern Europe Region; Soviet Union; Cyprus*, pp. 324–25).

[2] For developments see no. 1276.

1267

*EM, WHCF,
Official File 133-B*

To Nelson Aldrich Rockefeller

July 29, 1959

Dear Nelson: Thank you for sending me the report of your Special Task Force on Protection from Radioactive Fallout.[1]

I was gratified both by the content of the report, which conforms to the National Plan for Civil Defense and Defense Mobilization, and by your prompt action in support of its recommendations.[2]

In recognizing your State's responsibility in the field of civil defense you have set a splendid example. Civil defense requires the combined effort of individual citizens and government at the Federal, State and local levels.

The problem of civil defense in the United States is a difficult one. We have been spared from warfare on our own soil for so long that the psychological climate in our country is not favorable to the voluntary basis for home defense. Nevertheless, the problem is there and must be faced.

You certainly have met the potential threat in your State forthrightly. Your action has done much to focus public attention on the vital importance of individual responsibility in civil defense.

I count on you to continue your efforts to help the people of your

State and of the Nation to prepare themselves better for the possibilities of the future.³

With warm regard, *Sincerely*

¹ New York Governor Rockefeller had sent the report, dated July 6, the same day it had been issued—after he and Eisenhower had discussed it on the telephone (AWF/A; see also Eisenhower to Rockefeller, July 6, 1959, *ibid.*, and *New York Times*, July 7, 1959). Both the report and a draft of this letter showing Eisenhower's handwritten emendations are in AWF/A, Rockefeller Corr.

The task force had submitted a three-point program that urged legislation requiring shelters in both new and existing buildings; recommended educational programs on the effects of radioactive fallout; and advocated the development of survival kits to allow survivors to stay in shelters for at least two weeks after an attack.
² In July 1958 the President had established the Office of Civil and Defense Mobilization, and Congress had enacted a bill vesting responsibility for civil defense jointly in the federal government and the states. In October of that year, Eisenhower had signed the first national plan for civil and defense mobilization (Hoegh to Eisenhower, Dec. 28, 1960, AWF/A; *Congressional Quarterly Almanac*, vol. XIV, *1958*, p. 63; *Public Papers of the Presidents: Eisenhower, 1958*, p. 498; and *New York Times*, Oct. 28, 1958). At Eisenhower's request the Director of the Office of Civil and Defense Mobilization had studied Rockefeller's report, and, since it was similar to the national plan, had endorsed it (Eisenhower to Hoegh, July 7, 1959, Hoegh to Eisenhower, July 28, 1959, and other papers in AWF/A, Rockefeller Corr.; Hoegh to Eisenhower, July 7, 1959, and other papers in same file as document). In New York Rockefeller had already begun to map an early educational program and to develop a cost analysis.
³ Rockefeller would thank the President for his supporting letter on August 14 (same file as document). They would discuss the civil defense program further at a White House meeting on August 18 (*New York Times*, Aug. 19, 1959). For developments see no. 1279.

1268   *EM, AWF, Administration Series*

To FREDERICK ANDREW SEATON   *July 29, 1959*

*Dear Fred:*¹ The attached copy of a letter from Doug Dillon proves without doubt that you have extraordinary talents on the diplomatic, as well as the domestic, front.² Congratulations on a job well done!

I know you are just as pleased as I am by today's news of the election results in Hawaii.³ I am sure that a large share of the credit for success there belongs to you.⁴

With warm regard, *As ever*

¹ Secretary of the Interior Seaton had represented the President at the July 23 inauguration ceremonies of the Khmer-American Friendship Highway. The 133-mile highway, linking Phnom Penh to the Gulf of Siam, was a major feature of the United States aid program in Cambodia. The road took two years to build and cost more than $32 million (see no. 1152; and *New York Times*, July 21, 24, 27, 1959).

[2] On July 28 Dillon, who had recommended Seaton for the post, had written to say he had received reports that Seaton's "bearing and personality" evoked "auspicious responses" from the highest level of Cambodian officials (AWF/A). Dillon concluded that Seaton's "highly effective manner" had advanced U.S. foreign policy objectives in Southeast Asia (see also Dillon to Eisenhower, July 11, 1959, and Eisenhower to Suramarit, July 13, 1959, both in AWF/I: Cambodia). On this same day Eisenhower would thank Dillon for the report (AWF/A).

[3] Eisenhower had signed the Hawaii Statehood Bill (P.L. 86-3) providing for the admission of Hawaii into the union on March 18 (see *Public Papers of the Presidents: Eisenhower, 1959*, p. 286, and *New York Times*, Mar. 19, 1959).

Hawaiians had elected a Republican governor, lieutenant governor, and senator. At his news conference of this same day Eisenhower would express gratification for the GOP victory, and add that he was most pleased with the election of two men of Asian ancestry in the three-member delegation in Congress. The President called it "a very fine example of democracy at work . . ." (*Public Papers of the Presidents: Eisenhower, 1959*, p. 550, and *New York Times*, July 30, 1959).

[4] Seaton long had advocated statehood for Hawaii. On his return trip from the Far East he had stopped in Hawaii on the day of the election (*New York Times*, July 30, 1959).

1269   *EM, AWF, Dulles-Herter Series*

To Christian Archibald Herter   *July 30, 1959*
Cable. Top secret

Dear Chris: Thank you for your report.[1] I am glad to hear that we finally seem to be making some dent in Gromyko. I may say your conduct of these long, difficult and tiresome negotiations has been a real comfort to me.[2]

Please remember me kindly to Mrs. Herter. *With warm personal regard*

[1] Two days earlier the Western foreign ministers had presented to Gromyko a slightly modified proposal for settlement of the Berlin situation. Total Western forces in Berlin would be limited to 11,000, with further reductions possible; no atomic weapons or missile installations would be located in West Berlin; freedom of access to West Berlin for all persons, goods, and communications would be maintained; and no propaganda activities would be allowed. In the absence of reunification, the arrangements could be reviewed at any time after five years at the request of any of the four governments. The Soviets had countered with proposals to limit Western garrisons to not more than 3,000 to 4,000 men and their previously stated requirement for an all-German committee to work out solutions to the Berlin problem and a peace treaty with Germany. In a private meeting on the preceding day Gromyko had given Herter the impression that he was under pressure to receive a commitment on the reduction of Western troops and might be willing to drop the link between the all-German committee and an interim settlement of the Berlin issue. Gromyko had also indicated that he wanted to reach an agreement before Herter left Geneva on August 5 for Santiago, Chile, and the foreign ministers' meeting of

the Organization of American States (State, *Foreign Relations, 1958–1960*, vol. VIII, *Berlin Crisis 1958–1959*, pp. 1080–88).

Herter had told Eisenhower that he and his colleagues thought it was "foolhardy" to make concessions regarding troop levels until the other questions were satisfactorily resolved. He was not as optimistic as the others but told Eisenhower that he thought there was "an outside chance" of "some simple deal involving three principal points: (1) some troop reduction; (2) access to Berlin as at present for both military and civilian personnel; (3) duration of agreement with rights protected when negotiations resumed for something between three and five years" (Herter to Eisenhower, July 29, 1959, AWF/D-H).

[2] For developments see no. 1272.

1270   *EM, WHCF, Official File 51*

TO GORDON HARRY SCHERER   *July 30, 1959*

Dear Mr. Scherer: Thank you very much for giving me your thoughts on HR 3460. My associates and I have been studying this bill intensively and your views will of course be seriously considered.[1]

One point that I should like to make, however, is that in your predictions as to the development of the TVA pattern, you seem to assume that all future Presidents and all future Congresses will be ready to approve each move that you see as practically inevitable.[2] I personally believe that the future pattern of TVA development will conform to public thinking and decisions as these evolve over the years, and that these will determine the nature of future legislation in this field.

Having made this observation, I assure you that I share your concern about that portion of the bill that you discuss in your second paragraph. This portion, in my opinion, is a serious error.[3]

I assure you again of my appreciation of your readiness to give me your views on this important subject.

With warm regard, *Sincerely*

[1] Scherer (LL.B. Salmon P. Chase College of Law 1929), a Republican Congressman from Ohio since 1953, had written concerning the failure of the Tennessee Valley Authority bill (H.R. 3460) to provide for executive or congressional approval of TVA projects. Scherer was also concerned that the territorial limitations for the TVA were inadequate. For background see no. 1250. See Scherer to Eisenhower, July 28, 1959, and other correspondence in the same file as the document.

[2] Scherer believed that "the proponents of socialized power have no intention whatsoever of acquiescing in a territorial limitation for TVA," and that given the authority to issue bonds, the agency would expand throughout the South. "The illusory fence placed around TVA's service area in this bill will fall like a stack of cards." He predicted "a rash of bills which will permit other government power agencies all over the United States to do the same thing."

[3] Scherer had discussed a part of the legislation that directed that the TVA's annual construction program be sent to the President, who was in turn to transmit it to Congress. Although the President could recommend changes, the program was to be considered approved unless Congress by concurrent resolution rejected or modified it within ninety days. "This provision," Scherer said, had "the practical effect of removing from the President and the Congress any real control over the construction program of this wholly-owned government corporation." On signing the legislation on August 6, the President would declare this provision "a clear invasion of the prerogatives of the Chief Executive." He signed the legislation with the understanding that legislation would be "passed swiftly by both Houses deleting this objectionable feature" (*Public Papers of the Presidents: Eisenhower, 1959*, p. 566). On that same day the Senate would pass and send to the House legislation to repeal the provision to which Eisenhower objected. The House would pass the bill on August 11, and Eisenhower would sign it on August 14 (see *Congressional Quarterly Almanac*, vol. XV, *1959*, pp. 261–65). For developments see no. 1385.

1271   *EM, AWF, DDE Diaries Series*

To Charles J. Solomon   *July 30, 1959*
Personal

Dear Mr. Solomon: When the Great Gruenther returned from Chicago on Sunday morning, I can assure you that he had a great deal of difficulty in explaining his low standing in the game with you Saturday afternoon.[1] His explanations were not very convincing. Your very amusing telegram, which arrived this morning, will assist somewhat in restoring his shattered self-confidence.

I can well understand your failure to comprehend the Eisenhower-Gruenther System in a single session. We have been playing it for years, usually about twice a month, and we still don't understand it.[2] I am inclined to think now that we should change to the Solomon System! At least I congratulate Mrs. Solomon and you and your other teammates on your fine victory.

Best of luck to you in the remaining events of the Summer Nationals. *Sincerely*

[1] Solomon, president of the American Contract Bridge League, had persuaded Gruenther, well-known as a pioneer in the "scientific" direction of contract bridge tournaments and Eisenhower's usual partner, to play bridge in the American Contract Bridge League's national tournament in Chicago. Gruenther also was president of the American Red Cross, which would receive the benefits of the Bridge League's charities this year. On July 25 in the Mid-Atlantic Pair event Gruenther and Solomon had finished 248th out of 992 of the world's best bridge players (*New York Times*, 24, 26–29, 1959).

[2] On July 29 Solomon had wired that he and his wife had won a bridge tournament using the Eisenhower-Gruenther system. Although he had not been able to learn the

system in the single session with Gruenther, Solomon said that he now understood it "perfectly." "Many thanks," he added (WHCF/PPF 1-A-7 Favorite Hobbies–Bridge; see also Andy [Goodpaster] to Ann [Whitman], July 30, 1959, *ibid.*).

1272   *EM, AWF, Dulles-Herter Series*

To CHRISTIAN ARCHIBALD HERTER   *July 31, 1959*
Cable. Top secret

Dear Chris: I agree with you that it is essential to obtain agreements satisfactory to us on points one and three of your CAHTO 183.[1] Provided we have obtained firm agreement on these two items, I would be prepared to accept a unilateral statement by Western powers that they would limit their forces in Berlin to a figure such as that mentioned by Couve.[2] In my opinion this is clearly a political and psychological matter and has no military importance. A modest reduction of this order should not cause lasting discouragement in Berlin. If such a modest reduction in forces becomes necessary we should make every effort to put it in its true light to the Berliners and the West Germans and be willing to accept some temporary discouragement as the price for a sound agreement on the issues of basic importance to us.[3] *With warm regard*

[1] For background see no. 1269. Herter had told Eisenhower that an agreement would be difficult to reach on three major unresolved points: Soviet guarantees regarding the continuation of Western rights in Berlin; the increasing Soviet insistence on the reduction of troop levels in Berlin; and the linkage, demanded by the Soviets, of all-German talks with the duration of any temporary agreement. The first point, Herter said, was "a practical necessity," and the third was impossible to accept (Herter to Eisenhower, July 30, 1959, AWF/D-H; see also State, *Foreign Relations, 1958–1960*, vol. VIII, *Berlin Crisis 1958–1959*, pp. 1092–95).

[2] French Foreign Minister Couve de Murville believed that the allies could achieve an agreement at a level of between 8,000 and 10,000. All his advisors, Pentagon and NATO officials, and West German leaders "strongly opposed any reduction," Herter told Eisenhower, and he was "personally terribly reluctant to make any concessions [on] this point." He recalled that Eisenhower and Secretary Dulles had agreed that troop numbers in Berlin were negotiable, and he asked for the President's personal reaction.

[3] Following two days of fruitless talks between Gromyko and the Western foreign ministers, Herter would cable Eisenhower that the time remaining before his departure for the United States would be devoted to finding "a satisfactory method of disengaging." Although no one was happy with the results of the conference, Herter said, "the one cheering thing" was that the four Western ministers were "in complete agreement with respect to our position" (Herter to Eisenhower, Aug. 3, 1959, AWF/D-H; see also State, *Foreign Relations, 1958–1960*, vol. VIII, *Berlin Crisis 1958–1959*, pp. 1102–3, 1105–7). For developments see no. 1276.

To CHRISTIAN ARCHIBALD HERTER   *July 31, 1959*
Personal and confidential

Memorandum for the Secretary of State: I send you herewith a memorandum prepared by a man, outside of government, who is knowledgeable in the business of collecting and disseminating information in the world. He is likewise very deeply interested in the international events of the day and the methods by which America can lead other parts of the free world in combined efforts to defeat the international communist conspiracy.[1]

In effect the memorandum talks about what, for a time, we called psychological warfare. I have been deeply interested in this subject from the early days of General Donovan's assignment as the Chief of the "Office of Strategic Services," and I have attempted in many ways to emphasize the importance of developing public opinion of a positive kind both at home and throughout the world.[2]

At the beginning of my first Administration, I established a Special Assistant to advise me on "Psychological Warfare." In practice there was generated some resentment in the State Department and the opposition was sufficiently great that finally I thought it best to abolish the office.[3]

This new memorandum tries to point out that the purpose to be achieved cannot be done wholly within the State Department. In fact, this is so clearly recognized throughout the government that we gave the function to the OCB. Thereafter, however, the OCB has become so busy in the original functions for which it was set up— the examination of how our various policies are operating in other countries and how well our separate departments are coordinating in implementing appropriate Security Council policies as approved by the President—that the psychological or public opinion objective has seemed to suffer from neglect in all portions of government.[4]

I should like this paper studied very carefully by someone appointed from your Department who can view it and analyze it objectively and without any preconception that it would necessarily create an interference with the State Department function. In the same way I am asking that it be studied by George Allen, of USIA, Karl Harr of OCB, and Allen Dulles of CIA. In all cases I desire that the paper be closely held and that it receives attention only from senior individuals that you may specifically designate. Routine staff comments on the idea would not be valuable and could result only in undesirable leaks. In all cases I should like the comments to be submitted to the White House, on a confidential basis, by September first, and handed personally to General Persons for transmission to me.[5]

P.S. Incidentally, just recently C.D. Jackson got in touch with me about his concern that our efforts in this field should be evaluated. He felt that we should get our targets more specifically outlined and the methods we use greatly improved—and that such policies as we have did not percolate down to "Ambassadors and Indians." He suggested—and I agreed—that when you returned a small group of us would meet at the White House at a stag dinner to discuss the whole question.[6]

[1] Eisenhower was referring to a memorandum titled "Strategy For Peace" (AWF/A, Lawrence Corr.) which may have been authored by David Lawrence, president and editor of *U.S. News and World Report*. The lengthy memorandum was critical of American efforts to mold public opinion on both sides of the Iron Curtain. It called for a vigorous and well-coordinated media attack designed to win the cold war: "It is a battle of ideas, and we have all the ammunition necessary, but we do not have the means to transport that ammunition to its targets." The memorandum concluded that a new White House office, headed by a Special Assistant to the President, was necessary. Although the office's publicly stated purpose would be to gather information, its real tasks would involve "careful direction as well as advisory activities in order to carry out the objectives of the United States on the 'information front' generally."

[2] For background on Brigadier General William J. Donovan, the former U.S. Ambassador to Thailand and special-warfare pioneer, who had died on February 8, 1959, see Galambos, *Chief of Staff*, no. 608. See also nos. 1556 and 1863, *ibid.*, for Eisenhower's interest in psychological warfare; on his views regarding informed public opinion see, in these volumes, no. 1240.

[3] C. D. Jackson, vice-president of Time, Inc., had served as Eisenhower's psychological warfare adviser in 1953–1954; see Galambos and van Ee, *The Middle Way*, nos. 8 and 188.

[4] For background on the Operations Coordinating Board, established in 1953 and incorporated into the National Security Council structure in 1957, see *ibid.*, nos. 8, 481, 1095, and 2158.

[5] For responses to the memorandum see Dillon to Persons September 10; Allen to Eisenhower, August 20; Dulles to Persons, August 27; Harr to Eisenhower, September 1, 1959, and additional documents, all in AWF/A, Lawrence Corr. Secretary Herter would try to discourage "the establishment of yet another committee or office such as a Special Assistant to the President." "This," he said, had "been tried many times in the past, and we know it has not brought a solution" (Sept. 10, *ibid.*).

[6] See no. 1237. Jackson had made this remark during a telephone conversation following up on plans for the stag dinner (Telephone conversation, C. D. Jackson to White House, n.d., AWF/A). At a stag dinner hosted by Eisenhower on September 10, 1959, the guests would include Jackson, Vice-President Nixon, Deputy Assistant Secretary of State for European Affairs Livingston Merchant, Staff Secretary to the President General Andrew Goodpaster, Jr., Major John Eisenhower, Press Secretary to the President James Hagerty, Secretary of Commerce Frederick Mueller, and George Kistiakowsky, who had been appointed on July 15 as Special Assistant to the President for Science and Technology. Herter, having accompanied the President on his goodwill trip to Europe, was resting at his summer home in Manchester, Massa-

chusetts, and would not attend (see no. 1276; *New York Times*, Sept. 6, 9, 1959). Jackson would thank the President after the dinner, commenting that he thought it had opened up an honest dialogue and prevented a "real crisis" from "boiling up" (Sept. 11, 1959, AWF/A). Ann Whitman would note that while "C.D. thought it valuable," Jim Hagerty thought it was a "complete waste of time" (Ann Whitman memorandum, Sept. 10, 1959, AWF/AWD). For developments see no. 1320.

1274   *EM, AWF, Administration Series*

To WILLIAM BIRRELL FRANKE   *July 31, 1959*

Dear Mr. Secretary:[1] I have your letter of July 23, 1959, in which you recommend that the three currently unnamed fleet ballistic missile submarines be named the "Nathan Hale,"[2] "Sam Houston," and "John Marshall."

While all these names seem fine to me, I would prefer to save the name Nathan Hale for future use and to name that particular submarine the Thomas A. Edison.[3]

With warm regard, *Sincerely*

[1] Former Under Secretary of the Navy Franke had been sworn in as Secretary of the Navy on June 8 (*New York Times*, June 4, 9, 1959). In 1948 Franke had been a member of the United States Army Controller's panel. He later served as Assistant to the Secretary of Defense and Assistant Secretary of the Navy for Financial Management.
[2] Franke's letter is in AWF/A: Navy. American Revolutionary War officer Nathan Hale, who had been apprehended while attempting to spy on the British, had been hanged. Before his death he reportedly said that he regretted he had only one life to give for his country.
[3] On August 14 the Navy would announce that three more Polaris submarines, numbers seven, eight and nine, would be named for distinguished Americans Sam Houston, the one-time president of the Republic of Texas; John Marshall, the Virginian who served thirty-four years as Chief Justice of the United States; and Thomas A. Edison, the inventor (*New York Times*, Aug. 15, 1959). The ballistic missile submarine *Nathan Hale* would be launched and commissioned in 1963.

1275   *EM, WHCF,*
                              President's Personal File 239

To WILLARD STEWART PAUL   *July 31, 1959*

Dear Stewart: Art Nevins has been under the weather recently and therefore my Gettysburg information has been limited.[1] Only today did I learn, from a newspaper source, that you have been hospitalized with what I am told is a heart difficulty.[2] I hope very much that the attack is minor in character and that your recovery will be swift and sure.

Incidentally, you might be amused to know that at my press conference on Wednesday I had a question regarding a rumor that I might, after 1961, become President of Gettysburg College.[3] I had no trouble in squelching that one by saying that Gettysburg College already had an able man at the head, and a man younger than I![4]

With warm regard, *Sincerely*

[1] Earlier in July Nevins had been hospitalized in Walter Reed Army Medical Center (see no. 1242).
[2] Paul had suffered a heart attack and was in West Side Hospital in York, Pennsylvania (Peterson to Hagerty, n.d., same file as document).
[3] For the full text of Eisenhower's remarks see *Public Papers of the Presidents: Eisenhower, 1959*, p. 553.
[4] Paul, who was four years younger than Eisenhower, had been President of Gettysburg College since 1956. Paul would retire in 1961 (*New York Times*, June 6, 1961).

1276   *EM, AWF, International Series:*
                                                        Macmillan

To Harold Macmillan   *August 1, 1959*
Cable. Top secret

Dear Harold: I have received another message from Khrushchev confirming our agreement for an exchange of personal visits. I now expect there will be simultaneous announcements in Washington and Moscow about this early next week, probably on Monday, August third.[1]

I am also communicating the substance of these arrangements to de Gaulle and Adenauer, adding the suggestion that if they consider it useful I would be glad to come over for a Western Summit toward the end of August. I am suggesting in addition to de Gaulle that I might pay him an individual visit in Paris on August 27. That is the 15th Anniversary of my meeting with him incident to the liberation of Paris.[2] Since de Gaulle apparently has misgivings about a Western Summit, it is my thought that if agreeable to you I could come to London immediately after seeing de Gaulle for the Western Summit, or in any event to meet with you and Adenauer.[3]

With warm regard, *As ever*

[1] For background on the exchange of visits see no. 1266. Khrushchev had told Eisenhower that he was pleased that the Geneva negotiations had brought the two sides

"somewhat closer." However, he reiterated his position that the problems facing the foreign ministers were too much to resolve, making a meeting of the heads of government "even more urgent" (State, *Foreign Relations, 1958–1960*, vol. X, pt. 1, *Eastern Europe Region; Soviet Union; Cyprus*, pp. 375–76). For Eisenhower's announcement on August 3 see *Public Papers of the Presidents: Eisenhower, 1959*, pp. 560–64.

[2] The President's cable to West German Chancellor Adenauer is the following document; his letter to French President de Gaulle appears in State, *Foreign Relations, 1958–1960*, vol. VII, pt. 2, *Western Europe*, pp. 238–40; see also no. 1255. On Eisenhower's 1944 meeting with de Gaulle see Chandler, *War Years*, no. 1916; and Eisenhower, *Crusade in Europe*, p. 297.

[3] Secretary Herter had reported that de Gaulle "would neither invite nor attend" a Western summit meeting before Khrushchev's visit to the United States. He believed that such a meeting could be interpreted as "giving four-power negotiating power to [the] President" in his meetings with the Soviet leader (Herter to Dillon, July 29, 1959, AWF/D-H).

For developments see no. 1278.

1277   *EM, AWF, International Series: Adenauer*

To Konrad Adenauer   *August 1, 1959*
Cable. Top secret

Dear Mr. Chancellor: For some time it has appeared unlikely that the Foreign Ministers would reach a sufficient measure of agreement at Geneva to justify a Summit Meeting.[1] I think you will agree that in a situation where our hope for minimum progress has not yet been met a Summit Meeting would risk failure. With this in mind I have been in communication with Mr. Khrushchev about a visit to the United States.[2] It seems to me that this would be a logical next step. Certainly a tour by Mr. Khrushchev through the U.S. would provide him with a better picture of our strength and way of life. It would also serve to reduce the atmosphere of crisis should the Foreign Ministers recess without progress. If I were to follow this up with a briefer visit to Moscow this might stimulate further progress at the Foreign Ministers level which could well lead to a Summit Meeting later in the fall.

I would intend in my informal talks with Mr. Khrushchev to do whatever I can to assure that he obtains a clearer understanding of American attitudes, power and resources. I do not want to over estimate the value of my conversations with, and the impact on, him of an exposure to the people and the facts of life in the U.S. Nevertheless I cannot help but believe that the effect might be considerable.

I hope that the foregoing will appeal to you as a sensible view. I expect that the announcement of the visit of Mr. Khrushchev to the

U.S., which probably will take place in mid-September, and of my later visit to the Soviet Union will be made early next week, very likely on Monday, August third.[3]

I am sure that I do not need to tell you that my chief purpose in inviting Mr. Khrushchev to this country is to impress on him the strength and determination of the Western countries to maintain their rights against all forms of Communist aggression. Prime Minister Macmillan has indicated that he feels a Summit Meeting of the four Western Heads of Government would be helpful prior to my meeting with Mr. Khrushchev. Of course I shall be glad to come to Europe for such a meeting. This would also give me the opportunity I have been seeking for a bilateral talk with de Gaulle which should be helpful in smoothing out some of our recent problems in NATO.[4]

With warm personal regard, *Sincerely*

[1] For background see no. 1269.
[2] See no. 1266.
[3] Khrushchev would arrive in the United States on September 15. For Eisenhower's announcement on August 3 see *Public Papers of the Presidents: Eisenhower, 1959*, pp. 560–64.
[4] Eisenhower had sent a similar message to the French president on this same day, suggesting a visit that would coincide with the fifteenth anniversary of the liberation of Paris (State, *Foreign Relations, 1958–1960*, vol. VII, pt. 2, *Western Europe*, pp. 238–40). For developments see the following document.

1278   *EM, AWF, Dulles-Herter Series*

To Christian Archibald Herter   *August 4, 1959*
Cable. Secret

Dear Chris: As you may know, there has been some difficulty in arranging with General de Gaulle a meeting date that will be convenient for both of us. However, I think that possibly this will soon be accomplished.[1]

Referring to Harold's message through Selwyn, I would be the last one to occasion the Queen any inconvenience or discomfort. Consequently, if he thinks that the Queen and Prince Philip really want me to pay a brief visit to Balmoral, I would be glad to take the extra time to do so, even if the visit were shortened to a luncheon date with the entire trip consuming only a single day.[2]

The duration of the present Congressional session is undetermined, but it appears that no adjournment date earlier than September 15th is in the cards. Therefore it seems to me that the earlier I go to Europe the better, so far as my duties here are concerned.[3]

Of course I shall be available to see you on Thursday afternoon. I understand that you are to reach here about five o'clock. We might have a tentative meeting hour of six o'clock.[4]

With warm regard, *As ever*

[1] On the President's goodwill visit to Europe see no. 1276. In a State Department letter to de Gaulle Eisenhower had proposed meeting on August 27—the fifteenth anniversary of their meeting in Paris, after that city had been liberated by the Allies. De Gaulle would reply that he would be out of the country at the end of August. He would offer to change his plans if the President could not meet with him early in September (see State, *Foreign Relations, 1958–1960*, vol. VII, pt. 2, *Western Europe*, pp. 238–41, and Eisenhower, *Waging Peace*, pp. 413–14). For developments see nos. 1282 and 1285.

[2] Herter and British Foreign Secretary Selwyn Lloyd were in Geneva attending the foreign ministers' conference (see nos. 1269 and 1272). Macmillan had suggested that the President spend August 28 and 29 at Balmoral Castle in Scotland with Queen Elizabeth, who was expecting her third child in February (Herter to Eisenhower, Aug. 3, 1959, WHO/OSS: Subject [State] State Department). News of the Queen's pregnancy would be announced on August 7 (see no. 1282). For developments on Eisenhower's visit see no. 1301.

[3] The first session of the Eighty-sixth Congress would adjourn on September 15 (*Congressional Quarterly Almanac*, vol. XV, *1959*, p. 24; see also no. 1238).

[4] On August 6 Herter would arrive at Andrews Air Force Base at 4:14 P.M. and would immediately motor to the White House for a discussion with the President (*New York Times*, Aug. 7, 1959).

1279

EM, AWF,
Administration Series

To Nelson Aldrich Rockefeller

August 5, 1959

Dear Nelson: Thank you for your message from Puerto Rico.[1] I am delighted that the Governors' Conference unanimously adopted the Civil Defense Committee Report and Recommendations on Fallout Protection Program. As you so well know, I have long wanted the states and communities to take the initiative in this vital area.[2]

Incidentally, Mamie and I are just as pleased as everyone in the country seems to be by the story-book romance of your son and Miss Rasmussen.[3] I understand that you and Tod will go to Norway for the wedding; I hope that you will give the young couple our very best wishes for a long and happy life together.[4]

With warm regard, *As ever*

[1] Rockefeller's August 4 telegram is in AWF/A.

[2] At the fifty-first annual Governors' Conference in San Juan Rockefeller had chaired a civil defense panel discussion on survival in the atomic age (*New York Times*, Aug.

2, 3, 6, 1959). For background on Rockefeller's special task force on protection from radioactive fallout see no. 1267. The governors would adopt four resolutions. First, they pledged to initiate a campaign to educate citizens in each state on fallout and the "crucial importance of affirmative action" to protect against "nuclear blackmail." Second, the Governors Conference Committee on Civil Defense would meet with the President, military leaders, and representatives of the executive and legislative branches to review the nature of the nuclear hazard and to define the steps available to governments for the protection of U.S. citizens. Third, each state would survey all state-owned or operated facilities to determine their adequacy as shelters. Fourth, each state would take steps to protect their seats of government to assure continued leadership during and after a nuclear attack (Resolution of Civil Defense Committee, Aug. 5, 1959, AWF/A, Rockefeller Corr.).

[3] On August 22 Steven Clark Rockefeller would marry Norwegian-born Anne-Marie Rasmussen in her home town of Kristiansand (*New York Times*, Aug. 3, 22, 1959).

[4] Tod was Rockefeller's wife, the former Mary Todhunter Clark.

1280   *EM, AWF, Administration Series:*
                                                                          Gray Corr.

To Karl Gotleib Harr, Jr.   *August 6, 1959*
Memorandum

I am keeping in mind the matter that we talked about some time back and to which you allude in your memorandum of August fourth.[1]

I think it would not be feasible for me to make any projected trip to the uncommitted nations unless there was some factor that I could present as logically limiting the extent of my tour and the length of any visit. However, since there are one or two nations that seem to loom up more importantly than most others I am still considering the matter.[2]

[1] Special Assistant to the President Harr had referred to an earlier conversation with Eisenhower "conferring in a general and informal way" with heads of government, from Asia and the Middle East, "with a view to identifying common problems and jointly seeking ways and means of solving those problems" (AWF/A, Gray Corr.). He warned the President that "failure to indicate concern for the attitudes and aspirations of the principal non-European free world leaders" might "reaffirm their latent suspicions that the only areas that truly matter to us are those of the Western 'club.'"

[2] For background on the announcement of the exchange of visits between Soviet Premier Khrushchev and Eisenhower see no. 1266; on the President's upcoming goodwill tour of Western Europe see no. 1276. Harr thought that the autumn's "schedule of momentous events" had created "a favorable climate within which to try some relatively bold overtures" in areas where the United States was not making progress.

Despite the President's reservations, he would embark in December on an eleven-nation goodwill tour of Europe, the Middle East, and Asia (see no. 1384).

To DAVID LAWRENCE   *August 6, 1959*
Personal

Dear David: Your article on a "Day's Work" in the life of President Wilson intrigued me greatly. Of course I constantly compared it with my own routine.[1] Out of curiosity I asked Bill Hopkins, our efficient Chief Clerk, who has been in the White House since the days of President Hoover, what the comparison of the mail load might be.[2] No records are easily available for Wilson's day, but eight or nine hundred letters a week was considered a "heavy" mail during the days that President Hoover was in the White House. Just for the record, the White House mail for the first four years of my administration averaged roughly fifteen thousand pieces a week, with eleven thousand addressed to me personally!

Thank you also for sending me your two recent pieces on the burdens of the Presidency.[3] I note your statement, "The people should be able at will to remove the Cabinet, the President, or Congress." I assume that you would suggest, in effect, a parliamentary form of government.[4]

I am grateful for your thoughtfulness in sending me the articles. With warm regard, *Sincerely*

[1] On August 5 Lawrence had sent the President an article entitled, "The President and his Day's Work," which he had written for the March 1917 issue of *The Century* magazine (Lawrence to Eisenhower, same file as document). The paradox of the presidency, Lawrence explained, was that while holding the most powerful office in the world, the President was the most restricted person in the country. The Constitution defines the president's legal powers, Lawrence said, and society imposes proscriptions on the president's personal liberty.

[2] William J. Hopkins had served on the White House institutional staff since Herbert C. Hoover's inauguration in 1929.

[3] The articles, "The Presidency is Too Big for One Man" and "The Need for Cabinet Government," had appeared respectively in the October 7, 1955, and November 22, 1957, issues of *U.S. News & World Report*. Eisenhower was attentive to these kinds of structural questions; for background on the President's Advisory Committee on Government Organization see, for example, nos. 381 and 538.

[4] Modern chief executives could give only cursory attention to vital national and international problems, Lawrence had written. Heads of the major departments, not the President, conducted the business of the federal government, and therefore they, as well as the leaders of the majority party in Congress, should share the President's responsibility for policy-making. Lawrence suggested that a cabinet of ten or more members should devote most of its time to advising the President.

To Harold Macmillan   *August 7, 1959*
Cable. Secret

Dear Harold: Quite naturally my wife and I are delighted with the news about The Queen.[1] If you find it possible we should like for you to extend to Her our felicitations, as well as assurances of continued respect and devotion.

I fully concur with your idea about the character of the visit we should have together when I get to London. I think Chequers would be fine.[2]

During my visit I should like to have an informal get-together, if time permits, with some of my old war time friends, possibly through a dinner that Jock Whitney could arrange at the Embassy.[3] If this would become possible at all, it would have to be a very hastily arranged affair since business could always intervene and I would not want to cancel out something already arranged. Nevertheless I would hope that you and people like Alanbrooke, Portal, Tedder, Alexander, de Guingand, Dempsey and a dozen or so more might be able to attend.[4] Of course I would want to invite Winston but would not expect him to attend unless he felt up to such an evening.[5] I would hope we could fit something together on very short notice.

NEW SUBJECT. My planning for the exact dates that I shall be in Britain is upset this morning by the receipt of a message from Adenauer. He seems to think that my request for him to come to London implies an intention on my part to consider Germany as a second class nation.[6]

Frankly I have tried hard to arrange things so that I could not possibly hurt the feelings or be guilty of any slight to an ally. So, I am a bit annoyed. Of course your own readiness to understand some of my problems and difficulties and to meet me either in France or in Britain has been perfect. You know how grateful I am.[7]

After some correspondence with General de Gaulle, he expressed his very keen delight that I could come to Paris on September second. He suggests that I stay in Paris through September fourth. But I'd like to leave by the evening of the third. I must return here no later than the fourth or fifth.[8] To reassure Adenauer I may have to pay him a short visit and then come back to you in London. Geographically it would be more logical to come first to you, but what I am trying to do is to save the maximum amount of time for my visit to Britain. By going first to Bonn I may be able to keep that visit to a matter of twelve hours. Tentatively I am thinking of suggesting that I spend Thursday, the twenty-seventh, with him, then come to Britain on the twenty-eighth.[9]

Regarding the possibility of a trip to Balmoral to pay my respects to The Queen, I am completely at her and your disposal. We could work out a day somewhere along the line where I could fly up to Scotland and stay a few hours with The Queen and The Prince and come back to London. Or I might land first at Prestwick and then go on to Bonn. Another solution might be that I stop a second time in your country on my return from Paris and visit Balmoral and from there take off for the States. Finally if The Queen should prefer to postpone my visit to a later time, I would understand completely. I hope that she will think only of her own convenience and health.[10]

With warm regard, *As ever*

[1] On August 6 Macmillan had wired the President that Queen Elizabeth II was expecting her third child in February (PREM 11 [2687]). The State Department would send the text of this letter to London for Macmillan on this same day (AWF/I: Macmillan).

[2] For background on Eisenhower's goodwill tour in Europe see no. 1276. Macmillan had suggested a meeting at Chequers, the British Prime Minister's country estate. For developments see no. 1285.

[3] On September 1 Eisenhower would host a stag dinner at U.S. Ambassador Whitney's home in London (see no. 1294). On the earlier plans for a somewhat different get-together see no. 1229.

[4] Field Marshal Alan Francis Brooke (Alanbrooke), Marshal of the Royal Air Force Viscount Charles Portal, Marshal of the Royal Air Force Lord Arthur Tedder, Field Marshal Harold Alexander, and Major General Francis de Guingand would be among the President's twenty-eight guests. General Sir Miles Christopher Dempsey would not attend (see no. 1229, *New York Times*, Sept. 2, 1959, and the Chronology).

[5] Former Prime Minister Churchill would indeed attend the stag affair (Eisenhower to Churchill, Sept. 1, 1959, and Churchill to Eisenhower, Sept. 16, 1959, both in AWF/I: Churchill, and *New York Times*, Sept. 2, 1959).

[6] German Chancellor Adenauer had declared that a presidential visit to Paris and London, leaving out Bonn, would hurt his prestige (Memorandum of Conversation with the President, Aug. 7, 1959, AWF/D). See n. 9 below.

[7] See also no. 1285.

[8] For background see no. 1278. Eisenhower had proposed to make Paris his first stop on the European tour. Instead, he would arrive in Paris on September 2, after flying to Germany and the United Kingdom. He would depart on September 4 (Eisenhower to de Gaulle, Aug. 5, 7, 1959, AWF/I: de Gaulle). On the discussions with de Gaulle see no. 1309, and Merriman Smith, *A President's Odyssey* [New York, 1961], pp. 48, 61–71.

[9] On August 26 the President would meet with West German Chancellor Adenauer in Bonn (see no. 1285). On their discussions see no. 1304.

[10] The President would spend August 28 and 29 at Balmoral Castle in Scotland with the Queen. Eisenhower's thank-you letter to her is no. 1301.

Dear Ezra: Your August fourth letter is so general in character that I hardly know how to reply. I realize that actions in the field of foreign trade, implemented by Departments other than your own, can result in reductions in agricultural exports.[1] The reverse is also true. Actions of the Department of Agriculture can work to the disadvantage of other Departments.

This is the reason for the network of interagency consultation. You yourself work with other members of the Cabinet. Your Department is represented in the Council on Foreign Economic Policy, in the Trade Policy Committee, in the Trade Agreements Committee, in the Interagency Committee on Agricultural Surplus Disposal and in other less formal groups.

So far as I am aware, it is exceptional for decisions to be taken in the foreign economic field without full interagency consultation. I hope the Departments can continue to adhere to such consultation. This may not always be possible, but it is my belief that we have been most successful when established procedures have been followed.

It is perfectly appropriate for Cabinet officials and their subordinates to present their views vigorously in interagency meetings. There is always the opportunity to appeal from decisions reached in these groups.[2]

If there are specific decisions that now seem to you to have been unwise, I hope you will call them to my attention.

With warm regard, *As ever*

[1] Benson had complained that the foreign trade policies of some unspecified executive departments were harming American agricultural exports and programs. When U.S. government policies resulted in actions that caused "an interference with a reasonable flow of trade," other countries retaliated against those policies by restricting agricultural imports. He was also unhappy about agencies that interfered with agricultural import controls and felt that agriculture had thus suffered for the benefit of other economic sectors. He pointed out that some of the same leaders of the major farm organizations who had supported trade legislation last year were now "seeing serious difficulties ahead unless we can get more balance in our foreign trade policies." Benson's letter is in AWF/A; for further background on trade legislation see *Congressional Quarterly Almanac*, vol. XIV, *1958*, pp. 165–76.

[2] On open debate in Cabinet meetings as part of Eisenhower's managerial style see Greenstein, *The Hidden-Hand Presidency*, pp. 100–51. The President would tell Under Secretary of State C. Douglas Dillon on August 11 that Benson had objected to interference with his efforts to dispose of surplus agricultural products overseas. Dillon would reply that he had been unaware of any complaints from the Department of Agriculture (John S. D. Eisenhower, Memorandum of Conference, Aug. 11, 1959, AWF/D). Benson would meet with Eisenhower in Gettysburg on August 19, but this subject apparently was not discussed (John S. D. Eisenhower, Memorandum of Conference, Aug. 19, 1959, *ibid.*). There is no further correspondence in AWF regarding this matter.

To Benjamin Franklin Fairless   *August 7, 1959*

Dear Ben: With a great deal of trepidation and only at the insistent and inexplicable urging of Bob Woodruff, I am sending to you a sample of my amateurish "painting." My effort is supposed to be representative of Benjamin Franklin. As my model I used a lithograph made from an original painting by Duplessis.[1]

My diffidence in sending this to you is accompanied by a quit claim deed that allows you (without prejudice) to store the thing in a blazing furnace or in the ash can. But in defense of my temerity I plead the fact that you bear the name of Benjamin Franklin and that, like him, you fall within my own classification of "distinguished citizens." *As ever*

P.S. Another suggestion from Bob is that this work of art should finally find its resting place in the Fairless Library.[2] His contention is that this might symbolize your leadership in the development of the Eisenhower Library in Kansas.[3] My own feeling is that this would be merely adding super-egotism on top of egotism!

[1] Fairless, former president of U.S. Steel and coordinator of the President's Citizens Advisors on the Mutual Security Program, was a member of the Western Pennsylvania Arts League. Robert W. Woodruff was president of the Coca-Cola Company. The painting of Benjamin Franklin by French painter Joseph-Siffred Duplessis (1725–1802) is said to convey Franklin's intelligence and was among many diverse compositions the artist exhibited in the Salon Carré of the Louvre in 1779.

[2] Fairless would hang the painting in his library (Eisenhower to Fairless, Sept. 11, 1959, AWF/D).

[3] On October 13, 1959, Eisenhower and Fairless would attend the groundbreaking ceremonies of the Eisenhower Presidential Library in Abilene (for background see no. 899). In a thank-you letter to the President Fairless would say it was a "great honor and a distinct pleasure" to be connected with the project (Oct. 16, 1959, AWF/D).

To Harold Macmillan   *August 10, 1959*
Cable. Secret

Dear Harold: Your message clearly evidences your deep understanding of some of the problems that, because of my position, beset me whenever I contemplate a visit outside of this country. I am truly grateful that you have written in the fashion that you did. It is exactly what I should expect from such an old and valued friend.[1]

I am more than flattered by the hope that you and The Queen

have expressed that my wife and I can make a State visit to your country some time later this fall. I assure you that our own desire has been no less keen than yours, but of course there are certain obvious obstacles to be overcome. Some of these I should like to talk over with you when we meet later this month. But no matter how important these difficulties may prove to be, I assure you that they will not be made more so by any informal visit that I may be privileged to make upon The Queen and Prince Philip. This was one of the reasons that I was determined to schedule my stay in Britain at somewhat greater length than pure business would demand.[2] Additionally, of course, I plan that one day out of the five will be without engagements or work of any kind. Since I am already scheduling a meeting with the Chancellor in his Capital, the day that I had planned to give to him in London can now be my own.[3]

As you know, I expect to reach London in the evening of the 27th, and from that time on I will be quite available for making the journey to Balmoral according to any schedule that you may think desirable. I should think if we planned to use one day for the purpose this should provide the time to make the round trip as well as to have a few hours at Balmoral. Nothing could please me more than to make such a visit provided that you have no fear that I should occasion any unnecessary fatigue to the Queen.[4]

Another thing: I cannot tell you how much I am looking forward to revisiting some of the scenes that came to mean so much to me in your great country, and even more how hopeful I am of having a real opportunity to see and talk with some of the fine friends with whom I then lived and worked.[5]

With warm regard, *As ever*

[1] Macmillan had written (Aug. 6, PREM 11/2687) that he wanted to meet Eisenhower at Chequers, the British Prime Minister's country estate, where they could talk with a "minimum of publicity." He understood, he added, that the dates were still tentative. For background on the President's goodwill visits to Bonn, Paris, and London see nos. 1276 and 1282, and *London Times*, Aug. 8, 27, 28, Sept. 1, 1959, and *New York Times*, Aug. 26–Sept. 8, 1959. The State Department would send the text of this message to London on this same day (AWF/I: Macmillan).

[2] Macmillan had written that Queen Elizabeth, who was expecting her third child in February, was resting at Balmoral Castle in Scotland (see no. 1282). She had invited the President to make a State visit when she returned to Buckingham Palace in the fall. In December the President would embark on an eleven-nation goodwill tour; Great Britain would not, however, be on the itinerary (see no. 1359).

[3] Eisenhower would meet with West German Chancellor Adenauer in Bonn on August 26 (*London Times*, Aug. 27, 1959, and *New York Times*, Aug. 26, 27, 1959).

[4] Macmillan also had asked the President if he would be interested in visiting the Queen in Scotland if she "felt well enough." Macmillan would suggest that Eisenhower schedule the Balmoral visit on August 28–29. Although the President would express concern about imposing upon the Queen for more than a few hours, he would spend the afternoon and night of August 28–29 at Balmoral (see Macmillan

to Eisenhower, Aug. 11, 1959, and Eisenhower to Macmillan, Aug. 11 and 13, 1959, in AWF/I: Macmillan; on the visit see no. 1301 and *New York Times,* Aug. 29, 1959).
[5] In addition to attending conferences and delivering speeches in London, the President would host a stag dinner for his wartime associates (*London Times,* Aug. 28, Sept. 1, 1959, and *New York Times,* Aug. 26–Sept. 8, 1959; on the stag dinner see no. 1294).

1286   *EM, AWF, Name Series*

To Arthur William Tedder   *August 10, 1959*

Dear Arthur: I can't tell you how much I enjoyed your letter.[1] It looks now as though I shall be in Britain for a few days toward the end of the month and if there is any break at all in the official discussions, I want of course to see you and others of our wartime association. As a matter of fact, I have already been in touch with Harold Macmillan about such a possibility. The business at hand must have priority, quite naturally, and any such affair would have to be arranged at the last minute.[2]

It is hard for me, too, to realize that Richard is no longer a child but that he is, in fact, ready for public school.[3] Time passes much too quickly, especially in this job where there is scarcely an hour, and never a day, that I can call wholly my own.

I shall save any comments about "our" author until we see each other![4] *All the best*

P.S. Mamie and I most definitely want you to come to see us next spring. When your plans are definite, please give me some advance notice.[5]

[1] Tedder's August 2 letter is in AWF/N. He had praised the "great and courageous initiative" that Eisenhower had taken in offering to meet with Soviet Premier Khrushchev. He had added that the President would have "the support and confidence" of the people of the United Kingdom.
    Ann Whitman drafted this letter for Eisenhower.
[2] On the President's upcoming goodwill trip to Europe see the preceding document.
[3] Eisenhower's godson, Richard Seton Tedder, was born on May 22, 1946. In September he would attend Glenalmond public school in the Scottish highlands.
[4] Eisenhower was referring to British Field Marshal Bernard Law Montgomery, who recently had published his memoirs. Tedder said that he had been "sorely provoked" by Montgomery's recent "antics." On the President's reaction to the volume see, for example, nos. 1012 and 1104.
[5] Tedder had said he planned to visit the United States and "—perhaps?—" could call on the Eisenhowers. For developments see no. 1436.

To George Magoffin Humphrey   *August 11, 1959*

Dear George: What I am trying to say below is not to be interpreted as any effort to inject the government into the current strike situation in the steel industry.[1] I merely have put together in my own mind a "formula" that makes sense to me. Admittedly I have no intimate acquaintanceship with the steel business, but I do necessarily study daily a whole list of reports and I do have a good many indications of differing convictions and opinions which have induced me to set forth the bare bones of what would seem to be fair to everybody.

1. A firm agreement for correction of local labor practices which do not seem to accord with the need for efficiency and fairness.[2]

2. To give the average worker about six cents raise an hour either in the form of fringe benefits or in cash. While the pattern of increases for all industry so far this year has been on the order of a nine cents an hour minimum, yet the statistics show that the steel workers have been somewhat ahead of the average, and a six cent raise would seem to be somewhat fairer.[3]

3. To give the public some slight benefit arising out of the high steel income by granting a reduction, say, of about $2 per ton. This would have, in my opinion, a more salutary effect in keeping down inflation than the mere announcement of a "hold the line" policy.[4]

This letter needs no answer or acknowledgment—indeed I hope you will do nothing but read and consider it merely as an honest personal opinion of my own, based upon such information as I can obtain and the interpretations that I make of the facts. I rather feel that neither side would accept such a suggestion, which could be some evidence that it at least has some minimum value.[5]

Give my love to Pam, *As ever*

P.S. Do *not* answer.

---

[1] Steel industry executive Humphrey, who had served as Treasury Secretary from 1953 until 1957, was board chairman of the National Steel Corporation and a director and member of the executive committee of Consolidated Coal Company. On July 15, 1959, 500,000 steel workers had walked off the job, marking the failure of months of labor-management negotiations in an effort to head off a steel strike. At issue were union demands for a package of improvements equal to approximately a fifteen to twenty cents an hour pay raise, and an industry call for greater management authority to change local work rules to increase efficiency and prevent "featherbedding." The Eisenhower Administration had rejected suggestions that the government should "settle" the steel conflict. "Let the federal government fix wages," Eisenhower argued, "and it will next have to fix hours and work rules, moderate

grievances, and finally set prices. Once it regulated wages and prices in major industries, it can run the entire economy—and will soon run it for political, not economic, advantage" (Eisenhower, *Waging Peace*, p. 454; see also *New York Times*, July 13, 14, 15, 1959; Paul A. Tiffany, *The Decline of American Steel: How Management, Labor, and Government Went Wrong* [New York, 1988], pp. 153–66).

[2] See Saulnier, *Constructive Years*, pp. 116–19, and *New York Times*, May 3, 1959.

[3] Government statistics showed that the average steel wage of $3.03 an hour was 84 cents higher than the average for all factory workers. During the previous five years wages in the steel industry had risen faster than either productivity or living costs (*New York Times*, Apr. 19, 1959).

[4] On the impact of steel prices on the inflationary problems of 1958 see Tiffany, *The Decline of American Steel*, pp. 158–59.

[5] For developments see no. 1367.

1288   *EM, AWF, DDE Diaries Series*

To Neil Hosler McElroy   *August 13, 1959*
Secret

Dear Neil: With respect to your memorandum of August fifth, I agree with the position you have taken.[1] I agree also with your conclusion that it will be some time before we can, either in concert with other nations or unilaterally, determine the character of tests, if any, we may undertake in the future.[2] As you know, I feel that world opinion is very definitely swinging against tests that involve any additional contamination of the atmosphere.[3]

I am not certain what the effect would be of an underwater test, but this is one of the things I shall learn from Dr. Kistiakowsky.[4] *As ever*

[1] Secretary of Defense McElroy's memorandum concerning the resumption of nuclear testing after the expiration of the suspension period (October 31, 1958, through October 31, 1959) is in AWF/A. For background on the moratorium and the Geneva Conference on Discontinuance of Nuclear Tests see nos. 718 and 737. McElroy had directed the Department of Defense, which had cut back preparations for future tests, to make modest plans to resume nuclear testing. He felt that very high altitude tests, in particular, were needed "to obtain information on interruptions or blackouts of communications and other effects of nuclear explosions in a hitherto relatively unexplored environment." These tests would also help gauge the effectiveness of the available detection systems.

In the meantime, McElroy had asked for the views of the Joint Chiefs of Staff. The JCS had maintained that it was contrary to the interests of the United States to impose restrictions on the development of its armaments in the absence of enforceable agreements that would impose equivalent restrictions on the Soviet Union (Twining to McElroy, Aug. 13, 1959, AWF/A, McElroy Corr.; see also McElroy to Eisenhower, Aug. 14, 1959, *ibid.*).

[2] McElroy had concluded that it would be unwise to embark on the expensive prepa-

rations required for testing until the outcome of the Geneva negotiations and its implications for future U.S. policy became known.

[3] On the growing world-wide fear of radiation hazards from atomic war and the hazards of nuclear weapons testing see no. 1267, and *Congressional Quarterly Almanac,* vol. XV, *1959,* pp. 746–48. See also Divine, *Blowing on the Wind,* pp. 262–80; Eisenhower, *Waging Peace,* p. 474; Hewlett and Holl, *Atoms for War and Peace,* pp. 295–99; and George Bogdan Kistiakowsky, *A Scientist at the White House: The Private Diary of President Eisenhower's Special Assistant for Science and Technology* (Cambridge, 1976), pp. 249, 263–64, 291, 295, 325–27.

[4] McElroy had said he was issuing instructions to continue preparations for one or more underground tests in 1960. He added that preparations for more extensive tests, including underwater and high altitude tests, would be limited to maintaining test plans in a current status and to the procurement of very long lead time items only.

On this same day the Joint Chiefs of Staff would question the ability of existing control systems to detect and identify underwater nuclear explosions. The Joint Chiefs had forwarded the memorandum to the Under Secretary of State with a request that the President's recently appointed Special Assistant for Science and Technology, George Bogdan Kistiakowsky, assess the technical aspects (Twining to McElroy, Aug. 13, 1959, and McElroy to Eisenhower, Aug. 20, 1959, AWF/A, McElroy Corr.).

Kistiakowsky (Ph.D. University of Berlin 1914) had immigrated from Kiev, the Ukraine, in 1926. He had been teaching chemistry at Harvard since 1930 and had been instrumental in the development of the atomic bomb. He had also served on Eisenhower's Science Advisory Committee since its inception in 1957.

On August 26 the State Department would announce that the President had ordered a two-month extension of the moratorium on testing, to begin on October 31 (*U.S. Department of State Bulletin* 41, no. 1055 [September 14, 1959], p. 399; *Congressional Quarterly Almanac,* vol. XV, *1959,* p. 73; Kistiakowsky, *Diary,* pp. 140–43, 214; and *New York Times,* Aug. 27, 1959). For developments see nos. 1326 and 1327.

1289   *EM, WHCF, Official File 101-Y*

TO PHILIP DUNHAM REED   *August 13, 1959*

Dear Phil: Many thanks for your letter. I am glad that you feel there has been an amazing upsurge of support for certain of the Administration policies. I'd like to talk to you about it sometime; I really think I attribute it to the essential soundness in thinking of the American people. (And what frightens me sometimes is that I feel the people are more often than not ahead of the government in determining what is best for the country.)[1]

But we will discuss all this later, interspersed with those golf and bridge games of 1961. Of course I shall see you long before then, but an analysis of the phenomenon must await a little leisure.[2] Incidentally, I see very little leisure in my personal crystal ball—for the next few months at least![3]

With warm regard, *As ever*

[1] On August 11 Reed had written in praise of the President's nationwide appeal for a new labor-management relations law (same file as document). (On the August 6 address see *Public Papers of the Presidents: Eisenhower, 1959*, pp. 567–71, and *New York Times*, Aug. 7, 1959). Reed had noted that despite the election results in November 1958, Eisenhower's positions on economical government, balanced budgets, and solid resistance to inflationary action by labor or management had become political assets. If the current national demand for a stable dollar continued to grow, Reed wrote, "a political posture aligned with that objective will become essential." He attributed "this amazing turnabout in public attitude" to Eisenhower's "courageous leadership."

[2] Reed had cautioned Eisenhower to take care as he was planning to play both golf and bridge with the President in 1961 and did not "want to be disappointed." As it turned out, Eisenhower and Reed would not get together during the rest of Eisenhower's Administration.

[3] Later in the summer the President would travel to England, France, and Germany (see nos. 1276 and 1282); in the fall he would host Soviet Chairman Khrushchev (see no. 1265); and in December he would make a goodwill tour of Europe, the Middle East, and Asia (see no. 1384).

1290   *EM, AWF, Name Series*

To Malcolm Charles Moos   *August 14, 1959*

Dear Malcolm: I have done a bit of editing on the draft for the Brown speech. Ann will send you a clean copy with this note.[1]

What I think this piece lacks is a distinct theme that sets forth the dimensions of a basic purpose and the vital importance of that purpose to the world. Throughout it there are found references to the importance of raising living standards for the masses of the world, of whom so many are hungry. I believe that we ought in unequivocal language state that there is an inescapable requirement for the so-called civilized nations to make this a mandatory purpose, taking priority over all others.[2]

A part of the theme would be that such nations must mobilize together if they are going to do the job well and efficiently. Against the background of this statement of purpose and the need to co-operate among governments to achieve that purpose, there should be shown that compared to this problem that of East-West relationships, arms races, and even the most important of domestic issues pale into insignificance.

I believe that if some such thought as this could be stated succinctly and unequivocally in the talk, the whole piece would hang together better because each of the things that we would talk about in the political, economic and intellectual worlds would fall into place.

As I say, I have worked over the thing editorially only. But I have not attempted to introduce the thought which is so inadequately expressed in this memorandum.

However, if we could do this, then I feel that it would be worth the time and trouble I might take to go to Brown to deliver this speech. Otherwise I think I should cancel.

I believe also that we have to make sure of our satisfaction with the Harvard talk because I cannot possibly cancel one without cancelling the other.[3]

As soon as you come back, I think we ought to get busy on both of these.[4]

[1] For background on the President's invitation to receive an honorary degree and deliver the opening address at a three-day convocation on "Man in a Contracting World in an Expanding Universe" at Brown University see no. 1198. The copy of the second suggested draft (Aug. 12, 1959), containing Eisenhower's extensive handwritten emendations, is in AWF/N.

On May 22 Eisenhower had met with Moos and other advisers to discuss major presidential speeches and speech commitments over the next eighteen months. Following the meeting Moos had suggested that the speech at Brown should be about education and "the need for understanding" (Moos to Dwight Eisenhower and Milton Eisenhower, May 24, 1959, AWF/N, Milton Eisenhower Corr.; see also no. 1172).

[2] Moos had begun the eleven-page draft by stressing the relationship between the university and government in a world simultaneously contracting and expanding due to increased power, people, knowledge, and communication. The world population was growing by 45 million each year, Moos wrote, and most of them went hungry. More people would demand more food, goods, and individual rights. Broadly stated, Moos said, economic and political progress had failed to keep up with technology and no amount of technical improvising could fix the new social and moral landscape. Solving the world's problems involved "patiently and painstakingly" allowing people to provide adequately for themselves through their own efforts.

[3] Eisenhower had been invited to speak at the dedication ceremonies of the International Law School Building at Harvard University (Moos to Dwight Eisenhower and Milton Eisenhower, May 24, 1959, AWF/N, Milton Eisenhower Corr.).

[4] The President and Moos would meet on September 8. On that same day the President would cancel the speeches at Brown and Harvard in order, he said, to keep his schedule free for diplomacy. He would send a message to Brown University expressing confidence that the conference would bring about efforts to restore "'the kind of world God meant all mankind to enjoy'" (New York Times, Sept. 9, Oct. 22, 1959).

1291   *EM, WHCF, Official File 124*

TO CHARLES S. JONES   *August 14, 1959*

Dear Charlie: Your telegram was on my desk this morning when I arrived at my office (incidently, after a sparkling round of golf with Pete, Cliff and Bill Robinson). Thank you so much.[1]

The final labor bill must of course await the action of the conference committee, but we are hopeful it will come out of conference in substantially the same form as the Landrum-Griffin bill passed yesterday by the House.[2] At any rate, we have made a good start toward a real reform bill.

You know, of course, that the four of us are here in Gettysburg, with golf and bridge the order of the day (and as a sobering influence, a little paper work each day for me). I hope the others are having as good a time as I am, and I only wish you were in the vicinity to join us.

With warm regard, *As ever*

P.S. What is this outlandish story about Freeman Gosden?[3] If true he must be insufferable.

[1] Jones's August 13 telegram congratulating the President on the passage in the House of Representatives of anti-corruption labor legislation is in the same file as the document. For background see nos. 536 and 897. For Eisenhower's address to the nation calling for an effective labor bill see *Public Papers of the Presidents: Eisenhower, 1959*, pp. 567–71.

Eisenhower's Gettysburg vacation would last from August 11 through August 18. On this day he had played golf with friends W. Alton "Pete" Jones, William Robinson, and Clifford Roberts.

[2] On August 14, 1959, the House of Representatives had passed H.R. 8342, the Landrum-Griffin Labor Reform bill. The vote represented a major victory for the Eisenhower Administration, which had sought to stiffen the labor legislation originally introduced in the Senate by Massachusetts Democrat John F. Kennedy. The new law closed the "no-man's land" gap in the Taft-Hartley Act (see no. 905) by letting states take jurisdiction over interstate commerce labor disputes that the National Labor Relations Board would not handle. It also increased restrictions on secondary boycotts and imposed new curbs on certain types of union picketing (see *Congressional Quarterly Almanac*, vol. XV, *1959*, pp. 156–72; *New York Times*, Aug. 14, 15, 1959; see also Eisenhower, *Waging Peace*, pp. 388–89; and Lee, *Eisenhower and Landrum-Griffin*).

The final version of the legislation as agreed to by Congress in early September would mirror the House bill, except for a few minor changes. Eisenhower would sign the bill into law on September 14.

[3] On Gosden's hole-in-one see no. 1313.

1292   *EM, WHCF, Official File 225-E*

To HENRY AGARD WALLACE   *August 15, 1959*
Personal

Dear Mr. Wallace: Thank you for your letter concerning the exchange of visits with Mr. Khrushchev.[1] I am interested in your thesis that he wants to talk with me concerning the question of China—if so I suspect he will want to discuss not only the economic potential of that country but also their very evident desire to be one of the "nuclear" nations.[2]

I much appreciate your good wishes that something tangible may come from the talks. My own feeling is that no harm can result and that just possibly something positive might emerge; at any rate both of us will have a much better understanding of each other and of the peoples of our respective countries.[3]

With warm regard, *Sincerely*

---

[1] The former agriculture secretary and vice-president under Roosevelt and commerce secretary under Truman had written on August 10 (same file as document). On the upcoming exchange visits between Eisenhower and Khrushchev see nos. 1236, 1258, 1276, and 1277.

[2] Wallace had said that China's rapidly growing population, was the most significant fact in Russia's future. He predicted that China could "gallop into modern times" faster than Russia. In the long run, Wallace wrote, the Soviets were "far more threatened" by China than by the United States because of the "unique capacities of China." For background on Sino-Soviet relations see nos. 168, 404, and 944.

In 1957 Wallace and the President had corresponded on the subject of creating "divisive" influences between China and the Soviets (see no. 187; see also State, *Foreign Relations, 1958–1960*, vol. XIX, *China* [1996], pp. 591–93).

According to the CIA's National Intelligence Estimate, Soviet and Chinese Communist interests in nuclear weaponry were incompatible. As Communist China grew in strength and stature, differences of view would appear with regard to nuclear weapons, attitudes and tactics toward the West, and patterns of economic and social development. Communist China wanted nuclear weapons, and a test ban would seriously impair its chances of developing and producing them (State, *Foreign Relations, 1958–1960*, vol. XIX, *China*, pp. 577–81). On the Soviet position on disarmament see no. 1200.

On September 26 and 27 Eisenhower and Khrushchev would discuss China at Camp David (see Eisenhower, *Waging Peace*, p. 445; State, *Foreign Relations, 1958–1960*, vol. XIX, *China*, pp. 595–98; and Morton H. Halperin, ed., *Sino-Soviet Relations and Arms Control* [Cambridge, Mass., 1967], pp. 122–23, 124, 135, 140–43). For Eisenhower's summary of the talks see no. 1329. For developments see nos. 1327, 1328, and 1332.

[3] Wallace had written of his belief that Eisenhower would "give tangible and lasting expression to that which I have always felt was within your heart"—his desire for world peace. See no. 1295.

1293   *EM, AWF, Administration Series*

TO RICHARD MILHOUS NIXON   *August 18, 1959*
Personal and confidential. Secret

Dear Dick: Your secretary telephoned to Mrs. Whitman a couple of days ago expressing some astonishment and irritation about a report that Nelson Rockefeller had publicly expressed disapproval of the invitation to Khrushchev, and allegedly putting the responsibility of the invitation at your door.[1] I felt that we should find out what the facts were, but I did not want to put the matter in writing.

This morning I had a chance to talk to Nelson. He stated clearly and without equivocation that the story that disturbed you is without any foundation in fact. Nelson branded it as a "complete lie." He has already volunteered to the State Department the services of himself and of his state organization for whatever help they can be in promoting the purpose of the Khrushchev visit. Moreover, a day or so ago at a press conference he was asked about what he thought about the Khrushchev visit and stated about as follows: "I have absolute confidence in the judgment and purposes of the President. Whatever purposes he has in mind in inviting Khrushchev to this country are worthy ones and are designed to promote the best interests of the United States."[2]

On the other hand, I gave to Nelson a short account of the correspondence between myself and Khrushchev and told him that you had been informed of my invitation just before you went to Russia and therefore you were obviously innocent of any purpose of your own in urging a visit of Khrushchev to this country.[3]

My concern about the matter is that two people—even if they should both become candidates for the same nomination—who have supported me so long and faithfully through the years I have been in this office, should find themselves publicly at odds about an issue that in fact does not exist. My own opinion is that people can be politically ambitious if they so desire without necessarily becoming personal antagonists.[4]

I went out of my way to repeat to Nelson how appreciative I was of the work you had done, which work was performed on a voluntary basis since the Vice President is an elected official in his own right.

I think perhaps some enthusiasts, possibly both in Nelson's group and your own, are seeing things that don't exist. In any event, I would have asked you to come to the office to talk the matter. But since I find you are in Virginia Beach I would prefer to write a letter than to call you to the phone, and I am sending the letter on the most secret possible basis.[5]

Give my love to Pat and, of course, warm regard to yourself. *As ever*

---

[1] Vice-President Nixon's personal secretary, Rose Mary Woods, had told Ann Whitman that the Vice-President had obtained his information from a "totally unimpeachable source" (Whitman to Eisenhower, Aug. 14, 1959, AWF/AWD; see also *New York Times*, Aug. 15, 1959). According to this report, Rockefeller was "very critical" of the visit and had vowed to "stay away unless ordered not to do so by the President

or the State Department." On Khrushchev's upcoming visit to the United States see nos. 1258 and 1310; see also *Public Papers of the Presidents: Eisenhower, 1959*, pp. 560–65, 573–83, and *New York Times*, August 4, 1959.

[2] The President had met privately with Governor Rockefeller from 12:30 to 12:47 P.M. After Eisenhower had announced his invitation to Khrushchev, Rockefeller had been among several U.S. governors who expressed fear that it would be misconstrued by neutrals and allies as a change in American foreign policy. On September 18, by State Department arrangement, Rockefeller and Khrushchev would meet in New York (*New York Times*, Aug. 6, 15, Sept. 19, 1959, and Joe Alex Morris, *Nelson Rockefeller: A Biography* [New York, 1960], pp. 351–54).

[3] Eisenhower's invitation to Khrushchev is no. 1236. On Nixon's visit to the Soviet Union (July 22–Aug. 5) see no. 1254; see also Ambrose, *Nixon*, vol. I, *The Education of a Politician, 1913–1963*, p. 528.

[4] For background on Eisenhower's views regarding the possible candidacy of Nixon and Rockefeller see, for example, no. 1222. Throughout the summer and fall Rockefeller would continue to challenge Nixon for the Republican nomination. On December 26 Rockefeller would withdraw from the campaign (*New York Times*, Aug. 15, 18, Dec. 27, 1959; Morris, *Rockefeller*, pp. 346–57; and Ambrose, *Eisenhower*, vol. II, *The President*, pp. 545–46).

[5] The Nixons were probably vacationing in Virginia Beach, Virginia.

1294   *EM, AWF, Name Series*

To Francis Wilfred de Guingand   *August 18, 1959*
Personal

Our last two letters crossed.[1] In mine I mentioned that I hoped to have a stag dinner some time when I was in London.[2] You will hear from Jock Whitney about it; Jock will act as host at the dinner where I hope to meet many of my old comrades. So far as Monty is concerned, I have instructed the Ambassador to include him on the guest list because I am not going to appear before the British public as one who is overly concerned with biased opinion.[3]

Of course there will be very little opportunity for private conversation at such a dinner—I believe the total number will be something on the order of twenty-eight or thirty.[4] But possibly I can get hold of you for a few minutes in order to hear what you have been able to accomplish in the way of developing any interest in our tenuous project for next year.[5]

With warm regard,

[1] De Guingand had written on August 14 (AWF/N; see also de Guingand to Whitman, Aug. 14, 1959, AWF/N). We have been unable to locate a copy of Eisenhower's letter. His last message to de Guingand is no. 1229.

[2] On the President's goodwill tour to Europe see no. 1285.

³ On the recent publication of Montgomery's memoirs see no. 1012. De Guingand, Field Marshal Montgomery's former Chief of Staff for Intelligence and Operations, sympathized with Eisenhower's feelings regarding Montgomery's volume. He had urged the President to meet with Montgomery, however, in order to produce an entirely "favourable" effect.

⁴ On September 1 the President would host a stag dinner at Winfield House, the U.S. Ambassador's residence in London, for twenty-eight of his wartime associates (*New York Times*, Sept. 2, 1959). De Guingand would say he had never witnessed "such genuine warmth being shewn by old comrades to their old Commander." He added that it was "big" of Eisenhower to invite Montgomery and that Montgomery had appreciated the gesture (Sept. 14, 1959, AWF/N).

⁵ Montgomery's memoir had prompted Eisenhower to plan with de Guingand a reunion of wartime colleagues in order to renew valued friendships and write a joint history of the European phase of World War II (for background see nos. 989, 991, and 1229).

In a September 14 letter de Guingand would congratulate the President on his successful visit to Europe. He would add that although they did not discuss Eisenhower's history project, he would continue to work on it (AWF/N; see also de Guingand to Whitman, Sept. 14, and Telephone calls, Sept. 4, 1959, both in AWF/N). For developments see no. 1436.

1295   *EM, WHCF, Confidential File: Russia*

To Cola Godden Parker   *August 22, 1959*
Personal and confidential

*Dear Mr. Parker:*¹ Thank you for your letter of August eleventh expressing your views on the forthcoming visit of Mr. Khrushchev to the United States and my plan to visit the Soviet Union. Frank and constructive expressions of this type from men who have held positions of responsibility are, of course, highly useful to me.²

I am a little chagrined that my efforts, both oral and written, to set forth my purposes and objectives in this exchange of visits have failed to clarify my position to you. Basically, my feeling is that the world is headed toward an arms race of such magnitude as can culminate only in unbearable burdens on our peoples at best, or general war at worst. No efforts should be spared to find some way out of this grim prospect. Face to face talks with Mr. Khrushchev, while I expect very little from them, represent nearly the only course left now to this end. Such action does not involve approval of Mr. Khrushchev himself or his methods, nor does it, to my mind, represent any act of appeasement whatsoever.

Since I would like you to develop a better understanding of the reasoning behind this decision, I have asked Under Secretary of State Robert Murphy to contact you on his forthcoming trip to the Middle West, and to give you a chance to talk the matter over with him personally. You are, I know, acquainted with him through your work in the ILO.[3] *Sincerely*

[1] Cola Godden Parker (J.D. University of Chicago 1912), former president of the Kimberly Clark Corporation, was a delegate to the International Labor Organization and chairman of the finance committee of the National Association of Manufacturers. Eisenhower had appointed Parker to the Commission on Foreign Economic Policy in 1953 (see Galambos and van Ee, *The Middle Way*, no. 170). For background on the Khrushchev visit see no. 1266.

[2] Parker had told Eisenhower that he found the Khrushchev invitation "utterly incomprehensible." Based on his many contacts with Communist members of the ILO, he believed that any attempt to change the mind of any Communist was "pure wishful thinking" (Parker to Eisenhower, Aug. 11, 1959, same file as document).

[3] Eisenhower had objected to the State Department draft of this letter as "too defensive and too lengthy." He and State Department officials then agreed that Murphy would see Parker and "set him straight" (Memorandum of Conference, Aug. 24, 1959, AWF/D).

Murphy would tell John Eisenhower that he had spoken by telephone with Parker, then vacationing in New Hampshire. Parker had stressed that he was principally concerned with the effect that Khrushchev's visit might have on "some of our 'soft minded' friends in places like England." He agreed, however, that the advantages had to be weighed against the obvious disadvantages (Murphy to John Eisenhower, Aug. 26, 1959, same file as document). Parker would subsequently write Eisenhower that he had not intended to criticize the purposes and objectives of the exchange of visits. "I did not doubt your sincerity in this effort," he wrote, "but I did feel that I must express to you why it seemed to me to be a mistake" (Parker to Eisenhower, Sept. 16, 1959, *ibid.*). For developments on the Khrushchev visit see no. 1325.

1296   *EM, WHCF, Official File 72-B*

TO MAURICE HUBERT STANS   *August 22, 1959*
Personal

Dear Maury: I am impressed with your article in the *Reader's Digest* and grateful to you for calling it to my attention.[1]

I shall be interested to learn whether Arthur Summerfield's efforts are successful. Some time ago it was reported to me that DeWitt Wallace was "afraid" that the name of the magazine might be confused, in the minds of the public with "Republican Digest."[2]

With warm regard, *As ever*

[1] The Director of the Bureau of the Budget had written to the President on August 21. Stans had enclosed a reprint of the article, entitled "Must We Delude Ourselves into Disaster?" which had appeared in July 1959. Without a balanced budget, Stans had warned, Americans would "face certain hard inevitabilities"—tax increases, a mounting national debt and growing inflation with "disastrous" rises in the cost of

living and a weakening of national strength. Stans urged Americans to "halt this ru-
inous race toward calamity" (both in same file as document).

[2] Stans had said that Postmaster General Summerfield was going to try to induce
Reader's Digest publisher Wallace to run similar articles each month written by Cabinet members. For background on Eisenhower's efforts to persuade Wallace to publish an essay on the accomplishments of his Administration see no. 1120.

1297   *EM, AWF, DDE Diaries Series*

To Elivera Carlson Doud   *August 22, 1959*

Dear Min: Mamie has been home for two days and has given me a
long account of her visit with you.[1] Although I know that you cannot be very active, it is satisfying to your two daughters to have the
opportunity to visit you occasionally and talk over the many things
of common family interest.[2] I hope that the Good Lord will give you
enough strength to enjoy those visits at shorter periods and of longer
length.

Here in Gettysburg I have been enjoying, although not on a complete vacation, a period of comparative quiet due to the absence of
persistent callers of all types.[3] I keep in touch with major events of
foreign and domestic importance and keep up with my correspondence, of course through Mrs. Whitman's efforts.

Now I am about to embark on a European trip to reaffirm the
understanding between the leaders of the Allied countries and myself.[4] Except for the fact that Mamie does not feel she can go along,
I would somewhat look forward to the trip. My two days in France
will be difficult; the other part should be relatively easy.[5] However,
I think Mamie is right in refusing to go because she becomes so ner-
vous in airplanes that she gets really ill.[6] But I shall not be gone too
long—in the meantime she will probably spend some time at the
farm and will unquestionably have some of her friends up to visit
her.

I know that the doctors and Mrs. Bonebrake and others are watching out for you very carefully, a fact that gives us all real satisfaction.[7] Take care of yourself and one of these days we will have again
a real reunion—one with everybody present. That would surely be
a lot of fun.[8]

Please remember me to Aksel and Mrs. Bonebrake and the others that you see from time to time and, of course, deepest love to
yourself.[9] *Devotedly*

[1] Mrs. Eisenhower had left for Denver on August 13 (*New York Times*, Aug. 14, 16, 20,
1959). Mrs. Doud had been in poor health since 1957 (for background see no. 612).

[2] The First Lady's sister was Mabel "Mike" Moore.

[3] While staying at his Pennsylvania farm the President had been occupying offices at the Gettysburg Hotel (*New York Times*, Aug. 14, 1959).

[4] On August 26 Eisenhower would depart for Bonn, Paris, and London (for background see no. 1276).

[5] On the talks in Paris see no. 1276.

[6] On Mrs. Eisenhower's dislike of long flights see Galambos and van Ee, *The Middle Way*, no. 1916; see also Susan Eisenhower, *Mrs. Ike*, p. 196.

[7] Mrs. Bonebrake apparently was Mrs. Doud's companion.

[8] The President would visit his mother-in-law in February and August 1960. Mrs. Doud would die on September 29, 1960 (*New York Times*, Sept. 30, Oct. 1, 1959).

[9] This was Eisenhower's friend and investment adviser Aksel Nielsen, a real estate developer.

1298   *EM, AWF, DDE Diaries Series*

To Mary Keane Allen   *August 24, 1959*

Dear Mary: I shall envy you and Mamie any time you can spend at Gettysburg during the ten days that I plan to be cast in the role of the "drummer" in the Western European region.[1]

I am sorry that I didn't get a chance to say "goodbye" to you and George Sunday; for some reason or other I thought George was going to be here today.[2]

With affectionate regard, *As ever*

[1] Eisenhower had been in Gettysburg since August 12; Mrs. Eisenhower had joined him on August 20 (see the preceding document). George and Mary Allen owned eighty-eight acres in Gettysburg and had been visiting since August 18 (for background on the Eisenhower-Allen farming enterprise see Galambos and van Ee, *The Middle Way*, nos. 892 and 1321). On August 26 the President would depart for Europe in an effort to unify Western policies toward the Soviet Union (for background see no. 1276).

[2] The Eisenhowers had returned to the White House the evening of August 23 (see also *New York Times*, Aug. 26, 27, 1959). Allen was counsel for Alvord and Alvord, a Washington, D.C., law firm.

1299   *EM, AWF, DDE Diaries Series*

To Patricia Riley Aurand   *August 25, 1959*

Dear Patty:[1] This morning we had a tragedy in the Eisenhower family, with the real burden of grief falling on poor little Susie. "Me Too", while racing around the pasture with the other horses, slipped and fell, breaking his leg just above the knee. He had to be chloroformed and destroyed instantly, because the veterinarian said that in view of his age and a progressively developing blindness, it would be hopeless to try to bring him back into riding condition.[2]

Susie is heartbroken, but I shall try to find immediately another small horse or large pony that has been fairly well trained in horse show practices. I intended to bring in at once the Arab that is still held in Minnesota for me. However, I had word today that the mare would need another year's training before she was really suitable for young children.[3]

I was anxious for you to know about the matter at once because I thought you might be wondering why Susie had to cancel some of her scheduled appearances in the Gettysburg-Emmitsburg area.[4]

From all I hear about Pete, he is on the job in London.[5]
Affectionately

[1] The former Patricia Riley was the wife of Captain Evan "Pete" Aurand (USNA 1938), the President's naval aide since 1957 (*New York Times*, Jan. 25, 1957).

[2] In late June, John Eisenhower and his family had moved to Gettysburg (see no. 1238). Seven-year-old Susan had been eager to move her pony to the country (Telephone calls, Susan Eisenhower and Eisenhower, June 22, 1959, AWF/D; see also Eisenhower to Allam, Sept. 15, 1959, AWF/D).

[3] The Arabian filly was nearly four years old (see Galambos and van Ee, *The Middle Way*, no. 1749).

[4] For developments on Susan's equestrian skills see no. 1313.

[5] Aurand, the son of the President's West Point classmate Henry Spiese Aurand, apparently had gone to Europe ahead of Eisenhower, who was scheduled to depart on August 26 (for background on the trip see no. 1276).

1300   *EM, WHCF, Confidential File:*
State Department

To Ngo Dinh Diem   *August 29, 1959*

Dear Mr. President: I am prompted to write to you personally as a result of recent allegations which reflected adversely on the United States aid program in Viet-Nam and on Viet-Nam itself.[1] I want you to know that I regret these charges and the accompanying reflections on your government and people who have worked so valiantly under your leadership.

If there have been deficiencies in the administration of the aid program attributable to American officials, they will be corrected, and I am sure you would take the same action as to matters under your control. I am pleased to note that in the investigations thus far concluded there have in fact been no findings of serious deficiencies of any kind. So far as the United States is concerned, the inquiries which have been held by two Committees of our Congress represent a useful means of bringing deficiencies to light. They also afford an opportunity to demonstrate instances where unwarranted allegations are not supported by the facts. I am confident that the inquiries in the case of the Viet-Nam program will in particular serve this latter purpose and that the base for our cooperation in the aid program and on other matters will rest on yet firmer ground.[2] I trust that this will be as welcome to you as it is to me, and will compensate for the unpleasant aspects of what must have seemed to you a disheartening and inexplicable development.

Ambassador Durbrow has now returned to Viet-Nam; he has brought with him my renewed confidence and also my good wishes to you and your countrymen.[3] I recall very well our frank discussions of mutual problems, and feel much the richer in my appreciation of the problems of the people of Southeast Asia and Viet-Nam for having discussed them with you.[4] It is a source of great satisfaction to know, as I do, that the Free World in general and the United States in particular have such a staunch friend as yourself in free Viet-Nam.[5]

With warm regard, *Sincerely*

---

[1] A six-part series appearing in the Scripps-Howard newspaper chain from July 20 to July 25, had criticized the administration of the American aid program and had charged the Diem government with corruption and authoritarianism (State, *Foreign Relations, 1958–1960,* vol. I, *Vietnam,* p. 225, and *New York Times,* July 25, 31, 1959). The Secretary of State, mindful of President Diem's "stout anti-communism" and his "well-known role as a good friend of the United States," had suggested that the President reassure Diem and the Vietnamese people of his "continuing warm regard" for them (Herter to Eisenhower, Aug. 25, 1959, same file as document).

A copy of the State Department draft containing Eisenhower's handwritten emendations is in *ibid.* A portion of this sentence, deleted from the draft, had stated that the allegation had "received somewhat sensational treatment in a section of our press."

[2] The Scripps-Howard allegations of "serious waste" and "outrageous scandal" had prompted a congressional investigation of the aid program. The Senate Foreign Relations Subcommittee on State Department Organization and Public Affairs had held hearings on the charges July 30–31. The House Foreign Affairs Subcommittee No. 2 had held similar hearings August 11–14. Both subcommittees would order on-the-spot investigations of the administration of foreign aid in Vietnam (*Congressional Quarterly Almanac,* vol. XV, *1959,* p. 730, and *New York Times,* Aug. 5, 14, 15, 1959; on the U.S. aid program in Vietnam see Ronald H. Spector, *Advice and Support: The Early Years 1941–1960,* in *The United States Army in Vietnam,* edited by David F. Trask [Washington, D.C., 1985], pp. 306–10).

[3] Ambassador Durbrow had been recalled to the United States for the investigation (State, *Foreign Relations, 1958–1960,* vol. I, *Vietnam,* pp. 225–26, 239–42, and *New York Times,* July 31, 1959).

[4] President Diem had visited the United States in 1957 (see no. 710).

[5] For developments see no. 1371.

To Elizabeth II, Queen of England   *August 30, 1959*

Dear Queen Elizabeth: As I think was quite evident to you, the trip to Balmoral was perfect in every respect, and provided precisely the relaxing twenty-four hours that I needed to break up the continuity of official appearances on this European swing.[1] I cannot tell you how privileged and delighted I was to be with you, Prince Philip, and members of your lovely family.

I particularly appreciate the warm hospitality that you extended to me and my party.[2] For all of us our visit was both memorable and enjoyable.

Here at Chequers the Prime Minister and I are having the kind of satisfying talks that are possible between good friends.[3] All in all I can only say that every moment of my visit to Britain has served to re-emphasize the depth of my admiration and respect for you and the people of your country and to renew and refresh the real love I have for this Island.[4] And, as I told both your mother and your sister, my wife and I are delighted about the coming "event," as is everyone in your Kingdom.[5]

With affectionate regard to you and all the members of your family, *Sincerely*

P.S. Many thanks for the grouse—we are having them tonight for dinner.[6]

---

[1] The President had visited the Queen at Balmoral Castle in Scotland on August 28 and 29 (for background see nos. 1276, 1282, and 1285).

[2] John S. D. Eisenhower, General Howard McC. Snyder, and Eisenhower's orderly, Sergeant John Moaney, had accompanied the President to Balmoral (see John S. D. Eisenhower, *Strictly Personal,* pp. 237–38, 243–48).

[3] On the meeting at Chequers see no. 1285.

[4] In his memoir, *Waging Peace,* the President would say he had been "happily overwhelmed" by the reception accorded his party (pp. 419–20; see also Smith, *President's Odyssey,* pp. 52–58).

[5] The Queen was expecting her third child in February (see no. 1282).

[6] The Queen had sent five brace of grouse from Balmoral; see Smith, *President's Odyssey,* p. 57.

VIII

"Friends and Foes"

SEPTEMBER 1959 TO FEBRUARY 1960

19

Khrushchev in America

To JOHN GEORGE DIEFENBAKER   *September 1, 1959*
Cable. Top secret

Dear John: Since leaving Washington I learned of the decision of your
Government to withhold its approval for the air defense exercise
known as Sky Hawk which had been scheduled for early next
month.[1] As I am sure you have been told, I personally reviewed and
approved the military training plans last month before the formal
approval of the Canadian Government was requested.[2] It seems to
me of great importance to both of us that the defense of our continent should be maintained in good order. The purpose of exercises such as Sky Hawk is to give ourselves realistic assurance on this
score. I do not myself see anything provocative in such a defensive
exercise, and from the point of view of my coming talks with Mr.
Khrushchev, they should have no adverse effect. Indeed, the knowledge on his part and ours that we are determined and able to resist
an attack certainly tends to provide an essential foundation for serious and, I hope, productive discussions.[3]

I do hope, therefore, that you will again consider your decision
in the light of these thoughts.[4]

With warm regard, *Sincerely*

[1] The President sent this message to Canadian Prime Minister Diefenbaker from London, where he had stopped during his tour of Europe (for background see no. 1276).
The Canadian embassy had notified the State Department on August 28 that plans
to proceed with operation Sky Hawk were "unwise" at this time. Diefenbaker had objected to the late date on which he received information regarding the project, and
the Canadian government had criticized the U.S. military for making decisions
"which are shoved down throats of Canadian civil officials" (State, *Foreign Relations*,
vol. VII, pt. 1, *Western European Integration and Security; Canada*, pp. 763–66).
[2] The President had approved the exercise on August 5 (*ibid.*, p. 765).
[3] Canadian officials believed that grounding civil air transport while Soviet Premier
Khrushchev was in the United States could be interpreted by the Soviets as "provocative" (*ibid.*). Khrushchev would visit the United States September 15–27 (see nos.
1276 and 1326).
[4] For developments see no. 1314.

To Harold Macmillan   *September 1, 1959*

Dear Harold: You and I have had many memorable meetings but
none, as far as I am concerned, has been more fruitful or more enjoyable than this one I am now reluctantly concluding.[1] By virtue of
your American mother, you can rightfully claim a kind of dual citizenship; but I sometimes feel a right to be an adopted son of Great
Britain.[2] Certainly I feel completely at home here, and the welcome
given to me by you—and by so many of the wonderful people of
this Island—has warmed and touched my heart beyond any words
at my command.[3]

It seems inadequate to say "thank you" for the courtesies, the kind-
nesses, and the attention to details to assure my comfort and pleasure. I know that essentially all of the direction for the trip emanated
from you; I can only say that everything has been perfect.

Won't you please convey to the fine members of your staff my
warm gratitude for the assistance they gave so willingly and freely to
me and to the members of the party travelling with me?

With deepest thanks and warm personal regard, *As ever*

[1] For background on the President's trip to Western Europe see nos. 1276 and 1277.
Eisenhower and Macmillan had met in London and at Chequers, the Prime Minister's country estate, on several occasions between August 27 and September 2. On
their discussions see nos. 1304, 1309, 1323, and Eisenhower to Adenauer, September 3, 1959, AWF/I: Adenauer.
[2] Macmillan's mother was the former Helen Artie Belles of Spencer, Indiana. Macmillan would reply (Sept. 3, AWF/I: Macmillan) that the British people had "long ago
adopted" Eisenhower and the visit had been "just the occasion for them to show
this." Macmillan would add that the President's visit had given "a new reality to the
friendship and alliance" of Great Britain and the United States.
[3] In his memoir *Waging Peace* (p. 419) Eisenhower would say he was "happily overwhelmed by the reception" accorded his party by the British (see no. 1301).

To Jawaharlal Nehru   *September 2, 1959*
Cable. Secret

Dear Mr. Prime Minister: As you know, I am currently engaged in a
round of visits in Europe, prior to receiving Chairman Khrushchev
in the United States.[1]

I am pleased to be able to tell you that my talks with Chancellor

Adenauer and Prime Minister Macmillan have been most useful, as I expect will be my talks with President de Gaulle.[2] I have been strengthened and heartened in my determination to explore every possible avenue which might lead to a just and lasting peace by the first hand reaffirmation of common aims and basic unity which my trip is providing.

In the midst of these talks, I have been distressed to learn from your statements in Parliament that India is experiencing serious trouble with the Chinese Communist regime over border incursions and certain matters concerning Tibet. These difficulties are of concern to India's friends and, indeed, to all peace-loving countries.[3]

Last September 11 in a speech to the American people, I had occasion to comment on other actions then being taken by the Chinese Communist regime. I said that we, on our part, believe that we should never abandon negotiations and conciliation in favor of force and strife. It is distressing, now, to observe that once again the Chinese Communist regime is acting in disregard of that principle.[4]

I would like you to know that I am personally following these events with concern, and that I fully appreciate the problems which they have created for you.

I appreciated very much my opportunity to see Madame Pandit yesterday and to learn directly from her some of the circumstances of these border violations.[5] During our talk, I was especially grateful for your cordial invitation to me to come to India, which she conveyed.[6]

With expression of my high esteem, warm regard, *Sincerely*

[1] See no. 1276.

[2] See nos. 1301 and 1309.

[3] Responding to a March 1959 revolt in Chinese-occupied Tibet, the Peking government had sent troops to the disputed Sino-India border. On August 31, following a series of border incidents, 400 Chinese troops had invaded and occupied several square miles in the semi-independent state of Bhutan (*New York Times*, Sept. 1, 1959; John S. D. Eisenhower, synopsis of State and Intelligence material, Apr. 29, May 1, May 26, 1959, AWF/D). For background see Steven A. Hoffmann, *India and the China Crisis* (Berkeley, 1990), pp. 31–74; and Neville Maxwell, *India's China War* (New York, 1970), pp. 89–143; see also State, *Foreign Relations, 1958–1960*, vol. XV, *South and Southeast Asia*, pp. 513–14.

[4] On September 11, 1958, the President had addressed the American people regarding the situation in the Formosa Straits (see *Public Papers of the Presidents: Eisenhower, 1958*, pp. 694–700; for background see no. 838; for a discussion of Eisenhower's speech see no. 852). In response to questions about what India intended to do regarding the Chinese incursions, the Prime Minister had responded: "We hope this will be settled by discussions and conferences, and we do not propose to go to war." Nehru's statement contrasted with earlier claims that India had no choice but to defend its borders and that any aggression against Bhutan and Sikkim would be considered "an aggression against India" (*New York Times*, Sept. 1, 1959; see also *ibid.*, Sept. 4, 5, 10).

⁵ Vijaya Lakshmi Pandit was Nehru's sister and the Indian High Commissioner in the United Kingdom, Ambassador to Ireland, and Ambassador to Spain.
⁶ There is no record of this conversation in AWF. For developments see no. 1315.

1305   *EM, AWF, International Series:*
                                                                    Macmillan

TO HAROLD MACMILLAN   *September 5, 1959*

Dear Harold: Thank you so much for the note that Jock Whitney brought to me yesterday when we both arrived at Culzean Castle. (I shall return this the same way). You express far better than can I the unique and friendly character of this latest of our conferences, a character that I am certain was engendered not so much by the warm welcome of the English people—heartwarming as it was, but by the close relationship between the two of us that seemingly grows stronger every time we meet.¹

This part of Scotland has never been lovelier. The weather is absolutely perfect. Unfortunately I see that my golf score of yesterday was published in the press, so you will know that my game was certainly not on a par with the weather and the surroundings.² But it is delightful to be here, and today I was joined by two of my friends from the States.³ With Jock we will have the best possible weekend before I have to go back to wrestling with the Congress and numerous other frustrating duties.

I shall be pulling for you in the weeks ahead, as I am sure you know.⁴

Once again, my deepest gratitude to you and your associates, and my warm personal regard to yourself, *As ever*

¹ Macmillan's letter of September 3 is in AWF/I: Macmillan. Professing himself "glad that the chances of fortune" had enabled him "to lead Her Majesty's Government at this time and to be spokesman of the feelings of the whole country," he had told Eisenhower that the affection demonstrated during his visit had been "a tribute to you as President of the United States, our great ally and friend and firm rock of the Alliance; yet it was a real personal triumph for you."

Following conferences in Bonn, London, and Paris, the President had flown to his private apartment in Culzean Castle in Ayrshire, Scotland (for background on the goodwill tour see no. 1303; on the castle see no. 55). U.S. Ambassador to Britain John Hay Whitney would remain with Eisenhower throughout the weekend. The President would return to the United States on September 7 (*New York Times,* Sept. 5, 6, 7, 1959).

² Eisenhower had shot an 89 on his first round of golf at Turnberry golf course, which was five miles from Culzean.

³ These friends were W. Alton Jones and William E. Robinson.

Eisenhower was referring to the upcoming British elections. On October 9 the President would congratulate Macmillan on his victory. Macmillan would reply the following day (both in AWF/I: Macmillan; see also *New York Times,* Oct. 10, 1959).

1306   *EM, AWF, DDE Diaries Series*

To John Hay Whitney   *September 8, 1959*

Dear Jock: I talked to Doug Dillon about his experience as Ambassador to France, with particular reference to the charging off of Ambassadorial entertainment expenses against annual income.[1]

He informed me that with the entire approval of his lawyers and the Internal Revenue people, he did this all the time he was Ambassador and that Amory Houghton is doing the same thing. He said that no item that he ever included of this kind was ever challenged by the Internal Revenue people. He did, of course, submit vouchers to substantiate his claims.

I think that this is some information that you will want to pass on to the accountants who handle your own tax affairs.[2]

We had a smooth and uneventful trip back to the United States, passing the time in a bridge game in which the three of us recruited John as a fourth.[3] I sadly report that I was the big loser, with a maximum of five points.

Please tell Betsey that Mamie was highly pleased with the selection of sweaters and that am I *feverishly* awaiting the duplicate bill.[4] Mrs. Whitman has confessed that she managed to lose the one Miss Gainsford gave her just before we left Winfield House.[5]

With warm regard,[6] *As ever*

[1] On September 7 Eisenhower had returned from his tour in Western Europe; see no. 1276. While in London and Scotland he and U.S. Ambassador to Great Britain Whitney had met on several occasions (see Kahn, *Jock,* pp. 242–44). Eisenhower had met with Under Secretary of State Dillon this same day. Dillon had served as Ambassador to France 1953–1957, and Houghton had succeeded him (see no. 95).

[2] During the meeting with Dillon the President had reported that last year Whitney, whom he did not name, had spent $110,000 of his own money on entertainment. Eisenhower wanted the Treasury Department to rule on whether the expenses were deductible from income taxes (see Goodpaster, Memorandum of Conference, Sept. 11, 1959, AWF/D, and Ann Whitman memorandum, Sept. 8, 1959, AWF/AWD).

[3] Whitney had been among the President's British guests at his apartment in Culzean Castle in Ayrshire, Scotland. On September 4 William E. Robinson and W. Alton Jones had joined them for a few days of recreation (see the preceding document; Eisenhower, *Waging Peace,* p. 431; and John S. D. Eisenhower, *Strictly Personal,* p. 253).

[4] Apparently Mrs. Whitney had purchased the sweaters for the First Lady at Eisenhower's request.

[5] Miss Gainsford was probably employed at Winfield House, the U.S. Ambassador's residence in London.
[6] For developments see no. 1337.

1307   *EM, WHCF, Official File 85-II*

TO JOHN GEORGE DIEFENBAKER   *September 10, 1959*

Dear John: We have been giving much thought to the Conference on the Law of the Sea to be convened at Geneva next spring because the issues before the Conference are of especial importance. In our view every effort should be made to assure that the Conference achieves general agreement on a narrow territorial sea. A simultaneous solution must also be found to the complex and important problems of fishery jurisdiction in a contiguous zone.[1]

I believe that our two countries recognize the importance of agreement on a narrow territorial sea to our common defenses, to the security of the Western Hemisphere and to the entire free world. We both realize that failure of the Conference to achieve agreement will encourage various countries to claim wider territorial seas by unilateral acts. This would be contrary to our common interests.[2]

In the area of fisheries, however, our two countries have so far not seen eye to eye. The fact that Canada and the United States advocated different proposals at the first Conference contributed to a voting division of the free world and to the resulting failure to achieve the majority required for success.[3] Clearly the prospects of agreement would be improved were Canada and the United States to approach the next Conference with an agreed position. We therefore welcome the approach made through your Embassy suggesting certain language to amend the Canadian proposal as put forward by the Geneva Conference of 1958. However, before seeking to work out specific language at the technical level I thought it would be helpful to have further discussion regarding both the security considerations and the possibilities of finding some acceptable compromise on fishery problems. Such discussion should facilitate the search for precise language.

Accordingly, I have asked Mr. Dillon, the Under Secretary of State, to go to Ottawa to discuss this matter with you and your associates in an attempt to find the outlines of a common ground on which we can develop a mutually agreed proposal that could lead to the success of the Conference which we both desire.[4]

If you agree, a mere note of assent would suffice.[5]

With warm personal regard, *Sincerely*

[1] For background see nos. 589, 609, and 671. On December 10, 1958, the United Nations General Assembly had agreed to convene a second Law of the Sea Conference during March–April 1960 to settle questions involving the extent of territorial seas and exclusive fishery rights in a contiguous zone (State, *Foreign Relations, 1958–1960*, vol. II, *United Nations and General International Matters*, pp. 715–16, 730–31).

The State Department draft of this letter is in the same file as the document.

[2] In June 1959 the Canadian government had proposed a territorial sea of six miles with an exclusive six-mile zone subject to the exercise of historic rights for five years. The United States historically had supported the concept of a three-mile territorial sea as established by previous international law, but had offered to compromise in an effort to obtain agreement on principles that would not drastically curtail rights of navigation (see no. 589, and State, *Foreign Relations, 1958–1960*, vol. II, *United Nations and General International Matters*, pp. 716, 722).

[3] The Canadians had proposed a nine-mile fishing zone; the United States had proposed a six-mile fishing zone (see nos. 589 and 609).

[4] On September 8 Acting Secretary of State Dillon had told the President that the possibilities of achieving agreement at the conference would be improved if the United States and Canada could work together. Dillon proposed that he go to Ottawa for preliminary talks (same file as document; Goodpaster, Memorandum of Conversation, Sept. 11, 1959, AWF/D; and Ann Whitman memorandum, Sept. 7, 8, 1959, *ibid.*).

[5] Diefenbaker would reply that he could meet Dillon on October 23 (see Dillon to Eisenhower, Sept. 22, 1959, Eisenhower to Diefenbaker, Sept. 23, 1959, and related correspondence all in AWF/I: Canada; see also State, *Foreign Relations, 1958–1960*, vol. II, *United Nations and General International Matters*, pp. 730–31). The two nations would agree to work for a bilateral agreement on the exercise of traditional fishing rights, conditional on the adoption by the conference of a six-mile territorial sea plus an outer six-mile fishing zone. The United States would attempt to gain the support of European countries for this solution, and Canada would approach Norway, Denmark, Ireland, and possibly Iceland for the same purpose (State, *Foreign Relations, 1958–1960*, vol. II, *United Nations and General International Matters*, p. 733).

Eisenhower added the last sentence and the complimentary close by hand to the State Department draft. For developments see no. 1509.

1308   *EM, AWF, Ann Whitman Diary Series*

DIARY[1]   *September 10, 1959*

Today, 15 years ago I met Monty at Brussels Air Field.[2] I was accompanied by Gale and Tedder.[3] He made his preposterous proposal to go to Berlin. I asked him first to get across the Rhine and gave him all he asked for this operation. I told him that when he was across he must clear out opposition to Antwerp because of our extended supply position. He failed even to get the bridgehead!![4]

[1] The President had written this note in pencil on the covering page of a television and radio talk to the nation about his recent trip to Europe. For background on the trip see no. 1276. The text of the speech is in *Public Papers of the Presidents: Eisenhower, 1959*, pp. 648–52.

² On the conference with Field Marshal Bernard Law Montgomery see Chandler, *War Years*, no. 1941.

³ Lieutenant General Sir Humfrey Myddleton Gale had served as General Eisenhower's Deputy Chief of Staff and as his Chief Administrative Officer from 1942 to 1945. Marshal of the Royal Air Force Arthur William Tedder had served as the Supreme Commander's deputy.

⁴ On Montgomery's role during the invasion of Normandy (OVERLORD), the advance on Berlin, and the crossing of the Rhine see Chandler, *War Years*, nos. 1979, 2032, 2040, 2247, 2448, and Eisenhower, *Crusade in Europe*, pp. 305, 306, 399. For Montgomery's account of his role see his *Memoirs*, pp. 68, 240, 244, 257. On the controversy surrounding Montgomery's volume see, for example, nos. 1012 and 1197 in these volumes.

1309   *EM, AWF, International Series:*
                                                              Macmillan

To Harold Macmillan   *September 11, 1959*
Cable. Secret

*Dear Harold:*¹ My talks with General de Gaulle went very well, I believe. The discussions were completely friendly and open, and it seemed to me that each succeeded in putting across to the other exactly what we had in mind, although the time available was so short that I was obliged to leave one or two items to be covered in a written communication with him.²

As anticipated, the question of Algeria, and of U.S. support for France on this issue, was uppermost in his mind.³ I made it clear that we wanted to support our French friends and hoped they would take a course which would make this possible. His thought is that when the rebellion is over, Algeria will be able to make its choice as to whether to remain completely French, to have a certain degree of autonomy, or to have complete independence. He will make a public statement on this within the next few days, and seemed confident that it will be one both you and I could support.⁴

We discussed very frankly the difficulties that are ahead in the United Nations. The French do not wish to discuss Algeria in the U.N., holding that this is an internal affair. We pointed out that someone should speak for France, and make a good presentation of what France has done for Algeria in the economic, social and other spheres. If this is done early there will be time to round up other delegations. We are hopeful that his public statement will give the basis we need.

It is clear that he has given a great deal of thought and attention to the problems in Africa, believing that the countries there should sooner or later be able to decide their own future. He said that France has started this process within the French Community, with members deciding of their own free will whether to work in common with France on matters of defense, foreign affairs and economic activity. He noted that Guinea alone has chosen to be independent, but still wants, and is receiving, French help. He expressed a great deal of concern over the threat of communism in the area, and the efforts of the Soviet bloc to "buy" their way into various countries through extending aid to them. (Incidentally, he said flatly that Sekou Toure is a Communist.)[5]

We discussed my suggestion regarding aid to underdeveloped countries primarily. Of course he, again, is concerned most with the French Community.[6] I believe he will agree that it is vital for the Western countries to work together.

Our discussions regarding tri-partite consultations were relatively brief, ending in clear agreement on the idea of conferring informally among ourselves regarding matters that lie beyond NATO.[7] I mentioned that ad hoc staff committees could be established, but that I thought it unwise to establish institutions of a formal or permanent character, and he agreed.

He expressed himself as heartily in favor of the North Atlantic alliance, which he felt should be maintained and developed. He raised several questions, all well known, in a very restrained fashion. He questioned the integration of forces as taking from the people a sense of responsibility for their defense, and losing the impetus of patriotism. On this I simply pointed out the necessity of integrated control for effective military operations in the present era, and some of the difficulties that would be inescapable in a coalition of purely national forces—not only for effective combat, but also in failing to provide a basis for the presence of U.S. forces in Europe. Both with him, and in my brief remarks at NATO and SHAPE, I stressed the need to develop a dedication to Western ideas, extending beyond the traditional national patriotism of the past.[8]

He seemed to be satisfied with our discussion regarding the decision to use atomic weapons. I made the point, as we had discussed at Chequers, that unless the situation were one of surprise attack, with bombers overhead, we would of course never unleash the use of nuclear weapons without consulting our principal allies.[9] With respect to atomic weapons, General de Gaulle said that France will continue to develop its own. I explained the difficulties deriving from our legislation to him, and he seemed quite aware of them. He did not press for more liberal action on our part, and said he is not asking for anything in this regard.[10]

Finally, with respect to German questions and the visit of Khrushchev and a possible summit meeting, I found a close identity of views. On Berlin we reached complete agreement to remain entirely firm on the principle of not abandoning Berlin but to examine with flexibility such changes as might be possible in the present arrangements. He showed no concern regarding the Khrushchev visit—but no optimism either. He did not think a summit meeting would be helpful unless some constructive result might be anticipated. He felt that some advance assurance of this is essential.

All in all, I believe the visit and the discussions were of real value in demonstrating that we are joined in common purposes. Incidentally, I think General de Gaulle was highly pleased that the ceremonies he had arranged succeeded in showing me such courtesy and so warm a welcome.[11] I was encouraged to find him confident, cooperative, and clearly in command of the affairs of his government.

Thanks very much for the character sketch of Mr. Khrushchev that you sent, and for your ideas as to the line I might take in discussions with him. I am grateful for all the help I can get.[12]

With warm regard, *As ever*

[1] A draft of this letter, with Eisenhower's handwritten emendations, is in AWF/M:G. State Department officials cabled the message to the American embassy in London for immediate delivery to Macmillan.

[2] Eisenhower had met with the French president in Paris on September 2 and at the palace of Rambouillet on September 3 and 4 (see State, *Foreign Relations, 1958–1960*, vol. VII, pt. 2, *Western Europe*, pp. 255–74; see also Eisenhower, *Waging Peace*, pp. 424–30; and Eisenhower to Macmillan, Sept. 4, 1959, AWF/I: Great Britain). Eisenhower's later communication to de Gaulle is no. 1318.

[3] For background see nos. 451 and 860.

[4] On September 16 de Gaulle would announce that Algeria could determine its future in an election to be held no more than four years after peace was restored to the region. Algerians could choose either independence, integration into the French Republic, or a form of federal autonomy with close ties to France (State, *Foreign Relations, 1958–1960*, vol. XIII, *Arab-Israeli Dispute; United Arab Republic; North Africa*, pp. 670–72; and State, *American Foreign Policy; Current Documents, 1959*, pp. 1096–99; see also NSC meeting minutes, July 1, 1960, AWF/NSC). For Eisenhower's comments on de Gaulle's proposal see *Public Papers of the Presidents: Eisenhower, 1959*, p. 665).

[5] Sékou Touré was president of the Republic of Guinea. On September 28, 1958, Guinea had declared its independence by voting against the draft constitution of the Fifth Republic, and in October Touré had written Eisenhower asking for U.S. recognition. On concerns regarding Guinea's acceptance of aid from Communist countries see State, *Foreign Relations, 1958–1960*, vol. XIV, *Africa*, pp. 689–91; see also R. W. Johnson, "Sekou Touré and the Guinean Revolution," in *African Nationalism and Independence*, edited by Timothy K. Welliver (New York, 1993), pp. 120–35. Touré would visit the United States in October (see State, *Foreign Relations, 1958–1960*, vol. XIV, *Africa*, pp. 693–706; State, *Foreign Relations, 1958–1960*, vol. VII, pt. 2, *Western Europe*, pp. 256–57; and no. 1502).

[6] Eisenhower had added this sentence to the State Department draft. The French Community, established in September 1958 with the approval of the constitution of the Fifth Republic, included the majority of the citizens of France, nineteen over-

seas departments, five overseas territories, and twelve autonomous republics (State, *Foreign Relations, 1958–1960*, vol. VII, pt. 2, *Western Europe*, p. 256).

[7] For background on these consultations see no. 1106.

[8] Eisenhower's remarks to the North Atlantic Council and at SHAPE headquarters on September 3 are in *Public Papers of the Presidents: Eisenhower, 1959*, pp. 636–68; see also State, *Foreign Relations, 1958–1960*, vol. VII, pt. 1, *Western European Integration and Security; Canada*, pp. 480–84.

[9] For the Eisenhower-Macmillan talks at Chequers on August 29 see State, *Foreign Relations, 1958–1960*, vol. VII, pt. 2, *Western Europe*, pp. 850–58.

[10] On restrictions placed on the sharing of atomic information by the Atomic Energy Act of 1954 see nos. 718 and 725.

[11] Close to one million Parisians had welcomed Eisenhower on September 2 (see *New York Times*, Sept. 3, 1959).

[12] Macmillan had told Eisenhower that although Khrushchev was "undoubtedly a clever and calculating politician," the Soviet leader was "more like a human being" than Stalin had been. He wanted to be considered as "the responsible leader of a great bloc of countries," Macmillan said, and less of "the odd man out in international affairs." Although the Soviet leader would be "on his best behavior" during his upcoming visit to the United States, Macmillan advised that Eisenhower calmly accept any manifestations of Khrushchev's "personal touchiness." He also told the President that an awkward scene might result if Khrushchev thought that Eisenhower "had decided definitely against a comprehensive agreement on tests." Macmillan urged Eisenhower "to play this matter as gently and slowly as possible" (Macmillan to Eisenhower, Sept. 4, 1959, PREM 11/2675; see also no. 1254). For developments see no. 1323.

1310   *EM, AWF, Name Series*

To Milton Stover Eisenhower   *September 11, 1959*

Dear Milton: I have just realized that the arrival of Chairman Khrushchev coincides with another very important date, at least in the annals of the Eisenhower family.[1] But I promise you that I shan't let the sound and the fury of Tuesday overshadow, in my mind at least "your" day.[2]

Have a Happy Birthday, and know as always that I wish for you the best of everything and—also—that I am lastingly grateful for all you do for me, both officially and personally.

With warm regard, *As ever*

[1] Soviet Premier Nikita Khrushchev's two-week tour of the United States would begin on Tuesday, September 15 (see no. 1265 and *New York Times*, Sept. 13, 15, 16, 1959). For developments see no. 1326.

[2] Milton Eisenhower would celebrate his sixtieth birthday on September 15.

To Konrad Adenauer   *September 12, 1959*
Suggested message[1]

On the tenth anniversary of the assumption of your duties as Chancellor of the Federal Republic of Germany, I send most cordial personal greetings.[2] On behalf of the American people I congratulate you for your historic contribution not only to the affairs of your own country but to those of the European community as a whole. Through your dedication and inspiring leadership, the Federal Republic has risen out of the chaos of war to a position of influence and responsibility in the community of free nations.[3] Moreover, there has been developed in Germany a government guided by the principles of democracy and motivated by a sincere desire to play a positive role in the great movement toward European cooperation and integration. Your effective work in developing understanding between our two peoples has also been a contribution of major significance.[4] It was a most valued and enjoyable opportunity to confer with you in Bonn recently, and I wish you many more productive years in the interests of your own country and those of the free world.[5]
    With assurances of my continued esteem and friendship.[6]

[1] Eisenhower's handwritten emendations appear on the State Department's draft of this letter (AWF/I: Germany). See also *Public Papers of the Presidents: Eisenhower, 1959*, p. 659.
[2] Military government in occupied West Germany had formally ended with Adenauer's election as West Germany's first chancellor on September 15, 1949. In 1952 the Federal Republic of Germany had joined both the North Atlantic Treaty Organization and the seven-nation Western European Union (WEU). Germany had not become fully sovereign, however, until 1955 (see Konrad Adenauer, *Memoirs 1945–53* [Chicago, 1966]; Eisenhower, *Mandate for Change*, pp. 399, 506; Galambos, *Columbia University*, no. 1129, and *NATO and the Campaign of 1952*, nos. 577 and 816; Galambos and van Ee, *The Middle Way*, no. 1340; and *New York Times*, Sept. 16, 18, 22, 1949, Apr. 8, Sept. 16, 1959).
[3] The State Department's original draft had noted that West Germany had risen out of "despair and destruction" to a position of "respect and responsibility" in the Free World.
[4] Adenauer would reply on September 18 that credit for the Federal Republic's development as a "healthy and vigorous nation" was due "to a considerable degree to the generous help given by the American people" (AWF/I: Adenauer).
[5] The President had met with Adenauer on August 26 during his trip to Europe (see no. 1282). Adenauer would tell Eisenhower that his visit had demonstrated "the growing friendship" between West Germany and the United States. He added that he was committed to "further strengthen and deepen the friendship" that connected his country to the other free nations (Sept. 18, 1959, AWF/I: Adenauer). See also the related correspondence between American and West German officials in AWF/I: Germany.
[6] For developments on the relationship between Eisenhower and Adenauer see, for example, no. 1433.

To Lewis Lichtenstein Strauss　　　　　　　*September 13, 1959*
Personal

Dear Lewis: Last evening I felt an urge to talk to you, but the operator reported that she could not locate you or Alice. I hope this means that you are somewhere enjoying a rest this beautiful weekend.[1]

I had nothing specifically on my mind, except perhaps to complain about an indifferent showing our bulls made in a Maryland show held last week. The heifers did well.[2]

I did want to report a little on the results of the talks I had with our friends in Germany, Britain and France.[3] All in all, I feel the entire trip went very well. The Chancellor went out of his way to be friendly and was, I thought, in fine health and spirits.[4] Harold, of course, was his old self, and the talks with him were no strain at all.[5] Plowden and others send you their special regard.[6] Incidentally, I await the events of the ten days just ahead with something less than the assurance that I had on my European trip.[7]

My schedule is uncertain, to say the least, for the next weeks, but whenever you are in town do give either Tom Stephens or Ann Whitman a ring. You know that I always want to see you, if possible.[8]

Give my affectionate regard to Alice and, of course, all the best to yourself. *As ever*

[1] The President had attempted to reach Strauss at his home in Culpeper, Virginia (Telephone Calls, Sept. 12, 1959, AWF/D).
[2] Eisenhower probably was referring to competitions at the Maryland State Fair, held annually the week preceding the Labor Day holiday.
[3] On the President's recent trip to Europe see no. 1276.
[4] This was German Chancellor Konrad Adenauer.
[5] This was British Prime Minister Harold Macmillan.
[6] Edwin Noel Plowden was chairman of the British Atomic Energy Authority. Strauss had chaired the U.S. Atomic Energy Commission from 1953–1958. For background on the Plowden-Strauss relationship see no. 718.
[7] Eisenhower was referring to the upcoming visit to the United States by Soviet Premier Nikita Khrushchev (see no. 1265).
[8] Strauss would visit the White House the afternoon of September 22.

To Freeman F. Gosden   *September 13, 1959*

Dear Freeman: Last night I felt an urge to talk to you (not to brag about any hole-in-one that *I* had made, I assure you), but the operator reported that your phones did not answer.[1] Incidentally, one member of the Eisenhower family did do very well yesterday in another field of competition—young Susie, aged seven, won a blue ribbon for horsemanship in a show held near Gettysburg yesterday afternoon.[2] The whole family is bursting with pride, of course.

Bill, Pete and I had two fine days on the golf course near Culzean Castle, and many times wished that you and our other Augusta friends could have joined us—and that the time there could have been indefinitely prolonged.[3] The weather was just about perfect, and the golf not too bad, all things considered.

It has been much too long since I have seen you, and I do hope you will pay Washington that promised visit some time this fall.[4] My own fall plans are indefinite (which is definitely the under statement of the year), and I am not at all sure that I shall be able to work in my usual November visit to Augusta. But of that I have not given up all hope.[5]

Do let me hear from you. And give my affectionate regard to Jane with, of course, all the best to yourself. *As ever*

[1] The President had attempted to telephone Gosden at his home in Los Angeles (Telephone conversations, Sept. 12, 1959, AWF/D). Gosden recently had shot a hole-in-one (see Eisenhower to Gosden, Aug. 14, 1959, Gosden to Whitman, Aug. 17, 1959, and Whitman to Gosden, Aug. 19, 1959, all in same file as document).

[2] Susan had taken a first prize at the South Mountain Fair in Arendtsville, Pennsylvania. She had ridden the President's two-year-old chestnut filly, Goldie, at a walk, canter, and trot in a children's pleasure horse class (*New York Times*, Sept. 13, 1959).

[3] Following his trip to Germany, France, and England, Eisenhower had visited Scotland. William E. Robinson and W. Alton Jones had joined him on September 5 and they had played golf at Turnberry Golf Course (see no. 1305).

[4] Gosden would be among several friends who would join the President on his vacation in La Quinta, California, September 30–October 8. Gosden next would visit the White House on April 22, 1960.

[5] On the upcoming visit to the United States by Soviet Premier Nikita Khrushchev see nos. 1265 and 1326. On December 3 Eisenhower would embark on a goodwill tour to Italy, Turkey, Pakistan, Afghanistan, India, Greece, Tunisia, France, Spain, and Morocco. He would vacation in Augusta, Georgia, October 21–25 and November 12–23.

To John George Diefenbaker   *September 15, 1959*
Secret

Dear John: On receiving your message of September sixth concerning the projected air defense exercise SKY HAWK, I asked for an urgent report on the possibility of modifying it along the lines you suggested.[1] My advisers have indicated there would be little purpose or
value in an exercise modified to confine its scope to the air space
of the United States alone, or, alternatively, to limit it so as to avoid
the grounding of civil aircraft. These possibilities were apparently
examined by the military authorities of our two countries when the
exercise was being planned and developed. In light of this, I have
felt obliged to accept the cancellation of the exercise.[2]

There is little I can add to my former message regarding this exercise and similar test and training activities. I am informed that,
because of the multiplicity of factors to be coordinated, it will be at
least several months before an exercise of this type could be resched-
uled, but I believe it is important that our two governments, through
appropriate representatives, consider together the anticipated political and psychological results of such an exercise. I think that our
combined military staffs are convinced of its value and even of its
necessity. Should the governments agree on this future need, the
exercise, I understand, would again be planned by the integrated
United States-Canada staff of NORAD.[3]

I hope that at such later time arrangements satisfactory to us both
can be made.[4]

With warm regard, *Sincerely*

---

[1] For background on Canada and Sky Hawk see no. 1302. Diefenbaker had expressed
concern that public opinion in Canada would be "unduly alarmed" by the scope and
timing of the exercise, at a time when improvement in East-West relations was expected (State, *Foreign Relations*, vol. VII, pt. 1, *Western European Integration and Security; Canada*, pp. 768–69). A draft of this letter, containing Eisenhower's handwritten
emendations, is in AWF/I: Canada. The American ambassador to Canada would send
an advance text of this letter to the Prime Minister (Wigglesworth to Diefenbaker,
Sept. 16, 1959, Diefenbaker Papers).

[2] At a White House conference on September 8 Eisenhower had recalled an earlier
arrangement by which the Canadians were notified at the political level of upcoming projects before the specifics were decided. The Secretary of State had agreed to
reinstate the procedure which, he said, could eliminate what the State Department
believed was a defect in communications between Canadian military authorities and
civilian officials. At the conclusion of the conference the President had decided to
cancel the exercise (Goodpaster, Memorandum of Conference, Sept. 11, 1959, AWF/
D; Ann Whitman memorandum, Sept. 8, 1959, AWF/AWD; and State, *Foreign Relations*, vol. VII, pt. 1, *Western European Integration and Security; Canada*, pp. 769–72).

[3] The North American Air Defense Command (NORAD) had been established in 1957. It comprised parts of all the American armed services and Canada's Air Defence Command and was charged with defending the entire North American continent (*U.S. Department of State Bulletin* 37, no. 940 [August 19, 1957], 306; State, *Foreign Relations, 1955–1957*, vol. XXVII, *Western Europe and Canada*, pp. 897, 906; see also *Public Papers of the Presidents: Eisenhower, 1960–61*, p. 54).

The Canada-United States Ministerial Committee on Joint Defense would meet November 8–9, and the Canada-United States Permanent Joint Board on Defense would meet January 18–21, 1960. An air defense exercise would be among the topics discussed by both groups (State, *Foreign Relations*, vol. VII, pt. 1, *Western European Integration and Security; Canada*, p. 772; *U.S. Department of State Bulletin* 41, no. 1066 [November 30, 1959], 788–89, and *New York Times*, Sept. 20, Nov. 9, 10, 1959).

On June 3, 1960, the President and the Canadian Prime Minister would discuss another proposed air defense exercise, Sky Shield. Diefenbaker would agree to further joint examination of the project at the military level. On June 16 the Canadian Cabinet would approve the exercise (State, *Foreign Relations*, vol. VII, pt. 1, *Western European Integration and Security; Canada*, p. 804, and *New York Times*, July 13, 14, 1960).
[4] On September 10, 1960, the United States and Canada would participate in exercise Sky Shield. Civilian air traffic in both countries would be grounded for six hours during the mock battle. Canadian and American officials would conclude that the experience had benefitted the joint United States-Canadian radar-interceptor-missile forces (State, *Foreign Relations*, vol. VII, *Western European Integration and Security; Canada*, p. 811, and *New York Times*, July 27, Aug. 4, 28, Sept. 10, 11, 1960).

1315   *EM, AWF, International Series: Nehru*

To Jawaharlal Nehru   *September 16, 1959*
Secret

Dear Prime Minister: I found your letter of the thirteenth to be most interesting to me and to this government.[1] I of course hope that your difficulties with Red China can be settled amicably and justly. Unfortunately there seems to be a growing amount of evidence that the Chinese Communists are embarking on a more aggressive policy, apparently in the hope that through force and the threat of force they may weaken their neighbors.[2] I applaud your determination to adhere strictly to peaceful methods in solving your own difficulty with them, unless your country is attacked.[3]

As you know, Mr. Khrushchev is now in our country.[4] My invitation to him was sent, of course, in the prayerful hope that he could show a more conciliatory spirit than has been apparent in his public statements and in the instructions that he has obviously given to his representatives in Geneva and elsewhere. I could think of no better way to explore the possibility that, in a personal meeting, he may be ready to move somewhat more in the direction of peace than toward increased irritation and possible conflict.

I treasure your invitation to visit India. The prospect has been much on my mind and I am sure you are aware that I have long wanted to make such a visit. The principal deterrent is the considerable number of governments that apparently might take amiss such a journey unless I could include each of their countries in my itinerary. However, I am still working on a program that might possibly eliminate this difficulty. I should think I could give you a definite answer within the next few weeks.[5]

With assurances of my highest esteem and warm personal regard, *Sincerely*

[1] Nehru's letter remains classified.

[2] See no. 1304.

[3] Nehru had reaffirmed his commitment to the principles of nonalignment and peaceful coexistence agreed to by India and China in 1954 as part of an agreement on trade in Tibet, and again in 1955 at the Bandung Conference (see *New York Times*, Sept. 14, 16, Oct. 4, 1959; see also Harold Hinton, *China's Turbulent Quest* [Bloomington, Ind., 1972], pp. 73–102; and Richard L. Jackson, *The Non-Aligned, the UN, and the Superpowers* [New York, 1983], pp. 12 -15).

[4] On Khrushchev's visit see nos. 1310 and 1326.

[5] On December 3, 1959, the President would begin a world tour taking him to eleven countries in three weeks, including India, Pakistan, and Afghanistan. Eisenhower would visit India from December 9–14; see no. 1389.

1316   *EM, WHCF, Official File 117-V*

To Isidor Schwaner Ravdin   *September 19, 1959*
Personal and private

Dear Rav: On September eleventh I acknowledged your note to me of the second. But I felt the urge to tell you a little more about some of the thoughts that plague me about this matter of Federal financing.[1]

To start with, Federal funds for medical research have doubled since 1956 and have quadrupled since the levels of 1953, the year I came to this office.[2] This *rate* of expansion seems not only to be establishing a pattern for research in this particular field, but in our habits in other types of Federal expenditures as well. Most of these have to do with the "welfare" of our people.

No part of our Federal activity can be considered in a vacuum, apart from other essential activities.

Federal spending is one of the inciting causes of uneasiness about the soundness of our money and government bonds. This creates a trend away from investment in debentures and bonds and toward excessive investment in equities and in hazardly speculative ventures. Federal expenditures continue to increase our debt and have been one of the reasons for the rise in interest rates. With expenditures increasing and the rates going up, we find that for the current fiscal year we must spend about a billion more for interest alone than we had anticipated. This figure should startle every citizen.[3]

I am most respectful of the serious study that you and your associates have been making on these matters and for the conclusions you have reached.[4] But in my special seat I feel that it is not enough to know that an activity and its expenditure are merely *desirable*. We must be quite clear in the establishment of priorities so that these things can be done at a *rate* and in a sequence that will conform to the fiscal facts, as well as the clear requirements, of a nation that operates, primarily, on the *free enterprise system*. Water power developments, sewage disposal, many other types of public works, new educational responsibilities, farm subsidies that seem always to grow, grants of every possible kind to states and cities, research of all kinds including space travel—all these and other expenditures are piled on top of the inescapable costs for defense and for assisting our allies to contain the Communist aggression. All this means, I think, that it is not enough to allocate appropriations wisely. It is additionally necessary to consider how much that appropriation is needed as compared to others projected. Each expenditure is increasing fiscal difficulties, cheapening our dollar, pushing up prices (including medical prices) and in time this process may defeat the very purposes for which these great sums are appropriated.

Within a matter of months I shall be leaving this office. By no means do I want to be neglectful of any important need of our people. Among these is access to medical facilities and assisting in the conduct of research so that our health standards may steadily be improved. But it would be futile to allow the aggregate expenditures of the Federal government to reach the point where we might, for example, have conquered one or more of the diseases that are so terrifying to mankind, but at the same time, through our improvidence, either stagnated our economy and again experienced the existence of block-long bread lines and suffering akin to that of the early 30s, or to turn to the kind of governmental control that might solve both fiscal and expenditure problems but at the loss of much of the personal freedom and liberty that we so deeply value.

By no means do I mean to paint a picture of disaster "just around the corner." I do want to convey to our people in and out of government a conviction of the need for good husbandry in all our activities—particularly those in which the Federal government itself is involved. If I can leave to all our people, as a legacy out of these eight years, a better understanding of all these things, then indeed the entire effort will have been worth while.

With warm regard, *As ever*

[1] On August 14, 1959, Eisenhower had signed into law the final version of H.R. 6769, the fiscal 1960 funding bill for the Departments of Labor and Health, Education and Welfare. Ravdin had written on September 2 (same file as document) expressing his support of the legislation and assuring the President that the increased appropriation to the Institutes of Health was "wisely allocated." He told Eisenhower that he could consider "as a safeguard" the fact that most of the money had gone to "universities and other well organized research institutions." Ravdin did not believe "that any other type of institution in our country" had a "higher sense of integrity and desire for widening the span of knowledge, without self-interest." We have been unable to locate the President's note of September 11.

[2] The 1960 appropriation bill provided $259 million more than had been requested by the Administration. Most of the increase had gone to health and education programs. The $400,000,000 appropriation for the National Institutes of Health marked an increase of $105,700,000 over that of the previous year. The additional amount was in response to charges by congressional Democrats that the medical research budget was totally inadequate to meet the nation's needs, and that the Administration had "gone so far as to set back the medical research program in a desperate attempt to present, on paper, a balanced budget" (*New York Times*, Apr. 29, 1959). In signing the bill, Eisenhower had countered that there was "a limit to the rate at which medical research can grow and yet grow soundly." On increases in 1958 see *Congressional Quarterly Almanac*, vol. XIV, *1958*, pp. 341–42.

[3] On Eisenhower's efforts on behalf of a balanced budget see nos. 1040, 1042, and 1114.

[4] Ravdin had written that in his years serving on scholarly committees he had "never met with more thoughtful groups" than the committees established to advise the Secretary of Health, Education and Welfare and the Surgeon General on the best uses for the additional appropriations. He believed that he and many of the men he respected most in the medical sciences had not given their time "to unwise considerations of requests for grants."

1317   *EM, WHCF, Official File 155*

To Kenneth Allison Roberts   *September 19, 1959*

Dear Mr. Roberts: Upon receipt of your and your colleagues' letter of September fifth, I requested a detailed report from the interested agencies concerning your suggestion that funds be recommended in the fiscal year 1961 budget for the construction of the Millers Ferry lock and dam.[1]

First, let me say that we are just beginning to develop the budget for fiscal year 1961, and of course my decisions on individual items must await further analysis of the overall fiscal situation and a careful weighing of all the many competing demands for the available revenues. Specifically regarding the Millers Ferry lock and dam, I understand that this structure would be only the first of three major structures needed to provide a nine-foot channel from the mouth of the Alabama River to Montgomery. The total cost of these structures at today's prices would be something in excess of $120 million.[2]

As for development by the Alabama Power Company of several dams on the Coosa River above Montgomery, I find that in 1954 when the Congress authorized non-Federal construction of these hydro-electric dams it made no definite commitment concerning the Federal structures below Montgomery which are planned for navigation and flood control purposes. However, the legislation did provide for compensation of the private company for allocated navigation and flood control benefits of these dams when Federal work on other phases of the Alabama-Coosa River development occurred. This represented the partnership phase of the development to which I referred in my 1955 State of the Union Message.[3]

You correctly infer that wherever possible I have encouraged non-Federal interests to develop portions of our vast water resource program, and I certainly welcomed the decision of Congress to permit non-Federal interests to develop the hydro-electric power facilities on the Coosa River. However, I doubt that there is a direct relationship between these hydro-electric projects and a decision concerning a series of Federal dams designed largely for navigation and flood control purposes.

However, you may be assured that your views will be carefully considered as we develop the fiscal year 1961 budget. I hope you will pass these views along to your colleagues who joined in your letter to me,[4] *Sincerely*

<hr>

[1] On September 5, 1959, Alabama Democratic Congressman Roberts (LL.B. University of Alabama 1935), president of the Piedmont Development Company from 1945–1950 and a member of Congress since 1951, had been joined by both Alabama senators and nine members of Congress in a letter requesting funding for the Millers Ferry lock and dam. These structures were to be part of an authorized project to provide a nine-foot navigation channel up the Alabama River to Montgomery, Alabama, and from there up the Coosa River to Rome, Georgia. Eisenhower had told White House Special Assistant Wilton B. Persons on September 8 that if this was "truly the kind of partnership project that it purports to be," then he was "sympathetic." The President had requested that his staff prepare a draft response.

[2] Congress had authorized the development of the Alabama-Coosa River system for navigation, flood control, hydroelectric power and other purposes as part of the River and Harbor Act of 1945. Authorization for federal development was suspended in 1954 to permit non-federal interests to construct a series of power dams. The Federal Power Commission licensed the Alabama Power Company to build four new dams; the firm started construction of the first in July 1958. Planning appropriations for the initial phase of federal development of the Alabama River had been made in 1956. These included $700,000 out of a project total cost of $125.4 million towards construction of Jones Bluff and Millers Ferry multipurpose improvements,

Claiborne lock and dam, and a supplemental channel to Montgomery (Staats to Merriam [Sept. 10, 1959] WHCF/OF 155).

[3] The President had called for the treatment of resource development as a "partnership undertaking" in which "the participation of private citizens and State and local governments is as necessary as is Federal participation" (*Public Papers of the Presidents: Eisenhower, 1955*, p. 18. See also *U.S. Statutes At Large*, vol. 68, pt. 1 [1954], pp. 302–3).

[4] Roberts and his colleagues would write on November 12 again urging funding for the Millers Dam project. Eisenhower would reply (Nov. 19) that he would bear their "interest in mind as the fiscal 1961 budget is developed, while considering also, as of course I must, the many other public programs that require Federal attention." A November 16, 1959, memorandum to Bryce Harlow would note that the Millers Ferry project would not be included in the new starts for 1961 "because it is a very low priority project compared, for example, with the need to replace locks and dams on the Ohio river where *present* navigation is, as we know, very heavy." All correspondence is in the same file as the document.

1318

EM, AWF, International Series: de Gaulle

To Charles André Joseph Marie De Gaulle

September 21, 1959

Secret

Dear General De Gaulle:[1] As I reflect on my visit and my discussions with you in Paris and Rambouillet, my feeling of gratitude—both for your hospitality and for the opportunity of considering with you questions that concern us both—continues to increase.[2] I look forward to the time when we can renew our talks.

The limitations of time did not permit me to cover adequately several subjects of common interest. I would like at this time to comment on two particular points.[3] The first is the Mediterranean fleet. We have discussed this previously, and I believe that it should be possible to attain a satisfactory understanding.[4] I do not propose for the United States any special or favored status for its naval forces in the Mediterranean, and I think our naval experts should be able to devise arrangements which would place on the same footing the British, French and U.S. fleets—both in peacetime and wartime. With this in mind, I would suggest that both our people raise this matter with our British friends with a view to having the Standing Group consider with SACEUR and SACLANT arrangements that, when approved by the two of us and Mr. Macmillan, would meet the NATO needs in the Mediterranean as regards the naval forces of our three countries, while at the same time satisfying the particular needs of each nation.

Secondly, I would like to mention the question of storage of nuclear weapons in France for the use of both U.S. and French forces assigned to NATO.[5] I start from the belief that the purpose of storing these weapons in France would be to assure the most effective common defense of Western Europe, of course including France. If the arrangements were properly worked out, I cannot believe there would need to be any impairment of national sovereignty for either of us. The arrangements could rest on a firm agreement that the consent of the French Government would be required prior to the use of such weapons by either U.S. or French forces. There should of course be some advance agreement covering the case of general attack upon us with no advance warning.

This form of close cooperation is, to me, a logical necessity arising out of modern military technology, as is the whole concept of integrated commands. As I indicated when we were together, my own effort to reconcile the needs of modern weapons and techniques with the traditions of national patriotism and esprit led me in 1951 to the concept of joining national forces together into integrated commands. Developments since that time have tended, in my opinion, to strengthen this need. I believe the American forces in Europe, for example, while serving in their own national uniforms and under their own flag, feel also a considerable—and a growing—attachment to their collective force and to the North Atlantic Community.

Our talks clarified again, I think, the degree to which we both are attached to common ideals and ideas of Western security. I do not believe that there is any divergence in our objectives, and I present these thoughts as my ideas concerning the best means, in these special fields, of achieving them. I remain convinced that we can so solve these problems that NATO will function the better for it.

As you may have seen, at my press conference on September seventeenth, I took the opportunity to say I am greatly encouraged by your courageous and statesmanlike declaration on Algeria, and hope that it will lead to an early peace.[6]

Please accept, Mr. President, the expression of my highest consideration and sincere friendship.[7]

With warm personal regard, *Sincerely*

---

[1] Eisenhower had asked Under Secretary Dillon to prepare a draft of this letter to the French president. It was reviewed by Secretary Herter, Defense Department officials, the U.S. Ambassador to France, and NATO officials in Paris before the President approved it and sent it to de Gaulle on September 23 (see State, *Foreign Relations, 1958–1960*, vol. VII, pt. 2, *Western Europe*, p. 283).

[2] On Eisenhower's discussions with de Gaulle see no. 1309.

[3] At the suggestion of U.S. officials in Paris these sentences were revised to avoid the implication that the points of common interest were limited to two (Dillon to Houghton, Sept. 21, 1959, AWF/I: de Gaulle).

⁴ On de Gaulle's decision to remove the French Mediterranean fleet from NATO control see nos. 1106 and 1112.

⁵ De Gaulle had previously told Eisenhower that France would no longer agree to store atomic weapons on her soil without complete control over them (see no. 1192).

⁶ For de Gaulle's Algerian declaration see no. 1909. Eisenhower's comments are in *Public Papers of the Presidents: Eisenhower, 1959*, p. 665.

⁷ De Gaulle would agree with Eisenhower's suggestions regarding the naval forces and would instruct the French representative of the Standing Group in Washington to enter into discussions on the issue. He added that arrangements were possible regarding the stockpiling of atomic weapons in France "as soon as we can agree that the launching of an atomic war by the West anywhere in the world would require the joint decision of the United States, Great Britain, and France" (de Gaulle to Eisenhower, Oct. 6, 1959, AWF/I: de Gaulle).

On the issue of command structure, after paying tribute to the "cohesive force" that the American presence supplied to the alliance, de Gaulle would remind Eisenhower that both the international NATO forces and the forces defending the territory of the United States were under American command. The French forces defending their homeland, however, were not under their own national leaders. Although he admitted that it was "not advisable" to restructure NATO's defenses at that time, de Gaulle would say that he hoped "to see rectified some day" the "disadvantages inherent in this system." Eisenhower and de Gaulle would continue to discuss these issues at the Western Heads of Government meeting in Paris on December 19–21 (see State, *Foreign Relations, 1958–1960*, vol. VII, pt. 2, *Western Europe*, p. 319).

1319   *EM, AWF, Administration Series*

To Clarence Douglas Dillon   *September 21, 1959*
Confidential

Dear Doug: I have a suggestion that I should make an address to the United Nations General Assembly immediately after Khrushchev's visit.¹ The idea is that if we make no progress whatsoever in conversations with Mr. K., I should tell the world—through the UN—exactly what were the differences encountered. On the other hand, if any progress is made, this fact itself would be a good topic for a talk and as a vehicle through which our own views could be clearly expounded.²

In this connection you might be interested in reading a report on what a well-known minister said in New York on Sunday.³ *As ever*

¹ Former Chairman of the Atomic Energy Commission Lewis Strauss had made this suggestion. For background on the Khrushchev visit see no. 1266; see also Goodpaster, Memorandum of Conference, September 26, 1959, AWF/D.

² Eisenhower would not address the United Nations following Khrushchev's visit. The two men would issue a joint communiqué on September 27, and Eisenhower would discuss the visit at his news conference on the following day (*Public Papers of the Presidents: Eisenhower, 1959*, pp. 694–702). For memorandums of the discussions see State,

Foreign Relations, 1958–1960, vol. X, pt. 1, *Eastern Europe Region; Soviet Union; Cyprus*, pp. 392–402, 409–10, 459–69, 477–83.
[3] We have been unable to clarify this reference. Eisenhower had added the handwritten postscript: "What do you think?" to the end of this message. There is no response in AWF.

1320   *EM, AWF, Administration Series*

TO CHARLES DOUGLAS JACKSON   *September 23, 1959*
Personal

Dear C. D.: Your note with its enclosure reached me this morning. Already I have twice read your draft. I believe that what you have suggested for a public talk needs to be said but that by itself it would not satisfy a number of questions that must be in the minds of the American people.[1] By this I mean that while we should be sure to set the record straight on

1. Our attitude toward the captive European peoples
2. Total disarmament
3. Our faith in the strength and vitality of the free way of life,

not even the most emphatic reiteration of our position on these generalities can substitute for some homely truths about the threats against Berlin, the fighting in Laos, and abusive propaganda.[2] These are matters that are with us now, and each has its part in preventing what Mr. Khrushchev so glibly calls "easing of tensions."

So, while I suspect that later developments during Mr. Khrushchev's visit will have quite an influence in determining the character of what, if any, public report I should make, I think that your clear exposition of a sound American attitude in important general areas must be buttressed by a few specifics.[3]

Of course, if miraculously our visitor chooses to make any real concessions in some of his more rigid positions, the tone of my report would be modified. In this I'm a pessimist.

You made one statement in the middle of page seven of your draft that is somewhat incorrect. I refer to the sentence beginning "And I would remind Mr. K. . . ."[4] Mr. Khrushchev did not, himself, react favorably either initially or later, to my "Open Skies" proposal. Bulganin did—but the first word of Mr. Khrushchev on the subject was—"I do not agree with our Chairman." That was when I found out, beyond all question, who was the real boss in the delegation!

Many thanks for your effort. I know it will be useful to me.[5]

With warm regard, *As ever*

[1] Jackson had urged Eisenhower to address the American people immediately after Soviet Premier Khrushchev's visit to the United States, and he had enclosed a draft for the President's approval. After reviewing the preliminary plans for the visit and Khrushchev's itinerary, Jackson, in his draft, had stated the three main themes of the Soviet leader's talks: maintaining the status quo in Eastern Europe; seeking total disarmament as the best solution to coexistence; and anticipating the triumph of communism over capitalism. Jackson wanted Eisenhower to review the Western position on these three issues and to encourage the Russians to improve their living standards in peaceful competition with the United States (Jackson to Eisenhower, Sept. 23, 1959, AWF/A; Jackson's draft, with Eisenhower's handwritten emendations, is in AWF/A, Jackson Corr.).

[2] For background on the Berlin situation and anti-Western propaganda see no. 1187. On September 5 the State Department had cabled Eisenhower, then vacationing in Scotland, about the situation in Laos (see no. 404). Communist Pathet Lao rebels had attacked government forces near the North Vietnamese border; many American officials suspected that the rebels had been supported by the North Vietnamese. The JCS had warned that unless the United States took decisive action, the President would have to send in American military units (Eisenhower, *Waging Peace*, pp. 421, 431; State, *Foreign Relations, 1958–1960*, vol. XVI, *East Asia–Pacific Region; Cambodia; Laos*, pp. 588–89, 598–600, 602–5, 624–26; see also NSC meeting minutes, July 30, Aug. 6, 1959, AWF/NSC; and Synopses of State and Intelligence Material Reported to the President, July 7–8, 14, Aug. 4, 5, 6, and Sept. 8–9, 1959, AWF/D). After returning to the United States, Eisenhower had increased aid to the Laotian government, and the Pathet Lao had scaled back their military activity. For developments see no. 1749.

[3] Khrushchev had arrived in Washington on September 15. Two days later he had left for a tour of New York, California, Iowa, and Pennsylvania and would return for meetings with Eisenhower at Camp David on September 26 (see State, *Foreign Relations, 1958–1960*, vol. X, pt. 1, *Eastern Europe Region; Soviet Union; Cyprus*, pp. 388–92).

[4] Jackson had written: "And I would remind Mr. Khrushchev of his own initial reaction in Geneva in 1955, when I proposed the "Open Skies" policy as a practical step in this direction." On Eisenhower's proposal and Khrushchev's reaction see Galambos and van Ee, *The Middle Way*, no. 1523.

[5] Eisenhower would not make the speech that Jackson had suggested. For the joint communiqué issued at the conclusion of the visit and the President's remarks at his news conference see *Public Papers of the Presidents: Eisenhower, 1959*, pp. 694–702. For developments see no. 1332.

1321   *EM, AWF, Administration Series*

To Frederick Henry Mueller   *September 23, 1959*

Memorandum for the Secretary of Commerce: I enclose a copy of a note I have just sent to Mr. Canham, who visited me in my office this morning. Present also were Clarence Randall and Mr. Paarlberg of my staff.[1]

My note to Mr. Canham makes mention of the subject in which

he is interested; Clarence Randall has promised to have a talk with you to describe it more fully.

I think you know of my great interest in expanding trade and in getting ourselves better prepared to meet the mounting economic offensive of the Sino-Soviet bloc.[2] Since Mr. Canham believes the Chamber of Commerce can be helpful by making available to the businessmen information now available within the government, I think that your office is the natural one to provide the focal point for his contact. I am sure you can do this on a very informal basis.

Clearly the State Department, Department of Agriculture, Labor Department, Council of Economic Advisers and even the CIA would have some interest in the matter. There may be others.

[1] Erwin Dain Canham (B.A. Bates College 1925), president of the U.S. Chamber of Commerce and head of the Manpower Council, had served with the *Christian Science Monitor* since 1925 as a correspondent, head of its Washington bureau, general news editor, managing editor, and editor since 1945. The Chamber of Commerce had set forth a proposal for helping American businessmen deal more effectively with the Communist economic offensive by making available more government information, particularly from the Department of Commerce. Eisenhower had written Canham that he was "delighted that you are planning to make available to the American businessman the kind of information that will be helpful to him in increasing profitable foreign trade" (AWF/D). See *New York Times*, September 24, 1959.
[2] See nos. 168, 768, and 1107; see also *New York Times*, November 10, 14, 15, 1959. There is no further correspondence on this subject in AWF.

1322   *EM, WHCF, Official File 3-A-17*

To Stuyvesant Wainwright II   *September 23, 1959*

Dear Stuyve: I have just had a report from Defense in respect to our exchange of letters about the possibility of converting the Boards of Visitors to the Service Academies into Boards of Trustees. The suggestion has been quite carefully evaluated.[1]

The study points up certain significant differences between a private and a public institution, the necessity to maintain close contact between the Academies and the Services in which the graduates serve, and the strong position of the present Boards of Visitors due to their direct access to the President. In the light of these considerations the study concludes that the Board of Trustees concept would be impracticable and that the Boards of Visitors can, upon request, provide any additional information to the President and the Congress.[2]

I incline to agree with the study's findings. If it occurs to you that more definitive instructions might be given to the Boards of Visitors, in the light of your own experience with Board procedures, please forward your suggestions and I will see that they are kept at hand for possible future use.[3]

With warm regard, *Sincerely*

[1] Congressman Wainwright (Rep., New York), had asked the President to have a study made of the functions of the boards of visitors attached to each service academy. He suggested that these investigating committees be replaced by boards of trustees, similar to those found at Yale, Harvard, and Columbia universities. Each of the current boards was "no more than a rubber stamp for an Academy Superintendent," and he felt that Eisenhower, as a West Point graduate and past president of Columbia University, should be apprised of this "defect" (Wainwright to Eisenhower, May 26, 1959). Eisenhower had replied, in a letter drafted by Goodpaster, that he thought the idea was "interesting" and that he would make the request (Eisenhower to Wainwright, June 2, 1959). Goodpaster, also a graduate of West Point, suggested that the Department of Defense should study the matter (Eisenhower to Wainwright, June 2, 1959; Goodpaster to Harlow, n.d.; Harlow to Persons, n.d.).

[2] Eisenhower's letter was based on a report submitted by the Department of the Army, in collaboration with the Departments of the Navy and Air Force. The Army report had pointed out that the university boards had decision-making powers, while the United States Military Academy's Board of Visitors (established in 1816) could only inspect and make recommendations; the ultimate authority rested with the military departments, Congress and the President (Hogue to Goodpaster, June 18, Short to Assistant Secretary of Defense for Manpower, Personnel, and Reserve; Harlow to Persons, n.d.; and Roche to Goodpaster, Sept. 11, 1959). All correspondence is in the same file as the document. For background on the Board of Visitors see Ambrose, *Duty, Honor, Country*, p. 56 and *passim*.

[3] Wainwright currently served as a rotating member of the U.S. Military Academy Board of Visitors.

1323   *EM, AWF, International Series:*
                                                        Macmillan

To Harold Macmillan   *September 24, 1959*
Cable. Secret

Dear Harold:[1] Thank you for your letter of September sixteenth.[2] Since I wrote to you on the eleventh an event has, of course, occurred which is of capital importance—the de Gaulle announcement of the Algerian program.[3] While we still have not had time to make a detailed analysis of this complex plan, and it is apparent immediately that there will be difficulties involved (as is inevitable in a matter of this delicacy), you have possibly noted that I publicly stated it is a program which deserves our support.[4] Secretary Herter also made a statement on behalf of our UN delegation in an effort to be helpful to the de Gaulle program.[5]

I have seen the supporting statement of the Foreign Office in London and the favorable London press reaction to the de Gaulle plan which matches the generally favorable attitude of our own press. I believe that you and ourselves should keep in the closest possible touch on this whole Algerian problem and specifically with reference to the tactical problems which are bound to arise in the UNGA debate on the subject, where we wish to avoid a repetition of the situation which developed last year when French sensibilities became injured.[6]

With regard to the difficulties which we have encountered in achieving our NATO objectives, I have written General de Gaulle a letter, in which I outlined my views on the principal outstanding issues, such as the French Mediterranean Fleet, the questions of stockpiling atomic weapons, and the broader concept of integrated defense in the NATO area.[7] All of these views are of course well known to you. I feel sure my letter will be read sympathetically by General de Gaulle even if he does not agree fully.[8] I hope it may be useful in convincing him that in our NATO defense concepts, we are merely trying to achieve the maximum security for us all.

On the subject of tripartite consultations, we will probably be moving ahead shortly, since you indicate in your letter of September sixteenth that you are willing to participate in informal talks on matters of interest outside the NATO area, on the understanding of course that no new institutions are created.[9] It is our understanding that the French wish talks to begin, perhaps in the first instance on Moroccan and Tunisian subjects, and our people will be in touch with yours on this subject.

Finally, I want to thank you again for your kind words about my trip to Europe from which I derived the greatest pleasure and which was, I hope, useful.[10] I shall soon be in touch with you again to tell you about the substance of the current visit of Chairman Khrushchev to the United States. What a pity we cannot talk to him without an interpreter. I have the feeling that if each of us could talk to him, alone, in a common language, we could do better.[11]

With warm regard, *As ever*

---

[1] A draft of this letter with Eisenhower's handwritten emendations is in AWF/M: G.

[2] Macmillan's letter is in PREM 11/3002. Taking note of the French people's "most enthusiastic reception" for Eisenhower on his European trip (see no. 1282), Macmillan had written that he had "never believed the tales of French hostility."

[3] On de Gaulle's program for Algeria see no. 1309.

[4] For Eisenhower's positive comments on de Gaulle's proposal see *Public Papers of the Presidents: Eisenhower, 1959*, p. 665.

[5] Herter had made his remarks to the United Nations Correspondents Association in New York on September 22 (see "The U.N. as a Peace Mechanism," *U.S. Department of State Bulletin* 41, no. 1059 [October 12, 1959], 502–4; see also *ibid.*, 500–501).

[6] The French had objected when the United States had abstained from voting on a

December 1958 resolution for Algerian independence in the United Nations (see nos. 974 and 1309; see also State, *Foreign Relations, 1958–1960,* vol. XIII, *Arab-Israeli Dispute; United Arab Republic; North Africa,* pp. 646–47).

[7] Eisenhower's letter to de Gaulle is no. 1318.

[8] Eisenhower had substituted this sentence for one in the draft that began: "I do not believe this letter is so phrased that it will cause any trouble. . . ."

[9] For background on tripartite discussions among Great Britain, France, and the United States see no. 1106. The consultations could be between military experts, Macmillan had written, "always provided that no new formal institutions are created. After all," he added, "our Governments are free to have private discussions with what other governments they choose, on an informal basis" (PREM 11/3002; see also Draft Message to the President, n.d., PREM 11/2997).

[10] Macmillan had written that Eisenhower's European trip had strengthened the unity of the West. "Of course no member of a democratic alliance thinks exactly like every other member on every point," Macmillan said. "But your journey will have made people realize that any differences ought to be reconciled in view of the great issues at stake."

[11] Eisenhower added the previous two sentences to the original draft. For developments see no. 1328.

1324   *EM, AWF, DDE Diaries Series*

To ROBERT BERNERD ANDERSON   *September 25, 1959*

Dear Bob: I have done a bit of editing on your draft.[1] As you will see, I have shortened it some by eliminating the percentages and other statistics. I did this because I am quite certain that these figures and percentages will be discussed by other speakers, and I think the Governors will not expect me to deal in specifics.

I invite your particular attention to one short paragraph I have inserted. It is the third from the end, beginning "Clearly, by such action . . .".[2] I think this is an obvious statement, but I think also it might be a useful one to make for the simple reason that we want the other nations to know that we expect greater contributions from them both as a matter of a more stable free world and also as a matter of the self-interest of each.

I hope you will return the draft to Mrs. Whitman as quickly as possible, together with any comments you want to make. *As ever*

[1] The Secretary of the Treasury had drafted a welcoming speech for Eisenhower to give at the annual meeting of the Boards of Governors of the International Bank for Reconstruction and Development (the World Bank), the International Monetary Fund, and the International Finance Corporation. The draft is not in EM. At the meeting held on September 29, 1959, Eisenhower would mention the improved state of the U.S. economy, the stable consumer price index, and the balanced federal budget. All these, he would say, were "significant signs of the progress that can be made if we pursue the right policies in strengthening the financial bases of our economy

and achieving inflation free economic growth." The final draft of the speech is in AWF/A; see also *Public Papers of the Presidents: Eisenhower, 1959*, pp. 702–4.

[2] In his speech Eisenhower would state that taking steps to increase international capital investment was important for less-developed nations as well as for industrialized countries, and he would conclude that "clearly, by such actions there will result a stronger and more stable free world to the material benefits of every participating nation, both the helper and the helped." Eisenhower would also express his support for the proposed International Development Association (*ibid.*; see no. 831).

1325   *EM, AWF, International Series: Germany*

To Konrad Adenauer   *September 28, 1959*
Confidential

Dear Mr. Chancellor: I know how interested you are in the results of my meetings with Mr. Khrushchev.[1] I expect very shortly to send you a summary of all that occurred and follow that up with my more considered personal impressions of the man and what the visit so far may have accomplished.[2]

Meanwhile, however, I want to send you immediate word concerning my discussions with Mr. Khrushchev regarding West Berlin. I do so particularly because some confusion seems to have arisen out of one question posed in my press conference this morning.[3]

At the outset let me say that I made the situation of Berlin and the removal by the Soviet Government of any appearance of a threat or time limit to the settlement of this problem the touchstone of my talks with the Chairman. Indeed, the fact that we did not cover the list of items which we had informally agreed we would try to cover at Camp David was due to the prolongation of our discussions on the subject of Berlin and my insistence that any hint of duress must be specifically removed before I was prepared to talk about anything else.[4]

Mr. Khrushchev finally accepted the fact of our determination to insure the security and freedom of the people of West Berlin. This I told him was a responsibility and an obligation which we had accepted and from which we would not be driven. I told him that we were prepared to resume negotiations on the Berlin question subject, of course, to agreement by the others directly concerned—the British, the French, and yourself. I told him that we would negotiate in good faith for a solution which would assure the freedom and security of West Berliners. I said that we had no intention of prolonging those negotiations indefinitely but that we would not enter upon them if there was to be any time limit fixed for their conclusion. He agreed to this and I so stated publicly this morning. Mr.

Khrushchev also assured me that he would publicly confirm this understanding, and I am momentarily awaiting word that he has done so.[5]

The problem of a divided Berlin, as you and I have agreed, is like the problem of a divided Germany, abnormal and unjust. The logical solution is the reunification of Germany and this remains our objective. But the attainment of that objective may, and it seems probably will, be postponed for a considerable time and I feel that we must seek a firm arrangement under which the people of West Berlin are secure in their freedom and from any harassment against themselves, their economy and their communications, and are not interfered with in their movement to and from the city and the Federal Republic. Such an arrangement or solution we will do our best to find, one that is fair to all, so far as this may be achieved within a divided Germany. Meanwhile, I know I don't have to tell you after our talks in Bonn last month that the United States is resolved together with its allies to safeguard the freedom and security of the people of West Berlin, so long as this may be necessary.[6]

With warm regard, *From your friend*

[1] On the Khrushchev visit see no. 1320.

[2] Eisenhower's subsequent letter to the West German leader is no. 1333.

[3] The Berlin discussions, which took place at Camp David on September 26–27, are in State, *Foreign Relations, 1958–1960*, vol. IX, *Berlin Crisis 1959–1960; Germany; Austria*, pp. 35–45.

A correspondent had asked Eisenhower whether any solution to the Berlin problem would guarantee allied rights in the city and protect the freedom of the citizens in West Berlin. "I can't guarantee anything of this kind," Eisenhower had answered, "for the simple reason I don't know what kind of a solution may finally prove acceptable." His response had raised concerns in Bonn that the allied position on West Berlin was weakening. The White House later released a statement declaring that any Berlin agreement had to be acceptable to the people of West Berlin and the West German government (*Public Papers of the Presidents: Eisenhower, 1959*, p. 702; Goodpaster, Memorandum of Conference, Sept. 30, 1959, AWF/D; Telephone conversation, Hagerty to Herter, Sept. 29, 1959, Herter Papers, Telephone Conversations; and *New York Times*, Sept. 29, 1959).

According to Secretary Herter, the State Department had prepared the draft of this letter to "dispel any uneasiness which alarmist newspaper reports might arouse" (Herter to Eisenhower, Sept. 28, 1959, AWF/D-H).

[4] For the list of agenda items see State, *Foreign Relations, 1958–1960*, vol. X, pt. 1, *Eastern Europe Region; Soviet Union; Cyprus*, pp. 467–68. On Khrushchev's ultimatum regarding Berlin see no. 983.

[5] On his arrival in Moscow on this same day Khrushchev would tell the Soviet people that he had the impression that Eisenhower "sincerely wanted to liquidate the 'cold war' and to improve relations between our two great countries." He would also deny that there had ever been any ultimatum regarding Berlin (*New York Times*, Sept. 29, 1959; see also Eisenhower, *Waging Peace*, p. 447).

[6] For developments see no. 1333.

1326
EM, AWF,
International Series:
Khrushchev

To Nikita Sergeyevich Khrushchev   *September 28, 1959*
Cable

Dear Mr. Chairman: I am grateful for the cordial message you sent
to me from your plane, as you left the United States, and glad that
you found both pleasant and interesting the brief visit to our country by yourself, your family and members of your official party.[1] For
my part I found the meetings with you most interesting, instructive
and pleasant.

It is gratifying to know that you feel our discussions may constitute
some small step in the promotion of mutual understanding and the
reduction of the causes of those international tensions which have
brought us great difficulty in the past. We share the hope that concrete and meaningful progress in the important field of disarmament
can be made. Nothing could be more useful than progressive and mutually fair discussions in the promotion of the just and durable peace
which I am sure the peoples of both our countries earnestly seek.

The members of my family join me in greetings to you and your
family, and the assurance that we look forward to our later visit to
your country.[2]

With the prayerful hope that such meetings as this will prove of
real benefit to the world, and with personal wishes for the health
and well-being of yourself, your family, and the people of the Soviet
Union. *Sincerely*

[1] In his letter of thanks Khrushchev had told Eisenhower that the exchange of views
had shown that the desire to end the cold war in an atmosphere of confidence and
mutual understanding was "steadily gaining the upper hand" (Khrushchev to Eisenhower, Sept. 28, 1959, AWF/I: Khrushchev).
[2] For developments regarding Eisenhower's proposed trip to the Soviet Union see
no. 1386.

1327
EM, AWF,
International Series:
Khrushchev

To Nikita Sergeyevich Khrushchev   *September 29, 1959*

Dear Mr. Chairman: I have been thinking over what you were saying
to me on Sunday at Camp David in regard to the question of China.

In view of the number of subjects on which our thinking seemed to be coming closer together, the exposition of your views on this one point disturbs me. Consequently, I felt the need to give to you immediately our views in somewhat more detail than was possible at Camp David, and in the spirit of frank exchange of views which we both agreed would be valuable.[1]

You left me with the clear impression that you thought the People's Republic of China had the right to seek to take territory of the Republic of China, that is to say Taiwan, the Pescadores and other islands, by force of arms. If I understood you correctly, you further thought that this was a question of civil war and that the Government of the Republic of China under President Chiang Kai-shek should in fact be regarded as a rebel defying the legitimate government of the country. You emphasized that in your view this grave question relating to China was a domestic question and not an international question.[2]

I feel that in the interest of understanding between us I must state in all frankness that I cannot agree that this is purely a domestic question. The China question is important to our common interest in the peace of the world. Some 45 countries including the United States recognize the Republic of China as the legitimate government of that country. As for the United States, we have a formal treaty of mutual defense with the Republic of China. Under these circumstances, the proposition that the People's Republic is entitled to enforce its will on the Republic of China by force of arms is inconsistent with the needs of peace and is at variance with our common objectives.[3]

The world in which we live is in a sense an indivisible one. I must say that I find a disturbing contrast between what you said to me on China toward the close of our talks and what you said to me with regard to the question of Germany, which is also a great—and divided—country.[4] You spoke of the need for a peaceful solution of the German question but you said the People's Republic could legitimately use force in China. We, of course, disagree with this view. In my view both are international matters. I have expressed my willingness to discuss the German question seriously with you and the other interested parties in the hope of reaching a peaceful conclusion in the interest of our two countries and mankind as a whole. I think that the question of China can, in time, be resolved the same way. At the same time, I agree with you that this question has not, at this moment, matured to the point where rapid progress through negotiation could be foreseen. I feel, however, that this fact makes all the more necessary a policy of restraint and moderation, in order to prevent further exacerbation and threat to peace.

You have also stressed to me that the central question of our times is disarmament and I have agreed with you both privately and publicly.[5] I cannot think of any way in which to destroy our common objective, disarmament, more effectively than to endorse the use of force against the Republic of China. In the case of all the other countries so tragically divided in the post-war years, there has been a renunciation of the use of force on both sides, either as a result of an armistice, an agreement or some other act having practical effect, but in the sole case of China one side continues to insist that the use of force is legitimate.

Having in mind the great effort which you and I have made to take a step which would lessen the chance of international conflict, and having in mind how much the peoples of all countries look to you and me at this time in this regard, I await your reply in the hope that, even with regard to the strained situation that exists in China, we can guide our respective courses in such a way as to help safeguard peace.

In sending this message directly to you, I am sure you will understand that I feel that strictly personal exchanges of views between us can at times be of value in the continuation of the type of frank discussion which we held together at Camp David.[6] *Sincerely*

[1] On Khrushchev's visit see nos. 1320 and 1326. The substance of Eisenhower's discussions with Khrushchev on China are reviewed in the following document (see no. 1328). See also State, *Foreign Relations, 1958–1960*, vol. X, pt. 1, *Eastern Europe Region; Soviet Union; Cyprus*, pp. 388–92, 477–82. For background see no. 1292; Chang, *Friends and Enemies*, pp. 208–13.

[2] Khrushchev had told the President that the Soviet Union agreed with the Chinese position that Taiwan was a province of China. The determination of the future of Taiwan was part of the process of the Chinese revolution, and the Soviet Union fully understood China's aspirations in that respect. Khrushchev said that he believed that the Chinese Communists had the right to liberate Taiwan "from a Chinese general who has mutinied against the Government" (*ibid.*, p. 480). Secretary of State Christian Herter had responded to Khrushchev's comments with a memorandum to the President and a draft of this letter to the Soviet Premier. "All day I have been haunted by the statements made by Mr. Khrushchev with regard to Taiwan," Herter wrote Eisenhower. "They are so completely contrary to the spirit of the things for which you, and ostensibly he, are working" (Herter memorandum, Sept. 28, 1959, Herter Papers).

Eisenhower would discuss the issue with Herter on the afternoon of September 29. He told Herter that he redrafted the letter, shortened it, and slightly changed its tone to make it more in keeping with his talks with Khrushchev. Herter was worried that Khrushchev was going to claim that Taiwan was not an "international question," and he reiterated the importance of including language regarding "outstanding international questions being settled peacefully." Eisenhower agreed and noted that he had changed the tone rather than the meaning of Herter's letter (Telephone conversation, Eisenhower and Herter, Sept. 29, 1959, Herter Papers, Telephone Conversations; see also Herter memorandum, Oct. 28, 1959, AWF/D-H).

[3] See Chang, *Friends and Enemies*, pp. 12–42, 81–115.

[4] See nos. 1325 and 1333.

[5] For the disarmament discussions see State, *Foreign Relations, 1958–1960*, vol. III, *National Security Policy; Arms Control and Disarmament*, pp. 776–77; see also no. 1332.
[6] For further discussions on the China question see the following document.

1328   *EM, AWF, International Series:*
                                                              Macmillan

To HAROLD MACMILLAN   *September 29, 1959*
Top secret

Dear Harold: Thank you very much for your two notes.[1] Only time will tell whether congratulations are in order. The most I can say at this moment is that the meeting with Mr. Khrushchev did not end up on the truly sour note that it well could have. I believe he is sincere in his desire for helping arrange a program of disarmament. He talked to me at great length about costs in armaments and the sacrifices that their manufacture demands of citizens everywhere. Moreover, I believe he is genuine in his anxiety that there should be no general war.[2]

It was difficult for him to get off his initially rigid position respecting Berlin, but he finally did it in the proposal of a sentence to the effect that "negotiations should not be prolonged indefinitely, but no time limit is fixed upon them."[3]

The one place where he has taken a very strong position, with no deviation is respecting China. He likens Chiang Kai-shek to a rebellious general fighting against his own proper government. In other words, he is a traitor and a brigand and the whole China-Formosa dispute is an "internal matter." He apparently sees no connection whatsoever between a divided Germany and a divided China. In all cases he urges that we have peaceful negotiations to settle our international affairs, except as to China—in this affair he says that China has a right to "complete its revolution."[4]

On this matter I merely told him that our views were diametrically opposed on every point and there was little use of his arguing the matter. However, after reflecting on some of his extraordinary statements about China, I sent him a letter which, though friendly in tone, should leave him no doubt as to the firmness of our attitude in supporting the Nationalist Chinese.[5] After all, forty-two nations have recognized that country.

I have not heard further from General de Gaulle, although I sent him a very friendly letter respecting NATO affairs.[6] While I don't assume for a moment that this will settle these matters, I do think our approval of his enlightened approach to the Algeria question will do something to make him see things in a broader light. Incidentally, my personal conferences with him were interesting and even enjoyable.[7]

If I get any positive reaction from any quarter respecting my recent conference, I shall keep you advised.[8]

With warm regard, *As ever*

[1] Macmillan had written in response to Eisenhower's September 24 letter regarding French President de Gaulle's program for Algeria (no. 1323; on the Algerian proposals see no. 1309). Macmillan had endorsed the proposals and had stressed the importance of the forthcoming debate on Algeria in the United Nations. Although the best result would be a resolution endorsing de Gaulle's plan, Macmillan wrote, he hoped the General Assembly would do nothing that would jeopardize the chances for success. He also welcomed Eisenhower's suggestion that the U.S. and British delegations at the United Nations work together on the issue.

Macmillan told Eisenhower that he thought he had "handled" Soviet Premier Khrushchev "splendidly" and hoped that "his occasional outbursts of rage" had not given the President too much trouble (Macmillan to Eisenhower, Sept. 28, 1959, PREM 11/2687).

In a second message Macmillan had congratulated Eisenhower on his visits to London, Bonn, and Paris and had told the President that he had made "an immense contribution to the understanding between the Western allies" (Macmillan to Eisenhower, Sept. 28, 1959, PREM 11/2675; see also no. 1309).

[2] For the disarmament discussions see State, *Foreign Relations, 1958–1960,* vol. III, *National Security Policy; Arms Control and Disarmament,* pp. 776–77.

[3] On these discussions see no. 1325.

[4] See the preceding document. The discussions regarding China are in State, *Foreign Relations, 1958–1960,* vol. X, pt. 1, *Eastern Europe Region; Soviet Union; Cyprus,* pp. 479–82.

[5] See no. 1327.

[6] Eisenhower's letter to de Gaulle is no. 1318.

[7] See no. 1309.

[8] For developments see no. 1332.

1329   *EM, AWF, Dulles-Herter Series*

To CHRISTIAN ARCHIBALD HERTER   *September 29, 1959*
Personal

Dear Chris: I think we should keep on the ball with respect to all the subjects that we considered in our recent conferences.[1] Wherever any of these, and particularly those with Khrushchev, suggest or indicate some needed action on our part, I think we should act as promptly as we can get the particular points studied and decisions made.

For example, I am thinking of such things as exchanges on peaceful uses of atomic energy, trade in general, broadening of other kinds of contacts, Mr. K's statement that they would be glad to avoid jamming of everything except appeals made to the Soviet peoples over the head of the government (in other words, the kind of thing that he regards as an attempt to set his people against him) and any other subjects which we should follow up rapidly.[2]

In any case where we have to use diplomatic channels, I suggest that we use our Ambassador to Moscow rather than the Soviet Ambassador to this country. The reason for this should be obvious.[3] *As ever*

---

[1] Memorandums of conversations between Eisenhower and Khrushchev and among other U.S. and Soviet officials are in State, *Foreign Relations, 1958–1960*, vol. X, pt. 1, *Eastern Europe Region; Soviet Union; Cyprus*, pp. 392–428, 432–39, 442–44, 448–54, 459–83; and *ibid.*, vol. IX, *Berlin Crisis 1959–1960; Germany; Austria*, pp. 35–45, 47–49. Memorandums of conferences among Eisenhower and State Department officials are in AWF/D.

[2] U.N. Ambassador Lodge, who had accompanied Khrushchev on his cross-country tour of the United States, had told Eisenhower of the Soviet leader's willingness to "ease up" on the jamming of certain Voice of America broadcasts (State, *Foreign Relations, 1958–1960*, vol. X, pt. 1, *Eastern Europe Region; Soviet Union; Cyprus*, p. 455).

[3] Llewellyn E. Thompson, the U.S. Ambassador to the Soviet Union, had also accompanied Khrushchev on his travels. For background on Soviet Ambassador Mikhail Menshikov and Eisenhower's first impressions of the diplomat see no. 580. According to Thompson, Menshikov "was constantly feeding poison to Khrushchev throughout the trip." This was confirmed by Lodge, who said that Menshikov had taken every opportunity he could to criticize the United States. Eisenhower indicated that he considered Menshikov "evil and stupid" (Goodpaster, Memorandum of Conference, Sept. 28, 1959, AWF/D; see also Henry Cabot Lodge, *The Storm Has Many Eyes* [New York, 1973], pp. 157–81).

Herter would agree to moving ahead promptly on the subjects discussed and added that he "thoroughly understood" Eisenhower's remark regarding Thompson. He also noted the urgency Eisenhower had attached to the jamming of VOA broadcasts and agreed to "get to work immediately" on the issue (Herter to Eisenhower, Oct. 1, 1959, AWF/D-H). In the first status report on matters discussed by the two leaders, Herter would tell Eisenhower that the State Department had been in close touch with the United States Information Agency and that the VOA had been instructed "to watch its programs carefully with a view to eliminating as much provocative material as possible" (Herter to Eisenhower, Oct. 8, 1959, AWF/D-H; see also Herter to Eisenhower, Nov. 14, 1959, *ibid.*). For developments see no. 1338.

1330   *EM, AWF, Administration Series*

To Henry Cabot Lodge   *September 29, 1959*

Dear Cabot: It is always difficult for any male of the Anglo-Saxon strain to pay a direct tribute or compliment to another of the same sex and the same blood. We have never adopted the Latin customs of the "abrazo" or the kiss on both cheeks. Consequently I was not very successful in telling you how impressed I was by your performance during Chairman Khrushchev's visit to the United States and how grateful I am for the skill you displayed.[1]

I admired your patience and self-control, as did I your diplomatic proficiency and the easy and friendly manner you exhibited throughout the tour.[2] In all of this, of course, I include Mrs. Lodge, who went out of her way, I know, to assure that Mrs. Khrushcheva and her daughters had an enjoyable and successful visit to our country.[3]

In short, I am deeply appreciative of the efforts of both of you, and I do hope that now you will manage, despite your UN duties, to get a little well-deserved rest.

With warm regard, *As ever*

[1] The President had selected Lodge as his personal representative and host in order to facilitate Soviet Premier Khrushchev's tour of seven U.S. cities (*New York Times*, Aug. 23, 1959). Eisenhower had thanked Lodge at a White House conference on September 25 (Memorandum of Conversation with the President, Sept. 28, 1959, AWF/D). For background on Khrushchev's visit see no. 1265.

[2] Lodge's role is discussed in Eisenhower, *Waging Peace*, pp. 432–49; Khrushchev, *Khrushchev Remembers*, pp. 368–416, esp. pp. 379–80, 403, 489; and Lodge, *The Storm has Many Eyes*, pp. 158–59, 162, 181.

[3] Mrs. Lodge was the former Emily Sears. The family members in the Soviet leader's party were his wife Nina Petrovna Khrushchev, his son Sergei, daughters Yuliya Gontar and Rada Adzhubei, and his son-in-law Alexis I. Adzhubei (see also *New York Times*, Sept. 18, 1959).

1331   *EM, WHCF, President's Personal File 350*

To Charles R. Yates   *September 29, 1959*

Dear Charlie: I never thought I would make such an assertion, but it is a relief, after ten days of Mr. Khrushchev, to get back to some of the politiking that goes on in the United States, as illustrated by the letter from your Democratic friend.[1]

Many thanks for your own efforts, which I note are intensive and subtle!

With warm regard, *As ever*

[1] On Soviet Premier Nikita Khrushchev's tour of the United States see, for example, nos. 1265 and 1326. Yates had sent the letter through Presidential Secretary Ann Whitman suggesting that it may give her "wonderful boss" a reason to "chuckle." Yates had received a note in reply to a mail solicitation in connection with a Republican fund-raising dinner to be held in Georgia. The author of the letter, a Democrat, had described himself as not on Yates's list of "fat cats," but he admitted that

he had purchased a ticket because he felt the President merited the "support of all Americans." He had added that the Democrats' recent political misfortunes had left them "as confused as bastards on Fathers Day" (see Milstead to Yates, Sept. 12, 1959, and Yates to Whitman, Sept. 23, 1959, both in same file as document).

1332

EM, AWF, International Series:
Macmillan

To HAROLD MACMILLAN
Cable. Secret

September 30, 1959

Dear Harold: The enclosed memorandum describes in greater detail than my letter of yesterday the course taken by the talks with Mr. Khrushchev at Camp David last week end.[1] In conjunction with the final communique and the reports of my press conference, it gives a rather complete picture of the nature of the conversations.[2]

The range of our talks turned out to be quite limited—simply because of the amount of time we spent on Berlin. From the outset, I tried to make clear to Mr. Khrushchev my conviction that there would be no profit in detailed discussions of other matters while the Berlin problem remained in its present unsatisfactory situation.[3]

With warm regard, *As ever*

[1] Eisenhower's previous letter is no. 1328. The President would send similar letters and the memorandum to German Chancellor Adenauer and French President de Gaulle (see the following document and Eisenhower to de Gaulle, Sept. 30, 1959, AWF/I: de Gaulle).

According to the memorandum, the talks were "carried out in a generally dispassionate, objective, and calm tone" with "no harangues or outbursts" from Khrushchev. Khrushchev had denied any attempt to take unilateral action in Berlin and said that although the Soviets wanted to solve the German problem through negotiation, he could accept no agreement that would perpetuate the occupation of Berlin indefinitely. Eisenhower and Khrushchev agreed that the negotiations on Berlin would not be prolonged indefinitely but that they would set no fixed time limit on their duration.

The two men discussed the issue of arms limitation only in general terms. Both agreed that extravagant costs and inherent dangers were involved in the arms race and that disarmament was the most serious issue facing the international community.

Eisenhower told Khrushchev that because of their busy schedules that his proposed visit to the Soviet Union might be postponed. Khrushchev agreed and suggested that the best time for a visit would be May or June.

After Khrushchev had suggested that a summit conference be held before the President's visit to the Soviet Union, Eisenhower stated that he would have to consult with U.S. allies on this question. In any event, he said, a summit conference could not take place as long as threats to Berlin remained.

Khrushchev had raised the issue of Communist China in view of his forthcoming visit to that country. He compared a divided Germany with a divided China and charged the United States with inconsistency in its insistence on reunification on the one hand and support of a separate government on the other. Although Eisenhower "admitted some comparison was possible," he stressed the importance of peaceful solutions in both cases. The two men concluded that further discussion of the Chinese situation was pointless.

Although Eisenhower and Khrushchev had not discussed exchanges in detail, they reaffirmed their support of reciprocal agreements in scientific, technical, and cultural areas.

In addition to the discussions between the President and the Soviet leader, State Department and Atomic Energy Commission officials and members the Soviet delegation had discussed a non-aggression treaty, trade restrictions, peaceful uses of atomic energy, travel restrictions, and the establishment of consulates in Leningrad and New York (Memorandum—President Eisenhower's Talks with Chairman Khrushchev at Camp David, Sept. 30, 1959, AWF/I: Macmillan; for Eisenhower's account of these conversations see Eisenhower, *Waging Peace,* pp. 405–13; see also John S. D. Eisenhower, *Strictly Personal,* pp. 254–64; Lodge, *The Storm Has Many Eyes,* pp. 157–81; and Khrushchev, *Khrushchev Remembers,* pp. 368–416).

[2] For both Eisenhower's news conference remarks and the communiqué see *Public Papers of the Presidents: Eisenhower, 1959,* pp. 694–702.

[3] For developments see no. 1338.

1333   *EM, AWF, International Series: Adenauer*

TO KONRAD ADENAUER   *September 30, 1959*

Secret

My good friend: The summary of my conversations with Chairman Khrushchev is now completed and, as I promised in my communication of September twenty-eighth, I am sending it along to you for your confidential information.[1]

You will also be able to glean some of the atmosphere of our talks from the communique which was issued and from the press conference which I held on Monday.[2] As I indicated to you when I saw you last at the end of August, I did not consider my meetings with Mr. Khrushchev as an occasion for negotiation since the issues between the United States and the Soviet Union largely involve the interest of the Allies of the United States.[3] You will have gathered that no detailed negotiations of any kind have in fact taken place.

I shall be in touch with you further as to the form and timing of our future negotiations with the Soviets. On balance, I think that the visit of Mr. Khrushchev to this country was advantageous. We did not expect any concrete result to emerge from the trip. I think that the visit has had an impact which will favorably affect the course of affairs in the future.[4]

With warm regard, *Sincerely*

[1] For the summary of the conversations see the preceding document. Eisenhower's earlier message to Adenauer is no. 1325. The text of this letter was cabled to the American ambassador in Bonn for delivery to Adenauer on this same date.
[2] For Eisenhower's news conference remarks and the communiqué see *Public Papers of the Presidents: Eisenhower, 1959*, pp. 694–702.
[3] Eisenhower had visited the German leader on August 27 (see State, *Foreign Relations, 1958–1960*, vol. IX, *Berlin Crisis 1959–1960; Germany; Austria*, pp. 10–13, 19–25).
[4] For developments see no. 1338.

1334

EM, AWF,
International Series:
Khrushchev

To Nikita Sergeyevich Khrushchev

October 1, 1959

Dear Mr. Chairman: I am writing to you to raise one question which, in our concentration on other matters, I did not take up with you during our talks at Camp David.[1] This is the question of the fate of the eleven men who are still missing since September 2, 1958 from the C-130 United States Air Force transport aircraft.[2]

I know you will understand the deep concern of the families of these men who continue to hope that some indication of their fate will yet be uncovered. I know of Vice President Nixon's exchange of letters with you about this case, and I want to express my own hope that the appropriate Soviet services will again look into this question to see if there is further information which I can provide to the families of the missing airmen.[3] I am encouraged to renew this personal appeal because of the fine and understanding attitude you took toward such human problems during our talks at Camp David.[4] *Sincerely*

[1] Premier Khrushchev had visited the United States September 11–25. On the talks at the presidential retreat see no. 1332.
[2] On September 13 the Soviet Union had reported that the missing C-130 Hercules turboprop plane, carrying seventeen persons, had crashed in Soviet Armenia, killing six of its crew. The State Department had sent instructions to the U.S. embassy in Moscow to press the Soviets on an "urgent basis" to locate and return the remaining airmen. Moscow had failed to release information concerning the missing eleven and had ignored a State Department request to inspect the site of the crash (*New York Times*, Sept. 4, 5, 7, 13, 14, 1958).
[3] On August 1 Vice-President Nixon had queried Khrushchev about the fate of the missing men. Khrushchev had replied on August 22 that raising the question after the Soviet Government had done "everything in its power" to cooperate in the investigation was "regarded as . . . an attempt to set up artificial barriers in the way of an improvement in American-Soviet relations." Khrushchev denied that the Soviets

had shot down the plane, contended that the remains of the six men had been returned to the United States, and declined to address the question of the remaining eleven (both in AWF/I: Khrushchev).

[4] In view of the public interest in the case, Secretary Herter had suggested that the President write "a brief and non-contentious inquiry" about the matter to Khrushchev (Herter to Eisenhower, Sept. 30, 1959, AWF/I: Khrushchev).

According to Herter, Khrushchev's October 10 reply would provide "nothing new," and it was "'highly unlikely'" that information would be given on the fate of the eleven men. On October 29 the President would send personal messages of sympathy to their families (State, *Foreign Relations, 1958–1960*, vol. X, pt. 1, *Eastern Europe Region; Soviet Union; Cyprus*, pp. 186–89).

1335   *EM, WHCF, Official File 106-I*

To James Churchill Oliver   *October 1, 1959*

Dear Mr. Oliver: I have your recent letter regarding the food needs of unfortunate people in Maine and in other parts of the country.

You propose the implementation of the Food Stamp Plan, which was authorized, though not made mandatory, in the recent session of the Congress.[1]

I indicated, in signing the legislation to which you refer, that the Food Stamp Plan would not result in providing additional supplies of food to our needy people.[2] If there is a serious question as to whether needy persons in your District are receiving adequate supplies of food, the program presently operating should be reviewed.

I am asking for a report from the Department of Agriculture on the status of the program in your area. When this has been supplied I shall see that you are informed.[3] *Sincerely*

[1] Representative Oliver (A.B. Bowdoin College 1917) was a former real estate developer from Maine. A Democrat, Oliver had been elected to Congress in 1958 and served on the House Merchant Marine and Fisheries Committee. He had asked the President to implement the new pilot food stamp program in the economically depressed areas of his district (Oliver to Eisenhower, Sept. 25, 1959, same file as document). Eisenhower, who had not favored the congressional plan for the distribution of surplus commodities to the poor, had reluctantly approved it on September 2. The provision had been passed as part of a law extending the Agricultural Trade and Assistance Act of 1954 (P.L. 480). Under this legislation, surplus agricultural commodities were to be sold for foreign currencies, bartered for certain materials, or distributed for foreign or domestic relief operations (for background see Galambos and van Ee, *The Middle Way*, nos. 652 and 787).

The food stamp program was to be implemented at the discretion of the Secretary of Agriculture and only when requested by state or local governments. Oliver was concerned that Eisenhower had not chosen to utilize it. The present system, Oliver said, failed to provide the needy with adequate food supplies for a balanced diet. He argued that no one should "shrink" from the responsibility of meeting minimum standards because of "ideological reasons," and he implied that Eisenhower was unfamiliar with the limitations of his own program: "Of course, you have never stood in one of these food lines and observed the inadequacies and the indecencies of the present distribution plan" (see Jeffrey M. Berry, *Feeding Hungry People: Rulemaking in the Food Stamp Program* [New Brunswick, N.J., 1984], pp. 21–23; Trudy Huskamp Peterson, *Agricultural Exports, Farm Income, and the Eisenhower Administration* [Lincoln, Neb., 1979], pp. 70–98).

White House Aide Bryce Harlow probably drafted this letter for the President. See Eisenhower's note to him in the same file as the document.

[2] Oliver had referred to the comments Eisenhower had made upon signing the bill into law. The President had complained that the food stamp plan, if implemented, would not only be ineffective but would also increase the already disproportionate federal share of welfare expense (*Congressional Quarterly Almanac*, vol. XV, *1959*, pp. 230–36).

[3] We were unable to locate any further correspondence regarding this matter in EM. The Administration would not implement the food stamp program.

1336   *Prime Minister's Office Records,*
                                                    PREM 11/2990

To Harold Macmillan   *October 2, 1959*
Cable. Top secret

Dear Harold: I appreciate greatly your letter of October 1 containing your comments on the visit of Mr. Khrushchev.[1] As you have correctly inferred in your public statements I feel that the way toward a Summit has now been cleared.[2] However, no specific times for the holding of a Summit were discussed with Mr. Khrushchev nor was there any discussion as to whether such a meeting should be asked for by any individual State. It is my own feeling that the time and the place should be arranged by diplomatic negotiation leading to a simultaneous announcement from the four capitals rather than that the initiative should be taken by myself. This procedure will of course take some time because of the necessity of concerting our positions. However, I can see no possible objection to your pursuing the lines that you have already taken with respect to the strong possibility of a Summit meeting as long as no specific agreement is indicated.[3]

With warm regard, *As ever*

[1] Macmillan had told Eisenhower that "the single most important point" gained in the Khrushchev talks was the Soviet leader's agreement to remove the threat from the Berlin situation, thus clearing the way to a summit meeting. "Personally," Macmillan stated, "I believe that this ought to take place soon and without another meeting of the foreign ministers. An early Summit, proposed by you, would keep the initiative with the West and prevent the Russians going back to the position of threat"

(same file as document; see also Telephone conversation, Herter and Goodpaster, Oct. 1, 1959, Herter Papers, Telephone Conversations).
² For Macmillan's public statements see the *London Times*, September 29, 1959.
³ For developments see no. 1338.

1337

To John Hay Whitney *October 3, 1959*

Dear Jock: Many thanks for your note of the twenty-eighth. You have properly impressed all the amateurs here in the desert (especially Bill) by the report of your prowess at St. Andrews.¹ But I should still like to know your score for the entire eighteen.

At the moment I just don't know where I shall be on the sixteenth, but if I am in Washington I shall, of course, be delighted to see you.² Ann will expect a call from you upon your arrival.

It goes without saying that we are watching the progress of the campaign in Great Britain with greatest interest. But when I stop to realize that the United States has already a bit of the frenzy that 1960 will produce, I again reflect on the great virtue of limiting the electioneering to three weeks.³

With affectionate regard to Betsey and, as always, the best to yourself. *As ever*

¹ Whitney had written following a week's vacation in Scotland (AWF/A). While playing golf at the fabled St. Andrews course, he had suddenly realized that he was in the process of posting a very low score on his round. The realization caused him to "four-putt and then take a seven at the next hole, but it was a big moment." The President and several friends, including William E. Robinson, were vacationing near Palm Springs, California (see no. 1313 and Ann Whitman memorandum, Oct. 8, 1959, AWF/AWD).
² Whitney would be in the United States to attend the marriage of his adopted stepdaughter, Kate Roosevelt, on October 17 (*New York Times*, Oct. 14, 18, 1959). As it turned out, Eisenhower would play golf with Whitney on October 16.
³ Whitney said he had watched "a lot of political television." He criticized the Conservatives for running a "very amateurish campaign." The Labor Party, on the other hand, had been "professional, almost to a fault," which contrasted with the "deadly smugness on the other side." Whitney concluded that the election would be close (see no. 1305; Macmillan, *Riding the Storm*, pp. 744–47, 750; and *London Times*, Sept. 17, 19, 23, Oct. 9, 1959). Members of Great Britain's House of Commons served maximum terms of five years. At any time during those five years, the prime minister had the right to dissolve Parliament and call a general election. Only three weeks notice had to be given for a general election.

To Harold Macmillan   *October 9, 1959*
Cable. Secret

Dear Harold: You will recall that in my account to you of my conversations with Mr. Khrushchev at Camp David I said that I had made
it clear to him that as far as a Summit conference was concerned I
could make no commitments without prior consultation with the
others concerned.[1] Accordingly I should like very much to learn
your present thoughts with respect to Mr. Khrushchev's proposal
that a Summit meeting be held before I visit the Soviet Union in
the Spring. I am also writing in this same vein to President de Gaulle
and Chancellor Adenauer.[2]

As a result of my discussions with Mr. Khrushchev at Camp David
I now have, as I indicated to you earlier, fewer objections to a Summit conference. The appearance of threat and duress in negotiating on the Berlin problem has in my opinion now been sufficiently
altered that I, for my part, would feel able to meet jointly in such a
conference with the Soviet Chairman. Although Mr. Khrushchev
certainly did not modify any of the substantive positions of the Soviet Government regarding Berlin, German reunification, disarmament or other major international questions during our talks, there
was sufficient indication of a change of tone to lead me to believe
that further exploration would now be desirable. Indeed I believe
we would be assuming a heavy responsibility if we now refused to
meet him at the Summit.

I know you will agree with me that in such a meeting we on our
side must clearly be united regarding the limits which our national
interests place upon us. There is a possibility that we will find ourselves under severe pressure to accept proposals dangerous to our
interests under the threat of a total breakdown of negotiations. This
is a pressure under which we were placed at Geneva. I have no doubt
about the West's ability to resist it. If it proves that no acceptable
agreements can be worked out at the Summit, however, I now believe we will be better able to win world support of Western positions than if we refused to meet at all.

Knowing that you feel that a Summit meeting should be held, we
must therefore now consider the complicated question of a timetable which will permit the preliminary inter-allied consultation
clearly required.

I feel that there would be some advantage to a Summit meeting
in December, which, if agreements in principle are reached, would
make it possible to hold more detailed negotiations at the Foreign

Minister or expert level before the Spring. If a meeting is held in December it would have to precede the NATO Ministerial Meeting scheduled for December 15, and therefore should probably commence near the beginning of the month.[3]

I believe that we should meet with our French and German colleagues before a Summit meeting. For my part, I should be delighted to act as host to a pre-Summit meeting in the United States with our Western colleagues but would be prepared to go to Europe before the conference with the Soviets depending on the site selected for that conference and on what seems to be the most convenient arrangements for the others.

I await with the greatest interest your views on these questions, including possible sites for our meetings.[4]

With warm regard, *As ever*

[1] For background see no. 1336.

[2] See Eisenhower to de Gaulle, October 9, 1959, AWF/I: de Gaulle; and Eisenhower to Adenauer, October 9, 1959, AWF/I: Adenauer.

[3] The ministerial meeting of the North Atlantic Council, attended by the foreign ministers and the permanent representatives of the fifteen NATO countries, would be held in Paris on December 15–17 (see State, *Foreign Relations, 1958–1960*, vol. VII, pt. 1, *Western European Integration and Security; Canada*, pp. 527–52).

[4] For developments see no. 1343. In a second letter on this same day Eisenhower would congratulate Macmillan on the large majority of parliamentary seats his Conservative party had won in the British elections held on October 8. "I want to tell you how much I look forward to the continuation of that spirit of close friendship and cooperation which has made our association so rewarding in the past," he wrote (Eisenhower to Macmillan, Oct. 9, 1959, AWF/I: Macmillan; see also Macmillan to Eisenhower, Oct. 10, 1959, *ibid.*; and *New York Times*, Oct. 9, 1959).

1339   *EM, AWF, Dulles-Herter Series*

To CHRISTIAN ARCHIBALD HERTER   *October 9, 1959*
Secret

Dear Chris: Admiral Mountbatten, Chairman of the British Chiefs of Staff, called to my attention certain incidents which constitute, in his opinion, breaches of security.[1] One of these I understand is alleged to be of British origin—the others, American. I understand also that Ambassador Caccia has sent to you a letter on this matter.

This matter should be thoroughly examined. I think that Defense, C.I.A., and the Attorney General should be consulted. There is always the possibility that we should try, once more, to obtain better legislation in this field.[2]

I should like for you to keep me informed.[3] *Sincerely*

[1] The President had hosted a small dinner party in Mountbatten's honor on October 8 (see no. 823).

[2] On October 16 (AWF/D-H) Herter would reply that he had discussed the subject of security breaches with Caccia and Mountbatten on October 9. Herter said the State Department had a copy of Caccia's letter and the matter was being "urgently" investigated by the United States Intelligence Board, on which the Departments of State and Defense, and the CIA were represented.

[3] We have been unable to locate any further correspondence on this matter in AWF.

1340   *EM, AWF, Dulles-Herter Series*

MEMORANDUM FOR THE RECORD   *October 9, 1959*

Because of the very close personal relations I have been trying to develop with the President of Mexico, and knowing the latter's penchant for making gifts of a very personal character, I have decided that in the present case—as I did in others such as the Japanese and Thailand Prime Ministers—to make the gifts that Mrs. Eisenhower and I will give purely personal and on our own responsibility.[1]

The Ford Company had offered to make available to me, without cost, a small car (Falcon) for me to deliver as a present to the Mexican President. I declined to accept it on this basis, but stated that I would be willing to accept it if I could pay $1,000. This seems to be agreeable.[2] Mrs. Eisenhower is obtaining some kind of a fitted case for the daughter and I think is having an autographed picture framed for the President's wife.[3] I am giving to all of them a copy of one of my personal "amateur's" paintings.

[1] The President sent this memorandum to the Secretary of State (see Eisenhower to Herter, Oct. 9, 1959, AWF/D). Mexican President Adolfo López Mateos had arrived in the United States on October 9 and would remain in Washington until October 13 (State, *Foreign Relations, 1958–1960*, vol. V, *American Republics*, pp. 884–89, Eisenhower to López Mateos, Sept. 19, Oct. 17, 1959, AWF/I: Mexico, President Adolfo López Mateos, and *New York Times*, Oct. 10, 11, 12, 13, 1959). López Mateos would give Eisenhower a life-size bronze bust of the President made by a Mexican sculptor (*ibid.*, Oct. 13, 1959).

During Japanese Prime Minister Nobusuke Kishi's visit to the United States in July 1957, Eisenhower had given him a set of golf clubs (see no. 207, and Kishi to Eisenhower, June 21, 1957, AWF/I: Japan). Eisenhower had sent Thai Premier P. Pibul Songgram an album of photographs taken during his U.S. visit in 1955 (Galambos and van Ee, *The Middle Way*, no. 1415, and Pibul Songgram to Eisenhower, Jan. 28, 1956, AWF/I: Thailand).

[2] Eisenhower would present the Mexican president with a Ford Falcon sedan, which usually sold for $2,300. The Falcon, a new model, was one of the first of a series of American compact cars (*New York Times*, Oct. 13, 1959).

[3] The López Mateoses had a seventeen-year-old daughter Evita. Senora López Mateos was the former Eva Samano.

To Robert Gordon Menzies   *October 12, 1959*
Confidential

Dear Prime Minister:[1] Thank you for letting me have your thoughts on the visit of Chairman Khrushchev.[2] I believe that our discussions, although they were not intended to and did not involve negotiations on specific international issues, were useful and that the visit itself may have some impact on Chairman Khrushchev's views when he considers future courses of action.

As Secretary Herter pointed out in his meeting with the SEATO members, we made it a central objective to convince the Chairman that the prospects for fruitful negotiations were remote so long as there seemed to hang over us some threat of unilateral Soviet action in Berlin.[3] It was agreed during the talks that negotiations on Berlin would not be prolonged indefinitely, but that there could be no fixed time limit for them. The Soviets did not wish to include this in the communique, but agreement was reached that I would announce this in a press conference and the Chairman said that he would confirm it publicly. As you know, he did so in a public statement September twenty-ninth. I believe that this has removed a major impediment to negotiations with the Soviets and improved somewhat the prospects for mutually acceptable agreements with the Soviet Union.

As to disarmament, I believe as you do in its great importance. The thorough review of disarmament policy we are presently conducting reflects this belief.[4] The problem grows in importance as the range and power and velocity of modern weapons is extended. We must not let the failures of the past discourage our search for real solutions to these problems.

As to Mr. Khrushchev's proposal of September eighteenth, I can say that we share the ultimate goal of comprehensive disarmament and are, therefore, studying with care this proposal along with other possible measures.[5] We have already noted the very general character of the proposal. It has little detail on the control measures by which commitments would be verified or the stages by which the goal will be reached. It does not propose an international police force or recognize the problem of maintaining international order during and after the period of reduction of armaments. Neither does it concern itself with any relationship between disarmament and the settlement of political issues, which deeply influence national attitudes toward disarmament. Whether these matters will present practical difficulties, however, can only be judged when detailed negotiations on the proposal begin in the ten-power disarmament committee next year.[6]

I have myself concluded that the best hope for immediate progress in disarmament lies in negotiations on partial measures, such as those on a discontinuance of nuclear weapons tests. We have gone far in these negotiations; but there remains a variety of important issues to be resolved. The foremost of these is to reach agreement, in the light of all the relevant data, on the amount of on-site inspection which is required for effective control. Thus far the Soviet representatives have refused to join in scientific discussions of significant new data which recent research has disclosed. I hope that this problem will be overcome and that further progress in these negotiations can be registered when the negotiations resume on October twenty-seventh.[7]

I am convinced that confidence in any disarmament measures, certainly as far as Americans are concerned, can only be assured if effective and reliable control measures are made integral parts of any agreements for the reduction and limitation of armaments. I believe that progress toward disarmament is possible if the principle of control is thus accepted and I would hope that we could move forward in this direction through discussions in all forums, including a possible summit meeting.

As I stated in my press conference on September twenty-eighth, the conversations which I had with Chairman Khrushchev removed many of the objections to a summit conference that I have heretofore held, but the question of whether or not to hold a summit conference is a matter for negotiation and consultation with our allies.[8]

With warm personal regard, *Sincerely*

[1] This letter, drafted by State Department officials, was sent to the American embassy in Canberra for delivery to Australian Prime Minister Menzies (Herter to Eisenhower, Oct. 11, 1959, AWF/I: Australia; see also Telephone conversation, Sept. 29, 1959, Herter Papers, Telephone Conversations).

[2] For background see no. 1332. Menzies had told Eisenhower that all countries were indebted to him for providing an opportunity for "true negotiation." "I feel that the world situation is now such that public opinion expects that no opportunity should be missed for attempting to negotiate an improvement in relations between East and West." He told Eisenhower that he hoped the Khrushchev meetings would make possible a discussion of "the principles of controlled disarmament" at a future summit meeting (Menzies to Eisenhower, Sept. 29, 1959, AWF/I: Australia).

[3] Members of the council of the Southeast Asia Treaty Organization had met informally in Washington on September 28 (see State, *Foreign Relations, 1958–1960*, vol. XVI, *East Asia–Pacific Region; Cambodia; Laos*, Microfiche Supplement no. 287; see also *New York Times*, Sept. 29, 1959).

[4] In July Eisenhower had established a group to study arms control and reduction. The study, on behalf of the Departments of State and Defense, was to prepare U.S. officials for questions they would face in future disarmament negotiations (see NSC meeting minutes, Jan. 26, 1960, AWF/NSC; Telephone conversations, Herter and

Berkner, Aug. 10, 1959; Herter and Lawrence Rockefeller, Herter and Goodpaster, Sept. 30, 1959, Herter Papers, Telephone Conversations; and *New York Times,* July 30, 1959).

[5] An extract of Khrushchev's disarmament speech to the United Nations General Assembly, in which he proposed the abolishment of all weapons and armed forces within four years, is in State, *Documents on Disarmament, 1945–1959,* vol. II, *1957–1959,* pp. 1452–60; see also Goodpaster, Memorandum of Conference, September 26, 1959, AWF/D; and *New York Times,* September 19, 1959.

[6] The Ten-Nation Committee on Disarmament consisted of the United States, Great Britain, France, Canada, and Italy for the West; and the Soviet Union, Poland, Romania, Czechoslovakia, and Bulgaria for the Soviet bloc. The committee would begin negotiations in Geneva on March 15, 1960 (see State, *Foreign Relations, 1958–1960,* vol. III, *National Security Policy; Arms Control and Disarmament,* pp. 832–33, 836–46).

[7] For background on the Geneva meetings on the suspension of nuclear testing see no. 1127. The talks had recessed on August 27 because of the Khrushchev visit (see State, *Foreign Relations, 1958–1960,* vol. III, *National Security Policy; Arms Control and Disarmament,* pp. 766–67).

[8] On the President's news conference see *Public Papers of the Presidents: Eisenhower, 1959,* pp. 694–702. For developments see no. 1343.

1342   *EM, AWF, DDE Diaries Series*

To Christian Archibald Herter   *October 13, 1959*
Personal

Memorandum for the Secretary of State: In a conversation with Joyce Hall of Kansas City (Hallmark Cards), he told me of a project he has that he hopes would be helpful in promoting greater knowledge of all the American people with foreign countries.[1]

The project is, in brief, that by arrangement with the City, he would obtain a section of the park area and on this area provide plots for the erection of native houses, with authentic types of furniture and appointments from each of the countries that might be ready to cooperate.

He, and a Foundation which he controls, would be quite ready to pay all overhead and other expenses that would be necessary over and above those borne by the several nations placing their exhibit in this region.[2]

He has been in touch with one of your assistants, Mr. Thayer, I believe, who seems to be quite enthused about this project.[3]

If Mr. Hall is to proceed without making useless and possibly costly mistakes, he needs someone who can deal through diplomatic channels with the other countries and who could, at the same time, keep Mr. Hall informed as to possibilities in this line. Among other things he would like to know, for example, is whether any attempt should be made to induce Iron Curtain countries to participate in this way.[4]

On the surface, at least, the project looks to me to be a very fine one—especially in this central region where foreign travel is not one of common practice. If you think well of the general idea, I hope you will direct some one of your assistants to take the initiative in keeping in touch with Mr. Hall and with the countries interested in cooperating.[5]

[1] The President had been in Abilene, Kansas, to attend the ground-breaking ceremonies for the Eisenhower Library (see the following document). He had met with Hall earlier this same day. For background on Hall's interest in the People-to-People Program see no. 546.

[2] In 1954 the Hallmark Educational Foundation, incorporated in 1943 in Missouri, had combined funds with the Hallmark Education Foundation of Kansas (see *ibid.*, and Margaret Mary Feczko, and Elizabeth H. Rich, eds., *The Foundation Directory 1995 Edition*, New York, 1995, p. 755).

[3] Robert Helyer Thayer (A.B. Harvard 1922; LL.B. Harvard 1926) had been the State Department's Special Assistant for the Coordination of International Educational and Cultural Relations since 1958. He had served the U.S. government since 1951 as a special assistant to the Ambassador to France, Minister to Rumania, and as officer in charge of Western European Affairs on the Operations Coordinating Board (OCB).

[4] The question of inviting the countries of Eastern Europe, Herter would reply (Oct. 23, 1959, AWF/D-H), was under careful consideration. It was assumed, he wrote, that representation in the International Village project would be limited to nations with which the United States maintained diplomatic relations.

[5] Thayer and Hall had been discussing the Hallmark Foundation since May, Herter would report. Thayer had brought Hall's representative together with the cultural attachés of a selected group of countries to discuss the proposal. All had expressed "great interest in the project," and the State Department was awaiting official comment after the diplomats consulted with their governments. Herter promised that Thayer would keep in "close touch" with Hall.

On October 19, at an informal meeting at the White House, Eisenhower would tell a group of People-to-People committee chairmen that their kind of contacts represented "the only way" to advance international understanding (Memorandum of conference, Oct. 19, 1959, AWF/D; Ann Whitman memorandum, Oct. 19, 1959, AWF/AWD; and *New York Times*, Oct. 20, 1959. See also Supplement to Staff Notes, Dec. 31, 1959, AWF/D, and *New York Times*, Oct. 3, Dec. 11, 12, 1959).

1343

EM, AWF, International Series: Macmillan

To HAROLD MACMILLAN
Cable. Secret

October 16, 1959

Dear Harold:[1] I am glad to have your prompt reply of October 12 on the question of a Summit meeting.[2] I think our views are essentially not far apart. My own feeling is that we owe it to the free world and to ourselves to take every opportunity to explore further the attitude of the Soviets. However, I feel strongly that we cannot do this until we know that we have a concerted point of view among ourselves.[3]

President de Gaulle, in responding to my letter to him on my talks with the Soviet Chairman, has already expressed to me some of his views on a prospective Summit meeting. He is plainly lukewarm to the idea of holding one at all, and certainly has no wish to see a meeting take place as early as December.[4] Chancellor Adenauer has indicated to me that early December would be acceptable provided the necessary concerting of our positions is possible in advance. As suggested above, this is really my view, too.[5]

One reason that I regard an early meeting with you, General de Gaulle and the Chancellor desirable is the fact that I am not at all sure that my evaluation and yours of the possibility of agreeing on a modus vivendi on Berlin with the Soviets at a Summit meeting are the same. It seems to me that when the Foreign Ministers adjourned their sessions at Geneva in August there was still a wide gulf between us and the Russians.[6] I quite agree that the elements of an agreement and the position of the two sides were clearly revealed. On some of the less important elements of our positions there was a varying measure of agreement. But on the vital question of where we would stand with respect to our rights at the end of the period we made no progress at all in spite of heroic efforts by the Western ministers. I do not think we should underestimate the difficulties with which we are likely to be confronted when we take up this thorny subject again in a formal negotiation.

Another point on which we must reach agreement among ourselves revolves around the problem of dealing with suggestions that the Summit meeting should include representation of countries other than the four which met at Geneva in 1955.[7] Since the subject of disarmament is almost certain to come up, the other side will very likely propose the admission of other participants in our meeting, citing the precedent of our acceptance of the Committee of Ten for Disarmament.[8] The Soviets can in any event be expected to raise the question of East German participation. I think we must make every effort to keep the meting on a Four Power basis as we did at the Summit conference in Geneva in 1955.

Both the question of what we would talk about at a Summit meeting and the possible differences as to its desirability, composition and dates indicate to me that we of the West must get together at the Heads of Government level at the earliest possible moment. I have reviewed my own schedule and find that with some readjustment I could free myself for the purpose for a few days at the end of this month. Paris would seem to me to be the logical place to meet in light of the difficulty which General de Gaulle would presumably find in visiting either London or Washington in advance of his state visits. For my part Paris would be entirely acceptable. I would envisage such a meeting as involving no ceremonies, no social affairs, and devoted purely to business.

I should welcome your views on all these matters. We seem to be in basic agreement already on the main questions and with the pressure of time under which we are laboring I have asked Chris to take this matter up at once with Harold Caccia and with Ambassador Grewe and Ambassador Alphand as well.[9] If you agree in principle, I think we can leave the arrangements to be worked out by them through diplomatic channels.

On this strictly personal side may I thank you for your letter of October 10 which reached me just before I went out to Kansas for a ceremony in connection with the ground breaking of the Eisenhower Library there.[10] I am more than grateful for your good wishes for my anniversary and I hope with you that together we shall be able to do even more in the next twelve months toward the goals we both so earnestly seek.[11]

With warm regard, *As ever*

[1] Eisenhower would send similar letters on this same day to French President de Gaulle and West German Chancellor Konrad Adenauer (see AWF/I: de Gaulle and AWF/I: Adenauer).

[2] For background see no. 1338. Macmillan had reiterated his desire for a summit meeting with Khrushchev "at the earliest practicable moment" and agreed to an early December date. He also agreed to a meeting with French President de Gaulle and West German Chancellor Adenauer immediately preceding the main meeting. Although he was prepared to leave most of the details of any understanding reached to the respective countries' foreign ministers, Macmillan argued that the heads of government should try to formulate personally at least one specific agreement, such as an interim agreement on Berlin. In this way they would be certain to preserve "the good work" that Eisenhower had accomplished when he had persuaded Khrushchev to withdraw the Berlin ultimatum (Macmillan to Eisenhower, Oct. 12, 1959, PREM 11/2996).

[3] After reading the State Department drafts of this letter and those to de Gaulle and Adenauer, Eisenhower had told Secretary Herter that any message to the three leaders must stress the importance of a concerted viewpoint on major problems (see Goodpaster, Memorandums of Conference, Oct. 21, 22, 1959, AWF/D).

[4] For Eisenhower's earlier letter to de Gaulle see no. 1338. In his October 8 letter, which crossed in the mail with Eisenhower's, de Gaulle had said that the Khrushchev conversations had shown that the Soviet leader wanted to relax tensions without modifying the Soviet positions that had caused the problems. He advised waiting for specific actions that would indicate a general international détente before agreeing to a summit conference (AWF/I: de Gaulle).

[5] See Adenauer to Eisenhower, October 13, 1959, AWF/I: Adenauer.

[6] For background on the Geneva meetings see no. 1269.

[7] The countries meeting in 1955 were the United States, Great Britain, France, and the Soviet Union (see Galambos and van Ee, *The Middle Way*, no. 1523).

[8] On the Ten-Nation Committee on Disarmament see no. 1341.

[9] Harold Caccia, Wilhelm C. Grewe, and Hervé Alphand were the British, West German, and French Ambassadors to the United States.

[10] Eisenhower had left Washington on October 13 and returned the following day. For background on the Abilene ground breaking see no. 899.

[11] Macmillan had told Eisenhower that he could look back "with pride" on all he had accomplished during the year, and he believed that the year to come would be even better (AWF/I: Macmillan). For developments see no. 1349.

1344   *EM, AWF, Administration Series*

To Joseph Morrell Dodge   *October 16, 1959*
Personal

Dear Joe: The problem described in your letter of the thirteenth is one that has worried me for a long time, as you well know.[1] Every time that I feel we have made some step toward its correction, I have finally to conclude that progress, if any, is far from noticeable.[2]

As a result, our foreign economic programs have too many internal conflicts and are too little understood within the government, to say nothing by the people in general. And an informed public opinion is the only thing that can be counted upon to make these programs effective as we try to build a peaceful world.[3]

But the economic part of our foreign operations is inextricably bound up with other portions. To assist in better coordination in this whole field, I have been studying for some years the establishment of a top assistant to the President, who would be given specific delegated authority and a title that would be commensurate with his functions and responsibilities.[4]

At this point it might be well to recall that the Hoover Commission felt that in addition to the Constitutional Vice President, there should be two others appointed under the authority of law. Of these one was to take cognizance of foreign affairs in all its aspects.[5]

I believe that the designation of additional Vice Presidents would be confusing to our people. I would like to give an individual occupying a position of coordinator for all foreign affairs the title of "First Secretary of the Government." The title "First Secretary" would describe many of the functions of the Prime Minister in a parliamentary form of government. It would describe *all* of his functions insofar as they touch on foreign affairs.

It seems to me that such an individual could coordinate, daily, on behalf of the President questions involving our foreign policy and foreign operations. In effect he would act for the President as Deputy Chairman of the National Security Council. The difference would be that he would not have to bother his head with national finances, business matters, or any domestic problem of any kind. But insofar as the Department of State, and the foreign operation functions of the Treasury Department, Defense Department, Agriculture Department, Labor Department, Commerce Department, the ICA and USIA, such a man would have the delegated authority from the President to coordinate and direct activities in accordance with policies approved by the President. As usual, unreconcilable conflicts between Departments would be brought before the President, but only after specific points of difference had been carefully analyzed by the First Secretary.

The person occupying this position would rank with but [sit] at the head of the entire Cabinet. He would have a very small staff and would of course have more daily business with the Secretary of State than with any other individual. But his authority would be so much more broadly based than that of the Secretary of State that he could be most helpful in keeping things better coordinated and would certainly take a lot of detailed work off the President.

A whole detailed plan for bringing about such coordination has been under study for some years. Foster Dulles finally became quite keen on the idea—although at first opposed—and he and I agreed that we would place it before the Congress, both as a reorganizational plan and as a legislative request (the latter to provide the small staff, position and salary of the incumbent) during the final session of the Congress in my Administration.[6] The reason I held off until this coming year was so that there could be no charge that self-glorifying motives were involved. The scheme would be for use by later Presidents.

This is a very rough description of what I have had in mind; some day when you are here you and I could chat about it. Moreover, I might have one of the members of my "Organizational Study Committee" talk to you about its details to see whether or not our ideas are roughly similar.[7]

Thank you a lot for your letter, and with warm personal regard,
As ever

[1] Dodge's letter, marked "personal," is in AWF/A. He had asked Eisenhower's "indulgence" in offering "the only unsolicited comment about the Government's affairs" that he had made since he left the Administration in 1954. Dodge reminded the President that in 1954 he had asked Dodge to investigate the foreign economic assistance programs. Dodge had outlined the wide dispersion of authority and activities among the federal departments and agencies, and he had recommended the creation of the Council on Foreign Economic Policy (for background see Galambos and van Ee, *The Middle Way*, no. 1020).

Although the work of the council, Dodge wrote, had been of "some constructive benefit," the situation had worsened. He thought that the government had no mechanism for review of foreign military and economic assistance programs, their objectives and inter-relationships. Dodge argued that properly coordinated foreign aid programs would save money and prevent further criticism.

² The Reorganization Act of 1949 authorized the President to reorganize executive agencies subject to the veto of either the Senate or the House. But progress had been difficult to achieve. In June the House had failed to approve a plan to shift certain functions of the Secretary of the Interior to the Secretary of Agriculture, and the Senate failed to act on a bill (H.R. 5140) to extend the Reorganization Act for two years. Therefore the legislation had lapsed (*Congressional Quarterly Almanac*, vol. XV, *1959*, pp. 81, 308, and Memorandum, President's Advisory Committee on Government Reorganization, June 8, 1959, AWF/A). See also J. S. D. Eisenhower, Memorandum of Conference, July 30, 1959, AWF/D.

³ For the President's emphasis on an informed public see no. 1240.

⁴ In 1957 Eisenhower had begun discussing the creation of a position within the State Department for coordinating the activities of the State Department, the U.S. Information Agency, and the International Cooperation Administration. The coordinator would also assist in establishing policies, for the international activities of the Departments of Defense and Commerce (see nos. 538 and 555).

⁵ On the Hoover Commission's recommendations see no. 157.

⁶ According to John S. D. Eisenhower, the late Secretary of State Dulles "had abhorred the idea" at first, but had later become "somewhat reconciled" toward the end of his tenure (see J. S. D. Eisenhower, Memorandum of Conference, July 30, 1959, AWF/D; and Eisenhower, *Waging Peace*, p. 637).

⁷ On November 6 the President would meet with his Advisory Committee on Government Organization to discuss the creation of the First Secretary post and the reorganization of the State Department. At the meeting the President would decide to discuss the First Secretary proposal with the Cabinet in January, and to postpone planning the State Department reorganization (see Memorandums for Record, Nov. 12, 21, 1959, AWF/D).

At a legislative leaders' meeting on January 12, 1960, Eisenhower would propose the creation of a new business manager post in the Executive Branch and a First Secretary of the Government to assist the President in national security and international affairs (AWF/D). The National Policy Machinery Subcommittee of the Senate Government Operations Committee would hold hearings from February to July 1960 on the subject of a First Secretary. On November 22, 1960, the subcommittee would reject the proposal, saying its creation would lower the prestige of existing Cabinet posts (*Congressional Quarterly Almanac*, vol. XVI, *1960*, pp. 721–27, and Eisenhower, *Waging Peace*, pp. 633–38).

1345   *EM, AWF, Administration Series, Flemming Corr.*

MEMORANDUM   *October 16, 1959*

Memorandum for Files: Attached is a memorandum discussed with me this morning by Bob Burroughs.¹ I have asked him to see the Secretary of HEW with a copy of this document. Secretary Flemming, when convenient, is to give me his reactions to it and any recommendations he may have in the circumstances.

In case Secretary Flemming does not bring up the matter in the next couple of weeks, acw should remind the President.²

[1] Robert Philips Burroughs, a pension plan engineer and former presidential advisor, had met with the President in the White House (President's daily appointments, Oct. 16, 1959; see Galambos and van Ee, *The Middle Way*, nos. 110 and 779). He had prepared a statement on the inadequacies of health care for the elderly, arguing that many were unable to afford high hospital and medical care costs or private insurance plans. Burroughs advocated a compulsory, contributory federal health insurance plan implemented through the social security system. He urged the Administration to "take the lead in bringing this protection to retired people," an action which would be popular with the general public although not with medical, insurance, and conservative business groups (Oct. 16, 1959, AWF/A).

In July 1959 the House had held hearings on a controversial bill, sponsored by the Democrats, that included medical care among the benefits provided by Social Security Old Age and Survivors Insurance; no further action would be taken on the proposal (*New York Times*, July 15, 1959). A special Senate subcommittee had also conducted investigatory hearings throughout the year on problems of the aged and would issue a report in February 1960. Although the social security approach was gaining support in some quarters, Eisenhower was opposed to compulsory insurance and continued to favor voluntary private insurance. In 1960 the question of medical care for the elderly would again be raised in Congress and would become an issue in the 1960 presidential campaign. For background see no. 826; *Congressional Quarterly Almanac*, vol. XV, *1959*, p. 67, and vol. XVI, *1960*, pp. 148ff.; Edward D. Berkowitz and Kim McQuaid, *Creating the Welfare State: The Political Economy of 20th-Century Reform*, 4th ed., (Lawrence, Kans., 1992), pp. 165–92, and Edward D. Berkowitz, *America's Welfare State from Roosevelt to Reagan* (Baltimore, 1991), pp. 153–86. For developments see no. 1516.

[2] The President would meet with Arthur Flemming, the Secretary of Health, Education and Welfare, and with General Goodpaster on October 20 (AWF/AWD); "acw" is Ann Cook Whitman, Eisenhower's personal secretary. There is no record of the discussion in AWF.

1346   *EM, AWF, Name Series*

To Katherine Boyce Tupper Marshall   *October 16, 1959*

Dear Mrs. Marshall: I cannot possibly describe to you the sense of loss I feel in the knowledge that George has passed to the Great Beyond.[1] I looked to him for guidance, direction and counsel ever since I first had the great privilege of meeting him late in 1941.[2] The country has lost one of its most distinguished citizens who was both an eminent soldier and an outstanding statesman.[3]

Mamie joins me in deepest sympathy,[4] *Sincerely*

[1] General of the Army George Catlett Marshall had passed away at 6:08 P.M. at Walter Reed Army Hospital. He had suffered two strokes earlier in 1959 and had entered Walter Reed on March 11. The President had visited him on three occasions. Eisenhower would attend the funeral services on October 20 (*New York Times*, Oct. 17, 21, 1959, and Ann Whitman memorandums, Oct. 16, 20, 1959, AWF/AWD; see

also Ed Cray, *General of the Army: George C. Marshall, Soldier and Statesman* [New York, 1990], pp. 734–35).

[2] On December 14, 1941, Eisenhower had joined the War Plans Division of the War Department as Deputy Chief for the Pacific and Far East. On that same day he had reported to Chief of Staff Marshall, who had asked him to outline a general line of action in the western Pacific (see Chandler, *War Years*, no. 1, and Eisenhower, *Crusade in Europe*, pp. 14–22). On the President's relationship with Marshall see *Eisenhower Papers*, vols. I–XVII, and Forrest C. Pogue, *George C. Marshall*, 4 vols. (New York, 1963–87), vol. IV, *Statesman, 1945–1959* (1987), pp. 496–501, 504–5, 507, 509–10, 516.

[3] Following World War II Marshall had initiated and had given his name to the aid program that helped bring recovery to Western Europe—the Marshall Plan. He had been awarded the Nobel Peace Prize in 1953. He had also served as Secretary of State from 1942–1948 and as Secretary of Defense from 1950–1951.

[4] Mrs. Marshall would thank the President on November 12 (AWF/N).

1347   *EM, WHCF, Official File 116-WW*

To Victor Emanuel   *October 20, 1959*

Dear Victor: First, let me thank you deeply for your note and for your more than generous comments, on the occasion of my birthday anniversary.[1]

I have just now had an opportunity for a careful reading of your letter of the seventh, and only wish I could find the time to answer it in the detail it deserves. With much of what you report I agree.[2] I think it is only natural that the people of Great Britain should feel some resentment of their "richer" cousins.[3] Also, I can quite understand their desire to avoid, at whatever cost, atomic war that could mean the end of their nation—as indeed, atomic war could mean the end of all civilization, including our own.[4]

Perhaps the situation changed a little bit for the better by the time I was in London, at the end of August.[5] But I did not discern any unfriendliness in the press then and I thought that, within reason, their coverage of our news was adequate.[6]

These are just rambling comments. As I say, I should like to talk all these matters over with you; failing that, I shall have to appoint George my diplomatic representative (although I have no great confidence that he won't get Very Speedy mixed up with Selwyn Lloyd) to discuss my reactions with you.[7] But, at the very least, I do thank you very much for your interesting, provocative and challenging letter.[8]

With warm regard, *Sincerely*

[1] Avco Manufacturing Corporation President Emanuel had sent birthday greetings on October 12, adding that Eisenhower "stood higher in the affections of the Amer-

ican people, if not a good part of the free world, than any President we have ever had."

[2] Emanuel's six-page letter had recounted "only the most disturbing" impressions he observed while visiting Great Britain in March. Emanuel had discussed various subjects with his British friends and had been "simply shocked" to learn that the British were more concerned with economic conditions in the United States than with international issues.

[3] Emanuel had observed a "deep-rooted jealousy of the United States" for "having become the leading power in the world."

[4] "The English people do not want war," Emanuel wrote, "in fact . . . some favor appeasement at any price."

[5] On Eisenhower's trip to Europe see nos. 1301 and 1303.

[6] Emanuel had said his "second greatest shock in England" was that the British daily newspapers carried little American news—"perhaps on average two articles daily."

[7] In a September 5 letter to George Allen, Emanuel had related the reaction of his son, who lived in Great Britain, to the British television program that featured the President and Prime Minister Macmillan. The younger Emanuel said Eisenhower was "magnificent" and had changed the feelings of Englishmen about the United States. Allen had forwarded Emanuel's letter to Eisenhower. "Very Speedy" was probably one of Allen's thoroughbred horses; Selwyn Lloyd was the British Defense Minister. All correspondence is in the same file as the document.

[8] For developments see no. 1717.

1348   *EM, WHCF, President's Personal File 182*

To Frank McCarthy   *October 20, 1959*

Dear Frank: I have your letter of October sixteenth in which you propose to cast in bronze an excerpt from the talk I made last June to the Virginia Military Institute Glee Club and to place the plaque in the Marshall Arch at that school. I am of course delighted to give permission to do this.[1]

Because the passage has been taken out of context, I have reworded it slightly in accordance with your suggestions, as you will see from the attachment.[2]

Although I understand that your letter was written and mailed before General Marshall's death, I note that it bears the same date. Today I will have the sad experience of attending the funeral of this great man, held so much in reverence by all who cherish freedom.[3]

With warm regard, *Sincerely*

[1] McCarthy (A.B. Virginia Military Institute 1933; A.M. University of Virginia 1940) was director of public relations at Twentieth Century-Fox Film Corporation. During World War II he had served in the War Department as military secretary to Chief of Staff George C. Marshall. McCarthy's letter is in the same file as the document.

    On June 18 the President had attended a dinner at the Sheraton Park Hotel in

Washington, marking the occasion of the twenty-fifth anniversary of the Federal Housing Administration. The V.M.I. Glee Club had provided the entertainment.
[2] The President's statement would read:

> VMI is a school that has given to the United States and to the armed services many of its most distinguished members. Among these is a man who in World War II stood out as one of the great soldiers, and later as one of the great statesmen, of our time—George Catlett Marshall.
> He is a patriot, a distinguished soldier, and the most selfless public servant I have ever met. Any school that can boast graduates like General Marshall—and all his associates who have been so valuable in wartime and peacetime service to this country—is indeed a distinguished institution and one that we certainly will nourish as long as there is an America.

On October 23 (same file as document) McCarthy would say he had met with the superintendent of V.M.I., who had been enthusiastic about the bronze plate. On October 22, 1960, the plaque would be placed at eye-level on the wall of a barracks building near the Marshall Arch (*New York Times*, Oct. 23, 1960).
[3] On Marshall's death and funeral see no. 1346.

1349   *EM, AWF, International Series:*
                                                                 De Gaulle

To CHARLES ANDRÉ JOSEPH MARIE DE GAULLE
Cable. Secret   *October 21, 1959*

Dear General de Gaulle: I have received your letter of October 20 with regard to my suggestion for an early Western Summit meeting.[1] I understand the reasoning behind your letter; however, I must say that I cannot, in all frankness, agree with all the conclusions which you reach regarding timing and other matters. I have certainly tried in all my contacts with both Western and Soviet leaders to describe accurately the American determination that we should not retreat or surrender on any vital point. But to show a readiness to negotiate is not to demonstrate weakness.[2]

As I mentioned before, I believe that we have achieved a somewhat better atmosphere in East-West relations and I believe that we would be derelict in our duty if we of the West did not promptly explore further the possibilities for producing an agreed program for making some significant steps toward disarmament as well as a *modus vivendi* on Berlin in the light of their action in removing the time limit for Berlin negotiations.[3]

I am certainly not seeking to impose any fixed date for a summit meeting with the Soviets although I had previously suggested the possibility of December. I would not envisage in any event that a summit meeting would lead to any extended series of concrete agreements.

I do believe that the views of Prime Minister Macmillan, Chancellor Adenauer and yourself are sufficiently diverse so that an early meeting among the four of us becomes more rather than less urgent. In any case I do not believe such a meeting should be put off until the spring. To do so, and thus to present to the world a picture of Western inaction, would not, in my view, lead to a more forthcoming attitude on the part of Mr. Khrushchev. On the contrary I fear it would lead to a renewed hardening of his attitudes. Therefore, I conclude this is another reason bespeaking a reasonably early meeting among the four Western leaders.

I see no real reason why an early Western Summit would lead to harmful speculation in the press and in public opinion regarding an immediately following meeting with the Soviets. Indeed this would be one of the questions to be discussed by Western leaders. I now suggest that a Western summit should take place well before the mid-December NATO ministerial meeting. I think that the four of us should consider among ourselves our present thinking about the NATO posture in advance of that meeting.[4]

I believe that our correspondence, like our thorough and frank discussions in Paris have revealed a large community of views in these vital matters. I feel confident we can iron out these purely procedural matters so that a fruitful Western coordination can occur before we attempt any discussions with the Soviets.[5]

With warm regard, *Sincerely*

[1] For background see no. 1343. De Gaulle had agreed with Eisenhower that there was an urgent need to end East-West tensions. He had "strong reservations," however, about the benefits of a summit conference. Only on the subject of Berlin had Khrushchev indicated any willingness to cooperate, de Gaulle wrote, yet a solution to the problem seemed "more uncertain than ever." "I wonder what, in this situation, a summit meeting at this time could accomplish besides highlighting a fundamental disagreement between East and West or surrendering more or less to Soviet claims to Berlin. In the first case, the cold war would very likely be aggravated; in the second, the world might consider such a retreat on the part of the West the beginning of a series of retreats, and the firmness of the Atlantic Alliance would suffer grave consequences." He recommended a summit conference in May or June, only after the Soviet Union had indicated in deeds and words a willingness to cooperate. He also recommended "a leisurely preliminary meeting" among the Western powers in early spring (AWF/I: de Gaulle).

[2] After reading the de Gaulle letter, Eisenhower had told Secretary Herter that the French president evidently saw any agreement on Berlin as a "retreat" (Goodpaster, Memorandum of Conference, Oct. 23, 1959, AWF/D).

[3] For Eisenhower's earlier letter to de Gaulle see no. 1343. Eisenhower told Herter that the draft of this letter was focused too heavily on a summit meeting and "should be tied more to the need for the development of an agreed Western program and approach on disarmament, Berlin and other questions" (*ibid.*).

4 Eisenhower had asked Herter to include in the draft a statement to the effect that a Western summit meeting would be an opportunity to review NATO positions (*ibid.*). As it turned out, the Western heads of government would begin their meetings on December 19, four days after the beginning of the NATO meetings.
5 Eisenhower had met with the French president on September 2–4 (see no. 1309). For developments see no. 1354.

1350   *EM, AWF, International Series:*
                                                          Macmillan

To Harold Macmillan   *October 22, 1959*
Cable. Top secret

Dear Harold: In my latest letter to General de Gaulle I did not mention an East-West meeting.[1] I merely pointed out what I thought to be the great advantages of a Western summit. It is quite clear that he is hopeful of postponing any direct contact with Mr. Khrushchev pending what he calls clear evidence of a changed Soviet attitude. Apparently such a change of attitude will be evidenced by a "correct" Soviet vote in the UN about Algeria.[2] However, I have no theory covering his reasons for believing that a Western conference would be a mistake. We shall have to wait and see what his answer is to my most recent letter.[3]

With warm regard, *As ever*

[1] See the preceding document.
[2] De Gaulle had told Eisenhower that during the upcoming United Nations debate on the French plan for Algerian independence (see no. 1309) the French government would "observe Soviet conduct closely." "I should certainly not participate in a summit conference with Mr. Khrushchev at a time when his representatives in New York were speaking out against my country or joining those who were" (de Gaulle to Eisenhower, Oct. 20, 1959, AWF/I: de Gaulle; see also State, *Foreign Relations, 1958–1960*, vol. XIII, *Arab-Israeli Dispute; United Arab Republic; North Africa*, pp. 682–85).
[3] For developments see no. 1354.

1351   *EM, AWF, Dulles-Herter Series*

To Christian Archibald Herter   *October 26, 1959*

Memorandum for the Secretary of State: It occurs to me that there may be valid and adequate reason to give permanent status to a unit of government dealing with disarmament. I recently received a suggestion to this effect which seems to me to carry a good deal of weight.[1]

In all probability the unit should be in the State Department. Our own experience tends to support this. One specific solution would be to have a Special Assistant to the Secretary of State (or possibly an Assistant Secretary of State) charged with disarmament responsibilities, with a suitable permanent staff, library, and other necessary support.

When convenient, would you let me have your comments concerning this?[2]

[1] On October 25 the President had returned from a vacation in Augusta, Georgia, where he may have received the suggestion (see *New York Times*, Oct. 21–26, 1959, and Slater, *The Ike I Knew*, pp. 202–7).

[2] Herter would reply on November 12 (AWF/D-H) that the Department of State was the logical place to put the responsibility for leadership in disarmament. He proposed strengthening the present office of the Special Assistant to the Secretary of State for Disarmament and Atomic Energy. The State Department, Herter promised, would continue to solicit the active participation and support of other agencies in formulating and carrying out a sound and vigorous armaments control policy.

On September 9, 1960, the Department of State would announce the establishment of the U.S. Disarmament Administration to develop policies and coordinate activities in the field of arms limitation and control (State, *Foreign Relations, 1958–1960*, vol. III, *National Security Policy; Arms Control and Disarmament*, p. 905, and *New York Times*, Sept. 10, 1960).

In 1961 Congress would create the independent Arms Control and Disarmament Agency. Later the agency would merge with the State Department in accordance with the Foreign Affairs Agencies Consolidation Act of 1998 (see *Public Papers of the Presidents: John F. Kennedy, 1961*, pp. 646–47; *New York Times*, September 27, 1961; and *Congressional Quarterly Almanac*, vol. LIV, *1998*, pp. 16–19). See also Ernest W. Lefever, ed., *Arms and Arms Control: A Symposium* (New York, 1962), pp. 109–13.

1352 *EM, AWF, DDE Diaries Series*

TO ROBERT TYRE JONES, JR. *October 26, 1959*

Dear Bob: I have just received the copy of the article that you wrote in 1934 on "good putting."[1] It seems to me that where I have been making my greatest error is in the violation of your paragraph 2(a).

When I went to Augusta last Wednesday I found there the "working model" of Calamity Jane.[2] Without practice I took it out for my first round and my first three greens were one-putters. This statement loses a bit of its glamor when I say that two of them were under three feet.

There was one difficulty I had that I could not overcome in spite of four days on the course. I simply could not get used to the heavy greens. Until the last day they could not be mowed. The Bermuda was heavy and stiff, and some of the rye was just beginning to come up through the Bermuda. In this situation I began to "freeze up" because I had formerly been using a much heavier putter. My fairway shots, both irons and woods, were fairly good for me, but except for one day my driving was terrible. I think the cold weather and the wind had something to do with this because I simply could not feel relaxed. With driving and putting both in a sad state of disrepair my scores were less than satisfactory.

In the latter part of my stay Charlie Yates was my partner.[3] He was putting about as well as could be imagined, but the ball simply would not go into the hole. He has no trouble whatever with the distance factor. Whereas it was nothing at all for me to be short six feet or over by ten, he was rarely more than from six inches to a foot in error in this matter.

In any event I accomplished one thing—which was to get out of this office for four days. Now I am looking for good weather and a chance to exercise "Jane."[4]

Give my love to Mary—and of course all the best to yourself. *As ever*

---

[1] We have been unable to find Jones's article.

[2] In 1930 Jones had retired from competitive golf and had given Calamity Jane, his special putter, to the British Museum. In March 1934, however, he had come out of retirement to play at the first Masters Invitational Golf Tournament in Augusta, Georgia. He had used a duplicate putter and had finished thirteenth (*Newsweek*, Mar. 31, 1934, pp. 22–23). Eisenhower had used the replica.

[3] This was Charles R. Yates of Atlanta.

[4] The President had vacationed in Augusta, Georgia, October 21–25 (see Slater, *The Ike I Knew*, p. 206). He would practice golf on the south grounds of the White House three times and play full rounds of golf four times before returning to Augusta on November 12. He would remain in Georgia until November 23.

1353   *EM, AWF, International Series: Haiti*

To Francois Duvalier   *October 27, 1959*

Dear Mr. President: I was happy to learn from your letter of October eighth of the encouraging progress in the joint efforts of our two Governments to alleviate the economic and financial crisis Haiti has undergone in recent months.[1] I thank you especially for your generous words of praise for the officials of this Government who are cooperating with officials of your Government in this endeavor.[2]

I know that the well-being of the Haitian people is your constant concern. Your determination to find solutions to the problems still confronting them is apparent in your letter.[3] You may be confident of the continuing desire of the United States to assist you and your people in every appropriate way.

I assume by now you have received a report from your Minister of Finance on his recent detailed discussions with officials of this Government concerning present conditions in Haiti and ways in which the United States assistance might be employed in the solution of specific problems.[4] Among the subjects discussed with him were technical assistance in budgetary and other administrative matters, proposals now before the Development Loan Fund for financing development projects, and the importance of orderly constitutional processes as a basis for real economic progress.[5]

You have just passed the second anniversary of your inauguration as Constitutional President of Haiti. This fact recalls to me the period preceding your Government, when the lack of a regularly-constituted governmental authority seriously impeded economic progress.[6] The United States continues to wish you all success in the efforts of your Government to strengthen constitutional processes and safeguards, which are of such incalculable importance to real economic and social progress.[7]

I assure you, Mr. President, of my sincere interest in your struggle to provide a greater measure of well-being for the Haitian people. In closing, I wish again to express appreciation for your generous offer of military facilities and your assurances that Haiti and the United States continue to share the same views on international questions.[8] *Sincerely*

[1] For background on Haiti's relationship with the United States see nos. 811 and 1214. Duvalier, Haiti's President, had expressed appreciation for the technical and financial assistance the United States and various loan agencies had provided his country over the past year. Among these measures had been a six million dollar emergency grant, advice on reorganizing fiscal operations and departments, and three loans approved by the Development Loan Fund (Duvalier to Eisenhower, Oct. 8, 1959).

[2] Duvalier had commended the U.S. Ambassador to Haiti, the First Secretary to the Embassy of the United States, the Director of the International Cooperation Administration program in Haiti, and the United States Operations Mission Adviser to the Minister of Finance for their assistance.

[3] Duvalier had described a range of political and economic problems: governmental inefficiency and mismanagement of funds; financial losses from poor coffee crops; poor roads; an obsolescent airport that made it difficult to attract tourism; and inadequate shipping facilities.

[4] Fritz St. Firmin Thebaud had been appointed Minister of Finance in June 1958. In February 1959 Thebaud had met with officials in Washington to discuss Duvalier's appeals for help with his country's dire economic situation (Duvalier to Eisenhower, Jan. 12, and Herter to Eisenhower, Feb. 2, 1959). Eisenhower had asked a number

of agencies to study Haiti's specific problems and to discuss their findings with Haitian officials (Eisenhower to Duvalier, Feb. 4, 1959).

Disapproval of Duvalier's dictatorial rule had affected U.S. aid decisions. Political instability elsewhere in the Caribbean region and an unsuccessful, small-scale Cuban invasion of Haiti in May 1959, however, had convinced officials that it was in the best interest of the United States to protect Duvalier's regime. Military and financial assistance would be granted to Haiti in 1960 (Herter to Eisenhower, July 27, 1960; additional correspondence in AWF/I: Haiti; and State, *Foreign Relations*, vol. V, *American Republics*, pp. 817–19, and Microfiche Supplement, HA-19–29).

[5] Duvalier had described a number of projects for which Haiti was seeking additional Development Loan funding. Among these were construction of a new international airport, modernization of a major shipping wharf, and road construction. Duvalier had asked Eisenhower to help expedite these loans and had warned "that conditions in the Caribbean have been dangerously aggravated by belligerent attitudes and a contemptuous disregard for international rights and agreements—presumably motivated by the East" (Duvalier to Eisenhower, Oct. 8, 1959).

[6] See no. 811. Military leader Paul Eugene Magliore had preceded Duvalier as President (1950–1956) until a military junta had forced him to resign. A series of provisional governments had followed until Duvalier's election to the office in 1957.

[7] Upon assuming the presidency, Duvalier had written, he had instituted several constitutional and administrative reforms. With assistance from U.S. development agencies, he had cut government spending, attempted to balance the budget, and begun to modernize and reorder several government departments. He had assured Eisenhower that new procedures for handling monetary aid would in the future prevent the graft and misappropriation that had occurred in the past (Duvalier to Eisenhower, Oct. 8, 1959).

[8] Duvalier had several times offered to make land available for the United States military to construct guided missile facilities, training camps, or a submarine base in Haiti (Briefing Memorandum for Conversation with Haitian Ambassador, n.d.; Duvalier to Eisenhower, July 13, 1959). In a meeting with Eisenhower on August 4, the Haitian Ambassador had voiced another offer (Memorandum of Conversation, Aug. 4, 1959). On September 19, 1959, Eisenhower had sent a State-drafted memorandum concluding that the United States did not need permanent military installations in Haiti, but that it would be useful on occasion to have access to sites suitable for amphibious training (State, *Foreign Relations*, vol. V, *American Republics*, Microfiche Supplement, HA-18). In his letter of October 8, 1959, Duvalier had assured Eisenhower that any site needed would be made available immediately and that Haiti would vote with the United States in the United Nations. All correspondence is in AWF/I: Haiti.

1354

EM, AWF, International Series:
De Gaulle

To Charles André Joseph Marie de Gaulle
Secret   *October 28, 1959*

Dear General de Gaulle: Thank you for your letter of October twenty-sixth in which you say that you would be agreeable to a Western summit meeting in Paris on December nineteenth.[1] I will be happy to be there on that date. Meanwhile I have asked Secretary of State

Herter to inaugurate in Washington without delay talks with your Ambassador and the Ambassadors of the Federal Republic and Great Britain for the purpose of preparing for our discussions.[2] I believe that we have no time to waste and this thought, as you know, was behind my hope that we Western Heads of Government would be able to meet at an early date. Needless to say we will remain in close and continuous touch with your Government through diplomatic channels.[3] *Sincerely*

---

[1] For background see no. 1350. De Gaulle had repeated his reservations regarding a summit conference "that would be limited to banal declarations of a general nature without positive results." He was also concerned about a "disorderly retreat" on the German problem by the Western powers, which, he said, "would be a severe blow to our Atlantic Alliance." The talks between Eisenhower and Khrushchev and the latter's acceptance of an invitation to visit France, however, had eased the tensions, de Gaulle wrote, and he agreed to a meeting of the Western powers to begin preparations for a summit meeting to be held preferably in April (AWF/I: de Gaulle).
[2] Hervé Alphand was the French Ambassador to the United States. Wilhelm C. Grewe and Harold Caccia were the West German and British ambassadors.
[3] For developments see no. 1377.

1355   *EM, AWF, International Series:*
Panama

To ERNESTO DE LA GUARDIA, JR.   *October 28, 1959*

Dear Mr. President: Since receiving your letter of March seventh, I have given careful consideration to the course of relations between our two countries. I have been particularly encouraged to receive recent information that our representatives have been making progress toward reducing points of divergence in the application of the Treaty of Mutual Understanding and Cooperation of 1955.[1]

The pending issues between our two countries arising in the course of implementation of that Treaty have been and are under continuing study by the responsible officers of this government, including myself.[2] It is clear to me by now that further discussion of the intent and meaning of certain aspects of our treaty undertakings is unlikely to bring about full agreement. However, I do not think that this should deter our efforts to achieve ever-increasing understanding between our two countries. For my part, accordingly, I have approved a number of revisions in operating policies of the Canal Zone authorities which resulted from a meeting of representatives of our two Governments in which you actively participated.[3] I trust that these actions, the substance of which will be communicated to you by Ambassador Harrington, will redound to the benefit of the people of Panama.[4]

I am confident that it is your desire, as it is mine, that our two countries should continue their traditionally close cooperation to insure the efficient operation of the Panama Canal for the benefit of the entire world.[5] *Sincerely*

[1] In his letter of March 7, 1959, the President of Panama had charged that the United States had violated both the Treaty and the understandings reached by the two nations in January 1955 (for background on the Treaty see Galambos and van Ee, *The Middle Way*, no. 753). He alleged that U.S. officials had failed to implement a promised uniform wage scale, and had not eased the unnecessarily stringent security restrictions excluding Panamanian workers from skilled jobs (de la Guardia to Eisenhower, same file as document). On July 25, 1958, Eisenhower had ordered U.S. government agencies to conform to the treaty agreements (P.L. 85-550), and in December, he had issued new employment regulations by executive order (Howe to Goodpaster, Aug. 13, 1958; *Congressional Quarterly* Almanac, vol. XIV, *1958*, p. 475; *U.S. Federal Register*, vol. 23, Nov.–Dec. 1958, p. 10974). De la Guardia, however, maintained that the new regulations only perpetuated the "old system of discrimination" against Panamanian workers and continued to deprive them of "equality of opportunity." Arguing that the deterioration in U.S.-Panamanian relations encouraged their common adversaries and threatened "the principles and ideals of democracy, equality, and respect for human dignity," he had threatened to take the matter to an international court (de la Guardia to Eisenhower, Mar. 7, 1959, AWF/I: Panama). For background on the wage issue see Galambos and van Ee, *The Middle Way*, nos. 1926 and 2020.

In an initial response Eisenhower had assured de laGuardia that he was "deeply interested" in U.S.-Panamanian relations and that he would request a detailed government study (Eisenhower to de la Guardia, Apr. 6, 1959; see also Herter to Eisenhower, Apr. 2, 1959, AWF/I: Panama). Panama's Foreign Minister had rejected the study's proposals in July 1959 (Dillon to Eisenhower, July 11, 1959; Eisenhower to de la Guardia, July 13, 1959, *ibid.*).

Secretary of State Herter had suggested that Eisenhower send this letter in the hope that it would provide a "written record of good faith in cooperating" should Panama carry out the threats to take its accusations to the International Court of Justice (Herter to Eisenhower, Oct. 28, 1959, AWF/I: Panama). On October 12, at an interdepartmental meeting, Eisenhower asked that steps be taken to improve the employment and wage system and to implement a housing loan project. Stressing that the Panama Canal had "deep impact" on foreign relations, he suggested that officials from the Army and State Department work closely together on resolving the issues of conflict (Memorandum for Record, Oct. 12, 1959, and Memorandum of Conference for Record, Oct. 13, 1959, both in AWF/D; see also Memorandum for S/S, Oct. 19, 1959, Herter Papers, Chronological Series). Also on October 12 the President had met with Ambassador Ricardo Arias of Panama and had told him that recent public criticism made by the Panamanians would not help relations. He had hoped Arias would not use his presidential campaign as a vehicle to attack the United States and suggested that another location for the canal might have to be found if satisfactory relations could not be maintained (Memorandum of Conversation, Oct. 12, 1959, AWF/D). For additional background see *New York Times*, December 2, 1959.

[2] After ratification of the 1955 treaties, de la Guardia and other officials had complained that Panamanian business suffered unfair competition from Canal Zone sales

outlets. They also pressed hard for an increase in Panama's share of the profits from canal toll receipts and for the right to fly the country's flag within the Zone (Walter LaFeber, *The Panama Canal: The Crisis in Historical Perspective* [New York, 1978], pp. 115–31; Thomas M. Leonard, *Panama, The Canal and the United States* [Claremont, Cal., 1993], pp. 73–84; and J. Michael Hogan, *The Panama Canal in American Politics* [Carbondale, Ill., 1986], pp. 69–75). For background see State, *Foreign Relations, 1958–1960*, vol. V, *American Republics*, pp. 908–10.

[3] Eisenhower was referring to a September 1 meeting between Panamanian and American officials attended by de la Guardia. Herter had reported that Canal Zone authorities had begun to reduce purchases of goods from third countries and to limit the sale of duty-free luxury items. He suggested that this information could be conveyed orally to the Panamanian President when this letter was delivered to the Ambassador and that information on other issues could be communicated later (Herter to Eisenhower, Oct. 28, 1959, AWF/I: Panama; for developments see nos. 1380, 1443, and 1645).

[4] Julian Fiske Harrington had been appointed U.S. Ambassador to Panama in 1955.

[5] This letter was drafted by the State Department and approved by the President without any changes. The State Department had received the signed original on November 2, 1959, and transmitted it for delivery. On November 4, 1959, Ambassador Harrington had advised withholding the letter in view of the riots in Panama City the previous day. The State Department instructed the Ambassador to return the President's letter to the Department via air pouch (Herter to Eisenhower, Oct. 28, 1959, AWF/I: Panama, State, *Foreign Relations, 1958–1960*, vol. V, *America Republics* Microfiche Supplement, P-22. For developments see no. 1380.

1356 EM, WHCF, Official File 8

TO ROBERT DANIEL MURPHY *October 28, 1959*

Dear Bob: I accept with deep regret, but with complete understanding, your decision to retire from the Foreign Service on October 31, 1959, and at the same time I accept your resignation as Under Secretary of State for Political Affairs, and Chairman, Operations Coordinating Board, as of December 3, 1959.[1]

For more than forty years you have served with great effectiveness and distinction in various capacities in that most difficult and most important area—our relationships with other countries. You have skillfully carried out the most difficult negotiations and well earned your unofficial title of our number one "trouble shooter." Though you have consistently played down your own accomplishments, I am aware, as I am sure many Americans are, of the vast contribution you have made, on behalf of all of us, in your efforts to advance a just and secure peace.[2]

It has been my privilege to work with you on many an assignment since early 1941, when we were together in Algeria.[3] I have always respected your judgment, admired your effectiveness, and valued highly your friendship. I hope that, if need be, Secretary Herter and I may call upon you from time to time for the special advice that you, because of your experience, training and sensitive perception, can so ably give.[4]

Along with your associates in the government, Mrs. Eisenhower and I wish for you and Mildred much happiness in the many years that lie ahead.[5]

With warm personal regard, *As ever*

[1] Murphy had tendered his resignation on October 27 (same file as document). He had served as Deputy Under Secretary of State before his appointment to his current position on August 14 (*New York Times*, July 31, Aug. 15, 1959).

[2] Murphy had begun his diplomatic career in 1917 as a member of the American Legation in Bern, Switzerland. Among the several posts he held were Vice-Consul in Zurich and Munich, American Consul in Paris from 1930 to 1936, and chargé d'affaires to the Vichy government. For further background on Murphy's diplomatic career see Chandler, *War Years*, no. 471; Galambos, *NATO and the Campaign of 1952*, no. 16; and Galambos and van Ee, *The Middle Way*, no. 865.

[3] In 1941, at President Roosevelt's request, Murphy had investigated conditions in French North Africa in preparation for the Allied landings—operation TORCH, the first major Allied ground offensive during World War II. He was appointed the President's personal representative with the rank of Minister to French North Africa.

Eisenhower and Murphy had first met in London in September 1942. After Allied Force Headquarters (AFHQ) moved to North Africa in November Murphy became Eisenhower's Chief of the Civil Affairs Section. See Chandler, *War Years*, vol. II; Eisenhower, *Crusade in Europe*, pp. 85–88, 95–114; and Murphy, *Diplomat Among Warriors*, pp. 99–134.

[4] Murphy would accompany the President on a goodwill tour in December (see no. 1395 and *New York Times*, Nov. 6, 1959).

[5] Murphy's wife was the former Mildred Claire Taylor.

1357   *EM, AWF, Administration Series*

To Arthur Frank Burns   *October 29, 1959*

Dear Arthur: Thank you very much for your letter of October twenty-first and for the account of your conversation with the Russian economists.[1]

I was very much interested in learning what their line of talk is and what you think about it. I am quite in agreement with the Russians' view that we could accomplish a transition to a lower level of defense spending without serious economic dislocation.[2] It seems to me we proved that after the Second World War and again after Korea. But, in my opinion, the Russians' views on our growth prospects underestimate considerably the growth potential of our economy.

I am also interested in your comment that our growth rate has been too low recently.[3] If you have thoughts as to how we could step it up, in addition to what you say in your letter, I should be very glad to know of them.

With warm regard, *Sincerely*

[1] Burns had reported that the Soviet economists had emphasized the problems faced by the American economy due to military spending (AWF/A). Burns believed that this new "party line" was designed to fit neatly into Khrushchev's "new peace offensive." "My guess is that Khrushchev really believes that Russia can beat us soon on the economic front, that the uncommitted areas will go communist when they see this happen, that Russia could move ahead faster on the economic front if some disarmament took place, and that they will know how to disarm 10 per cent when they agree to disarm 20 per cent and get us to do so."

[2] The Soviet economists had said that although the rate of growth of the American economy, which they believed to be less than two percent a year, was low, the rate of improvement of living standards could be raised if a smaller percentage of resources went into defense production. Because Americans had learned how to control the business cycle, partial or complete disarmament could be accomplished without leading to significant unemployment.

[3] In a postscript Burns had disputed the Russian claim that the U.S. economy had been growing at an average rate of less than two percent a year since 1953. "In fact, the average rate shown by official figures is 2.7 per cent and there are some cogent reasons for considering this an understatement." Burns felt that the recent rate of growth had been too low, and that it was "highly important" that a strenuous effort be made to raise it. "Among other things," he said, "we can no longer afford the luxury of a shorter work week or the continuation of feather bedding."

1358   *EM, AWF, Administration Series*

To EMMET JOHN HUGHES   *October 31, 1959*
Personal and confidential

Dear Emmet: Thank you very much for your letter telling me about your forthcoming book.[1] Of course I respect your right to express your own views, no matter how much they differ from my own and even though our sources of information are necessarily far from being the same both as to origin and in detail of content.[2]

There is only one clause in your letter to which I seriously object, because it shows a misconception on your part. It reads ". . . the spirit and direction of foreign policy as conceived and executed by the Department of State over these years." The basic conception and direction of foreign policy is my responsibility and not one of any other Department or individual.[3]

With warm regard, *Sincerely*

[1] Hughes had written on October 22 (AWF/A) about the publication of his critical study of U.S. foreign policy, *America the Vincible* (New York, 1959). See also *New York Times*, November 10, 1959.

[2] Hughes had explained that the letter had not been an "easy letter to write." He acknowledged that Eisenhower would neither "approve of, nor concur with" much of what he had written. He believed, however that "open and honest dissent" was vital to healthy government.

[3] Hughes had explained that he had written the book to express his "increasing anxieties and fears" with regard to the State Department's execution of foreign policy.

1359

EM, AWF,
International Series:
Khrushchev

To Nikita Sergeyevich Khrushchev   *November 2, 1959*

Dear Mr. Chairman:[1] I think you might like to know that Prime Minister Nehru has invited me to visit India, which I have long desired to do.[2] I now find it possible to go to New Delhi early in December. The specific occasion for the visit will be the opening of the American Exhibit at the Agricultural Fair at New Delhi. I shall be making courtesy visits to other countries en route. The full schedule is not yet worked out with the countries concerned, but I expect that an announcement will be made in a few days.[3]

You will recall that during our discussions at Camp David on the question of a future meeting of the Heads of Government, I pointed out that it would be necessary for me to consult with our allies. Since our talks, I have had correspondence with President de Gaulle, Prime Minister Macmillan and Chancellor Adenauer and, as you are aware from news reports, we have agreed to meet together in Paris on December nineteenth.[4] I had hoped that our process of consultation might have been somewhat speedier, but as it turned out the date of December nineteenth was the only one found convenient to all.

I have asked Ambassador Thompson, who is returning to Moscow on November seventh, to see you at your convenience to discuss developments which have occurred since our meeting at Camp David.[5] With best wishes to you and your family, *Sincerely*

[1] State Department officials drafted this letter in response to Eisenhower's suggestion that an opportunity be found to let Soviet Premier Khrushchev know that the United States was working on the problems discussed at Camp David (see Goodpaster, Memorandum of Conference, Nov. 3, 1959, AWF/D; on the Camp David meetings see no. 1332). The text of this message was cabled to Moscow for delivery to Khrushchev on this same day.

² On the Nehru invitation see no. 1304; Herter to Eisenhower, October 21, 1959, AWF/D-H; and Memorandum of Conversation, October 28, 1959, AWF/D; see also State, *Foreign Relations, 1958–1960,* vol. XV, *South and Southeast Asia,* pp. 521–26.

³ Eisenhower would leave on December 3 for visits to Italy, Turkey, Pakistan, Afghanistan, India, Iran, Greece, and Tunisia before the Western summit meeting in Paris on the nineteenth. He would visit Spain and Morocco on his way back to the United States (see Goodpaster, Memorandum of Conference, Nov. 3, 1959, AWF/D; Herter to Eisenhower, Oct. 28, 1959, AWF/D-H; and *Public Papers of the Presidents: Eisenhower, 1959,* p. 766; for Eisenhower's December 11 remarks at the opening of the fair see *ibid.,* pp. 839–42; see also Khrushchev to Eisenhower [Dec. 9, 1959], AWF/I: Khrushchev).

⁴ On the de Gaulle correspondence see no. 1354; on the Macmillan and Adenauer correspondence see no. 1343.

⁵ For developments see no. 1377.

1360   *EM, WHCF, Official File 138-C-1-F*

To CHARLES HARTING PERCY   *November 3, 1959*

Dear Chuck: Only within the past couple of days have I seen any actual copies of the four reports made by the Task Force of your "Committee on Program and Progress."¹ I think it is my own fault that I have not sought out these documents, but I think also that I have possibly been living in the comforting thought that one of these days you would be coming to see me to talk to me about the report, its content and the most practical use to make of it.

Even yet I have not had the chance to give the four pamphlets the study and careful attention that they deserve, but it is easy to see that your group must be credited with a real accomplishment; I think I shall write a short note of thanks to each member of the Task Force.

In the meantime I shall follow up to see that the attention of each of the Department Heads has been directed to the report or reports that has most to do with that particular agency. Indeed, I hope that the distribution can be such that each head of agency can make certain that his higher subordinates have considered carefully the contents of the pamphlets. For example, I think that Reports #1 and #2 would be of special interest to State and to Defense, while #4 should certainly incite the interest of everybody in government.²

I still should like to see you and talk over with you the whole affair.³

With warm regard, *As ever*
P.S.: And I add—congratulations and thanks!

¹ For background see nos. 963 and 982. The four task force reports on "Decisions for a Better America," prepared by the Republican Committee on Program and

Progress (No. 1, "The Impact of Science & Technology"; No. 2, "National Security & Peace"; No. 3., "Human Rights & Needs"; and No. 4, "Economic Opportunity & Progress"), are in the same file as the document.

[2] The science and technology pamphlet argued that "freedom, personal economic opportunities, and material survival" depended on excellence in science and technology. The report urged support for programs at all levels of government and in private organizations. The national security paper called for a defense adequate to "insure our security as a nation," without being "wasteful." The report advised support for efforts at "effective disarmament and control of weapons of mass destruction." The panel recommended that the United States take a leadership role in "protecting freedom where it now exists" and "nurturing it where it can readily develop," and it called for the demilitarization of outer space. "Human Rights & Needs" called for government support to "stimulate the pursuit of excellence" in the schools. The study on economic opportunity and progress reaffirmed the Republican belief that the economic role of government was to "help solve those problems which generally obstruct and interfere with the individual citizen's opportunity to achieve his fullest potential."

[3] Percy would meet with Eisenhower on February 8, 1960, and would follow the meeting with a summary of the report (Percy to Eisenhower, Feb. 8, 1960, same file as document). Noting that the report was a "political document," Percy would emphasize that the purpose of the committee was to "make known to every citizen the Republican approach to broad problem areas and to further make it a matter of record that the Republican party looks forward—indeed forward to 1976—rather than backwards."

1361   *EM, AWF, DDE Diaries Series*

To Samuel Taliaferro Rayburn   *November 3, 1959*

Dear Mr. Sam: It is indeed difficult for me to decline to go along with a personal suggestion of yours affecting an individual in government. Indeed, I cannot recall any case of doing so during the past seven years.[1]

Respecting your note about Judge Witt, I have consistently abided by the laws and regulations governing the retirement of members of the Executive Department and related agencies. I am informed that Judge Witt is over eighty years of age and has more than fifteen years of service. According to the statute, anyone who has achieved the age of seventy, with fifteen years of service, *must* be retired. Frankly, I have very great misgivings about keeping anyone in appointive office who has attained this number of years. I am sorry that in this instance I must differ with your suggestion.

With warm personal regard, *Sincerely*

[1] House Speaker Sam Rayburn had written the President on October 28, 1959 (WHCF/OF 26), to recommend the retention of Judge Edgar E. Witt on the Indian Claims Commission beyond the normal retirement age. "I have known Edgar Witt

for forty years and know him to be an outstanding and capable man," Rayburn wrote. "Many people who practice before that court have written me that they have great confidence in him and that his age is not interfering with his ability to do a good job." In a note to Bryce Harlow, Ann Whitman indicated that this letter was "dictated personally by the President" (Ann Whitman memorandum, n.d., *ibid.*).

1362 *EM, AWF, Name Series*

To William Pierce Rogers *November 4, 1959*
Personal

Dear Bill: Attached is a letter from my brother about Judge John R. Dethmers of Michigan, together with a copy of my reply (which was prepared on the basis of information secured from the Deputy Attorney General).[1]

It is my understanding that Judge Walsh assumes Ed's information is incorrect, since no inquiry has been made by you to the American Bar Association regarding Judge Dethmers.[2] Even so, I still think there is a possibility that Ed may be right in his report on the conclusion of the ABA.[3]

At any rate, here's the exchange of letters.

With warm regard, *As ever*

[1] Edgar Eisenhower had written on October 30 (AWF/N) in support of the appointment of Judge Dethmers to the Michigan Sixth Circuit Court of Appeals. Dethmers (LL.B. University of Michigan 1927) had served as Michigan Attorney General from 1945–1946, when he was appointed to the Michigan Superior Court. Edgar had said that the American Bar Association's committee on the selection of federal judges had told him that Dethmers was their first choice for that appointment. Eisenhower's November 4 reply to Edgar, promising to discuss the appointment with the Attorney General, is in AWF/N.

[2] Eisenhower was referring to Judge Lawrence Edward Walsh (LL.B. Columbia University 1935), who had been appointed U.S. Deputy Attorney General in 1957. Walsh had served as a district court judge in the Southern District of New York from 1954–1957. A memorandum from Ann Whitman (n.d., AWF/N) stated that: "Jerry Morgan says that Ed's information must be incorrect; that Justice has never submitted Dethmers' name to the Bar Association. He also said Dethmers organized a group of state supreme court justices to criticize the Supreme Court a few years ago." As it turned out, Dethmers would not receive the appointment; he would instead be appointed Chief Justice of the Michigan Supreme Court (see *New York Times,* Jan. 15, 1960).

[3] Eisenhower had written on the memorandum from Whitman: "In any event send Ed's letter for Atty Gen. attention. He deserves as much courtesy as we give anyone else. I don't see why the ABA could not say this—even if Justice has not made an inquiry."

LEONARD DUDLEY HEATON   *November 5, 1959*

Dear Leonard: As quickly as I came back from the hospital I meant to send you a package of the new "Super" Gillette blades. I am now experimenting with my own. I find that on the first day the shave is absolutely perfect. The second day there is little difference. On the third I begin to notice some deterioration, but even so I think the shave is still better than it was with the old "Blue Blades." Tentatively I am adopting the schedule of throwing the blade away after three days.[1]

I shall be interested to see what you conclude after using this package.[2]

Give my best to Sara Hill.[3] *As ever*

[1] On September 9 Heaton, Commanding General of Walter Reed Army Hospital, had been promoted to the rank of Lieutenant General and had been appointed Surgeon General of the U.S. Army (*New York Times*, Sept. 10, 1959). On the evening of October 29 the President had entered his suite at Walter Reed for his annual exam and had dined with Heaton in the hospital dining room. The following morning Eisenhower had undergone a complete physical examination. The President had received sample packages of the improved razor blades from an executive of the Gillette Safety Razor Company (see Eisenhower to Brownlee, Nov. 5, 1959, AWF/D).
[2] Although we have been unable to find a reply from Heaton, Eisenhower received favorable reports from the other friends to whom he had given the samples (*ibid.*).
[3] The former Sara Hill Richardson was Heaton's wife.

1364   *EM, AWF,*
                                                        Administration Series

TO GEORGE MAGOFFIN HUMPHREY   *November 6, 1959*
Personal

Dear George: When we were talking on the phone last evening, there was a matter that I intended to take up but allowed it to slip my mind. It was your feeling, as expressed to Al Gruenther, that the individuals that I have selected to head what I call my "Coordinated Policy" or "Goals" Committee are not up to the job.[1]

The selection of people for this kind of thing is a very tricky and tough business. First of all, if it were headed by a big businessman, I think it would probably be boycotted by labor—the reverse of this statement is probably also true. In these circumstances I decided to go into the educational field to find a man of the professional qualifications and national standing who could fill the bill as Chairman.

I think my own personal choice would have been my younger brother—but, he has the wrong name. There were two college presidents that I thought of, but upon approaching them found that they were so heavily committed for the next year and a half that it was impossible for them to undertake the job.[2]

Arthur Burns has established for himself a national name and he is known as one of the sounder and more realistic economists.[3] While he is not pure "Adam Smith," he is certainly a long way from the Schlichter school.[4]

Since he was in my Administration for a long time, he of course is known as a Republican and I found it necessary to hunt for a Deputy Chairman who was known to be a Democrat and an intelligent man. I went to Frank Pace.[5] I understand clearly that he heads a company whose principal business is with the government, but the only thing I am doing in the whole business is to try to get the show on the road—there will be *no government influence or connection with the matter* except as the different Task Forces want to get from the different Departments facts and statistics. I discussed these two names with a number of my friends and while, as I say, there seemed to be no ideal solution, these two seemed to fit the bill fairly well. At the same time I approached Clark Kerr, President of the University of California, who has a very fine reputation in this country and who has been known as a sort of champion of labor.[6] His tentative acceptance gave me a counterbalance for Frank Pace in what might be called the purely economic field. With these three men I hope—once we can see that private financing has been made adequate—to consult together in order to get two or possibly four more members of the Board. I do not want anyone who is carrying a torch for any "ism" or is too much controversial. On the other hand, I would like to get a very fine lawyer—possibly a lawyer who has acted in some capacity as a mediator in labor-management disputes, is known as a "Constitutional" lawyer. Alongside him I would like also to get a solid businessman who has a good name and reputation, but who is not easily classified as "big business."

Now, to be a bit more specific about the purpose I have in mind. Every day there come questions to my desk that deal with matters that are more than merely transitory and temporary. It would be a great help to me if I could have the results of a study that tries to visualize the future of America, both at home and internationally, and what we should be doing to realize those hopes. What we are talking about here is the coordination of the policies that should guide us as a people. These would of course deal with education, health and well-being of our people at home, the growth of our economy, the soundness of our fiscal arrangements, and all matters that are related to these fundamental subjects. Our success in going forward on these lines will be affected by our standing in the world and what we do to make the world a place in which our national ambitions can be realized. Such a study would therefore involve the coordination of policy, domestic and foreign, to achieve these goals. So I have referred to the Committee, for convenience, as a "Goals" Committee.

The final report must be such as to command the confidence of our people. The result would be far wider than merely giving some guidance to the political officials. We would hope to have it so publicized that thinking people in every walk of life and in every corner of our country would see that their daily decisions will be more often correct if they conform generally to the great policies and goals we have set for ourselves extending on for the next eight to ten years.

This does not mean that the study, no matter how well executed, will be perfect. But it will provide a series of logical conclusions useful to the busy Executive, whether in business or in government, to ponder and consider. From such an effort it seems some good would almost certainly result.

I should like to point out that we are talking about such practical matters as the cost of the Atomic Energy Commission, of the Defense Department, of the mutual security program, the cost to the Federal government of every kind of domestic program, many of which include grants to states, the building of roads, and assistance to farmers. If we could get a better national understanding and better executive decisions in any one of these areas, we could in a single year possibly save ten times the amount that the study itself would cost, even though that cost would not be negligible.

Such a project could not be carried out except through a series of Task Forces and the men on the Task Forces would have to be assisted by researchers and analysts.

I am quite certain that the project is worthwhile. While it is quite possible that I have not obtained the ideal personnel, I still think they are people that could turn out a good honest result.[7]

*   *   *   *   *

Needless to say, I am sorry I can't see my way clear to a visit to the Cedar Point Club but it just seems impossible in view of the schedule I have laid out for myself.

Give my love to Pam and all the best to yourself. *As ever*

[1] On June 15, 1959, Eisenhower had named Arthur F. Burns, former chairman of the Council of Economic Advisors (1953–1956), and Frank Pace, president of General Dynamics and former Director of the Bureau of the Budget, as cochairmen of the National Goals Committee (see nos. 999, 1059, and 1185; *New York Times,* June 15, 1959).

² Eisenhower was probably referring to Dr. Lawrence A. Kimpton, chancellor of the University of Chicago and Dr. James Lewis Morrill, president of the University of Minnesota. Both apparently were willing to serve, but neither could obtain leave from their respective universities (see Merriam, Memorandum for Record, Robert E. Merriam, Mar. 18 and 19; *New York Times,* Apr. 20, 1959).

³ In addition to serving in the Administration, Burns had published several books and was at this time president of the National Bureau of Economic Research.

⁴ Dr. Sumner Huber S/ichter (A.B. University of Wisconsin 1913), a noted economist and specialist in industrial relations at Harvard University, was known for his unorthodox economic views. Unlike Eisenhower, he had favored an unbalanced budget and maintained that moderate inflation was necessary for maximum economic growth; he also thought wage increases would benefit the economy. Slichter had died on September 28 (*New York Times,* Mar. 21 and Sept. 29, 1959).

⁵ For background on Pace see no. 1185.

⁶ A specialist in labor economics, Dr. Clark Kerr (B.A. Swarthmore 1932) had served as director of the Institute for Industrial Relations at Berkeley before becoming President of the University of California at Berkeley in 1952. He had also been active in labor arbitration. See also Memorandum for Record, Robert E. Merriam, June 15, 1959, AWF/D.

⁷ For developments see no. 1428.

1365   *EM, AWF, International Series:*
                                                              Paraguay

To Alfredo Stroessner   *November 7, 1959*

Dear Mr. President: I have received your letter of September twenty-third, which was delivered by the Paraguayan Minister of Finance.¹

I have noted your request for various transport aircraft and have instructed appropriate agencies of the Government to begin an immediate study of the request. Let me assure you that this matter will be accorded most careful consideration and that the result of the study will be communicated to your Government, through normal diplomatic channels, as soon as possible.²

Your vivid account of Paraguay's heroic past and of her people's dedication to peace, work and progress refers to a notable chapter in the history of the Americas. With respect to more recent times, I extend most sincere congratulations on what Paraguay has done, and continues to do, to promote economic and financial stability in order to build a solid foundation for the progress to which Paraguayans aspire and which they rightly merit. I appreciate your sending me the album of photographs showing the public works that are under way throughout the country.

That Paraguay and the United States have been good friends and neighbors for a long time is evidenced by the fact that this year marks the one hundredth anniversary of the signing of the Treaty of Friendship, Commerce and Navigation between the two countries. We have, particularly in recent years, been endeavoring to cooperate with the Paraguayan people in their efforts to overcome the economic and social problems which have stood in the way of their aspirations to a better life. I am confident that this cooperation will continue to characterize relations between the peoples of our two countries.

Permit me to extend my best wishes for the continued prosperity and progress of Paraguay, and for the enduring friendship which unites our two nations.[3] *Sincerely*

[1] This letter, drafted by State Department officials, was sent to the American embassy in Paraguay for delivery to President Stroessner on November 9 (see Herter to Eisenhower, Oct. 27, 1959, AWF/I: Paraguay). Stroessner had recounted the history of Paraguay, its struggle to survive after a devastating nineteenth-century war, its dedication to Pan-Americanism, and its friendship with the United States. He followed these pleasantries by asking Eisenhower for four DC-4 airplanes, six DC-3 airplanes, and six AT-6 training planes (AWF/I: Paraguay). César Barrientos was Paraguay's finance minister.

[2] For background on U.S. aid to Paraguay see Galambos and van Ee, *The Middle Way*, nos. 660 and 1925; see also State, *Foreign Relations, 1958–1960*, vol. V, *American Republics*, Microfiche Supplement, PA 3–5, 7. Eisenhower had told Secretary Herter that he doubted any of these old planes were still available. He also told Herter that "he would rather just say no than to give this sort of soft-soap reply which cast [him] in the role of a Pontius Pilate." For his part, Herter was particularly concerned about Paraguay's ability to use the planes and wanted to return this kind of correspondence to the usual diplomatic channels (*ibid.*, PA 9).

This paragraph was expanded from the original draft to reflect Eisenhower's desire to give Stroessner "a somewhat more definite commitment subject to further study" (AWF/I: Paraguay).

[3] Although the United States would not provide the planes, the State Department would recommend that Paraguay be given a loan from the International Bank for Reconstruction and Development (IBRD, the World Bank) for the establishment of an economic development bank (Rubottom to Brand, Nov. 17, 1959, State, *Foreign Relations, 1958–1960*, vol. V, *American Republics*, Microfiche Supplement, PA 10; see also *ibid.*, PA 12). Later, economic setbacks would prompt the Paraguayan government to ask for additional aid in the form of loans (*New York Times*, Feb. 20, 1960).

1366   *EM, AWF, Name Series*

To Aksel Nielsen   *November 7, 1959*

Dear Aks: Don't you realize that in this new moral era into which television has plunged us that there is no, repeat no, effort to conceal the facts?[1] In other words, what were all the scores as a result of your Pebble Beach game?[2]

A fairly formal letter is going off to you today to express my official thanks for your participation in the recommendation for the World's Fair. I need only add that I am grateful, as always, for your willingness to undertake any chore on which I need help.[3]

With warm regard, *As ever*

P.S. I'll keep in mind that Reverend Miller will deliver the sermon at the National Presbyterian Church on January tenth.[4]

[1] The reference is to the quiz-show scandals (see no. 1368).

[2] Nielsen had written on November 3 that he was becoming "a full-fledged-golfer." He had played golf with three friends, and while he did not do as well as one of them, he did better than the other two. He did not wish to "embarrass" the losers, he said, because his score had been 121.

[3] The official letter is not in AWF. In early October the President had appointed Nielsen to serve on a three-man committee to select the site for the 1964 World's Fair. On October 28 the commission took testimony from the three major aspirants—New York, Washington, D.C., and Los Angeles—and chose New York. Eisenhower approved the report the following day (*New York Times*, Aug. 10, 12, 13, Oct. 30, 1959). For developments see no. 1708.

[4] Arthur Lemoine Miller (A.B. Indiana University 1922; B.D. McCormick Theological Seminary 1925) had been pastor of Montview Boulevard Presbyterian Church in Denver since 1947. As the current moderator of the United Presbyterian Church of the United States of America, Miller was scheduled to preach in Washington, D.C. The Eisenhowers would, however, spend the weekend of January 8–10 at their Gettysburg farm.

1367   *EM, AWF, Ann Whitman Diary Series*

MEMORANDUM   *November 9, 1959*

Memorandum for the Record: On Saturday morning, November 7th, the Supreme Court approved the injunction ordering the steel workers back to their jobs for a period of eighty days.[1]

From the very beginning of negotiations between steel management and the union, I have been indirectly—or even occasionally directly—in contact with some of the participating individuals, so as to keep in touch with the issues that seemed to be primarily at stake. My principal informant has been Secretary Mitchell.[2]

What seems to be involved primarily is different convictions concerning the so-called "work rules."[3]

The management seems to believe that these rules are antiquated and in themselves compel an inefficient type of operation that helps to price their products out of the market, especially foreign markets.

On the other hand, the union labels as trust-busting any attempt to change these so-called work rules.

Secretary Mitchell and I believe that the management does not comprehend how seriously the union membership takes this matter. The management seems to believe that the issues are raised merely to achieve a better wage settlement. On the other hand, the union asserts that it has never stood in the way of improved technology and in achieving automation. It insists that it is quite ready to submit arguments on this point to arbitration.

On Friday evening, November sixth, Mr. McDonald came to see me, off the record.[4] He was accompanied by Secretary Mitchell. He professed himself as being very anxious for a fair and just and non-inflationary settlement, and he seemed to believe that Mr. Cooper, the negotiator for the steel management, is not only very rigid and stupid but is obsessed with a distorted conviction as to the importance of these so-called work rules.[5] I sent Secretary Mitchell to see Mr. Blough, President of U. S. Steel and to keep in very close touch with the matter to see whether something might be done.[6] Mr. Blough and Mr. McDonald met either Saturday or Sunday for a two hour meeting and have agreed to meet again on Wednesday.

I earnestly hope that something will be done promptly.[7]

[1] For background see no. 1287. On November 7, 1959, the Supreme Court had upheld, in an 8 to 1 ruling, the constitutionality of the Taft-Hartley injunction (invoked by Eisenhower on October 19) and its application to the steel strike (*New York Times,* Oct. 10, 20, Nov. 8, 1959).

[2] See Eisenhower, *Waging Peace,* pp. 453–59.

[3] The steel industry had demanded greater authority over work practices at the plant level in order to end "featherbedding," and had made agreement to such changes a precondition to any pay raise. The union held that the old rules did not obstruct maximum output and that the industry sought new rules only to restore "industrial dictatorship." It had offered to guarantee that work rules were not intended to block progress, or to leave the issue to future study by a joint committee (*New York Times,* Oct. 10, 1959).

[4] David John McDonald (Carnegie Institute of Technology 1932) had served as president of the United Steelworkers of America since 1953. He was concurrently vice-president of the AFL-CIO. Eisenhower had met with McDonald for 70 minutes on the evening of November 5. Following the meeting the President called Secretary of Labor Mitchell to say that McDonald "really wants to settle. He really wants to compromise. He has a political problem and he does not quite know how to handle it with his own union" (see Ann Whitman memorandum, Nov. 5, 1959, AWF/AWD).

[5] Richard Conrad Cooper (B.S. University of Minnesota 1926) had served as U.S. Steel executive vice-president for administration and planning since 1955. For more on Cooper's bargaining position see Tiffany, *The Decline of American Steel,* pp. 162–65.

[6] Roger M. Blough (A.B. Susquehanna University 1925; LL.B. Yale 1931) had joined U.S. Steel as general solicitor in 1942, becoming executive vice-president for law in 1951. He had succeeded Benjamin Fairless as chairman in 1955 and was currently U.S. Steel's chief executive officer.

[7] For developments see no. 1375.

President Eisenhower holds a special meeting of legislative leaders in his White House office March 6, 1959. *Front row, L to R:* House Minority Leader Charles A. Halleck, Senate Majority Leader Everett M. Dirksen, Speaker of the House Samuel T. Rayburn, President Eisenhower, Senate Majority Leader Lyndon B. Johnson, Vice-President Richard M. Nixon. *Back row, L to R:* Central Intelligence Agency Director Allen W. Dulles, Under Secretary of State Christian A. Herter, and Secretary of Defense Neil H. McElroy.

President Eisenhower jokes with Secretary of the Navy Thomas S. Gates, Jr. (*right*), prior to his being named Deputy Secretary of Defense, May 19, 1959. Secretary of Defense Neil H. McElroy stands to the left.

President Eisenhower meets with (*L to R*) Britain's Prime Minister Harold Macmillan, Under Secretary of State Christian A. Herter, and British Foreign Affairs Secretary Selwyn Lloyd at Camp David, Maryland, March 20–22, 1959.

President Eisenhower and His Imperial Majesty
Shah Mohammed Reza Pahlavi meet in the Marble
Palace following the President's address to a joint
session of the Iranian Senate and Majlis (lower
house), December 14, 1959.

President Eisenhower greets Prime Minister David Ben-Gurion of Israel (*left*)
and Under Secretary of State C. Douglas Dillon (*right*) at the White House,
March 10, 1960.

Sir Winston Churchill and President Eisenhower pause for a moment during the former Prime Minister's visit to Washington, D.C., May 4–6, 1959.

Eisenhower motorcades in Paris with General de Gaulle at the beginning of the President's tour of Europe, September 2, 1959.

President Eisenhower hosts a stag dinner for his wartime colleagues at Winfield House, September 1, 1959. *Front row, L to R:* Field Marshal Viscount Bernard L. Montgomery, Viscount Alan Francis Brooke, Sir Winston Churchill, President Eisenhower, Field Marshal Earl Harold Alexander, Prime Minister Harold Macmillan. *Back row, L to R:* Major General Sir Francis de Guingand, Marshal of the R.A.F. Viscount Charles Portal, Marshal of the R.A.F. Lord Arthur Tedder, Lieutenant General Sir Brian Horrocks, General Lord Hastings Ismay, Marshal of the R.A.F. Sir Arthur Harris, Brigadier General Andrew J. Goodpaster.

President Eisenhower poses with Soviet Premier Nikita Sergeyevich Khrushchev in front of the Aspen cottage at Camp David, Maryland, September 25, 1959.

Khrushchev inspects the remains of the downed U-2 plane, May 1960.

President Eisenhower lifts a gavel made of Kansas pecan wood
at the Republican Convention in Chicago, July 1960.

To WILLIAM D. KERR   *November 9, 1959*

Dear Bill:[1] Thank you very much for your note of the sixth.[2]

I am attaching a letter from a gentleman who wrote to his Congressman as a result of a suggestion from you. (I am happy to say that his views and yours do not coincide). But I thought you would be interested to see at least one comment provoked by the speech you gave in New York on October fourteenth.[3]

As far as the television situation goes, I am in agreement with much of what you say, but I do not think that the President or the government can get into the business of deciding what kind of programs should be presented. As I said in my press conference the other day, the Justice Department is undertaking a study to see what laws, if any, have been broken, and the FTC is also conducting an independent investigation. But I do think that moral pressure upon the networks for the proper kind of programs for youngsters should come from the homes, schools, churches, and the many organizations in America who are dedicated to making our country a better place to live.[4]

With warm regard, *Sincerely*

[1] William D. Kerr was an investment banker with Bacon, Whipple and Company in Chicago (for background see Galambos and van Ee, *The Middle Way*, no. 680). He was president of the Investment Bankers Association of America.

[2] Kerr had written regarding a talk on inflation that Eisenhower had given to a breakfast meeting of representatives from forty-eight business and industrial organizations. The President had emphasized the importance of public opinion in an expanding but sound economy. The inspiration that the group received was "substantial," Kerr had written (Kerr to Eisenhower, Nov. 6, 1959, same file as document; see also *Public Papers of the Presidents: Eisenhower, 1959*, pp. 760–74).

[3] The letter is not in AWF. In a speech at the annual dinner of the bankers association Kerr had urged a change in federal economic policy, calling for a balanced budget with a provision for debt retirement, an increase in the ceiling on interest rates on long-term federal debt, and an end to the upward wage-price spiral (*New York Times*, Oct. 15, 1959).

[4] On November 2 an investigation of television quiz shows had culminated in the disclosure that contestants had been given the questions and answers in advance. Kerr had told Eisenhower that the situation was "a mess and must be corrected." He also asked Eisenhower to address the subject of the material presented on TV programs. "There are few things that menace the youth of our country to the extent that everyday television does," he wrote (see *Public Papers of the Presidents: Eisenhower, 1959*, p. 769; see also Galambos and van Ee, *The Middle Way*, no. 1751; and *New York Times*, Nov. 2, 3, 1959).

To Douglas McRae Black   *November 9, 1959*
Personal and confidential

Dear Doug: Because I have an intermittent correspondence with Pug
Ismay, I have known for some time that he has been working on his
memoirs. I thought—perhaps I merely assumed—that he already
had a publisher.[1]

As for the suggestion that Pug might write an introduction to a
new edition of *Crusade in Europe*, to be published in London, my
confidential thoughts run along this line. From the days of the war
he was a man I admired and since that time he has devoted a great
deal of time to useful work for his country and in furthering the
purposes of the Western world. I have for him a warm and staunch
friendship. Should Pug, at your request, feel it fitting for him to
write a short foreword to the reprint of *Crusade in Europe*, I assure
you that I would have no objection.

He has long known that I have never allowed anyone to "defend"
me against any public charge. Indeed, if you will look at page 428
of *Crusade*, you will find a little paragraph quoted from my Victory
Order of the Day, written on May 8, 1945. The paragraph to which
I refer begins "Let us have no part in the profitless quarrels . . .". So
far as I know I have not, myself, consciously violated the exhorta-
tion I then delivered to the command. The paragraph might just as
well have contained the word "individual" as well as "country" and
"service."[2]

If a foreword should be added, I *think* it might be helpful if this
short little paragraph be included, and that there be *no further mention* of quarrels, charges, counter-charges, individual criticisms, and
so on.[3]

As you know, I have long believed—in fact I told you this emphatically way back in 1947—that a soldier should confine his memoirs to a simple narrative account of those affairs in which he was a
part. A soldier is not a trained historian and he does not have the
time or possibly the qualifications to dig through all of the records
across the board to learn what others were *thinking, believing* and *doing.*

With this conviction you can well understand that I would not
want anyone to hold up *Crusade* as anything more than what it purports to be—a simple and, I hope, honest account of the war activities with which I had to deal. Moreover, wherever there is given in
the book any impression of mine concerning an individual, it invariably winds up with an expression of respect and even admiration.

I have given you these personal impressions because I would not want to feel that any friend, no matter how devoted, would find a compulsion or reaction for defending and explaining my past decisions and actions. Whatever their quality, the record must stand for itself.[4]

With warm personal regard, *As ever*

[1] Black, president of Doubleday & Company, had written on November 4 (AWF/N) that he had been talking to a British publisher about publishing Lord Ismay's memoirs. On the memoirs see no. 1012.

[2] Alexander S. Frere, who in 1947 had been responsible for publishing Eisenhower's memoir in London, had made the suggestion as a result of the recent flurry of attacks by British generals "sniping" at the President. The publisher said it annoyed him, and Ismay, who was "more than annoyed," and had been "sharpening his pen" (Frere to Black, Nov. 2, 1959; see also Black to Frere, Nov. 4, 1959 and Frere to Black, Nov. 10, 1959, all in AWF/N, Black Corr.). On the controversy over some of the publications see, for example, nos. 1104, 1197, and 1286; Alanbrooke to Eisenhower, n.d., and Eisenhower to Alanbrooke, Nov. 20, 1959, both in AWF/N).

[3] Eisenhower quotes the paragraph in the following document.

[4] Black would reply on November 12 that if the re-issue of *Crusade in Europe* would "aggravate the situation in London" then it should be dropped. That same day Black would write his London associate that "good taste and human dignity" do not permit self-respecting people "to engage in 'profitless quarrels.'" "Long after the event," he said, "pettiness and ... quite crude and bald innuendo is directed against the President of the United States who is continuing his major part in helping to solve the problems of our civilization. Let us have no part in it" (Black to Frere, Nov. 12, 1959, both in AWF/N).

1370

*EM, WHCF,
Confidential File:
State Department*

To Cornelius Wendell Wickersham   *November 9, 1959*

Dear Neil:[1] Thank you for your memorandum on the Cuban situation. I shall take the liberty of sending it along to Chris Herter, on a confidential basis. For the moment about all I can say is that we have been and shall continue to watch developments there closely.[2]

As for your comment about Alanbrooke, may I refer you, with all modesty of course, to the following paragraph from my Victory Order of the Day (May 8, 1945):

"Let us have no part in the profitless quarrels in which other men will inevitably engage as to what country, what service, won the European war. Every man, every woman, of every nation here represented has served according to his or her ability, and the efforts of each have contributed to the outcome. This we shall remember—and in doing so we shall be revering each honored grave, and be sending comfort to the loved ones of comrades who could not live to see this day."

I prefer to look on the positive side of all quarrels, and I do think most of us have lived up to what I thought, and still think, was the only right course of action.[3]

With warm regard, *As ever*

---

[1] For background on Cornelius Wendell Wickersham, who had served with Eisenhower in Europe during World War II and was a partner in the New York law firm Cadwalader, Wickersham and Taft, see Chandler and Galambos, *Occupation, 1945*, no. 313; and Galambos, *NATO and the Campaign of 1952*, no. 483.

[2] For background on the Cuban situation see nos. 1142 and 1265. In the past six months a number of developments had prompted the U.S. government to reevaluate its attitude toward Fidel Castro's government and the course of the Cuban revolution. Castro had authorized land confiscations as well as the seizure of records belonging to foreign companies that had been prospecting for oil in Cuba. Controls were placed on imports from the United States, and Communists had moved into positions of power in the National Agrarian Reform Institute, the universities, the media, and organized labor. Anti-American sentiment in Cuba had reached a new high when on October 21 an airplane, apparently based in Florida, had flown over Havana and dropped leaflets attacking Castro and his moves toward communism. At his news conference on October 28 Eisenhower had discussed the situation in Cuba and the difficulties in controlling flights that could originate from any one of the two hundred airfields in Florida (State, *Foreign Relations, 1958–1960*, vol. VI, *Cuba*, pp. 509–16, 524–34, 537–41, 543–44, 564–74, 595–605, 611–23, 627–58; *Public Papers of the Presidents: Eisenhower, 1959*, pp. 751, 753; NSC meeting minutes, Oct. 29, 1959, AWF/NSC; Eisenhower, *Waging Peace*, pp. 523–24; Bonsal, *Cuba, Castro, and the United States*, pp. 70–109; Rabe, *Eisenhower and Latin America*, pp. 124–27; and Quirk, *Fidel Castro*, pp. 254–72).

Wickersham had told Eisenhower that the U.S. government should take action to prevent "the chaos and barbarism" that was rapidly developing in Cuba. In his memorandum he had cited many alleged abuses of power by the Castro government, including the recently announced suspension of the writ of *habeas corpus*. He wanted the government to protect the rights and property of American citizens as well as the citizens of other countries and asked for measures to prevent the further proliferation of Communist policies (Wickersham to Eisenhower, and Memorandum Regarding Cuba, Nov. 6, 1959, same file as document). For developments see no. 1516.

[3] For background on Alanbrooke, chief of the British Imperial General Staff during World War II, and the controversy surrounding the first volume of Alanbrooke's wartime diaries, see no. 550. Wickersham had referred to the recently-published second volume of Arthur Bryant's, *Triumph in the West*, in which Alanbrooke had been quoted as saying that Eisenhower was "no commander . . . had no strategic vision, was incapable of making a plan or of running operations when started." Shortly before the Battle of the Bulge, Alanbrooke recounted, Eisenhower was "on the golf links at Rheims—entirely detached and taking practically no part in running the war" (pp. 254, 255; see also *New York Times*, Oct. 31, 1959). Wickersham had told Eisenhower that he was "disgusted with Alanbrooke's remarks" and that "such idle gossip should never have escaped [the] editorial pen" (Wickersham to Eisenhower, Nov. 6, 1959, same file as document).

To Michael Joseph Mansfield   *November 10, 1959*

Dear Mr. Chairman: I am advised that on October 8, 1959, there was delivered to the Office of the Director of the International Cooperation Administration your written request that you be furnished with that agency's evaluation report of the program in Viet-Nam.[1]

As I have stated on other occasions, it is the established policy of the Executive Branch to provide the Congress and the public with the fullest possible information consistent with the national interest. This policy has guided, and will continue to guide, the Executive Branch in carrying out the Mutual Security Program so that there may be a full understanding of the program and its vital importance to the national security.

At the same time, however, under the historic doctrine of the separation of powers between the three great branches of our Government, the Executive has a recognized Constitutional duty and power with respect to the disclosure of information, documents and other materials relating to its operations. The President has throughout our history, in compliance with his duty in this regard, withheld information when he found that the disclosure of what was sought would be incompatible with the national interest.

It is essential to effective administration that employees of the Executive Branch be in a position to be fully candid in advising with each other on official matters, and that the broadest range of individual opinions and advice be available in the formulation of decisions and policy. It is similarly essential that those who have the responsibility for making decisions be able to act with the knowledge that a decision or action will be judged on its merits and not on whether it happened to conform to or differ from the opinions or advice of subordinates. The disclosure of conversations, communications or documents embodying or concerning such opinions and advice can accordingly tend to impair or inhibit essential reporting and decision-making processes, and such disclosure has therefore been forbidden in the past, as contrary to the national interest, where that was deemed necessary for the protection of orderly and effective operation of the Executive Branch.

The ICA evaluation report which you have requested, which I understand is the August 15, 1957 report entitled "Evaluation of Viet-Nam Program", is an internal Executive Branch communication comprising opinion and advice on official matters.[2] It is one of a class of reports prepared by small teams of senior officers on the basis of extensive study in the field and in Washington. The purpose of each such report is to examine basic ICA program objectives and program content in a particular country from the standpoint of determining whether the ICA program in that country is effectively carrying out our foreign policy objectives. Such reports contain the candid personal opinions, suggestions and recommendations of the officers who prepare them, and are prepared for submission directly to the Director of the ICA for his information and use. Reports such as the one which you requested have been an important factor in the decision-making process within the agency, and requests for their release have consistently been denied.

Since the disclosure of the report requested by you would not be compatible with the national interest, I have forbidden that it be furnished pursuant to such request and hereby so certify in accordance with Section 111(d) of the Mutual Security Appropriation Act, 1960.[3]

Although I have forbidden the furnishing of the evaluation report requested by you, I wish to make it clear that this has not been done for the purpose of preventing the disclosure of any facts shown by the report. Such facts will be made available to you as promptly as possible.[4] *Sincerely*

[1] See no. 1300 for background on the congressional investigation of the foreign aid program in Vietnam. Mansfield was chairman of the Senate Foreign Relations Subcommittee on State Department Organization and Public Affairs and the Committee on Foreign Affairs (see Dillon to Eisenhower, Nov. 7, 1959, same file as document). A State Department draft of this letter is in the same file as the document.

[2] The International Cooperation Administration (ICA) evaluation of the aid program in Vietnam and related correspondence are in *ibid.*

[3] The President had signed P.L. 86-383, the Mutual Security Appropriations Act of 1960, on September 28. Section 111(d) required the President to respond within thirty-five days to any authorized congressional request for material relating to the administration of any provision of the Mutual Security Act by the ICA, except military assistance. The ICA was required to furnish either the material or a certification by the President that he had denied the request, together with his reasons for doing so (*U.S. Statutes at Large*, vol. 73 [1959], p. 720).

[4] Staff members of Mansfield's subcommittee would spend three weeks in Vietnam investigating the program. On December 17 Mansfield would write the President that he had not received the information respecting the ICA evaluation and that his subcommittee was in the process of preparing its report. On December 28 Presidential Aide Bryce Harlow would apologize for the delay and would confirm that a report had been submitted (Harlow to Mansfield, both in same file as document). The subcommittee would release its report on February 26 (see U.S. Congress, Senate, Committee on Foreign Relations, Subcommittee on State Department Organization and Public Affairs, *United States Aid in Vietnam*, 86th Cong., 2d sess., 1960). The report, although mildly worded, would criticize the non-military aspects of the aid program (see State, *Foreign Relations, 1958–1960*, vol. I, *Vietnam*, pp. 274, 289; *Congressional Quarterly Almanac*, vol. XV, *1959*, p. 730; and *New York Times*, Dec. 24, 1959, Feb. 27, Sept. 25, 1960).

In December and again in August 1960 Eisenhower would invoke Section 111(d) of the Mutual Security Appropriation Act, 1960 (see Eisenhower to Campbell, Dec.

15, 1959; Eisenhower to Campbell, Aug. 31, 1960; and other correspondence in same file as document).

1372

EM, AWF, International Series: Nehru

To Jawaharlal Nehru

November 10, 1959

Dear Prime Minister: I am particularly delighted, on this occasion of your seventieth birthday, to send my congratulations and best wishes for continued health and long life.[1]

This important milestone in your career offers me the opportunity to felicitate you on your many accomplishments during the long service that you have devoted to India and its people. Your leadership over many years, especially in the office of Prime Minister, has inspired your own people as well as millions outside of India. Through your writings, moreover, you have shared with others, including many Americans, your appreciation of India's noble past and the bright hope of its future.

Although any man could well be proud of this record of achievement, I know that your thoughts are not directed to the past but to the present and the future. You have devoted your life to the realization of a just and peaceful world order; but many problems remain to be solved before this goal can be reached.

I am looking forward to seeing you in a few weeks.[2]

With warm personal regard, *Sincerely*

[1] State Department officials and the American ambassador to India had suggested that Eisenhower send this message to Nehru. Much would be made of the prime minister's birthday, Secretary Herter had told Eisenhower, and many heads of state would send him personal greetings. The message was sent by cable to the American embassy for delivery to Nehru, with the request that it be released only on the Indian leader's initiative (Herter to Eisenhower, Nov. 6, 1959, AWF/I: Nehru). A State Department draft with Eisenhower's handwritten emendations is in *ibid.*

[2] For background on Eisenhower's trip to India and ten other countries see no. 1359. He would arrive in New Delhi on December 9 (see no. 1315; see also Prasad to Eisenhower, Nov. 5, 1959; Herter to Eisenhower, Nov. 12, 1959; and Eisenhower to Prasad, Nov. 14, 1959; all in AWF/I: Nehru).

Thanking the President for his message, Nehru would express optimism regarding the international scene and attribute "its brighter aspect" to Eisenhower's "personal efforts and initiative." Although the goal was still distant, he wrote, "the results already achieved hold promise of progressive advance towards ultimate success" (Nehru to Eisenhower, Nov. 27, 1959, *ibid.*).

1373

To Hugh Arthur Parker   *November 10, 1959*

Dear Lefty: I must admit to a certain feeling of nostalgia as well as surprise when I learned today of your retirement this coming November twenty-third from the United States Air Force.[1]

Inevitably, I think of our close association, over twenty years ago, when we saw service together in the Philippines when you, Bill Lee and I were engaged in the task of helping build the air strength of the Philippine Army.[2] Particularly, I often wonder how you found the patience to pursue your effort to teach me some of the "mysteries" of piloting a Stearman Trainer.[3]

I send my congratulations to you on the termination of a successful and highly useful career in the Air Force. More than that, however, I want to wish the very best to you and Janet in all the years that lie ahead.[4]

Mamie joins me in sending our warmest regard, *Sincerely*

[1] Parker had been commander of Continental Air Defense Command Forces, Western Continental Air Defense Region and Western Air Defense Forces at Hamilton Air Force Base in California since 1957. As one of the first two flight instructors assigned to the Philippines (1935–1938), Parker had organized the Philippine Army Air Corps. Eisenhower had met him in 1935. A note from Ann Whitman indicates that the President revised this letter and sent a copy to his Air Force aide, William G. Draper (same file as document).

[2] William L. Lee also had been a flying instructor with the Philippine Air Corps. In August Lee had retired with the rank of Brigadier General (see no. 1015).

[3] For Eisenhower's account of his flight training see *At Ease,* p. 226, and Daniel D. Holt and James W. Leyerzaph, *Eisenhower: The Prewar Diaries and Selected Papers, 1905–1941* (Baltimore, 1998), p. 421.

[4] Parker's wife was the former Janet L. Baker. For developments see the following document.

1374   *EM, AWF, Administration Series*

To Thomas Dresser White   *[November 11, 1959]*

Dear Tommy: I hope you didn't take me too seriously on my tirade about Lefty Parker's retirement.[1] I was mainly trying to express my astonishment that all other people must have been less aware of his abilities than I.[2] *Sincerely*

[1] The President had written this undated longhand note after the November 11 National Security Council meeting. Air Force Chief of Staff White had attended the

meeting in place of the Chairman of the Joint Chiefs of Staff. During the meeting the council had discussed military force reductions (NSC meeting minutes, Nov. 11, 1959, AWF/NSC). The subject of General Hugh Arthur Parker's retirement undoubtedly came up during or after the meeting (see the preceding document).

[2] White would reply (Nov. 12, AWF/N) that he also was acquainted with Parker and had "most poignant regrets" that he and "people of his ilk" were retiring. He added, however, that there was no room at the top for all the good people, and that there were "literally thousands of really top-notch colonels coming along."

1375   *EM, AWF, Administration Series*

To James Paul Mitchell   *November 12, 1959*
Personal

Dear Jim: There appears frequently in the press speculation concerning the kind of labor-management laws that Congress will be proposing, considering and possibly passing in the event that the steel strike resumes after the eighty day period of work required under the Taft-Hartley Act.[1] Congressional activity of this kind would be much intensified if a resumed steel strike were accompanied by others, including the railroads, Can companies and so on.[2]

Some time back I requested that you, with the Attorney General, Secretary of Labor, Chairman of the Council of Economic Advisers and others study this whole field to see whether or not there was anything of a practical character that could be suggested and enacted into law *without* sooner or later starting a definite trend toward governmental control of the entire economy.[3]

One thing that crossed my mind was inspired by some of the projects under study which look toward partial disposal of accumulated surpluses in stock piles of copper, aluminum, rubber and other commodities.[4]

The Taft-Hartley Act can be invoked only when the continuation of a strike endangers or threatens to endanger the national security or health. What this means is that the Taft-Hartley injunctive process is presumably invoked when the strike becomes not merely an internecine warfare between labor and management, but which *really becomes an attack on the welfare of the entire nation.* On this basic assumption the government intervenes to protect the public.

Now, assume that the government had, as a matter of policy, acquired a considerable stock of inventories in the types of steel that are essential to the Defense Department and to those portions of the industry that necessarily satisfy the fundamental requirements of the public. A new law could provide that these inventories might be used under stated conditions prescribed by law and thus tend to make both parties more amenable to conciliation.

Inventories are, of course, of a fixed and static character and the point might be made that they would be useful for a matter of sixty days or something of that kind. The law might then provide that ten days after production in any essential industry had been stopped by strike, the government could authorize the lowering or elimination of tariffs on steel and invite an inflow of the kind of things we need.

Of course we realize that no industry in any country is geared up to a sudden increase of output. But if we had the authority of which I speak on the books, probably most of the steel exporting countries would somewhat enlarge their own inventories in the hope of making quick and large sales to the United States. Our cost and price structure in this country is such that whatever these companies throughout the world might have on hand would be immediately on the road toward our shores. The effect of this would probably be to lower prices here at home and both the steel companies and the unions would be on notice that their position could not longer be regarded as completely monopolistic. Of course it is possible that some companies using steel products brought in from abroad would be hit by secondary boycotts. In such cases the law should be so broad as to allow the tariff to be removed from the articles produced by that particular company from such steel products.

I realize that there would be many practical obstacles (and perhaps even more serious political ones) to getting such laws on the books, but I am quite sure that if such authority did exist, we might see a great diminution in the number of strikes. Certainly such a position would discourage the continuation of any long strike.

Of course any such authority would cease the moment the strike was settled. But foreign steel already contracted for and shipped would come in. Since I think there would be a great rush on the part of industrial nations to take advantage of our prices, the shipments could reach a considerable amount. Knowledge on the part of companies and unions would have a great influence in keeping domestic industry from attempting to become the master of the people.

*   *   *   *   *

I think this is not too brilliant a thought. I have not even developed in my own mind anything that I could call a real idea. The only thing I am trying to say is that I am searching to see what kind of thing the United States can do to protect itself against these disruptive strikes brought about by the selfishness and stupidity of both sides and which at the same time violate our principles of free economic practices.[5]

With warm regard, *As ever*

[1] For background on the steel strike and Eisenhower's invocation of the Taft-Hartley Act see no. 1367. A handwritten note by Ann Whitman on another copy of this document (AWF/D) indicates that Eisenhower dictated this letter but later decided not to send it.

[2] On the issues involved in a potential railroad strike see *New York Times*, November 1, 1959. On September 30 a strike by 32,500 employees of the two largest American can manufacturers was averted when the union and companies agreed to extend their contracts until thirty days after settlement of the national steel strike or until January 1, 1960, whichever came first (see *ibid.*, Sept. 30, Oct. 1, 1959).

[3] See no. 806.

[4] See no. 700.

[5] Announcement of agreement on the issues in the steel strike would be made on January 4, 1960. The contract would be seen as a major victory for the United Steelworkers, who would receive increases averaging 41 cents an hour over thirty months, from January 1, 1959, through July 1, 1962. The issue of work rules would be referred to a committee for recommendations. See *New York Times*, January 5, 1960.

1376   *EM, AWF, Administration Series*

To Ezra Taft Benson   *November 14, 1959*

Dear Ezra: Thanks for your note of the twelfth.[1] I do not remember that I promised to make a television appearance.[2] My impression was that I said I would consider the matter. In addition, of course, I have to make the earlier decision as to whether or not I feel that my appearance on such a show would be necessary or desirable.

With all the rest of your note I of course agree.[3]

With warm regard, *As ever*

[1] The Secretary of Agriculture had thanked Eisenhower for meeting with him and Presidential Assistant Don Paarlberg on November 10, 1959, to discuss farm legislation (Nov. 12, 1959, AWF/A). On that same day the Administration had unveiled the five-point farm program it planned to present to the next congressional session. Benson had told the press that the new proposal relating price supports on storable commodities to market prices was chiefly directed toward alleviating the wheat surplus problem (*New York Times*, Nov. 11, 1959). For background see no. 1263, and for developments see no. 1498; see also Benson, *Cross Fire*, pp. 459–66, 500–509.

[2] Benson had apparently asked the President to discuss the new farm program on television. He had written that Eisenhower's "sympathetic interest" and "promise of a TV appearance" would be helpful, especially in light of opponents who had quipped, "'Benson's gall bladder has finally done what his critics have been unable to do: side lined him from all speech making tours for the rest of the year'" (Benson to Eisenhower, Nov. 12, 1959, AWF/A). Benson had been briefly hospitalized for treatment of his gall bladder, which he would have removed on December 4 (*New York Times*, Oct. 31, Nov. 1, Dec. 3, 1959). While public reports had circulated for several months that Eisenhower would discuss the wheat situation on television and radio, he would choose not to do so (*New York Times*, Aug. 20, 1959). He would briefly

express concern about the agricultural situation during a news conference on December 2, 1959 (*Public Papers of the Presidents: Eisenhower, 1959*, p. 788).
[3] In his letter Benson had criticized the government's high costs for storing surplus wheat. He said that he was studying a possible option for sending more wheat abroad.

1377 *EM, AWF, International Series:*
de Gaulle

To Charles André Joseph Marie de Gaulle
Secret   *November 17, 1959*

Dear General de Gaulle:[1] I have scrutinized carefully your statement and your answers to press questions on November tenth and would like to take the liberty of commenting on certain portions thereof.

With regard to the holding of a summit meeting, I am inclined to agree with your reasoning and your analysis of the situation.[2] I believe there is one additional point worth mentioning and that is Khrushchev's conviction that time is on his side and his growing confidence that a detente will work to the advantage of the Soviet Union. I believe our own approach to a summit meeting should reflect our own profound belief in the inherent strength of our own cause, and the belief which I have, that on the contrary time will work to our advantage, especially in the event that the Soviet Union is further opened to Western influences. Therefore, we believe probing operations of the type envisaged at the summit meeting have a definitely useful role in our relations with the Soviet Union.

In view of our long, and what I consider close, friendship I was somewhat astonished to find in your remarks certain passages that seem to imply a lack of confidence in the good faith of this nation and its Government. I hope, of course, that there is some other explanation that does not seem apparent to me. I should be less than frank if I did not express quite bluntly the concern which I feel. The passage I quote comes from the text handed to the State Department by Ambassador Alphand: "Who can say that, for example, some sudden advances in development, especially for space rockets, will not provide one of the camps with so great an advantage that its peaceful inclinations will not be able to resist it?

"Who can say that if in the future, the political background having changed completely—that is something that has already happened on earth—the two powers having the nuclear monopoly will not agree to divide the world?

"Who can say that if the occasion arises the two, while each deciding not to launch its missiles at the main enemy so that it should itself be spared, will not crush the others? It is possible to imagine that on some awful day Western Europe should be wiped out from Moscow and Central Europe from Washington.

"And who can even say that the two rivals, after I know not what political and social upheaval, will not unite?"[3]

While I am sure this was not your intention, I am disturbed by the implication in these remarks that you might consider the United States to be on such a low moral plane as to be disregardful of its commitments to its allies. I need hardly add how profoundly the United States is attached to its commitments in Europe reflected in NATO. Likewise I am greatly astonished by your apparent implication that the United States would be with the Soviets, a party to "dividing the world". I am sure you did not mean this conclusion to be drawn because you are certainly aware of how profoundly contrary it would be to the most fundamental tenets of United States policy. Furthermore this policy is not based on any transitory features but is fixed by our Constitution and is firmly rooted in the very nature of the American people.

The equation you appear to have drawn between my country and the Soviet Union is one which I feel unjustified,[4] and I should appreciate a word from you that it was in fact not your intention to place the United States in the same category of nations with the Soviet Union insofar as the upholding of moral commitments and dedication to peace are concerned.

I do not wish to close without likewise mentioning the most interesting portions of your press conference dealing with Algeria and the Community. Your remarks dealing with Algeria appear to be a further courageous step forward on your part, on which I congratulate you, and which we all hope will assist your country in solving this most difficult problem. As you know I welcomed your declaration of September sixteenth on Algeria and continue to support your Algerian policy. I was likewise happy to note your reiteration of the principles of freedom of choice of their political status by the members of the Community.[5]

With warm regard, *Sincerely*

---

[1] The State Department draft of this letter, with Eisenhower's handwritten emendations, is in AWF/I: de Gaulle. The text was sent by cable to the American embassy in Paris for immediate delivery to de Gaulle.

[2] De Gaulle had stated that France was in favor of a summit meeting. "But precisely because she hopes that the proposed meeting will result in something positive, she believes it necessary not to rush into talks which might be superficial . . . or which might end in some botched-up arrangement which would be regretted the very next day." He argued that three conditions must be satisfied before the first meeting: continued improvement in international relations during the coming months; an un-

derstanding among the Western heads of government on the issues involved; and personal contact between Soviet Premier Khrushchev and himself (Statement by General de Gaulle, Feb. 10, 1959, *ibid.*).

[3] This response by de Gaulle was in answer to a reporter's question regarding French plans to test nuclear weapons in the Sahara (*New York Times,* Nov. 11, 1959; see also Goodpaster, Memorandum of Conference, Nov. 13, 1959, AWF/D).

[4] Eisenhower had substituted the previous three words for the words "is most unpalatable to me" in the State Department draft.

[5] For background on the French Community and de Gaulle's Algerian policy see nos. 1309 and 1323. The Algerians would decide their own destiny, de Gaulle had stated, in a choice that would be "entirely free." France would also provide as much aid as possible to the African countries in the French Community. "France's policy toward these countries is to respect and recognize their free disposal of themselves, and even to offer them the opportunity of forming with her a group in which they will find her aid, and in which we shall invite them to take part in world-wide activities" (*New York Times,* Nov. 11, 1959). For developments see no. 1387.

1378   *EM, WHCF, Official File 3-C-8*

TO WINSTON LEWIS PROUTY   *November 17, 1959*

Dear Senator Prouty:[1] I have carefully read your letter of November thirteenth, and I assure you that I am completely sympathetic in the concern you express.[2] Manifestly I have to depend upon the several agencies of government to locate their installations in such manner and to carry on their operations as to assure the general taxpayer the maximum return for his expenditure.

Since alteration of great organizational patterns, including the geographical location of major installations, is a most expensive business, I have throughout my career urged always that original planning should be carefully done so that later changes do not become necessary, and bring in their wake added expense to the government and distress to the localities. The Secretary of the Air Force is as aware of these general considerations as I am.

Nevertheless, it is inevitable that shifts do have to be made from time to time because of changing techniques and requirements in the world situation. Because of the extremely compelling nature of your letter and your emphasis upon the distress being caused in certain communities in Vermont as well as in the State in general if the proposed action, as now evidently planned, is taken, I am taking the liberty of sending your letter directly to the Secretary of the Air Force. I again express my confidence that he will re-examine this particular question and will communicate with you further.[3]

With warm regard, *Sincerely*

¹ Republican Senator Winston Lewis Prouty, former mayor of Newport, Vermont, and speaker of the Vermont House of Representatives, had served five terms in the U.S. Congress. He had been elected to the Senate in 1958.

² Prouty had first written Eisenhower on October 30 regarding the decision, announced by the Air Force two days earlier, to close the Ethan Allen Air Force Base in Burlington, Vermont, in March 1960. He claimed to have received "indications virtually amounting to assurances" in July and August from the Department of the Air Force that the base would remain active for the next two years. The "complete reversal" would have a great impact on the small state of Vermont, Prouty had written, and he had asked that Eisenhower give the matter, which had "been handled badly from beginning to end," his personal attention. On November 5 Presidential Assistant Bryce Harlow told Eisenhower that defense officials had spoken with Prouty and had moved the decision date from March to May of 1960. The senator, Harlow said, had seemed "reasonably satisfied with this arrangement" (see Prouty to Eisenhower, Oct. 30, 1959; Aiken to Eisenhower, Oct. 29, 1959; Harlow to Eisenhower, Nov. 5, 1959; Eisenhower to Aiken and Prouty, Nov. 5, 1959; all in the same file as this document).

In his November 13 letter Prouty had told Eisenhower that the decision to continue operating the base for two additional months would "not begin to mitigate the problems" facing the area. Although a large metropolitan area could withstand a loss of two hundred jobs and twelve to fifteen million dollars in federal spending, Prouty said, the consequences for Burlington would be "devastating" (Prouty to Eisenhower, Nov. 13, 1959; and *Advantages of Ethan Allen Air Force Base*, both in the same file as this document).

³ In his memorandum accompanying a copy of this letter Harlow would point out to Air Force Secretary James H. Douglas that Eisenhower had dictated the concluding paragraph, committing the secretary to communicate further with Prouty. The decision to close the base remained unchanged, prompting petitions from 15,000 Vermont citizens in protest. Eisenhower would again ask Douglas about the closing and would later state that all aspects of the problem had been investigated. The decision was based "solely on military considerations," he said; "to continue its use would involve expenditures which would not effectively contribute to our national defense" (Harlow to Douglas, Nov. 21, 1959; Aiken to Eisenhower, Jan. 27, 1960; Eisenhower to Aiken, Feb. 3, 1960, all in the same file as this document).

1379   *EM, WHCF, Official File 116-XX*

To Thomas Joseph Dodd   *November 18, 1959*

*Dear Senator Dodd:*¹ I welcome your suggestion that a leader of the Democratic Party join with me on my early December trip abroad.² Much about your proposal appeals to me, but the practical arrangements for a mission such as I am undertaking, with its daily schedules crowded to the minute, require that the personnel accompanying me be limited to staff assistants, with minimum State Department representation.

More useful, in my view, would be a pre-departure discussion with various of the Congressional leaders of both parties, an arrangement

I have already proposed. A bipartisan discussion of this kind should serve, in some measure, the purpose you had in mind.[3]

Thank you again for your letter and the suggestion it brought to me.

With best wishes, Sincerely

[1] Thomas Joseph Dodd (LL.B. Yale University 1933), former Democratic Congressman from Connecticut, had been elected to the Senate in 1958. He had been assistant to five successive U.S. attorneys general and had served as chief trial counsel at the Nuremberg trials of Nazi war criminals.

[2] For background on Eisenhower's trip see no. 1359. Dodd had suggested that Eisenhower invite one or more Democrats with wide experience in international affairs to accompany him. "I believe that this would emphasize the fact that you carry with you the full support and backing of the American people," he wrote (Dodd to Eisenhower, Nov. 12, 1959, same file as document).

[3] Noting that Secretary Herter and U.N. Ambassador Lodge had received and rejected similar suggestions, Presidential Assistant Bryce Harlow had recommended that Eisenhower invite congressional leaders of both parties to a White House breakfast to "prevent any subsequent Democratic caterwauling over having had their requests to go along declined by the Administration" (Harlow to Whitman, Nov. 13, 1959, *ibid.*).

Eisenhower and Vice-President Nixon would meet with State Department officials and congressional leaders on November 30. Eisenhower would tell the group that because there was doubt and suspicion in the world regarding American armaments and the country's support of peace, he was going abroad to pay the leaders of the eleven countries the "compliment of visiting them in person and to tell them in person what our true beliefs are, rather than seeking to achieve anything else" (Harlow, Memorandum for the Record, Dec. 5, 1959, AWF/D; see also Harlow to Stephens, Dec. 19, 1959, *ibid.*).

1380   *EM, WHCF, Confidential File:*
                                              State Department

To Elva Whitman Fairchild   *November 20, 1959*
Cable. Personal and Confidential

Dear Mrs. Fairchild: I am deeply appreciative of your taking the trouble to write me so frankly of your deep concern over the situation in Panama, a concern that I wholeheartedly share.[1] Even more I share the basic conviction expressed in your letter, namely that in the presence of the weak, the strong should always be humble. Humility comprises politeness, courtesy and an effort to understand.[2] I assure you I shall ponder carefully what you say, and I am taking the liberty of sending a copy of your letter and its enclosure to the Secretary of State.[3]

Undoubtedly you know that Under Secretary of State Livingston

Merchant is now on his way to Panama, coming as my personal emissary to discuss with the Panamanian Government the difficulties between us. He is a sensitive and capable individual, and I feel will be helpful in the current situation.[4] If you would like to talk to him, the Embassy will be glad to arrange an appointment for you.[5]

When next you write to your mother-in-law, please tell her that Mrs. Eisenhower and I think often and affectionately of her and send her, as we do you, our best wishes.[6] *Sincerely*

P.S. Because of the time element, I send you this as a cable in order to be sure you will receive it during Mr. Merchant's stay in Panama.

[1] See no. 1355 for background. Mrs. Fairchild (B.S. Boston Teachers College 1936) was a portrait artist who had lived in Panama since 1938 with her husband Alexander Graham Bell Fairchild, an entomologist (and grandson of the inventor Alexander Graham Bell). She was the daughter-in-law of David Galveston Fairchild, a prominent botanist. The President had met David Fairchild during his combined convalescence and vacation in 1947 (Galambos, *Chief of Staff*, nos. 1234 and 1241). Eisenhower, she wrote, had "spent many an evening" sitting upon Fairchild's porch in Coconut Grove, Florida. She was critical of the manner in which the Canal Zone authorities had handled the November 3 riots in Panama City and Colon. Canal Zone police and U.S. military troops had beaten back Panamanian students in their attempts to enter the Zone and plant the Panamanian flag. Fairchild maintained that the Canal Zone governor had exacerbated tensions and placed the United States in a "position of ridicule" by situating "armed soldiers in gas masks with bayonets and firemen with hoses on our exact boundaries." If the Zone authorities had instead chosen to celebrate with Panama on her Independence Day by flying the flag within the Canal Zone, the United States could have "easily struck a blow for democracy and astounded those simple minded university students who had been misled" (Fairchild to Eisenhower, Nov. 20, 1959, in same file as document). For background see LaFeber, *The Panama Canal*, pp. 90–131; Hogan, *The Panama Canal in American Politics*; and *New York Times*, Nov. 3, 4, 6, 7, 9, 10, 15, 1959).

[2] Fairchild had asserted that the United States, as a stronger, wealthier, and "on the whole, more intelligent" nation, could afford to offer friendship to a country led by a weak government and corrupt politicians. She had also criticized the recent increase in fees that made it difficult for middle class Panamanians to attend the Canal Zone schools. She thought schooling Panamanian and American children together was a good investment that helped cultivate close relations between the two countries (Fairchild to Eisenhower, Nov. 20, 1959, in same file as document).

[3] In relaying the President's request to the U.S. embassy in Panama the Secretary of State had reported that "the President remarked orally that he agreed entirely with Mrs. Fairchild's letter" (Herter to American Embassy in Panama, Nov. 20, 1959, *ibid.*).

[4] Eisenhower had sent Deputy Under Secretary of State Merchant to Panama to meet with President de la Guardia and other officials (Telephone conversation, Herter and Goodpaster, Nov. 16, 1959, Herter Papers, Telephone Conversations). On October 21 Eisenhower had appointed Merchant to succeed the retiring Robert Murphy as Under Secretary of State for Political Affairs. He was subsequently confirmed by the Senate (*New York Times*, Nov. 1, 21, 22, 24, 26, Jan. 28, 1960).

Merchant would meet with Eisenhower on November 27, 1959, and report that although his trip to Panama had been productive, there was still risk of further anti-American demonstrations. He had told Panamanian officials that the United States was prepared to take certain ameliorative actions that had been decided upon prior to the riots, after calm had been restored. On completing the talks with the Panamanians, Merchant had released a press statement declaring that the United States recognized titular sovereignty over the Canal Zone ("Panama Reassured on Titular Sovereignty in Canal Zone," *U.S. Department of State Bulletin* 41, no. 1068 [December 14, 1959], 859; *New York Times*, Nov. 25, 1959; for additional background see State, *Foreign Relations, 1958–1960*, vol. V, *American Republics*, Microfiche Supplement, P-20– 25).

Eisenhower would tell Merchant that after the 1956 Suez Canal crisis, he had discussed preventing a similar crisis from occurring in Panama. He also stated that not enough had been done under the agreements of 1955 regarding wage discrepancies and that he was eager to have the question of third country purchases settled and to begin a training and apprentice program for Panamanian workers (see no. 1355). He would ask Merchant to make sure there was no "footdragging" by the Department of Defense, and that the Panamanians' requests were considered constructively and sympathetically. He also said he would like to announce that the Panamanian flag would fly at some appropriate place in the Zone (Memorandum of Conversation, Nov. 27, 1959, AWF/I; see also *New York Times*, Nov. 28, 29, 30, 1959). For developments see nos. 1425, 1443, and 1450.

[5] Merchant would visit with the Fairchilds in the U.S. embassy on November 23 (Merchant to Goodpaster, Nov. 25, 1959, and Merchant to Whitman, Dec. 31, 1959, both in the same file as document).

[6] Fairchild's mother-in-law was Marian "Daisy" Hubbard Fairchild, the daughter of Alexander Graham Bell.

1381   *EM, AWF, DDE Diaries Series*

DIARY   *November 28, 1959*
Personal and confidential

Candidacy for President: The possibility that I might one day become a candidate for the Presidency was first suggested to me about June, 1943.[1] My reaction was of course completely negative, and my feeling was that the matter was never seriously considered even by the proposers. Actually the hard military campaigns of the war were at that time obviously still ahead of us, and any diverting of our attention to political matters would have been more than ridiculous.

The subject was again brought up in the middle of 1945.[2] By this time the war was over in Europe and there was more than idle speculation on the part of visiting friends, newspaper representatives and non-career soldiers. I cannot recall, at that time, of any career soldier who mentioned the matter, possibly because they had concern, all being my juniors, as to the character of my reaction. This subject became one of more lively interest when, with a number of military associates of all services, I made a tour, at the direction of the President and the War Department, through several American cities. The purpose of the tour was to establish a more personal connection between the victorious army, navy and air force in Europe, and the people at home. Incidentally, the party accompanying me had representatives of all ranks from private upward.

We visited Washington, New York, West Point, Kansas City and Abilene, Kansas. For the first time newspaper representatives began quizzing me in public press conferences, in an effort to determine my attitude. I continued, as always before, to reply in completely negative terms.[3]

There was no question that I felt a very great sense of pride in the success of the invading forces in Western Europe. When we arrived at D-Day, June 6, 1945, there was no universal confidence in a completely successful outcome. Indeed most people thought that even should we, in some two or three years, eventually win, we would pay a ghastly price in battling our way toward Germany in the pattern of World War I, with its terrible memories of Passchendale, Vimy Ridge, Verdun and the like.[4]

Some newspapers went so far as to predict 90% loss on the beaches themselves. Even Winston Churchill, normally a fairly optimistic individual, never hesitated to voice his forebodings about the venture. He frequently repeated that if we were successful, that we could count any advance on the Allied part that would seize and hold Paris by mid-winter as one of the greatest and most successful military operations of all time.

Consequently, when on May 8, 1945 the confidence and enthusiasm of my own headquarters proved justified by completing the entire campaign in eleven months, I felt that the climax of my own personal career had clearly been attained.[5] Anything that could happen to me thereafter would, in my opinion, be anti-climatic. I had some conversations with General Marshall and others about my desire to retire, but I did agree to remain temporarily as Military Governor of the American Zone in Germany, although at that time constantly recommending to the War Department, to the President and to Secretary of State Byrnes that as quickly as possible a civilian should be appointed to this post.[6] My superiors expressed sympathy for the idea, but said that this could not be done until the Allies, including the Russians, would agree. I kept pounding away on this matter because of my feeling that after wars are over and matters of civil government come to the fore, the executive head of all organizations governing civilians should be, under the Western tradition, a civilian.

In any event, the Armistice in Europe provided an opportunity for many American visitors to come into the area. In the tradition of the past these people almost inevitably revised the proposition that a successful general should be considered as a possible candidate for the Presidency. I always had the feeling that most of these, at that time, had no interest in my possible qualifications or my personal philosophy of government. They were merely voicing interest in an individual who, because of the circumstances of the war, might finally develop into a popular public figure. At the same time, I think that they were very little impressed by my denials of any interest in politics or of any intention to get involved in political affairs. In these circumstances, while the matter never completely died out, it never reached a real crescendo of discussion and debate. One of the reasons for this was because President Truman was still in his first year of incumbency of the office.

At the end of the year, I was ordered back to Washington to become Chief of Staff of the Army. I informed the President of my hope to retire and unless he had a positive desire that I take over the office for a period, I should like to decline the appointment. He told me that the only other individual he could consider to take General Marshall's place was General Bradley, who at that time was serving as the Head of the Veterans' Bureau. He informed me also that he would need General Bradley in that post for at least two years, but stated that if I was still of the same mind at that time, he would accept my resignation and appoint Bradley to the post of Chief of Staff of the Army.

Under this circumstance, I retained the post of Chief of Staff until early 1948.[7]

By mid-1947 the pressure brought to bear upon me to secure my consent for seeking the Presidency had many times intensified. The nature of the argument presented underwent a change. No longer was the matter completely personal; it now began to involve also governmental philosophy. Since I continued to maintain my negative attitude toward the entire matter, I declined also to outline in specific terms my own conception as to the functions of government and my own satisfaction or dissatisfaction with the political scene as I viewed it.

While my appointment book would of course give a record of those individuals visiting my office to discuss this matter, I cannot now recall many of them to my mind. Three that did stick out in my memory were Douglas Freeman, the historian, Walter Winchell, the columnist and commentator, and Mr. Wadsworth, a Congressman.[8] Each of these had a different type of approach. Douglas Freeman was deeply religious and opened his conversation with a prayer. He believed that government needed a shake-up; in his opinion complacency had overtaken the party which had been in power ever since 1932. Because of this he felt that the Democratic Party was neglectful of self-examination and as a result there was becoming evident examples of carelessness and, even worse,[9] in the conduct of governmental affairs. He was very earnest and he placed his accent on the word "duty." He said that recent history would show that only a popular figure could defeat any Democratic candidate—and that I had the duty to make the race. He played upon this theme for a considerable time; as I recall he stayed more than an hour and called upon history to provide examples of the need for change. I had met Dr. Freeman several times earlier and had long talks with him. He paid me the compliment of saying that he knew I was not only reluctant to accept his counsel but that the whole idea of political involvement was distasteful. But he added that because I had a sense of duty and since he believed that I was both disinterested and honest and had shown good administrative capacity, he was sure I would see my duty and perform it. These thoughts were the subject of the prayer with which he opened the conversation.

Walter Winchell put the whole matter on a personal basis. He didn't like the government then existing, he wanted it changed. He thought I was the only one that could do it. He didn't care whether I was a Democrat or a Republican.

Mr. Wadsworth was more analytical, but he was fully as thoughtfully serious as Douglas Freeman. As in the prior cases, I told him that I had decided to do nothing whatsoever about the matter.

A few others who talked to me at that time were some from the newspaper world, Senator Vandenberg, and so on. The whole affair became more difficult. At a Republican dinner, which I had *supposed* to be entirely social and non-partisan, an attempt was made to portray me as an extreme New Dealer. The purpose of this was to show me as unacceptable as a Republican candidate. Whether traveling outside of Washington or in my office in the Pentagon, every day brought some new recommendation, conviction or opinion. The purport of each was that I simply had to run for the Presidency.[10]

Finally, in January of 1948 there came a letter from a man named Finder, one of the publishers of a newspaper in New Hampshire, saying that a group of which he was a part intended to enter my name in the New Hampshire primary of that year. I knew that I was going to refuse, but I also felt a compulsion to inform the public, through my answer, of why I would not allow my name to be used. A copy of that letter is attached to this memorandum. I still believe it was sound. After its writing, I felt that I had removed myself from the political scene for once and all, and thereafter I could feel free to do as I pleased since within a month or so I was to leave the office of Chief of Staff.[11]

I had already accepted an invitation to become President of Columbia University, the effective date to be the one on which my term as Chief of Staff officially was to end—I think it was about May 5th or 6th.[12]

Very quickly my belief that I had removed myself forever from politics was shattered. Suddenly there came to me a multitude of new suggestions, recommendations and importunities, this time almost exclusively from Democratic Party members. Up until the time I had written the letter in January the pressure had come largely from the Republicans. Now it seemed that the whole experience was to be repeated, but with the other Party. Numerous governors, United States senators, private citizens and others joined the campaign. Since I had already made my position clear—and in my letter I had not mentioned Party—I saw no necessity for repeating anything further. Nevertheless, as the late spring of 1948 rolled by, the pressure became almost unbearable. A telegram reaching me about July first seemed to demand an answer. I made another statement, which I did through the Public Relations Officer of the University, Mr. Herron. It was again negative and is on record—I assume a copy is now in the hands of Colonel Schulz.[13]

This had the effect of stopping, for the moment, most of the pressure from the Democratic side. Strangely enough, a new flurry came from the Republicans during the course of their National Convention, held that year in Philadelphia. Numerous telephone calls came into the office to the effect that certain individuals wanted to come over to New York at once to urge me to reconsider my decision and, as reported to me, to stop the trend toward Dewey. I refused to receive any calls or to discuss the matter further.

Quite naturally, after Dewey's defeat in the fall of 1948, I again began to feel the pressure.[14]

With Dewey's failure against Truman, who was then popularly supposed to be the weakest candidate that the Democrats could put into the field, the cry began to be heard that "We must find some new faces in the Republican Party if ever we are going to win a national election." Since we were again in the beginning of a Presidential cycle, most of the suggestions and arguments could be pushed off without trouble. But before many months the campaign began again to intensify. When Mr. Dewey ran for re-election to the Governorship of New York, he stated, in order to answer a charge that he was running again merely to enhance his standing as a candidate for the Presidency, that he favored me as the Republican candidate in '52.[15] This really put fresh fuel on the fire—and every day contributed something new to its heat.

Finally, in December of 1950 President Truman called me on the phone to ask whether I would undertake the duty of commanding the allied forces to be established under the North Atlantic Treaty Organization.[16] He and I both knew that this was a thankless job, but I was in complete agreement with the President that collective security arrangements for Western Europe had to be worked out in the least possible time and that America had to participate in the effort. By this time I had become deeply interested in my work at

Columbia University and it was a tremendous personal disappointment to me to have to give it up. But I reminded him that I was a soldier and subject to his orders. But he emphasized that he wanted to persuade me that undertaking this duty would be a great public service. I felt that the European post was of such importance that, so long as he thought me best fitted for the job, I should have to undertake it at least until we had worked out its programs of raising, organizing, training and deploying troops. It was a demanding effort.

My first move was to make a "reconnaissance" visit to every capital involved. Since I did this in mid-winter, the task was difficult, but I met with the governments of the twelve countries involved and completed the trip in some eighteen or twenty days.[17] I came back to report to the President, made a television speech to the public, and reported also to an informal Joint Session of the Congress held in the auditorium of the Congressional Library.[18] Just before departing again for Europe, I called in a couple of members of my staff and told them that I was going to make a personal move and a statement which, if successful in its preliminary parts, would take me forever, and beyond any question, out of the political scene.

My purpose was to invite Senator Taft to come to my office to discuss what we were trying to do in Europe, and I told my associates that if Senator Taft would pledge his support to the idea of collective security in Europe, I would immediately make a statement to the effect that my return to active military service precluded any future speculation about the possibility that I would ever enter the political arena and that my answer, in advance, to any further importuning along this line would be a flat negative.

I invited the Senator to my office in the Pentagon and he came one evening around 5:00 or 5:30. My conversation with him was exclusively on the subject of NATO. I went through the whole history of the war and later developments in Europe, the operation of the Marshall Plan, the responsibilities and opportunities now lying before the Western World, and how necessary it was that we strengthen Western European defenses by welding them together in one machine. I thought also that American contingents and troops would have to be employed in Europe but as to their number I was not certain.

It happened, at that moment, there was an argument going on between the President and the Congress as to the President's unrestricted right to station American troops wherever he decided they should go in the world. Congress was further pre-occupied with a debate as to whether there should be four or six divisions sent to NATO.

I told the Senator that with the details either of the Constitutional question or with the amount of forces to be sent abroad I had no interest at the moment. I said that until I could survey the situation more closely, I would not have any recommendation as to the size of the American forces that should come to Europe. I simply asked the Senator *whether he could not agree that the collective security of Western Europe, with some American help, had to be assured.* He declined to commit himself on the matter, repeating words to the effect that he was not sure whether he would vote for four or six divisions. I argued that this was of no interest to me whatsoever. I simply wanted to get his assurance of support in the work for which I was called back to active duty. He repeated his refusal to make the point clear and so finally we parted and, of course, I did not go through with the part of my plan that would have depended upon his affirmative reply.[19]

*　　*　　*　　*　　*

For the next few months the whole matter seemed to lie fairly dormant, although now and then individuals of more or less importance arrived in Paris from America to give me their views about the forthcoming campaign. Starting in the fall of '51, the whole matter came to the fore once again and this time the clamor was more intensified than ever before. Since I had never made public my particular political affiliations, the pressure came from both parties. However, it was more pronounced on the Republican side than the Democratic. One reason for this was a speech that I had made before the American Bar Association in St. Louis on September 3, 1949.[20] In that talk I analyzed and discussed the so-called "Middle-of-the-Road" approach to political activity. This represented a profound conviction on my part and I repudiated any thought that the idea comprised any namby-pamby or fence-straddling viewpoint. Indeed, I argued that in great human affairs the middle-of-the-road approach was the only one that provided any avenue for progress and the extremists both of reaction and of so-called liberalism should be abjured like the plague.

A good many people remember this talk and felt that as opposed to the New Deal-Fair Deal philosophies of the 30s and 40s, it was sound Republicanism.

These Republicans all had one battle cry, "We must win or the two-party system as we know it will be destroyed." Behind this pronouncement was always one of a secondary character which was "Only a new, respected figure can carry us to victory. Of all the figures in sight you are the one that can do this without question."

There was every conceivable kind of variation on which this theme was played and many tangential streams of argument went along with it.

As the months wore on, I stood my ground and kept on file in my office the letter I had written to Mr. Finder in January of 1948 and would insist always that the visitors familiarize themselves with the language I used in that letter.

I think the argument that began to carry for me the greatest possible force was that the landslide victories of '36, '40 and '44 and Truman's victory over Dewey in '48 were all achieved under a doctrine of "Spend and spend, and elect and elect." It seemed to me that this had to be stopped or our country would deviate badly from the precepts on which we had placed so much faith—the courage and self-dependence of each citizen, the importance of opportunity as opposed to mere material security, and our belief that American progress depended upon the work and sweat of all our citizens, each trying to satisfy the needs and desires of himself and his family, and that instead we were coming to the point where we looked toward a paternalistic state to guide our steps from cradle to grave.

I believed this most profoundly, but I still hoped and believed that someone else could lead the Republican Party much more effectively and to a better result than I could. But because I did believe the basic truth I did go so far, in January '52, to admit that I had always been Republican in leanings, and had always voted that ticket when given the opportunity to do so.[21] On the second point, the identity of the individual who could lead the Republican Party to victory was the place where all argument was now focused. Rallies were held around the country—cables and letters told me about their purpose. A group of about twenty Congressmen sent me a petition in February to become a candidate—and so on and so on. What impressed me more than anything else was the extent of real grass roots sentiment for me to become a candidate.[22] I had seen enough of the Presidency to realize that any serious-minded incumbent of that office is bound to feel the weight of his burdens and soon come to feel that its frustrations and disappointments far outweigh any possible personal satisfaction any one could have in holding the position. Consequently I had no struggle with any personal ambition of my own. Beyond this, it was clear that by next election time I would have passed my sixty-second birthday. Ever since the end of 1941, I had been occupying posts both in war and in peace of great importance and I was eagerly looking forward to a period when I could, with my family, live a somewhat more restful and leisurely life.

Always with friends I brought out these points; always they were brushed aside by people who had become in some instances almost fanatical in their conviction as to my duty to become a candidate for the Presidency.

Respecting every other candidate then campaigning actively or passively for the office, those who came to see me were pessimistic, if not even scornful, of their ability to win the national election.

Bit by bit my confidence that I alone should make a negative decision was worn away—I have always been particularly sensitive to any insinuation that I might recoil from performance of any duty, no matter how onerous. But to persuade me that it was a duty to stand for election was an entirely different matter.[23] I cannot at this moment remember the names of all those who came to see me. Among them were Lodge, Clay, Bill Robinson, Jacqueline Cochran (who brought with her a two-hour film of a Madison Square Garden Rally gotten up by private citizens), Herb Brownell—and many others.[24] On the Democratic side, the man I remember best was Senator Brian McMahon, who came to see me in the late fall of 1951 and who used much the same arguments that the Republicans did.[25]

Finally one thing became clear. Either I had to decline flatly and unequivocally to stand for the nomination or I had to leave my present post. Our work at NATO had progressed satisfactorily and in the past fifteen or sixteen months we had gotten command and staff systems well set-up, training schools started, the EDC Treaty initialed by all the governments, and finally I decided to resign my present post and turn it over to another soldier.[26]

I reached the United States on June first and informed my friends that if the Republicans and their supporters saw fit to nominate me, I would make the race. I refused to seek delegates—in fact to this day I have never consciously requested any individual in the world to vote for me. But I did make myself available for people who wanted to see me. This compelled me to make a number of talks— the first of which was on a rainy day in Abilene about the first week of June; thereafter I was stampeded by invitations to speak but went back to 60 Morningside at Columbia to spend a few weeks.[27] There, and later in Denver, when I went about the middle of June, a number of delegations visited me and we had discussions about the political scene, but there was no "electioneering" as such.[28]

As time for the convention approached, I told my friends that I did not want to go to Chicago. I felt that the business of nominating a candidate belonged to the convention and its delegates. The whole prospect was completely distasteful to me. But all the friends that I have mentioned and hundreds more kept hammering that it was my duty to allow myself to be seen, to receive visitors at my hotel suite and to chat with them on a friendly basis. This I did. By the time the voting for candidates rolled around I was completely worn out and heartily sick of the whole business.[29]

When the balloting was all done, I was the Republican candidate for the President, but I still was not completely confident that my decision to allow this effort to go forward was a wise one.

[1] In his memoir *Mandate for Change* (pp. 4–5) Eisenhower recalled that the earliest suggestion that he become a presidential candidate was made by newspaper correspondent Virgil Pinkley (see also Chandler, *War Years*, nos. 422, 936, 1324). Several copies of this diary entry, containing Eisenhower's extensive handwritten emendations, are in AWF/D.

[2] By Eisenhower's account, President Harry Truman had offered to help him win the presidency in 1948 (see Eisenhower, *Crusade in Europe*, p. 444; and *Mandate for Change*, pp. 5, 10).

[3] General Eisenhower had toured the United States June 18–July 9, 1945 (see Chandler and Galambos, *Occupation, 1945*, nos. 161 and 164). On the speculation regarding an Eisenhower candidacy see, for example, *ibid.*, nos. 233 and 441.

[4] The Normandy invasion took place on June 6, 1944. During World War I the battles of Verdun (1916), Vimy Ridge (1917), and the Third Battle of Ypres, or Passchendaele (1917), resulted in terrible casualties without securing their strategic objectives.

[5] The Germans had surrendered on May 7, 1945, at 2:45 A.M. All hostilities were supposed to have ceased at midnight May 8 (see Chandler, *War Years*, no. 2499, and Eisenhower, *Crusade in Europe*, pp. 424–28).

[6] James Francis Byrnes had served as Secretary of State from 1945–1947 (see also no. 1177). For Eisenhower's views toward creating an organization which could be administered by an appropriate civilian see Chandler and Galambos, *Occupation, 1945*, no. 209.

[7] Marshall had suggested Eisenhower as his successor in an August 20, 1945, letter to President Truman. Eisenhower would resign his post as Chief of Staff and administer the oath of office to his successor, General Omar Nelson Bradley, on February 7, 1948 (see Chandler and Galambos, *Occupation, 1945*, nos. 287 and 311, and Galambos, *Chief of Staff*, no. 2056).

[8] Douglas Southall Freeman had visited Eisenhower in Washington on November 18, 1946 (Galambos, *Chief of Staff*, no. 1152). Walter Winchell had used his column and radio program to speculate on Eisenhower's candidacy (see Galambos, *Columbia University*, no. 798). The late James Wolcott Wadsworth, Jr., Republican from the Forty-first District of New York, had served in the House of Representatives from 1933–1951 (for background see *ibid.*, no. 845).

[9] The commas setting off the words "even worse" may have been placed in the text inadvertently.

[10] The late Arthur Hendrick Vandenberg had represented Michigan in the U.S. Senate between 1928–1951 (for background see also Galambos, *Chief of Staff*, nos. 694 and 1815). On Vandenberg's views of Eisenhower as a possible political candidate in the 1952 presidential election see Arthur H. Vandenberg, Jr., *The Private Papers of Senator Vandenberg* (Boston, 1952), pp. 573–76. On Eisenhower's experience at the 1925 F Street Club dinner in 1947, see Galambos, *NATO and the Campaign of 1952*, no. 1926.

[11] Leonard V. Finder, publisher of the Manchester, New Hampshire, *Union Leader*, had written on January 12, 1948. Eisenhower's reply to Finder is in AWF/D; it is published in Galambos, *Chief of Staff*, as no. 1998.

[12] General Eisenhower had received formal notice from the Trustees of Columbia University on July 15, 1947 (Galambos, *Chief of Staff*, nos. 1640 and 1757). The Eisenhowers had moved into 60 Morningside Heights, the Columbia University president's house, on May 2, and the General had officially taken office on June 7. A formal inaugural ceremony had taken place on October 12, 1948 (see Galambos, *Columbia University*, no. 191).

[13] On July 3, 1948, a group of Democratic party leaders sent telegrams to the more than 1,500 delegates to the Democratic National Convention inviting them to attend a caucus in Philadelphia to find the ablest and strongest man available. Although

Eisenhower was not mentioned as a potential nominee, it had been widely understood that he was their choice to replace Truman. On Eisenhower's statement, made through the Director of Public Information at Columbia University, Robert Harron, see Galambos, *Columbia University*, no. 106.

[14] The election results had shocked many people; Truman had won by a decisive majority in the electoral college (see *ibid.*, no. 245).

[15] On Dewey's efforts to persuade Eisenhower to enter politics see *ibid.*, no. 491.

[16] President Truman first had approached Eisenhower on October 28. The official notification from Truman would appear in the form of a letter on December 19, 1950 (see *ibid.*, nos. 1045 and 1136).

[17] The General traveled in Europe January 6–27, 1951.

[18] See Eisenhower, *Mandate for Change*, p. 13, and Galambos, *NATO and the Campaign of 1952*, no. 23.

[19] Seeking to retain "whatever political influence" he had in order to keep American policy makers "on the right track," the General had destroyed the statement (Eisenhower, *At Ease*, pp. 371–72; *Mandate for Change*, pp. 13–14; and Galambos, *NATO and the Campaign of 1952*, no. 196).

[20] On September 5, 1949, Labor Day, Eisenhower had addressed more than thirty-five hundred members and friends of the American Bar Association (see Galambos, *Columbia University*, no. 532). The text of the speech is reprinted in *New York Times*, September 6, 1949 (see also Eisenhower, *Mandate for Change*, pp. 11–12, and *New York Times*, Sept. 4, 6, 1949).

[21] On the General's statement, delivered January 7, 1952, see Galambos, *NATO and the Campaign of 1952*, nos. 583 and 592.

[22] On the popular and congressional support for the Eisenhower-for-President movement see, for example, *ibid.*, no. 706.

[23] In the Minnesota primary (Mar. 18, 1952) Eisenhower had received more than one hundred thousand write-in votes. On March 20 he had released an informal statement to the press that he would "re-examine" his personal position regarding participation in a preconvention campaign (*ibid.*, no. 743).

[24] These were Senator Henry Cabot Lodge, Jr., *New York Herald Tribune* publisher William E. Robinson, pioneer aviator Jacqueline Cochran, and former Republican National Committee Chairman Herbert Brownell. On the Madison Square Garden Rally, held February 8, and Eisenhower's reaction to it see Galambos, *NATO and the Campaign of 1952*, no. 667.

[25] This was Connecticut Senator Brien McMahon.

[26] The General had requested relief from his post as Supreme Allied Commander, Europe on April 2, 1952. General Matthew Bunker Ridgway had been appointed Eisenhower's successor, effective June 1 (see *ibid.*, nos. 725, 784, 785, and 847).

[27] Eisenhower had delivered the speech launching his campaign for the Republican nomination on June 4 (see Eisenhower, *Mandate for Change*, pp. 33–36, and Galambos, *NATO and the Campaign of 1952*, nos. 848 and 849).

[28] On the General's political activities up to this point see *ibid.*, nos. 854, 855, and 856.

[29] For Eisenhower's account of the Republican National Convention and his nomination on July 7 see *Mandate for Change*, pp. 40–47; see also Galambos, *NATO and the Campaign of 1952*, no. 867.

To Nikita Sergeyevich Khrushchev

Secret

Dear Mr. Chairman: I much appreciated your letter of November sixth and share your thought that your meeting with the President of France should be useful in increasing the possibilities for future settlement of outstanding international problems.[1] You will thus have had the opportunity for direct discussion with the three other Heads of Government who will participate with you in the forthcoming Summit meeting, which possibly compensates for any delay it occasions in that meeting as we had envisaged it at Camp David.[2] Possibly the meeting could be arranged on a date soon after your visit to France. I shall discuss this with President de Gaulle and Prime Minister Macmillan when I meet with them in Paris next month.[3]

Since other events are also being planned, I am anxious to begin to think in more concrete terms about the date and arrangements for my return of your visit to the United States. I have reviewed my schedule and, having in mind your suggestion with respect to the timing of my visit, i.e., May or June, I would now plan to leave this country on the night of June 9 to stay a week to ten days in your country.

I am also tentatively thinking of a two-day visit to Tokyo following my stay in the Soviet Union. This would be in response to an invitation I have received to visit Japan during the early part of June in connection with centennial observations of Japanese-American diplomatic relations.[4]

It would be most convenient if I could proceed to Japan direct from the Soviet Union and thus return to the United States via the Pacific. Perhaps I could visit some of the points of interest in the central and eastern parts of your country, continuing on to Japan and home.

This would, of course, involve the travel of the party accompanying me and our aircraft across the Soviet Union, something that I would suggest only if it would present no problem from your point of view.

I should be grateful for your thoughts on these matters.[5]

With greetings and best wishes to you and your family, *Sincerely*

---

[1] Khrushchev had received an invitation from President de Gaulle to visit France in February or March 1960. Concerned about the possibility of bad weather, he had elected to make the visit in the middle of March and told Eisenhower that he thought his talks with de Gaulle would be useful in eliminating tension and ensuring peace

(Khrushchev to Eisenhower, Nov. 6, 1959, AWF/I: Khrushchev). The President made several changes in the State Department draft of this letter.

[2] Khrushchev had met with British Prime Minister Macmillan in Moscow the previous February and had visited the United States from September 15–27 (see nos. 1074 and 1332). On the Camp David talks and discussions regarding a summit meeting see nos. 1332 and 1338.

[3] For discussions among the Western leaders regarding possible dates for the summit meeting see State, *Foreign Relations, 1958–1960*, vol. IX, *Berlin Crisis 1959–1960; Germany; Austria*, pp. 136–38, 140, 153. For developments see no. 1397.

[4] The Japanese finance minister had first suggested such a visit to Secretary Herter. It was later enthusiastically endorsed by the American ambassador to Japan as a way to indicate that the United States did not consider its interests in the Far East as secondary to those in Europe (State, *Foreign Relations, 1958–1960*, vol. XVIII, *Japan; Korea*, pp. 223–24; and *ibid.*, Microfiche Supplement no. 496). The trip, however, would not take place (see nos. 1564 and 1568).

[5] For developments see no. 1408.

20

"No substitute for personal contact"

To John George Diefenbaker   *December 1, 1959*
Personal

Dear John: Before leaving on my forthcoming tour to Europe, the Mediterranean and the Near East, I have found it desirable to write the various Presidents of the Latin American Republics to try to afford them some perspective regarding my plans and objectives in these various visits.[1] I know that very little explanation is necessary in your case, but I do desire to drop you one more line of correspondence before leaving.[2]

My visit will take me to Rome, Ankara, Karachi, Kabul, New Delhi, Tehran, Athens, Tunis, Paris, Madrid, and Casablanca. In each country I will of course have an opportunity to visit with the head of government and exchange views, as well as to participate in ceremonial occasions. Accordingly, I have every hope that at least some good may come from this undertaking.

Whenever one undertakes a project of this sort, there is the danger that his motives and objectives will be widely misinterpreted. Most prevalent, of course, is the concern held by many that I will be attempting to negotiate on this trip, to represent the views of other members of the North Atlantic Alliance, and possibly even to further the cause of the interests of the United States in some parts of the world, as against those of our friends. I need not assure you that nothing could be further from the truth. My purpose in making these visits is simply to do what I can to strengthen the ties which bind the nations of the Free World together. You and I have found from experience that there is no substitute for personal contact in furthering understanding and good will.

I think it is desirable also to take all possible steps to allay the fears of those in underdeveloped countries regarding the objectives and ambitions of the West, and the United States in particular. I am especially anxious to convince our friends that the vast military power, including the nuclear deterrent which is maintained by the West, serves, in our view, one purpose only—a defensive purpose to deter aggression.

The tour will be fatiguing, to say the least, and when we couple this with commitments for a Summit meeting and a return visit to Moscow, my schedule would appear full indeed for my remaining time in office. I still count, however, on the opportunity of seeing you in the months ahead.

I leave Thursday evening. That time is almost upon us, but if you would want to suggest anything to me before departure, I would, as always, welcome a phone call from you.[3]

With warm personal regard, *Sincerely*

[1] For background on Eisenhower's eleven-nation tour see no. 1359. On his letters to the presidents of the Latin American republics see the following document.

[2] For Eisenhower's previous correspondence with the Canadian leader see no. 1314.

[3] Eisenhower would leave on December 3 for Rome. There is no response from Diefenbaker in AWF.

1383   *EM, AWF, International Series:*
                                                                    Mateos

To Adolfo López Mateos   *December 1, 1959*
Personal

Dear Mr. President: I have received your courteous letters of October twentieth and October twenty-eighth containing your expressions of appreciation for the efforts made to reciprocate the gracious and cordial hospitality you and the Mexican people displayed during our meeting at Acapulco.[1] I agree that the problems that remain to be solved between our two countries are susceptible of solution in the spirit of mutual understanding and respect that characterize our relations, and that this collaboration between our countries can have favorable effects on hemispheric relations and can set an example for nations everywhere.

As you undoubtedly know by this time, I am planning, in conjunction with my attendance at the Western summit meeting in Paris on December nineteenth, a visit to several countries of the Mediterranean and the Near and Middle East.[2]

It seems to me possible that the heads of our sister American Republics with whom the United States maintains close and cordial ties might like to be apprised of the reasons for my undertaking this project. Accordingly, I am taking the liberty of writing to you directly with this in view.

My visit will take me to Rome, Ankara, Karachi, Kabul, New Delhi, Tehran, Athens, Tunis, Paris, Madrid, and Casablanca. Basically, my purpose in visiting these nations is to do what I can to strengthen the ties which bind the nations of the Free World together. I have found from experience that there is no substitute for personal contact in furthering understanding and good will.

I think it is very worthwhile to take every step possible to allay the fears held by many in the far-flung reaches of the world as to the intentions and the ambitions of the West. While you and I know that the vast military power possessed by the Free World in its various alliances is maintained in readiness for *defensive* purposes only, on behalf of the principles in which we all believe, this fact, so obvious to us, is not always apparent to our friends. I assure you, Mr. President, that I will do everything in my power to convince our friends around the world that this is so. The Organization of American States is dedicated to the pursuit of peace with justice for all; I hope to impress upon each government I visit that this purpose is a basic aspiration among all the peoples of our entire Continent.[3]

The tour will, of course, represent a strenuous undertaking. It will fill my time from now to the end of the year. Subsequent to that, there are various other commitments, such as a summit meeting and a return visit to Moscow, which will crowd considerably my time left in office. I want to assure you, however, that though these commitments are made outside the American sphere, it is my profound hope that all the American States will approve of the effort I am making and of the results, if any, that I may be able to achieve.[4] I hope that an opportunity may still be afforded me to meet again with the leaders of those countries which comprise the Organization of American States.[5]

Please be assured of my continuing high esteem.[6] *Sincerely*

---

[1] This letter was sent by cable to the American embassy in Mexico City for delivery to President López Mateos. The White House requested that the ambassador "tactfully stress" that the message remain confidential. The Mexican president had visited the United States on October 9–19 (State, *Foreign Relations, 1958–1960*, vol. V, *American Republics*, pp. 884–85). López Mateos's second letter was an acknowledgment of Eisenhower's thanks for a painting the Mexican leader had presented to the American people during his visit (both letters are in AWF/I: Mateos). On the Acapulco meeting the previous February see no. 1062.

[2] For background on Eisenhower's trip see no. 1359. This paragraph and the remainder of this message were also cabled to the presidents of Argentina, Bolivia, Brazil, Chile, Costa Rica, Ecuador, El Salvador, Guatemala, Haiti, Honduras, Nicaragua, Panama, Paraguay, Peru, Uruguay, and Venezuela (AWF/I). The State Department draft with Eisenhower's extensive handwritten emendations is in AWF/I: Brazil. Eisenhower would write again to the Latin American leaders after the collapse of the summit meeting in May 1960 (see no. 1541; see also Eisenhower to Herter, May 9, 1960, AWF/D).

[3] Eisenhower had added the preceding sentence to the draft of this letter.

[4] Before Eisenhower's changes, this sentence had originally read: "I want to assure you, however, that the fact of these commitments, being as they are outside the American sphere, do not at all indicate a diminished interest in the affairs of our own hemisphere."

[5] From February 23 to March 3, 1960, Eisenhower would visit the four southernmost countries in South America (Argentina, Chile, Uruguay, and Brazil; see no. 1403).

[6] Eisenhower handwrote the words "and with warm personal regard from your friend" at the end of this letter.

To ARLEIGH ALBERT BURKE   *December 1, 1959*

Dear Arleigh: There is nothing that I like more than a "writ of exception", especially when it provides a break in the disciplinary barriers normally confounding human instinct. I shall take plentiful, even self-indulgent, advantage of the dispensation, if for no other reason than because of reverential awe of the extraordinary power possessed by any one authorized, legally, to issue such a writ—and make it stick.[1]

My thanks for your welcome present, and even more for the escape you have provided from ordinary rules of naval behavior. Your thoughtfulness already has done much to lighten some of the forebodings that have clouded anticipations of my impending tour.[2]

With warm personal regard, *Sincerely*

[1] Admiral Burke, in his third term as Chief of Naval Operations, had sent the President a gift of "liquid stimulant" in anticipation of Eisenhower's visit aboard the U.S.S. *Des Moines* in the Mediterranean, during his twenty-day good will tour of Europe, the Middle East, and Asia. (On the tour see nos. 1382 and 1395.) Since alcohol was prohibited on Navy vessels, Burke wrote that he had resorted to "legal subterfuge" in effecting a "writ of exception" that applied only to "Presidents, Royalty, and those excepted by their express invitation." Burke said that he hoped that Eisenhower's "inner man" might benefit from "this extraordinary remedy at law" (Nov. 23, 1959, AWF/N).

In February Eisenhower had congratulated Burke on the success of the Vanguard missile program and had sent along a bottle of Burke's favorite scotch whiskey (see John S. D. Eisenhower, *Strictly Personal,* pp. 200–201; on the Vanguard program see no. 548).

[2] Eisenhower would board the U.S.S. *Des Moines* on December 15 (*New York Times,* Nov. 8, Dec. 14, 16–19, 1959).

To JOHN WILLIAM BYRNES   *December 2, 1959*

Dear John: In answer to your letter of November twenty-fourth concerning the Tennessee Valley Authority, I would first like to affirm your understanding of arrangements which have been made with the Tennessee Valley Authority for review by the President of its annual construction program. As was indicated at the time of debate on the financing bill, I will submit to the Congress each year my recommendations concerning this program for the ensuing fiscal year, starting with the fiscal year 1961.[1]

The new plant in Western Kentucky about which you have inquired, is to be located in an area where it could best serve the existing system and where coal is readily and economically available.[2] While I can understand your concern about expansion of the TVA area, I am sure you realize that the new legislation places rather severe restrictions on the power service area of the Corporation.[3] I would doubt that the simple location of a plant which is providing additional power for that system would either add to or detract from any pressures for geographical expansion. As a matter of fact, I am told that even the addition of this power unit will not meet all the anticipated power demands within this TVA area itself.

Concerning your suggestion that the site be reviewed by the Congress, you may recall that as finally enacted, the financing bill specifically exempted from the requirement for Congressional review the first power project to be built after enactment of the legislation.[4] In the light of this mandate I do not believe it would be appropriate to prohibit TVA from proceeding with work on this first new site.

You may be assured of my intention to require continuing close review of TVA's development plans. I am satisfied that the arrangements which have been worked out for this review will prove to be ample.

With warm regard, *Sincerely*

[1] For background see no. 1270. John William Byrnes (LL.B. University of Wisconsin 1938) had served as Republican Congressman from Wisconsin since 1945. He had written the President on November 24, 1959 (same file as document) regarding the expansion of the territorial limits of the Tennessee Valley Authority. Eisenhower's letter may have been drafted by White House aide Gerald Morgan.

[2] On October 1, 1959, the TVA had announced plans to build the world's largest steam turbine, to be located in Muhlenberg County in western Kentucky (see *New York Times*, Oct. 2, 1959).

[3] Byrnes had written that the large capacity of the new plant would influence communities outside the TVA service area boundary to make a strong effort to be supplied with TVA power. "Thus, irresistible pressures for geographical expansion will be created with inevitable harmful effects on Federal, State and local tax sources and on existing business enterprises." The new Tennessee Valley legislation had specified that the corporation was to make no contracts for the sale or delivery of power which would make it "directly or indirectly, a source of power supply outside the area for which the Corporation or its distributors were the primary source of power supply on July 1, 1957 . . ." (*U.S. Statutes at Large*, vol. 73 [1959], pp. 280–85).

[4] Byrnes had suggested that the President "order the TVA corporation to cease carrying out plans for construction of a plant at this location until the President and the Congress have had an opportunity to review this far-reaching decision." The legislation had specified that "Neither bond proceeds nor power revenues received by the Corporation shall be used to initiate the construction of new power producing projects (except for replacement purposes and except the first such project begun after the effective date of this section) until the construction program of the Corporation shall have been before Congress in session for ninety calendar days" (see *U.S. Statutes at Large, ibid.*).

To Nikita Sergeyevich Khrushchev   *December 3, 1959*
Cable. Secret

Dear Mr. Chairman:[1] Thank you for your letter telling me of your gift of seedlings of some of the trees and shrubs which grow in your country, as well as the book about your visit to the United States.[2] I am very pleased by your kind gesture, and will be glad to have these enduring souvenirs of your visit and of our talks.

I understand that the trees and shrubs should arrive here about December 8. I am sorry that I will not be here to receive them personally at that time, but shall look forward to finding them on my return.[3] As for the Russian toys, I am sure they will contribute to making a happy Christmas for the grandchildren but, in accordance with tradition, these presents will remain a secret until discovered by them on Christmas morning.

As Ambassador Thompson has perhaps told you by now, Admiral Strauss is now back in Washington and we are arranging to send the bull and two heifers to you by plane in January.[4]

Mrs. Eisenhower joins me in this expression of our appreciation, and in sending best wishes to you, to Mrs. Khrushchev and the other members of your family for the New Year.

I am grateful for your consideration of my suggestion that I might, on my visit to Russia, go out through Siberia. There is no hurry about the matter, and I shall await your further decision. I do want to assure you personally that I had no military consideration of any kind in mind, but made the suggestion simply as what seemed to be the best way to get most easily to Tokyo.[5]

Again, with best wishes. *Sincerely*

[1] This letter was sent by cable to the American embassy in Moscow for delivery to Khrushchev.

[2] Khrushchev had visited the United States in September (see no. 1332). Impressed with the trees Eisenhower was raising at his Gettysburg farm, he had told the President that it was a good tradition "when, as a token of friendship and remembered events, people plant trees which serve as a reminder of those events" (Khrushchev to Eisenhower, Nov. 30, 1959, AWF/I: Khrushchev; see also Thompson to Herter, Nov. 13, 1959, *ibid.*).

[3] Eisenhower would leave on this same day for his eleven-nation trip and the Western summit, which was to begin in Paris on December 19 (see no. 1382).

[4] During Khrushchev's visit to the Gettysburg farm Eisenhower had presented the Soviet leader with a black Angus heifer. Lewis Strauss, former head of the Atomic Energy Commission and Secretary of Commerce, had promised Khrushchev another Angus heifer and bull. The livestock would arrive in Moscow on January 16 (Herter to Eisenhower, Jan. 25, 1960, AWF/D-H; and *New York Times*, Jan. 14, 17, 1960).

[5] Eisenhower's earlier letter to the Soviet leader, suggesting that he leave the Soviet Union through Siberia is no. 1381-A. According to Soviet regulations, no American was permitted to visit the seaport of Vladivostok, on the eastern coast of Siberia (see Murphy, *Diplomat Among Warriors*, p. 439). For developments see no. 1408.

1387   *EM, AWF, Dulles-Herter Series*

To CHRISTIAN ARCHIBALD HERTER   *December 7, 1959*
Cable. Secret

Dear Chris:[1] I note in the *New York Times* of 5 December a speculative piece by Bruson. He dwells on the alleged opinion of De Gaulle that an American withdrawal from Europe is a distinct probability.[2] While I consider that in this instance a whole cloak has been woven out of an insignificant piece of lint, I think that it may be desirable for us to move promptly to squelch such irresponsible rumors or manufactured straw-men. The article goes on to say that this conviction of De Gaulle is another reason that he opposes integration of NATO forces.[3]

There obviously has been leakage at Bonn and possibly a lot of misinterpretation regarding these remarks attributed to De Gaulle in his recent conversations with Adenauer.[4] Perhaps best way of squelching story would be for French to issue some form of denial concurrently with whatever you decide we might appropriately say in Washington.

As agreed among members of our government, we are interested in strengthening NATO forces and believe that Britain, Belgium, Germany and France have especially important obligations to study this matter. Even though we believe their proportional contributions should be increased, we have never hinted at withdrawal.

Do you think it might be wise even prior to your arrival in Paris that our Ambassador to France be instructed to inform the French that we believe that such false rumors and assumptions as these mentioned should be emphatically squelched by the French Government. If you approve, you may act with no additional communication to me.

These are my thoughts on the matter but you will have to decide on most effective way of handling, or indeed if anything at all should be done.[5]

With warm regard, *as ever*

[1] This message was sent to Secretary Herter by cable from Karachi, Pakistan, the third country Eisenhower visited on his eleven-nation tour. The President had earlier sent a brief cable about his trip to Herter from Rome (AWF/D-H).

[2] The writer Sidney *Gruson*, former reporter and foreign correspondent for the *Canadian Press* in Toronto and a staff member of the *New York Times* since 1944, had said that for the first time since the end of World War II the prospect of an eventual withdrawal of U.S. forces from Western Europe was being openly discussed on the Continent (*New York Times*, Dec. 5, 1959).

[3] For de Gaulle's decision to withdraw French forces from the NATO Mediterranean fleet see nos. 1106 and 1112.

[4] Gruson had included quotations from a German newspaperman who had written an article after West German Chancellor Adenauer had concluded two days of talks with de Gaulle in Paris on December 2 (see State, *Foreign Relations, 1958–1960*, vol. IX, *Berlin Crisis 1959–1960; Germany; Austria*, p. 118).

[5] Herter would arrive in Paris on December 13 in preparation for the ministerial meeting of the North Atlantic Council. Agreeing that the Gruson story "was not helpful," he would tell Eisenhower that he had informed the British, French, and West Germans that the United States was determined to maintain its "fair share of the over-all NATO defense effort in Europe" as long as the Soviet threat remained. He also said that he would strengthen the appropriate portions of the speech he would deliver at the opening meeting of the council "to counteract speculation of the type contained in the Gruson story" (see State, *Foreign Relations, 1958–1960*, vol. VII, pt. 1, *Western European Integration and Security; Canada*, pp. 537–38). He urged Eisenhower to consider presenting the U.S. position at the Western summit. "Indeed it is my conviction that this is the only fully adequate means for coping with this problem at the present time" (Herter to Eisenhower, Dec. 8, 1959, AWF/D-H).

1388   *EM, AWF, Administration Series*

To Richard Milhous Nixon   *December 8, 1959*
Cable. Confidential

Dear Dick: While of course I cannot have any idea of the reaction in the American press, everything seems to be going reasonably well.[1] The weather was bad in Rome and consequently dampened the public reaction. But the talks there were friendly and amiable. The reception in Turkey was colorful and outstandingly warm. Here in Karachi, however, I was literally overwhelmed by the sheer numbers of people on the street. Everywhere there is evidence that they look to America as a sort of father-nation, and that they feel we will be able to help them achieve the fulfillment of their desires. I am greatly impressed here, as I was in Turkey, by the giant strides they have made in the past few years.[2]

My most outstanding impressions in each of the three countries I have visited so far are, first, the determination of the Italians to take a greater role in the formation of Western policy;[3] second, the dedication of the Turks to the economic improvement of their country and their pressing need for assistance from us in order to carry that out; and, in Pakistan, the strong and forward looking leadership being given by President Ayub, who has clear recognition of the needs of his country.⁴ In both Turkey and Pakistan, leaders and people alike leave no doubt of their courage and resolution.

With warm regard, *As ever*

¹ Eisenhower was writing from Pakistan, the third country on his eleven-nation good-will tour (for background see no. 1382).

² Eisenhower had arrived in Rome on December 4, accompanied by his son and daughter-in-law and Under Secretary of State Robert Murphy. On his meetings with Italian officials see State, *Foreign Relations, 1958–1960*, vol. VII, pt. 2, *Western Europe*, pp. 574–81; on his one-day visit to Turkey see State, *Foreign Relations, 1958–1960*, vol. X, pt. 2, *Eastern Europe; Finland; Greece; Turkey*, pp. 819–24; and on his activities in Pakistan see Smith, *A President's Odyssey*, pp. 85–95; and State, *Foreign Relations, 1958–1960*, vol. XV, *South and Southeast Asia*, pp. 781–94; see also Eisenhower, *Waging Peace*, pp. 485–96; John S. D. Eisenhower, *Strictly Personal*, pp. 264–69; and *New York Times*, December 5, 7, 13, 1959.

³ Italian President Giovanni Gronchi had told Eisenhower that Italy's commitments as a NATO member nation made it necessary that the Italians should be brought into Western summit discussions regarding Germany. He also said that Italy should participate in disarmament talks whenever specific proposals relating to limitations in certain areas were discussed (State, *Foreign Relations, 1958–1960*, vol. VII, pt. 2, *Western Europe*, pp. 580–81).

⁴ Mohammed Ayub Khan had been commander-in-chief of the Pakistani army and chief martial law administrator. He became president and minister of defense of Pakistan in October 1958. For developments see the following document.

1389   *EM, AWF, Dulles-Herter Series*

To Christian Archibald Herter   *December 12, 1959*
Cable. Secret

Dear Chris: Today I am having, and enjoying, something of a "breather"—the first of the trip.¹ During the breather I have only the signing of dozens of autographs and well over fifty letters, work on two speeches, an informal luncheon, an "Open House" at 4:30 and a formal dinner. The schedules each day until now have been full, as I am sure yours will be in Paris.²

With regard to your NATO discussions, I fully concur in the actions you suggest to counteract the stories that we are thinking of withdrawing our troops from Europe. There are one or two changes I would suggest in the statement you propose to make at the NATO Ministerial meeting. Bob Murphy will wire these to you.³

My trip continues to give every appearance that it is serving the purposes we had in mind. The reception here in India has been friendly almost beyond words (as I know you have already heard, from your press conference statement quoted in the papers here this morning) and the response to the statements I have been making seems to be satisfactory.[4] Though formal discussions with Nehru and his associates have been limited, I have had opportunity to talk with him at some length, and always in a most cordial vein, at luncheons and other social functions. I am to have a dinner with him alone Sunday evening.[5]

With warm regard, *Sincerely*

[1] Eisenhower had arrived in New Delhi on December 9 after visits to Italy, Turkey, Pakistan, and Afghanistan (see the preceding document). He would remain in India until December 14. This message was sent to the American embassy in Paris, where Secretary Herter was preparing for the ministerial meeting of the North Atlantic Council.

[2] Eisenhower's letters to government officials in Italy, Turkey, Afghanistan, and Pakistan, as well as the American ambassadors in those countries, are in AWF/I. Eisenhower and the president of India would greet selected guests at a reception for 5,000 people in the Mogul gardens in New Delhi. In the evening Eisenhower would give a formal dinner at the American ambassador's residence in honor of Prime Minister Nehru (see the President's daily appointments, AWF/D; and Smith, *A President's Odyssey*, pp. 112–13).

[3] On the issue of the rumored U.S. troop withdrawal and Herter's statement see no. 1387. Under Secretary Murphy's cable is not in AWF.

[4] In his news conference two days earlier Herter had stated that the President's trip had "categorically" exceeded expectations. The "genuine enthusiasm" of the people had indicated a deep feeling for the United States and for Eisenhower as an individual. Although discussions with heads of state had not touched upon matters of detailed substance, Herter said, the President had been able to emphasize the general philosophy of the United States and its attitude toward world problems (*U.S. Department of State Bulletin* 41, no. 1070 [December 28, 1959], p. 396; and *New York Times*, Dec. 11, 1959. For press reports of the trip see USIA, Special Staff Note, December 17, 23, 1959, AWF/D).

[5] On Eisenhower's meetings with Nehru see State, *Foreign Relations, 1958–1960*, vol. XV, *South and Southeast Asia*, pp. 520–25. For developments see no. 1393.

1390   *EM, AWF,*
                                                                    Name Series

To Louis Francis Albert Mountbatten   *December 12, 1959*

Dear Dickie: Yesterday I was donning my academic robes at Delhi University, in a room in which I noticed a plaque.[1] I read the inscription, which was part of a statement from you detailing some facts concerning the history of the University and your marriage to Edwina, including the circumstances of your engagement to her, all of which recounted quite a long chain of coincidences.[2]

Of course I was interested and, indeed, was able to add to this coincidental history one small item of a ridiculous character. I found after coming to Delhi that the mornings were quite chilly and I have been in the habit of riding at that time in an open car, sometimes rather rapidly. The result has been that I got cold, particularly around the feet and legs. Yesterday morning I solved my problem by putting on a pair of the socks that you gave to me right after you visited Washington a few months back.[3] So there I was in the room where you proposed to Edwina, standing in the socks that you sent to me as a present so many years later. I rather felt that it was time that the room ought to be called the "Dickie Mountbatten Room" of Delhi University.

As you many know, Mamie is not with me because of the arduous character of the airplane trip.[4] I am accompanied, however, by my son and daughter-in-law, and the three of us, together with some of the most important members of my staff, are living in the Rashtrapati Bhavan.[5] I am on the second floor—you being British would probably call it the first—but at least one flight up from the ground floor.

I have the suite on the south wing. We are extremely comfortable and vastly intrigued by the atmosphere and history of the building.

Give my warm greetings to Edwina and, of course, all the best to yourself.[6] *As ever*

[1] As part of his tour of Europe, the Middle East and Asia (see no. 1384), Eisenhower was visiting India, where he would receive an honorary Doctor of Laws degree from the university. In his address he stressed the need for young people of all nations to "concern themselves with the problems, possibilities, the resources and the rewards of a common destiny" (see Rao to Eisenhower, Nov. 28, 1959, and Eisenhower to Rao, Dec. 12, 1959, in AWF/1: India; *New York Times*, Dec. 11, 1959; *Public Papers of the Presidents: Eisenhower, 1957*, p. 836; and Smith, *A President's Odyssey*, pp. 31–32, 110–11).

[2] On February 14, 1922, Mountbatten had proposed to the former Edwina Cynthia Annette Ashley in her sitting room at Delhi University, which had been founded that same year as a residential university. At the time he was serving as an aide to the Prince of Wales, then on a tour of the British Commonwealth. Mountbatten later served as Supreme Allied Commander, South East Asia (SACSEA), as Viceroy and subsequently as Governor-General of India (John Terraine, ed., *The Life and Times of Lord Mountbatten* [London, 1969], pp. 32–40, 100–101, 145–65; see also Galambos, *Columbia University*, no. 1087).

[3] Eisenhower had hosted a small dinner party for Mountbatten on October 8 (see nos. 823 and 1339).

[4] The First Lady had gone to Denver to visit her ailing mother (Susan Eisenhower, *Mrs. Ike*, pp. 298–99, and *New York Times*, Dec. 5, 7, 9, 19, 1959).

[5] On Barbara Eisenhower's role during the tour see Susan Eisenhower, *Mrs. Ike*, pp. 298–99; Smith, *A President's Odyssey*, pp. 16–17; and *New York Times*, December 5, 7, 8, 13, 14, 20, 21. The Rashtrapati Bhavan was the official home of India's president.

[6] Mountbatten would reply (Jan. 21, AWF/N) that it was "fascinating" that Eisenhower would have dressed in his academic robes wearing Mountbatten's "patent Ten-

ova" socks in the same room in which he had proposed to his wife. He added that he had heard from many friends in India of the overwhelming success of Eisenhower's visit. "How wonderful," he concluded, "to end up a victorious soldier's career as a great man of peace."

1391   *EM, AWF, International Series: Nehru*

To Jawaharlal Nehru   *December 14, 1959*
Cable. Secret

Dear Prime Minister:[1] I recall to you your observation about the opportunity of the Shah of Iran to strengthen his position politically, by initiating real land reform.[2] He informed me today that he is, within the next two or three days, to introduce a bill to his Parliament, which he says will pass, and of which the following are the highlights. Already of course, as you are well aware, he has initiated a token land reform by dividing up a great portion of his own private estates. But he is now moving in a much more radical direction. First of all, the limit for land holdings in the country will be 700 acres. The second point is that the land holders will have to sell their land to the government at the assessed value on which they have been paying taxes. Thirdly, the government will pay off the indebtedness in fifteen years, initially issuing bonds on which they will pay 3%. The holdings allowed to each peasant will vary somewhat according to the nature of the terrain and the climatic conditions, as well as population density. The land will be sold to the peasants on a twenty year basis, with 4% interest, and at an amount not greater than its cost to the government. The plan calls for completion of the distribution within a space of two years. He thinks that some little more time may be required in certain instances because of complications as to current number of tenant farmers, and so on.

The Shah gladly gave me his permission to pass this information to you personally to be kept confidential until after the bill has been submitted to the Parliament.

With respect to the possible opposition of the land holders, he said, "Well, after all there are about one hundred of them. What can they do? In my opinion this move will be approved by the public and the land holders themselves will make no kick whatsoever."[3]

With warm personal regard, *Sincerely*

---

[1] This message was sent to the Indian prime minister by cable from Athens, Greece, the seventh country Eisenhower had visited on his eleven-nation tour. The President had just met with Shah Reza Pahlavi during a six-hour stop in Tehran (see State, *For-*

eign Relations, 1958–1960, vol. XII, *Near East Region; Iraq; Iran; Arabian Peninsula*, pp. 658–59).

[2] On the conversations between Eisenhower and Nehru during the President's four-day visit to India see State, *Foreign Relations, 1958–1960*, vol. XV, *South and Southeast Asia*, pp. 521–26; see also Eisenhower to Nehru, December 13, 1959, AWF/I: India, Goodwill Tour.

[3] Nehru would express his gratitude for Eisenhower's message and his pleasure in the fact that Iran was taking effective steps toward land reform. "For several years," he wrote, "I have thought that this was the most urgently needed reform in Iran." Nehru would also tell Eisenhower that his visit had "powerfully" affected the Indian people and that he would always welcome any communication from Eisenhower that would help him "understand the great developments that are taking place on the world scene" (Nehru to Eisenhower, Dec. 16, 1959, AWF/I: Nehru). For more on Eisenhower's meeting with the Shah see the following document.

1392   *EM, AWF, International Series:*
                                                                              Iran

To Mohammed Reza Pahlavi   *December 14, 1959*
Cable. Secret

Your Majesty: I deeply regret that our conversation, which I found intensely interesting, had to be terminated because of the requirements of my personal schedule.[1] I was especially interested in your views of the possible intentions and moves of the Eurasian forces and the measures that you consider most applicable for countering.[2] I received the maps giving diagrammatic dispositions of forces in neighboring countries and will have these, together with your conceptions of the proper organizing and equipping of your own forces, studied by our military groups.

Again I assure you of my appreciation of your welcome to me and the reception given to me by your people. It was an unforgettable and heartwarming experience. I shall write you a little later to try more adequately to express my gratitude of all that you did for me and my party, but in the meantime this hurried note, dictated on my plane, brings you the assurance of my deep thanks.[3]

With expressions of my high esteem and warm regard, *Sincerely*

[1] Eisenhower had met with Shah Reza Pahlavi during a six-hour stop in Tehran, before traveling on to Greece. This message, sent by cable from Athens, was followed by a personal letter from Eisenhower thanking the Shah for the gracious reception he had received in Iran (Eisenhower to Pahlavi, Dec. 14, 1959, AWF/I: Iran, Goodwill Tour; see also Pahlavi to Eisenhower, Dec. 14, 1959, *ibid.*).

[2] The Shah had told Eisenhower of the dangers to Iran from Iraq and Afghanistan. Both countries, he believed, were "acting as proxies for Soviet aggression." He had determined that Iran needed a "crash program" to build up its armaments, includ-

ing highly mobile forces equipped with atomic weapons, long-range missiles, additional air bases, and improved aircraft (State, *Foreign Relations, 1958–1960*, vol. XII, *Near East Region; Iraq; Iran; Arabian Peninsula*, pp. 658–59).

[3] The Shah would write Eisenhower that he was grateful for the President's interest in his plans for Iran and would communicate his ideas more extensively in later correspondence (Pahlavi to Eisenhower, Dec. 20, 1959, AWF/I: Iran). For developments see no. 1400.

1393   *EM, AWF, Dulles-Herter Series*

To Christian Archibald Herter   *December 14, 1959*
Cable. Secret

Dear Chris: The following message, which I have drafted to send to our Ambassadors in Karachi and New Delhi, conforms to the facts of my conversations with Ayub and Nehru.[1] In order to keep this properly on the communication tracks, I would like to have you transmit it to Rountree and Bunker if it meets with your concurrence. If you see any objection, please hold up on transmitting it and send me a message on the matter on the *Des Moines*.[2]

Proposed message to Karachi and New Delhi follows.

"Following message to you is from the President:

During the course of my conversations in Delhi with Nehru, a good deal of time was devoted to Indo-Pakistani relations.[3] I stressed the importance which we attach to this question and the hope we entertain that the improvement which has already occurred will develop further into a close and confident working relationship. I expressed the opinion that such improvement would be in the interest not only of the parties directly concerned but of the entire free world. I would be glad to be helpful if that were needed and welcome, but made clear that I could not be in the position of a mediator. I mentioned that in our Mutual Security Program for Pakistan I was often perplexed between a desire to see Pakistan well equipped militarily, and an equal wish not to cause embarrassment or anxiety in India. I told Mr. Nehru that we regarded the deployment of Pakistan and Indian troops on the Kashmir cease-fire line as wasteful and as tending to weaken the front that the free world presented to the Communists. Incidentally, I said to Mr. Nehru that President Ayub personally expressed his great desire for consideration of differences, saying that, at the very least, he and the Indians should not continue to find it necessary to deploy forces on the Kashmir line. I also told Mr. Nehru that so far as any risk or danger that Pakistan might attack India is concerned, I could not believe there is even a remote possibility, and furthermore I believe the United States could be effective in preventing it.

While Mr. Nehru in the first instance dwelt briefly on his apprehension at one time of a Pakistan "stab in the back," in our conversation Sunday evening he expressed a desire for an approach in the form of either a joint declaration by himself and Ayub or separate statements to the effect that all questions between India and Pakistan would be settled for the indefinite future by peaceful negotiations. Resort to force and war would be excluded. In reply to a question of mine, Nehru said that this declaration should apply to all questions, both present and future, i.e., including those now existing (e.g. Kashmir).

If this were done, Nehru indicated—without being precise about it—that he would then be less opposed to our assisting Pakistan in modernizing its army. He clearly left the road open for further communication with me on this matter should his proposal find any favorable reaction in Karachi.

For Karachi:

Rountree is instructed to talk with Ayub on a secret and personal basis. Likewise he should make an exploratory effort to obtain reaction. He should not show this message to him or other Pakistanis. Our purpose would be to make sure that President Ayub understands the great opportunity this could give him in modernization of his army. I would appreciate a report as promptly as possible in your EYES ONLY series.[4]

For Delhi:

It would be appreciated if Bunker would deliver to Nehru personally the following message:

After reflecting on our last evening's conversation I have instructed my Ambassador in Karachi to discuss with Ayub personally on a strictly confidential basis the thought you expressed regarding the possibility of a joint declaration or separate statement by India and Pakistan. This would be to the effect that all questions between them for the indefinite future will be settled by peaceful negotiations, i.e., without resort to force or war. As I told you I am not trying to be a mediator but I also said I should like to repeat to President Ayub your feelings on the matter, as I told you of his. My Ambassador will stress to Ayub the great importance attaching to such an initiative not only to the parties directly concerned but to the entire free world. I am sure President Ayub will understand the importance this might have in respect of United States assistance to Pakistan in the future, particularly as to his hope of modernizing his regular forces.[5]

I shall hope to inform you as soon as possible of Ayub's reaction or other development. It does seem to me that your inspiration could lead to a substantial step forward; but I do not minimize your difficulties in this field. I know they are many. Should any type of useful information come to my notice I shall *inform you* promptly.[6] With warm personal regard, Dwight D. Eisenhower."

End of proposed message. *As ever*

[1] This message was cabled to Paris, where Secretary Herter was attending the ministerial meeting of the North Atlantic Council. William M. Rountree and Ellsworth Bunker were the American ambassadors to Pakistan and India. For Eisenhower's conversations with Pakistani President Mohammed Ayub Khan, Indian Prime Minister Nehru, and other government officials see State, *Foreign Relations, 1958–1960*, vol. XV, *South and Southeast Asia*, pp. 781–94, 521–26; see also nos. 1392 and 1389.

[2] In his transmitting message Herter would tell the two ambassadors that he had reviewed Eisenhower's proposal and concurred "wholeheartedly" (Dec. 16, 1959, AWF/D-H; see also Herter to Eisenhower, Dec. 15, 1959, *ibid.*). Eisenhower would leave on this day from Piraeus, Greece, aboard the U.S.S. *Des Moines*, the flagship of the U.S. Sixth Fleet, en route to Tunisia.

[3] For background on the Indo-Pakistani conflict over Kashmir see no. 113; see also Eisenhower, *Waging Peace*, pp. 494–95.

[4] In a December 22 meeting President Ayub would tell Rountree that he appreciated U.S. objectives in pursuing the matter. He believed, however, that Nehru was seeking assurance that he could continue to hold vital areas of Kashmir without Pakistani resistance. Signing the declaration that Nehru had suggested "without certain accompanying steps," Ayub said, would be like handing "Kashmir to India on a silver platter." He thought that Nehru should formulate an agreement on the basic principles of a Kashmir settlement before their countries could undertake a "no war-no force" statement. Rountree thought that it was "highly unlikely" that the Pakistanis would agree to Nehru's declaration without relating it to a solution of the Kashmir problem and that the Pakistani people were already concerned about moves toward rapprochement with India. Eisenhower's visits with Ayub and Nehru had much improved the atmosphere between the two countries, Rountree said, and he urged the State Department to explore all avenues that might lead to a settlement of the Kashmir issue (State, *Foreign Relations, 1958–1960*, vol. XV, *South and Southeast Asia*, pp. 197–201).

[5] Eisenhower had added the last ten words of this sentence to the draft of this letter (AWF/D-H).

[6] For developments see no. 1516.

1394   *EM, AWF, Names Series*

To Robert Winship Woodruff   *December 26, 1959*
Personal. Top Secret

Dear Bob: For the first time I find you somewhat less than understanding. When I tip up a bottle of Coca Cola for a good drink it lasts only seconds—with a straw, a lot of talk and more walking, I was able to contact more photographs and newspaper correspondents than I could possibly otherwise have done![1] *As ever*

¹ The word "photographs" in the second sentence should probably be "photographers." The Eisenhowers would vacation in Augusta, Georgia, December 27–January 5 (see Slater, *The Ike I Knew*, pp. 213–19, and *New York Times*, Dec. 25, 26, 28–31, 1959, Jan. 1–4, 6, 1960). The President and former director of the Coca-Cola Company Woodruff would play golf on December 30. On January 7, 1960, Woodruff would confirm his "verbal acknowledgment" of this letter. "I have nothing more to say and anything I have said I take back," he would write (AWF/N). There is no further correspondence on this subject in AWF.

1395   *EM, AWF, Administration Series*

To CHARLES DOUGLAS JACKSON   *December 27, 1959*
Personal

Dear C.D.: Of course your suggestion is no way "impertinent." But whatever the interpretation made by the press, the fact is that I made no "promises" whatever in the various countries that I visited.¹ Of course I did discuss with the leaders of those countries various problems of common interest, and certain suggestions that were made on both sides will be given adequately and full follow-up treatment. As you know Bob Murphy was with me and present during most of the official conferences, and he is taking care of this particular piece of business for me.²

Thank you for my "part-time" Christmas gift. I shall without question enjoy Churchill's World War II—and I am grateful for your thoughtfulness in sending me a copy.

With many thanks for your generous praise of what I tried to do on the trip just concluded, and warm personal regard.³ *As ever*

P.S. And, of course, best wishes for a Happy New Year to you and Mrs. Jackson.⁴

¹ Eisenhower had returned on December 22 from his eleven-nation tour. Jackson had congratulated him on his "triumphal" visits "in some very tricky areas where there were plenty of leaks." The leaders of these countries would inevitably feel that Eisenhower's hopeful words outlining a better future "were construed as pretty definite promises," Jackson said. He suggested that Eisenhower have someone make a list of what might have been considered promises and then take fast action on as many of them as possible. "The effect," he said, "would be electrifying." He did not want his letter to seem impertinent, but "could not help thinking that after your sensational and statesmanlike performance, it would be a crime to have the opportunities that you have created nibbled to death by the bureaucracy" (Jackson to Eisenhower, Dec. 21, 1959, AWF/A; see also Jackson to Whitman, Dec. 21, 1959, *ibid.*).
² Robert D. Murphy was Under Secretary of State for Political Affairs. He had delayed his retirement, after forty years of government service, to accompany Eisenhower on his trip (see Murphy, *Diplomat Among Warriors*, pp. 444–46).

[3] For developments see the following document.
[4] Jackson's wife was the former Grace Bristed.

1396

EM, AWF,
Miscellaneous Series:
President's Goodwill Trip

To CHRISTIAN ARCHIBALD HERTER   *December 27, 1959*
Personal

Dear Chris: There seems to be some press comment expressing the fear that I have promised "many things" to each nation I visited on my recent tour.[1] I thought it might be well to put myself on record with you as to what actually I did do.

Whenever the matter of additional help to the various countries came up, I contented myself with saying "We would be glad to study the suggestions made.["] In those instances where I knew we had commitments to countries, I indicated that we intended to keep them.

In one case, in Pakistan, I agreed with President Ayub that it would be a very good thing to have his regular army modernized. By no means, however, did I suggest that America would be ready to pay the bill.[2]

I have already asked General Goodpaster to collect the minutes of each conference I held with any Head of State or Government throughout my travels. I think it would be wise to have everyone concerned very clear on these conversations. Possibly each of our Ambassadors should also be told the bare facts.[3]

With warm regard, *As ever*

[1] See the preceding document; see also *New York Times,* December 24, 1959.
[2] On Eisenhower's meetings with the Pakistani President Mohammed Ayub Khan see no. 1393; see also State, *Foreign Relations, 1958–1960,* vol. XV, *South and Southeast Asia,* pp. 781–92.
[3] For Eisenhower's discussions with the foreign leaders see State, *Foreign Relations, 1958–1960,* vol. VII, pt. 1, *Western European Integration and Security; Canada,* pp. 318–48; vol. VII, pt. 2, *Western Europe,* pp. 574–81; vol. X, pt. 2, *Eastern Europe; Finland; Greece; Turkey,* pp. 688–94, 819–24; vol. XII, *Near East Region; Iraq; Iran; Arabian Peninsula,* pp. 658–59; vol. XIII, *Arab-Israeli Dispute; United Arab Republic; North Africa,* pp. 795–800, 878–85; and vol. XV, *South and Southeast Asia,* pp. 521–26; see also nos. 1388 and 1393, and Eisenhower, *Waging Peace,* pp. 490–513.

To Nikita Sergeyevich Khrushchev   *December 29, 1959*

Dear Mr. Chairman: I note with satisfaction that you have agreed to participate in a Summit meeting of the Four Powers in Paris which Prime Minister Macmillan, President de Gaulle and myself proposed to you. I can well understand the difficulty of arriving at a date commonly acceptable to the four of us.[1]

I have been in touch with Prime Minister Macmillan and President de Gaulle in regard to the alternative dates which you suggest. Unfortunately, due to other engagements, both President de Gaulle and I would not find it possible to meet on April twenty-first. I further understand that Prime Minister Macmillan has prior commitments which run from May third until mid-May.[2]

Provided that this is acceptable to you, the best arrangement would seem to be for the meeting of the Four Powers to open in Paris on May sixteenth.[3]

I trust, Mr. Chairman, that this will not present any difficulties to you and that we may agree to meet in Paris on that date.[4] *Sincerely*

[1] The Western heads of government, at their first meeting in Paris on December 19, had agreed to extend to the Soviet Union an invitation to an East-West summit meeting in Paris from April 27 to May 1, 1960. Among the possible agenda items proposed for discussion were aid to underdeveloped nations, Berlin and Germany, and disarmament and related questions. Two days later representatives from the three Western embassies in Moscow had presented the invitation to Soviet Foreign Minister Gromyko for delivery to Khrushchev (State, *Foreign Relations, 1958–1960*, vol. IX, *Berlin Crisis 1959–1960; Germany; Austria*, pp. 136–38, 140–49, 151–54). Khrushchev had welcomed the proposal and had told Eisenhower that only through "the personal meetings of statesmen at the highest level" could urgent international problems be resolved. The date, however, was inconvenient for him, and he had suggested either April 21 or May 4 (Khrushchev to Eisenhower, Dec. 25, 1959, AWF/I: Khrushchev).

[2] Both de Gaulle and the King of Nepal had planned visits to the United States in April; Macmillan was to meet with the commonwealth prime ministers on May 3–14.

[3] On the selection of this date see Merchant to Eisenhower, and Draft Telegram to American Embassies, Dec. 26, 1959, AWF/D-H; see also State, *Foreign Relations, 1958–1960*, vol. IX, *Berlin Crisis 1959–1960; Germany; Austria*, pp. 153–54.

[4] Khrushchev would agree to convening the summit meeting in Paris on May 16 (Khrushchev to Eisenhower, Dec. 30, 1959, AWF/I: Khrushchev). For developments see no. 1433.

To Henry Robinson Luce   *December 29, 1959*

Dear Harry: When I returned from my recent trip, Jerry Persons proudly presented to me, as a gift from you, the portrait that Andrew Wyeth did of me and that was used as a cover on one of the issues of TIME.[1] I am, as you probably know, a great admirer of Mr. Wyeth's work and I do think he did as well as could be expected with the material at hand. Needless to say, I am greatly indebted to you.

Thank you, too, for the copy of Churchill's World War II; I cannot fail to find it highly interesting.[2]

With my deep appreciation of your thoughtfulness come my good wishes to you and Clare for a Happy New Year, and, as always, my warm personal regard. *As ever*

[1] On the President's goodwill tour of Europe, the Middle East, and Asia see no. 1382. Persons and Luce had arranged for Eisenhower to receive the painting as a Christmas gift. Wyeth and his photographer had visited Eisenhower's Gettysburg farm on August 16. Wyeth's painting of the President had been featured on the cover of *Time* on September 7, 1959 (see Luce to Persons, Dec. 4, 1959, Persons to Luce, Dec. 10, 1959, and King to Luce, Dec. 18, 1959, all in same file as document).

[2] On December 11 (*ibid.*) Luce had written that *Life* had had the "honor of publishing this year" Churchill's two-volume memoir, *The Second World War*. The work, which was an abridgement of Churchill's six-volume series of the same title, included photographs, paintings and maps from *Life*'s own collection. Two sets had been "specially bound and boxed for two distinguished friends of the editors," Luce wrote. One copy would go to the author and the other to Eisenhower.

To Milton Stover Eisenhower   *December 31, 1959*

Dear Milton: Just as I was about to send you a formal letter of thanks for all you have done throughout these years for me, and particularly these last twelve months, your note of the twenty-eighth arrived—and I promptly tore my effort up.[1] By no means have you any right to feel that you haven't been of much "help" recently to me; quite the contrary. In addition to the concrete things you have done, I always find invaluable any few minutes I can spend with you.

And don't worry—I shall certainly call upon you often during the remaining twelve months and twenty days of the Administration![2]

Mamie joins me in best wishes to you and Ruth for a Happy New Year. *Devotedly*

P.S. I purposely haven't mentioned the South American trip since, despite the New York Times, plans are still very much in the tentative stage.[3]

[1] In 1953 the President had appointed his brother Milton as his personal representative and special ambassador on matters affecting Latin America. On Milton's recent efforts to improve U.S.-Mexican relations see, for example, nos. 1163 and 1170. His letter is in AWF/N.

[2] Milton had admitted that his duties as president of Johns Hopkins University were "arduous," but he promised that he could "always find time to be of assistance" if his brother desired his service. On the President's relationship with Milton see Eisenhower, *Waging Peace*, pp. 16–18, and Galambos and van Ee, *The Middle Way*, nos. 85, 188, and 827. See also Milton Eisenhower, *The President is Calling*, and *The Wine is Bitter*, and Ewald, *Eisenhower the President*, p. 189.

[3] On this same day the *New York Times* had printed a front-page story on Eisenhower's upcoming plans to visit four nations in South America. In his letter, Milton had offered to accompany him: "I want to go along, and I'm sure that I can earn my keep on that trip." For developments see no. 1403.

1400   *EM, AWF, Administration Series:*
                                                              Dillon Corr.

To Mohammed Reza Pahlavi   *January 2, 1960*
Secret

Your Majesty:[1] I appreciate very much the kind thoughts expressed in your recent letter. I would also like to thank you again for the warm welcome that you and your people extended to me in the course of my recent visit to your beautiful country. The stimulating and informative discussions that we had on our many mutual problems were among the highlights of my trip, and I am awaiting with interest the further thoughts and plans that you have promised to send to me.[2]

As I indicated to you during our talks, I believe that now and in the foreseeable future, the principal threat to our mutual interests is most likely to come from the Soviet Union[3] and that our mutual efforts to maintain appropriate defense postures should continue to be directed primarily toward that threat. Should any other country in the region become clearly controlled and directed by the U.S.S.R. the nature of the defensive situation would be, of course, greatly altered. It will be in the light of the current situation that your thoughts will be given by our Defense officials the full and careful consideration that I promised while in your capital. As I understood your presentation to me at Tehran, your chief preoccupation is a modernization of your forces even if such a process should require a diminution in total numbers.[4]

In considering your plans, we will have to take account of our capabilities. I know that I need not tell you that the resources of my country, as well as yours, are limited, and that we shall fail in our larger objectives if we impose too great a burden our on economies. These basic considerations are limiting factors to any sound planning.

We must keep in touch with one another and continue our constructive discussions. I have come to value these highly.

I would also like you to know that during my all-too-short visit in your lovely city I was impressed again with the courageous and enlightened leadership that Your Majesty is giving to the great Iranian nation. At a time and in an area so beset with troubles, it is particularly reassuring to find the Iranian people and their leaders so staunchly dedicated to our mutual goal of freedom with justice.[5]

With warm regard, *Sincerely*

[1] A State Department draft of this letter to the Shah of Iran with Eisenhower's handwritten emendations is in AWF/I: Iran; see also State, *Foreign Relations, 1958–1960*, vol. XII, *Near East Region; Iraq; Iran; Arabian Peninsula*, pp. 660–61. The text of the letter was cabled to Tehran on January 4.

[2] For background see no. 1392. Eisenhower had visited Tehran on December 14. The Shah had written Eisenhower that he hoped to send the President a more extensive summary of his needs by mid-January (Pahlavi to Eisenhower, Dec. 20, 1959, AWF/I: Iran).

[3] Eisenhower had deleted the words "directly or indirectly" at this point in the draft (see the following document).

[4] Of the preceding three sentences, Eisenhower had added the first and third and had revised the second (see the following document).

[5] The Shah would send Eisenhower a detailed outline of his plans on January 12 (see no. 1455; see also Eisenhower to Pahlavi, Jan. 14, 1959, AWF/I: Iran).

1401   *EM, AWF, Administration Series*

To Clarence Douglas Dillon   *January 2, 1960*
Secret

Dear Doug: I have somewhat changed the draft of the suggested letter to the Shah of Iran. I was anxious to make certain that there was no misunderstanding of what I said in Tehran.[1]

I eliminated the expression in the second paragraph "directly or indirectly" because it was precisely on this point that the Shah bases his plans for revision. By this I mean that he thinks the *in*direct threat now much greater than the direct and believes that all of us should recognize this.

Another purpose of my revision of your draft is to assure him that we are making our studies on the basis of the current situation, even though future political developments may require a revision of our defensive system.[2] *As ever*

[1] Eisenhower's letter to Mohammed Reza Pahlavi is the preceding document.
[2] For developments see no. 1455.

1402   *EM, WHCF, President's Personal File 1771*

To Lorraine P. Knox   *January 2, 1960*

Dear Lorraine: Thank you so much for your Christmas card and, particularly, for your personal note. I am, as always, cheered and gratified by the knowledge of your good wishes and your prayers.[1]

I only wish you could have been with us on this last trip. Twenty-two thousand miles, I discover, is nothing in a jet—actually there was not sufficient time between stops for the paper work that is necessary in such an undertaking. And the crowds, while at times exhausting, were still tremendously heartwarming, and demonstrated to my real satisfaction, the amount of good will held by people all over the world, not for me, but for America and Americans.[2] My discussions with the distinguished leaders I met were friendly, informative and valuable; incidentally, I came back with renewed conviction that our "People to People" program ought to be intensified and strengthened as one of the best bases for developing understanding between peoples and countries.[3]

Mrs. Eisenhower is here with me in Augusta and in between long sessions of work and a certain amount of bad weather, I have managed to get some rest and relaxation in preparation for the opening of the Congressional session, which is always a particularly busy time for me.[4]

Again my thanks for your thoughts of me, my best wishes for a Happy New Year and, as always, my personal and warm regard, *Sincerely*

[1] Eisenhower had continued to correspond with Captain Knox, one of the Fitzsimons Army Hospital nurses who had attended him after his heart attack in 1955 (see Galambos and van Ee, *The Middle Way*, no. 1625). Knox had written on the inside of the greeting card that although she knew the President was "so terribly busy (but magnificent)" she wanted to wish him a happy holiday "—with a prayer that the happiness may continue throughout the year."
[2] On Eisenhower's world tour (Dec. 3–22) see no. 1389.
[3] On the People-to-People program, initiated by Eisenhower in 1956, see no. 546.
[4] The Eisenhowers had arrived in Augusta on December 27; they would return to

Washington on January 5 (*New York Times*, Dec. 25, 26, 28–31, 1959, Jan. 1–4, 6, 1960). The Second Session of the Eighty-sixth Congress would convene on January 6 (*Congressional Quarterly Almanac*, vol. XVI, *1960*, p. 24).

1403   *EM, AWF, International Series:*
                                                                Mateos

To Adolfo López Mateos   *January 6, 1960*
Confidential

Dear Mr. President:[1] Your gracious communications of December sixteenth and December twenty-fourth regarding my recent visit to Asia and Europe were indeed most delightful Christmas remembrances for me.[2] I trust my recent tour was helpful in promoting international understanding and in reducing world tensions, and it was most gratifying to hear that you have concluded that the trip achieved some success.[3]

The extensive tour that you will soon undertake to countries of South America will be enjoyable, I am sure, as well as fruitful for Mexico and productive in drawing the countries of this hemisphere even more closely together.[4] I am delighted that you find it possible to make this journey.[5] I wish you, Mrs. Lopez Mateos and the others who will accompany you Godspeed and best wishes.

During the latter part of February, I, myself, plan to visit a few countries of Latin America, on a tour which will necessarily be less extensive than your own, but which will be a further demonstration of the deep interest, both of myself and of my country, in the concerns and aspirations of our partners in the inter-American system.[6] I am happy that you and I will be pursuing parallel objectives in so similar a manner during the early months of 1960.[7]

With warm personal regard, *Sincerely*

[1] This message, drafted by State Department officials and edited by Eisenhower, was cabled to the American embassy in Mexico City for delivery to President López Mateos.
[2] On Eisenhower's eleven-nation goodwill tour see no. 1383. In his December 16 letter López Mateos had congratulated Eisenhower for his efforts to convince the people in the countries he had visited "of the peaceful spirit that unites the nations of the free world, and of the fact that the military power which they possess is solely for the purpose of defending their high principles." He shared Eisenhower's conviction that personal contact between chiefs of state was "an element of very singular importance in creating understanding and strengthening good will" and noted that for the leaders of the Americas such contacts were "almost always easy and agreeable" (AWF/I: Mateos).
[3] Before Eisenhower's changes, the end of the preceding sentence had read, "you have reached a like conclusion."

4 López Mateos had told Eisenhower that, in response to friendly invitations, he was planning to visit Argentina, Bolivia, Brazil, Chile, Peru, and Venezuela. He would discuss "the intensification of trade relations, cultural exchanges, the possibilities of mutual technical assistance, and, in general, all those other questions that either temporarily or permanently affect the inter-American community."

5 Eisenhower had added this sentence to the State Department draft.

6 From February 23 to March 3 Eisenhower would visit Brazil, Argentina, Chile, and Uruguay (see State, *Foreign Relations, 1958–1960*, vol. V, *American Republics*, pp. 267–86, 607–24, 757–68, 801, 915–16; and *New York Times*, Feb. 23, 1960). He would decline invitations to visit Bolivia, Ecuador, El Salvador, Peru, Venezuela, and Colombia (see Eisenhower to Silas Zuarzo, Jan. 6, 1960; and Silas Zuarzo to Eisenhower, Jan. 18, 1969, AWF/I: Bolivia; Eisenhower to Ponce Enriquez, Jan. 6, 1960, AWF/I: Ecuador; Eisenhower to Lemus, Jan. 6, 1960; and Dillon to Eisenhower, Dec. 31, 1959, AWF/I: El Salvador; Eisenhower to Prado, Jan. 11, 1960, AWF/I: Peru; Eisenhower to Betancourt, Jan. 11, 1960; and Dillon to Eisenhower, Jan. 9, 1960, AWF/I: Venezuela; and Eisenhower to Lleras Camargo, Jan. 13, 1960; Lleras Camargo to Eisenhower, Dec. 29, 1959; and Merchant to Eisenhower, Jan. 12, 1960, AWF/I: Colombia).

7 In February Eisenhower would commend the Mexican president on his successful South American tour and the efforts he had made to enhance unity among the American nations. "Your profession of faith in the great destiny of this continent," he said, "has stirred the hearts of freedom-loving peoples who wish to live a fuller life in peace and justice" (Eisenhower to López Mateos, and Hill to Herter, Feb. 5, 1960, AWF/I: Mateos).

1404   *EM, AWF, Administration Series*

TO LAURIS NORSTAD   *January 11, 1960*
Secret

Dear Larry: Thank you very much for your letter of the seventh. I think that in replying I can do no better than to give you a brief record of the impressions I formed after my talk with General De Gaulle on the subjects that your letter brings up.[1]

The item that the General and I discussed at greatest length was that of coordinating the air defense in the NATO area. I told him that, as far back as World War II, I found it was necessary to develop a system for effective coordination in this field. I pointed out that with the improvement of weapon systems, both interceptors as well as the ground to air weapons, and with the reduction of the time element, single control was far more important than ever before. I said that unless we had a single control in this vital field, it would be impossible to concentrate available defensive forces at the point of greatest danger; for example, if France were the principal target, we could not, without pre-arranged defense plans under single control, concentrate available forces from other nations to help in the battle.

To this kind of presentation he countered with the hypothetical case that Italy might be attacked, and then all of the French aircraft would be sent to that place, leaving the whole of France defenseless. I argued that a commander responsible for operations along a great front had two things to do: to keep in place those formations that would always be necessary for local defense, particularly his short-range interceptors and air defense missiles, and secondly, to keep abreast of all intelligence so as to concentrate in timely fashion at the point most seriously threatened.

Beyond all this, I talked to him about the great need for coordination between the missile and the interceptor. I think that as far as technique is concerned, he knows that the theory of a single command is correct; he commented that operations conducted under the authority of a "Council of War" had always been inefficient.

His great preoccupation is the glory and prestige of France. He argued, among other things, that no man in uniform can develop real enthusiasm for serving in any such amorphous organization as an "Allied Command." He said that patriotism and morale are built around nationalistic considerations. Because of this he said that the "defense of France is a French responsibility." Finally, he argued that what you were asking in what he called your "new" plan of air organization was something in addition to what you already had. He said that he was quite ready to let the matter stand as it is now arranged; he was objecting, however, to any further integration of French forces into NATO.[2]

In this matter as well as in that of the Fleet, I argued that all nations and forces should be on an equal footing.[3] I pointed out that American forces were in Europe as a result of a multilateral treaty providing for common defense. Unless we had a coordinated defense system, it was rather silly for American forces to be in Europe.

I urged that France take action tending to solidify NATO's determination, morale and organization, and should, by no means, do anything that would tend to set up centrifugal forces, which would inevitably work toward the weakening or even the destruction of the alliance.

I asked him to see you personally. He said that this he could not do until some time around the middle of January because of a very heavy schedule involving different types of work. Debre told me the same.[4]

In any event, I hope you can make some impression on him but I must admit that he seems to be singularly blind to the fact that if each nation is going its own way, this automatically destroys NATO. I am quite sure he would not want that—at least he says he does not so desire. He is, on the other hand, very keen on promoting the closer union and ties with Germany. It is possible that his objective in this line may be diminishing his respect for NATO. In any event, good luck![5]

Give my warm greeting to Isabelle, and, of course, all the best to yourself, *As ever*

[1] Norstad, Supreme Allied Commander, Europe, had written regarding discussions at the December meeting of the North Atlantic Council on a unified air defense system. The issue, Norstad said, was raised not because it was either the greatest or most urgent military problem facing the alliance, but because "it was a symbol of the principle of collective security." The French representatives had agreed to consider the technical aspects of a unified system and report their findings to the council two months later. On a ministerial level the French seemed cooperative, Norstad told Eisenhower, but he was not optimistic. Eisenhower had met with de Gaulle on December 19 (Norstad to Eisenhower, Jan. 7, 1959, AWF/A; and State, *Foreign Relations, 1958–1960*, vol. VII, pt. 2, *Western Europe*, pp. 317–18; see also *ibid.*, pp. 315–16; State, *Foreign Relations, 1958–1960*, vol. VII, pt. 1, *Western European Integration and Security; Canada*, pp. 546, 551–52; and Norstad to Twining, Jan. 7, 1960, AWF/A, Norstad Corr.).

[2] For more on de Gaulle's assessment of the French position in the NATO alliance see Charles de Gaulle, *Memoirs of Hope: Renewal and Endeavor* (New York, 1971), pp. 199–215.

[3] In March 1959 the French had removed their Mediterranean fleet from NATO control (see no. 1112).

[4] Michel Debré was prime minister of France.

[5] For developments see no. 1435.

1405   *EM, WHCF, Official File 108-A*

TO WILLIAM HENRY MEYER   *January 11, 1960*

Dear Mr. Congressman:[1] I have long been aware of the impression of some that the bodies and groups which advise the President reach their decisions by majority vote. This impression is highlighted by your comment that some believe that Secretary of State Herter had been outvoted by the AEC and the Pentagon.[2]

Decisions of the type to which your letter refers are made, however, and Constitutionally they must always be, by the President and the President alone. In reaching such decisions, a frank statement of varying views is always helpful rather than a hindrance to sound decision. I want to make it clear that in the instance you have cited, my advisers have been unanimous on the essence of their advice to me and on the decisions reached.

It is unnecessary to say that I share your deep conviction that there is no satisfactory alternative to working for peace; in fact I have been devoting a great portion of my energies ever since 1945 to the seeking of some progress towards this goal. At the same time, a man carrying the responsibilities of this office must seek for the greatest possible knowledge of all the currents and drifts of international affairs, and cannot afford to give way to mass emotion or sentiment, no matter how noble these may be.

My own actions, I assure you, are determined on the basis of my judgment as to what is good for the United States and peace in the world.[3]

Thank you for your letter. *Sincerely*

---

[1] Meyer (B.S. Pennsylvania State College) had been a Democratic Representative from Vermont since 1959 and was a member of the House Foreign Affairs Committee. He also had been active in the Soil Conservation Services in Vermont and at one time had been executive director of the Vermont Forest and Farmland Foundation. Eisenhower dictated this letter and sent it to Meyer after he had consulted with Under Secretary of State Douglas Dillon (see Whitman to Harlow, and Harlow to Eisenhower, n.d., same file as document).

[2] For background on the Geneva negotiations for a test ban treaty see nos. 1127 and 1288. The talks, which had been suspended because of Soviet Premier Khrushchev's visit to the United States, had resumed on October 27. Citing Soviet rejection of the reservations held by U.S. scientists regarding the ability to detect underground tests (see no. 1095), Eisenhower had announced on December 29 that the United States would reserve the right to resume testing after the voluntary moratorium expired on December 31 (*Public Papers of the Presidents: Eisenhower, 1959*, p. 883; and *New York Times*, Dec. 30, 1959, and Jan. 2, 3, 1960).

Meyer had written that he was disappointed with Eisenhower's decision, even though he understood that the United States would refrain from testing for the present and that the decision was made to pressure the Soviet Union to reach a decision at Geneva for a permanent agreement. "Unfortunately," he said, "the background to the negotiations suggests that the Administration did not prepare adequately in a technical and psychological sense for a successful effort." He felt that the Atomic Energy Commission and the Pentagon had concentrated on proving that a system of controls would not work and, therefore, that testing should resume. Meyer had acknowledged, however, that Eisenhower had "spoken out clearly and wisely for the kind of peace that the peoples of the world want and need" (Meyer to Eisenhower, Jan. 6, 1959, same file as document; for discussions between Eisenhower and State and Defense Department and Atomic Energy Commission officials regarding the decision see Goodpaster, Memorandum of Conference, Dec. 31, 1959; see also State, *Foreign Relations, 1958–1960*, vol. III, *National Security Policy; Arms Control and Disarmament*, pp. 816–19; and Kistiakowsky, *Diary*, pp. 212–14).

[3] For more on the U.S. decision see no. 1413.

1406   *EM, WHCF, Official File 101-R*

TO WILLIAM PIERCE ROGERS   *January 11, 1960*

Dear Bill: In view of the alleged difficulty of getting any section of the Department of Justice to discuss the Winn et al case, I wonder if you would be good enough to have one of your associates who is familiar with the matter call Mr. Whipple. Attached is a second letter from Mr. Kerr on the subject.[1] *As ever*

[1] William D. Kerr, a partner in the Chicago investment firm of Bacon, Whipple & Company, had written on December 14, 1959, and again on January 5, 1960, at the behest of another partner, Jay N. Whipple. Whipple was concerned about what he believed were excessively severe jail sentences imposed on F. Bliss Winn and three other men who had pled *nolo contendere* to charges of having violated the Sherman Antitrust Act in a conspiracy to fix prices on garden tools. Each of the defendants had been sentenced to ninety days in jail and fined $5,000 (see *New York Times*, Oct. 14, 15, 1959, Aug. 18, 1960). Kerr had asked Eisenhower "to arrange to have the proper authorities in your Administration investigate this case and report to you on the equity of the proceedings." Eisenhower had responded (Dec. 26, 1959) that he would have one of his associates look into the matter at once. On this same day he would write Kerr that he had meant to speak to him about the subject over the New Year at Augusta (see no. 1394), but instead, he had asked the Attorney General to have the Justice Department contact Whipple.

Rogers would write the President on January 14 that the Pardon Attorney had called Whipple, who had professed himself satisfied with the Justice Department's actions. Rogers would also assure the President that "during the time that the petition has been under consideration by the Department, neither the Antitrust Division nor the Pardon Attorney has refused to discuss the matter with the counsel for these defendants." Rogers added that "the representation made by Mr. Kerr in his letter to you that the Pardon Attorney was unaware of the application for commutation is either incorrect, or else refers to a period of time before the petition was received by the Pardon Attorney." Executive clemency would be denied on January 19, 1960. All correspondence is in the same file as the document.

1407

EM, WHCF,
President's Personal File 1324

To Lewis Lichtenstein Strauss   *January 11, 1960*

Dear Lewis: It just occurs to me that I should transfer back to you the third interest you gave me a couple of years ago in Brockmere 10.[1] Since you have told me that Amandale Eileenmere 492-8 is a better specimen that Brockmere, you might possibly want to dispose of the latter (and I assure you I can have no use for more than one bull). Obviously it would simplify matters very much if Brockmere should be registered exclusively in your name.[2]

It is not necessary for me to express again the very deep sense of obligation I feel to you for your courtesy in making available to me the opportunity of procuring semen from some of the fine animals in your herd.[3]

Incidentally I noted Saturday morning that you were reelected to the Boards of NBC and RCA.[4] I am sure that membership on these Boards is an interesting experience; I hope you enjoy it.

Please give my warm greetings to Alice and, of course, all the best to yourself. *As ever*

P.S. Except for a possible trip to the farm this coming weekend, I shall be in town steadily until the twenty-seventh. Can you find some convenient time to call Tom Stephens with a view to making me a visit? For my part any time from breakfast onward would be okay.[5]

---

[1] For background on the arrangements of the one-third interest, transferred in 1958, see nos. 697 and 736.

[2] Eisenhower and Strauss probably had discussed the bulls during a telephone conversation the morning of December 26 (Telephone calls, Eisenhower and Strauss, AWF/D; see also Walker to Whitman, Oct. 9, 1959, AWF/A). Strauss would reply that Amandale Eileenmere 492–8 stood seventh in his class of 25 and his first calves "look very good indeed" (Jan. 13, 1960, AWF/A).

[3] On Strauss's original offer to provide a herdsire for the Eisenhower Farms see Galambos and van Ee, *The Middle Way*, no. 1215; no. 96 in these volumes; see also Nevins, *Five-Star Farmer*, p. 125.

[4] Strauss had served on the boards of the Radio Corporation of America and of the National Broadcasting Company, an R.C.A. subsidiary, before he had resigned to become chairman of the Atomic Energy Commission in 1953 (*New York Times*, Jan. 9, 1960).

[5] The Eisenhowers would not make the trip to their Gettysburg farm over the weekend. Strauss would reply that he had arranged with White House Appointments Secretary Stephens to meet with the President on the morning of January 22 (Jan. 13, 1960, AWF/A).

1408

EM, AWF,
International Series:
Khrushchev

To Nikita Sergeyevich Khrushchev   *January 12, 1960*

Dear Mr. Chairman: I am deeply grateful for your personal message, conveyed to me verbally by Ambassador Menshikov.[1] Moreover, he brought to me an additional list of Soviet films and informed me that a new one on Ivan the Terrible was already on the way to the White House. Responding to his invitation, I told him that I would like to see the one entitled "Hunting in Siberia," which has English language subtitles. Then, of course, I thank you for the wines and caviar. For your continued courtesies, I assure you I am most appreciative.

Since the date for the Heads of Government meeting has now been fixed for mid-May, I have been able to examine carefully my calendar to plan for the period during which I would return your memorable visit to this country. I have selected June ninth as the date of my departure from the United States, and propose to stay in the Soviet Union from June tenth to June nineteenth. If this is agreeable to you, I suggest that on January seventeenth, at 9:00 A. M. Washington time, we make a joint announcement of the visit.[2]

Without appearing to be importunate, I should like to recall to you the request that I made in my letter of November twenty-eighth, seeking permission for my departure from the Soviet Union through an Eastern exit in order that I might pay a visit to Tokyo on my way back to the United States.[3] I shall ask Ambassador Thompson to communicate to you my reasons for the request, but I assure you that I will accept without question any decision you may make. I think you will understand that I am asking for a decision at this early date merely so that I can plan the remaining portion of my journey after leaving the Soviet Union.

I am told that at long last the three Aberdeen Angus cattle, two from Admiral Strauss and one from me, are to leave the United States by airplane tomorrow, to be delivered in Moscow. I hope that they prove to be good breeders and suited to your particular climate and conditions. The attendant accompanying them is an agricultural specialist. He will deliver the registration papers of the animals, and will be ready to provide to your herdsmen any information concerning the habits and characteristics of the animals that may be desired.[4]

Please convey my warm greetings to your family, and best wishes to yourself, *Sincerely*

[1] This letter was sent by cable to the American embassy in Moscow for delivery to the Soviet leader (see Eisenhower to Merchant, Jan. 12, 1960, AWF/D). For background see nos. 1381-A and 1386. Mikhail A. Menshikov, Soviet ambassador to the United States, had met with Eisenhower on the preceding day and brought New Year greetings and presents for the President (Memorandum of Conversation, Jan. 11, 1960, AWF/I: Khrushchev).
[2] For background on the summit meeting date see no. 1397. For the announcement see *New York Times*, January 18, 1960.
[3] See no. 1381-A.
[4] On the gift of cattle see no. 1386; see also Khrushchev, *Khrushchev Remembers*, pp. 48, 408. For developments see no. 1422.

1409   *EM, AWF, Name Series*

To HASTINGS LIONEL ISMAY   *January 12, 1960*
Personal

[*Dear Pug:*] I cannot tell you how much I value your letter of December thirtieth.[1]

My trip to Asia provided me with one of the most valuable experiences I have ever had. As far as your specific point is concerned, there are encouraging signs that some of the bitterness is going out of the relations between India and Pakistan—and that both Nehru and Ayub think so. Their success in negotiating a settlement of the border dispute between India and East Pakistan has heartened them.[2]

Do take care of yourself, and if the doctors advise Southern France, by all means go. And let me hear from you from time to time.[3]

With warm greetings to Kathleen and all the best to yourself,

[1] Ismay had sent his "warmest congratulations" on Eisenhower's "incredible journey around the world." Having spent much of his life in India, Ismay was particularly concerned about what Prime Minister Nehru would have to say about Kashmir. "I always regard that apparently petty squabble as one of the great tragedies of my lifetime," he wrote. An Indian official had told him that "Nehru, being a Kashmiri Brahman, had a blind spot where Kashmir was concerned, and that had it not been so, the problem could have been settled in half an hour" (Ismay to Eisenhower, Dec. 30, 1959, AWF/N; see also Lionel Hastings Ismay, *The Memoirs of General Lord Ismay* [New York, 1960], pp. 64–68, 409–46).

[2] Negotiations earlier in the month between Pakistani and Indian officials had led to the settlement of four of the five pending border disputes between the two countries. Eisenhower had asked that the U.S. ambassadors in both India and Pakistan congratulate both Nehru and Ayub on the successful resolution of the boundary difficulties (State, *Foreign Relations, 1958–1960*, vol. XV, *South and Southeast Asia*, pp. 201–2).

[3] Ismay had suffered from recurring bouts of pneumonia over the years. For developments see no. 1679.

1410   *EM, AWF,*
                                              Administration Series

TO GEORGE MAGOFFIN HUMPHREY   *January 12, 1960*

Dear George: I have reluctantly decided that this year I must give up all thought of a visit to Milestone, disappointed though I am to have to make such a statement.[1] Perhaps you know that I am to be in Los Angeles on the twenty-seventh, and plan to spend a few days in the nearby area.[2] Then I hope—as I have hoped for a long time—to work in a trip to Cape Canaveral.[3] On top of this comes the South American tour, beginning on February twenty-second.[4] All this, in addition to my regular work, means that the schedule must give somewhere, and I am afraid it is the trip to Thomasville that must be put aside.

In any event, Mamie would be unable to come with me, since at that period she would want to be in Washington getting her clothes and such things ready for South America.[5] So, all in all, I decided I must forego for the time being the search for quail—and, of course, for large wild turkeys—in addition to the joy of being with you once again.[6]

I know you will understand and realize, too, my deep gratitude for your invitation.

With affectionate regard to Pam and all the best, of course, to yourself, *As ever*

[1] For background on the President's frequent midwinter visits to Humphrey's Milestone Plantation near Thomasville, Georgia, see no. 578.

[2] On January 27 Eisenhower would fly to Los Angeles to attend one of the nationwide Republican "Dinner with Ike" rallies. He would stress the Republican conviction to uphold the personal, political, and economic freedoms of the individual, and he would say that a healthy, free society required a wide diffusion of power and responsibility. The President also would review the Republican record over the last seven years (*Public Papers of the Presidents: Eisenhower, 1960–61*, pp. 137–43, and *New York Times*, Jan. 28, 1960). Eisenhower would then take a four-day golf holiday at the home of George E. Allen in La Quinta, California (*New York Times*, Jan. 29–31, Feb. 1, 2, 1960).

[3] On February 10 Eisenhower would instead visit Cape Canaveral, Florida, to inspect the missile test center (see *Public Papers of the Presidents: Eisenhower, 1960–61*, p. 166, and *New York Times*, Feb. 10, 11, 1960).

[4] On the President's South American tour (Feb. 23–Mar. 3) see no. 1403, and *New York Times*, February 23–March 8, 1960.

[5] Although the First Lady had planned to accompany the President on the South American trip, on medical advice she would decide not to take the tour. She would visit her ailing mother in Denver January 28–February 1 (*New York Times*, Jan. 7, 28, 30, Feb. 2, 22, 1960).

[6] Despite his tight schedule, the President would be able to travel to Albany, Georgia, on January 16 for a weekend of quail hunting. Humphrey would join him the following day (*New York Times*, Jan. 16, 17, 1960).

1411   *EM, AWF, Ann Whitman Diary Series*

[MEMORANDUM]   *January 13, 1960*
Secret

In the conduct of a national political campaign there are two distinct parts: (1) The support of the Presidential ticket; (2) The effort to elect all other candidates, both on the Congressional level and on the state and local level.[1]

The National Chairman is of course concerned with both these purposes, but principal responsibility for the conduct of the Presidential campaign must be borne by the Presidential nominee—or his designated representative. Many speakers may be available for both divisions of the campaign, but the nominee for the Presidency should himself make sure that there is a group of speakers to support him and the Vice Presidential candidate. I believe the candidate should choose these men from among people who have the knowledge and qualifications expected for one or more of the Cabinet posts.

The man nominated for Vice President should, of course, have the qualifications to take over the Presidency whenever circumstances might compel him to do so, and should be able to speak from this broad base.[2] Men who might qualify are, among others, Anderson, Lodge, Mitchell, McElroy, Rockefeller, Rogers, Morton, Halleck and, if he could be induced to go into political life, General Gruenther.[3] (In this list, I have not tried to arrange names in any order of priority).

To speak in the field of Foreign Affairs, likely selections would be: Lodge, Dillon, Secretary of the Treasury Anderson, possibly Dillon Anderson.[4] (Herter not mentioned because of office)[5]. (a)

To discuss finance and the duties of the Secretary of the Treasury are such men as Anderson, Stans, Dillon, Hauge, Baird, Scribner and George Humphrey.[6]

In the field of Defense there are Gates, McElroy, Seaton and Dillon Anderson. Possibly others could be added from among the civilians now holding appointive office in the Defense Department. Brucker might be good.[7] (a)

(a) Speeches in these fields should never be strictly partisan, but they can properly extol Republican record and policies.

Post Office Department: Arthur Summerfield, Charlie Hook, Stans, Sessions.[8]

Agriculture: The man who stands highest, so far as knowledge of this subject and integrity of purpose are concerned, is, of course, Secretary Benson. Many Republicans think that any public appearance by him would be a detriment in the Middle West. Nevertheless it is possible that he could be used efficiently in the metropolitan areas because his viewpoint is that of the nation and not of the local voters. Individuals who would be listened to respectfully in the farm areas would include Allen Kline, W. I. Myers (Cornell), Les Arends, Charlie Hoeven and, if he could be induced to participate in the political campaign, Milton Eisenhower.[9]

Attorney General: There might be Rogers, Brownell, Walsh, Barnes, Dewey, and others.[10]

In Interior are: Seaton, Governor Hatfield, Walter Williams.[11]

Commerce: Chuck Percy, Secretary Mueller, Hauge, Walter Williams, Harold Boeschenstein, Stephen Bechtel.

Labor: Jim Mitchell, Rocco Siciliano, and selected members of the labor committees in both the Senate and the House.[12]

H.E.W.: Flemming, Oveta Hobby, Chuck Percy, Hauge.

Two subjects not to be neglected are Housing and Budget. A number of men, in and out of public life, could meet the requirements.[13] Housing could well be handled by Mason and Aksel Nielsen.[14]

Each of the individuals named above is sufficiently well informed to talk on the whole general field of political philosophy, and in each talk his major theme should be the field assigned by the candidate. The idea of segregating these according to Cabinet Department is so that none of the qualifications, in the aggregate, of the Speaker's Bureau will be overlooked.

[1] The President had made extensive handwritten comments on the draft of this memorandum (AWF/AWD). A note on the text indicates that this document was given to Vice-President Richard Nixon on February 12.

[2] See nos. 58, 107, and 566.

[3] Eisenhower was referring to Treasury Secretary Robert B. Anderson, Labor Secretary James P. Mitchell, Attorney General William P. Rogers, and former Defense Secretary Neil H. McElroy, who had resigned in December 1959. Henry Cabot Lodge was U.N. Ambassador; Nelson Rockefeller was New York State Governor; Charles Halleck was Republican Congressman from Indiana; Thruston Morton was serving as Republican Senator from Kentucky, and Eisenhower's close friend Alfred Gruenther was currently president of the American Red Cross.

[4] C. Douglas Dillon had been Under Secretary of State since June 12, 1959, after having served as Under Secretary of State for Economic Affairs from July 1, 1958, to June 12, 1959. Dillon Anderson had served as Special Assistant to the President for National Security Affairs from 1955 to 1956.

[5] Someone had added this sentence to the draft memorandum; the handwriting is not Eisenhower's.

[6] Maurice Stans had been Director of the Bureau of the Budget since March 18, 1958; Julian Baird had served as Under Secretary of Treasury for Monetary Affairs since 1957; Fred C. Scribner, Jr. was appointed Under Secretary of the Treasury in August 1957.

[7] Fred Seaton had served as Secretary of the Interior since 1956, and Wilber Brucker had been Secretary of the Army since 1955.

[8] Charles Hook, executive vice-president of the Kudner Agency, had served as Deputy Postmaster General from January 1953 to October 1955; Edson Oliver Session (B.S. Harvard 1925), Deputy Postmaster General from September 1957 to October 1959, had been appointed U.S. Ambassador to Finland in October 1959.

[9] Allan Blair Kline (B.A. Morningside College 1915) had served with the American Farm Bureau Federation, as vice-president from 1945 to 1947, and as president from 1947–1954; William Irving Myers was professor of farm finance at Cornell from 1920 to 1959. Eisenhower's list also included two Republican Congressmen: Leslie Arends (Ill.) and Charles Hoeven (Ia.).

[10] Eisenhower probably was referring to Stanley Nelson Barnes (A.B. University of California 1922; J.D. 1925), who had been appointed judge of the U.S. 9th Circuit Court of Appeals in 1956. Barnes had previously served as assistant attorney general in the antitrust division of the Department of Justice from 1953–1956, and as a member of the President's Conference on Administrative Procedures in 1953. Eisenhower had added Dewey's name to this list in the draft memorandum.

[11] Walter Williams, Under Secretary of Commerce from 1953–1958, was chairman of Continental, Inc., mortgage bankers.
[12] Rocco Carmine Siciliano (B.A. University of Utah 1944; LL.B. Georgetown 1948) had served as Eisenhower's assistant for personnel management until 1959, when he became a partner in the law firm of Wilkinson, Cragun & Barker.
[13] Eisenhower had added these two sentences by hand to the draft of this memorandum.
[14] Norman Peirce Mason had been FHA commissioner between 1954–1959. In 1959 he had been appointed director of the U.S. Housing and Home Finance Agency.

1412   *EM, AWF, International Series: Adenauer*

To Konrad Adenauer   *January 13, 1960*
Cable. Confidential

Dear Mr. Chancellor: I have received your letter of January ninth, which referred to our conversation at Paris about the matter of vested German assets in the United States.[1] You will recall that I pointed out the very considerable political and legislative difficulties we have encountered in developing a program which would provide for the rather substantial return of assets proceeds as proposed by your Government. I should also mention that the latest German suggestions, of which you spoke in your letter, do not appear to resolve all of the obstacles which remain in the way of a final settlement of this matter at the present time.[2] However, this problem is receiving very careful consideration in the light of these proposals and as soon as our studies are completed the Department of State will be in touch with your Ambassador here.[3]

With warm regard, from your friend, *Sincerely*

[1] For background on the issue of German assets see no. 134; see also State, *Foreign Relations, 1958–1960*, vol. IX, *Berlin Crisis 1959–1960; Germany; Austria*, p. 653. Adenauer had reminded Eisenhower of the "political importance to be attached to an early settlement of the question" and had told the President that he would like to resolve the issue during Eisenhower's final year in office (Adenauer to Eisenhower, Jan. 9, 1960, AWF/I: Adenauer; for the Paris conversations see State, *Foreign Relations, 1958–1960*, vol. IX, *Berlin Crisis 1959–1960; Germany; Austria*, pp. 149–51).
[2] Adenauer's letter had not included the specifics of the latest German suggestions.
[3] Eisenhower would tell Adenauer, during the German leader's March visit to Washington, that for seven years he had tried to settle the matter, "negotiating not only with Germany, but also with his friends on the Hill." The matter had turned out to be "a sort of three-cornered problem," with Eisenhower "caught in the middle." He urged the foreign ministers to work toward a solution (Memorandum of Conversation, Mar. 15, 1960, AWF/I: Adenauer Visit).

Under Secretary of State Dillon would later tell Adenauer that the problem of American claims against Germany had to be resolved before the return of assets could be considered. Once a bill dealing with claims had been passed, Dillon said, Congress might then consider the return of assets. In June, however, the German government would concede that the chances of being reimbursed by the U.S. government were unrealistic and agreed to compensate its citizens for the seizure of their property (State, *Foreign Relations, 1958–1960*, vol. IX, *Berlin Crisis 1959–1960; Germany; Austria*, pp. 672–74; and *New York Times,* Jan. 16, 17, 20, June 3, 1960).

1413   *EM, WHCF, Official File 108-A*

To Albert Arnold Gore   *January 13, 1960*

Dear Senator Gore:[1] I appreciate your telegram urging renewed consideration of your earlier proposal concerning unilateral action by the United States in halting atmospheric tests.[2]

I do want you to know that before I decided, as announced on December 29, to permit our 14-month voluntary moratorium to expire on December 31, 1959, and to place our suspension on a voluntary, indeterminate basis, various other courses of action were most carefully weighed. My conclusion was that a unilateral commitment of any nature at this juncture would not further our objective of reaching, at the Geneva test ban negotiations, an agreement providing for a ban on nuclear weapons tests which can be adequately monitored and controlled.

While we have no immediate intention of resuming nuclear weapons tests, I wished to make clear that we are free to conduct such tests if we deem it necessary, unless, or until, a mutual, safeguarded agreement is reached.[3]

With warm regard, *Sincerely*

[1] For background on Gore, a Tennessee Democrat, see Galambos and van Ee, *The Middle Way*, no. 1458.

[2] In a November 1958 meeting Senator Gore had urged Eisenhower to seize the propaganda initiative by approving a unilateral cessation of atomic testing in the atmosphere for at least three years. Eisenhower had asked Gore to submit a memorandum of concepts that could be studied by his advisors. Gore's telegram (Dec. 28, 1959) had come one day before Eisenhower had announced that the United States would allow the voluntary moratorium on nuclear testing to expire on December 31 (see no. 1405; see also Gore to Eisenhower, Dec. 28, 1959; Harlow, Memorandum for the Record, Nov. 18, 1958; Gore to Eisenhower, Nov. 19, 1958; and Harlow to Gore, Jan. 15, 1959).

Acting Secretary Dillon suggested that a reply over the Secretary of State's signature might reduce the possibility that Senator Gore would make a public appeal for further consideration of his earlier proposal. Presidential Assistant Bryce Harlow, however, had subsequently recommended that Eisenhower sign the letter. He had told the President that Gore was still grateful for the "gracious reception" Eisenhower had given him in November. "Having his telegram answered by someone else would tend to weaken this personal feeling that Senator Gore very strongly holds," Harlow had written (see Dillon to Eisenhower, Jan. 8, 1959; Calhoun to Goodpaster, Jan. 9, 1960; and Harlow to Eisenhower, Jan. 13, 1960). All papers are in the same file as this document.

[3] For developments see no. 1429.

1414   *EM, AWF, Administration Series*

To Thomas Keith Glennan   *January 14, 1960*

Dear Dr. Glennan: As we have agreed, it is essential to press forward vigorously to increase our capability in high thrust space vehicles.[1]

You are hereby directed to make a study, to be completed at the earliest date practicable, of the possible need for additional funds for the balance of FY 1960 and for FY 1961 to accelerate the super booster program for which your agency recently was given technical and management responsibility.

Consistent with my decision to assign a high priority to the Saturn development, you are directed, as an immediate measure, to use such additional overtime as you may deem necessary on this project.[2] *Sincerely*

[1] For background on the Administration's space policy see nos. 548 and 574. Glennan (B.S. Yale 1927), a former sound engineer, was head of the National Aeronautics and Space Administration, organized in 1958. He was on leave of absence from the presidency of the Case Institute of Technology, Cleveland, Ohio. Eisenhower was referring to the Saturn rocket, a launch vehicle designed to surpass Soviet capabilities by generating enough thrust to lift very heavy space crafts into the earth's orbit. Eisenhower had transferred the Saturn project from the Department of Army to NASA in October (*Public Papers of the Presidents: Eisenhower, 1959*, pp. 731 and 733).

Over the past several days, Eisenhower had met with Glennan and other space officials to discuss funding for Saturn, the transfers from the Department of Army, and proposed changes in the National Aeronautics and Space Act of 1958 to reorganize military and non-military space programs into separate agencies (Goodpaster, Memoranda of Conferences, Nov. 17, Jan. 8, 11, and 12, 1960; Harlow, Memorandum of Conference, Jan. 13 and 14, all in AWF/D; President's daily appointments, Jan. 14, 1960). On this day Eisenhower formally notified Congress of the transfers. He also sent a special message asking Congress to amend the Space Act, specifically requesting that all responsibility for non-military space activities be placed under NASA (*New York Times*, Jan. 15, 1960; *Public Papers of the Presidents: Eisenhower, 1960–61*, pp. 32–37; *Congressional Quarterly Almanac*, vol. XV, *1959*, p. 259). For background see Glennan, *The Birth of NASA*, pp. 20–47; *The History of Rocket Technology: Essays on Research, Development, and Utility*, ed. Eugene M. Emme (Detroit, 1964), pp. 119–21; Medaris, *Countdown for Decision*, pp. 237–69; Kistakowsky, *A Scientist at the White House*, pp. 125–26, 229; McDougall, *The Heavens and the Earth*, pp. 196–204, 222–23. For developments see no. 1746 and Goodpaster, Memorandum of Conference, Apr. 8, 1960, AWF/D.

² Glennan would report back to the President that he had authorized an additional $1.5 million to be used for overtime work and that his study recommended that additional funds be assigned to the project (Feb. 24, 1960, AWF/A). Eisenhower had originally asked for $802 million for the effort in his budget for FY 1961. In February 1961 he would request another $113 million to speed Saturn's development. Congress would appropriate the full $915 million (*Congressional Quarterly Almanac*, vol. XVI, *1960*, p. 71; *New York Times*, Feb. 9, 1960, July 2, 1960).

1415   *EM, AWF, DDE Diaries Series*

To Clarence Douglas Dillon   *January 14, 1960*

Dear Doug: Many thanks for your telegram. I am delighted to have your account of the discussions. I realize that the outcome represents a lot of work on your part.¹

Incidentally, I was a little disturbed that there was no indication of a mention of Japan as yet. I hope that something regarding this phase of our ideas can also be worked out.²

Good luck, and warm regard,

¹ This note would be sent by cable to Under Secretary of State Dillon, who was in Paris attending a special economic committee meeting of representatives of thirteen countries and the European Economic Community Commission. The meeting, which preceded the regularly scheduled meeting of the Organization for European Economic Cooperation (OEEC), had been recommended by Eisenhower, Macmillan, de Gaulle, and Adenauer at their meetings in December. At that time the four men had expressed concern regarding the growing differences in the trade policies of the two European trade blocs: the six countries of the European Economic Community (Common Market), formed by treaty in 1957, and the European Free Trade Association (Outer Seven), established in 1959 by Great Britain and six other European countries outside the Common Market.

Dillon had previously told the National Security Council that differences between the two groups could present a danger to the Western alliance and could lead to bilateral agreements between European countries harmful to the United States. To deal with the rival trade blocs and provide better economic aid to the less developed nations, Eisenhower had suggested the expansion of the OEEC to include the United States and Canada, with some provision for the inclusion of Japan (State, *Foreign Relations, 1958–1960*, vol. IV, *Foreign Economic Policy*, pp. 242–43, 367–68; State, *Foreign Relations, 1958–1960*, vol. VII, pt. 1, *Western European Integration and Security; Canada*, pp. 205–23; State, *American Foreign Policy; Current Documents, 1959*, pp. 570–72, 574–75, 576–77; State, *American Foreign Policy; Current Documents, 1960* [Washington, D.C., 1964], pp. 319–26; *U.S. Department of State Bulletin* 42, no. 1072 [January 11, 1960], 43; "United States Participates in Economic Talks at Paris," *ibid.*, no. 1075 [February 1, 1960], 139–47; *Public Papers of the Presidents: Eisenhower, 1960–61*, pp. 6–8; and NSC meeting minutes, Dec. 16, 1959, AWF/NSC; see also Kaufman, *Trade and Aid*, pp. 182–85; and Eisenhower, *Waging Peace*, p. 125. For background on the formation of the EEC see no. 753).

In his cable Dillon had told Eisenhower that in the committee meeting on the preceding day the representatives from Switzerland and Sweden had "used every opportunity to attempt to gain some tactical advantage for the Outer Seven as against the Common Market." Despite these tactics, Dillon said, the committee had finally agreed on the three U.S. objectives: the appointment of a small group (the Four Wise Men) to study the reorganization of the OEEC; the establishment of a working committee to discuss the trade problems of the Common Market and the Outer Seven; and the establishment of a small group of exporting countries to coordinate assistance to less developed countries (Dillon to Eisenhower, Jan. 14, 1960, AWF/D-H; and *New York Times,* Jan. 13, 14, 15, 1960).

[2] In a cable on the following day Dillon would tell Eisenhower that the representatives of the OEEC governments had approved the recommendations of the special committee and that "the spirit of jealousy and petty animosity . . . had completely disappeared." Even though final solutions would not be immediate, Dillon told Eisenhower, the two groups had agreed that their differences could be settled "by submerging them in a larger program of cooperation including the U.S. and Canada." Dillon also told the President that the Europeans were reluctant to mention Japan in the resolutions because of a number of unresolved trade problems. The group of capital exporting countries had agreed unofficially, however, to include Japan in its meetings on the coordination of aid to other countries (State, *Foreign Relations, 1958–1960,* vol. VII, pt. 1, *Western European Integration and Security; Canada,* p. 236; for background on trade with Japan see no. 1133).

In April the Four Wise Men would publish their report, calling for the establishment of a new organization, the Organization for Economic Cooperation and Development (OECD), which would include the United States and Canada and would take the place of the OEEC (State, *Foreign Relations, 1958–1960,* vol. VII, pt. 1, *Western European Integration and Security; Canada,* pp. 252–56, 282; State, *American Foreign Policy; Current Documents, 1960,* pp. 328–29; see also Kaufman, *Trade and Aid,* pp. 185–86). After approving the draft of a convention for the new organization in July, the twenty OEEC nations would sign the treaty in December. Eisenhower would ask for approval of the OECD in his State of the Union message in January 1961 (State, *Foreign Relations, 1958–1960,* vol. VII, pt. 1, *Western European Integration and Security; Canada,* pp. 282, 284–85, 313; *Public Papers of the Presidents: Eisenhower, 1960–61,* pp. 913–30).

1416   *EM, AWF, DDE Diaries Series*

TO AKSEL NIELSEN   *January 18, 1960*

Dear Aks: In your recent letter you talk about the strength of the "entire" ICA organization. When you talked to me you were concerned about the strength of the organization in Washington. I have no doubt that possibly some six thousand people are employed on a program that involves as much money as the ICA does.[1]

However, I am delighted that the BAC is going into the matter thoroughly.[2]

With warm regard, *As ever*

P.S. And many thanks for taking time out to visit Mrs. Havens.[3]

P.P.S. Do you still use and want that 1873 model rifle? I have no

use for it, but a friend asked me whether I could give him any sport-
ing rifle that could shoot deer.[4]

[1] For background on the International Cooperation Administration see no. 76.
Nielsen had written on January 11, 1960 (AWF/Name Series) to continue a discussion with the President on the size of the ICA. Eisenhower had told Nielsen that the
agency had 1,700 employees. Nielsen had again checked on the personnel totals for
ICA and had repeated his assertion that it had more than 6,000 employees, including the people in the ICA Overseas Missions Program. For developments regarding
the ICA see no. 1515.

[2] For background on the Business Advisory Council see no. 612. Nielsen had written
that the problems of overseas financing were complicated. It was extremely important that a program be set up "where people can go one place to find out what assistance is available, through what channel, and not be working with the various agencies at the same time, and thereby waste much effort and get very easily discouraged."
The BAC was working on this problem, he reported.

[3] We have been unable to identify Mrs. Havens.

[4] The President would call Nielsen on January 19, and they may have discussed the
rifle then. There is no further information on this matter in AWF.

1417   *EM, AWF, DDE Diaries Series*

To Henry Robinson Luce   *January 20, 1960*

Dear Harry: While I would not object to making the recording of
which you speak, I find that Jim Hagerty's notes of the talk I made
on January sixth are most fragmentary.[1] The only sentences that he
quoted from it are:

> "To my mind the project which these plans set forth is a mon-
> ument to our belief that man's dignity is something that we
> ought to talk about just as much as the Russians talk about sput-
> niks. Our religious beliefs and convictions should be held be-
> fore the world as one of the truly basic values on which we have
> established our civilization and government."

Since my memory is never accurate concerning statements that I
have made extemporaneously, it would be somewhat difficult for me
to reconstruct the few sentences I delivered that day. If you could
give me a brief account of your own recollections, I might try to put
together something of two or three minutes duration that I could
put on tape. Incidentally, the quotation that I give you above was
apparently taken from the end of the talk.[2]

With warm regard, *As ever*

[1] Eisenhower had made an impromptu talk at the National Presbyterian Church following the service of Intercession and Holy Communion held in connection with

the reconvening of the Eighty-sixth Congress. He had spoken at the presentation of plans for the proposed new National Presbyterian Church Center. Luce, a member of the Executive Committee of the Sponsors Committee for the new center, had told Eisenhower that his "little talk . . . was an inspiration." He asked the President to make a short tape-recording that could be used to promote the center (Luce to Eisenhower, Jan. 15, 1960, WHCF/OF 144-B-1-A).

[2] Luce would refer Eisenhower's request to the executive secretary of the Sponsors Committee, who would send her recollections of the speech to Presidential Assistant Frederic Ewing Fox. Luce would send a copy of *Time*'s story, a dispatch from the magazine's Washington bureau, and Associated Press releases. After reconstructing the speech, the White House would send the tape to Luce on February 19 (Livingston to Fox, Jan. 26, 1960; Nollen to Elson, Jan. 22, 1960; Luce to Fox, Jan. 23, 1960; and Whitman to Nollen, Feb. 19, 1960, all in *ibid.*).

1418   *EM, AWF, Ann Whitman Diary Series*

MEMORANDUM   *January 20, 1960*

Memorandum for the record: It has been suggested, directly in the case of Charlie McAdams of the McNaught Syndicate,[1] and indirectly, through the *Saturday Evening Post*,[2] and by letter from Harry Luce of TIME-LIFE, that I should do some writing after leaving this office.[3]

My response has never gone further than to say that I would never engage myself to do this without letting the individual or company know of my intention.[4]

[1] McAdam may have asked the President to write for the McNaught Syndicate at their meeting on August 3, 1959 (see McAdam to Eisenhower, Aug. 11, 1960, and President's daily appointments, Aug. 3, 1959). Eisenhower would write to McAdam on August 15 (see no. 1613).
[2] On the President's interest in writing for the *Saturday Evening Post* see no. 1751.
[3] Luce had written on January 16 (AWF/N). Eisenhower's reply to him is no. 1424.
[4] Throughout 1960 the President would receive other invitations to write after leaving the White House; see nos. 1430 and 1643. For developments see nos. 1650, 1737, and 1751.

1419   *EM, AWF, Administration Series*

TO EZRA TAFT BENSON   *January 20, 1960*

Dear Ezra: I have thought very earnestly about your request that I write a foreword for a forthcoming book of yours on agriculture.[1]

For several reasons I feel compelled to decline, even though my views and yours respecting the basic difficulties with agriculture coincide almost exactly.

First: in spite of many requests I have received, since I have been President I have refused to write any foreword or introduction for any document written by another, other than for official reports.

Second: we have got a difficult struggle ahead of us in attempting to get needed legislation during this session. It would seem probable that any plan we might propose may have to undergo some revision or even some compromise.[2]

Third: there is a very important political campaign coming up, during which the Republican nominee for my present office will be the individual responsible for detailing a legislative program affecting agriculture. I do not believe that I should be a party to tying his hands completely.

Finally: I do not know how I could explain my position to others—some of them my good friends—who have requested me to write an endorsement of a document intended for publication.[3]

For all these reasons I do not feel I should comply with your request—indeed, if I could make you a gratuitous suggestion it would be that your book should not be published until the election has been held.[4]

I am sorry to give you this negative reply, but I hope you will understand that my reasons are not personal.

With warm regard, *As ever*

[1] Benson had asked the President to write the foreword to his forthcoming book, *Freedom to Farm*, and had sent a draft for him to review. The volume, he said, described the record of the Eisenhower Administration in agriculture—a record "based on sound economic principle and not political expediency" (Benson to Eisenhower; Benson to Whitman, both Dec. 2, 1959, AWF/A).

[2] For background see no. 1263; for developments see no. 1498. In 1960 the Eisenhower Administration would continue to battle with Congress over price and production controls, particularly in regards to wheat, which was creating the nation's most serious farm surplus problem. In February Eisenhower would appeal to Congress to enact "constructive" legislation following the guidelines he suggested. Congress, however, would fail to pass any general farm legislation (*Public Papers of the Presidents: Eisenhower, 1959*, pp. 162–64, 77, 80; Benson, *Cross Fire*, pp. 500–48 *passim*; *Congressional Quarterly Almanac*, vol. XVI, *1960*, p. 325).

[3] For a similar refusal see no. 1420.

[4] *Freedom to Farm*, published by Doubleday & Company, would be released on July 15, 1960, with an introduction by Benson (*New York Times*, July 16, 1959).

To Henry Pitney Van Dusen   *January 20, 1960*

Dear Dr. Van Dusen:[1] I have your request, brought to me by Mr. Fox, that I write some kind of a foreword for a forthcoming publication of some of Foster Dulles' statements.[2]

My admiration, respect and affection for Foster Dulles are well known; on this score I would, of course, feel honored and privileged to contribute whatever I could to a book of which he was, in effect, the author.[3] However, as President I have consistently declined to write forewords or introductions for any publications.[4] While I realize that the present case might be somewhat exceptional, the fact is that it would be difficult to make any explanation to many others, some of them my good friends, who have requested me to do something of this kind.

Should the book that you are intending to publish come out no earlier than January 20, 1961, I would gladly reverse this decision, but I assume that you are thinking of early publication.[5]

With warm regard, *Sincerely*

[1] Van Dusen (Ph.D. Edinburgh University 1932), a professor of systematic theology, had been president of Union Theological Seminary in New York since 1945. Van Dusen had edited a manuscript that would be published as *The Spiritual Legacy of John Foster Dulles: Selections From his Articles and Addresses* (Phila., 1960).
[2] During World War II Frederic Ewing Fox (B.D. Union Theological Seminary 1948; D.D. Defiance College 1952) had served in the European Theater of Operations as a Captain in the Army Signal Corps. In July 1956 he had become Special Assistant in the White House and the following year he had become Staff Assistant to the President.
[3] On Eisenhower's esteem for the late Secretary of State see, for example, nos. 203 and 1137.
[4] See, for example, the preceding document.
[5] The publisher would instead reprint a tribute to Dulles that Eisenhower had delivered on May 24, 1959—the date of Dulles's death (see no. 1167). It would appear in Van Dusen's book before the editor's preface. In 1963 Eisenhower would write the foreword to Eleanor Lansing Dulles's *John Foster Dulles: The Last Year.*

1421   *EM, AWF, Name Series*

To Natalie Brush Gates   *January 20, 1960*
Personal

Dear Natalie: Proving that forty-five years of knocking about the world has done something, on the surface at least, to overcome my 1914 shyness, I am addressing you by the name that I have always re-membered you by—Natalie.[1]

When my secretary put on my desk this morning your nice note, together with the enclosure, I assure you that for a few moments I was completely removed from my current problems and transported instantly back to West Point days.[2] Thank you for giving me such a welcome break, for telling me of your current whereabouts, and for your assurance that the letter of an obviously self-conscious twenty-four year old will not reach the public, at least during our lifetimes.[3]

With best wishes and much gratitude. *Sincerely*

[1] The former Natalie Brush and First Class Cadet Eisenhower had attended the an-nual Army-Navy game at Franklin Field in Philadelphia on November 28, 1914.

[2] Mrs. Gates had sent Eisenhower a copy of his letter to her, dated December 1, 1914, along with a note describing the letter as "so ingenuous and charming" that she thought he would enjoy reading it (AWF/N). She was "honored," she wrote, to have been "mildly pleasing . . . at such an early age, to so distinguished a man."

The letter read:

My Dear Miss Brush:

It was a great day and a greater game. The only thing I regretted was that I couldn't inflict my presence on that delightful party after the game—but fate, the hussy, interfered.

I told Pat I was going to write to you, and he said, "you know you have no legitimate reason for writing her."

—Just a second, my skag went out—all lit up once more.

I looked for you between halves, but couldn't see you. *I* was very sorry.

Pat will kid me for a week for writing to a girl—but I believe in this case I like the kidding—

The whole purpose of this letter was to ask you to write me, and since I got up the courage to do it, I reckon I'd better stop. But somehow that seems to me to be an awfully poor ending, so I'll rave on.

As an aftermath of the game, what do you think of Hodgson, the man that made that long run at the beginning of the game. Some boy, and he's my "roomie". I'm some proud!

And now good night, in case you've forgotten my name, it is D. D. Eisenhower"

We have not been able to identify "Pat." "Skag" was a slang term for cigarette. Paul Alfred ("P.A.") Hodgson, Eisenhower's roommate and longtime friend, had carried the ball for a thirty-five yard gain, helping Army defeat Navy 20–0 (*New York Times*, Nov. 29, 1914). For background on Hodgson, who had died in 1955, see Galambos and van Ee, *The Middle Way*, no. 1638.

[3] Mrs. Gates said that Eisenhower's original letter was in her safety deposit box and she assured the President that it would not be published.

To Nikita Sergeyevich Khrushchev   *January 21, 1960*
Secret

Dear Mr. Chairman:[1] Ambassador Menshikov has handed me your letter of January thirteenth, and I discussed with him some of the questions related to my visit to the Soviet Union.[2]

I was pleased to learn that you were able to arrange for the use of my personal plane in the Soviet Union.[3] This must have presented some problems for you, and I am grateful for your efforts to accommodate my request. I assume from our previous correspondence that the press and members of the party not traveling in my plane will proceed to Khabarovsk by Soviet aircraft and there transfer to American planes for the trip to Tokyo.

As I informed Ambassador Menshikov, it will probably be impossible to bring the grandchildren along. To bring the younger ones along on such an extended trip does not seem wise, either for them or for us. I fear that should we try to bring some and not the others there would be real family upheaval.[4] However, Mrs. Eisenhower and my son and daughter-in-law will accompany me. I would hope that official formalities can, to the extent feasible, be kept to a minimum so that we can have more opportunity to become acquainted with your country, its people and each other.[5]

I regret that it was not possible to arrange to spend more than ten days in your country, but with Congress in session, it was quite difficult to work it out so that I could be gone as long as I shall.

With regard to my itinerary during the visit, you are probably the best judge of what it would be desirable and useful for me to see, and I would be grateful for your suggestions. For my part, I should particularly like to see, in addition to Moscow, Kiev and, in the Lake Baikal region, Irkutsk. Of course, if time would permit I would also like very much to go back briefly to Leningrad, but would omit that visit if in your judgment some other area would be better.

I have asked Ambassador Thompson to discuss further arrangements for the visit with anyone whom you designate.[6]

Please convey my warm greetings to your family, and with best wishes to yourself, *Sincerely*

---

[1] A copy of the State Department draft of this letter with Eisenhower's handwritten emendations is in AWF/I: Khrushchev. The text of this message was sent by cable to U.S. Ambassador Llewellyn Thompson for delivery to the Soviet leader (see Herter to Eisenhower, Jan. 20, 1960, *ibid.*).

[2] For background see no. 1408. Khrushchev had welcomed Eisenhower's decision to

make a ten-day visit to the Soviet Union beginning on June 10. He had regretted, however, that the visit would be so short (Khrushchev to Eisenhower, Jan. 12, 1960, AWF/I: Khrushchev; on Eisenhower's meeting with Menshikov see Memorandum of Conversation, Jan. 14, 1960, *ibid.*).

[3] Khrushchev had told Eisenhower that he had consulted his military advisors and had "finally . . . succeeded in convincing them" that Eisenhower could use his personal plane on the flight eastward across the Soviet Union en route to Japan. Secretary Herter had instructed Ambassador Thompson to leave the "clear impression" with Khrushchev that the President would fly in his own plane on the entire itinerary, since previous correspondence had referred only to the use of Eisenhower's plane across Siberia (Herter to Thompson, Jan. 21, 1960, *ibid.*).

[4] Eisenhower had added this sentence to the State Department draft.

[5] The President had added the words "and each other" to the draft.

[6] For developments see no. 1454.

1423   *EM, AWF, DDE Diaries Series*

TO ED EDSTROM   *January 21, 1960*

Dear Mr. Edstrom: It is a pleasure to welcome you as a member of the "Club of Presidents."[1] But, as always, this too shall pass—and I understand that for both of us that passing will take place on the same day in 1961.

It would be an additional pleasure to be present personally at your inauguration at the National Press Club. This I cannot do.[2]

But I can express the hope that you will enjoy the experiences, prerogatives and perquisites of your Presidency, and will always find them much heavier in the scales than the absorbing and demanding obligations pertaining to your office.

You have my good wishes for your 1960 Administration. I am confident that we can meet our common fate of "One Year to Go" with equanimity.

With warm regard, *Sincerely*

[1] Edstrom, Washington correspondent for the Hearst newspapers since 1957, would be inaugurated as president of the National Press Club on January 30 (*New York Times*, Jan. 31, 1960). He had been assistant Sunday editor of the *Louisville Courier-Journal* from 1941 to 1950, when he became the paper's Washington correspondent.

[2] The President would be in California (see no. 1410).

To Henry Robinson Luce   *January 22, 1960*
Personal

Dear Harry: You pay me a great compliment in expressing such a deep and practical interest in any book that I might write after January, 1961.[1]

Of course it is much too early to say whether or not I shall ever attempt the writing of another book. Certainly I would want to take a "breather" before I should make such a decision. Also, I might add that I am quite sure I could not complete such a work in one year.

It is true that other publishers have expressed an interest in developing some kind of connection with me on the assumption that I might feel an urge to produce something for the public. I have invariably refrained from allowing my reply to go any further than the mere statement of "I am grateful for your courteous suggestion."[2]

When I think of the real problem that I shall have in assembling and transferring my records, making certain that they are organized and accessible, undertaking the exploratory work that would be required in making a selection of material, and, finally, combing my mind—or what is at that time left of my mind—all of which would be necessary in preparation for writing a book, I am almost appalled at the prospect.

But should this particular kind of ambition awaken in me, I shall apprise you of the fact, at the very least.[3]

Thank you again for your kind thought.

With warm greetings to Clare, and, of course, all the best to yourself, *As ever*

---

[1] Luce had written on January 16 that the editors of LIFE hoped that the President would proceed to write a book in the year following his departure from office (AWF/N). Luce asked that Eisenhower consider his note as a "formal application on behalf of LIFE for the honor of presenting the magazine serialization of the book." He added that although LIFE was among many aspirants for the honor, his magazine yielded "to no competitor in its willingness and ability to put full resources behind such a presentation."

[2] See, for example, nos. 1418 and 1430.

[3] For developments see nos. 1650, 1737, and 1751.

To Edgar Newton Eisenhower   *January 23, 1960*
Personal

Dear Ed: It is easy to understand the resentment expressed in the letter you wrote on your birthday.[1] Perhaps that was your way of cele-
brating.

It would take too long to explain, in a letter, all of the factors that
have a bearing—pro and con—upon our relationships with Panama.[2] I shall have to wait for some opportunity when we can talk on
the subject for an hour or so.

I would observe this one thing. You are contemplating a trip to
Costa Rica. Should we use the old method of sending marines into
any Latin American country as a means of asserting and enforcing
our interpretation of any difficulty that might arise, any North American would have a most unpleasant time if he should undertake such
a journey.[3]

But I do assure you that at times my temper gets almost out of
control because of the implication that we have, all too often, in this
situation, a case of "biting the hand that feeds."[4]

Give my love to Lucy, and all the best to yourself. *As ever*

[1] Edgar Eisenhower's birthday was January 19. His letter of that date to the President
is in AWF/N.

[2] Edgar Eisenhower had criticized the willingness of the United States to compromise over Panama's demands regarding the Canal. He had written that he was disturbed that the United States had surrendered its "rights to the present communistic element in Panama," by increasing payments and relinquishing railroad terminals.
He was also upset by demands that the Panamanian flag be flown within the Canal
Zone and by Panama's assertions of sovereignty over the territory that the United
States, he said, had "bought and paid for." Following the November anti-American
riots in Panama, Eisenhower had acknowledged at a news conference (Dec. 2) that
there should be "some sort of visual evidence" that Panama had "titular sovereignty"
over the region (*Public Papers of the Presidents: Eisenhower, 1959*, p. 288). For background see nos. 1355 and 1380; for developments see no. 1443.

[3] "Personally," Edgar had written, "I would send a contingent of Marines into Panama
and tell the damn communists" that the United States would "run them all out of
the country" if they continued to create disturbances. He added, "It seems to me
somebody has got to assert American rights or otherwise we end up as a vassal to Mr.
K" (Jan. 19, 1960, AWF/N).

[4] The President had penned on the margin of Edgar's letter, "Would you like to apply for the job of Secstate?" (*ibid.*). For background see no. 1380.

To Barry Morris Goldwater　　　　　　　　　*January 26, 1960*
Personal

Dear Barry: Of this you are perhaps aware, but I want you to know, respecting your January 14th letter, that the B-70 program has had my close attention for a considerable time. The B-70 is not cancelled, as your letter seems to imply; the program goes forward as an active research project, and two of these aircraft are being carried at my personal direction, despite vigorously expressed opposition.[1]

I respect your desire to increase this effort, but it seems to me that an all-out B-70 program, if carried to its logical ultimate and applied to the host of other weapons, could in due course create a great and costly duplication of weapons systems. Tough decisions have to be made continuously on each of these immensely costly systems and I believe, of course, that the decisions reached have been the right ones. It is very difficult to see how the B-70 system could possibly become militarily useful to our country in view of now predictable progress of other long-range weapons. However, as an insurance against unforeseen difficulties in missile programs, I have decided as indicated above.[2]

I am bringing your letter to Secretary Gates' attention.[3]

With warm regard, *Sincerely*

[1] Arizona Senator Goldwater's January 14 letter is in the same file as the document. Goldwater had complemented the President on his "fine presentation to the American people of the degree of accuracy we have achieved with the Atlas missile," in his recent State of the Union Address. But Goldwater was concerned about cuts in funding for the new long-range supersonic B-70 bomber (see *New York Times*, Dec. 2, 3, 1959; Jan. 12, 14, 1960). He had urged that the B-70 "should be built regardless of what its ultimate mission might be. It is a new concept in aerodynamics and would offer American aviation the opportunity of learning the possibilities of this configuration being used in the development of transport."

[2] For background see Watson, *Into the Missile Age*, pp. 338–41, 431. On the debate over the defense budget see no. 1503; see also *Congressional Quarterly Almanac*, vol. XVI, *1960*, pp. 373–79; and McDougall, *The Heavens and the Earth*, pp. 126–29.

[3] On December 1, 1959, Eisenhower had appointed Deputy Secretary of Defense Thomas S. Gates, Jr. to succeed Neil McElroy as Secretary of Defense (see *New York Times*, Dec. 2, 1959). Congress would approve a defense budget that was $780.7 million more than the Defense Department's revised requests; the increase included an additional $190 million for the B-70 program (see *New York Times*, July 1, 11, 1960). For developments see no. 1693.

To Charles André Joseph Marie de Gaulle
Cable. Secret *February 2, 1960*

Dear General de Gaulle: I have hesitated to write to you before, knowing full well how preoccupied you have been during this past week.[1] As you may know, we asked your government if it believed that some positive act or statement on our part could be of assistance to you. Learning that your government believed official silence was the preferable course of action, we have maintained such a governmental position. Our attitude, however, was reflected in the unanimously warm and full support given you and France by our press and our people.

I do want you to know that you have and maintain our full confidence in this troubled period. In re-affirming your forward looking policy for Algeria you have once again demonstrated the faith and courage which have always marked your actions. As we know it must, France under your leadership guards unshaken its strength and unity.[2]

With warm regard, *Sincerely*

[1] For background on the Algerian situation see no. 1309. The dismissal on January 22 of the commander of the Algerian Army Corps, thought to have opposed de Gaulle's Algerian policy, had led French residents in Algeria to barricade parts of the city, call for a general strike, and demand that de Gaulle publicly support a "French Algeria." Sporadic fighting had developed between the European insurgents and French security forces, and the French army's loyalty to de Gaulle was in doubt. Facing a possible civil war, de Gaulle had pledged to restore order and had ordered the army to end the insurrection. In addition, he had reiterated his program for Algerian self-determination as the "only policy worthy of France." The crisis had ended on February 1 with the surrender of the insurgents (State, *Foreign Relations, 1958–1960*, vol. XIII, *Arab-Israeli Dispute; United Arab Republic; North Africa*, pp. 685–86; Synopsis of State and Intelligence Material Reported to the President, Jan. 27, Feb. 2, 1960, AWF/D; and *New York Times,* Jan. 30, 31, 1960).

Secretary Herter had thought about sending a message to de Gaulle "while the crisis was still on," he had told Eisenhower, "but had decided against recommending this since the question was essentially an internal problem. He now thought that a message could be sent "with good effect." Eisenhower approved the draft of this message and told Herter "that he thought de Gaulle would appreciate such a note" (Goodpaster, Memorandum of Conference, Feb. 8, 1960, AWF/D). Herter instructed the U.S. Ambassador to France to deliver the message "in person to de Gaulle if at all possible" and cautioned him that it was "NOT RPT NOT for publication."

[2] "I have been deeply touched by the friendly attitude and support which you and the people of the United States have shown toward France during the recent events," de Gaulle would respond. "This is an additional manifestation of the solidarity that causes all the countries of the Free World to feel deeply anything that affects one of them" (De Gaulle to Eisenhower, Feb. 6, 1960, AWF/I: de Gaulle). For developments see no. 1525.

To William Alton Jones   *February 2, 1960*

Dear Pete: The Goals Commission is apparently on the road, after a year of agonizing effort.[1] We have got hold of eleven men, and I am sure that all are men of whom you would approve, with the possible exception of two or three. But we do have to have all kinds.

Henry Wriston has accepted the Chairmanship.[2] Frank Pace is Vice Chairman. In addition we have Crawford Greenewalt, Colgate Darden, Jim Conant, George Meany (invited but not yet responded), Clark Kerr, Erwin Canham, Jim Killian and Al Gruenther.[3] The name of the other individual escapes me at the moment, and I do not have the file immediately in front of me.[4] In any event, we have followed your suggestion and the whole affair will be handled through the American Assembly under the direction of Wriston.[5]

I am told that Ford is turning in $200,000 and Mr. Sloan at least $100,000. A few of the private foundations are contributing relatively small amounts.[6]

While you and Bob, I understood, were quite ready to help, particularly if the matter was handled through the American Assembly, whatever you do in this line I would prefer would be between you and Henry Wriston.[7] If you would communicate with him I would be most appreciative.

The announcement of the membership will be made in a day or two.[8] After this is done, I shall try to become completely invisible so far as this matter is concerned because of my anxiety that the matter be handled on a completely bipartisan basis and without any taint of political direction or influence.

In my estimation this is one great thing we can do for the country, and we should have some results that would interest the man in the street as well as the businessman and the egg-head.[9]

I cannot tell you how grateful I am for the suggestions you and Bob made.

We had a fine time for four days in the desert.[10] Charlie was with us during the entire period and, indeed, in order to make a bridge game across the continent, he made a special trip to Washington.[11] It was hardly worth it from his standpoint because he lost a total of $2 for the day!

Give my love to Nettie and, of course, all the best to yourself. *As ever*

[1] For background see nos. 1059, 1185, and 1364.
[2] Henry M. Wriston was president of the American Assembly and former president of Brown University. Both Robert Woodruff and Pete Jones had recommended Wris-

ton (Eisenhower to Woodruff, Feb. 2, 1960, AWF/N). Eisenhower would announce the chairmanship on February 3 (*New York Times*, Feb. 4, 1960).

[3] Frank Pace was president of General Dynamics Corporation; Crawford H. Greenewalt (B.S. Massachusetts Institute of Technology 1922) was president of E. I. duPont de Nemours & Company; Colgate Darden, Jr. (A.B. University of Virginia 1897) was former Governor of Virginia and retired president of the University of Virginia; James B. Conant was a noted educator and former president of Harvard University; George Meany, who would join the committee was president of the American Federation of Labor and Congress of Industrial Organizations; Clark Kerr was president of the University of California at Berkeley; Erwin D. Canham was editor of *The Christian Science Monitor* and president of the U.S. Chamber of Commerce; James R. Killian, Jr., was chairman of the Corporation, Massachusetts Institute of Technology and a former Special Assistant to the President for Science and Technology; and Alfred M. Gruenther was currently president of the American Red Cross (Report of the President's Commission of National Goals, 1960, AWF/A: Commission on National Goals).

[4] Eisenhower was referring to Learned Hand (A.B. Harvard 1893), a distinguished former U.S. Circuit Judge in New York.

[5] The American Assembly was a national, nonpartisan educational organization established by Eisenhower at Columbia University in 1950 (Galambos, *Columbia University*, no. 1165).

[6] The committee would be financed by the Ford, Alfred P. Sloan, Rockefeller, Maurice and Laura Falk, Richardson, Carnegie Corporation, Johnson, and U.S. Steel foundations (Fact Sheet, 1960, AWF/A: Commission on National Goals).

[7] Eisenhower was referring to Robert Woodruff. See also Eisenhower to Woodruff, February 2, 1960, AWF/N.

[8] Eisenhower would announce the names of the committee members on February 6 (*New York Times*, Feb. 7 and 8, 1960).

[9] The committee would issue its report on November 27, 1960 (a copy is in AWF/A; see *New York Times*, Nov. 28, 1960), and the President would host a luncheon for committee members at the White House on December 5 (President's daily appointments).

[10] Eisenhower had met with California Republican leaders in Los Angeles, and then spent several vacation days at La Quinta, California, where he played golf with George E. Allen, Freeman F. Gosden, and William E. Robinson (President's daily appointments, Jan. 27–Feb. 1, 1960).

[11] Eisenhower was referring to Charles S. Jones.

1429

To HAROLD EDWARD STASSEN   *February 3, 1960*
Secret

Dear Harold: Thank you for your letter.[1] Its most interesting feature is your suggestion that any treaty respecting cessation of nuclear testing should provide that "on the spot" inspection would be authorized by the United Nations or the treaty would automatically terminate. I shall have the idea thoroughly studied.

Your further suggestion that the treaty might well provide for underground testing for small bombs is what we call the "threshold" concept. So far as I know, the Soviet position seems to be that of all or nothing.[2]

With warm regard, *Sincerely*

[1] For background on the negotiations to formulate a treaty on nuclear testing see no. 1341. Stassen, who had resigned his position as Special Assistant to the President for Disarmament in February 1958, had written Eisenhower regarding the upcoming summit meeting and the opportunity it presented for "the important first step" of establishing inspection posts to verify the cessation of nuclear testing. Stassen explained that under the treaty as he envisioned it, "the power to terminate the agreement, contained within its own clauses, would be the sanction to prevent the extensive frustration of inspections on the one hand, or the extensive abuse of the power of inspection for intelligence purposes on the other" (Stassen to Eisenhower, Jan. 27, 1960, AWF/D).

[2] The Geneva negotiations on the cessation of testing had reached an impasse over the relationship between the kiloton equivalent of an underground explosion and the strength of the seismic signal generated. George Kistiakowsky, Eisenhower's Special Assistant for Science and Technology, had proposed that the definition of a threshold in the treaty be measured in terms of seismic signal strength on the Richter scale (earthquake equivalents rather than TNT kiloton equivalents). Explosions below the threshold, being unidentifiable by seismic means, would be permitted by implication; explosions above the threshold would call for an on-site inspection. A measure of 4.75 on the Richter scale, Kistiakowsky believed, would allow for effective monitoring and approximately ten on-site inspections a year. Improvements in detection methods would permit the gradual reduction in the threshold (Goodpaster, Memorandums of Conference, Dec. 31, 1959, Feb. 3, 8, 1960, AWF/D; State, *Foreign Relations, 1958–1960*, vol. III, *National Security Policy; Arms Control and Disarmament*, pp. 820–33; and Kistiakowsky, *A Scientist at the White House*, pp. 201, 210–11).

For developments see no. 1445.

1430   *EM, AWF, Administration Series*

To John Hay Whitney   *February 4, 1960*
Personal

Dear Jock: Of course I am deeply complimented by your suggestion that, after you and I both shall have laid down the duties incident to our current activities, I might be interested in taking some part in your publishing ventures.[1] As you might possibly assume, other publishing firms have suggested something of this kind, but I have not yet turned my mind to the matter in any specific or definite sense.[2] It goes without saying that there would be a great personal pleasure in some kind of association with you.[3]

I think I shall have great difficulty in deciding upon the kind of thing I might be able to do, which I could feel to be both useful to the public and satisfying to myself. Suggestions have been made to me by both weekly magazines and newspaper associates, but I have talked seriously to no one about the subject. I am sure of one thing: for some months,* at least, I shall not want to be tied down rigidly to a "production" task.

The next time you come to the States we may have an opportunity to chat about the matter.[4] But in the meantime I must tell you again of my gratification that you thought of me in such a connection.

Please give my best love to Betsey and, of course, warm regard to yourself. *As ever*

*after next January

---

[1] Ambassador Whitney had written on January 29 (AWF/A) following his meeting with the President earlier in the week in Washington, D.C. He and Eisenhower had discussed the possibility of the President's publishing his ideas on "subjects of particular importance." Whitney said he had "developed a real enthusiasm" for the project and he hoped that when and if Eisenhower considered the idea he would explore the existing possibilities in the Whitney Communications Corporation (for background see nos. 759 and 799).

[2] For background see no. 418.

[3] On Eisenhower's interest in Whitney's acquisition of the *New York Herald Tribune* see, for example, nos. 825 and 1026.

[4] Eisenhower and Whitney would meet the evening of June 8 at the White House.

1431   *EM, WHCF, Official File 102-R*

To Mason K. Knuckles   *February 4, 1960*

Dear Mason: Needless to say, I am sympathetic to your problem. However, I was not aware of the fact that you so urgently desired some position in the Federal government.[1]

Presidential appointments, of course, have to be made on my personal decision, but there is a very long and thorough procedure followed before applications reach my desk. The appropriate staffs of the various Departments and Agencies determine the special requirements of a position and then try to fit into those requirements the man they deem best qualified.

I shall ask my principal staff officers to survey any present or prospective vacancies to determine whether or not there is any place where you could logically be appointed.[2]

With personal regard, *Sincerely*

[1] Knuckles, an insurance agent in Denver, Colorado, was a member of the board of trustees of the University of Denver, and president of the Republican Club of Denver. He had met Eisenhower in 1952 when the President-elect was vacationing in Denver (for background see Galambos and van Ee, *The Middle Way*, no. 462). He had written on February 1 (same file as document) that a mutual friend had nominated him for a position in Eisenhower's Administration, but the friend had been told that nothing was available for a man of his "talents." He had spent his entire adult life serving the Republican party, and now, he wrote, "Like the Master 'He came unto His own, and His own received Him not.'"

[2] There is no further correspondence on this subject in EM, and there is no indication that Knuckles received an appointment.

1432

EM, AWF,
DDE Diaries Series

To Elizabeth II, Queen of England

February 4, 1960

Dear Queen Elizabeth: I am truly grateful for your kindness in sending me the recipe for the scones.[1] I hope we may soon use it.

You will understand my rather woeful ignorance of culinary practices when I tell you that I did not recognize the term "caster" as a type of sugar.[2] But when I called the British Embassy for help, the problem was promptly solved for me.

May I ask that you convey warm greetings from my wife and me to Prince Philip, to the Queen Mother, to Princess Margaret and to your children? Quite naturally we both send you our affectionate regard as well as our prayers that all will be well with you in the arrival of the expected addition to your charming family.[3]

With great respect and high esteem, *Sincerely*

[1] Queen Elizabeth had sent the recipe with a longhand note on January 24 (AWF/I: Queen Elizabeth). She recently had remembered that she had promised the recipe to the President when he visited her in Scotland (on the visit see no. 1285).

[2] The recipe had called for four tablespoons of caster sugar. Caster sugar is sugar dispensed from a container with a perforated top.

[3] The Queen would give birth to a son, Andrew Albert Christian Edward, on February 19 at Buckingham Palace (*New York Times*, Feb. 20, Mar. 23, 1960; *London Times*, Feb. 20, 1960). Eisenhower would send an official congratulatory message to Queen Elizabeth and Prince Philip on February 19 (*Public Papers of the Presidents: Eisenhower, 1960–61*, p. 202; see also the draft letter to Queen Elizabeth [Feb. 16, 1960] in AWF/ D).

To Konrad Adenauer   *February 5, 1960*
Confidential

Dear Mr. Chancellor: I have just had an opportunity to study your recently released letter of January eighth to Mr. Khrushchev and I want you to know how much it impressed me. Both in its substance and in its tone, I found it a model of statesmanlike communication.[1]

Your ability to hold to a course of patience, reasonableness and dignity in the face of numerous provocative, not to say scurrilous, attacks made on you personally in recent months from a variety of Communist sources will surely do much to persuade world opinion of your strength of purpose in a just cause.[2]

May I also express my gratification at the cooperative contribution you made to resolving the very perplexing question of organization for the preparation on the Western side for the summit conference. Let me assure you that no matter what the procedural forms adopted may be, we always have in mind the essential interest of the Federal Republic in the issues to be discussed with the Soviets. It is self-evident that we will continue, as before, to work out our policies in the closest cooperation with your Government.

I look forward to seeing you here in March. We will then have the opportunity to discuss at some length the problems that concern us both.[3]

With warm regard, from your friend, *Sincerely*

[1] Adenauer had written Khrushchev in response to an earlier letter in which the Russian leader had accused him of obstructing disarmament by raising such issues as the signing of a German peace treaty and the establishment of a "free city" of West Berlin. Khrushchev more recently had accused Adenauer of making an agreement on disarmament a precondition for the resolution of the political issues. The Federal Republic never intended "to make our tasks more difficult by raising preliminary conditions and priorities," Adenauer had written. Although disarmament could not be completely separated from other international concerns, "it would be unrealistic to lay down from the outset a rigid sequence for the solution of the problem facing us." Adenauer had also urged Khrushchev to consent to the right of the German people to self-determination. At such time as the Germans could freely chart their own course, he said, then "the way to the conclusion of a peace treaty will be free and the Berlin problem will settle itself" (State, *Documents on Germany 1945– 1985*, pp. 688–90).

In a memorandum accompanying the State Department draft of this message, Secretary Herter had told Eisenhower that Adenauer's letter was "remarkably good for its carefully reasoned substance and its patient and dignified tone." Herter also had told Eisenhower that Adenauer had agreed to the elimination of the Western nations' Steering Committee that was preparing for the summit, even though the Germans were members, in order to end the quarrels regarding German representation that had divided the West. He had taken this step, Herter said, regardless of the possible reaction among the West Germans and his fear that he would not be kept informed of the summit preparations (Herter to Eisenhower, Feb. 4, 1960, AWF/I: Adenauer; for more on the problem of representation on the Steering Committee see State, *Foreign Relations, 1958–1960*, vol. IX, *Berlin Crisis 1959–1960; Germany; Austria*, pp. 175–77, 186). The State Department would cable the text of this message to the American embassy in Bonn for delivery to Adenauer.

[2] The Soviet Union also had criticized the Federal Republic for trying to establish a West German radio station in West Berlin. The action was illegal, Soviet authorities stated, and would intensify hostile activity against the German Democratic Republic (State, *Documents on Germany 1945–1985*, pp. 686–87).

[3] Adenauer would tell the President that his message had strengthened him in his "endeavors, through continuing the correspondence with Mr. Khrushchev, to explore in every justifiable manner a possibility to get one step ahead with him" (Adenauer to Eisenhower, Feb. 12, 1960, AWF/I: Adenauer). The German leader would make an informal visit to Washington on a trip to the West Coast to receive an honorary degree from the University of California. He would meet with Eisenhower on March 15 (see no. 1459).

1434   *EM, AWF, International Series: Adenauer*

To JAWAHARLAL NEHRU   *February 5, 1960*
Cable. Confidential

Dear Prime Minister: You will recall that, during our talks in New Delhi last December,[1] I mentioned the forthcoming conference in Geneva on the Law of the Sea.[2] I expressed the hope that you would be able to support a compromise formula of a six-mile territorial sea, coupled with a six-mile contiguous fishing zone. With the gratifying support of the Indian Government, such a proposal came close to adoption at the last conference in 1958.[3]

You were good enough to say that you saw no objection to India's giving renewed support to such a compromise, but added that you could not commit yourself without discussing the matter with your cabinet colleagues.

I understand that since our talks the United States position has been explained to the Indian Government in some detail by Ambassador Bunker and other American officials.[4] I know that Mr. Bunker would be glad to talk to you further if you so desire.

I am writing to you now, as the time for the conference approaches, because it seems to me especially important that our two governments work together for its success. I hope that, since the occasion of our talks, the Indian Government will have found it possible to support such a compromise proposal as I mentioned. Our information indicates that a formula along some such lines affords the only probable basis for a conference agreement.

The Law of the Sea is a troubled area of international law, where much can be accomplished in removing a serious cause of international tensions if agreement is reached. The contribution which India can make in securing conference agreement is enormous. I hope that your government's delegation will work, as will mine, for the adoption of a sound and realistic limit to the territorial seas and a successful Conference.[5]

With best wishes and warm personal regard, *Sincerely*

[1] This message, drafted by the State Department, would not be made public (Herter to Eisenhower, Feb. 4, 1960, AWF/I: India, Nehru, and State, *Foreign Relations, 1958–1960*, vol. II, *United Nations and General International Matters*, pp. 746–50). For background on the President's twenty-day trip to Europe, the Middle East, and Asia see no. 1384.

[2] On the upcoming second Law of the Sea Conference see no. 1307.

[3] On the first Law of the Sea Conference, held February 24–April 27, 1958, see nos. 589 and 609. On the position of India's government regarding the proposal see State, *Foreign Relations, 1958–1960*, vol. II, *United Nations and General International Matters*, pp. 643, 656, 660, 663, 683, 684, and 721.

[4] Bunker had reported that the Indian Cabinet was about to choose the position it would take at the conference. Meanwhile the State Department had learned that India might support a formula that included a three-mile territorial sea and a twelve-mile contiguous fishing zone (State, *Foreign Relations, 1958–1960*, vol. II, *United Nations and General International Matters*, pp. 747–49).

[5] Nehru would express regret for giving Eisenhower the impression that India would support any particular formula for the size of the territorial sea. He indicated that his government probably would support the twelve-mile formula (Herter to Eisenhower, Mar. 10, 1960, AWF/I: India, Nehru). The President later would apologize for the misunderstanding, adding that he was gratified that Nehru was "in full accord for reaching a settlement acceptable to the great majority of the countries of the world" (Mar. 11, 1960, AWF/I: India, Nehru). For developments see no. 1509.

1435   *EM, AWF, Administration Series:*
                                           NATO-Norstad-De Gaulle

To Lauris Norstad   *February 5, 1960*

Dear Larry: Many thanks for your letter reporting your talks with General de Gaulle and Prime Minister Debre. They cannot fail to be of value in creating a better understanding of major aspects of the air defense and naval problems in the allied command area in Western Europe.[1] Hopefully, they should bring about some progress on the part of General de Gaulle, in particular, in accepting sensible command and organizational arrangements.

All in all, I think the talks represent a good step forward, not in the least because they have put you in effective contact with Gen-

eral de Gaulle himself on the military specifics of these questions.
I am glad that Walters was of such help to you.[2]

With warm regard, *Sincerely*

[1] For background see no. 1404. Norstad had met with de Gaulle on January 21 and
with Prime Minister Michel Debré two days later. The meeting with de Gaulle had
taken place "in a friendly and constructive atmosphere," Norstad had written, and
he believed that de Gaulle desired "an accommodation of views which would put an
end to further dissension on the question of air defense." De Gaulle had told Norstad
that he wanted the French Territorial Air Defense to have the same status as the
British Fighter Command, which was under the command of SHAPE but required a
national agreement to be transferred outside the United Kingdom. Although Norstad
argued that such an arrangement did not make military sense, he agreed to support
the proposal before NATO's military committee if de Gaulle insisted. The Debré
meeting had encouraged Norstad to hope for a return of the French fleet to NATO
"in exchange for at least the appearance of a little more independence and a somewhat more important role" (Norstad to Eisenhower, Jan. 27, 1960, AWF/A, NATO-
Norstad–de Gaulle; see also State, *Foreign Relations, 1958–1960*, vol. VII, pt. 1, *Western European Integration and Security; Canada*, pp. 567–77).

[2] Vernon A. Walters had accompanied Norstad on both visits as an interpreter and a
recorder of the conversations (see Walters, *Silent Missions*, pp. 502–3). For developments see no. 1522.

1436   *EM, AWF, Name Series:*
                                                        War Reunion

To Arthur William Tedder   *February 5, 1960*

Dear Arthur: Your letter of January twenty-second just came to my
desk and I fear that you are already on your round-the-world tour.[1]
Possibly this note can catch up with you some time during your journey.

Your feeling that you should avoid controversy with authors is in
complete accord with my own convictions and practice. No matter
what the provocation I always refuse to comment.[2]

On the other hand, I think it is perfectly justifiable and appropriate to seize any opportunity that is offered to make truthful and
logical statements involving any phase or incident of the war as we
knew it. To state such things factually is not, as I see it, to argue.
Moreover, I am quite intrigued by your thought that there might be
a chance, some day, for a number of us, both British and American,
to get together for several days during which we could talk over the
war as we remember it, or as our own personal records may show it
to have been.[3] In fact I made a suggestion along this line to Freddie de Guingand when he was here some months back. I said that

I would be delighted to have a number of my British friends as my personal guests at Camp David some time during the coming fall and that I could provide recording machines and even some staff assistants to get the conversational results edited and coherently organized.[4] I dropped the matter when Freddie informed me that a number of British officers that he had in mind might find it embarrassing to provide the transportation costs of such a trip.[5] However, we might, on a more modest basis than I had originally envisioned, go ahead with something of this kind. I would hope to have such a group as my personal guests and I assure you that the place would be conducive both to concentrated work and to some relaxation.

I am sure that you and Toppy will have a wonderful time on your tour.[6] I do not know how long you will be in New York in April. As far as my own plans go, I expect to be in Augusta, Georgia, from about April ninth or tenth to about the twentieth, at which time I have to be back here to greet and entertain General De Gaulle.[7] I think, however, if you could give me the details of your American itinerary, we ought to be able to get together for a brief talk. If not, I can always telephone you.[8]

Give my love to Toppy, and of course all the best to yourself. *As ever*

[1] Marshall of the Royal Air Force Tedder's letter is in AWF/N: War Reunion. The Tedders had left their trip at the end of January.

[2] For background on the publication of Field Marshal Bernard Law Montgomery's controversial memoir see nos. 933, 948, and 970. Lord Tedder said he had been pressed by others to tell his own story of the Allied forces during World War II. His instincts, however, inclined him toward silence. "On the other hand," he had added, "it can be argued with some force, if the myth is repeated often enough and strongly enough, it may well end up being regarded as gospel."

[3] Tedder had suggested that if four or five men would spend a few days together to "pool" their memories of the main phases of the Mediterranean and European operations, maybe something "approaching the real truth" would emerge.

[4] For background on the President's idea, which had been prompted primarily by reaction to Montgomery's memoir, see nos. 989, 1229, and 1294.

[5] See no. 1229.

[6] Lady Tedder was the former Marie de Seton Black.

[7] The Tedders planned to arrive in New York on April 16. The Eisenhowers would vacation in Augusta April 11–21. French President de Gaulle would visit April 22–26 (see nos. 1516 and 1522).

[8] For developments see no. 150.

To John Stanley Rice   *February 5, 1960*
Personal

Dear Mr. Rice: Shortly before I left for California, George Allen handed me your more than kind letter of January eighteenth, suggesting again that Gettysburg College would be happy to make available to me, at the conclusion of my present responsibilities, office space at the College.[1] The idea has great personal appeal and, needless to say, I am grateful.

My difficulty is this. Up to this moment I have had no real opportunity to decide upon what, if any, activity will be engaging my time after next January. While I expect that I shall need a Gettysburg office as my main headquarters, there is always the possibility that I might find it necessary to establish my principal place of work in some other locality.

If you could hold the matter in abeyance until late March, I think that I could confer with several people who have exhibited some interest in my future activities and that by this time I should be able to give you a definite answer.[2] By no means do I want to appear lacking in consideration for the very generous offer made by you, the trustees and officials of the College, and if my request for this much time to give you a definite answer would impede the prosecution of your plans, you should proceed without any regard whatsoever for the difficulty that I have tried to describe.

I assure you that such a decision on your part will be fully understood by me and I shall feel none the less grateful for your offer, even if you should feel it necessary, under these conditions, to withdraw it.[3]

With deep appreciation and personal regard, *Sincerely*

[1] The President had vacationed in California January 27–February 1 (see no. 1410). Rice, chairman of the board of trustees of Gettysburg College and Secretary (since 1958) of the Commonwealth of Pennsylvania, had enclosed his letter to Eisenhower with a letter of the same date to Allen (both in AWF/D). For background on the offer of a suite of offices see nos. 544 and 1242.

[2] The President would tour South America from February 23 to March 3 (see no. 1403).

[3] As it turned out, the President would occupy a suite of offices in the house traditionally assigned to the president of Gettysburg College. The building, erected in 1915, currently houses the Admissions Office and is called "Eisenhower House" (see John S. D. Eisenhower, *Strictly Personal*, pp. 280–84; Ann Whitman memorandum, Jan. 20, 1960, AWF/AWD; and *New York Times*, Dec. 28, 1960). For developments see no. 1720.

To ADNAN MENDERES   *February 9, 1960*

Dear Mr. Prime Minister: I am grateful for your cordial letter concerning the recent visit to Turkey of a group of representatives of the Development Loan Fund.[1]

I have had an opportunity to discuss with the Managing Director of the Development Loan Fund the results of his discussions with Your Excellency and with officers of your Government and representatives of Turkish private industry. I am glad to note the extent to which cooperation between private American industry and Turkish private investors has proceeded with assistance from your Government. The helpful attitude displayed by all concerned in this mutual endeavor truly reflects the warm friendship of our two countries.[2]

Thank you for the generous reception you accorded to our representatives. May I again stress the great admiration the people of my country feel for the courage of the Turkish people and their determination to solve their economic problems in a constructive and progressive manner.[3]

With warm personal regard, *Sincerely*

[1] Turkish prime minster Menderes, with whom Eisenhower had met during his world tour in December (see no. 1382; Eisenhower, *Waging Peace*, p. 497; President's daily appointments, Dec. 6, 1959), had written to express his appreciation for the visit from the loan officials (for background see nos. 746 and 814).

[2] Menderes was pleased with the progress in negotiations on funding for the construction of a steel mill, an enterprise jointly sponsored by private interests from the United States, Turkey, and France, the Development Loan Fund, and the Turkish government (Menderes to Eisenhower, Jan. 28, 1960; Herter to Eisenhower, Feb. 8, 1960, both in AWF/I: Turkey; State, *Foreign Relations, 1958–1960*, vol. X, pt. 2, *Eastern Europe; Finland; Greece; Turkey*, p. 887). Although a military coup in 1960 would result in Menderes's removal and execution, negotiations would go forward as part of the international efforts to stabilize the inflation-ridden Turkish economy. An agreement on an aid package was to be announced on January 5, 1961 (*New York Times*, Dec. 30, 1960).

[3] For developments see no. 1536.

1439   *EM, AWF, Name Series*

To EDGAR NEWTON EISENHOWER   *February 9, 1960*

Dear Edgar: You just don't read my public pronouncements! I refer you to the following quotation from the State of the Union Message for this year:

"In the same message I stated that our efforts would include a reexamination of our own relation to the International Court of Justice. The Court was established by the United Nations to decide international legal disputes between nations. In 1946 we accepted the Court's jurisdiction, but subject to a reservation of the right to determine unilaterally whether a matter lies essentially within domestic jurisdiction. There is pending before the Senate a resolution which would repeal our present self-judging reservation. I support that resolution and urge its prompt passage. If this is done, I intend to urge similar acceptance of the Court's jurisdiction by every member of the United Nations."

You may gather that I am in complete disagreement, not for the first time, with you.[1]

With warm regard, *As ever*

[1] Edgar Eisenhower had written of his opposition to congressional efforts to alter the arrangements under which the United States had agreed to participate in the World Court: "I am opposed to this country surrendering any more of its sovereign rights to any outside group and I don't give a damn who they are." He asked Eisenhower to use the power of his office "to sustain the present position in spite of what Bill Rogers or the State Department says" (Edgar Eisenhower to Eisenhower, Feb. 3, 1960, AWF/N). The brothers were referring to the Connally Resolution, which allowed the United States to reject adjudication by the court if a dispute was determined to be a domestic issue. Eisenhower had supported the repeal of the restriction in his message on January 7, and on January 27 Secretary of State Herter and Attorney General Rogers had urged the repeal before the Senate Foreign Relations Committee (*Public Papers of the Presidents: Eisenhower, 1960–61*, p. 15; *Congressional Quarterly Almanac*, vol. XVI, *1960*, pp. 230–31; see also *New York Times*, Jan. 28, 31, Feb. 24, 1960).

On March 29 the Senate Foreign Relations Committee would vote to defer consideration of the resolution indefinitely (*Congressional Quarterly Almanac*, vol. XVI, *1960*, p. 230).

1440   *EM, AWF, Administration Series*

TO JAMES PAUL MITCHELL   *February 11, 1960*

Dear Jim: During my trip to California, I met Dave McDonald and had a conversation with him one morning at breakfast.[1] He spoke about a speech made by Roger Blough in Miami Beach, on January eighteenth.[2] While I cannot recall the exact words he used in describing the talk, he did most earnestly deplore its tenor and content, alleging that Roger had mis-stated the case and was impeding any progress toward true cooperation between labor and management in the steel industry.

I have now read the text of Roger's speech. To me it seems reasonable and factual.

Would you please mark for me the passages in the attached copy that present an unfair picture of labor, and which seem to you to be distorted or unreasonable?

Better than this, I would really like for you to get Dave McDonald to do the same thing for you, which you could pass on to me for my edification, if you so desire.[3]

Obviously I am not going to have in the remainder of my term of service a steel controversy such as the one we experienced in 1959. But I hope to continue as long as I can be sure I am not approaching senility my interest in such matters and will probably have something to say about them from time to time. This accounts for my hope for a little enlightenment in this particular case.

With warm regard, *As ever*

[1] Eisenhower had met with McDonald, head of the United Steelworkers of America, in Palm Springs on January 30, 1931. They had discussed the recent steel strike settlement and its effect on prices (*New York Times*, Jan. 31, 1960). For background see no. 1375.

[2] The chairman of U.S. Steel had denied Democratic charges that the steel companies had made a deal with White House mediators to delay raising prices until after the presidential elections (*New York Times*, Jan. 19, 1960).

[3] The Secretary of Labor would reply that he also had not found anything "unfair, distorted or unreasonable" in Blough's speech. Mitchell had asked McDonald about the talk, and the labor leader had stated that he had not read a printed version of the speech and that his opinion was based on a comment made by one of his associates (Mitchell to Eisenhower, Feb. 29, 1960). McDonald would later tell Mitchell that a close reading of the address had reaffirmed the opinion he had already expressed; Blough, he said, had only reiterated old arguments about inflation, imports, and product competition and had failed to advance any progressive thoughts (McDonald to Mitchell, Mar. 1, 1960, and Mitchell to Eisenhower, Mar. 4, 1960, all in AWF/A).

1441   *EM, AWF, DDE Diaries Series*

TO THEODORE MARTIN HESBURGH   *February 15, 1960*
Personal

I am most grateful for the telegram you sent to Jim Hagerty.[1] It is entirely possible that I could personally be responsible for the leaking of this story; unavoidably I have talked to several individuals about the rather complicated schedule and circumstances with which I must plan to conform before I can accept your invitation for June fifth.[2]

If I am responsible, it is entirely inadvertent. I share your chagrin because I realize that if I should be forced to refuse your most complimentary suggestion, there would be a measure of embarrassment for you and the University.[3]

Again I thank you for your message. *With warm regard*

[1] The Reverend Hesburgh (Ph.D. Gregorian University 1940) had been president of the University of Notre Dame since 1952. He also was the Vatican's representative on the International Atomic Energy Authority. Hesburgh's telegram, which apparently had informed the White House about a news story concerning the possibility of a presidential visit to Notre Dame, is not in AWF.

[2] On February 3 the President and his advisors had discussed Hesburgh's invitation to receive an honorary degree and to deliver the commencement address at Notre Dame (see memorandum of conference with the president, AWF/D).

[3] For developments see no. 1449.

1442   *EM, AWF, DDE Diaries Series*

TO RALPH EMERSON MCGILL   *February 15, 1960*
Personal

Dear Ralph: During the past weekend I had my first opportunity to devote a few hours to the excellent book by Wiley and Milhollen that you sent to me as a Christmas present.[1] I was tremendously impressed by it. The simplicity of its picture-and-text presentation brought home to me a better sensing of the opposing armies, their equipment, their morale and their convictions than I have ever before achieved—and this in spite of the fact that my reading concerning the conflict between the States spreads over many years and that it has been one of my favorite subjects.[2]

I also had a chance to read your Cooper Union speech. You said a number of things which of course you have said before: through iteration and reiteration you are helping to bring before the consciousness of America some of our important problems.[3]

I so frequently find myself wanting to say "hurrah" after reading one of your pieces that I am in danger of being one of your most annoying fans. In any event, keep up the good work!

With warm regard, *As ever*

[1] McGill was editor of the *Atlantic Constitution.* The book to which Eisenhower referred is *They Who Fought Here* (New York, 1959). Bell Irvin Wiley had written the text and Hirst Dillon Milhollen had selected the illustrations.

[2] For Eisenhower's account of his interest in the Civil War see his memoir, *At Ease,* pp. 43–50.

[3] McGill's speech, delivered February 12, was entitled "The Meaning of Lincoln To-

day: Idea of a National Dialogue a Critical One Then and Now." Citing ideas expressed in Lincoln's February 27, 1860, speech at Cooper Union regarding Americans' moral responsibilities and slavery, McGill had addressed the urgent need for honest national dialogue on the subject of civil rights (*Vital Speeches of the Day* 26, no. 11 [1960], 328–32). On McGill's articles on states' rights and desegregation see, for example, nos. 840 and 879. For developments see no. 1670.

1443   *EM, AWF, Dulles-Herter Series*

To Christian Archibald Herter   *February 16, 1960*

Memorandum for the Secretary of State: Attached is a summation of some of the complaints leveled against us by the Panamanians, together with what are alleged to be the facts.[1] It does seem to me that we should be able to make some moves which would tend to lessen the tensions between our two countries and at the same time would not damage America's basic interest.[2]

I am sending a copy of this same document to the Secretary of the Army and after our return from South America,[3] I will hope to have a conference at which these matters can be properly discussed with a view to finding some better answers than so far have been developed.[4]

[1] For background see nos. 1355 and 1380. The report was written by insurance executive and former political adviser Robert P. Burroughs. Among the most serious grievances, Burroughs stated, was the belief that the United States had violated the 1955 treaty agreements to eliminate job and wage discrimination against Panamanians, working for the Panama Canal Company. Americans, he noted, were paid four times as much as Panamanians and he advocated an immediate wage increase of at least five cents per hour for local workers (Confidential Report to the President Regarding Panama, February 16, 1960, AWF/D).

[2] In his memoirs, Eisenhower would note that he agreed with some of the Panamanian complaints and that he had thought as far back as 1934 the "United States should make some reasonable changes"(Eisenhower, *Waging Peace*, p. 518).

[3] On Eisenhower's trip see nos. 1403 and 1452.

[4] Wilber M. Brucker, who as Secretary of the Army supervised the administration of the Canal Zone government, would prepare a memorandum outlining a program to redress Panamanian complaints. The President would write on the document "this memo is to be used as a basis for beginning action except for those things needing Congressional authority" (Memorandum for the President, [March 1960], AWF/A: Army). On March 21, 1960, Eisenhower would meet with Brucker and State Department officials to discuss the proposals, and on April 19 he would announce his plans to improve relations with Panama (Memorandum for Record, Mar. 21, 1960, AWF/AWD). While the President's program would not cover the increasingly contentious issue of raising the Panamanian flag within the Zone (NSC meeting minutes, Feb. 18, 1960), it would address other grievances. Eisenhower wanted to raise the pay of Panamanian workers and teachers at Latin American schools within the

Zone; to provide for the replacement of substandard housing, the reduction of water rates, and the construction of a new water main; and to expand the skilled job apprentice program. Eisenhower would also express his intent to support legislation for new disability rates and retirement payments for Panamanian workers (*New York Times*, Apr. 20, 1960; *Congressional Quarterly Almanac*, vol. XVI, *1960*, p. 219). For developments see nos. 1450 and 1645.

1444   *EM, WHCF, Official File 111-J-1*

To Eric A. Johnston   *February 16, 1960*

Dear Eric: As I told you, I had promised Bob Burroughs to communicate with the movie executives to see whether it was not possible to distribute films in Africa, as a habitual practice, which would, in broad cross section, give a fairly accurate picture of America. Your coming to my office made it possible to give you this commission—one that I truly believe is important to the interests of the United States.[1]

In doing so, you will of course run into numbers of my friends. Please give to each my warm greetings.[2] *As ever*

[1] Life insurance executive Robert P. Burroughs had met with Eisenhower at noon on this same day (see the preceding document). Johnston, president of the Motion Picture Association of America, Inc., had seen Eisenhower immediately afterward (President's daily appointments). Eisenhower had asked Ann Whitman to send a copy of this message to Burroughs (see Whitman to Burroughs, Feb. 16, 1960, same file as document).

[2] Johnston would write Eisenhower after meeting with the movie company executives on April 7. The proposal had received a warm response, he said, and all of those present wanted to cooperate fully. They had agreed on procedures that Johnston believed would "bring about steady and continuing improvements in the times ahead." Johnston had also returned the greetings of Eisenhower's friends (Johnston to Eisenhower, Apr. 8, 1960, *ibid.*).

1445   *Prime Minister's Office Records,*
                                          PREM 11/2997

To Harold Macmillan   *February 18, 1960*
Cable. Secret

Dear Harold: Of course I share your concern about the nuclear test negotiations. We are now studying the latest Russian proposal.[1]

As to my own suggestion, the scheme was one on which we had been working for a long time and we felt it would stand any kind of critical examination as long as the analysis was fairly made.[2] I am very much afraid that the Soviets are back at the old game of disarming by "pronouncement". The fact that they imply that only a very limited number of on-site inspections would be permitted is seemingly throwing a road block in the way of real progress.

Respecting the matter we discussed at Rambouillet, I am quite astonished at the atmosphere of formality with which the French seem to view the matter and the difficulties they see of putting the simple plan into action. You will recall that General de Gaulle wanted to have some way of conducting three-way consultations on any subject of common interest. I suggested that we might have one or two junior but capable staff officers from each country keeping abreast of the questions that might call for such consultation and that when the occasion so demanded, conferees at higher level could get into the picture. But such consultations would always be so conducted as to avoid even the appearance of venturing unjustifiably into the affairs of others. When our conversation took place, I thought that General de Gaulle was in complete accord and seemed to agree that the scheme could be set afoot without fanfare and without trouble. Just where it jumped the track I do not know.[3]

I quite agree with your statement that we should get away from the arguments about the memorandum and what it did or did not mean, and try to concentrate on practical discussions of current interest.[4]

I am glad that you accepted General de Gaulle's invitation to meet with him for a couple of days at some spot in the country. It appears from my informal reports that the negotiations looking toward the clarification of command structures in NATO show signs of improvement. It would be good to get that problem out of the way.[5]

I am not clear as to your exact meaning in referring to the "defense question and the deterrent". In our own case the measures we are taking seem to us to be sound and though the circumstances of an upcoming Presidential campaign have stimulated a lot of demagogic shrieks and cries of alarm, the fact is that our defenses and our deterrent are not only strong but grow more powerful day by day. On the other hand I am very much worried that the Congress will again cut back on the amounts we can devote to military assistance to our allies. If they do, I think the Western powers will be faced with a very difficult situation.[6]

In my family and, indeed, I think in all Washington, we are examining news bulletins every hour, on the hour, in our anxiety to learn that the new member has joined the Queen's family. I do most sincerely pray that all goes well.[7]

It is good to have you back in London where we can get in touch whenever we choose.[8]

With warm regard, *As ever*

P.S. Before I could get this off, I was able to send to Her Majesty a cable of congratulations. I know that all England is very happy as indeed we are.[9]

[1] For background on the Geneva test ban negotiations see no. 1429. Two days earlier the Soviet Union had proposed giving the West a limited number of inspections per year of any suspicious explosion on Soviet territory. For two or three years the Soviets would accept scientific standards, originally proposed by the West, that allowed inspection of a variety of seismic disturbances (State, *Documents on Disarmament, 1960* [Washington, D.C., 1961], pp. 40–44).

"As you know," Macmillan had told Eisenhower, "I feel very deeply what a frightful responsibility you and I have to prevent the spread of these weapons and I am sure that we must really not lose the chance of calling a halt" (Macmillan to Eisenhower, Feb. 17, 1960, PREM 11/2997).

[2] On February 11 U.S. negotiators at Geneva had presented a proposal for a treaty that would ban all nuclear weapons testing in the atmosphere, in the oceans, and in space. Only small-scale underground tests below the threshold of detection would be allowed. In addition, the plan included a program of research by the United States, Great Britain, and the Soviet Union to improve the detection of small underground tests in order to extend the ban. The Soviet Union immediately rejected the proposal because of the clause allowing underground testing (State, *Documents on Disarmament, 1960,* pp. 31–39; see also *Public Papers of the Presidents: Eisenhower, 1960–61,* pp. 193–94; and no. 1429).

[3] For the meetings with French President de Gaulle in December 1959 see State, *Foreign Relations, 1958–1960,* vol. VII, pt. 1, *Western European Integration and Security; Canada,* pp. 319–23; see also no. 1404.

Macmillan had referred to recent correspondence among the British, French, and U.S. foreign ministers regarding topics for discussion in the tripartite consultations and particularly to a reference by the French foreign minister to de Gaulle's memorandum of 1958. This memorandum had criticized the NATO alliance and had questioned France's future role in the organization (see no. 901; see also no. 974; and State, *Foreign Relations, 1958–1960,* vol. VII, pt. 1, *Western European Integration and Security; Canada,* pp. 82–83, 326–27).

[4] Macmillan had told Eisenhower that he believed the tripartite talks provided a way to deal with the memorandum and that the agendas for the meetings would take form as the consultations progressed.

[5] Macmillan's acceptance of de Gaulle's invitation would, he said, give him "an opportunity to explore his mind." He asked Eisenhower for his thoughts on any problems de Gaulle was likely to raise. On the issue of the NATO command structure see no. 1435.

[6] Macmillan had told Eisenhower among other problems "the defence question and the deterrent" matter were "quite difficult." He had hoped to make some progress on the issue within the week and suggested that the two countries discuss the problem before the NATO defense ministers met at the end of March. On U.S. defense spending see no. 1426.

[7] On the birth of Prince Andrew see no. 1432.

[8] Macmillan had just returned from a six-week tour of four African nations (see Macmillan, *Pointing the Way,* pp. 119–31, 143–63; see also Eisenhower to Macmillan, Feb. 12, 1960, AWF/I: Macmillan).

[9] See no. 1432.

To Dwight David Eisenhower II   *February 19, 1960*

Dear David: Attached, in rhyme, is "The Code of the Shooter."[1]

In the fourth couplet, you will see the words "stops and beaters." Beaters are the men that beat through the woods to drive the game towards the huntsmen. I am not sure about the functions of the "stops."[2]

In the third to last couplet, you will see the expression "Follow not across the line." This means that if you are shooting with a partner, you must not let your gun swing toward him so that it will point beyond an imaginary line that divides your shooting zone from his.

If you will learn this little code, it will remind you always to be careful with your gun. *Affectionately*

[1] The President had received a linen tablecloth and napkins displaying the seasons for hunting and fishing in the British Isles, together with verses for youngsters to learn before using firearms. In the cover letter the donor had enclosed the entire text of the "Code of the Shooter" (see Cordle to Eisenhower, [Feb. 18, 1960]; and Eisenhower to Cordle, Feb. 20, 1960; and related material, all in WHCF/PPF 1-L Gifts). The verse reads:

> If a sportsman true you'd be
> Listen carefully to me:——
> Never never let your gun
> Pointed be at anyone.
> That it may unloaded be
> matters not the least to me.
> Stops & beaters oft unseen
> Look behind some leafy screen
> Calm & steady always be
> *Never* shoot where you can't see
> When a hedge or fence you cross
> Though of time it cause a loss
> From the gun the cartridge take
> For the greater safety's sake
> If twixt you & neighboring gun
> Bird may fly, or beast may run
> Let this maxim e'er be thine
> Follow not across the line
> You may kill or you may miss
> But at all times think of this
> All the pheasants ever bred
> Won't repay for one man dead.

[2] In hunting, a "stop" is an individual posted to prevent game animals from leaving the area after being located.

To Jacob Koppel Javits

Dear Jack: Early this winter you wrote me to suggest a major White House Labor-Management Conference on Productivity, to be held in 1960, looking toward the development of labor-management productivity councils.[1]

I regarded the continuing improvement of productivity as one of the most important of our national economic goals, and I want to do everything that is practicable to promote it. I doubt, however, that it would be wise to try to hold a White House Conference on Productivity this year. A great deal of preparatory work is required for any technical conference, and there is question whether there would be sufficient time to complete all the detailed preparations which would be necessary.[2]

Moreover I have some reservations about a national conference directed solely to the improvement of productivity. It seems to me that this is only one phase—a very important one, to be sure—of the broader problem of labor-management relations, and can best be discussed in that setting.[3]

I believe that we should do all we can to encourage labor-management discussions away from the bargaining table, especially at the plant level where, after all, the real work is done. Such discussions hold much promise in working out improvements and adaptations in specific work situations, which would lead to greater productivity. The organization of formal "Productivity Councils" might prove to be too limiting. I understand that experience with productivity committees or councils, both here and abroad, has not been particularly impressive.[4]

I shall continue to stress, as I know you will, the urgent need both for continued gains in productivity and for more frequent discussions by labor and management at all levels to explore their mutual problems.

I appreciate your having made this suggestion.[5]

With warm regard, *Sincerely*

[1] New York Republican Senator Javits had written on November 19, 1959 (same file as document) to propose that the departments of Labor and Commerce sponsor a major White House Labor-Management Conference on Productivity. Javits's proposal was inspired by testimony given by Allen Dulles before the Subcommittee on Economic Statistics of the 1960 Congressional Joint Economic Committee. Eisenhower had sent Javits's letter to the Secretaries of Labor and Commerce and to the Chairman of the Council of Economic Advisors, Raymond Saulnier, for comment. This letter was based upon a draft prepared by the Department of Labor (Feb. 12, 1960, same file as document).

[2] The Department of Labor had stated that while "continuing improvement in the

productivity of our economy is vital both to national security and to a further gradual rise in the standard of living," it was doubtful whether it was "possible to get ready for a full-scale conference on the subject of productivity."

[3] The Labor Department had warned the President that it "would be unwise to hold a conference on such a controversial subject in an election year. The question of growth of the American economy in relation to that of other countries is already a political issue, and productivity would hardly be discussed dispassionately."

[4] Javits had proposed the development of local labor-management productivity councils, "benefitting from our experience with such councils during World War II." The Labor Department, however, had advised Eisenhower that "a number of experienced American observers have concluded that the productivity councils, as such, accomplished comparatively little."

[5] The Administration would not hold a White House Conference on Productivity during the remainder of Eisenhower's term in office.

Shattered Dreams

MARCH 1960 TO JULY 1960

21

"Progress in a knotty problem"

To WILTON BURTON PERSONS   *March 9, 1960*

Memorandum for General Persons: Here is a letter sent by Tom Murray of the Post Office Committee to General Summerfield. Please note the marked paragraph.[1] It would seem to me that there is so much partisan politics involved in Post Office affairs that it would be difficult to have a profitable bipartisan meeting.[2]
    What do you think?

[1] We have been unable to locate this letter from Thomas Jefferson Murray, the Democratic chairman of the House Post Office and Civil Service Committee, to Postmaster General Summerfield. The letter almost certainly addressed Eisenhower's request for postal rate increases. In his budget message the President had urged Congress to raise rates in order to eliminate the large postal service deficit (for background see nos. 784 and 930). He would send a special message to Congress on March 11, and, after an unenthusiastic Congress failed to enact legislation, would again request the increase in his budget message for FY 1962 (*Public Papers of the Presidents: Eisenhower, 1960–61*, pp. 65, 71, 288–89, 977–78).
[2] On this day Summerfield had met with Eisenhower to discuss scheduling a bipartisan conference on the postal deficit, an idea that he said came from Murray. While the President felt the situation had become "too political now," he had referred the proposal to General Persons for consideration (Ann Whitman memorandum, Mar. 9, 1960, AWF/AWD). On May 10, the day Congress would begin hearings on a rate increase, Eisenhower would discuss postal services and the Post Office budget with legislative leaders. Since improvements in the two areas were incompatible so long as Congress refused to raise rates, the President suggested that it might be a good idea for Summerfield "to inject some life into the situation by reducing service to the point justified by revenues" (Legislative leadership meeting notes, May 10, 1960, see also Feb. 16, AWF/LM; *New York Times*, Feb. 17, 23, and Mar. 12, 1960).
    Congress, however, was being pressured by the postal unions (see no. 1578 for developments) and was proposing and would eventually approve a pay raise for postal workers, a move that constituted a further setback to efforts to erase the deficit (*Congressional Quarterly Almanac*, vol. XVI, *1960*, pp. 240–46, 249). For more on Eisenhower's support for a balanced postal budget see Arthur E. Summerfield as told to Charles Hurd, *U.S. Mail: The Story of the United States Postal Service* (New York, 1960).

To THEODORE MARTIN HESBURGH   *March 9, 1960*

Dear Father Hesburgh: This note is to confirm my acceptance of your invitation for June fifth.[1] (If bad weather should unexpectedly intervene, I am completely devoid of any alibi to offer).
    I must tell you that I have always deplored long commencement addresses, beginning in the days when I, an unwilling captive, had

to listen to some rather ponderous deliveries. Later experience with young people merely emphasized to me how much they are thinking about the opportunity to get back to town, go to the theatre, or try out their new car, rather than to listen with avid interest to the VIP designated as the speaker of the day.

All this is to say that I am aiming at a twelve minute talk, and making my maximum fifteen minutes. My thought is that although my effort may be somewhat banal or boring, its brevity will still compensate for its lack of brilliance.[2]

Again my thanks for the compliment of your invitation, and my warm personal regard, *Sincerely*

[1] Hesburgh had invited Eisenhower to speak at the Notre Dame University commencement ceremonies and to receive an honorary degree (see no. 1441).
[2] On June 5 the President would interrupt his forty-fifth class reunion at the United States Military Academy to fly to South Bend, Indiana. In his speech Eisenhower would call upon the graduates to help the United States meet its responsibilities to the people in underdeveloped nations, who regarded America as a "beacon of freedom." He would also address the growing need for talented people in government service (see *Public Papers of the Presidents: Eisenhower, 1960–61*, pp. 461–67, and *New York Times*, June 6, 1960). See also Ann Whitman memorandum, April 25, 1960, AWF/AWD.

1450   *EM, WHCF, Official File 41*

To Ralph Harlan Cake   *March 10, 1960*
Personal

Dear Ralph: Thank you for your letter.[1]

I have been going into this Panama Canal business intermittently for something like seven years. I started out with the theory that we could "do something" to improve our relationships with the Panamanians, most particularly those that work for the Canal. Though many of the problems seemed fairly simple at first glance, the fact is that results have not been too startling.[2]

The idea that you bring up about medical training for doctors is a new one so far as I am concerned.[3] Since I now have an appointment with Governor Brucker, who is to come to my office with his principal associates concerned with the Panama affair, I will ask him to study this suggestion also.[4]

Should you discover, when you next come to Washington, that Tom Stephens can find a few minutes that would be available to us both, I would be, of course, more than happy to see you.[5]

With warm regard, *Sincerely*

[1] Cake's letter of March 10, 1960, is in the same file as this document. Cake (A.B. University of Oregon 1913), a savings and loan executive, was on the Board of Directors of the Panama Canal Company.

[2] For background see nos. 1355, 1380, 1443, and Galambos and van Ee, *The Middle Way*, no. 1926; G. Bernard Noble, *Christian A. Herter* in *American Secretaries of State and their Diplomacy*, 20 vols. (1927–85), vol. 18 (New York, 1970), pp. 205–16. For developments see no. 1645.

[3] Cake had suggested an idea, which he attributed to Canal Zone Governor Major General William Everett Potter, for starting an international medical teaching program at Gorgas Hospital, near Panama City. He had proposed bringing as many as 1,000 doctors from Central and South America to study different diseases over varying time periods. As a budget committee member, Cake was willing to have the Canal Company provide transportation and housing facilities. He knew of nothing, he wrote, that "would bring as much good will to the United States." Cake had also described the poor housing conditions in Panama, and he had proposed that the United States help finance and build up to two thousand homes. He argued that "you cannot expect anything but unrest and violence in places where you find the people huddled together four or five in a room . . . with no sanitary conditions" (Cake to Eisenhower, Mar. 10, 1960, same file as document).

[4] Eisenhower would meet with Brucker and other officials on March 21, 1960, to discuss various aspects of the Panama situation (see no. 1443; Stephens to Brucker, Mar. 14, 1960, same file as document).

Ann Whitman, the President's secretary, would note that "State" liked Cake's idea, and would have a study made (Memorandum for the Record, Mar. 21, 1960, AWF/AWD). Dillon would report to the President that the project would be feasible, that Governor Potter had agreed to start the program with a small number of participants, and that the U.S. Ambassador would secure cooperation from Panama's Foreign Ministry (Dillon to Eisenhower, Mar. 20 and Apr. 15, 1960, AWF/D-H).

[5] Thomas E. Stephens was Appointments Secretary to the President. Eisenhower would meet with Cake on April 27, 1960 (President's daily appointments).

1451   *EM, AWF, Administration Series*

To John Charles Doerfer   *March 10, 1960*

Dear Mr. Doerfer: I have your letter submitting your resignation as Member and Chairman of the Federal Communications Commission.[1]

I regret the circumstances which have led you to your conclusion but they do, in my opinion, indicate your decision to be a wise one.[2] Your resignation is, accordingly, accepted effective, as you suggest, at the close of business on Monday, March fourteenth.

In the discharge of your duties first as a member and then as Chairman of the Federal Communications Commission you have served tirelessly, loyally, effectively—and with dedication. For your public service over many years at local, State and Federal levels you have earned the appreciation of your fellow citizens and of the Administration.[3]

I wish you every success in your future undertakings.[4] *Sincerely*

¹ Doerfer (B.A. University of Wisconsin 1928) had resigned after testifying before a House investigating committee on March 4 that he had accepted a broadcaster's hospitality while on vacation in Florida (Doerfer to Eisenhower, Mar. 10, 1960, AWF/A). It was the second such investigation of inappropriate conduct since he had been appointed by Eisenhower to the commission in 1953 (see no. 219). On March 9 Eisenhower had called David W. Kendall, the President's Special Counsel, to his office to discuss the allegations of influence peddling. The President had said that Doerfer could meet with him if he wished and "have his day in court," but if the story was true, then the staff should immediately ask Doerfer to resign. Referring back to his 1952 campaign promise "not only to avoid evil, but the appearance of evil," the President said that members of regulatory commissions are in "the most sensitive spots in government and should control their affairs in such a way as to be above suspicion" (Ann Whitman diary, Mar. 9, 1960, AWF/A: FCC). Ann Whitman, the President's secretary, had written that the President had "literally demanded" that Doerfer resign, but the staff, in her opinion, took "its own sweet time" and the resignation did not take place until 48 hours later (Ann Whitman memorandum, Mar. 9, 1960, AWF/AWD).

² Doerfer had told the investigating committee that a commissioner ought to be free to choose his friends and social activities as he saw fit (*New York Times*, Mar. 3, 4, 5, 10, and 11, 1960). In his letter of resignation he had said that a commissioner's job required day-to-day contact with industry people, which did not imperil his integrity, or theirs, despite appearances.

³ Doerfer had served as a city attorney and chairman of the Wisconsin Public Service Commission before joining the FCC. His term was not due to expire until July 1, 1961.

⁴ Eisenhower would designate commission member Frederick W. Ford as chairman of the FCC and would appoint New Jersey lawyer Edward K. Mill, Jr., to replace Doerfer (*New York Times*, Mar. 11 and 24, 1960).

1452   *EM, WHCF, Official File 101-2*

To David Sarnoff   *March 10, 1960*

*Dear Dave:*¹ At the conclusion of my broadcast the other evening, I found that I had allowed myself to run one minute over the time allotted to me. Although I usually keep a watch at hand to pace myself, I had neglected to do so and had no idea that I was exceeding the fifteen minutes you had so kindly given me.²

The offense will not be repeated!³

With warm regard, *As ever*

¹ Sarnoff, chairman of the board of the Radio Corporation of America since 1947, had served as Eisenhower's communications consultant during the Normandy invasion in 1944 (for background see *Eisenhower Papers*, vols. X–XVII).

² On March 8, in a radio and television broadcast, the President had summarized his impressions gathered during a ten-day tour of Brazil, Argentina, Chile, and Uruguay (for background see no. 1403). In his address Eisenhower had declared that U.S.-Latin American relations had "reached an all time high." He urged his fellow citi-

zens to become better informed regarding Latin Americans, their institutions and traditions, and he advocated closer ties between North and South Americans (see *Public Papers of the Presidents: Eisenhower, 1960–61,* pp. 282–87, and *New York Times,* Mar. 9, 1960).

[3] Sarnoff would reply (Mar. 17, same file as document) that the additional time had caused no difficulty in the network operations. The National Broadcasting Company had scheduled fifteen minutes of news comment directly following Eisenhower's address so the extra minute "was not even noticeable."

On this same day the President would send similar letters to the chairmen of the boards of the Columbia Broadcasting System, Mutual Broadcasting System and the American Broadcasting System (see Eisenhower to Stanton; Eisenhower to Hurleigh; Eisenhower to Goldenson, and Goldenson to Eisenhower, both Mar. 18, and Hurleigh to Eisenhower, Mar. 24, all in same file as document).

1453   *EM, WHCF, President's Personal File 1494*

To David Lawrence   *March 10, 1960*

Dear David: When I returned to my desk recently, I found that someone had thoughtfully saved for me your column of February twenty-sixth entitled "There's a Gap in the Olympics." I merely wanted to tell you that I read it with much amusement and, as always, with admiration of your great talents.[1]

At the same time, just let me say that although I am hesitant to flood you with correspondence, there is many a day on which I say "bravo" when I read, as I always try to do, your column.[2]

With warm regard, *As ever*

[1] Syndicated columnist Lawrence had sent a clipping from the Washington, D.C., *Evening Star* to the President's press secretary on March 2 (Lawrence to Hagerty, same file as document). Likening a supposed "Olympic gap" to the U.S.-Soviet missile gap, Lawrence had explained in political terms why the U.S. winter Olympic teams were lagging behind the Russian teams. Lawrence had blamed poor American intelligence estimates and had called for a congressional investigation to ascertain Democratic administrations produced colder weather and therefore better American skaters and skiers. He also said that the U.S. government should subsidize ice-skating facilities in all congressional districts in order to minimize the Russian cold-weather advantage. While Eisenhower had saved us from the "golf gap," Lawrence concluded, many citizens might have preferred to have a few billions of dollars appropriated to close the Olympic "gap."

[2] Lawrence would thank the President for his comments on March 16 (same file as document).

To Nikita Sergeyevich Khrushchev   *March 12, 1960*

Dear Mr. Chairman:[1] I am grateful for your consideration in sending your letter of March third in which you share with me your views on matters which are indeed of great importance.[2] As indicated in your letter, we were in full agreement at Camp David, as was mentioned in the communique covering those discussions, that the question of general disarmament is the most important one facing the world today and that the Governments of the Union of Soviet Socialist Republics and the United States will make every effort to achieve a constructive solution of this problem.[3] To this I cannot fail to give my wholehearted and continued support.

In reply to the thoughts expressed in your letter, and in the same spirit of frank exchange of views I welcome this opportunity, as you requested, to set forth considerations which I think important.

First of all, while I do not wish to make extended comment on your remarks about the Federal Republic of Germany, I do consider that these reflect a misunderstanding of the nature of the post-war German state. An impartial appraisal would, I believe, show that the leaders of the Federal Republic, as well as the overwhelming sentiment of the population which elected these leaders to office, want peace as much as any of us and do not present an aggressive threat to any country. I can assure you from personal knowledge that this is the case, recognizing that, while memories of the past may justify caution, they should not blind us to the realities of the present.

Now, with regard to the basic questions raised in your letter, I should note that, as you yourself say, certain of the observations you make are based on interpretations arrived at in various parts of the world of the meaning of comments that Secretary Herter and I made in the course of press conferences during the month of February. If the interpretations of our comments to which you refer led you to believe that a change had taken place or was in progress in the policy of the United States as regards the transfer of nuclear weapons or information on the design and manufacture of nuclear weapons, they were in error. Neither Secretary Herter nor I had any intention of implying the existence of or plans for any such change; and upon re-reading carefully the transcript of our remarks I do not feel that an interpretation in this sense would be justifiable.

Your letter therefore, based as it seems to be on misinterpretation of remarks which I have made, seems to reflect fundamental misunderstanding regarding the policy of the United States Government. At the risk of being repetitious I should like to review this policy for you.

It is our policy to avoid the widening of the circle of nuclear powers. This policy is implemented in the actions of the United States and is reflected in our basic laws, in particular the Atomic Energy Act of 1954 as amended.[4] The United States does not transfer nuclear weapons to the custody of its allies in time of peace and we do not (with the exception of the United Kingdom which is already a nuclear power) provide to our allies or to others information on the design and manufacture of nuclear weapons. Our policy has been public knowledge since its inception and any change would become immediately known. On the other hand, we do not know whether or not the USSR places nuclear weapons at the disposal of the members of the Warsaw Pact or others of its allies.

It must be recognized that states with a major industrial capability in the present world cannot be expected to be satisfied indefinitely with a situation in which nuclear weapons are uncontrolled and they themselves do not have nuclear weapons for their own defense. As for our allies in NATO, it must further be recognized that they have a legitimate desire to defend themselves with the most modern weapons available. This desire is easily understood when it is realized that they must provide for defense against forces which, as you yourself have made very clear on numerous occasions, already possess the most modern and destructive armaments. It is to help meet the legitimate need of our allies for their own defense that we have established the NATO atomic stockpile system. Under this system, custody of atomic warheads remains in the United States alone as provided by law and they can be used only in defense against aggression. The circle of nuclear powers is not widened thereby. The legitimate needs of our allies for modern weapons to be used in self-defense are satisfied, but in a manner which does not require them to produce such weapons themselves.

You and I must recognize, however, that the secrets of the production of nuclear weapons to which you refer cannot long remain hidden from many of the states in the modern world which have advanced scientific and industrial resources. If the proliferation of nuclear weapons is to be prevented we cannot longer delay a start on the agreed international control of nuclear energy and a beginning on meaningful disarmament agreements covering both conventional and nuclear arms under verifiable conditions.

It is generally agreed that technical means are not now available for assuring the elimination of past and present stocks of nuclear weapons. This situation was officially recognized by the Soviet Government in its disarmament proposals of May 10, 1955 and reconfirmed in its declaration submitted to the General Assembly of the

United Nations on September 18, 1959. I believe you also acknowledged it in a speech made at Moscow on May 24, 1958.[5]

Nonetheless there are things which can be done now and I urge that we take the opportunities which are before us to agree to the measures which would bring to a halt immediately the possibility of the emergence of new nuclear powers.

What we can now do are the following three things:

1. We can, in the Geneva negotiations for discontinuance of nuclear weapons tests, stop all nuclear weapons tests which can now be effectively controlled. That done, we could through joint research move, as quickly as additional control measures could be proven and agreed, to the cessation of all weapons tests. The response of your representative to the proposals of the United States representative on February eleventh for immediate agreement on the presently achievable steps has thus far been negative.[6] But surely it is in the interests of our two countries and of the whole world to conclude now an agreement in all areas for which the problems of essential inspection have been resolved.

2. We can support, in the April meeting of the Board of Governors of the International Atomic Energy Agency, the adoption of safeguards procedures which will ensure that the future expansion of nuclear power production does not itself become the source for fissionable material for production of nuclear weapons. Both the United States and the Soviet Union are taking significant strides in the development of nuclear power and in the making available of this new energy resource for the benefit of other nations. Surely we have a common interest, as reflected in our adherence to the principles of the statute of the International Atomic Energy Agency, in seeing that the nuclear power reactors which are built in the future in many nations do not become the source of material for manufacture of weapons by new nuclear powers.[7]

3. We can, in the disarmament negotiations beginning March fifteenth in Geneva, agree to stop the production of fissionable material for use in nuclear weapons—thus stopping the accumulation of nuclear weapons stocks—as soon as effective inspection measures are agreed and operating.[8] Simultaneously we could begin to transfer fissionable materials now in weapons stocks to peaceful purposes with a view to the eventual elimination of these weapons from national arsenals. This practical and important step is one which I have urged repeatedly since my letter of March 1956 to Premier Bulganin.[9] The arguments which you bring forward in your letter of March third seem to me to reinforce the cogent reasons for proceeding promptly with this significant measure.

I think we are agreed that the surest method of dealing with the situation which concerns you, as indeed it does me, is to make progress toward effective disarmament measures. I think you will agree that there is little prospect of achieving much in this field at the summit unless we can base ourselves on solid progress already achieved in the Geneva negotiations. I hope that you will instruct your representatives, as I have done mine, to make every effort to eliminate differences to the point where we will have something real to deal with at Paris in May.[10]

I hope that this frank statement will clarify the policy and objectives of my Government and remove the misapprehensions of our purpose. Particularly I again assure you that my public statements, to which you refer, implied no change whatsoever in this nation's policies or their application. I appreciate your expression of the concerns which you feel. For my part, I express the hope that you will join with us in the negotiations to which I have referred, in undertaking now the concrete and effective measures which will make vast progress in dealing with the nuclear threat.[11] *Sincerely*

[1] A State Department draft of this letter with Eisenhower's handwritten emendations is in AWF/I: Khrushchev. The text was cabled in a confidential message to the American embassy in Moscow for delivery to the Soviet leader. Eisenhower had authorized the State Department to inform U.S. allies in NATO of the substance of Khrushchev's letter and this response. On the subsequent leak to the press of these messages see Eisenhower to Khrushchev, March 19, 1960, *ibid.*

[2] Khrushchev had criticized statements that Eisenhower and Secretary Herter had made regarding the sharing of secret nuclear information with U.S. allies. The statements, Khrushchev maintained, were interpreted "as an expression of the intention of the United States to equip with American nuclear weapons, within the framework of NATO in particular, those of its allies who do not have such weapons." Such a step "would enormously impede the solution of the problem of general and complete disarmament." Khrushchev cited the danger of providing nuclear weapons information to the German Federal Republic, where, he said, many people sought revenge for the defeat in World War II and where Chancellor Adenauer had himself stated that the German people were "charged with a 'special mission'" (Khrushchev to Eisenhower, Mar. 3, 1960, *ibid.*; on Eisenhower's news conferences see *Public Papers of the Presidents: Eisenhower, 1960–61*, pp. 147–48, 189–98; on Herter's news conference see *U.S. Department of State Bulletin* 42, no. 1079 [February 29, 1960], 321).

[3] On the Camp David talks and the communiqué see no. 1332.

[4] For background on the act and its amendments see no. 718.

[5] For the disarmament proposals see Galambos and van Ee, *The Middle Way*, no. 1523; on the declaration see State, *Documents on Disarmament, 1945–1959*, pp. 1452–60; and on Khrushchev's speech, *ibid.*, pp. 1041–43.

[6] On the February 11 proposals see no. 1445.

[7] On the agency's statute see Hewlett and Holl, *Atoms for Peace and War*, pp. 370–71. In September the General Conference of the IAEA would adopt a resolution, co-sponsored by the United States, that established general principles for safeguards against the diversion of nuclear materials for military uses. The safeguards, which the agency's board of governors had ratified provisionally, would involve approval of plant designs, systematic record keeping, periodic and special reporting procedures, and IAEA inspections ("Atomic Safeguards," *International Atomic Energy Agency Bulletin* 3, no. 1 [January, 1961], 10–13; see also Cabinet meeting minutes, Oct. 7, 1960, AWF/D).

[8] On the upcoming Geneva meetings see no. 1341.
[9] See Galambos and van Ee, *The Middle Way,* no. 1765.
[10] For background on the plans for a summit meeting see no. 1397.
[11] For developments see no. 1459.

1455

EM, AWF,
International Series: Iran

To Mohammed Reza Pahlavi
Secret

March 12, 1960

Your Imperial Majesty:[1] Thank you very much for your letter of January twelfth and its enclosures which outline the eventual goals you perceive for the Iranian forces.[2] I recall with great pleasure my recent talk with you and the clarity and forcefulness with which you expressed your views.[3] Of particular interest to me was your appreciation of the fact that it is illusory to believe that sheer numbers of men can provide an effective defense.

The papers you sent have been carefully studied here. I find that, as we see it, they overstate somewhat the threat to your country from Iraq and Afghanistan. I also find that your paper includes a number of complicated and advanced weapons which would involve a high initial cost, which would be very costly to maintain, and which would require an advanced level of technical training which could only be achieved over a considerable period in time.[4]

I think that there is no more difficult decision in the world for any country than that of deciding what weapons it should acquire at any time. In our own case, this is a dilemma with which we are continually faced. It involves an assessment of the extent to which the resources of this country can be devoted to our military programs without damaging our economy and hurting social progress. I have become convinced, moreover, that here and elsewhere sound military development of balanced forces is an evolutionary problem that requires time and cannot be arrived at by the sudden and large-scale introduction of advanced and complicated weapons.

While I can give you no specific undertaking for the future as regards any particular kind or quantity of weapons, I can assure you that in developing current and future programs we will bear in mind your desire for more modern weapons. We will continue to discuss with you and your military experts the possible introduction of these weapons into your armed forces. We also stand ready to discuss with you, as your requirements evolve, the balance between your army and your air forces in the light of new air developments and any organizational adjustments that you feel called for within your armed forces.

In commenting in this general way on your analysis of your current needs, I have constantly in mind the very broad commitments that my country has already made toward the defense of your country. You will recall, I am sure, my letters of July 19, 1958 and January 30, 1959 and, in a more formal way, our bilateral agreement of March 5, 1959 and the Joint Resolution to Promote Peace and Stability in the Middle East.[5] In this day and age it seems to me real security lies in working together and relying on each other. As I told you on earlier occasions, Iran can always count on the United States in meeting the threat of international communism.

I have also reviewed the actual course of our military assistance to Iran to date, and I have been much impressed by the progress made through our mutual efforts and cooperation.[6] I have been particularly impressed by the reports of the eagerness and facility with which the officers and men of your armed forces embrace new equipment and training concepts. I am confident that in close cooperation we will continue to move forward.

We must continue to exchange views. These exchanges, whether oral or written, are always of value and interest to me. My friendship is enhanced by my respect for your courage, perseverance and foresight.[7]

With warm regard, *Sincerely*

[1] A State Department draft of this letter with Eisenhower's handwritten emendations is in AWF/I: Iran. The message was cabled to the American embassy in Tehran for delivery to the Shah.

[2] For background see no. 1400; see also State, *Foreign Relations, 1958–1960*, vol. XII, *Near East Region; Iraq; Iran; Arabian Peninsula*, pp. 664–65. Pahlavi had written "of the need for urgent action" to meet the emergencies he believed neighboring countries were creating for Iran. Among his specific requests were improvements or new construction at six air bases, two new early warning radar stations, 150 high-performance fighter bombers, and two battalions of antiaircraft missiles. To reorganize and modernize his army he had proposed the creation of ten battle groups equipped with atomic-capable missiles, tanks, armored personnel carriers, and antiaircraft weapons. He had also requested additional minesweepers, patrol vessels, and gunboats for his navy (Pahlavi to Eisenhower, Jan. 12, 1960, AWF/I: Iran; see also NSC meeting minutes, Jan. 13, 1960, AWF/NSC; and Synopsis of State and Intelligence Material Reported to the President, Jan. 6, 7, 1960, AWF/D).

[3] Eisenhower had visited Iran on December 14 as part of his eleven-nation goodwill tour (see no. 1392; see also State, *Foreign Relations, 1958–1960*, vol. XII, *Near East Region; Iraq; Iran; Arabian Peninsula*, pp. 658–59).

[4] According to Defense Department officials who had reviewed the Shah's requests, the Iranian leader had "overstated the threat" to Iran from its neighbors and that his requests, estimated to cost $600 million, were not only excessive but beyond the Shah's capacity to use effectively (*ibid.*, pp. 666–69; see also NSC meeting minutes, Mar. 14, 1960, AWF/NSC).

[5] Eisenhower's letters to the Shah are nos. 779 and 1038. On the bilateral agreement

see State, *American Foreign Policy, Current Documents, 1959*, pp. 1020–22; see also State, *Foreign Relations, 1958–1960*, vol. XII, *Near East Region; Iraq; Iran; Arabian Peninsula*, pp. 635–37, 639–42; and NSC meeting minutes, Feb. 12, 1959, AWF/NSC. On the Middle East resolution see nos. 63 and 791.

⁶ For background see Galambos and van Ee, *The Middle Way*, nos. 1774 and 2133, and no. 779 in these volumes.

⁷ According to the U.S. ambassador, the Shah, although "calm and sensible," would be disappointed that his specific requests had been answered in a general manner. The Shah would conclude that most of Eisenhower's letter had actually been written by the Defense Department, because the letter had contradicted statements Eisenhower had made to him during their visit (Wailes to Herter, Mar. 14, 1959, AWF/I: Iran). For developments see no. 1653.

1456   *EM, AWF, Dulles-Herter Series*

To CHRISTIAN ARCHIBALD HERTER   *March 12, 1960*

Dear Chris: I think that early next week you and I should have a conference over the planned composition of our party for the Summit.¹ Likewise we should figure out exactly the individuals that it would be advisable to take on my goodwill trip to Russia.²

With warm regard, *As ever*

¹ For background on the summit meeting, to begin in Paris on May 16 see no. 1397. Among those attending, in addition to the members of Eisenhower's party (see President's daily appointments) and Secretary of State Herter, would be Secretary of Defense Thomas S. Gates, Jr., Under Secretary of State Livingston T. Merchant, Special Assistant Charles E. Bohlen, Ambassadors James J. Wadsworth, Amory Houghton, Llewellyn E. Thompson and other State and Defense Department officials.

² On March 17 Herter would discuss with Eisenhower his participation in the President's scheduled trip to the Soviet Union in June (see no. 1422). He expected to be present during the principal conversations with Soviet officials, he said, but after consulting with U.S. Ambassador Thompson, he had decided that he would not accompany Eisenhower on his visits to Kiev, Leningrad, or Irkutsk. The President agreed that, since the trip was primarily ceremonial, both men should not be absent together from Washington for a long period (Goodpaster, Memorandum of Conference, Mar. 18, 1960, AWF/D). For developments see no. 1486.

1457   *EM, WHCF,*
                                                        Official File 3-WW

To THOMAS SOVEREIGN GATES, JR.   *March 14, 1960*

Memorandum for the Secretary of Defense: Early in my first Administration I agreed with the Secretary of Defense that we should not designate the position of head of a service academy as a three-star position, believing that it would be better for that kind of a post to have a young, up-and-coming two-star man. For several reasons this policy was later altered, but I have never changed my conviction respecting it.[1]

Unless you see some cogent reason to the contrary, I wish you would notify the heads of the several services that as soon as any incumbent of one of these positions, who may now hold three-star rank, retires or is transferred to another post, he will be replaced by an individual of not higher than two-star rank. Thereafter, these positions will be removed from the lists of those authorized by the President for the higher rank.[2]

I should like to make sure that the appropriate actions agreeable to this instruction will be made before the end of the current calendar year.[3]

[1] See Galambos and van Ee, *The Middle Way*, nos. 737, 890, and 980.
[2] The next superintendent appointed during Eisenhower's Administration would be two-star Major General William C. Westmoreland, who would replace Lieutenant General Garrison H. Davidson at the United States Military Academy at West Point on May 13, 1960 (*New York Times*, May 14, 1960).
[3] There is no written reply from Gates in EM.

1458   *EM, WHCF, Official File 85-F*

To Jacob Koppel Javits   *March 16, 1960*

Dear Jack: On my return, I find your letter urging my further support of legislation before the Senate to repeal the Connally amendment.[1]

I am glad you are aware of my strong interest in this regard. My two statements in successive State of the Union Messages should leave no doubt as to my conviction and position.[2]

However, with these statements before the Congress, supported by testimony from the Secretary of State and the Attorney General, I am a little at a loss as to what more I should do.[3] It seems to me that sheer repetition can hardly strengthen the case.

At the same time, in my conversations with leaders of the Senate, and others, I intend of course to continue to evince my known interest.

Your own interest in this legislation is very much appreciated.[4]
With warm regard, *Sincerely*

[1] In 1946, when the Senate had voted to accept the jurisdiction of the International Court of Justice in various international matters, it had also enacted the so-called "Connally Amendment." This reservation curtailed the Court's jurisdiction in mat-

ters that involved essentially domestic concerns, "as determined by the United States of America." A resolution had been introduced in the Senate in 1959 to repeal the amendment; for background see no. 1439. Javits's March 4 letter (same file as document) urged action during the current session of Congress because the drive to repeal the amendment had "gathered a certain momentum which may be difficult to recapture in future years." Javits also said that repeal would help solidify the "trust and friendship" that Eisenhower had created during his recent foreign travels. (On Eisenhower's trip to South America see no. 1403.)

[2] See *Public Papers of the Presidents: Eisenhower, 1959*, p. 18; *Public Papers of the Presidents: Eisenhower, 1960*, p. 15.

[3] Attorney General William Rogers and Secretary of State Christian Herter had testified before Congress on January 27 in favor of repeal of the resolution. Herter had argued that the United States would retain jurisdiction over domestic matters even without the Connally Amendment, and that the reservation handicapped the United States in bringing other nations before the Court. The Attorney General supported Herter's testimony, and he added that the Connally reservation led other nations to doubt American "good faith" in accepting the Court's jurisdiction (see *Congressional Quarterly Almanac*, vol. XVI, *1960*, p. 231).

[4] On March 29, 1960, the Senate Foreign Relations Committee would vote to postpone indefinitely consideration of the repeal of the Connally Amendment.

1459   *EM, AWF, International Series:*
                                                              Macmillan

To Harold Macmillan   *March 18, 1960*
Top secret

Dear Harold: Thank you very much for your letter. Frankly, no prior tour of mine in the past fifteen years has been so tiring as the one I completed in South America.[1] The combination of dust, crowded days and summer heat persuaded me that I am not as young as I was when we were together in Algiers.[2]

I have not read General De Gaulle's memoirs—but I shall make an effort to get the third volume of which you speak.[3] It has been a source of amazement to me that he seems to be unable to fathom the methods by which our three governments could easily keep in close touch on main issues. I explained to him how you and ourselves used both normal diplomatic exchanges, personal communications and, in acute cases ad hoc committees to keep together.[4] I think that the difficulty may lie in his memory of the British-American "Combined Chiefs of Staff" of World War II days, and his resentment that the French staffs were not integrated into that body. In any event, I have always made it clear that I was ready to do anything reasonable to maintain contacts and mutual understandings among us three; I adhere to this policy. But I think I made it clear to him that it was impractical to have frequent "Heads of Government" Conferences and yet, as you say, he seems to prefer this kind of approach to any on our common problems.

The Chancellor and I got along famously.[5] While I had been informed, a day or so in advance of our meeting, that he had expressed a great deal of uneasiness to friends in New York concerning Western firmness in preserving our rights in Berlin, he did not raise this question with me.[6] I conversationally reassured him on the point, as I have often done before, and he seemed pleased that I had mentioned the matter. He did not show any concern about it. A day or so later, the Chancellor went to a dinner with Secretary Herter and I heard that some misunderstandings arose which seemed to annoy him. I do not believe, however, that the points of difference involved fundamentals.[7]

All of us—including Mr. K.—seem in accord on one subject: the need for progress in controlled disarmament. We seem to be as far apart, as between East and West, as we possibly can be, on the procedures for attaining the objective.[8] I would derive tremendous satisfaction out of seeing some specific practical step agreed upon at the Summit, and initiated as soon as practicable. Such an accomplishment would be tangible evidence of some real progress in a knotty problem that has engaged your effort and mine for a number of years. It would be a ray of light in a world that is bound to be weary of the tensions brought about by mutual suspicion, distrust and arms races. Strangely, I never lose my conviction that sooner or later in some fashion or other, we shall bring about some rift in the clouds. But at the same time I must confess at times to a great feeling of impatience.

I forgot to say that the Chancellor is very much preoccupied with the 1961 elections in his country.[9] He made a point of saying that even the opposition agrees with him that all of us, and particularly, all of Germany, must be adamant concerning the allied occupational rights in Berlin. Any seeming weakening of this position would, he believes, have a most damaging effect on his party's position next year.

When we finally get together, maybe we will have an opportunity to compare notes on these journeys that we have been making here and there about the world.[10] *With warm regard*

---

[1] For background on Eisenhower's visit to South America see no. 1403; see also Eisenhower, *Waging Peace,* pp. 525–33; State, *Foreign Relations, 1958–1960,* vol. V, *American Republics,* pp. 267–86. Macmillan had written that he hoped Eisenhower had recovered "from what must have been a most terribly wearying trip" (Macmillan to Eisenhower, Mar. 14, 1960, PREM 11/2998).

[2] See Chandler, *War Years,* no. 753.

[3] Macmillan had just returned from an informal one-day meeting with de Gaulle (see Macmillan, *Pointing the Way,* pp. 180–85). "He was relaxed and rather philosophical," he wrote Eisenhower, "but nevertheless quite firm in the part that France should play in Europe. His main themes remain unchanged." The latest volume of de

Gaulle's memoirs (*Salvation, 1944–1946*, translated by Richard Howard, [New York, 1960]) "was wonderfully written," Macmillan said, "and gives a picture of his rather mystical thinking on these great matters."

[4] On Eisenhower's meetings with de Gaulle in December see no. 1404; see also no. 1445.

[5] On a visit to the United States in order to receive an honorary degree from the University of California, West German Chancellor Adenauer had met with Eisenhower on March 15 (see State, *Foreign Relations, 1958–1960,* vol. IX, *Berlin Crisis 1959–1960; Germany; Austria,* pp. 658–71).

[6] Ambassador Lodge had reported to Secretary Herter that Adenauer had told him he had found a great deal of "unrest" in New York regarding the Berlin situation. He was also concerned that Eisenhower wanted to change the legal status of Berlin (*ibid.,* p. 224; see also Telephone Conversation, Lodge and Herter, Mar. 14, 1960, Herter Papers, Telephone Conversations).

[7] Herter had reported to Eisenhower that following dinner Adenauer had become "very difficult and contentious in his discussion." He had cited a report that the Soviets would surpass the United States in economic output by 1965, and he complained that Eisenhower had not mentioned Central Europe as an area to be covered by a proposed aerial inspection plan. Eisenhower told Herter that he had indeed mentioned Central Europe and that the interpreter had failed to give a complete translation. Adenauer had "become extremely suspicious," Herter said, "and ready to believe any rumor that the United States is doing something against the interest of himself or his party." Eisenhower had replied that there were "clear signs of growing senility particularly in Adenauer's tendency to focus on a single point, with loss of perspective on the whole range of considerations" (Goodpaster, Memorandum of Conference, Mar. 18, 1960, AWF/D; and State, *Foreign Relations, 1958–1960,* vol. IX, *Berlin Crisis 1959–1960; Germany; Austria,* pp. 225–26, 678–79).

[8] For background on the disarmament issue see no. 1454. Macmillan had told Eisenhower that he was comforted that the Western nations were able to agree on a disarmament position. "You know how deeply I feel our duty to the world."

[9] Elections in Germany would take place on September 17, 1961. Adenauer believed that his twelve-year administration would be subject to "review and criticism" and was particularly concerned about the subjects of vested German assets (see no. 1412) and unanimity within the West German Bundestag on the subject of disarmament (State, *Foreign Relations, 1958–1960,* vol. IX, *Berlin Crisis 1959–1960; Germany; Austria,* pp. 659–60, 671).

[10] In a telephone conversation between the two men on March 21, Macmillan would suggest a trip to Washington to discuss a new Soviet proposal for banning nuclear tests. He would arrive on March 26 for two days of meetings with Eisenhower at Camp David (State, *Foreign Relations, 1958–1960,* vol. VII, pt. 2, *Western Europe,* pp. 859–65; see also Goodpaster, Memorandum of Conference, Mar. 25, 1960, AWF/D; and Macmillan, *Pointing the Way,* pp. 188–93, 252–58). For developments see no. 1486.

1460   *EM, AWF, Administration Series*

To JAMES ALDEN NORELL   *March 18, 1960*

Dear General Norell:[1] Thank you very much for the memoranda on the advent of the Gold Bar as a mark of rank for the Second Lieutenant, and on the use of the term "Mister" as a form of address.[2] The information was provided at my request, and I am delighted to find that my understanding on the two matters was substantially correct.

Incidentally, I find that a number of our novelists talk about "gold barred second lieutenants" from the time of the Civil War onward—and I frequently run into the expression, reportedly used during the 70s and 80s, "Lieutenant, that is an order." In my entire life I have never heard such an expression used by another officer.[3]

I appreciate the trouble you took to get the information for me. With best wishes, *Sincerely*

[1] Brigadier General Norell (B.S. University of Idaho 1932; M.S. 1933), had become chief of military history in the Department of the Army on August 1, 1959. He had served in the G-1 Section of Headquarters, European Theater of Operation throughout the war and had been awarded the Bronze Star Medal and the Legion of Merit. As a member of the Office of the Assistant Secretary of Defense for Manpower, Personnel, and Reserve, Norell had participated in the formulation and presentation to Congress of the President's "National Reserve Plan," which had been enacted as the Reserve Forces Act of 1955.

[2] Norell's memorandum ([March 20, 1960]) is in AWF/D. In 1917 the gold bar was proposed because it offered the least possible change to the existing scheme of uniform and insignia. The junior officers acquired the insignia color representing the more precious metal, while the first lieutenants, senior in rank, retained the established silver color.

The practice of addressing certain officers as "Mister," rather than by specific rank, appeared to have developed as a matter of social custom and not of military regulation, Norell had explained. Between the two world wars the rank of warrant officer had been created; these officers were also addressed as "Mister," leading to some confusion.

[3] The practice of addressing Army lieutenants as "lieutenant" became official in 1942, Norell reported. The Navy had continued its practice of having officers below the rank of commander addressed as "Mister."

1461 *EM, AWF, Dulles-Herter Series*

To CHRISTIAN ARCHIBALD HERTER *March 21, 1960*
Personal

Dear Chris: The attached is self-explanatory.[1] I had not known of General Clark's intimate association with General Trujillo—or possibly I had just forgotten it. In any event, he seems to think that he can do some preliminary work that might later develop to a situation that would redound to the benefit of the United States.

Please let me know what you think about the matter. I suppose that Rubottom ought to be the one to study this, but I would like to keep it as confidential as possible.[2] *As ever*

[1] Former Brigadier General Edwin Norman Clark, a friend and adviser of Eisenhower, had sent the President a memorandum concerning the Dominican Republic. The situation, he said, was "of such a delicate nature that a bit of bad luck" could result in the disruption of Latin-American relations "and might be a prelude to the establishment of another Communist regime." Opposition to the rule of Generalissimo Raphael Leonidas Trujillo Molina, in power since 1930, had increased both inside and outside the country. Trujillo knew his days in power were numbered, Clark told Eisenhower; he wanted to retire but was "in a quandary as to how to do it" without sacrificing the welfare of his family and the country.

Because of his past association with the dictator, Clark believed he was in a unique position to persuade Trujillo to retire in a way that would further the establishment of a constitutional form of government. He suggested the creation of a philanthropic foundation to which Trujillo would transfer the sizable assets amassed by the dictator and his family. The foundation would be administered by internationally known U.S. and Latin American citizens for the benefit of the Dominican people. The Trujillo family could be given asylum in the United States, Clark said, until their return to the Dominican Republic would not provoke bloodshed (Clark to Eisenhower, Mar. 21, 1960, AWF/D-H). For background on Clark see Galambos and van Ee, *The Middle Way*, no. 754; on the Communist takeover in Cuba, no. 1370; and on relations between Cuba and the Dominican Republic, no. 1265. See also State, *Foreign Relations, 1958–1960*, vol. V, *American Republics*, Microfiche Supplement; Synopsis of Intelligence Material Reported to the President, Mar. 10, 1960, AWF/D-H; Eric Paul Roorda, *The Dictator Next Door: The Good Neighbor Policy and the Trujillo Regime in the Dominican Republic, 1930–1945* [Durham, N.C., 1998]; and Rabe, *Eisenhower and the Foreign Policy of Anticommunism and Latin America*, pp. 153–56).

The National Security Council had discussed the Dominican situation on January 14. State Department officials had reported that although an internal revolution against Trujillo was possible, there appeared to be little prospect of a Communist takeover. Assistant Secretary of State for Inter-American Affairs R. Roy Rubottom had told the NSC that the moderate elements in the Dominican Republic that were friendly to the United States were convinced "that a move against Trujillo must be made soon" (NSC meeting minutes, Mar. 31, 1960, AWF/NSC).

[2] In a subsequent meeting CIA Director Allen Dulles would tell Eisenhower and Secretary Herter that recent atrocities by Trujillo's government had strengthened opposition to the dictator and that the regime might fall within three weeks. Herter thought that Clark's plan was "worth trying" but that the United States should not offer asylum to the Dominican ruler. Eisenhower said that if Clark played a role, he should make clear that he was acting on his own with no authority from the President (Goodpaster, Memorandum of Conference, [Mar. 25, 1960], State, *Foreign Relations, 1958–1960*, vol. V, *American Republics*, Microfiche Supplement, DR-17).

For developments see no. 1516.

1462   *EM, WHCF, Official File 122-T*

To CARL AUGUST NORGREN   *March 22, 1960*
Personal

Dear Carl: You are perfectly correct that the problem you pose in our letter—and that is so dramatically brought to the fore in the article from the Rocky Mountain News—is close to my heart.[1]

First, regarding the report of the proceedings of the Second Air Force Academy Assembly. If the newspaper story is accurate, not only are the allegations of the young people incorrect, but the very fact that they were uttered shows a woeful lack of understanding on the part of the delegates to the Assembly. We of course have to make allowances for the enthusiasms of youth; but those enthusiasms will be better directed if we are more energetic in getting before the youth the facts of today's world and the truths of America's development.[2]

Presumably all of these youngsters want good jobs and, as you observe, if there are no profits there are not going to be any "good jobs."[3] A worthwhile idea, I think, would be to publish the complete history of Sweden's progress in socialization and some of the results now discernible in the population of that country.[4]

Thank you for your letter.

With warm regard, *As ever*

[1] Norgren, a Denver rancher, engineer, and manufacturer of pneumatic products (see Galambos and van Ee, *The Middle Way*, no. 386), had sent Eisenhower an article entitled, "Businessmen Given Rough Going Over by Collegians." The article, published by the Denver, Colorado *Rocky Mountain News* on March 11, had described a meeting of students at the Second Air Force Academy Assembly.

[2] Representatives from various colleges and the service academies had gathered to discuss the quality of U.S. representation abroad by tourists, businessmen, the government, and the military. According to the article, students had condemned the overseas practices of businessmen who were willing to do anything for a profit, including playing "footsie" with dictators. They also indicted the practice of appointing businessmen to high political positions, because their profit-seeking motivations often were opposed to the nation's best interests (Norgren to Eisenhower, Mar. 16, 1960, same file as the document).

[3] Norgren had described a recent poll of college students that indicated, he said, that students wanted jobs and security, but did not seem to care if they were provided by industry or government. He observed: "Socialism was not spelled out, but how better could one define it?" Norgren had also sent Eisenhower a copy of the letter outlining his concerns, a copy of which he had sent to the heads of all the universities represented at the assembly (*ibid.*; see for example, Norgren to Davidson, Mar. 15, 1960, same file as document).

[4] See no. 1666 for developments. At a Republican breakfast held in Chicago on July 27, Eisenhower would criticize the socialist philosophy and practices of an unnamed "'fairly friendly European country,'" suggesting they were related to the high rates of suicide and alcoholism there. It was understood that he was referring to Sweden, and his comments would cause a stir among Swedish officials and the media (*New York Times*, July 28, 29, and Aug. 6, 1960). In this letter to Norgren, Eisenhower was alluding to his views on the many social welfare, tax and institutional reforms that Sweden had adopted. In 1959, for example, the government had established a universal and compulsory supplementary pension system, one which had gone beyond basic social security provisions (Leif Lewin, *Ideology and Strategy: A Century of Swedish Politics* [New York, 1988], pp. 204–37).

To ERNEST FREDERICK HOLLINGS   March 22, 1960

Dear Governor Hollings: My friend, George Humphrey, has sent on to me a copy of the sketch which depicts a scene described as being "Near Barnwell, S.C."[1] In the correspondence that is attached I find no mention of the very great sense of distinction my companion and I feel in being selected for the kind of advertisement that only matinee idols ordinarily merit.[2] Personally I think I shall have a number of copies struck off in color and send them along to friends who, like myself, need the publicity.[3]

In any event, I share George Humphrey's gratification that South Carolina and Georgia have settled their differences by negotiation and found no need for seeking out any other kind of battlefield.[4]

With best wishes, *Sincerely*

---

[1] Hollings (B.A. The Citadel 1942; LL.B. University of South Carolina 1947) had been governor of South Carolina since 1959. He had served as a member of the South Carolina House of Representatives (1948–1954) and as lieutenant governor of South Carolina (1955–1959). The sketch had appeared in several well-known publications as an advertisement for industry and tourism in South Carolina. A South Carolina advertising agency had engaged a New York artist who apparently had photographed Humphrey and Eisenhower as they rode in a shooting buggy near Humphrey's Thomasville, Georgia, plantation; the artist had then used the photograph as the basis for the artwork in the ad (Hollings to Vandiver, Jan. 18, 1960). On this same day the President would send a similar letter to Georgia Governor Samuel Ernest Vandiver (A.B. University of Georgia; LL.B. 1942).

[2] On March 15 Humphrey had written to Governor Vandiver that he was sending the correspondence between Vandiver and Hollings to the "other gentleman" pictured [i.e., Eisenhower], who was sure to "get a great kick out of it" (Humphrey to Vandiver, AWF/D).

On January 18 Hollings had apologized to Vandiver and the people of Thomasville (AWF/D). He had been unaware of the origins of the sketch, but pointed out that the published caption "near Barnwell" was technically accurate: "We think Georgia and Thomasville are near Barnwell—thank the Lord." Hollings said he had canceled the advertisement and would do anything the Georgia governor suggested to correct the mistake.

On February 29 Vandiver had written Humphrey that he had "accosted" Hollings for "using Georgia scenery. . . ." Vandiver had enclosed Hollings's January 18 letter to him, a letter which he claimed was "proof of South Carolina's perfidy."

[3] In fact, the President had painted this same picture in 1959 (see Davis, *The Eisenhower College Collection*, plate 42). See also Ann Whitman memorandum, March 17, 1960, AWF/AWD.

[4] In his letter to Vandiver, Humphrey said he had been impressed by the apology from South Carolina's governor to Georgia's governor, an apology which had avoided "serious litigation and recriminations." Humphrey added that he had enjoyed the episode and had been grateful to Vandiver for the spirit in which it was accepted. All correspondence is in AWF/D.

To George Edward Allen   *March 22, 1960*

Dear George: Herewith a copy of a letter sent to me by Colonel Turner (which I believe you have already seen).[1] Also I am enclosing, in an unsealed envelope addressed to him, a proposed reply. I direct your attention particularly to the second paragraph.[2]

I leave it to you to determine the advisability of mailing this letter. By no means do I want to hurt his feelings, but at the same time I am clear in my mind that I should not want the La Quinta people to undertake the proposed project.

So—it's all yours! Just let me know *if* you mail the letter or what changes you would suggest.[3] *As ever*

[1] The President had vacationed at Allen's home in La Quinta, California, January 28–February 2 (*New York Times*, Jan. 13, 28, 29, 30, 31, Feb. 1, 2, 1960). Courtney S. Turner was vice-president of Montgomery and Sutter Building Company in San Francisco. On March 17 he had thanked Eisenhower for taking the time to tour the golf course at the new La Quinta Country Club (AWF/Misc.: Miscellaneous Corr.).
[2] During the tour Turner had suggested that a cottage be constructed for the Eisenhowers' personal use on the grounds of the country club. The President would reply (Mar. 23, 1960, AWF/D) that he was "deeply touched" by the offer, but he was forced to decline because he and Mrs. Eisenhower wished to spend vacation periods "in different areas and in different localities." He added that they wanted to visit the area from time to time and when there he hoped to use the playing privileges so kindly extended to him by the country club.
[3] There is no reply in AWF.

1465   *EM, AWF,*
                                           International Series: Chile

To Jorge Alessandri Rodríquez   *March 23, 1960*
Cable

The report of the agreement between the Governments of Chile and Argentina on procedures to deal with the outstanding boundary problems which you discussed with me is welcome news indeed.[1] This act of high statesmanship in settling international differences by peaceful and cooperative means is an example to all of the nations of the Americas. Please accept my congratulations and personal best wishes. *Sincerely*

[1] The governments of Chile and Argentina had announced they would submit to arbitration their border disputes involving a region in the southern Andes and the Bea-

gle Channel (*New York Times*, Mar. 23, 26, 30, 1960). He sent this same message by telegram to Argentinian President Arturo Frondizi (Mar. 23, 1960, AWF/I: Argentina), with whom he had discussed the issue during his trip (see no. 1403; see also State, *Foreign Relations, 1958–1960*, vol. V, *American Republics*, p. 621, and Microfiche Supplement CL-28). The full text of the agreement, which would not be released until March 30, stated that the British Queen would be asked to arbitrate one dispute and the Swiss president to arbitrate other disputes that might develop (excluding the Beagle Channel issue, which was to be decided by the International Court of Justice). The agreement also contained a surprise clause: in case either arbiter declined to serve, then the countries might appeal to the President of the United States to appoint a substitute. Secretary of State Herter would agree to Eisenhower giving his tacit acceptance, even though the State Department had not been consulted in advance and had not received official notification of the stipulation. Herter would suggest that it was unlikely that Eisenhower would be required to act, but that the clause was "evidently intended as recognition of the interest you demonstrated in this matter during your recent South American trip and as an expression of confidence in you" (Herter to Eisenhower, Apr. 14, 1960; see also Alessandri to Eisenhower, Mar. 24, 1960, both in AWF/I: Chile; Frondizi to Eisenhower, Apr. 20, 1960, AWF/I: Argentina; and Howe to Herter, Mar. 30, 1960, AWF/D-H).

1466   *EM, AWF, International Series: Mateos*

To Adolfo López Mateos   *March 23, 1960*

Dear Mr. President:[1] I have received your courteous letters of February tenth, February fifteenth, and March seventh.[2] The remarkable parallel of purpose in our two visits to South America, independently conceived and independently expressed, exemplifies the closeness of the relationship that exists between our two countries. The cordial welcome that attended both visits was evidence that this relationship is an important element in furthering the solidarity of the American system. Incidentally, wherever I went I heard only expressions of the most profound satisfaction that you found it possible to make the visit and of admiration for what you had to say.

In my own case, I took the opportunity, in discussions with leaders of Brazil, Argentina, Chile, and Uruguay, to assure them of the deep interest of the United States in the just aspirations of the peoples of the Americas, an interest we are prepared to show through existing institutions which we hope will be increasingly utilized by the countries of this hemisphere.[3]

Mrs. Eisenhower joins me in reciprocating the good wishes and cordial friendship you so graciously express.

With warm regard, *Sincerely*

[1] This message, drafted by State Department officials and edited by Eisenhower, was cabled to the American embassy in Mexico City for delivery to President López Ma-

teos. Secretary Herter recommended that the message be made public only on the initiative of the Mexican president (Herter to Eisenhower, Mar. 19, 1960, AWF/I: Mateos).

[2] In López Mateos's first letter the Mexican leader had thanked Eisenhower for his January 8 message commemorating the fiftieth anniversary of flight in Mexico (Eisenhower to López Mateos, Jan. 8, 1960; Calhoun to Fox, Jan. 7, 1960; and López Mateos to Eisenhower, Feb. 10, 1960, *ibid.*). His subsequent letters described his activities and accomplishments during his three-week trip to six South American countries, as well as the similarities in purpose between that trip and Eisenhower's (López Mateos to Eisenhower, Feb. 15, Mar. 7, 1960, *ibid.* For background on both trips see no. 1403; see also Eisenhower, *Waging Peace*, pp. 525–33).

[3] For Eisenhower's discussions with the South American leaders see State, *Foreign Relations, 1958–1960*, vol. V, *American Republics*, pp. 607–9, 619–24, 757–58, 764–66, and 801.

1467   *EM, AWF,*
                                                    Ann Whitman Diary Series

MEMORANDUM FOR THE RECORD   *March 23, 1960*

Governor Hatfield brought Senator Lusk to my office to call.[1] I promised Senator Lusk that at the first time I had an opportunity, I would arrange a chopper trip around the city, since he used to live here many, many years ago—in fact, he is a fourth generation Washingtonian. I told him I would try to do it when I was going to Gettysburg some day, he could go with me and after dropping me he could come back on the Eastern boundaries of Washington.[2]

Foreign Minister Castiella of Spain informed me very confidentially that Franco will soon give the Protestants freedom of worship in Spain, but it is taking some little bit of time to swing public opinion around to it. He seemed to think this would take place in three or four months.[3]

[1] Oregon governor Hatfield and Judge Hall Stoner Lusk (A.B. Georgetown University 1904), who had been appointed to fill a vacant Senate seat resulting from a death, were photographed with Eisenhower during their visit to the Oval Office. Lusk took the oath as Senator on this same day. A Democrat, the seventy-two year old Lusk had resigned from the State Supreme Court and would retire from the Senate after the November elections. (President's daily appointments, Mar. 23, 1960; *New York Times*, Mar. 16, 24, and Aug. 7, 1960).

[2] Eisenhower would not meet with Lusk again.

[3] Fernando Maria Castiella y Maiz (University of Madrid), Spain's foreign minster since 1957, was a professor of international law and a member of the Permanent Court of International Arbitration. He had previously served as ambassador to Peru and to the Vatican. Meeting with Castiella on this same day, Eisenhower had discussed the issue of religious freedom for Protestants (see *New York Times*, Mar. 24, 1960). Castiella had assured the President that the Spanish government was working

on a permanent solution to this "delicate problem," but that the opposition of "fa-natical extremists" had to be overcome. The President's initiative, he said, had been helpful, but it had to be evident that any measures taken by Spain were voluntary and not in response to pressure from an outside source. Eisenhower had discussed the matter during his meeting with Spanish dictator Francisco Franco y Bahamonde in Spain on December 22 (see nos. 1359 and 1382). The President had told Franco that he had been petitioned to address this subject because some Protestant groups were complaining that they were not permitted to use the churches they had built in Spain. The President had added that increased religious tolerance would strengthen U.S.-Spanish friendship (Memorandum of Conversation on the Situation of Spanish Protestants, Mar. 23, 1960, AWF/I: Spain; State, *Foreign Relations 1958–1960*, vol. VII, *Western Europe*, pt. 2, pp. 747–49, 763–65, 767). In April, the Spanish Foreign Ministry would respond with a memorandum that Herter would describe as a disappointing "apologia and statement of intent rather than an exposition of ac-tion already taken with regard to the status of non-Catholics in Spain." The Spanish authorities would again ask that the views expressed in the memo be kept secret pending action in order that it not appear they were responding to U.S. pressure (Herter to Eisenhower, Apr. 20, 1960, AWF/I: Spain). See no. 1479 for developments. Eisenhower would write in his memoirs that he later heard that restrictions had been loosened (Eisenhower, *Waging Peace*, pp. 509–10).

1468   *EM, WHCF,*
                                                        President's Personal File 196

To Robert Daniel Murphy   *March 23, 1960*

Dear Bob: Because you are one who has served in this Administra-tion, I am confident that you share with me beliefs about America's needs, now and in the years ahead. Your own efforts have con-tributed to seven years of honest, efficient, progressive government.[1] During this time we have nurtured our economy on sound princi-ples, appropriately ministered to human needs, and met the tremen-dous challenge posed by our leadership among nations. As a nation we are strong and devoted to peace throughout the world.

This is, in large part, a Republican record. I am of the conviction that if our country is to continue to enjoy the benefits of sound pro-gressive government, the best way is through the Republican Party. I believe that at this time in our history our Party is the only political instrument that can provide the united, cohesive leadership vital to an America that must continuingly grow in strength and health.

Only eight months remain before the 1960 elections. There is much work to be done by all of us who share political beliefs of the kind to which I have referred above. For us the job is to translate the Republican record of achievement since 1953 into a portrait that all Americans can understand. Our task is to present this record and our Party's programs reaching into the future so forcefully and cogently that they will command Republican victory in 1960. This job cannot wait—it must get under way now.

As a former member of this Administration, you are in a position to be particularly effective in this effort. I am asking you and others to participate as active Administration alumni in this work. This effort will include speaking in behalf of the Republican record and programs, fund raising, assisting the Republican organization in seeking qualified new candidates, and participation in other phases of the pre-election activities. If your schedule permits you to participate in this kind of work, I hope that you will promptly inform the Chairman of the National Committee.[2] He will furnish you details of planned activities.

Because this letter is addressed to a sizeable number of individuals who have held important positions in this Administration, it may seem somewhat formal.[3] But in your case, I trust that, in view of our close friendship and association, you will consider it more as a sharing with you of my thoughts on the coming campaign rather than as any attempt to point out the path of political duty.

With warm regard, *Sincerely*

[1] On former Under Secretary of State for Political Affairs Murphy's retirement from the Foreign Service and State Department see no. 1356.

[2] Senator Thruston B. Morton (Kentucky) had replaced the retiring Meade Alcorn as the Republican National Chairman on April 11, 1959 (*New York Times*, Apr. 12, 1959); he would be reelected to the position in July 1960. On Eisenhower's efforts to attain speakers for the 1960 campaign see no. 1411.

[3] See, for example, Eisenhower to Murray, March 17, 1960, same file as document. Eisenhower would continue to use Murphy for diplomatic tasks; see no. 1572 and Murphy, *Diplomat Among Warriors*, pp. 332–38. There is, however, no record that Murphy participated in the 1960 political campaign.

1469   *EM, WHCF, Official File 156-F*

To Sarah A. Ferguson   *March 23, 1960*

Dear Sarah: Thank you for your letter of the eighteenth.[1] I assure you that the Administration, and particularly the Secretary of Labor, have been very interested in problems involving workers who are denied rewarding employment because they happen to be over forty-five years of age.[2] This arbitrary bar to the full utilization of their abilities causes a waste of valuable skills and talents and must be eliminated. I am bringing to the attention of Secretary Mitchell the letter that you enclosed and asking that he write you in more detail regarding the matter.[3]

I hope all is well with you.
With warm regard, *Sincerely*

[1] Ferguson, Eisenhower's cousin (see Galambos and van Ee, *The Middle Way*, no. 981), had asked the President who to contact in Washington about age discrimination labor laws. She had enclosed a copy of a letter sent by an unemployed 49-year-old Californian to his congressman asking that laws and government contracts be amended to prevent age discrimination, in the same way they prohibited racial and religious discrimination (Ferguson to Eisenhower, Mar. 18, and Stoll to Hosmer, Mar. 15, 1960, both in the same file as the document).

[2] For Eisenhower's previous comments on this issue see Galambos and van Ee, *The Middle Way*, no. 1162.

[3] Eisenhower had handwritten in the margins of the letter a note to Secretary of Labor James Mitchell asking: "*Why* couldn't we put something in contract specifications (or conditions) of this kind?" (Whitman to Mitchell, Mar. 25, 1960, same file as the document). There is no reply from Mitchell in the file. This issue would not be resolved during Eisenhower's term.

1470   *EM, AWF, DDE Diaries Series*

TO WILLIAM SAMUEL PALEY   *March 23, 1960*

Dear Bill: Thank you very much for your note.[1] I am only sorry that the circumstances surrounding the suggestion I made to you some years back have given you concern. I assure you that in spite of my regret that you could not join me, I instantly and cheerfully accepted your decision.[2]

I, too, greatly enjoyed our breakfast conversation—and I hope I shall see you again in the not too distant future.[3]

With warm regard, *As ever*

P.S. And for goodness sake, never hesitate to let me have a message from you at any moment you have anything you'd like to communicate to me.

[1] Paley, chairman of the board of the Columbia Broadcasting Company, had written on March 19 (AWF/D).

[2] In October 1954 the President has asked Paley to join the White House staff to handle cold war matters (for background see Galambos and van Ee, *The Middle Way*, no. 1095). Paley had written that he was afraid he had declined "in an awkward way" and felt that he had suffered in Eisenhower's esteem. He said that in an earlier meeting with Eisenhower's "emissary," he had made it clear that he could not accept the assignment. Paley thought that his declination should have spared Eisenhower the "business of making the offer" and himself the "hardship and embarrassment of saying 'No.'" He added that he had declined for personal reasons and feared that he had appeared selfish and ungrateful. He wanted Eisenhower to know that he had been "most appreciative" of the offer, and would "always regret" that he had to decline.

³ On March 16 Eisenhower had hosted an off-the-record breakfast for Paley. The President next would meet with Paley on December 1.

1471   *EM, AWF, Ann Whitman Diary Series*

NOTE   *March 24, 1960*

The marked sentence evidences the lack of understanding of most people as to the reasons for sending soldiers to Little Rock. The soldiers were to (1) see that order of a federal court should not be obstructed by mob violence or (2) by improperly used authority of a state official.¹

¹ Eisenhower's comments were written on a newsletter sent by New Hampshire Republican Senator Norris Cotton to his constituents on March 24, 1960. The newsletter, which was forwarded to Ann Whitman by presidential aide Jack Z. Anderson, dealt with the congressional debate over strengthening the 1957 Civil Rights Act (see *Congressional Quarterly Almanac*, vol. XVI, *1960*, pp. 191–97). After explaining his support for congressional efforts to ensure voting rights, Cotton had taken up the question of school desegregation. He reported that 798 school districts in 17 states had already started desegregating, a record which he claimed was "surprisingly good" and was "a far cry from 90 years of frustration in the field of citizenship." The progress made in integration did not "support the belief that the law now on our books is 'too gentle'" and did not "justify resorting to the club and the bayonet." Eisenhower had underlined this last passage. For background see nos. 330, 357, and 359. For developments see no. 1519.

1472   *EM, AWF, DDE Diaries Series*

TO NELSON ALDRICH ROCKEFELLER   *March 24, 1960*

Dear Nelson: I know that you are involved in an effort to secure the approval of the New York Legislature for a fallout shelter program in your State.¹ This being the case, it would not only be improper but possibly counter-productive if I should attempt to make recommendations in a matter that the citizens of New York would naturally consider their own business. However, it is not out of place, I think, for me to recall to you personal statements of mine that I have heretofore made public. These include such examples as:²

    "Civil defense requires the combined effort of individual citizens and government at the Federal, State and local levels."

    "We have been spared from warfare on our own soil for so long that the psychological climate in our country is not favorable to the voluntary basis for home defense. Nevertheless the problem is there and must be faced."

In the spring of 1958 I said:[3]

"In the event of nuclear attack on this country, fallout shelters offer the best single non-military defense measure for the protection of the greatest numbers of our people."

And only last summer I had this to say:

"Along with our military defense and retaliatory forces, civil defense and defense mobilization are vital parts of the nation's total defense—together they stand as a strong deterrent to war."

In any event, your efforts help to focus public attention on the importance of this subject; if we can get all the facts before the public we can abide, with confidence, on the decision of our people.[4]

With warm regard, *As ever*

---

[1] For background on the radioactive fallout task force see no. 1267. Early in January New York Governor Rockefeller, fearing that nearly 5 million New Yorkers could be killed in the event of a nuclear war, had proposed legislation that would have required all homeowners in his state to spend at least $150 on the construction of fallout shelters in or near their houses or apartment buildings. The measure would also have required schools to teach about the dangers of radioactivity (*New York Times*, Jan. 7, Feb. 23, Apr. 1, 1960).

[2] The following two paragraphs were taken from an earlier letter (no. 1267) that Eisenhower had sent Rockefeller in support of his fallout shelter program.

[3] We have been unable to locate the source of the quotations in the next two paragraphs.

[4] Political pressure from state lawmakers facing reelection would force Rockefeller to accept modifications that would have made the shelter program voluntary, with tax benefits and reduced property assessments for those who chose to participate. The New York legislature, however, would adjourn without taking action on the bill (*New York Times*, Mar. 31, Apr. 1, 1960). For more on Eisenhower's views on fallout shelters see no. 1576.

1473   *EM, WHCF, President's Personal File 238*

To WILLIAM MYERS LEE   *March 24, 1960*

Dear Billy: Your letter poses a pretty big question, while at the same time I am pleased by the compliment implicit in your writing me.[1]

But to try to answer you specifically: I would, if I were you, learn just as much about our country and the world as you possibly can; I would concentrate particularly on our history and what made America the great nation that it is. I would want to take all the science courses that are available in order more adequately to understand the developments that are certain to be made in the new era just opening up. And I would want to become proficient in one or more languages other than our own.

Perhaps you mean by asking what you should "aim toward," what profession I would advise. That I cannot begin to suggest, but if I were you I would simply try to be the best possible citizen of the United States. To this end you need to be informed on both domestic and international issues, and be aware of and understand the events that take place every day in the world around us. And as to what you should "do," I suspect you can do no better than live by the high precepts I know your parents have taught you.

If you do all of this, you will do more for me and for the rest of the people of our country than you possibly can now realize.[2] I have no doubt that you will grow up to be a fine citizen in every respect.

With affectionate regard, *Sincerely*[3]

[1] Eleven-year-old Lee was the son of Ernest Rose ("Tex") Lee, Eisenhower's former aide (for background see Galambos, *Columbia University*, nos. 27 and 192). Lee had asked the President for advice on what a sixth-grade boy should "read, aim toward" and do "everyday to grow up to be as fine a person as you are."

[2] The boy also asked the President to request "one special thing" of him to do in Eisenhower's honor.

[3] Eisenhower signed the letter, "Uncle Ike."

1474   *EM, WHCF, Official File 115-D-2*

To Fred Lazarus, Jr.   *March 25, 1960*

Dear Fred: Your letter of March twenty-first proposes a highly appealing suggestion for dealing forthrightly with debt reduction.[1] Along with its merits, it presents some difficulties, not the least of which is the tendency for some people to look for a political motive in anything a President does in his last months in office.

I am having Bob Anderson and Maurice Stans take a careful look at your suggestion, and at the same time I am asking them to see if they can develop a method whereby a systematic annual payment on the debt could be made standard budgetary procedure. Legislation may be required to initiate this in the way you suggest.[2]

I believe this is the best way to deal with the matter for the present. I will ask one of them to write you further after their views are crystallized.[3]

You have my best wishes for a fine trip and, as always, my warm regard. *Sincerely*

¹ Lazarus, Chairman of Federated Department Stores, had written on March 21 (same file as document) to propose an alternative to Eisenhower's suggestion, made in the 1960 State of the Union Address, that $4 billion of the estimated 1960–61 federal budget surplus revenues should be kept intact and used later to pay down the national debt (see *Public Papers of the Presidents: Eisenhower, 1960–61*, p. 13). Director of the Bureau of the Budget Maurice Stans may have drafted this letter for the President (see Persons to Stans, Mar. 28, 1960, same file as document).

² Lazarus had suggested that Eisenhower should increase his budget by $4 billion, the estimated amount of the surplus, and that Congress should then appropriate $4 billion for debt reduction as part of a balanced budget. This procedure would, he believed, reduce the pressure for "unwise" congressional spending, reduce pressure for unwarranted tax cuts, and reinforce the position of the dollar in the world.

³ Stans would write the President on July 8, 1960 (AWF/A), that he supported Lazarus's idea and had, along with Treasury Secretary Robert Anderson, drafted a joint resolution of Congress to retire debt at the rate of one percent a year. He had, however, been advised by Chairman of the Council of Economic Advisors Raymond Saulnier and Presidential Assistant for Economic Affairs Don Paarlberg that this proposal was unwise. Saulnier had written (Saulnier to Stans, June 29, 1960, AWF/A) that although the basic objective of the proposal was "highly desirable," certain other aspects seemed to raise "serious problems." He was concerned that the proposal might reduce the "free and flexible use of fiscal policy." Stans would write: "Under the circumstances, it seems that, while some of us had hoped that an effective plan could be developed, there is such difference of opinion that nothing fruitful has been found. We will continue to try to find a solution, but I am not optimistic that an agreed course is possible." As it turned out, there would be a $3.3 billion budget deficit in 1960–61.

1475   *EM, AWF, DDE Diaries Series*

To George Champion   *March 25, 1960*

Dear George: I am much interested in your letter of the twenty-second, and I am grateful to you for taking the trouble to write me at such length.[1]

As to my visits to Pakistan and India, I can only say that the entire experience was infinitely rewarding. It helped me gain a greater understanding of the problems of those countries at first hand (and as you know, no amount of reports or documents can substitute for that first hand knowledge, even if [it] has to be gained in a short period of time). More importantly, the visits demonstrated vividly the great friendship that the peoples of those countries hold for our country and its citizens.

I shall ask the State Department to consider your suggestions, both as to Prime Minister Tunku Abdul Rahman and as to a stopover in the Philippines (which has been under advisement). Much as I should like to do both things, there is always a limit to what I can undertake with a reasonable chance of carrying it off successfully.[2]

Any time you are in Washington, I should like to see you—and I know Doug Dillon would, too. It occurs to me that you may be planning to be in Augusta after the Master's, at which time we could have a talk. But if you are here before then, just give my office a ring—I am sure we can work out a time convenient for us both.[3]

With warm regard, *As ever*

[1] Returning from a trip around the world, Champion, president of Chase Manhattan Bank and a golfing friend of Eisenhower, had told the President that people in Pakistan and India were still affected by his visit, which had had "a profound effect for good throughout both nations."

[2] Champion had praised the leadership of Malayan Prime Minister Tunku Abdul Rahman Putra al-Haj "in handling the Communists and in developing a program of freedom, education and economic well-being in his country." Rahman, former minister for Internal Defence and Security, had helped negotiate independence for the Federation of Malaya and had first become prime minister in August 1957. He would have a significant influence on other countries in Southeast Asia, Champion wrote, and he believed that an invitation to visit the United States would greatly enhance Rahman's position.

Champion had also reported on encouraging plans in the Philippines that he believed would help solve that country's economic problems. The people of the Philippines had "a deep affection" for Eisenhower, Champion wrote, and even a day's stop there during his Far Eastern trip would "be one of the greatest morale builders that that nation could possibly receive" (Champion to Eisenhower, Mar. 22, 1960, WHCF/OF 151-A; on Eisenhower's visits to Pakistan and India see nos. 1388 and 1389; see also State, *Foreign Relations, 1958–1960*, vol. XV, *South and Southeast Asia*, pp. 781–94, 521–26).

Eisenhower would visit the Philippines on June 14–16. For more on the Far Eastern trip see no. 1529.

[3] Eisenhower would be in Augusta on April 11–21. Champion would arrive for a two-day visit on April 11 (see Champion to Eisenhower, Apr. 1, 1960, WHCF/OF 151-A). For developments see no. 1500; see also Herter to Champion, Mar. 30, 1960, AWF/D-H.

1476   *EM, AWF, Name Series*

To SAMUEL GOLDWYN   *March 25, 1960*
Personal

Dear Sam: Thank you for your prompt repudiation of the attempt of TIME Magazine to put into your mouth words to the effect that you condemned "the United States foreign policy mess." Your wholehearted approval of this foreign policy is more than gratifying.[1]

Last evening my family and I saw "Porgy and Bess." It was beautifully done and all of us enjoyed it. Thank you very much for making the film available for our viewing.[2]

There is another point on which I should like to hear your comments. In recent weeks I have been repeatedly told by different people that Dick Nixon will be unable to obtain any significant portion of the Jewish vote. Time and again I have asked for an explanation, and the only one I get is that they "hate him."

I happen to know that several years ago Dick was honored by one or two of the Jewish organizations—either the Anti-Defamation League or B'nai B'rith, I cannot recall which.[3] He has spoken more than once in support of their annual fund raising affairs and, so far as I know, has had good relations with many members of the Jewish community.

Nevertheless, the frequency with which these allegations come to me prompts me to ask a question in three parts: (A) do you believe these charges; (b) if so, what is the reason for them; and (c) if they are true, what can Dick or you or I or any one else do to develop a better understanding between him and the community?[4]

Thanks again for your note.

With warm regard, *As ever*

[1] In its section on "People," the current issue of *Time* magazine (Mar. 28, 1960) had quoted Hollywood producer Samuel Goldwyn as having enumerated the problems faced by Nixon in the presidential contest as "The defense budget, the U.S. foreign policy mess, Castro. And that H-bomb. That's dynamite!" On March 24 Goldwyn had written the publisher of *Time* (AWF/N), complaining that "no such statement was ever made" and expressing his amazement that *Time* would publish it "without any attempt at verification." Goldwyn emphasized that he was a "great admirer of President Eisenhower, and wholeheartedly approve his foreign policy." He had asked for a retraction.

[2] On the troubled making of *Porgy and Bess*, released in June 1959, see A. Scott Berg, *Goldwyn: A Biography* (New York, 1989), pp. 478–87.

[3] Eisenhower may have been referring to Nixon's California Senate race against Helen Gahagan Douglas, during which Nixon faced accusations of anti-Semitism. These charges prompted the Anti-Defamation League of B'nai B'rith to issue a statement exonerating Nixon of religious bigotry (Roger Morris, *Richard Milhous Nixon: The Rise of An American Politician* [New York, 1990], p. 599; see also Irwin F. Gellman, *The Contender: Richard Nixon: The Congress Years, 1946–1952* [New York, 1999], pp. 317–18, 341).

[4] There is no written response from Goldwyn in EM.

1477   *EM, AWF, Name Series*

To JOHN REAGAN MCCRARY   *March 25, 1960*
Personal and confidential

Dear Tex: I scanned the ESQUIRE story as you requested. I have never before heard of the author, but I can tell you that almost every one of his sentences carries some distortion, misunderstanding or exaggeration. If it were possible for Dick to talk as freely as some of the Democratic hopefuls, there would of course be no possibility of such a story appearing in print. But it is quite difficult to be the single accepted "candidate" of a political party and at the same time have to abstain from acting like one who is already the "*nominee*."[1]

Incidentally, I am told, repeatedly, that the Jewish vote is all against Nixon. Everybody should get to work to change this.[2]

In view of the invisibility that is, for the moment, imposed upon Dick by circumstances, I believe that a bit of interest might be stirred up if we should get stories going about possible Vice Presidential nominees. Without even attempting to make a complete slate or to list the following in any priority, I think of such people as Cabot Lodge, Nelson Rockefeller, Bob Anderson, Thruston Morton, Jim Mitchell, Chuck Percy, Fred Seaton, Bill Rogers, Arthur Flemming, Jerry Ford, Charlie Halleck, Pres Bush, General Gruenther, Hugh Scott, Neil McElroy, and others of this same type and roughly of the same age group. I should think some stories and speculation on this subject might stir up some interest.[3]

With warm regard, *Sincerely*

[1] Eisenhower was referring to "Ike *vs.* Nixon," an article by Joseph Kraft in the April 1960 *Esquire*, which McCrary had enclosed in his letter of March 22, 1960 (AWF/N). After examining the differences in the background, education and experiences of the two men, he had found a "coolness" in their relationship. Kraft explored what he termed Eisenhower's two moves "to bar Mr. Nixon from the Vice-Presidency," and his failure to voice support for Nixon's presidential candidacy.

McCrary had said he was "deeply worried" about the tempo of Nixon's campaign as well as the stories planted by the "boys in the Kennedy camp" about the "'feud' between you and Dick." The President's endorsement of Nixon's candidacy on March 16, he believed, had come "just in time" (*New York Times*, Mar. 17, 1960).

[2] See the preceding document.

[3] On the suitability of Anderson, Lodge, Mitchell, McElroy, Rockefeller, Rogers, Morton, Halleck, and Gruenther for the vice-presidency see no. 1411. On Percy, Flemming and Seaton see *ibid*. Gerald Ford had been a Republican Congressman from Michigan since 1949; Prescott Bush had been Republican Senator from Connecticut since 1952; and Hugh Scott had been Republican Senator from Pennsylvania since 1959.

1478   *EM, AWF, DDE Diaries Series*

To Lester Markel   *March 25, 1960*

Dear Lester: I spoke to the Vice President about your desire to have a talk with him.[1] He is not only agreeable; he is anxious to make such an appointment with you. He told me that he would initiate the communication to you, but if you sense any delay I suggest that you drop him a note yourself.

I thoroughly enjoyed my talk with you the other day.

With warm regard, *Sincerely*

[1] Markel, Sunday editor for the *New York Times* since 1923, had met with Eisenhower and Press Secretary Jim Hagerty off the record for one hour and twenty minutes on March 14. There is no further communication on this subject in AWF. No Markel news story resulted from this meeting.

1479   *EM, AWF,*
International Series:
Spain

To Francisco Franco y Bahamonde   *March 26, 1960*
Confidential

Dear General Franco: Thank you for your interesting and cordial letter of March eighteenth delivered to me by your Foreign Minister when he called on me on March twenty-third.[1]

I was glad to meet Mr. Castiella again and to have the chance to exchange views with him on a number of topics.[2] He said some kind things about the lasting effects of my visit to Madrid, which I was gratified to hear. You already know how much I enjoyed my stay in your impressive capital.[3]

Your views on the international drive of Soviet communism are of considerable interest to me. I share your view that the communist offensive is not exclusively military and that the chief battleground today is in the field of politics and economics.[4] During my conversation with Mr. Castiella I agreed that U.S. economic assistance alone cannot enable the Latin American and other nations to achieve the economic growth and political stability that they desire. These objectives can be reached only through the willing efforts of the people of those countries themselves.[5] Incidentally, the Latin American officials with whom I talked themselves emphasized this truth.[6]

We are, of course, aware of the great interest recently shown by the Soviets and Chinese communists in Latin America, especially the new regime in Cuba; and this problem is receiving our close attention.[7]

I am convinced that the communist system cannot ultimately satisfy the urge of people for a better life under conditions of individual freedom and human dignity. It is encouraging to note that although communist dictatorship continues, the Soviet Government has made some changes which have resulted in a better life for the Soviet people than existed under Stalin. Our hope is that this trend will continue and that the Soviet regime ultimately will evolve into one which does not threaten the rest of the world. Our policy of exchanges of persons and ideas with Soviet Bloc countries is aimed at furthering this trend.

It is evident to me, however, that we cannot afford to relax our struggle against communism in the hope that eventually communism will reform itself into a system that we need not fear. We must, therefore, continue actively to implement our policy of collective security and related policies for checking communist expansion, while at the same time exploiting such opportunities as offer themselves to ascertain the readiness of the Soviet government to arrive at mutually acceptable solutions of at least some of the outstanding problems in our international relations.

I hope you will accept my thanks for the thought-provoking message which your letter contains. I send to you and Mrs. Franco my best wishes.[8] *Sincerely*

[1] See no. 1467.

[2] The President and Castiella had discussed Eisenhower's trip to South America (see no. 1403); religious tolerance of Protestants in Spain (see no. 1467); and the nation's economic stabilization efforts; mention was made of changes in the costs of living, and Spain's tourist industry (State, *Foreign Relations*, vol. VII, *Western Europe*, pt. 2, pp. 763–65).

[3] Castiella had told Eisenhower that the memory of his trip to Spain was still vivid in the minds of all Spaniards. Franco had written that the visit had been an occasion for Spain to demonstrate affection and enthusiasm for Eisenhower and the United States (*ibid.*, pp. 742–48, 751–53, 763).

[4] Franco had suggested that communism was waging a political campaign against the West, taking advantage of all the "weaknesses and faults in the Western political systems" and "exploiting with propaganda the natural longings for social betterment and a rise in the living standards which the popular masses so desire." Franco worried that many nations, without the economic and cultural advantages of the United States, would be unable to protect themselves against this propaganda. A second campaign, he said, was economic: the Soviet Union and its satellite countries were building up production and planned to flood world markets and create a catastrophe for the West. "Their experts were intensively working toward that end," he said, "as can be seen by examining the five-year plans being carried out in all those countries." Franco wanted to sound a "note of alarm" in these fields in which the West was "so trusting."

[5] Franco had noted Eisenhower's recent "offer of aid" to the nations of the Western hemisphere. He may have been referring to Eisenhower's statements about United States support made during his radio and television addresses to the nation on February 21 and March 4, 1960, in *Public Papers of the Presidents: Eisenhower, 1960–61*, pp. 202–7 and 282–87. Although Franco thought that outside aid could help ease economic difficulties, the heart of the problem lay in what the Latin American people themselves chose to do: they had to avoid civil strife; domestic disorder; and lax discipline (State, *Foreign Relations*, vol. VII, *Western Europe*, pt. 2, pp. 751–53, 756–58, 763).

[6] See no. 1403.

[7] The Soviets, Franco said, had failed repeatedly since 1935 in their attempts to subvert the Spanish people, and they were now attempting through Spanish communist agents to establish a Moscow-Havana axis aimed at subverting Hispanic America (State, *Foreign Relations*, vol. VII, *Western Europe*, pt. 2, pp. 751–53).

[8] Carmen Polo y Martínez Valdés de Franco, a staunch Roman Catholic, had married Franco in 1923 and was active in state matters.

1480   *EM, AWF, Administration Series*

TO FREDERICK HENRY MUELLER   *March 26, 1960*

Dear Fritz: I appreciate your consideration in sending me the information about your son's connection with and your lack of any interest in the Mueller Metals Corporation. It seems to me that you are in a good position to convince any fair-minded person that in this situation there is no conflict of interest.[1]

With warm regard, *As ever*

[1] Secretary of Commerce Mueller had written Eisenhower that Senator William Proxmire, a Democrat from Wisconsin, was questioning business dealings between his son's furniture company and the United States embassy in Caracas, Venezuela. Proxmire had written the State Department, he said, and had implied that the Secretary had been improperly involved in the transactions (Mueller to Eisenhower, Mar. 11, 1960, AWF/A). Mueller wrote the President that he had not used his influence to help his son gain the relevant contract, nor had he any financial interests in the Mueller Furniture Company. In June Proxmire, noting that the Secretary sat on the Foreign Service Buildings Committee that had let the contracts, would openly accuse Mueller and the State Department of improprieties. Publicly denying the accusation, Muelller would state that the committee had not met in ten years and had been stripped of its furniture buying power for twenty-five. Proxmire would admit that Mueller's son had not acted improperly (*New York Times,* June 14, 16, and 18, 1960).

1481   *EM, AWF, Administration Series*

TO GEORGE EDWARD ALLEN   *March 26, 1960*

Dear George: Enclosed is the material on cholesterol values.[1] Those items marked on the right are very satisfactory both from the standpoint of cholesterol and calories. Those marked "never" on the left are bad—nearly always—because of both high caloric and cholesterol content. The ones that are not marked at all can be used occasionally.[2] *As ever*

¹ The President had vacationed at Allen's home earlier this year (see no. 1464). For background on Eisenhower's interest in Allen's weight see, for example, nos. 1049 and 1053.

The material, copied from an article that had appeared in *Newsweek* on May 20, 1957, is in AWF/D. Eisenhower had enclosed an alphabetical list of food items and their caloric and cholesterol values; examples of unsaturated fats, semi-saturated fats, and saturated fats; a list of the cholesterol values in commonly used foods; and a picture chart.

² In addition to writing the word "never" next to such foods as butter and egg yolks, the President had placed check marks and comments next to specific items that Allen could eat or that seemed especially healthful.

1482   *EM, WHCF, Confidential File: FBI*

To Walter R. Drennan   *March 26, 1960*
Personal and Confidential

Dear Walter: Thank you for recalling to me our meeting, so many years ago, at Helen Gruber's home.¹

I have read Dr. Kraft's recent sermon, which I found attached to your letter.² I most heartily agree with him that security and peace are not to be found in arms alone. Nevertheless, in spite of this general agreement and, admitting some accuracy in a number of specific accusations he directs against many groups and organizations, I think he vastly weakens the persuasiveness of his arguments by couching his indictment in greatly exaggerated terms.

It is easy, for example, to condemn what he calls the "military mind." For my part I have never been able to define this term and, indeed, I find that my fairly heavy correspondence bears out the possibility that in many cases people wearing the uniform are far more broadminded than are many classes of civilians in expressing their conviction that our nation's safety is to be found in spiritual and economic strength rather than in military power alone.

In other portions of Dr. Kraft's discourse, I find insinuations or allegations made against American businessmen and firms that cannot be substantiated, in my judgment, when couched in such wide generalizations as he makes. The presidents and directors of large corporations are not all inhuman or wholly grasping. Dr. Kraft seemingly assumes that every businessman who invests in a foreign country is selfishly wicked. On the other hand, partially to refute this view, I cite some of my experiences with Latin American officials, both here in Washington and during my recent trip to that region.³ Without exception they seek—avidly—investment of American private capital in their countries. They much prefer private capital over public. These nations are ready to provide all sorts of guarantees that a North American dollar will be accorded the same protection and the same treatment as a domestic dollar in developing productive enterprises within their own areas.

On top of this, the minister implies that the Latin American community almost unanimously admires, respects and even likes Fidel Castro. I heard no such expression of approval of Castro's actions. One President said to me, "Castro the revolutionary enjoyed real prestige in Latin America; Castro the political leader has lost it all." On all sides I heard expressions of uneasiness born of the fear that Castro's excesses could seriously damage the solidarity of the Organization of American States, which so many have worked hard to promote. They deplore the extremist tone of most of his pronouncements.

Like most Americans, I was happy to see someone lead a movement that uprooted the old Batista dictatorship.[4] But I do not believe that any fair-minded man can find much to cheer about in the subsequent actions of the new ruler of Cuba.

There are many other statements made in the sermon that are at variance with the conclusions I have reached based upon all the information I can muster.

Enough of this. I simply wanted to point out why I applaud the underlying thought of Dr. Kraft's dissertation, even while I deplore the use of exaggerated or incorrect statements in supporting a thesis, no matter how worthy it may be.[5]

It was indeed good to hear from you after these many years.

With best wishes, *Sincerely*

[1] Drennan, a Chicago businessman, had written that he and his wife had met "Ike" in Washington long ago when they were visiting his sister, the former Helen L. Drennan, who was the wife of William Randolph Gruber (Mar. 18, 1960, same file as document). The President and Mrs. Eisenhower had first met Major and Mrs. Gruber when they were students at the Army Command and General Staff College at Fort Leavenworth, Kansas. The couples had toured Europe together in 1929 (Holt and Leyerzapf, *Eisenhower: The Prewar Diaries*, pp. 60, 84–97, and Susan E. Eisenhower, *Mrs. Ike*, pp. 100–108).
[2] Drennan had sent Eisenhower a copy of a sermon entitled, "Our Military Mania" which he said had been given by Virgil A. Kraft, Associate Pastor of the People's Church in Chicago, on March 6 (see no. 1483). Drennan had thought the sermon was "very complimentary" to the President. The sermon is not in EM.
[3] See no. 1403.
[4] For background on the Batista regime see no. 1142.
[5] For developments see the following document.

To J. Edgar Hoover   *March 28, 1960*
Confidential

Dear Edgar: I send to you, with no recommendation whatever, a sermon received by me from an acquaintance in Chicago. The sermon was delivered by Virgil A. Kraft, Associate Pastor of the "Peoples Church of Chicago." I think the individual who forwarded it thought I was going to be pleased by what he called the "complimentary" references to me.[1]

Please don't go to the trouble of making any detailed analysis, but I should very much like to have your general opinion of the tone of the document.[2] It seems to me that Mr. Kraft must be very gullible, to say the least.[3]

With warm regard, *As ever*

[1] See the preceding document.

[2] At the end of this letter, Eisenhower had handwritten "and, by no means, are you to look up Mr. Kraft himself."

[3] In his reply, FBI Director J. Edgar Hoover would agree with Eisenhower. He suggested that Kraft's statement that "'we are beginning to see red hobgoblins behind every tree'" showed an unrealistic appraisal of the fight against communism and that his demand for disarmament played directly into the hands of the Soviet enemy. Kraft's "utopian" assumption that the captive peoples behind the Iron Curtain would eventually "'break down the walls of economic and cultural regimentation'" by themselves indicated a "regrettable failure to face facts." Kraft had given a similar speech, Hoover reported, following his trip to the Soviet Union in 1958. FBI files showed that he "was also associated with a number of known Communist Party members" and was a member of groups that had been designated as Communist organizations by executive order (Hoover to Eisenhower, Mar. 30, 1960, same file as document). Eisenhower's brief thank-you note to Hoover (Mar. 31, 1960) is in *ibid.*

To William Edward Robinson   *March 28, 1960*

Dear Bill: Harold Macmillan and I may have problems—but they are as nothing compared to the chaos that would result if we let the erudite chairman of the board of a well-known soft drink company and/ or a supposedly well-informed White House press corps individual loose on the economy of our country.[1]

My only recommendation to you is to take the five cent machine out of the White House basement—but soon. We have too much talk of "discrimination" in this country as it is![2]

With warm regard, *As ever*

[1] On the international problems shared by British Prime Minister Macmillan and the President see, for example, no. 1459. Coca-Cola board chairman Robinson had sent Ann Whitman his "exposition of the Robinson Law of the Budget" by way of a series of letters between himself and senior White House correspondent Merriman Smith (see Galambos and van Ee, *The Middle Way*, no. 669) regarding prices of Coca-Cola in the White House. Making fun of Coca-Cola's business practices and Eisenhower Administration efforts to balance the federal budget, the correspondence had begun on March 18 when Smith wrote that Coca-Cola representatives had visited the White House press room to say that the price of soft drinks would be doubled—from a nickel to a dime. Smith said the representatives had explained that by doubling the price, profits on the machine would be three times greater. "Are dividends paid by your company also being tripled?" Smith had asked. Robinson had replied (Mar. 25) that a balanced budget was "sine qua non" in the fight against inflation. By doubling the prices, he explained, vending machine owners and the Coca-Cola Corporation made more profit and also paid more taxes; consequently, the stockholders received more dividends so they, too, had to pay more taxes. "How can the President miss balancing that budget," Robinson asked, "when with one Coke machine and a little ole thin dime we provide increased taxes from three different sources. This is what is known as replacing the vicious circle with a benign circumference. And you're complaining."
[2] In a later exchange (Mar. 27), Smith asked Robinson why the Coke machine in the White House basement (used by staff members) charged five cents and the machine in the press room upstairs charged ten cents. Robinson replied (Mar. 30) that either the bottler had forgotten about that machine or he thinks the "Democrats are going to get elected and he's waiting to raise the price on them, since they don't mind spending more—as everybody knows."

On April 5 Robinson would send the President a copy of his letter to Smith of the same date. All correspondence is in AWF/N, Robinson Corr.

1485   *EM, AWF, International Series: New Zealand*

TO WALTER NASH   *March 29, 1960*
Secret

Dear Prime Minister: I have learned with interest of your projected visit to the Soviet Union. It will offer opportunities for discussions between you and Mr. Khrushchev that can be most helpful, especially in connection with the forthcoming summit meeting.[1]

In the hope that some positive results may emerge from the meeting, I have been doing all that I could at Camp David and elsewhere to lay the foundations for it.[2] It occurs to me that there are a number of things which you might wish to do that would contribute to the accomplishment of some progress.

As a preliminary matter it is clear, I am sure you will agree, that the Soviet Union will be in a mood to engage in meaningful negotiations looking toward realistic solutions only if it is convinced that there is no opportunity for exploiting actual or seeming differences of views among the Free World countries. Anything that any of us can do to convince Khrushchev of the solidarity of the Free World in our current objectives will be most helpful.

One of the keys to progress in disarmament will be willingness by the Kremlin to agree to the Western view of inspection and control.[3] A willingness by the Soviet Union to match the West in permitting inspection and control arrangements as a necessary part of a disarmament program, and thus creating international confidence[,] would be a great step forward.

Possibly the greatest step which the Kremlin could take to lessen the tension which presently grips the world would be to agree to the fundamental principle of self-determination and the right of countries such as Germany and Hungary to determine their own political, economic, and social patterns.

If there could be an honest, sincere, and convincing agreement on these subjects, the opportunity for devoting to the aid of underdeveloped countries a substantial portion of the resources that currently go into armaments would be something that could make this the greatest of centuries.

I am looking forward to seeing you when you are in Washington and to discussing with you the results of the conversations which you will be holding in the course of your trip.[4]

With warm regard, *Sincerely*

[1] New Zealand's Prime Minister Nash would leave April 5 for a nine-nation world tour. He would arrive in Moscow on April 18 (*New York Times*, Apr. 6, 19, 24, 1960). For background on the summit meeting, to begin in Paris on May 16, see no. 1397.
[2] Eisenhower had met at Camp David with Soviet Premier Khrushchev in September 1959, and with German Chancellor Konrad Adenauer and British Prime Minister Macmillan in March (see nos. 1332 and 1459).
[3] For the latest Western proposals see no. 1445.
[4] Nash would be in Washington to attend meetings of the council of the South East Asia Treaty Organization on May 31, and he would meet with Eisenhower on the following day (State, *Foreign Relations, 1958–1960*, vol. XVI, *East Asia-Pacific Region; Cambodia; Laos*, pp. 184–86; see also Goodpaster, Memorandum of Conference, June 8, 1960, AWF/D).

1486   *EM, AWF, International Series: Macmillan*

To HAROLD MACMILLAN   *March 30, 1960*
Personal. Top secret

Dear Harold: For your personal information only, I am attaching a passage taken from a message I received from Mr. Khrushchev some time ago. This passage deals with the Russian attitude toward West Germany, a subject of which you and I have talked so much.[1] While we have no way of determining the sincerity of the statement, it seems to me obvious that this is the line he will take in any negotiations. Consequently, I thought it better to give you the exact language of his statement rather than to be content with the general tenor as I expressed it verbally to you.[2]

With warm regard, *As ever*

[1] For Khrushchev's March 21 letter see no. 1493. The Soviet leader had described the foreign policy of West Germany as characterized by "an unwillingness to conclude a peace treaty; a definite refusal to recognize the state boundaries in Europe which resulted from the defeat of Hitlerite Germany; a refusal to establish diplomatic relations with several European states, including those which, in the last war, were subjected to attack by Germany and whose territory at present is the object of Bonn's claims; the appointment of former active champions of Hitler's policy, including war criminals, to leading positions in the government and, especially, in the army; [and] a poorly concealed desire to gain possession of nuclear weapons as quickly as possible." Khrushchev also objected to what he felt was an attempt by West Germany to establish army bases in other European and African countries. To protect the interests of the Soviet Union and those of all nations, including Germany, the Soviet leader had urged the fulfillment of the allied postwar agreement to guarantee "that Germany shall never again threaten its neighbors or threaten the maintenance of peace throughout the world" (AWF/I: Macmillan; see also no. 1454).

[2] For the Camp David meetings between Eisenhower and Macmillan see no. 1459; see also State, *Foreign Relations, 1958–1960*, vol. IX, *Berlin Crisis 1959–1960; Germany; Austria*, pp. 258–62. For developments see no. 1493.

1487

EM, AWF,
Administration Series

To Lewis Lichtenstein Strauss

March 30, 1960

Dear Lewis: Many thanks for your note giving me your suggestion about nuclear test inspection.[1] I had not previously seen the idea of requesting the Swiss to do this while the permanent inspection system is being established, but it is an interesting possibility. I shall certainly keep it in mind as we try to work out safeguard arrangements.[2]

With warm personal regard, *As ever*

[1] Strauss had proposed that the United States should once again offer to cease the testing of atomic weapons in the oceans, the air, and outer space, and to cease underground tests of any size if certain conditions were met. During the time necessary to effect a mutually acceptable inspection system both the Soviet Union and the United States would agree to have teams of inspectors designated by the Swiss government stationed in each country. The teams, comprising only Swiss nationals,

would have "unquestioned immediate access to all areas" with their costs paid in equal shares by the participating governments. The idea, Strauss said, might resolve the differences between the United States and the British and at the same time be acceptable to the Soviets (Strauss to Eisenhower, Mar. 28, 1960, AWF/A; for background on the test ban negotiations and the British-American disagreement over inspections see nos. 1445).

[2] For developments see no. 1491.

1488

EM, AWF, International Series:
Philippine Islands

To Carlos Polestico Garcia   March 30, 1960
Cable

Dear Mr. President: I have received your telegram of March 17 asking that I increase the Philippine sugar quota. As you know, the sugar quotas are determined by Congress and any modification would require Congressional action. Since the Sugar Act of 1948 as amended in 1956 expires this year, Congress is expected to consider its extension during the present session.[1]

The Administration has been giving considerable thought to what recommendations it should make to Congress for its consideration. After weeks of most careful study of this problem, I have concluded that the time is not propitious to recommend any change in the present structure of quotas assigned to foreign countries.[2]

Accordingly, I have recommended to the Congress only certain minimum changes in the present Sugar Act. The most important of these would give me the authority to reduce the quota for a calendar year for any foreign country, except, of course, the Philippines, and to make required replacements from any source when I determine it to be in the national interest or necessary to insure adequate supplies of sugar. I have requested this authority primarily to enable me to protect our sugar consumers should our supplies of sugar from foreign sources be endangered for any reason. The final decision as to whether I am to be given this authority, however, rests with Congress.[3] I regret therefore that it has not been possible for me to comply with the wishes of the Philippine sugar producers. I wish to assure you, however, that the position of the Philippines has been given full consideration by the Administration in arriving at the position which I have recommended to Congress.[4]

With assurances of my continued esteem, Sincerely

[1] The Sugar Act determined a quota system for the amount of sugar that could be sold to the United States by both domestic and foreign producers (for background

see *Congressional Quarterly Almanac,* vol. XVI, *1960,* pp. 208–16). President Garcia had cabled Eisenhower asking that the Philippines' quota be increased by as much as two hundred thousand tons, which, he said, could help stabilize and boost his country's economy (Mar. 17, AWF/I: Philippine Islands).

[2] In the letter accompanying State's draft of this response, Herter had explained that a previous statement made by Eisenhower had led Philippine growers to assume that the United States would raise their country's quota. Since Garcia had released his request to the public, Herter had recommended that Eisenhower also make his response public, which he would do on April 4 (Herter to Eisenhower, Mar. 28, 1960, AWF/I: Philippine Islands; *Public Papers of the Presidents: Eisenhower, 1960–61,* pp. 331–32; *New York Times,* Mar. 17 and Apr. 5, 1960).

[3] The Administration had sent its bill to Congress on March 16. The request for discretionary authority was understood to be a response to increasingly tense relations with Cuba, the nation's largest foreign supplier of sugar (*Congressional Quarterly Almanac,* vol. XVI, *1960,* pp. 208–16). Eisenhower denied that this proposal was intended as a "reprisal" against Cuba's Castro regime and maintained that it provided means to protect the nation's sugar supply (*Public Papers of the Presidents: Eisenhower, 1960–61,* p. 298; see also pp. 452–53). For background on relations with Cuba see no. 1370, and Bonsal, *Cuba, Castro and the United States,* esp. pp. 136–37.

[4] Herter had advised that it was not considered feasible to raise the quota of any foreign country given the difficulty of the situation with Cuba (Herter to Eisenhower, Mar. 28, 1960, AWF/I: Philippine Islands). Eisenhower had initialed a memo written by Don Paarlberg, Special Assistant for Economic Affairs, explaining that although Garcia's request had merit, it could lead to demands from other countries to divide the Cuban allotment among themselves, a step that would be "unfortunate from a diplomatic standpoint" (Paarlberg to John S. D. Eisenhower, Mar. 31, 1961, AWF/I: Philippine Islands). For developments see nos. 1578 and 1582; see also State, *Foreign Relations, 1958–1960,* vol. XV, *South and Southeast Asia,* pp. 961–62.

1489   *EM, AWF, International Series: Morocco*

To Mohamed V   *March 30, 1960*
Secret

Your Majesty:[1] Events of great consequence have occurred since my memorable meeting with Your Majesty in Casablanca last December.[2] I have been deeply saddened at the thought of the terrible ordeal which Morocco has undergone in the disaster at Agadir.[3] I am glad to learn, however, that the rapidity with which the Moroccan authorities, under the direction of Your Majesty and the Crown Prince, have instituted relief efforts has mercifully spared further suffering and brought consolation to the unfortunate victims.[4]

On a happier note, I trust that your historic tour of the Arab world, with its high promise of greater international understanding, has fully met your expectations.[5] In this regard, my own visit to South America, I am glad to say, was very gratifying.[6] I believe that the opportunity to meet friendly chiefs of state personally, and to discuss problems frankly with them, contributes significantly to the pursuit of peace and mutually advantageous relations between states.

Certainly our meeting in Casablanca, of which I retain very pleasant memories indeed, was an unusually important event in this respect. Secretary Herter has informed me of the letter he received from your Prime Minister expressing particular satisfaction with our agreement about the bases operated by the United States in Morocco, as an example of the sincere cooperation which exists between our two countries.[7] I assure you that the United States shares this feeling. It is in this spirit that I now feel it desirable to write to Your Majesty about certain matters left in suspense by our conversation.

I recall Your Majesty's request that the United States assist in training Moroccan personnel to utilize the bases from which United States forces are to be withdrawn by the end of 1963, and my own assurances that the United States would give this matter sympathetic consideration. In connection with the recent withdrawal from Ben Slimane, I wish to confirm that the United States would be happy to provide such training assistance as may be agreed upon by our two Governments and would be pleased to received suggestions from your Government in this regard.[8]

I am, of course, confident I can count on Your Majesty's assurance that bases constructed by the United States will not be made accessible to any third power whose policies contain a threat to the security of my country. I feel free to anticipate Your Majesty's confirmation of this point because it seems an inevitable corollary of Moroccan-American friendship and entirely consistent with the principles of Moroccan policy which Your Majesty has expressed to me.

As for our reference to separate arrangements for certain communications facilities, I have asked the appropriate United States authorities to be prepared to discuss our needs for the period following 1963, and would be glad to learn Your Majesty's wishes concerning the negotiations we envisaged.[9]

Finally, I trust that any necessary clarifications of the status of the United States military forces during the remaining period of their presence in Morocco can be worked out to our mutual satisfaction by our respective representatives directly concerned.[10]

With my warmest personal good wishes, and with the highest respect, *Sincerely*

[1] A State Department draft of this message with Eisenhower's handwritten emendations is in AWF/I: Morocco. The text of the message was sent by cable to the American embassy in Rabat for delivery to King Mohamed.

[2] Eisenhower had met with the Moroccan ruler on December 22, at the end of his eleven-nation trip to Europe, Asia, and the Middle East (State, *Foreign Relations, 1958–1960*, vol. XIII, *Arab-Israeli Dispute; United Arab Republic; North Africa*, pp. 796–800; for background on the trip see no. 1382).

[3] On February 29 and March 1 approximately 15,000 people had been killed when two earthquakes, a tidal wave, and a fire destroyed the Atlantic port and resort city of Agadir.

[4] Crown Prince Moulay Hassan.

[5] King Mohamed had returned on February 7 from a month-long tour of the Middle East.

[6] On Eisenhower's South American trip see no. 1403.

[7] For background on U.S. air bases in Morocco see Galambos and van Ee, *The Middle Way*, no. 466; see also State, *Foreign Relations, 1955–1957*, vol. XVIII, *Africa*, pp. 531–38, 564–67, 577–80. Negotiations begun in May 1957 had culminated in the announcement, made after the meeting between Eisenhower and King Mohamed, that the United States would withdraw its forces from Morocco by the end of 1963. Secretary Herter had suggested that Eisenhower send this message to the Moroccan leader "to capitalize on the goodwill" produced by the agreement. Moroccan Prime Minister Moulay Abdullah Ibrahim had written to Herter on February 14 (Herter to Eisenhower, Mar. 24, 1960, AWF/I: Morocco; Herter to Ibrahim, Mar. 9, 1960, *ibid.*; State, *American Foreign Policy; Current Documents, 1959*, pp. 1106–7; and State, *Foreign Relations, 1958–1960*, vol. XIII, *Arab-Israeli Dispute; United Arab Republic; North Africa*, pp. 796–800, 803–6).

[8] As part of the evacuation agreement the air base at Ben Slimane would be relinquished by March 31, 1960.

[9] At the Casablanca meeting Mohamed had agreed to discuss separate arrangements for the status of U.S. communications centers in Morocco. Herter had suggested that reference to this point be included in the letter to determine how far Mohamed was prepared to go into the matter (State, *Foreign Relations, 1958–1960*, vol. XIII, *Arab-Israeli Dispute; United Arab Republic; North Africa*, pp. 803–4).

[10] Mohamed would tell the American ambassador on August 4 that he "was gratified U.S.-Moroccan relations were improving" and promised to reply in the near future. For developments see no. 1525.

1490   *EM, AWF, International Series: Chile*

To Patricio Fernández   *[March 30, 1960]*

Dear Mr. Fernández: I acknowledge with thanks the letter which you wrote to me on behalf of University Students of Chile. It reached me only a few minutes before I left the United States Embassy to keep the official engagements of the day. Hence I have had the opportunity only to glance through it hastily.[1]

At once I recognize that you are giving serious thought to hemispheric and world problems; that some of your critical comments are justified; but that other statements indicate a serious lack of comprehension of U.S. position and responsibilities.[2]

I shall have your letter completely analyzed and in due time you will receive a reply through the U.S. Ambassador, Mr. Walter Howe.[3]

Thank your organization for the interest you are taking in these important matters.

¹ Patricio Fernández was president of the Federation of Students of Chile. Eisenhower had been in Santiago, Chile, on February 29 during his visit to four South American countries. Although we have been unable to determine the exact date of this letter, it may have been sent before March 30 (see no. 1403; see also *U.S. Department of State Bulletin* 42, no. 1083 [March 28, 1960], 480–83; and State, *Foreign Relations, 1958–1960*, vol. V, *American Republics*, Microfiche Supplement, CI-29, 30).

² The university students had told Eisenhower that they were primarily Christians and were "firm supporters of democracy and in opposition to all types of dictatorship." They discussed the positive effects of the inter-American system but complained that the United States had more advantages than obligations. Reciprocity should be the moral basis of the system, the students maintained, and the United States should take the initiative as it had in Europe. They asked for fair prices, adequate remuneration for raw materials, and an end to the favoritism shown to the small group of privileged Latin Americans who exploited the poor people in their countries. The students supported the revolution in Cuba and, while applauding the U.S. government's declaration regarding the self-determination of the Cuban nation, deplored "the campaign of hatred, calumny and distortion" broadcast by U.S. news agencies (Federation of Students of Chile to Eisenhower, Feb. 24, 1960, AWF/I: Chile).

³ Secretary Herter had sent Eisenhower a State Department draft of the suggested reply on March 30. Upon the President's approval, Herter said, the letter would be sent to the American embassy in Santiago over the signature of Ambassador Howe. Herter recommended public release immediately. "By giving wide circulation to the letter from the students and to this reply," he told Eisenhower, "substantial progress will be made in countering and perhaps correcting some of the important misconceptions about the United States which are widely held in student circles in Latin America" (Herter to Eisenhower, Mar. 30, 1960, AWF/I: Chile; the draft of the reply with Eisenhower's handwritten emendations is in *ibid.*).

The reply would reiterate the U.S. position favoring democratic republics while refusing to enter into the internal affairs of others. Although the United States would not support dictators, actions taken in regard to them had to be "genuinely constructive" and should represent the consensus of the inter-American community. Emphasis was placed on the various agencies of the Organization of American States and the progress they had made in promoting economic and agricultural development, new housing initiatives, and child welfare. American businessmen and investors took their responsibilities toward their employees and the people of the countries of South America seriously, the reply argued. To say that the United States was only interested in exploitation was "a gross exaggeration and, in most cases patently untrue." The United States cooperated with primary producing countries to overcome violent fluctuations in the prices of raw materials and imposed low duties or, in some cases, none at all, upon these imports. Regarding Cuba, the reply stated that while supporting agrarian reform in that country, the United States had protested Cuban actions that disregarded the rights of its citizens (see "United States Replies to Chilean Students' Letter to President Eisenhower," *U.S. Department of State Bulletin* 42, no. 1087 [April 25, 1960], 648–58; see also *New York Times*, Apr. 9, 1960; Eisenhower, *Waging Peace*, pp. 528–29; and Milton S. Eisenhower, *The Wine is Bitter*, pp. 242–46).

1491   *EM, WHCF, Official File 108-A*

To John Fitzgerald Kennedy   *March 31, 1960*

Dear Senator Kennedy: Thank you sincerely for your letter and for the confidence it implies in the attempt I am making to achieve a fair and just agreement for the cessation of nuclear testing.[1] I note with satisfaction that you also support an effort to arrange a temporary moratorium of tests, for the purpose of providing opportunity to solve the inherent technical and other problems, and that you agree that I should act without regard to the coming national election.[2]

I assure you that I value your expression of dedication to the cause of world peace. *Sincerely*

[1] For background on Kennedy see Galambos and van Ee, *The Middle Way*, no. 1148. The Massachusetts senator had announced his candidacy for the Democratic nomination for president on January 2 (*New York Times*, Jan. 3, 1960). Kennedy had told Eisenhower that he was "greatly disturbed" that the Geneva test ban negotiations might be jeopardized by the upcoming presidential election. He could understand how Eisenhower might be reluctant to decide on a small-test moratorium that might restrict his successor. "Let me assure you," he wrote, "that, if elected President, I will undertake to carry out in good faith any moratorium extending beyond your term of office which you now decide to be in the best interests of the nation" (Kennedy to Eisenhower, Mar. 30, 1960, same file as document; for background on the negotiations see no. 1445).

[2] For developments see no. 1493.

1492   *EM, AWF, Dulles-Herter Series*

To Christian Archibald Herter   *March 31, 1960*

Dear Chris: The National Commander of the American Legion, Martin B. McKneally, and several of his associates have expressed a desire to go to Russia some time this fall.[1] I heartily approve of such visits and I have advised the Commander to make the request for the necessary visas at an early date to avoid the chance of being held up for any cause.

I would appreciate it if you would let the proper assistant know of my hope that the necessary Soviet visas will be forthcoming.[2] *As ever*

[1] Martin Boswell McKneally (LL.B. Fordam University) had become national commander of the American Legion in 1959. He and three other legion officials had met with Eisenhower on this same day (see President's daily appointments).

[2] McKneally would cancel the trip after the breakdown of the summit meeting and

Khrushchev's withdrawal of Eisenhower's invitation to visit the Soviet Union. "Where the President of the United States is not welcome, no American citizen should go," he said (*New York Times*, May 25, 1960; on the summit collapse see no. 1538).

1493

EM, AWF,
International Series:
Khrushchev

To Nikita Sergeyevich Khrushchev   *April 1, 1960*

Dear Mr. Chairman:[1] I have read your letter of March twenty-first with interest and great care. At the same time I have reviewed your earlier letter of March third and my response of March twelfth in order better to be able to understand where there may be points of difference to which I could address myself in order to make the position of the United States Government unmistakably clear to you.[2]

In my letter of March twelfth I tried to clarify for you the policy of the United States with regard to the transfer of nuclear weapons and information on the design and manufacture of nuclear weapons to other countries. I hope that I succeeded. It had been my hope that in response to this reaffirmation of United States policy in this regard you would find it possible to state equally clearly the policy of the Union of Soviet Socialist Republics. I was disappointed, therefore, not to find any mention of this in your most recent letter.

You come back in your letter to the foreign policy of the Federal Republic of Germany and the threat to the peace you believe to be implicit in that policy.[3]

I cannot forget, any more than you can, the immeasurable human suffering which was cruelly inflicted in the world by the Nazi dictatorship. I do not defend the government of the Federal Republic of Germany merely because it is allied with mine. I defend it from the charges and implications contained in your letter because it is my conviction, based on the most objective judgment, that the government of the Federal Republic is deeply committed to the achievement of its national goals without the use of force or the threat of force against any other country. This commitment is one which, after the disaster of the last war, the German people have accepted. Noteworthy is the fact that Germany is the only country in the world which has bound itself by formal international commitments not to manufacture nuclear weapons.

On the subject of the nuclear test negotiations which now have been in progress nearly a year and a half, you refer to the proposal submitted by your representative on March nineteenth.[4] This proposal takes into account for the first time the technical problems pointed out by the United States scientists and the need for additional research before adequate controls can be applied to a suspension of underground nuclear tests. It appears also to recognize that any agreement for the suspension of nuclear weapons tests must provide for underground nuclear tests in a manner different from other tests.[5]

This is a very significant and welcome development. Following as it does the general acceptance by your Government of the technical criteria for locating and identifying underground seismic events advanced by the United States scientists in technical working group II, it means that we now have an agreed framework for approaching the problem of concluding an agreement for suspension of nuclear weapons tests. I have instructed my representative in Geneva, along lines set forth in the communique issued March twenty-ninth by Prime Minister Macmillan and myself, to proceed vigorously in the negotiations to see whether an agreed arrangement can be mutually worked out.[6]

The objective of the United States continues to be the discontinuance of all nuclear weapons tests under effective controls. I recall that your position is similar, as expressed for example in the statement in your letter of April 23, 1959, that we must "establish such controls as would guarantee strict observance of the treaty."[7] We must also face the hard facts that at present there are technical limitations and uncertainties as far as the detection and identification of small underground seismic events is concerned. Of course, our position is not that these limitations and uncertainties mean that testing must be resumed in this area. It is rather that our negotiators must ascertain without delay what the best control arrangements are which are now obtainable, and whether these give each of us adequate assurance so that we can embark on an exploratory course of action of the kind outlined in our communique. I hope that this will prove to be the case.

I must point out however that elements of the Soviet proposal give us concern. The length of the proposed initial moratorium applying to small underground tests, which I understand to be four or five years, is excessive. It also is unacceptable to make commitments now that, if the research program were to be inconclusive or to show that control in this area is infeasible, the moratorium should even so be continued. Furthermore, jointly supervised nuclear explosions to test and prove the capabilities of control techniques should be a part of the coordinated research program which would be undertaken for the purpose of improving detection of underground seismic events.

There also remain a number of control issues which must be resolved in order to conclude a treaty such as my Government proposed on February eleventh.[8] The level of inspection on which we will be able to agree will be of the utmost importance in determining whether an adequate degree of control can be provided. I understand that your representative still refuses to give any indication of the number of inspections which your Government is prepared to permit annually. In this situation, Mr. Chairman, it is very difficult for us to assess the anticipated efficiency of the control system on which we are seeking agreement. While the other remaining issues are few, they are of great importance. The staffing of control posts and inspection teams must be such as to assure that they can fulfill adequately their function of control; the composition and voting procedures of the Control Commission must be such as to assure that it can function efficiently, impartially and without delay in its important functions; safeguarded procedures must be worked out under which nuclear detonations can be conducted for peaceful purposes; and clear and practical arrangements must be agreed on for the installation and geographic extension of the control system. The record of our ability to resolve other issues that seemed equally difficult at first gives reason for hope that these matters too can be settled, but they are not problems on which fundamental control principles can be compromised.

With regard to the broader problem of control of nuclear weapons, I must state that I cannot share your view that a cessation of production of fissionable material for weapons purposes would not by itself help contribute in any way toward lessening the danger of nuclear war. I believe that you consider that a cessation of nuclear weapons testing would by itself help to prevent the emergence of new nuclear powers and significantly retard the nuclear armaments race. To me it seems clear that the larger measure—the cessation of production of fissionable material for weapons purposes—would exert an even larger influence to these ends and is, indeed, indispensable if the eventual proliferation of nuclear capabilities is surely to be averted. This influence could be strengthened by commencing simultaneously the progressive and equitable transfers of such fissionable material to non-weapons purposes as I have repeatedly urged. I personally think that an agreement to stop the production of fissionable material for weapons purposes would be an important and constructive step.[9]

With regard to the safeguards of the International Atomic Energy Agency, I have never believed that such safeguards would solve completely the problem of avoiding the spread of nuclear weapons capabilities.[10] However, I continue to believe that support of such safeguards, both in the International Atomic Energy Agency and in bilateral arrangements, can contribute in a most important way to achievement of this goal.

The first steps to take on the road to general disarmament may look halting or small against the immense goal that we have set for ourselves. Nevertheless, the actual achievement of substantial initial measures of disarmament will I believe prove decisive in the long view of history.[11] *Sincerely*

[1] The text of this message was sent by cable to the American embassy in Moscow for delivery to the Soviet leader. A State Department draft, with Eisenhower's handwritten emendations, is in AWF/I: Khrushchev (see Herter to Eisenhower, Mar. 31, 1960, *ibid.*).
[2] For Khrushchev's previous letter and Eisenhower's response see no. 1454. Khrushchev's letter on March 21 is in AWF/I: Khrushchev.
[3] Eisenhower had previously sent Prime Minister Macmillan a copy of this portion of Khrushchev's letter (see no. 1486).
[4] For background on the negotiations see no. 1445. Semen K. Tsarapkin, the Soviet representative, had presented a proposal for a treaty on cessation of all nuclear weapons tests, including underground tests that produced seismographic readings of 4.75 or above on the Richter scale. For unidentified underground events below this level the Soviet Union proposed a joint program of experimentation and research together with Western officials during which time all parties would agree to suspend testing below the stipulated threshold (State, *Documents on Disarmament, 1960*, pp. 72–75; see also Goodpaster, Memorandums of Conference, Mar. 25, 1960, AWF/D). The proposal, Khrushchev had written, had considered the position of the Western powers and would "expedite and facilitate the achievement of agreement."
[5] For background on the perceived need for additional research see no. 1095.
[6] For the Camp David meetings between Eisenhower and Macmillan and the communiqué see no. 1459; see also State, *Foreign Relations, 1958–1960*, vol. IX, *Berlin Crisis 1959–1960; Germany; Austria*, pp. 258–62.
[7] See no. 1147.
[8] On the U.S. proposal see no. 1445.
[9] Eisenhower had substituted the preceding sentence for the original, which read: "I can think of no single agreement presently capable of being readily carried out which would have a more profound impact on the nuclear armaments race than an agreement to stop and then reverse the flow of fissionable material into weapons stockpiles."
[10] Khrushchev had referred to Eisenhower's earlier comment regarding the use of the IAEA to prevent the expansion of the number of states possessing nuclear weapons. "First," he had said, "the Agency can establish control only over those fissionable materials that it itself grants. And, secondly, the development of atomic energy in all countries cannot be placed under the control of the Agency without the banning of nuclear weapons."
[11] For developments see no. 1581.

1494   *EM, WHCF, Official File 133*

To Nancy Bierce   *April 4, 1960*
Personal

Dear Nancy: Your letter raises questions that go to the very depth of human nature and behavior; these are matters with which philosophers have wrestled throughout history and they are certainly ones that we are forced to ponder deeply as we read our Bibles.[1]

With the basic theme of your message—that both America's conscience and her own best interests require us to use our skills and our resources in helping the underdeveloped nations, I am in full agreement. Moreover, I believe that each of us should strive to do his or her part in helping America to remember and follow moral laws.[2]

But there is one statement you make that I cannot accept as completely accurate. You say, "If our faith in God is so slight that we must build huge defenses around us, we are going to deteriorate. . .".

All of us were created as creatures capable of independent decision. By this I mean that, while we should seek Divine Guidance, we cannot abandon our own responsibilities in a world of turmoil. I believe there is no mutual antagonism between a nation's faith in God and her determination to defend herself against attack particularly when she has been, over many years, the target of bitter attacks from an atheistic ideology, often threatening in their tone. I cannot agree that defenselessness is a virtue. I think that somewhere in St. Luke you will find a passage, admittedly taken out of context, which goes something like this, "When a strong man, armed, keepeth his palace, his goods are in peace."[3]

In such an observation there is no thought of aggressive or selfish intent—only self-protection.

In my own conviction, the purpose for which arms are developed is the determining factor as to whether their possession is good or evil. If we are dedicated to peace, if we make no threats against anyone else, if we refuse to attempt domination of others economically, politically or militarily, then I cannot see how we are, through possessing defensive armaments, guilty of violating moral law.

Of course every right-thinking person deplores the need for pouring into sterile mechanisms of war so much of our labor, skills and material resources. For this reason it is one of the principal duties of government to see that our defensive machinery is never more elaborate or extensive than is required. But I think we would be guilty of refusing to carry out our own responsibilities in this troubled world if we completely neglected the defenses of ourselves and other friendly nations who, like ourselves, are dedicated to freedom and human dignity.

Finally, I do applaud your conviction that all of us should unite in the fight for literacy, freedom and equality before the law.[4]

This reply is hastily written and is not intended to go to the very bottom of the questions you raise. I merely wanted to tell you promptly how I felt about your very nice and thoughtful letter.

With best wishes, *Sincerely*

[1] Bierce, a high school sophomore from New Jersey, had written the President on April 2, 1960 (same file as document) concerning questions that had arisen from her church and school discussions.

[2] Bierce had written that "All through the annals of history great nations have fallen because they have put their will above God's, they became egotistical and forgot the needs of those around them. We must be able and willing of mind to give up our identity as the richest nation with the highest standard of living, etcetera and by doing this we will have made a large step toward the Messianic Age both in our hearts and minds and in our daily actions." For Eisenhower's views on foreign aid see nos. 60 and 94.

[3] The quotation is from Luke 11:21.

[4] Bierce had written "We need an event, a crisis, to unite us in our fight for literacy, freedom, and equality in *all* the world."

1495   *EM, AWF, Name Series*

To Susan Elaine Eisenhower   *April 4, 1960*

Dear Susie: I have heard that you are the one who made up the very attractive invitation in which the entire family invited Mimi and me to Easter dinner.[1] As your father will tell you, Mimi and I have been planning for a long time to leave for Georgia on April 11th, and to stay there until about April 20th or 21st. For this reason we shall miss the dinner—and I cannot tell you how sorry we are.[2] I think it would be very nice if the entire family would come to Augusta for the weekend and have Easter Dinner with us down there![3]

Both of us congratulate you on the attractiveness of your invitation. I hope that your teacher gave you "A" in writing because it looks to me to be almost perfect.

Mimi and I sent our love to you and all the family. We hope you will tell all of them how much we appreciated your nice invitation.

Affectionately

[1] Eight-year-old Susan had written the invitation on lined, loose-leaf paper (AWF/N).

[2] For background on the Eisenhowers' traditional April vacation in Augusta, Georgia, see Galambos and van Ee, *The Middle Way*, no. 1730; nos. 106 and 659 in these volumes; and *New York Times*, April 11, 1960.

[3] The President and First Lady also sent their regrets to the rest of the family (n.d., AWF/D). As it turned out, on April 16 Major John S. D. Eisenhower and his family would join his parents in Augusta for the Easter holiday. The President, the John Eisenhowers and their four children would fly back to Washington on Monday, April 18. Later that same day the President and his son would return to Augusta, where they would remain until April 21 (Slater, *The Ike I Knew*, pp. 223–26, and *New York Times*, Apr. 11–14, 16–19, 22, 1960).

To Konrad Adenauer   *April 5, 1960*
Secret

Dear Mr. Chancellor:[1] I have read with great interest the paper, "The Spiritual Power of Communism," which you handed me at our meeting on March fifteenth.[2]

I share the view expressed in the paper that a most difficult problem facing the West in relations with the Communist bloc and in the struggle to keep the underdeveloped countries from coming under Communist domination is the bloc's widespread dissemination of propaganda extolling its economic and social system. Non-Communists will certainly be at a disadvantage unless they are aware of the strengths, as well as the weaknesses, of Communist ideology and practices.

However, I am convinced that Communist ideology can not for long satisfy the universal human urge for a better life under conditions of individual freedom. Our own prospects for freedom depend on widening the scope for this human urge and on the erosion of the totalitarian system in the Communist bloc. We view increased contact of persons and ideas with the peoples and leaders of the Communist countries as one means of hastening the latter process.

Yet, it is apparent that there is something in the nature of a race between the erosion process and the amassing of material power in the bloc which threatens our future security.

It is plain to me that the West cannot afford to relax the struggle against the threat which, in an earlier and cruder manifestation, resulted in the formation of NATO and other collective security arrangements.

I have asked the State Department to examine the proposal made in the paper you left with me concerning the establishment of an international institute for research on the impact of Soviet ideology on Soviet policy. The proposal seems to have considerable merit. However, we would want to explore carefully the effect such an institute would have on the underdeveloped countries, which are in great need of better understanding of Communism and which often are suspicious of Western moves in this field.[3] Perhaps representatives of your Embassy in Washington might wish to discuss this idea further with officers of the State Department.[4]

With warm personal regard, *Sincerely*

---

[1] The State Department cabled the text of this message to the American embassy in Bonn for delivery to the German chancellor.

[2] For Adenauer's visit to Washington see no. 1459. The paper, written by Dr. Hans Globke, German State Secretary since 1953, is in AWF/I: Adenauer. Globke had ar-

gued that since Communist ideology centered "around the creation of a new individual throughout the world," it ultimately compelled every person in the free world "to make a decision and to define his position."

[3] Secretary Herter had told Eisenhower that the paper pointed out "a great problem for the Western nations in their future relations with the Communists." Although the proposal for an international institute for research on communism was interesting, Herter thought, such a Western organization could not include representatives from the underdeveloped nations. "Not only are such countries in greatest need of a better understanding of communism, but they would probably view with great suspicion a Western institute of the type proposed" (Herter to Eisenhower, Mar. 31, 1960, AWF/ I: Adenauer). Herter also sent a draft of this letter for the President's approval.

[4] Adenauer would agree with Eisenhower's suggestion for further study and would ask his embassy to contact State Department officials about the matter (Adenauer to Eisenhower, Apr. 14, 1960, *ibid.*).

1497

EM, AWF, International Series:
Macmillan

To Harold Macmillan
Cable

April 5, 1960

Dear Harold: Pursuant to our conversations here in Washington the other day concerning the procedures to be followed at the Summit Meeting, with particular regard to the size of those meetings, I think it might be well if this question were clarified in advance with Chairman Khrushchev.[1]

I propose therefore to send a letter to him along the lines of the enclosure to this letter if you and General de Gaulle agree that this is desirable.[2]

There is a further matter which I think it might be well for us to take up through diplomatic channels with Chairman Khrushchev which derives from my own constitutional responsibilities. This has to do with reaching preliminary agreement on the probable duration of the Summit Meetings. If you agree I should like to have it made clear to him that the length of time I can be absent from this country is limited—in the present instance I must consider the fact that I plan to leave early in June for my visit to the Soviet Union as well as the probable early adjournment of Congress this year.[3] I propose to have our Ambassador at Moscow suggest to Chairman Khrushchev that we should agree the Paris meetings should end by the close of the week of May 16.[4]

I am communicating with General de Gaulle in the same sense and should be grateful for an early indication of your reaction to both of the foregoing suggestions.[5]

With warm personal regard, *As ever*

1894

[1] For background on Eisenhower's meetings with Macmillan on March 28 see no. 1459; see also State, *Foreign Relations, 1958–1960*, vol. IX, *Berlin Crisis 1959–1960; Germany; Austria*, pp. 258–62.

[2] Secretary Herter had recommended that Eisenhower first communicate with French President de Gaulle regarding a letter to Khrushchev "to avoid any implication that we are proceeding either unilaterally in a matter of concern to the three or as the result only of bilateral coordination with the British" (Herter to Eisenhower, Apr. 2, 1960, AWF/I: Paris-Summit Meeting). Later Herter had suggested that Eisenhower send the proposed letter to both Macmillan and French President de Gaulle, who was in London at the time for a three-day state visit (Goodpaster, Memorandum of Conference, Apr. 6, 1960, AWF/D; see also Macmillan, *Pointing the Way*, pp. 193–94; and de Gaulle, *Memoirs of Hope*, pp. 234–38).

Eisenhower had proposed to the Soviet leader that the four heads of government meet each morning in a private session on a "discussional rather than a negotiating basis." At an appropriate point they would be joined by the foreign ministers who would later prepare detailed analyses of the discussions. "In general," Eisenhower had written, "I think we would do well to plan one meeting a day. This would give all of us adequate time for reflection between our meetings and for such staff work among our delegations as might be helpful." A State Department draft of the letter to Khrushchev with Eisenhower's extensive handwritten emendations is in AWF/I: Paris-Summit Meeting.

[3] For background on Eisenhower's planned trip to the Soviet Union see no. 1456.

[4] Eisenhower would not send the proposed letter to Khrushchev. On April 16, however, U.S. Ambassador Llewellyn Thompson would deliver a message to the Soviet leader outlining the President's plan to leave Paris on May 23 (see no. 1508).

[5] Eisenhower's letter to de Gaulle is in AWF/I: Paris-Summit Meeting. Macmillan would agree that the size of the meetings should be manageable and that the entire summit should not last more than six days. He would recommend that at the restricted meetings of the heads of government the translators should provide each participant with the same translation. He added that he had discussed Eisenhower's letter briefly with General de Gaulle, who seemed to agree with the President's suggestions. Both Macmillan and de Gaulle thought that the three foreign ministers, who would begin meetings in Washington on April 12, could discuss the summit arrangements and agree on the draft of a letter that Eisenhower, as host of the foreign ministers' meeting, would then send to Khrushchev. "I am rather in favour of this plan myself, because de Gaulle will, after all, be the host of the Summit and it would, I think, be wiser for him to be closely associated with any letter which you send to Khrushchev on this subject" (Macmillan to Eisenhower, Apr. 8, 1960, AWF/I: Macmillan). For developments see no. 1506.

1498   *EM, WHCF, Confidential File:*
Agriculture-Farming

To Mary Conger   *April 5, 1960*
Personal and confidential

Dear Mrs. Conger: For a number of years I have been studying different aspects of the so-called farm problems of our country, trying to determine upon the proper and most useful function of government in connection therewith.

Your personal story, which I read and re-read last evening, seems to me to describe in better fashion than I have seen elsewhere some of the specific difficulties and frustrations of the commercial farmer.[1] My own farm is a specialized one and quite small. Worse than this, I get no time to learn about it from firsthand observation. But in your story I felt I was getting, from one experienced farmer, a clear account of your operations.[2]

I am quite sure that you are aware of the various facets of the agricultural dilemma; for example, the difficulties the government has in disposing of our surpluses to other countries without disturbing international markets, building up the size of surpluses in spite of "conservation reserves",[3] different types of restrictions and every kind of disposal plan that makes any sense whatsoever.

Your own problem deals, of course, with dairying. Concerning it, I hope you will permit me to ask a few questions. If my questions appear naive, please remember that I have had no experience with a dairy cow of any kind since boyhood days when I had the chore of milking two cows twice a day.

At one point in the article you suggest that the farmer might break the "cost-price squeeze" if he were allowed to organize, somewhat in the manner of labor unions. What is the specific reason you cannot do so?[4] I know of no law that would prohibit the practice.[5]

At another point you said that milk had gone from 11 cents a quart in 1952 to 8.1 cents a quart in 1959. I assume this was the price received from the wholesaler. Is this descending trend local or general for your region?

Governmental statistics show that, during the period 1952-59, middleman prices rose 2.7 per quart. They show further that in the United States, as a whole, dealers paid 12.4 cents a quart in 1952, as compared to 11.6 a quart in 1959. This appears to mean that in your locality the decline has been more than the average. Only the Middle Atlantic States have shown a slight improvement in the prices paid by dealers to farmers during these particular years.

To what particular factor do you attribute the unusual loss in your own area? Is local production too high? Is per capital consumption in your market decreasing? Is less milk being used for butter, ice cream and the like? Has the middleman's spread gone up, in your case, more than the national average of 2.7 cents?[6]

We know that farmers, except for the fortunate, many of whom are the big operators with a high degree of mechanization, have obviously been failing to share in the average increases in the nation's prosperity. For seven long years I have pondered this problem and every recommendation that I have been able to obtain from responsible parties. Every suggested cure seems to bring additional problems in its wake.

In this connection, one of the nation's most acute problems involves wheat.[7] Not only do we have more than three and a half billion dollars invested in wheat now in storage, but its storage and maintenance costs are getting most burdensome. But it is seemingly impossible to get any general agreement, among wheat farmers themselves, as to what measures are needed both to bring up net farm income in the wheat area and at the same time bring adverse factors under such control as will permit a maximum of freedom of action to the farmer and tend to reduce our tremendous Federal expenditures. This particular question seems relatively simple as compared to the one outlined in your own case. Yet I repeat that even for this one it seems impossible to reach any agreement as to what is the appropriate function of government or what measures would begin gradually to attain the objectives just mentioned.[8]

By no means do I want to ask you to give me any long reply. What I am really asking is—do you have any specific suggestions that you believe would be reasonable, practicable and which would, in the long run, tend to reduce rather than increase the Federal government's control over the farmer?[9]

I assure you that I found your article interesting. I have marked this letter "Personal and Confidential" because I merely seek a little information and a glimmer of light.[10]

With best wishes—and better milk prices! *Sincerely*

[1] Eisenhower was referring to Mary Conger's article, the "Farmer's Side of the Case," which would appear in the *Saturday Evening Post* on April 9, 1960. In it she described the pressures that she and her husband faced as owners of a dairy farm in southeastern Kansas, as well as those problems the dairy industry and agriculture as a whole confronted ("The Farmer's Side of the Case," *Saturday Evening Post*). Conger would explain that farmers were alarmed because misunderstanding of the true farm situation was so profound and widespread (Conger to Eisenhower, same file as the document, Apr. 14, 1960).

[2] On Eisenhower's Gettysburg farm, see, for example, in these volumes, no. 96; Galambos, *NATO and the Campaign of 1952*, nos. 170 and 770; and for general background see Nevins, *Gettysburg's Five-Star Farmer.*

[3] The soil bank provisions of the 1956 Agricultural Act had set up the "conservation reserve" program, an initiative under which farmers could enter into long-term contracts with the federal government to retire land out of productive use and devote it to conservation purposes. In exchange, participants received annual payments from the federal government (see Galambos and van Ee, *The Middle Way*, no. 1595, and *Congressional Quarterly Almanac*, vol. XII, *1956*, p. 375).

[4] Conger had described how dairy farmers, constantly under pressure to increase investments in order to make a profit, were caught in the squeeze between rising costs of production and lower income resulting from a downward trend in milk prices. Conger had suggested legislation that "would extend to farmers the same rights of collective bargaining, without antitrust penalties" that labor enjoyed. She had also suggested that farmers go on strike, be allowed to develop oligopolistic control over production and supply, and be given tax breaks such as those enjoyed by business ("The Farmer's Side of the Case," *Saturday Evening Post*, Apr. 9, 1960).

In her reply of April 14 to Eisenhower (same file as document), Conger, unable to give any specific reason why farmers could not organize, would allude to the dissension among existing organizations. She again referred to farmers' inability to eliminate the disparity in price ratios between agricultural and other products. The core of the farm problem, she explained, was that "most other groups are able to maintain or increase their prices, wages, and charges for services—and pass these costs on to us—while we [farmers] have no effective bargaining mechanism to force the consumer to pay comparable prices for our product."

[5] Before sending this letter, Eisenhower had called the Attorney General and had asked if any law prohibited farmers from organizing similarly to labor; the Attorney General had answered that there were none (Telephone conversation, Eisenhower and Rogers, Apr. 4, 1960, AWF/D).

[6] Conger would not answer these questions directly in her reply. The Secretary of Agriculture, however, would address the problem of milk prices in a letter to the President. The comparison Conger had made was not valid, Benson would state, because she had compared the high prices reached during the Korean War to those attained afterward, when price supports had been lowered to reflect declining markets and the huge expansion in production. Even so, the government had purchased its largest volume of dairy products during Eisenhower's presidency and had developed new methods of foreign disposal. In 1959, he said, producers were enjoying a record high in cash receipts. He added that Kansas farm real estate had "jumped 108 percent since the Congers purchased their farm in 1939" and thus "they could make a substantial capital gain if they sold out" (Benson's May 9 letter and Eisenhower's May 11, 1960, reply are both in AWF/A).

[7] For background on the wheat surplus see no. 1376; for developments see no. 1721.

[8] For Eisenhower's views on the difficulty of reconciling the costs of solving the agricultural dilemma with the need to limit government expenditures see no. 931.

[9] Conger would reply, "Farmers have reached a state of financial crisis in which they may not object to regulation by a benevolent government so much, as they fear the threat of liquidation." Farmers would look to the government for leadership, she thought, because they would need help in organizing some means of attaining equitable bargaining power and control over supply. If farmers could obtain "a fair return for feeding the nation's population, they could assume at least part of the responsibility of taking charge of their own surpluses." Specifically, she mentioned that a market regulation plan and the conservation reserve might help, and she observed that "taxpayers might feel they were getting more for their money" if the government bought the land for recreational purposes. "Let's explore the middle-of-the-road," she concluded: "There must be some course that lies between 'farm aid and subsidies' on the one hand and 'returning farmers to the free economy' on the other" (Conger to Eisenhower, Apr. 14, 1960, same file as document).

[10] Thanking Mrs. Conger for her reply, Eisenhower would note that she had not attempted to answer his specific questions: "Possibly they are not too important. In any event, the general tone of your letter indicates that in certain instances specific answers would not be possible" (Apr. 21, 1960, *ibid.*).

To William Edward Robinson   *April 5, 1960*
Personal

Dear Bill: This morning, at the Leadership meeting, one of the Congressmen present mentioned the apparently consistent criticism of the Administration that appears editorially both in the *Des Moines Register* and the *Minneapolis Journal-Tribune.* Both papers, as you know, are owned by the Cowles brothers who, in 1952 at any rate, counted themselves as "good Republicans."[1]

Have you been aware of this? Is it a result of any dissatisfaction on the part of John and Mike Cowles, or is it a matter their taking a "hands-off" policy as regards their editorial writers?[2] Is the criticism a blanket indictment of all Administration policies, or does it center around the farm problems. And do you have any suggestions?[3]

Once again, many thanks for interrupting your Augusta weekend to come up to Washington.[4]

With warm regard, *As ever*

[1] Eisenhower had first met the Cowles brothers in 1950 (see Galambos, *Columbia University,* no. 757). John Cowles was president of the Minneapolis Star and Tribune Company. Gardner ("Mike") Cowles was president of the Register and Tribune Company and Cowles Magazines of New York City. For background on their support of Eisenhower in 1952 see Galambos, *NATO and the Campaign of 1952,* nos. 308 and 879.

[2] Robinson would reply (Apr. 7, AWF/N) that both Cowles brothers were traveling. Robinson had been aware of their "lack of Administration support for some time." Mike Cowles's "sheer opportunism in his constant drive for circulation" was one reason, Robinson believed. He was "subtly attacking" the Administration and Republican philosophy in order to appeal to Democratic readers, Robinson said. Robinson had also heard that John Cowles had been "rabidly against Secretary Dulles" and had "disagreed with the Administration's Far Eastern policy" (for background see no. 944). With virtual newspaper monopolies in both Minneapolis and Des Moines, Robinson wrote, the Cowles brothers "obviously play both sides of the street as a means of preventing any competitive encroachment."

[3] Among the various subjects criticized in the editorials were the Administration's policies regarding civil rights, agriculture, and immigration (see, for example, *Minneapolis Journal-Tribune,* Mar. 23, 30, 1960, and *Des Moines Register,* Mar. 19–21, 24, 1960).

[4] Robinson, who had traveled to Washington on Saturday, February 20, said he planned to talk with both John and Mike Cowles. He suggested that Vice-President Nixon also take steps to correct the situation.

To CHRISTIAN ARCHIBALD HERTER   *April 12, 1960*
Personal

Memorandum for the Secretary of State: George Champion told me last
evening that within a few days he is to have an appointment with
you, during which he hopes to give you the impressions he formed
in the course of his trip through Asian countries.[1] He is particularly
anxious that we invite the Prime Minister of Malaya for a visit. As
you know, visits from Prime Ministers normally cause me very little
trouble, so if you should want to make such a gesture I would have
no objection.[2]

Incidentally, did you suggest anything to Diefenbaker about the
possibility of a visit to Washington between the Summit and my trip
to Russia and Japan?[3]

[1] For background see no. 1475. Eisenhower had seen Champion at the Augusta National Golf Club.

[2] Herter had reminded Eisenhower that Prime Minister Tunku Abdul Rahman had
received an invitation to visit the United States the previous January. "Unfortunately
his commitments were such that he could not accept at that time," Herter responded,
"but we have continued to hope that we might find an occasion to invite him later
this year" (Herter to Eisenhower, Apr. 19, 1960, AWF/D-H). Rahman would visit the
United States in October (see no. 1634; see also Rahman to Eisenhower, Apr. 20,
1960; Henderson to Eisenhower, Apr. 27, 1960; and Eisenhower to Rahman, Apr. 30,
1960, all in AWF/I: Malaya).

[3] On April 8 Eisenhower had told Secretary Herter that he had been reading about
deteriorating relations between the United States and Canada. Although neither had
been aware of specific problems, Eisenhower suggested that they give Diefenbaker
"a little more of the red carpet treatment" and invite him to visit the United States.
After discussing possible dates with Diefenbaker, the Canadian ambassador had told
Herter that a visit before the summit meeting in May would not be possible (Telephone conversations, Eisenhower and Herter; and Herter and Heeney, Apr. 8, 1960,
Herter Papers, Telephone Conversations, AWF/D, and State, *Foreign Relations, 1958–
1960*, vol. VII, pt. 1, *Western European Integration and Security; Canada*, p. 788; on Eisenhower's visits to the Soviet Union and Japan see nos. 1381-A and 1456).

Eisenhower would call Diefenbaker from Augusta three days later in order to establish a satisfactory date; the Canadian leader would meet with Eisenhower on June
3 for informal talks (Telephone conversation, Eisenhower and Diefenbaker, Apr. 15,
1960, AWF/D-H; see also State, *Foreign Relations, 1958–1960*, vol. VII, pt. 1, *Western
European Integration and Security; Canada*, pp. 800–807).

To Ruth Ann Couto   *April 13, 1960*
Personal and confidential

Dear Ruth Ann: Thank you for your thoughtful letter. I am delighted
to send you a personal reply, although I must request that you not
publish it, as you suggest, in your school paper.[1]

The question of whether we are "ahead" or "behind" the Russian
government is one, of course, that engages the attention of a great
number of people.[2] It is a popular—and an easy—topic of conversation. Certainly it is evident that currently the Russians have greater
power in their space engines, for instance, than have we; it is just as
evident that in other areas we have demonstrated our own scientific
superiority. But as to the basic question respecting our military
strength, I assure you that it is not only adequate, but is deeply respected by the Soviets.

You ask whether there will be another World War.[3] I can only repeat what I have said so many times; a war on a global basis, using
the awesome weapons of which many countries are now capable,
would, we all know, result in the annihilation of great portions of
the earth. I am sure Mr. Khrushchev is as anxious as am I, and as
are the leaders of other nations, to avoid such an unthinkable catastrophe. My own unshakeable belief is that under these conditions
our greatest danger is not military attack but exposure, throughout
the free world, to Communist subversion and penetration.

I recognize the concern that you and your classmates have about
these great issues; I hope you all appreciate the overwhelming advantage you have of living in freedom in a country where the individual's deeply held faith is paramount, as opposed to the atheistic
doctrines of the Soviets. Moreover, I venture to suggest that your
main job at the moment is to equip yourself, by education and all
other possible means, to be an informed citizen of tomorrow: in so
doing you and all the young people like you will be our country's
greatest asset in making progress toward a durable peace in freedom.

With best wishes, *Sincerely*

---

[1] Ruth Ann Couto, a thirteen-year-old eighth grader from North Westport, Massachusetts, had written Eisenhower that if he replied, her "other classmates would be
glad to know that K[h]rushchev isn't the only one who answers *fan* mail" (Mar. 27,
1960, AWF/D).
[2] Couto had asked about the relative strength of the Soviet Union and the United
States, writing "almost everyday you can find someone telling you that we are either
far ahead of Russia or far behind."
[3] Couto thought the possibility of war was the most important question and had also
asked under what circumstances a war with the Soviet Union might occur. She wrote:

"I have no personal hatred for Mr. K[h]rushchev but I think of him as a person. Any person, when given the choice, will choose to live rather than to die." "Mr. K[h]rushchev knows he could drop a bomb on the United States. . . . he also knows that before the United States would be totally destroyed that Russia would be well on her way too."

1502   *EM, AWF, International Series: Guinea*

To Sékou Touré   *April 13, 1960*
Cable. Confidential

Dear Mr. President: Thank you for the courtesy of your thoughtful letter of March nineteenth. I appreciate your taking the trouble to write me about certain aspects of the Republic of Guinea's foreign relations.[1]

During your visit to Washington last fall, I was impressed by your earnest explanation of Guinea's foreign policy.[2] I quite understand and respect your desire not to become involved in differences among other nations. In order for Guinea to be able to maintain this position, however, I assume that you would be anxious to avoid measures which by their nature would appear to place Guinea in a position which would tend to align her with either side.[3]

With regard to recognition of the North Viet-Namese regime, I would like to give you a frank expression of my opinions, not as any criticism of your own judgments, but to clarify the reasons which make such recognition for us an impossibility. In recognizing the Republic of Viet-Nam (which also emerged from the same colonial status as Guinea), the United States, along with fifty-two other non-Communist or neutral nations (including other independent African countries, and even such neutral nations as Iraq) has been guided by the principle that it, rather than the North Viet-Namese regime, represents the legitimate government of the entire country. Accordingly the United States is not signatory to the Geneva Agreements.[4]

I believe that our judgment in recognizing the Republic of Viet-Nam has been vindicated by the actions of her government, which include the holding of two national elections since the Geneva Agreements, during which time the North Viet-Namese regime has so far held none.

I sympathize with your desire to repatriate Guinean nationals in North Viet-Nam. I would like to point out, however, that this can be done by means other than recognition. In particular, I note that the International Red Cross has been very helpful in similar situations without recognition having been accorded to the country involved. Indeed, the North Viet-Namese regime has not been recognized up to this point by any nation outside the Communist bloc.[5] I should point out my concern that recognition on the part of Guinea, coming so soon after your announcement of Soviet assistance, will inevitably risk misinterpretation by some of Guinea's friends and association of Guinea in world opinion with countries of the Communist bloc.[6]

As far as Germany is concerned, I note with deep satisfaction your assurance that Guinea has not recognized the East German regime. You are, of course, familiar with the reasons why neither the United States nor any other non-Communist government regards East Germany as a separate State or the East German regime as a legitimate government and why we consider the German Federal Republic as the only government which may properly represent Germany in relations with other nations.[7]

Once again I assure you of the continued friendship of the United States and of our desire to cooperate and assist in Guinea's development. I was delighted to note the recent visit here by the Guinean youth delegation and look forward to welcoming more Guinean students to the United States and to sending English language teachers to your country. With such contacts between our two nations, the bonds, which you so ably established by your visit here, will continued to grow in strength.[8]

With assurances of my continued respect and esteem, *Sincerely*

[1] Touré's letter to Eisenhower is in WHO/OSS: International, Guinea.

[2] For background on Touré's visit and the concern over Guinea's political leanings see no. 1309, and E. Frederic Morrow, *Black Man in the White House*, pp. 288–90.

[3] Touré's letter had explained Guinea's neutrality to Eisenhower: "Our foreign policy prohibits our alignment with any bloc or interference in the internal affairs of peoples, nations, and governments" (Touré to Eisenhower, Mar. 19, 1960, WHO/OSS: International, Guinea).

[4] Touré had argued that the United States, which he said had played such a prominent role in ending the Indochina War and in negotiating and signing the Geneva Accords, should approve his country's diplomatic relations with North Vietnam.

[5] North Vietnam had been one of the first countries to propose diplomatic relations after Guinea's independence. Guinea had agreed, Touré explained, because the two countries faced similar problems and shared interests in dealing with the "aftereffects" of French colonization. He maintained that this course of action would help smooth the repatriation of Guinean nationals left in Vietnam after the Indochina Wars, as well as help those returned Guinean veterans who had married Vietnamese women.

[6] Touré had recently agreed to accept $35,000,000 in credit from the Soviet Union (*New York Times*, Mar. 5, 1960).

[7] Touré said that the press had mistakenly reported that Guinea had established relations with East Germany. While negotiations to establish relations had taken place, no official decision had yet been made (*New York Times*, Mar. 6, 9, 12, 17).

[8] Competing with the Soviet Bloc countries as well as China, the United States and

other western nations were attempting to gain credit with Touré (and the leaders of other former colonies) with offers of assistance. During Touré's visit to Washington, the U. S. government had offered 150 scholarships for Guinean students to study in the United States and abroad. In addition, the United States offered to provide teacher training for the country's English language program, which was a priority because Guinea had made English compulsory in its schools. The Eisenhower Administration would continue to face difficulties in negotiating an aid package with the Guineans (see Morrow to Herter, Mar. 21, 1960, WHO/OSS: International, Guinea), but an agreement would eventually be signed (*New York Times*, Oct. 31, 1960; for background, see State, *Foreign Relations, 1958–1960*, vol. XIV, *Africa*, pp. 698–710, and John H. Morrow, *First American Ambassador to Guinea* [New Brunswick, N. J., 1968], pp. 233–52). For developments see no. 1611.

1503   *EM, WHCF, Official File 99-V*

To Gerald Rudolph Ford, Jr.   *April 13, 1960*

Dear Jerry: I have just received in confidence a digest of the actions taken by the sub-committee. While of course you know my diverse views in certain details, it seems to me that you and your cohorts have achieved real successes in a difficult struggle. As we stick together and keep fighting we shall correct still more deficiencies. Congratulations to you and other friends in the sub-committee.[1]

With warm regard,

[1] In his February 16 message to Congress, Eisenhower had asked for $4,250,000,000 for the 1961 Mutual Security Program (see *Public Papers of the Presidents: Eisenhower, 1960–61*, pp. 177–88; for background see nos. 60, 94, and 1494). On March 7 the House Appropriations Foreign Operations Subcommittee had begun hearings on the appropriation legislation, which faced stiff opposition. Ford was a member of the subcommittee. For developments see no. 1536.

1504   *EM, WHCF, Official File 101-PP*

To Franklin G. Floete   *April 13, 1960*

Dear Mr. Floete:[1] The papers of a President, which from the time of George Washington have been regarded as the personal property of the President, have, inescapably, a direct and important association with the history of our country. Believing that they should be permanently and generally available for study, I desire that my papers should be made so available and believe that this can best be done through a Presidential archival depository, as provided by the Federal Property and Administrative Services Act of 1949, as amended.[2]

The Eisenhower Presidential Library Commission, an agency of the State of Kansas, now has under construction in the City of Abilene a library building, financed by public subscription, where it is proposed to house my Presidential and other papers. This building is appropriately situated on land adjacent to my boyhood home and to a museum, both of which are maintained by the Eisenhower Foundation, a non-profit corporation organized under the laws of Kansas.[3]

When the Library building has been completed, the Commission intends to present it, together with equipment and grounds, as a gift to the United States, on condition that the United States will maintain and operate this Library as a Presidential archival depository under the provisions of the above cited Act.[4]

Therefore, in furtherance of this plan and in accordance with the provisions of that Act, I now offer as a gift to the United States such of my papers and other documentary materials as are hereinafter described, on condition that these papers and materials will be accepted, preserved, and made available by the United States under the following terms:

1. Upon the close of my term in office, I shall cause to be transferred to the United States for deposit in the Library at Abilene the bulk of my papers in the White House office, estimated to include several million documents.

2. Other documents, still in my possession, including the remainder of my Presidential papers, the papers accumulated by me before my inauguration as President, and other documentary materials, including books, still pictures, motion pictures, and sound recordings, shall be transferred to the United States for deposit in said Library from time to time as shall be agreed upon by the Administrator of General Services or his representative and me or my representative, except those papers and other documentary materials which shall, before or after my leaving the Office of President, be determined by me or my representative to be excluded from this offer by reason of private or personal interest in such papers or materials on my part or on the part of a member of my family.

3. The offer of the papers and other materials described in paragraphs 1 and 2 hereof is conditioned upon acceptance by the United States of the offer of the land and buildings comprising the Eisenhower Library at Abilene, Kansas, and upon its agreement to maintain and operate the Library at all times thereafter as a Presidential archival depository for the storage of such papers and other materials, in accordance with the provisions of

the Federal Property and Administrative Services Act of 1949, as amended, such acceptance and agreement to be effected within 90 days after the end of the period described in the second proviso to section 507(f) (1) of said Act.

4. All papers and other documentary materials which shall be transferred to the United States pursuant to the foregoing shall be kept in the Library permanently, subject to the right of the Administrator of General Services in his discretion (*a*) to make temporary loans thereof to such persons, organizations, or institutions as he shall determine, (*b*) to dispose by sale, exchange, or otherwise of any such papers or documentary materials which the Archivist of the United Stats may determine to have no permanent or historical interest or to be surplus to the needs of said Library, and (*c*) to remove from said Library any or all such papers or documentary materials if he deems it necessary to preserve them from threatened destruction.

5. All papers and other documentary materials transferred to the United States pursuant to the foregoing shall be accessible at all reasonable times to me, my son, my representative, or to other persons authorized in writing by me or my son to have access to such papers.

6. It is my purpose to make the papers and other documentary materials donated to the United States by the terms of this instrument available for purposes of serious research as soon as possible and to the fullest extent possible. However, since the President of the United States is the recipient of many confidences from others, and since the inviolability of such confidences is essential to the functioning of the office of the Presidency, it will be necessary to withhold from public scrutiny certain papers and classes of papers for varying periods of time. In pursuance of this objective and in accordance with the provisions of Section 507(f) (3) of the Federal Property and Administrative Services Act of 1949, as amended, conditions are imposed on the use of my papers as provided in paragraphs 7 through 10 immediately following.

7. Subsequent to the execution of this instrument, the Administrator of General Services shall have the papers that are transferred to the United States reviewed and shall place under seal the following classes of materials:
    a. Papers that are security-classified pursuant to law or Executive Order, until such classification shall be removed.
    b. Papers the use of which may be prejudicial to the maintenance of good relations with foreign nations.
    c. Papers containing statements made by or to me in confidence.

d. Papers relating to my family or private business affairs, and papers relating to the families or private business affairs of persons who have had correspondence with me.

e. Papers containing statements about individuals which might be used to injure or harass them or members of their families.

f. Such other individual files as I, or my representative, or the Administrator of General Services may specify.

8. Papers placed under seal shall not be made available to anyone or their contents divulged to anyone (including public officials) except (a) persons authorized under the terms of paragraph 5 above, and (b) officials and employees of the National Archives and Records Service when performing essential archival work processes on such papers under the supervision of the Administrator of General Services.

9. All papers placed under seal in accordance with the foregoing provisions shall be reexamined from time to time by officials and employees of the National Archives and Records Service under the direction of the Administrator of General Services and, subject to approval by me or my representative, shall be opened to research use as soon as the passage of time or other circumstances have removed the conditions that required that they be put under seal.

10. All competent private persons interested in using my papers for serious scholarly research shall be granted equal access to those that are not withheld from use according to the foregoing, subject to the regulations issued by the Administrator of General Services governing the use of papers and other documentary materials in the Library.

11. Title to my papers and other documentary materials and the literary property rights in my papers, shall pass to the United States as such papers and materials are transferred to the United States under the terms and conditions herein expressed, except that I reserve to myself and my heirs (a) a right to make any use of any of these papers in writing for publication, and (b) literary property rights in any works that I have written or may hereafter write for publication. These reservations include the right to license any publisher of any such work.

12. My representative for purposes of paragraphs 2, 5, 7, 8 and 9 shall be such person or persons as I may designate in a letter filed with the Administrator of General Services. In the event that at any time after my death there should be no representative so designated, my representative shall be my son John Eisenhower, or such person or persons as he may designate in the same manner.[5]

The detailed conditions described in this letter have been drawn up in accordance with known precedents and with the cooperation of officials of your office and of the National Archives. Permit me to express my deep appreciation of the help that all these individuals have given me.[6]

With personal regard, *Sincerely*

[1] Floete was head of the General Services Administration.

[2] On August 12, 1955, the Federal Property and Administrative Services Act of 1949 was amended, by joint resolution, to include provision for the acceptance and maintenance of Presidential libraries. Federal approval of such offers to donate papers was assumed to be automatic, but the law required that the request rest before Congress for 60 working days (*U.S. Statutes at Large*, vol. 69 [1955], pp. 695–96; see also John S. D. Eisenhower, *Strictly Personal*, p. 283).

[3] For background on the Eisenhower Library see no. 1284; on the Eisenhower Museum see no. 899. See also no. 1556.

[4] Although the Eisenhower Library would be completed in October 1961, additional funds would be needed to provide it with the necessary equipment. On May 1, 1962, the State of Kansas would turn over the facility to the federal government. General Eisenhower would speak at the dedication (*New York Times*, Oct. 29, 1961, and May 2, 1962).

[5] See also John S. D. Eisenhower, *Strictly Personal*, pp. 282–84.

[6] Floete would accept Eisenhower's proposal on April 15 (same file as document), and subsequently would file a report on the proposal with Congress. The President's offer to the government and Floete's reply would be released on April 19 (see *Public Papers of the Presidents: Eisenhower, 1960–61*, pp. 348–52, and *New York Times*, Apr. 20, 1960).

The first truckload of the President's papers would arrive in Abilene on January 16, 1961 (*New York Times*, Jan. 17, 18, 20, 1961). The Dwight D. Eisenhower Library would formally open its manuscript collections for research on November 17, 1966 (see Wickman to Chandler, Oct. 24, and Chandler to Wickman, Oct. 31, 1966, EP).

1505   *EM, AWF, Name Series*

TO ARTHUR WILLIAM TEDDER   *April 13, 1960*
Telegram

Dear Arthur: I understand that the doctors want you to stay in the hospital at least until Sunday and then to rest for a few days before attempting the journey East and to England.[1] Much as I dislike throwing my vast hospital experience around, I do think you should obey their professional advice. The important thing is for you to get a thorough rest before attempting the not inconsequential rigors of the remainder of your trip. If you feel up to it and do not have to rush back, perhaps we can set up another date in Washington sometime after General de Gaulle leaves town.[2] I shall in the meantime hold Monday until I hear from Toppy.[3] But I strongly urge that you go direct to New York and on to London. I want very much to see you, but I shall be happier if you follow the doctors' orders without deviation. At any rate, I shall hope to see you in the not too distant future.

With love to Toppy and Richard[4] and all the best to yourself, *As ever*

[1] While traveling around the world Lord Tedder had suffered a stroke and had been hospitalized in California (see no. 1436, and Ann Whitman to Eisenhower, n.d., AWF/N, Tedder Corr.).

[2] See no. 1436. The Eisenhowers had planned to host a White House luncheon for Tedder and his wife on Monday, April 18 (Telephone conversation, Eisenhower and Mrs. Eisenhower, Apr. 6, 1960, AWF/AWD; and Tedder to Eisenhower, Mar. 16, 1960, AWF/N). On French President de Gaulle's visit to the United States (April 22–26) see nos. 1516 and 1522, and *New York Times*, Apr. 23, 30, 1960.

[3] Tedder would remain in California to recuperate. The President would telephone him shortly before noon on April 18 (Telephone conversation, Eisenhower and Tedder, AWF/AWD).

[4] Tedder's youngest son Richard, born May 22, 1946, was Eisenhower's godson.

1506   *EM, AWF, Dulles-Herter Series*

NOTE   *April 14, 1960*

I agree that DeGaulle should write the letter to Mr. K concerning procedures—pointing out, however, he did so after consultations.[1] Letter concerning V.P. is OK.[2]

[1] For background see no. 1497. Eisenhower had handwritten this note at the bottom of a memorandum to him from Secretary Herter regarding a proposed letter to Soviet Premier Khrushchev that dealt with summit procedures. Having discussed the draft letter with British Foreign Secretary Lloyd and French Foreign Secretary Couve de Murville, Herter had written: "While both of them were a little shy at the outset in talking frankly, they finally made it very clear that they felt De Gaulle's feelings would be greatly hurt if you did not hold up on this letter to discuss it with him when he arrives here at the end of next week. . . ." De Gaulle, according to Couve de Murville, was "in complete sympathy" with Eisenhower's suggestions and could then communicate, as host of the conference, the preferences of the three Western leaders to Khrushchev. Herter had enclosed a draft letter to the Russian leader "as a basis for a memorandum to present to de Gaulle for discussion, rather than as a letter you had proposed to send yourself" (Herter to Eisenhower, Apr. 14, 1960, AWF/D-H; see also State, *Foreign Relations, 1958–1960*, vol. IX, *Berlin Crisis 1959–1960; Germany; Austria*, pp. 331–32). For developments see no. 1516.

[2] For Eisenhower's letter to Khrushchev regarding Vice-President Nixon's possible role in the summit proceedings see no. 1508; see also Herter to Eisenhower, Apr. 14, 1960, AWF/D-H.

NOTE   *April 14, 1960*

I see little difference between senior advisors and advisors. As I understand it the members of the advisory group are all "on call."[1]

[1] Eisenhower had handwritten this note at the top of a memorandum from Secretary Herter regarding the makeup of the U.S. delegation to the summit conference scheduled to begin on May 16. Herter had attached a list of proposed participants divided into four categories: Delegation, including the President and the Secretary of State; Senior Advisers, including the American ambassadors to Great Britain, France, and the Soviet Union; Advisers, including other State Department officials; and Advisers on call for discussion of nuclear test suspension, including Defense Department officials and the chairman of the Atomic Energy Commission (Herter to Eisenhower, Apr. 14, 1960, AWF/D-H; see also Telephone conversation, Herter and Gates, Apr. 12, 1960, Herter Papers, Telephone Conversations).

    On the delegation see Telephone conversations, Herter and Goodpaster, April 20, 22, 1960, Herter Papers, Telephone Conversations). For developments on the conference see no. 1516.

1508   *EM, AWF,*
International Series:
Khrushchev

To NIKITA SERGEYEVICH KHRUSHCHEV   *April 16, 1960*

Dear Mr. Chairman:[1] As I know you fully realize, the length of time which I can stay away from this country in connection with our forthcoming Quadripartite Conference in Paris must, of necessity, be limited by my many responsibilities here, and by the fact that I shall again be out of the country on my visit to your country in the month of June.[2] I have laid out my schedule so as to be available in Paris for the whole week beginning May sixteenth, starting my return journey to the United States on Monday, the twenty-third of May, with a twenty-four hour stop-over in Lisbon.

    I am, of course, hopeful that our conversations can be concluded during the course of the week. However, should it seem advisable to carry them on beyond Sunday, and in the event that domestic responsibilities should then require my presence in the United States, I would designate[3] the Vice President to act in my place for the remainder of the meeting of the Heads of Government. I did want you to know of my projected plans so that you would understand my situation before any announcement was made of my twenty-four hour visit to Lisbon on May twenty-third.[4] *Sincerely*

[1] A State Department draft of this letter with Eisenhower's handwritten emendations is in AWF/D-H. The message was cabled to the American embassy in Moscow for delivery to Premier Khrushchev (see Herter to Eisenhower, Apr. 14, 1960, *ibid.*).
[2] For background on preparations for the Summit Conference and on Eisenhower's planned visit to the Soviet Union see nos. 1456 and 1506.
[3] In the State Department draft this word had originally been "request."
[4] The duration of the meeting should be contingent on its progress, Khrushchev would answer. "As to the question of the advisability of continuing the meeting without your participation, I feel that this should be decided at the meeting itself by agreement between all parties" (Khrushchev to Eisenhower, Apr. 20, 1960, AWF/I: Khrushchev). For developments see no. 1516.

1509

To Mohammed Reza Pahlavi   *April 16, 1960*
Cable. Confidential

Imperial Majesty: A situation has arisen at the Law of the Sea Conference in Geneva which deserves the urgent attention of all nations which cherish both their territorial integrity and free and unfettered intercourse among nations on the high seas.[1]

The United States and Canada have proposed a compromise solution to the question of territorial limits on contiguous international bodies of water which would seem to offer the optimum possible in terms of unilateral and international interests. I refer to the proposal that all countries recognize a six-mile territorial sea, with additional special fishing rights for a limited term of years with respect to an additional six miles. We earnestly solicit your support.

The United States is fully cognizant of the problems confronting Iran on this question. We know that Iran adopted a twelve-mile limit for territorial waters reluctantly and only after Iran's Persian Gulf neighbors had unilaterally claimed similar rights. We recognize that this limit has been approved by the Iranian Parliament and has become legally binding upon your government.

It is against this background that I, nevertheless, seek your support. From a legal viewpoint we believe that Iran could vote for the United States-Canadian proposal with suitable reservations as to the necessity of obtaining Parliamentary approval. In other words, assuming a two-thirds vote could be obtained for this proposal, Iran would be casting its affirmative vote subject to ratification by the Iranian Parliament and your signature. Since the vote would be taken ad referendum, Iran could reserve its final decision until the positions of the other Persian Gulf states became finally known.

If, for reasons which you consider imperative, your government cannot vote affirmatively for the United States-Canadian proposal, I hope that it will be possible for Iran to abstain at least under present circumstances.

We are convinced, after long deliberation, that if this conference fails, or reaches an unsatisfactory conclusion, the interests of all Free World countries will suffer material damage. It is in this vein that my government asks your support.[2]

With warm regard, *Sincerely*

[1] On the United Nations General Assembly's second Conference on the Law of Sea see no. 1307.

[2] On April 8 the United States and Canada had submitted a joint proposal. On April 13 the Committee of the Whole adopted the proposal with a vote of 43 in favor, 33 against, and 12 abstentions. That same day the delegation to the Conference on the Law of the Sea had telegramed the State Department that in order to get the necessary two-thirds majority it was necessary to reduce the number of opposed by at least six and to persuade the abstainees to support the joint proposal.

On April 15 the State Department had asked the President to send personal messages to the Shah of Iran, and to the leaders of India, Morocco, Ethiopia, and Tunisia requesting support for the U.S.-Canadian proposal (see McElhiney to Goodpaster, Apr. 15, 1960, WHO/OSS: Subject [State], State Department, and State, *Foreign Relations, 1958–1960*, vol. II, *United Nations and General International Matters*, pp. 792–93). The other messages, similar in content to this one, are in AWF/I: India, Nehru; AWF/I: Morocco; AWF/I: Ethiopia; and AWF/I: Tunisia. See also Eisenhower to Eyskens, Apr. 22, 1960, AWF/I: Belgium, and Eisenhower to King Idris, Apr. 25, 1960, AWF/I: Libya.

On April 26 the U.S.-Canadian proposal would fail by one vote; a motion to reconsider the proposal also failed. Discussions would go on throughout the spring and summer with no progress on the treaty (*Yearbook of the United Nations 1960* [New York, 1961], pp. 542–44; State, *Foreign Relations, 1958–1960*, vol. II, *United Nations and General International Matters*, pp. 777, 786, 792–93, 807–27; and *New York Times*, Mar. 9, 22, 23, 25, 30, Apr. 2, 9, 14, 17, 23, 26, 27, 1960).

In a memorandum (May 18) the Acting Secretary of State would explain that the Iranian delegation had not voted for the U.S.-Canadian proposal due to Iran's twelve-mile limit law. They had abstained, however, at the Shah's direction. On May 25 Eisenhower would thank the Shah for his "constructive contribution to the effort" (both in AWF/I: Iran).

A third Law of the Sea Conference would convene in 1982. By the time of its ratification in 1994, the much more complex treaty would extend coastal sovereignty from three to twelve miles, with full control of fishing and mining rights within a 200-mile zone (*Yearbook of the United Nations 1994* [New York, 1995], pp. 1301–17, and *New York Times*, Mar. 31, July 1, 12, 1994).

To George W. Woodruff   *April 20, 1960*

Dear George: One of my greatest problems these days is how to answer suggestions such as yours that I appear before the kick-off dinner, next February, for the fund-raising campaign for Agnes Scott College. Before I go into any lengthy explanation, let me assure you that I am appreciative of your cordial invitation.[1]

But I have, at this time, no specific plans beyond January twentieth of next year, nor do I have sufficient opportunity to give any real thought to what I shall want then to do. Actually, I think the prospect of being footloose (for the first time in fifty years) so intrigues me that I do not *want* to make any definite commitments.

As I told you, I might take a long trip or I might go to the West Coast. Equal possibilities are Gettysburg or coming down here, if the weather is sufficiently good.[2] Under the circumstances, and realizing full well that plans for an undertaking such as you have in mind must be formulated far in advance, I can only suggest that you look elsewhere for a major speaker for the event. However, I think it likely that if I am here at the Club and if you might want me to put in a mere appearance at the dinner, I would, at that time, make every effort to comply with your request.

I realize that this reply is totally unsatisfactory, but I doubt that even six months from now I could be any more definite. I am confident, however, that you understand both my mood and my dilemma.

Again, my thanks for the invitation.

With warm regard, *Sincerely*

---

[1] Woodruff, an Atlanta philanthropist, was the younger brother of Coca-Cola executive Robert W. Woodruff. He had served as a director of the Coca-Cola Company since 1936. Agnes Scott College in Decatur, Georgia, is a small, independent, four-year women's college established in 1889. No invitation or written reply by Woodruff is in EM.

[2] The President was vacationing in Augusta, Georgia, and probably had spoken to Woodruff there. During February, March, and April of 1961, the Eisenhowers would vacation in Thomasville, Georgia, and in Palm Springs, California. Eisenhower would not attend the fund-raising dinner at Agnes Scott (*New York Times*, Feb. 1, 7, and Apr. 15, 18, 1961).

To Ralph Thomas Reed   *April 20, 1960*

Dear Ralph: Through my own personal G-2—composed of friends
we have in common—I learn that you are retiring on May 1st as
President of the American Express Company.[1] Although I understand you will continue to have a senior position with the company,
I suspect now would be a good time for stocktaking, and in that effort you will find much of which to be proud.[2] In your sixteen years
of leadership, while building up the services and resources of the
American Express Company, you have advanced the welfare of your
fellow men and strengthened our relations with our neighbors overseas.[3] You have a splendid record of accomplishment, and I congratulate you most sincerely.

Knowing you, I know also that you have abundant talent and energy to continue to devote to your many interests. I trust that you
will continue to work toward the strengthening of our contacts (of
which you personally have so many) with the peoples of other countries, since I am more firmly convinced than ever of the importance
of such friendships.[4]

Incidentally, I shall myself join your enviable "society of the retired" in something like nine months. If I needed to be convinced,
the last ten days in Augusta have persuaded me completely that a
lot of good golf constitutes a fine prescription for a happy life![5]

With affectionate regard to Edna and Phyllis,[6] and all the best to
yourself, *As ever*

[1] The mutual friend was former Secretary of the Army Kenneth C. Royall (see Royall
to Eisenhower, Apr. 5, 1960, and Eisenhower to Royall, Apr. 8, 1960, both in same file
as document; see also *New York Times*, Apr. 27, 1960). Reed had joined the American
Express Company in 1919 as an assistant to the comptroller. A draft of this letter containing Eisenhower's handwritten emendations is in the same file as the document. In
a note on the incoming letter the President directed Special Counsel David Kendall to
add Reed's name to the "list of eligibles," presumably available for special federal tasks.
[2] Reed would reply (Apr. 26, same file as document) that he would continue as a director and chairman of the executive committee and would maintain his New York
office for consultation and advice.
[3] For background on Reed's efforts to strengthen relationships abroad see Galambos
and van Ee, *The Middle Way*, no. 1791.
[4] Reed and his wife planned to travel to Europe in May, Reed would write. He said
he would try to follow Eisenhower's advice about strengthening international relationships. He had been named chairman of the United States Council of the International Chamber of Commerce, he would add, and in that capacity he could play
a small part in improving relations with business leaders of other countries.
[5] At this point in the draft Eisenhower deleted language including "relief from responsibility" as part of a prescription for happiness. Reed would bid Eisenhower a
"premature welcome" to the ranks of the retired. He expected to spend more time

at Augusta, he wrote, and looked forward to seeing the Eisenhowers there. On the President's traditional April vacation in Augusta, Georgia, see no. 1495.

[6] Reed's wife was the former Edna May Young; Phyllis Ann was his daughter.

1512

EM, AWF,
Administration Series

To Robert Bernerd Anderson   *April 21, 1960*

Dear Bob: Attached is a letter from a Mr. Nielsen, in Omaha, which was forwarded to me by a personal friend.[1]

All of these people can't be wrong. No further communication need to be sent to Mr. Nielsen, but his letter does provide some information that might be valuable to your experts.[2]

I am leaving here this afternoon for Washington—sadly.[3] *As ever*

[1] N. Chris Nielsen owned Nielsen Violin Shop and dealt in high-grade string instruments. Eisenhower, who had received the letter through his son's mother-in-law, also sent a copy to his daughter-in-law because it contained "some very splendid observations about the value of music, both in the home and in the school" (Eisenhower to Barbara Eisenhower, Apr. 21, 1960, AWF/D).

[2] Nielsen had appealed to the President for help to eliminate the excise tax on musical instruments. Nielsen had close contact with music education in Omaha schools. School-purchased instruments were tax exempt, he wrote, but about 95% of the instruments used were purchased by students from music stores. Most string instruments, he said, were imported and carried a 20% duty. The excise tax was, in his view, an unnecessary burden that increased the price of the instruments.

In his budget message (Jan. 18, 1960), however, Eisenhower had already asked Congress to postpone reductions in excise and corporate income tax rates, and the House Ways and Means Committee had delayed taking up the request until May. No hearings would be held, but Secretary Anderson would testify in an executive session (May 24–25) in support of the President's request. Congress would approve the President's request for another one-year postponement in the scheduled reductions, and on June 30 Eisenhower would sign into law P.L. 86–564 (*Congressional Quarterly Almanac*, vol. XVI, *1960*, pp. 362–64).

[3] The President had been vacationing in Augusta, Georgia, since April 11 (see no. 1495).

1513   *EM, AWF, Administration Series*

To Charles Douglas Jackson   *April 22, 1960*

Dear C. D.: Yesterday on the plane I had an opportunity to read two of your letters of the eighteenth and, as always, found much of interest in your ideas (and in Mr. Patterson's suggestions). I shall discuss the various matters with the Secretary of State before he leaves town early next week.[1]

Meantime, the important thing is the congratulations that are deservedly due you. I can well understand that the job of publisher of LIFE will be a demanding one, but at the same time I know that you have energy abundant—and more—for such a task.[2]

Thanks so much, too, for the copy of Mr. Duncan's handsome book on the Kremlin. I shall send him a note of appreciation, too. As to the suggestion about Mr. Khrushchev, I'd be happy to take him a copy (if he has not already received one from the publishers or Mr. Duncan—or someone). Perhaps I should take it along with me to Paris, since I think half the pleasure of books like this one is the first glimpse.[3]

Needless to say, it gives me a great feeling of gratification to know that the "old fire horse" is in there pitching (if I may mix a metaphor).[4]

With warm regard, *As ever*

[1] Eisenhower had returned on the preceding day from an eleven-day golfing vacation in Augusta. One of three letters Jackson had written on that day referred to a conversation he had had with Morehead Patterson, former U.S. representative to the International Atomic Energy Agency. Patterson had suggested that Eisenhower tell Soviet Premier Khrushchev at the Summit Conference that he was just as interested in Atoms-for-Peace as he had been in December 1953 and that he would turn over the fissionable material of twenty-five stockpiled atomic bombs to the appropriate international agency for peaceful uses. Patterson also suggested that one or more of the obsolete bombs could be made into full-scale or miniature plowshares that Eisenhower could present to Khrushchev and other members of the Presidium during his visit to Moscow (Jackson to Eisenhower, Apr. 18, 1960, AWF/A). For background on Patterson see Galambos and van Ee, *The Middle Way*, no. 667; on Eisenhower's Atoms for Peace proposal see *ibid.*, no. 598; and on the President's scheduled visit to Moscow, no. 1456 in these volumes.

Secretary Herter would leave the United States on April 25 for pre-summit talks in London before attending meetings of the Central Treaty Organization in Tehran.
[2] On the preceding day, in a shift involving fifteen executives, Time, Inc., had announced the appointment of Jackson, formerly administrative vice-president, as publisher of *Life* (*New York Times*, Apr. 22, 1960).
[3] Jackson had written about the publication of a "truly extraordinary" book about the Kremlin and its art treasures by David Douglas Duncan, a former *Life* staff photographer. Duncan had asked Jackson to send Eisenhower "a specially inscribed copy" and had offered another copy for the President to give to Khrushchev when he visited Moscow (Jackson to Eisenhower, Apr. 18, 1960, AWF/A; see also David Douglas Duncan, *The Kremlin* [Greenwich, Conn., 1960]).

Jackson would respond that Duncan was arranging for a special copy of his book for Eisenhower to present to Khrushchev in Paris. Duncan would also offer to supply an unlimited number of copies for members of the U.S. delegation to present to their Russian friends (Jackson to Eisenhower, Apr. 29, 1960, AWF/A; see also Whitman to Goodpaster, [Apr. 29, 1960], AWF/A, Jackson Corr.).
[4] In a third letter, written on this same day, Jackson had told Eisenhower that "the

prospect of an epic international conference" had made him feel like "an old fire horse at the sound of the gong." He had enclosed a seven-page draft statement Eisenhower might make to Khrushchev at the Summit Conference, if the Soviet leader gave him "the appropriate cue." In his draft Jackson had emphasized the determination of the United States to do everything it could by peaceful means "to sustain and assist the aspirations of the people of Central and Eastern Europe for freedom." Eisenhower would send the memorandum, with his editorial changes, to Herter. According to Ann Whitman, Eisenhower had "found the ideas, at least some of them, interesting and stimulating" (*Draft Remarks by The President,* Apr. 6, 1960; and Whitman to Stilson, Apr. 25, 1960, both in AWF/A, Jackson Corr.).

1514   *EM, AWF, Name Series*

To Edgar Newton Eisenhower   *April 22, 1960*

Dear Edgar: Of course I was glad to sign the two affidavits attesting to your birth.[1] I hope you get your passport.

Your trip sounds very interesting. Would you like me to get in touch with the ambassadors in the various countries you and Lucy will visit, or would you prefer that I do nothing to agitate the "red carpet" treatment.[2]

While I did, at the request of Ezra Benson, consent to act as a patron of the Fifth World Forestry Congress, I did so with the understanding that I would not attend or be called upon for any special effort in connection with it. So, as far as I can now see, I shall not be making a trip to the West Coast around the first of September.[3] But I shall look forward to seeing you in August, if not before, and if I myself am in town at the time you are here.[4]

With warm regard, *As ever*

[1] Edgar had written (Apr. 18, 1960; see also Edgar Eisenhower to Ann Whitman, Apr. 18, 1960, both in AWF/N) that he had no official record of his birth and needed the affidavits signed by a family member.

[2] Edgar and Lucy Eisenhower planned to travel to Europe in June. On April 27 the President would urge his brother to extend the trip in order to see Athens and Rome (Ann Whitman memorandum, Apr. 27, 1960, AWF/AWD). For developments see no. 1528.

[3] Edgar wrote that he and his wife would be in Washington, D.C., for the American Bar Association meeting in late August, and they had hoped to "thumb a ride" to Seattle with the President if he was going to attend the World Forestry Congress meeting on August 28. Some 2,000 foresters from sixty nations had planned discussions on integrated use of timberlands (see *New York Times,* July 31, Aug. 28, Sept. 21, 1960).

[4] On August 26 the Edgar Eisenhowers would visit the President and First Lady at their home in Gettysburg.

To Christian Archibald Herter   *April 23, 1960*
Personal

Memorandum for the Secretary of State: I am interested in two subjects affecting our foreign operations that have come to my attention:

1. Ambassador Byroade told me of his conversations with Secretary Dillon regarding the need for better technical people in the field who gather the information for contracts for the construction of dams, roads, buildings, and so forth and so forth, under the aegis of ICA. He thinks that this contracting is done from the central office on the basis of inadequate information. The result is that facilities constructed are often not those that are desired by the country and in the case of roads, badly located. Moreover, he believes that if we could have better supervision in the field, we could eliminate criticism of peculation and waste. He advocates the use of Army engineers—and I must say the idea has some appeal.[1]

2. My second point concerns an article in the paper this morning, in which Governor Rockefeller (supposedly a Republican supporter) is advocating a "bold new program" for the United States in its leadership of the free world.[2] The article was not a detailed one, but by inference I gather he was talking about a new type of ICA operation.

I should like for you or Dillon to have a talk with him to see what he has in mind. It is easy to say the words "bold" and "new"—but this means nothing unless he has got a practical program that has escaped our attention. I assume he knows we have been trying to secure the cooperation of other industrial countries in the free world and that we have done everything possible to stir up greater cooperation and public interest in these necessary operations. However, it would be interesting to know just what he is insinuating.

---

[1] Former Brigadier General Henry Alfred Byroade (USMA 1937), currently U.S. Ambassador to Afghanistan, had served in several World War II theaters. In the Eisenhower Administration he had been Assistant Secretary of State for Near Eastern, South Asian, and African Affairs and the Ambassador, successively, to Egypt and to the Union of South Africa. Earlier this day Byroade had reminded Eisenhower that he had suggested the previous year that all major construction work overseas should be performed by the Corps of Engineers (Byroade had met with Eisenhower on February 24, 1959; see Ann Whitman memorandum, AWF/AWD). He thought such a solution might also appease congressional critics of the International Cooperation Administration. Eisenhower had asked Byroade to follow up on the idea, saying that he was tired of hearing complaints about the program's wastefulness, and alluding to congressmen who "spent all of their time trying to find mistakes overseas which could be used against the administration" (Byroade, Memorandum of Conversation, Apr. 23, 1960, and Calhoun to Goodpaster, May 4, 1960, both in AWF/I: Afghanistan; see also Ann Whitman memorandum, Apr. 23, 1960, AWF/AWD). On past congressional criticism of the ICA see no. 790; and for developments see no. 1744. Byroade's

initiative would result in reevaluation of ICA project execution and plans for better resource sharing among agencies, including the Corps of Engineers (State, *Foreign Relations, 1958–1960*, vol. IV, *Foreign Economic Policy*, pp. 496, 502–3).

[2] The article, published in the April 23, 1960, edition of the *New York Times*, had recounted Rockefeller's speech at a luncheon given by the Philadelphia World Affairs Council. The Governor of New York had stated that the United States was failing to give the world the hope of freedom because it had tried to "substitute military acts and economic acts for the vital and lacking political acts of creation." The Communist success at waging "political and psychological war" was a result of the nation's failure to "create larger political structures in which freedom could flourish." Americans, Rockefeller said, should become "political pioneers of peace," and he had outlined a ten-point program calling for the United States to take the initiative in creating a new world order rather than merely responding to Communist actions. Rockefeller had denied that he was criticizing any administration or individual, saying that his opinions were a result of his twenty-five years of experience in the nation and the world. For developments see no. 1527.

1516 *EM, AWF, Ann Whitman Diary Series*

Diary *April 25, 1960*

I started my day with a talk with Ambassador Bunker concerning some Indian problems in which America has some concern—for example, the success of the current development plan, assistance in building better communications in Northern India, better Indian relations with Pakistan, and other questions of importance.[1]

Ambassador Rountree, coming in from Pakistan, gave me a rather gloomy picture of certain portions of the Pakistan situation. Apparently relations between that country and Afghanistan are at the lowest ebb in many years; they mostly concern the Pushtunistan area. While President Ayub is grateful that we have been able to give him token amounts of modern weapons (some sidewinders, or air to air missiles, and about ten F-104 fighter planes), he is concerned that he is making so little progress with India in achieving a solution of the Kashmir problem.[2]

A little later Mr. Pawley came in to see me about our relationships with Cuba. He is very knowledgeable in this area and since he has divested himself of his commercial interests in the Latin American area, I find it profitable to talk with him. He seems to think that a modicum of sense is not characterizing some of Castro's grandiose programs and plans. He believes, as does Harry Guggenheim, that our relationship with the whole of Latin America would be much improved if we should appoint an Under Secretary with duties confined to this hemisphere.[3] I brought up this idea to the State Department many times over the past few years—the staffs there are always so bitterly opposed that I am becoming quite sure that I am right. This morning I told Secretary Herter that if I was to be put off in this matter again, I wanted to have some very convincing reason.[4]

The next appointment was with General Edwin Clark, who came in with the Secretary of State, to talk about the Dominican Republic and a plan for removing Trujillo from control of that country, and to establish in his position a controlling junta which could immediately call for free elections and make the attempt to get the country on a truly democratic basis.[5]

Any plan to be successful would have to be skillfully executed and would have to have the approval of a big majority of the members of the OAS. However, the Secretary of State has undertaken to follow through to determine whether something could be done that would not plunge the country into anarchy or throw it under communist control. Necessarily the plan should be one that would not place the United States in the role of "interventionists."[6]

Following that appointment, President de Gaulle came in for an hour and a half visit, accompanied by two or three of his important assistants. The conversation was intended to inform our Foreign Ministers of all that the two of us had talked about at Camp David yesterday, particularly planning procedures for the Summit and the subjects to be taken up at the Paris meeting. Any differences between us are matters of detail—almost minute detail. Although I initiated this matter of procedures by writing first to Macmillan and de Gaulle, I came to the conclusion that as the head of the host government, he should be the one to present our ideas to Khrushchev. I personally believe that Khrushchev will agree with them. In essence they are intended to make most of our meetings small and informal in the interests of progress and to avoid the appearance of a propaganda mill.[7]

After the President left I met with the National 4-H Conference in the Rose Garden. They are a fine bunch of youngsters and I enjoyed talking to them for a few minutes.

After luncheon I had a busy afternoon with the staff. First I was working on two speeches and a Message to the Congress. All were difficult and finally I gave up in despair and tried once more to pass the work to others.[8] The staff is preoccupied with bills dealing with health insurance for the aged and numerous other projects now before Congress that in some cases are so extreme as to practically demand a veto unless they are radically modified.[9]

The next item on my day was a state dinner at the French Embassy. General De Gaulle will pay his farewell call on me tomorrow morning at 8:30.[10]

[1] For background on these issues see nos. 656 and 1393. Eisenhower had told Ellsworth Bunker, U.S. Ambassador to India since March 1957, that he was pleased that India's relations with Pakistan had improved somewhat and that Prime Minister Nehru seemed to have "a more realistic view of world developments." The two men discussed the recent transfer of U.S. planes to Pakistan and India's fear that it would make the Indian air force obsolete. Eisenhower told Bunker that he saw no reason why the United States should not offer similar equipment to the Indians, and he asked him to inform the State Department of his views. India had greatly appreciated the scope of U.S. economic aid that provided assistance to both the public and private sectors, Bunker said, and both agreed that this policy should continue (State, *Foreign Relations, 1958–1960*, vol. XV, *South and Southeast Asia*, pp. 535–36, 809–10).

[2] William M. Rountree, former Assistant Secretary of State for Near Eastern and South Asian Affairs, had become U.S. Ambassador to Pakistan in August 1959. The dispute between Pakistan and Afghanistan involved a tribal group called Pathans or Pushtuns, who inhabited northwestern Pakistan and much of Afghanistan. A treaty in 1893 between Great Britain and Afghanistan had established a boundary between the two countries. After the 1947 partition of India and Pakistan, however, the Afghans had maintained that the treaty was no longer valid and had called for an independent country of Pushtunistan. Pakistan, fearing Afghan control over much of West Pakistan, maintained that it had replaced Britain as the contracting party and that the existing boundary between the two countries was valid.

Talks between Afghanistan's foreign minister and Pakistani president Mohammed Ayub Khan regarding Pushtunistan had broken down in January, and the Soviet Union had exploited the situation by supporting Afghanistan in the dispute. The U.S. Ambassador to Afghanistan had told Eisenhower that he and Ambassador Rountree would continue to look for a remedy to a situation that was "too serious to ignore." Rountree had told Eisenhower that although a solution would be difficult to reach, "the virulence of the propaganda campaign on both sides could be reduced" (State, *Foreign Relations, 1952–1954*, vol. XI, *Africa and South Asia*, pp. 1085, 1110, 1376–83, 1385–1428; State, *Foreign Relations, 1955–1957*, vol. VIII, *South Asia*, pp. 163–258; and State, *Foreign Relations, 1958–1960*, vol. XV, *South and Southeast Asia*, pp. 337–46; and NSC meeting minutes, Mar. 14, 1960, AWF/NSC; see also *New York Times*, Mar. 14, July 5, 1960). For more on U.S. aid to Pakistan and the Kashmir problem see State, *Foreign Relations, 1958–1960*, vol. XV, *South and Southeast Asia*, pp. 797–802; and no. 1393.

[3] For background on William Douglas Pawley, former U.S. Ambassador to Peru and Brazil, see Galambos and van Ee, *The Middle Way*, no. 369. On the Cuban situation see no. 1370. On Harry Frank Guggenheim, U.S. Ambassador to Cuba during the Hoover administration, and his interest in creating the position of "under secretary of state for Latin American affairs" see Galambos and van Ee, *The Middle Way*, no. 376.

[4] In discussing the position with Secretary Herter, Eisenhower had emphasized his interest in "someone of major reputation and influence" and mentioned Pawley as a suitable choice. Herter called the suggestion "timely" and said he would have the matter studied and legislation prepared (Goodpaster, Memorandum of Conference, Apr. 26, 1960, AWF/D; see also Goodpaster, Memorandum of Conference, Feb. 19, 1960, *ibid.*). For developments in the Cuban situation see no. 1578.

[5] For background see no. 1461; see also NSC meeting minutes, Apr. 7, 14, 1960; and Ann Whitman memorandum, Apr. 6, 1960, AWF/AWD. Clark had met with Trujillo on March 27. "I believe we can conclude," he had written Eisenhower on April 21, "that a) Generalissimo Trujillo is in real trouble and he knows it best of all; b) he desires to retire but at this moment does not quite know how to bring it off, and c) although Trujillo is disappointed that he has received no assistance from the United States in his present difficulties, he has not yet reached the point where he is resentful or angry at having to go it alone; however, these emotions, further aroused

by the pressure of events, may create an increasingly deteriorating situation so far as we are concerned" (State, *Foreign Relations, 1958–1960*, vol. V, *American Republics*, Microfiche Supplement DR-20).

[6] In the discussion on this day Herter had said that the junta was "the key to the situation" and that the United States "should be ready to back it very quickly." The big question, Eisenhower said, was the Organization of American States. He told Clark and Herter that he "knew of no alliance in which indecisiveness is so great, or in which it seems so hard to generate an initiative" (Goodpaster, Memorandum of Conference, Apr. 26, 1960, AWF/D).

Various U.S. emissaries, including Clark and Pawley, would fail to persuade Trujillo to step down and permit free elections. The Dominican leader reportedly told Pawley that the United States could bring all its armed forces into his country including the atomic bomb, and he would not leave except on a stretcher. In a meeting on May 13 Eisenhower would tell State Department officials that he had been "bombarded" by people opposed to Castro and Trujillo. He added that both leaders were involved in efforts to create disorder in Latin America and that he "would like to see them both sawed off." On June 10 Herter would tell Eisenhower that there were "various things being done which could result in a provisional government being set up for the Dominican Republic." The United States should recognize such a government quickly, Eisenhower said, and "then move in with troops on their request if need should arise" (Goodpaster, Memorandum of Conference, May 16, July 5, 1960, AWF/D; and Rabe, *Eisenhower and Latin America*, pp. 156–58). For developments see no. 1582.

[7] For background on the French president's visit and procedures for the Summit Conference see nos. 765 and 1506; see also Herter to Eisenhower, Apr. 19, 1960, Eisenhower to de Gaulle, Apr. 22, 1960, AWF/I: de Gaulle; and State, *Foreign Relations, 1958–1960*, vol. VII, pt. 2, *Western Europe*, pp. 339–42. De Gaulle had also met with Eisenhower on April 22, after his arrival in Washington, and on April 24 at Camp David. In those meetings the two men had discussed summit procedures, tripartite consultations, the Algerian situation, nuclear testing, and Western rights in Berlin. Both agreed that disarmament with effective inspection procedures would be the main topic of discussion. De Gaulle favored world-wide inspections of delivery systems that would open the entire Soviet Union to inspection. Eisenhower, who favored partial inspections, did not object to making the proposal but saw little chance of Khrushchev accepting it. He had previously told Herter that de Gaulle "was singularly unreceptive and immobile in thinking and did not see any great difference in the two proposals." French Foreign Minister Couve de Murville, Secretary Herter, Under Secretary Dillon, U.S. Ambassador Houghton, and French Ambassador Alphand also attended the meeting on this day (*ibid.*, pp. 343–58; State, *Foreign Relations, 1958–1960*, vol. IX, *Berlin Crisis 1959–1960; Germany; Austria*, pp. 346–57; Telephone conversation, Apr. 25, 1960, AWF/AWD; see also de Gaulle, *Memoirs of Hope*, pp. 242–47).

[8] Eisenhower is referring to a speech on the mutual security program, which he would deliver on May 2 at a dinner sponsored by the Committee for International Economic Growth and the Committee to Strengthen the Frontiers of Freedom, and to a commencement address that he would give on June 6 at the University of Notre Dame. According to Ann Whitman, Eisenhower had asked speech writer Malcolm Moos to go over the mutual security speech to make sure the paragraphs gave a logical development of the problem. He wanted every sentence to be "complete and logical and exact." The President, Whitman recorded, was "very weary of generalities." Eisenhower had also requested that Moos broaden the Notre Dame speech in order to emphasize the position of the United States in the world and the need to "take a decent stand that the world must be a place for all free proud people to live in." He would deliver a special message to Congress on the legislative program on May 3 (Ann Whitman memorandum, Apr. 25, 1960, AWF/AWD; see also *Public Papers of the Presidents: Eisenhower, 1960–61*, pp. 378–94, 461–67).

[9] For background on health insurance for the aged see no. 1345; see also Accomplishments of Department of Health, Education, and Welfare 1954–1960, and Social Security and Related Questions Currently Under Discussion, 1959, AWF/A. On March 22 Eisenhower had discussed with the Republican legislative leaders the Administration's stand against any program of compulsory health insurance. On May 4 Arthur Flemming, Secretary of Health, Education and Welfare, would announce the Administration's health coverage plan, under which the states, with some funds provided by the federal government, would pay 80 percent of the eligible medical expenses of low-income persons over sixty-five. The House Ways and Means Committee would approve a subsequent plan, which would be included in the Social Security amendments bill. Eisenhower would sign this measure on September 13 (Legislative leadership meeting minutes, Mar. 22, May 10, June 9, 21, Aug. 16, 23, 1960, AWF/LM; and *Congressional Quarterly Almanac*, vol. XVI, *1960*, pp. 153–65). For Eisenhower's discussion with Presidential Assistant Bryce Harlow regarding the issue see Ann Whitman memorandum, Apr. 25, 1960, AWF/AWD.

[10] The two leaders would discuss the tone of Khrushchev's recent speeches and the fact that the Soviet leader took extreme positions and then was forced to abide by them. Both agreed that at some time during the summit conference they would have to say "no" to him (State, *Foreign Relations, 1958–1960*, vol. VII, pt. 2, *Western Europe*, pp. 358–59). For developments see no. 1523.

1517   EM, AWF,
Ann Whitman Diary Series

To WILTON BURTON PERSONS   *April 25, 1960*
Memorandum

This is a little forehanded, but I want to make certain that when Victor Emanuel's term as a member of the Board of Visitors of the Air Force Academy expires (which I understand it does December 30th of this year), he is reappointed.[1]

[1] As it turned out, the sixty-two-year-old Emanuel, Chairman of the Board of the Avco Corporation, would die on November 26 (see no. 1717). For background on the boards of visitors for the United States service academies see no. 1322.

1518   EM, AWF, Name Series

To EDGAR NEWTON EISENHOWER   *April 25, 1960*

Dear Ed: I am astonished at your clairvoyant qualifications. Why won't you share your information with others? Or maybe you just read columnists.[1]
With warm regard, *As ever*

[1] On April 20 Edgar, obviously concerned by the Paris summit, had written (AWF/N) that there were "signs" that the United States would "ditch West Berlin." The "biggest murderer in all history" (i.e. Soviet Premier Krushchev) could not be trusted, Edgar warned. He said he "would rather die fighting than to become a government slave," which would happen "if Russia takes over." For developments see no. 1528.

1519   *EM, AWF, DDE Diaries Series*

To James Campbell Hagerty   *April 26, 1960*
Memorandum

Please give me a few simple statistics with which I could answer questions tomorrow regarding pay increases. For example, I need to know the increase in the cost of living over the past seven years, increase in direct pay, increase in fringe benefits, and so on.[1]

I should also like to have a very short statement giving credit to the Republican group regarding the passage of the civil rights bill.[2]

[1] Eisenhower would meet with Hagerty, Chairman of the Council of Economic Advisors Raymond Saulnier, and other members of his staff for forty-five minutes prior to his news conference on April 27. The reporters would not ask any questions about the economy or employee compensation (see *Public Papers of the Presidents: Eisenhower, 1960–61*, pp. 360–70).

[2] For background see nos. 248, 253, and 273. Facing growing charges of voting rights abuses, the Administration had moved again in February 1960 to seek legislation to protect African American voting rights in the South. In January 1960 the Attorney General had announced the Administration's intention to add to the civil rights legislative agenda a plan to place responsibility for guaranteeing voting rights in the courts through the appointment of "voting referees." The plan quickly became ensnarled in debate over the most effective approach to prevent abuses and over which party would get credit for the legislation. As passed by Congress on April 21, the Civil Rights Act of 1960 provided for a series of procedures to be used when the courts found a "pattern or practice" of depriving citizens of their voting rights. The legislation also provided for fines and/or imprisonment for persons who obstructed or interfered with federal court orders; made it a federal crime to cross states lines to avoid prosecution, punishment, or the giving of evidence on the bombing or burning of any building, facility or vehicle; required the preservation of voting records for twenty-two months; empowered the Civil Rights Commission to administer oaths and take sworn statements; and provided for the education of children of members of the armed forces when public schools had been closed to avoid integration (see *Congressional Quarterly Almanac*, vol. XVI, *1960*, pp. 185–207; see also Daniel M. Berman, *A Bill Becomes A Law: Congress Enacts Civil Rights Legislation* [New York, 1966]; and Steven F. Lawson, *Black Ballots: Voting Rights in the South, 1944–1969* [New York, 1976], pp. 140–249).

EM, WHCF,
                    Confidential File: Political Affairs

To Karl Earl Mundt   *April 26, 1960*
Personal and confidential

Dear Karl: Thank you for your letter of the fifteenth.[1]

While of course South Dakota will be a tremendously important state in the coming election, I believe that after the nominations, my part in the campaign should be very limited. Indeed, I have a very strong question in my mind as to the wisdom of any president appearing in the role of mentor or sponsor of the individual he hopes to be his successor.

With warm regard, *Sincerely*

[1] On April 6, 1960, South Dakota Republican Senator Mundt had invited the President to address the South Dakota Young Republican Convention in August. Eisenhower had declined the invitation on April 8, saying that he believed that South Dakota would be "a tremendously important state in the coming election." The President added that he was "going to try to save as much of August for myself as I can, since I suspect that the vacation I hope to get then will be the only break I can get this summer." Mundt had replied on April 15 that because of this statement he hoped that when Eisenhower was planning his "schedule of participation in the coming campaign" he would include South Dakota as one of the states in which he would make a "principal address." On Eisenhower's support for Nixon's presidential candidacy see no. 1477. All correspondence is in the same file as the document.

1521   *EM, AWF, Administration Series*

To Richard Milhous Nixon   *April 29, 1960*

Dear Dick: Attached to this note are the names and addresses of the three women of whom I spoke to you this morning. I think a brief note of encouragement to each, signed by you, would give them a lift that would keep them working forever in the cause of good Republicanism. As a rough suggestion, you might say something like this:

"The President has told me about your interest in working, through the Republican Party, for good government in Southern California (in the case of Mrs. Intemann, of course, in New York) and in the nation. It is inspiring to receive such a voluntary expression of your desire to fulfill the highest responsibility of citizenship. If there is anything which my own staff could do to provide you any details or information that you would consider helpful, please don't hesitate to communicate with my office.

"Possibly an opportunity may arise where I can express my thanks in more personal fashion.

"With best wishes, Sincerely",

I repeat, this is merely a suggestion![1] *As ever*

[1] Eisenhower and Nixon had met briefly on this same day. On April 26 the President had met with two of Mrs. Eisenhower's cousins, Mrs. Eugenie Intemann of New York and Mrs. Isabel Cochran of California. Following the meeting with Eisenhower, the women had asked to meet the Vice-President, but he had left his office (Ann Whitman memorandums, Apr. 26, 29, 1960, AWF/AWD). A third woman, Miss Eleanor Hall, had apparently accompanied Mrs. Cochran.

1522   *EM, AWF, Administration Series*

To Lauris Norstad   *April 29, 1960*
Secret

Dear Larry: It was a help to me to have, prior to my meeting with General de Gaulle, your letter giving me the status of military questions involving the French, and your recommendations concerning them.[1]

There was no good opportunity to press the matter of air defense organization. I did, however, discuss with him several times the idea of an inspection zone. His conception is to apply this on a world-wide basis covering the means of delivery—aircraft and missiles—of nuclear weapons. I emphasized to him the value of proposing a more limited project which would begin to test out the good faith of the Soviets, as well as the practical possibility of achieving effective inspection, and told him this proposal could be a fall-back position should his more comprehensive plan not be accepted. I must frankly admit that I cannot be sure of the extent to which this proposal really got through to him, his mind being so fixed on his own conception. At the least, however, he will be well aware of the idea if we should pursue it further at the Summit.[2]

With warm regard, *Sincerely*

[1] For background on negotiations with the French on air defense organization see no. 1435; on the de Gaulle meetings and the discussion of inspection zones see no. 1516. For Eisenhower's March meeting with Norstad regarding these issues see Goodpaster, Memorandum of Conference, March 15, 1960, AWF/D.

In an April 20 letter to Eisenhower (AWF/A) Norstad had written that an agreement in principle had been worked out whereby metropolitan France would be a separate air defense region under SHAPE and the French Territorial Air Defense would have the same relationship with NATO as the British Fighter Command. De

Gaulle had not yet considered the proposal, and Norstad had suggested that Eisenhower "apply a little pressure at this time." The stockpiling of atomic weapons in France was a dormant issue, Norstad thought, and one de Gaulle would not raise. He did think, however, that the French president would want to discuss atomic cooperation and the need for tripartite consultations.

[2] For more on the de Gaulle talks see the following document.

1523   *EM, AWF, International Series:*
Macmillan

To Harold Macmillan   *April 30, 1960*
Cable. Confidential

Dear Harold: In my talks with President de Gaulle, we agreed on arrangements for our meetings at Paris consistent with the suggestions which you outlined in your letter to me of April 8.[1] As you are aware, the details of these arrangements were also discussed between Secretary Herter and Foreign Ministers Lloyd and Couve de Murville, who I understand will again review this matter during their meetings at Istanbul.[2]

If at all possible, we hope to dispense with an opening plenary session and to aim at holding our first Summit meeting at the Elysee Palace on Monday, May 16 at 10:00 A.M. It is our expectation that this would be a short meeting, lasting perhaps an hour, restricted to the Heads of Government and devoted primarily to a discussion of procedural matters if that can be arranged. Immediately thereafter we would be joined by our Foreign Ministers.

We hope that subsequent meetings would take place each day at the same time and place and that we would be joined in these restricted meetings by our Foreign Ministers and two officials from each delegation who would be responsible for interpretation and note taking.

The question of interpretation which you raised in your letter was discussed between Secretary Herter, Foreign Minister Couve de Murville and Lord Hood of your Embassy here. I understand that a report on this subject has been forwarded to London by your Embassy.[3]

President de Gaulle, in his role as host, plans to write to Mr. Khrushchev outlining our proposals for Summit arrangements.[4]

I am reassured by our various exchanges that we are going into the Summit conference with substantial unity on our basic Western positions.[5]

With warm personal regard, *As ever*

¹ On the de Gaulle talks see no. 1516; on Macmillan's previous letter see no. 1497.
² The Western foreign ministers would be attending the NATO Ministerial Meeting in Istanbul on May 2–4 (see State, *Foreign Relations, 1958–1960,* vol. IX, *Berlin Crisis 1959–1960; Germany; Austria,* pp. 359–71).
³ Macmillan was referring to translations at the summit meeting and had suggested that they should be "either consecutive or simultaneous as we preferred, and the great advantage would be that we should know that all of us were having the same translation." However, Macmillan thought de Gaulle might prefer "whispered interpretation" (Macmillan to Eisenhower, Apr. 8, 1960, PREM 11/2992; see also no. 1497). Viscount Samuel Hood was minister of the British embassy. He had also headed the working group on Germany that had been meeting in Washington. The report is not in AWF.
⁴ See nos. 1497 and 1516.
⁵ For developments see no. 1538.

22

Disaster in Paris

To Christian Archibald Herter   *May 2, 1960*
Memorandum

Dear Chris: Many thanks for your message reporting the CENTO
meeting.[1] I have seen some of the accounts of the meeting, which
seem to have been held in a very good spirit. I particularly like the
point that the sessions were rather "relaxed," which suggested a welcome degree of self-assurance and confidence.

It was good also to know that the Shah is in a good frame of mind.
I appreciate his good wishes.[2]

I gather from reports of conditions in Istanbul that your meetings
there will not enjoy the same climate of relaxation—having in mind
the conditions in the city outside of the meetings.[3] Perhaps the presence of your group will lend a little steadiness to the situation there.
I hope so.

With warm regard, *Sincerely*

[1] Herter had met with delegations from Iran, Britain, Pakistan, and Turkey in Tehran,
Iran, for three days of "highly successful" Central European Treaty Organization
meetings (Herter to Eisenhower, Apr. 30, 1960, AWF/D-H). The United States was
not a full member of CENTO, but Americans participated in its various councils as
observers. For background see no. 1513 and Noble, *Christian A. Herter*, pp. 234–40.
[2] Herter had reported that he had spent an "intimate" evening with Mohammed Reza
Pahlavi, the Shah, who had been "most attentive" throughout all of the talks (Herter
to Eisenhower, Apr. 27 and 30, 1960, both in AWF/D-H). For background on U.S.
relations with Iran see no. 1455, and for developments see no. 1653.
[3] When he had sent his message, Herter had been airborne for Istanbul, Turkey, and
the NATO talks due to begin there on May 2. The city, however, was in turmoil: student-led mass demonstrations had broken out on April 27 in protest of the press censorship and other repressive measures the Turkish government had passed to muzzle
opposition. Violent confrontations between protestors and police would subsequently
lead to a declaration of martial law. The NATO meetings, however, would continue
as scheduled. On May 27 a military coup would oust the ruling government. For background on U.S. relations with Turkey see no. 1438, and State, *Foreign Relations, 1958–
1960*, vol. X, *Eastern Europe; Finland; Greece; Turkey*, pt. 2, pp. 832–35; *New York Times*,
Apr. 29, May 2, 3, 28, 29, 1960. For developments see nos. 1559 and 1578.

To King Mohamed V   *May 5, 1960*
Secret

Your Majesty:[1] I have reflected most carefully upon Your Majesty's letter of April twenty-second expressing eloquent concern over con-

tinuation of the Algerian conflict. In doing so I also recalled the thoughts Your Majesty conveyed to me on this subject at our meeting in Casablanca.[2]

The United States Government fervently hopes for an early end to this war, and to all the suffering and danger which it entails. Moreover, it continues to be alert to take any feasible step which could be a positive contribution to a just peace in Algeria.

I discussed this subject with President de Gaulle during his recent visit to Washington, and in particular I asked him whether his offer of self-determination to the Algerian people remains valid. The President assured me that he stands by this offer, and it remains the official policy of France.[3] Since there had been some reports that French policy might have changed, I was relieved to have the President's assurance, both because I believe that the principle of self-determination is the key to peace in Algeria, and because I repose such confidence in the sincerity and determination of President de Gaulle.

In addition, I am most grateful for Your Majesty's letter of April sixteenth. I have instructed Ambassador Yost to cooperate fully in the discussions which are envisaged.[4]

Allow me to express once again my personal esteem for Your Majesty and to restate the friendship which all Americans feel for the Moroccan people.[5] *Sincerely*

[1] This message, drafted by State Department officials, was sent by cable to the American embassy in Rabat for delivery to King Mohamed (see Dillon to Eisenhower, May 4, 1960, AWF/I: Morocco; see also *Public Papers of the Presidents: Eisenhower, 1960–61*, p. 363).

[2] For background on the Algerian conflict see no. 1427. In his message Mohamed had urged Eisenhower to intercede with de Gaulle to end the war in Algeria. "Your intervention with the French government will certainly be effective in putting an end to bloodshed, bringing about peace and stability to this part of the world and stopping fears and threats which are endured by many nations and peoples because of the Algerian war" (Mohamed to Eisenhower, Apr. 22, 1960, AWF/I: Morocco). During Eisenhower's visit to Morocco on December 22 the King had emphasized the importance of stability in Algeria, not only to Morocco but to the entire Arab and Moslem world. He supported self-determination for Algeria and said that Morocco was "always willing to act as a peacemaker" (State, *Foreign Relations, 1958–1960*, vol. XIII, *Arab-Israeli Dispute; United Arab Republic; North Africa*, pp. 795–96, 806–7; for more on Eisenhower's eleven-nation trip see no. 1382).

[3] On the Eisenhower-de Gaulle discussions see no. 1516; on the French president's proposal for Algerian independence see no. 1309.

[4] Mohamed had written in reply to Eisenhower's letter of March 30 regarding the dismantling of U.S. bases in Morocco (see no. 1489). The King had assured Eisenhower that Morocco would never allow a hostile third party to occupy the bases and had accepted the President's offer to train Moroccans to operate the facilities (Mohamed to Eisenhower, Apr. 16, 1960, AWF/I: Morocco).

[5] After reading this letter on May 9, King Mohamed would note that prompt action was needed to halt the deterioration of the Algerian situation. He also stated that

his foreign ministry would establish a commission to study the base problem and pursue negotiations with the United States (*ibid.*, p. 807). Eisenhower would discuss U.S.-Moroccan relations with Crown Prince Moulay Hassan in New York on September 27 (see John S. D. Eisenhower, Memorandum of Conference, Sept. 27, 1960, AWF/D).

1526   *EM, AWF, International Series: Rhee*

To Syngman Rhee   *May 5, 1960*

Dear Dr. Rhee: The vastness of the events which have taken place in Korea has claimed the attention of the entire world. I can assure you that no one has followed them with more anxious sympathy than I.[1]

With your voluntary withdrawal from political life, I am reminded ever more strongly of how much your country will remain in your debt. The rebirth of Korea in 1945 was the fruition of your long years of patient and arduous labor. Your tenacity and indomitable courage at a time when the Republic was the prey of Communist armies won the admiration of the entire Free World as well as the gratitude of all Koreans. Since then, under your guidance, Korea has recovered from the deepest wounds of that conflict and is today a monument to your life-long work.

I cannot but feel that your decision, momentous as it is, is yet another example of wisdom as well as selfless service. I assure you that the United States will continue to feel itself bound by strong ties of sympathy to Korea under your successors.

My best wishes for many years of health and happiness in the honored retirement which you have done so much to earn. *Sincerely*

[1] For several weeks Korea had been in a state of political turmoil. The announcement that Rhee had won reelection on March 15 by an overwhelming majority and that the incumbent vice-president, his political opponent, had been defeated by Rhee's candidate had provoked charges of election fraud. On April 19 there were bloody student-led riots in several Korean cities, resulting in demands for Rhee's resignation. On April 27 Rhee had stepped down, ending his twelve-year presidency and long political career. He had gone into exile in Hawaii. For background see no. 985; *New York Times*, April 23 and 27, 1960, and Quee-Young Kim, *The Fall of Syngman Rhee* (Berkeley, 1983), pp. 1–10. For developments see no. 1578. Eisenhower's letter would be released to the public on May 9, 1960 (*Public Papers of the Presidents: Eisenhower, 1960–61*, pp. 401–2, see also pp. 360–61, 407).

To Nelson Aldrich Rockefeller   *May 5, 1960*
Personal and confidential

Dear Nelson: I have read the texts of your Philadelphia and Chicago speeches. As a statement of basic values, in a free country, and as generalizations defining great objectives, I think they are admirable. Moreover, I think that every public figure owes it to himself and to others to make such a profession of faith and conviction.[1]

Difficulties arise, of course, when we begin to apply basic truths to human problems. This is natural because in almost every field of thought and action humans seem to distribute themselves almost according to a natural law, from one extreme to the other. The noticeable fact is that under what has been called "nature's curve," the extremes comprise small percentages of the whole; what might be called the compatible group is about two-thirds of the aggregate. Most people believe that in general they belong to the "middle-of-the-road" group.

While in the field of moral truth or basic principle a statement tends to be black or white, the task of the political leader is to devise plans along which humans can make constructive progress. This means that the plan or program itself tends to fall in the "gray" category even though an earnest attempt is made to apply the black and white values of moral truths. This is not because there is any challenge to the principle or to the moral truth, but because human nature itself is far from perfect.

It seems to me that the principal objective is to make progress along the lines that principle and truth point out. Perfection is not quickly reached; the plan is therefore "gray" or "middle-of-the-road." But it is *progressive!* Just as a tree does not instantly reach full stature when it is planted as a seedling, progress must be attained by steps, some of them at times discouragingly small. But as long as we do attain discernible progress and fight stagnation or recession with all our strength, I believe that we are on the right road—and people who seek to live by this doctrine should claim and deserve the name of progressives.

Respecting your idea about groupings of nations, I am not quite sure of your meaning.[2] We now have numerous political alliances and of course we are promoting in various areas international economic unions or "cooperatives." As of now the United Nations does not achieve the objectives you foresee for these groupings because of the intransigence of the Soviets—indeed, because your whole idea starts off with the transcendent value we ascribe to the human. This, of course, the Soviets deny.

However, I assume that from time to time you will be making additional speeches, based upon the truths and values described in the two I have just read. Constructive, progressive policies or solutions to specific problems will, I think, tend to follow the broad pattern of human thinking and behavior; that is, acceptable solutions will generally not be extreme in one direction or the other. I repeat, I think you have discussed the truths and values eloquently in the two speeches I have just read.

With warm regard, *As ever*

[1] New York Governor Rockefeller had addressed the Philadelphia World Affairs Council on April 22, 1960. On May 1 he had spoken about law and morality at the University of Chicago Law School, as part of a three-day ceremony dedicating the law center (see Nelson A. Rockefeller, *The Third Century: A Concept of American Foreign Policy* [New York, n.d.], and *Man and Law: An Appraisal of the Moral Foundations of Law in A Free Society* [New York, n.d.]; see also *New York Times*, Apr. 23, and May 2, 1960). In Philadelphia Rockefeller had called for a "bold new approach" to world leadership that did not "substitute military acts and economic acts for the vital and lacking political acts of creation." In Chicago the Governor had urged the United States to take the lead in "advancing civil rights both at home and in countries being developed abroad." For Eisenhower's immediate reaction to the speech on foreign policy see no. 1515.

[2] In his Philadelphia speech Rockefeller had said: "In the political arena, we must join with others to develop regional groupings of nations." He advised against resting on "old formulas of the nation-state," or rushing toward "the elusive formulas of some world-state." He pointed to the recent rise of "regional groups everywhere" from among the newest independent states of Africa, Asia, and the Middle East to the older states of Europe, and he proclaimed that "these regional associations and institutions—political, cultural and military—signal the hope of future international order that can be a home to freedom."

1528   *EM, AWF, Name Series*

TO LUCILLE DAWSON EISENHOWER   *May 6, 1960*
Personal and confidential

Dear Lucy: I received your series of May second letters and I will send to them a single reply.[1]

With respect to your trip: I note that you will stop in the following capitals: London, Dublin, Paris, Vienna, Bonn, and are passing through Bern and The Hague. Many Americans passing through any capital like to pay a brief call on the Ambassador. I shall send a brief note to each of the Ambassadors in the countries named to tell them that if you should make such a call, they will identify you and Ed as my brother and sister-in-law. This does not mean that I think you *should* call on the Ambassador, but if you have time, I think you might find it a rather smart thing to do because normally they can advise a visitor as to the most interesting things to see and so on.[2]

Regarding your second letter, I shall be glad to receive and read the two pamphlets you suggested. I of course depend primarily for my information as to Communist activities on the FBI, Intelligence agencies and the State Department.[3]

In another letter, you mention the short note I sent to Ed, advising him to pay less attention to columnists. My little note was in response to the following from him: "There are signs that we are getting ready to ditch West Berlin. If we do we are not entitled to survive as a nation."[4]

I know of no one in a position of responsibility who has even hinted at ditching West Berlin, so my first thought was to ask him where he got his information and please to share it with me!

Going on from there, you express disappointment about the untrustworthiness of so many of the things we see in the newspapers.[5]

I personally think there has been deterioration in the quality of the information given to the public and for this statement I have a very definite basis. In an apparent effort to "pep up" the news and gain larger circulation, newspapers have gone, in some cases, to very great extremes in the use of columnists, or correspondents who write under signed by-lines. These practices seem to justify the newspaper in saying that they present these stories as the views of the writer; implying, at least, that the paper itself has little responsibility for the accuracy of the story.[6] Added to this is the other factor of the weakness of our libel laws. Things are printed in American papers that, if printed in Britain, would occasion real punishment for the offender.

I agree with you that the Christian Science Monitor is an exception to the rule. Others are the Philadelphia Bulletin, the Philadelphia Inquirer, the Baltimore Sun and the Kansas City Star. There are of course others; I mention these as a few examples.

Normally when any AP story appears in your newspaper, it represents objective reporting. In other words, it rarely attempts to bring the opinions and judgments of the writer into the account. I think the UP generally follows the same pattern.

But I find that in almost every conference at the White House some individual quotes a columnist, apparently thinking that by doing so the speaker brings a matter of importance to the attention of the assembly. I never fail to reject such so-called information and insist that we deal in our works with the facts. The columnists they normally quote are Pearson, Doris Fleeson, Alsop, Reston, Marquis Childs, Lippman, Sokolsky, and so on.[7] There are many others. As a generalization you can say that any newspaper that carries an unusual number of these signed columnists is an untrustworthy peri-odical. Some of them are, of course, worse than others.

On the other hand, I note several people who do write columns that are in the main trustworthy. These writers do a lot of research before they write a story. The best two, I think, are Arthur Krock (who may write only for the New York Times, of this I am not sure) and Roscoe Drummond.[8] On most subjects, particularly in the for-eign field, David Lawrence is good.[9]

Respecting what you say about urging a greater sense of responsi-bility among editors and publishers, I assure you that in the past I have addressed many such groups and always in my talks I have brought in the necessity for this sense of responsibility as one of the most important matters that I wanted to emphasize.[10] Many other speakers have done the same, and by and large I think that most of the publishers and a good many of the editors feel this responsibility. But publishers, just like other heads of businesses, are plagued by the difficulties they have with personnel. You would think that reporting was a very individualistic occupation and a matter between the pub-lisher and the man doing the writing. But there are guilds that es-tablish rules that are, in the main, similar to those that govern unions.

Respecting what you say about the sit-ins in the South: I think you are mistaken if you think that Southerners are completely unaware of the occurrence of these incidents.[11] Within the last weeks I have been in Florida and Georgia at least three times. I have heard the matter discussed by my friends in those areas, often in a tone of amusement—at other times, resentment. None of them seemed to worry about the matter. I think most Southerners agree that we must make some progress toward achieving political and economic equal-ity among all individuals regardless of race. The trouble is that too often the possibility of an undesirable social mingling creeps into the thinking or fears of the individuals affected, and so the matter is distorted.[12]

Finally I refer to your concern about the Vice President's "liber-alism."[13] Just about eight years ago I finally decided I should come back to the United States to stand for the Presidency. I did so in the hope that I could stem what I thought was a clear drift toward pa-ternalism, if not socialism, in our government's relation to its peo-ple.[14] This has been a long, uphill struggle, and during the years I have learned some things.

The first of these is that this country is *not* going to the right—that the economic and political affairs of our people are not going to be so conducted as to take our nation back to the days of the 1890's. Indeed, this would be undesirable if we could do it. Our na-tion has become not only highly industrialized but highly interde-pendent among its several parts and classes.

Because of the great degree of specialization brought about largely by industrial progress, people find it much more difficult than formerly to change occupations, areas of employment, or modes of life. Workers, particularly those in the highly organized corporations, no longer find it possible to go from fireman to head of the organization, except in the most unusual circumstances. People are becoming more concerned about their future—as you know, the doctors have vastly lengthened the period of the so-called old age—and this concern is felt not only by the laborer, the skilled workman, the government employee, but even by professionals and in the groups that are classed as small businessmen. For example, I am constantly plagued by lawyer and doctor groups to permit the laying aside of annual sums for insuring comfortable old age without payment of taxes. All across the board, security has gotten to be foremost in our minds and a number of developments bring this kind of worry into acute focus. One of the inciting factors is the rising costs of medical care. The cost of catastrophic illnesses among the aged can create a calamity, unhappiness and the loss of self-respect. I have intimate knowledge of one case in which, for three years, it has cost $15,000 annually to take care of one person. (This is not an unusually high cost since private nurses are involved. The patient is at home; if hospitalization were necessary the cost, of course, would be much greater.) Fortunately in this case the means are available to take care of such expenses, but the same cannot be said of the great army of agricultural and industrial workers, clerks, and even more highly paid people who, after taking care of their income taxes and educating their children, are finding it increasingly difficult to carry insurance policies that are really adequate. Moreover, because of the constant erosion in the value of the dollar through inflation, these insurance policies tend to become a less and less trustworthy means of taking care of the aged.[15]

The greatest of all Republicans said that governments should always do for people what they cannot do at all, or so well do, for themselves. But Lincoln added that government should not interfere if the individual is perfectly capable of taking care of the matter himself.

I have pondered these things long and exhaustively, and I have come to the conclusion that the true middle-of-the road position is about as follows:

> Demand from the individual the maximum effort that he can make to take care of himself;
>
> The government at the city, state and Federal levels should participate in helping the individual over and above what he himself can do in providing adequate insurance policies, but this means, to be effective, sound money.

1938

(Right here I give you the difference between the Republican and Democratic candidates and philosophies—the Democrats have no apparent concern for the debasement of our currency. In the seven years just preceding 1953 I think the total cheapening of our dollar was about 40%. After seven years of sweat and work and fighting, we have done a great deal to stop the rate of increase, but nevertheless have had an additional 10% erosion during this period.

The real point I am making is that as a result of social and industrial revolutions and the breakdown of the so-called "laissez-faire" in industrial life, people are going to demand that the government do something to give them an opportunity to live out a satisfactory life.)

The big thing that the government and all of us should do is to act responsibly in our fiscal and financial affairs in order that the currency will not be debased and that the individual is given the opportunity thereby to participate actively in looking after his own future and the future of his family, in a manner such as to require the minimum of help from the community.

The principle can be expanded into many phases of our economic life. Above all other things it means the cutting down of Federal expenses in every possible way. Budgetary deficits will in the long run always cheapen the dollar and this hurts everybody. We must pay as we go, and we must try to keep our Federal expenditures at such levels that we can lower taxes. Once we can lower taxes, we can get every individual, no matter what his income, to do more to look after himself. This restores the feeling of self-dependence and self-respect, and enhances the value of the individual as an active citizen of our country. Paternalism and socialism are presented sometimes with an aura of righteousness. While I do believe that we truly must be "our brother's keeper," this does not mean that we should take away from him those great qualities of spirit which are of the deepest value to the individual by promising him some dole during his declining years. I repeat, the difference between the Republicans and the Democrats is not that either party fails to see the needs of the individual in our particular type of life; it is the fact that one wants to do this responsibly and in such fashion as to save the self-respect of the citizen and therefore the strength of our nation; the other refuses to face such a responsibility.

This is a long, rambling account of some of my feelings in these matters, but because I have so little time to write, I cannot possibly take the time to shorten it up and make it more emphatic.

I close by expressing the earnest feeling that the country must be made to see the difference between Nixon and any one of his prospective opponents and that it should rally to the cause of the policies and philosophies that he espouses.

1939

I have no patience whatsoever with the extremes in political thinking. Both are wrong, equally. We must have a constructive, useful program of action—but the great effort must be to place the maximum amount of responsibility on the individual.

Again I apologize for the length and lack of coherence of this letter; I am off to the country for the weekend—and a beautiful weekend it promises to be.

With affectionate regard to yourself, and all the best to Ed,[16] *As ever*

[1] Mrs. Edgar Eisenhower had written three letters (AWF/N; see also Edgar Eisenhower to Eisenhower, May 4, 1960, AWF/N). According to Ann Whitman, the President spent the better part of an hour dictating this letter (Ann Whitman memorandum, May 6, 1960, AWF/AWD).

[2] For background on the trip see no. 1514. Mrs. Eisenhower had enclosed a copy of an itinerary with one of the letters. The itinerary is not in EM.

[3] Mrs. Eisenhower had sent, under separate cover, an analysis of a trip to Russia made by an employee of the Boeing Aircraft Company and a study of "psycho politics as practiced by the communists." She suggested that the President read the latter pamphlet, called "Brain-washing," "with utmost concentration and undivided attention." She added that she wanted to "alert" the President so he could "observe how this technique is being used in America today."

[4] The President's reply to his brother is no. 1514.

[5] Mrs. Eisenhower said that millions of people "believe *everything* they read in the newspapers." The press is powerful, she wrote, and "should be exceedingly conscientious about printing both sides of a question. But do they do this?"

[6] See, for example, no. 1499.

[7] These were syndicated columnist Drew Pearson; United Feature Syndicate columnist Doris Fleeson; syndicated columnist Joseph Wright Alsop, Jr.; chief Washington correspondent for the Associated Press James Barrett Reston; chief correspondent with the *St. Louis Dispatch* Marquis William Childs; columnist and editor Walter Lippmann*n;* and author and syndicated columnist George Ephraim Sokolsky. For further examples of the President's distaste for newspapers columnists he considered irresponsible see nos. 807, 808, and 1218.

[8] On the President's esteem for Krock and Drummond see nos. 44 and 808, respectively.

[9] On Eisenhower's relationship with Lawrence see nos. 808 and 1010.

[10] The President's sister-in-law had suggested that in the future he should remind newspaper editors and publishers of their responsibility to the public to print facts rather than the opinions of the reporters. On April 17, 1958, Eisenhower had addressed the American Society of Newspaper Editors and the International Press Institute (see *Public Papers of the Presidents: Eisenhower, 1958*, pp. 325–34). On January 14, 1959, he had attended the National Press Club Conference (see no. 1037).

[11] Mrs. Eisenhower said that newspapers in the South reported the sit-ins as "minor incidents." The newspaper coverage on the West coast was considerably more extensive, she wrote, leading people to believe that "we were just about on the brink of another Civil War."

[12] The President had been in Cape Canaveral, Florida, on February 10 (see no. 1410). He had visited Fort Benning, Georgia, on May 3; Albany, Georgia, January 15–17 (see no. 1410); and Augusta, Georgia, December 27–January 5 and April 11–21 (see nos. 1402 and 1495).

For the President's position on civil rights see nos. 323, 840, and 1616. For background on Mrs. Edgar Eisenhower's views see no. 835.

[13] Mrs. Eisenhower said Nixon's "liberal me-too attitude" concerned and disappointed people on the West Coast. Both he and all the likely Democratic candidates, she wrote, were liberal so it made no difference which way one voted. On the President's support of Nixon see, for example, nos. 1293 and 1411.

[14] In June 1952 Eisenhower had resigned his position as Supreme Allied Commander, Europe, in order to launch his campaign for the Republican nomination (see Galambos, *NATO and the Campaign of 1952*, nos. 587, 784, 785). Eisenhower had laid out his middle-of-the-road political philosophy in a speech to the American Bar Association on September 5, 1949 (see Galambos, *Columbia University*, no. 532).

[15] The President had discussed the federal government's labor and welfare programs and the promotion of public health in his annual budget message to the Congress on January 18. He would address them again in his final budget message to the Congress on January 16, 1961 (see *Public Papers of the Presidents: Eisenhower, 1960–61*, pp. 37–112 and 934–1028).

[16] For developments see no. 1547.

1529   *EM, AWF, DDE Diaries Series*

To Arthur William Radford   *May 9, 1960*

Dear Raddy: It is never "presumptuous" of you to make any suggestion whatever to me; I think you know how much I value your opinions.[1]

As far as a visit to Taiwan and the Philippines is concerned, I can only say that this subject has been on my mind—and had been extensively discussed—ever since I decided to stop in Tokyo.[2] As you know, there is always a problem of the availability of time presented to any President who leaves the country during a session of the Congress. This is particularly true toward the end of the session. Dispositions and tempers are wearing thin and bills arrive at the White House with great frequency.[3]

My current plans call for my being out of the country from June ninth until somewhere around the twenty-sixth, although this did include a final thirty-six hours for rest in Hawaii. This is almost a must for the simple reason that only an individual who has been experienced in these matters knows the extent of the mental and physical exhaustion that a week or more of foreign "barnstorming" entails. However, I shall keep the matter on my mind and see if there is anything else I can work out.[4]

With warm regard, *As ever*

[1] Admiral Radford, former Chairman of the Joint Chiefs of Staff, had written on May 6 (WHCF/PPF 1-F-139). He had reminded the President that while he chaired the JCS, Eisenhower had encouraged him to "speak up" if he thought it was important. He had presumed to write, he said, "because of the seriousness of the situation" in the Far East.

² For background on Eisenhower's plan to visit Japan see no. 1381-A and *New York Times*, January 7, May 30, 1960. For developments on the trip see nos. 1564 and 1568. Radford had said that many Asian countries would not understand the President's visiting only Japan and Korea. Extending his journey by three days could "placate most if not all of the criticism" he wrote, and he proposed brief stops in Taipei, and Manila.

³ The second session of the Eighty-sixth Congress would recess temporarily on July 3. It would reconvene in August, and final adjournment *sine die* would come on September 1 (see *Congressional Quarterly Almanac*, vol. XVI, *1960*, p. 24).

⁴ The President would leave Washington on June 12. After stopping in Anchorage, he would arrive in Manila on June 14. On June 16 he would board the U.S.S. *St. Paul* for Taipei where he would stay until June 18. The following day he would travel to Okinawa and Seoul. On June 20 he would fly to Honolulu, where he would remain until June 25 (see Eisenhower, *Waging Peace*, pp. 562–66; nos. 1562, 1563, 1564, 1569 in these volumes; and *New York Times*, June 13–27, 1960).

1530

EM, AWF, Name Series:
DDE Politics 1960

To Oveta Culp Hobby
Personal and confidential

May 9, 1960

Dear Oveta: Would it get some Republican interest started up in Texas if the organization there should name Bob Anderson as a "favorite son"? Of course I realize that although he is qualified for any position in the entire government, such a Texas movement would be regarded largely in the nature of a complimentary action, because of the lack, in his case, of nationwide publicity and visibility. But who could more deserve a compliment![1]

Of course I have never mentioned this to Bob, but it occurs to me that if he would object, then we ought to be the first to name a lady as the "favorite *son*." How about it? In any event we ought to be having some real activity—the kind that will remind people that there are ladies as well as other leaders, such as Bob, who believe in moderate government, fiscal responsibility, and official and personal integrity. If you have any good hot ideas, I would like to hear them.[2]

Please give my warm greetings to the Governor, and my continued best wishes for the regaining of his health and strength.

With affectionate regard, *Sincerely*

[1] On Eisenhower's regard for Treasury Secretary Anderson see Galambos and van Ee, *The Middle Way*, no.1684. For the President's endorsement of Nixon's presidential candidacy see no. 1477.
[2] There is no response from Hobby in EM. See also no. 1560.

To Lyndon Baines Johnson   *May 10, 1960*

Dear Lyndon: I am profoundly appreciative of your telegram, bringing to me your generous assurance of support in the latest international incident. Such a statement could have been made only by an individual of strong conviction, deep understanding, and dedication to his country.[1]

With personal regard, *Sincerely*

[1] On May 7 Senate Majority Leader Johnson had sent the telegram containing his statement to the press (AWF/D; see also *New York Times*, May 11, 1960). Johnson's statement was the result of Soviet Premier Khrushchev's announcement (May 7) that parts of a United States U-2 reconnaissance airplane and its pilot were being held in Moscow. (For background on the secret flights, initiated in 1954 and code-named AQUATONE, see nos. 82 and 457.) Johnson had asked "all Americans to keep their heads" and to "dedicate themselves" to the unity of the United States at this time of "serious international crisis." Khrushchev, he said, was determined to exploit the incident; just how far he intended to "push his saber rattling" was not known. Johnson did think he knew, however, "just how far Americans intend to go to preserve their freedoms—right to the limit." All Americans, he said, Democrats and Republicans alike, would not permit their country to be terrorized, and both parties would solidly support the President when he spoke for the United States.

The U-2 plane had been missing since May 1. On May 5 Khrushchev had announced the downing of a U.S. plane that had penetrated deeply into Soviet territory. The CIA and JCS had assumed, incorrectly, that in the event of a mishap the plane could not withstand the stress and the pilot would not survive. Believing, therefore, that no proof of espionage existed, the White House had attempted to cover up the incident by announcing that an unarmed, weather-observation plane, flown by a civilian, had gone astray near the Turkish-Soviet border. To Eisenhower's consternation, however, Khrushchev had then revealed (May 7) that the Soviets had recovered not only the physical evidence that demonstrated conclusively the nature of the U-2's spy mission, but also its pilot, whom he described as "quite alive and kicking." On May 8 the President had admitted that he had been fully aware of the missions and had directed "information-gathering by every possible means to protect the United States and the Free World against surprise attack" (Eisenhower, *Waging Peace*, pp. 543–59; State, *Foreign Relations, 1958–1960*, vol. X, pt. 1, *Eastern Europe Region; Soviet Union; Cyprus*, pp. 510–21; Ambrose, *Eisenhower*, vol. II, *The President*, pp. 571–76; Beschloss, *Mayday: Eisenhower, Khrushchev, and the U-2 Affair*, pp. 243–57; Bissell, *Reflections of a Cold Warrior*, pp. 128–29; and *New York Times*, May 6, 7, 8, 1960). For developments see nos. 1538 and 1541.

To Clarence Douglas Dillon   *May 10, 1960*

Memorandum for the Under Secretary of State (Mr. Dillon) through the Secretary of State: In view of the importance we attach to the Inter-

American Bank and the desirability (I assume) of keeping the Development Loan Fund out of this area, why would it not be a good idea to transfer some of the capital we have been contemplating for the DLF to the Inter-American Bank?[1]

[1] Eisenhower was referring to funds planned for a new Latin American aid program that Dillon and other members of the National Advisory Committee on Inter-American Affairs were developing (on the Committee see no. 967). Eisenhower, convinced by his recent trip to Latin America (see no. 1403) that the region needed additional financial assistance, supported the proposal. In response to Eisenhower's query, Dillon would agree that it was best to channel the proposed funding through the newly-chartered Inter-American Development Bank, an institution designed to offer both hard and soft currency loans for economic and social development in the Western Hemisphere (for background see no. 1130). He thought using the IADB rather than the Development Loan Fund would avoid the appearance of competition with the Export-Import Bank or the World Bank, an issue that concerned the Administration. It would also allow the flexibility to make soft currency loans (as opposed to the hard loan policies of the two older banks). Dillon would recommend that since the IADB would not be fully operational until 1962, Eisenhower should request the special funds in the next budget. Alternatively, if the IADB was not used, he suggested that the DLF budget be increased with funds earmarked specifically for Latin America (Dillon to Eisenhower, May 17, 1960, AWF/D-H). For background see nos. 730 and 967; see also Kaufman, *Trade and Aid*, pp. 198–200; Noble, *Christian A. Herter*, pp. 220–25; Rabe, *Eisenhower and Latin America*, pp. 141–44; Milton S. Eisenhower, *The Wine is Bitter*, pp. 249–51.

Eisenhower would agree to follow Dillon's recommendation to use the IADB rather than the DLF for soft loans in Latin America (Goodpaster to Dillon, May 24, 1960, AWF/D-H). The aid package, subsequently called the Social Progress Trust Fund (or the Social Development Fund for Latin America), represented a shift in policy toward Latin America: funding assistance would now include loans aimed at political and social development, in addition to military aid. For developments see no. 1580; see also State, *Foreign Relations*, 1958–1960, vol. IV, *Foreign Economic Policy*, pp. 379–81.

1533   *EM, WHCF, Official File 7-C*

To Henry B. Jameson   *May 10, 1960*
Personal

Dear Mr. Jameson: Thank you for your letter.[1] I am glad you brought to my personal attention the matter of what the proposed new postal rates (second class category) would mean to the Abilene Chronicle and other similar papers throughout the country.[2]

I shall ask the Postmaster General to give you a more substantive reply than I possibly can at this moment. I do want, however, to assure you that I am, quite naturally, sympathetic with your problem— while at the same time I am desirous of doing everything possible to make the Post Office Department self-supporting on a basis equitable to all facets of our society.[3]

With warm regard, *Sincerely*

[1] Jameson, president and editor of the *Abilene Reflector-Chronicle*, had written on May 5 (same file as document). He noted that the "alarming increase" in costs to small-town newspapers combined with the elimination of the historic in-county mailing privilege (which allowed small newspapers to be mailed free within their home counties) could possibly put small publications out of business. At the bottom of Jameson's letter Eisenhower had written: "This is the first time I've heard of abolition of the 'free-in-county' privilege. How about it?"

[2] On March 11, in a special message to Congress, the President had requested a postal rate increase. The request had met strong opposition from business and newspaper groups (see *Public Papers of the Presidents: Eisenhower, 1960–61*, pp. 288–89; *Congressional Quarterly Almanac*, vol. XVI, *1960*, pp. 249, 628; and *New York Times*, Mar. 12, 1960).

[3] Postmaster General Summerfield would reply to Jameson on May 20 (same file as document). He explained that the Postal Policy Act of 1958 required that postal operations must be on a break-even basis. With a nearly $300 million revenue deficiency arising from the handling of newspapers and magazines, it was clear that the objective could not be met equitably unless a larger share of costs was borne by this class of users. The most recent second-class rate increases had affected only 'outside-the-county' matter and were primarily increases in pound rates. The heavier publications had automatically absorbed greater increases per copy than their lighter weight counterparts.

It was undoubtedly true that almost any up-dating in in-county rates would have to be "significant," Summerfield wrote, because the 80-year-old rates were so low in relation to current price levels. The Postmaster General went on to say that for a more specific analysis of Jameson's objections, the postal department had examined the postage records for the *Abilene Reflector-Chronicle*. On the basis of the Department's proposals, he reported, the average postage per copy would remain less than 0.9 cents per copy. Summerfield added that impact studies conducted for the Post Office Department had revealed that newspapers had experienced and adjusted to far greater cost increases in areas such as paper and wages.

On June 1 Summerfield would, however, withdraw the requested in-county rate increases for small circulation newspapers. No congressional action would be taken in 1960 on Eisenhower's request for an increase in postal rates (*Congressional Quarterly Almanac*, vol. XVI, *1960*, p. 249, and *New York Times*, June 2, 3, 1960).

1534   *EM, AWF, DDE Diaries Series*

To George Edward Allen   *May 12, 1960*

Dear George: Finally I had an opportunity to read all of your piece in the SATURDAY EVENING POST of April ninth. I can only say that I am greatly flattered.[1]

Particularly I am impressed that you neither criticized anyone— or attempted to change any opinion of others that you had previously expressed.

In other words, besides being highly complimented, I congratulate you not only on the famous Allen "style" but upon your use of the same technique that I tried to employ in CRUSADE IN EUROPE.[2]

With warm regard, *As ever*

[1] The article, entitled "My Friend the President," was an intimate portrait of Eisenhower and his reasons for entering politics. At the outset Allen warned his readers that there would be "no taint of objectivity" in anything he wrote about the President. Allen admitted to being so prejudiced in Eisenhower's favor that he even admired his faults. For developments see no. 1537.

[2] On April 25 Allen's best seller about Presidents Roosevelt and Truman, *Presidents Who Have Known Me* (New York, 1950), would be reissued and would include a chapter on Eisenhower. On Eisenhower's thoughts about his World War II memoir see, for example, nos. 1012 and 1369.

1535   *EM, WHCF, Official File 3-K*

To Louise Battle Caffey   *May 13, 1960*

Dear Louise: After receiving the letter you sent me on May eighth, I had a check made as to the proper procedure to be followed to obtain consideration for a physical disability determination.[1]

The first thing for Frank to do is to submit a request to the Department of the Army for such consideration, stating the grounds on which he bases his request. I am assured that there is an established procedure to handle the matter from that point forward.

If Frank desires to do this, and thinks that a statement from me concerning the physical difficulty he has experienced, to my personal knowledge, would be helpful, please let me know and I will be ready to provide one at once.[2]

With affectionate regard, *Sincerely*

[1] Mrs. Caffey had written that she had been distressed that her husband, Brigadier General Benjamin Franklin Caffey, Jr. (USA, ret.), who had recently undergone surgery at Walter Reed Army Hospital, had not had a chance to discuss "the urgent business" of his re-examination. For background on Eisenhower's friendship with Caffey, whom he had met while both were serving in the Philippines, see *Eisenhower Papers*, vols. I–XVII. Caffey had incurred a physical disability while he was serving as military attaché in Switzerland in 1949. At that time, he returned to the United States and entered Walter Reed Army Hospital for treatment. Six months later (March 1950), he retired voluntarily after having served in the U.S. Army more than thirty years.

Mrs. Caffey also had written to the President on May 1 and had explained that in 1950 the Army had advised Caffey that retiring on a physical disability basis would not benefit him. "No advice could have been worse." Her husband's condition had worsened, and now he sought a re-examination of his retirement status. At the bottom of that letter Eisenhower had asked General Goodpaster, "Is it possible for this case to be reviewed legally?" See also no. 1617.

[2] On September 15 (same file as document) General Caffey would write that a hearing on the status of his retirement would be held on September 28. All papers are in the same file as the document; there is no further correspondence on this subject in EM.

1536   *EM, WHCF, Official File 133-L-6*

To Thomas John Watson, Jr.   *May 14, 1960*

Dear Tom:[1] No doubt you saw in the press that Congress has just approved continuance of the mutual security program. This, however, merely gave authority to appropriate. The money itself has to be separately legislated.[2] In this latter respect, the mutual security program is so gravely endangered that I feel impelled to let you know of it, with the thought that you may wish to join me in an attempt to avoid irreparable damage to our country.

This situation reminds me of a similar challenge two years ago. You will recall that I then turned to you and other friends for cooperation in explaining to the Congress and the public the course of responsibility and wisdom on the reorganization of the Department of Defense. You and they, to my everlasting gratitude, responded magnificently. At the end the needed law was passed, and today all America is much the better for it.[3]

The mutual security problem is now in a similar status. The attached copy of a talk I made on May second to the Nation presents the situation in broad terms and deals with a number of the spurious arguments made by badly informed individuals against this program.[4]

Very shortly—probably within the next two weeks, and while I am in Paris—the level of appropriations for the mutual security program for the next fiscal year will be decided in the House of Representatives. If a crippling cut is made by the House, there will be little prospect of recouping in the Senate. As indicated in the enclosure, cuts of a billion to a billion and a half dollars are being forecast by powerfully placed House Members.[5]

I cannot but trouble over this possibility as I deal with the great issues confronting the free world, indeed all humanity, in the Summit Conferences in Paris.[6] It is incomprehensible to me that at this point in world affairs we should face the possibility of undermining, by our own hand, our buttressing of free nations and our partnerships in defense against communist imperialism. At stake here are the NATO and SEATO alliance structures, and the defense postures of South Korea, Taiwan, Turkey, Pakistan. Also at stake are the striving of hundreds of millions of people who look to us for cooperation in making it possible for them to grow in freedom rather than succumbing to an atheistic materialism bent upon domination of the world.

So crucial are these matters that I presume, once again, to suggest a crusade for our country. Those in Congress who support mutual security need active encouragement to lead this effort; those undecided need encouragement to place national and international need above parochial, political, and other lesser considerations; those opposed need indication that resistance to America's mutual security program, bipartisan since its very beginning, is, in these times, the course of retreat and, ultimately, national crisis.

The Congress, having just authorized continuance of this program, will take up the appropriations in just a few days.[7] To the extent that you share my concern over the announced intentions to slash these appropriations, and to the extent that you may be inclined to move constructively in connection therewith, I shall be at once gratified and grateful.[8]

With warm regard, *Sincerely*

[1] For background on Eisenhower's difficulty with his foreign aid program see no. 1503. Watson (A.B. Brown University 1937) had since 1952 been president of International Business Machines Corporation, a company built and controlled by his father, Thomas J. Watson, Sr. Watson, Jr., was also a member of the U.S. Department of Commerce's Business Advisory Council and, since 1949, had been a trustee and a member of the Executive Committee of the United States Council, International Chamber of Commerce. The President sent the same letter to numerous influential associates and friends. Included with the letter was a staff note explaining that Eisenhower had dictated the letter immediately before leaving for the Summit Conference in Paris, and that he had wanted it sent out even though he had not had time to sign it (the note was signed by Harlow, May 16, 1960, same file as document).

[2] On this day Eisenhower had signed the Mutual Security Act of 1960, which authorized $1,366,200,000. Added to the funds authorized in previous years, the combined total came to $4,186,300,000 (as opposed to the President's request of $4,250,000,000). After signing the bill, the President had issued a statement calling on Congress to continue its support and to appropriate the amounts he had requested (*Public Papers of the Presidents: Eisenhower, 1960–61*, p. 421, and *New York Times*, Apr. 17, 1960).

[3] See nos. 678 and 802, and Eisenhower, *Waging Peace*, p. 251.

[4] The President had spoken at a dinner sponsored by the Committee for International Economic Growth and the Committee to Strengthen the Frontiers of Freedom; see *Public Papers of the Presidents: Eisenhower, 1960–61*, pp. 378–84. The following day he had sent a special message urging Congress to appropriate the funds he had requested for the Mutual Security Program, as well as for his other legislative requests (*ibid.*, pp. 385–89).

[5] There were already indications that the President would encounter difficulties with his funding proposal, despite the Administration's strong appeals. The House Foreign Operations Subcommittee, led by the Democratic Chairman Otto E. Pass-

man, had begun hearings (held intermittently between March 7–May 19) on the 1961 mutual security appropriation even before the authorization bill had cleared. Passman had condemned the Mutual Security Program as riddled with "corruption, scandal and blackmail" and indicated his intention to cut the appropriations request by $1.5 billion (*Congressional Quarterly Almanac*, vol. XVI, *1960*, pp. 166–84, and *New York Times*, Apr. 1, 1960). On May 9 Eisenhower had invited Speaker of the House Rayburn to the White House to ask for his cooperation in dealing with Passman. Rayburn had responded that he would "'do his best'" to get the highest possible figure (Memorandum for Record, May 10, 1960, AWF/D, and Memorandum of the Effect on Mutual Security Program of a $1 Billion Reduction, May 7, 1960, AWF/D-H; see also Harlow to Eisenhower, May 9, 1960, both in AWF/D).

[6] See no. 1537 for current developments on the Summit.

[7] Congress would ultimately appropriate a combined total of $3,781,350,000. The legislation came through both a regular bill and a special supplemental appropriation resulting from a last-minute plea by Eisenhower for additional funds (*Congressional Quarterly Almanac*, vol. XVI, *1960*, pp. 166–84; State, *Foreign Relations, 1958–1960*, vol. IV, *Foreign Economic Policy*, pp. 498–504, 515–20; *Public Papers of the Presidents: Eisenhower, 1960–61*, pp. 659–61; *New York Times*, Sept. 3, 1960). For developments see nos. 1552 and 1571.

[8] Watson would reply (May 17) that he understood the importance of the President's program: "I want you to know I will do my utmost in its behalf." This and other written responses are in the same file as the document.

1537   *EM, WHCF,*
President's Personal File 1395

TO F. PEAVEY HEFFELFINGER   *May 14, 1960*
Personal

Dear Peavey: In the midst of all the problems that have presented themselves this last week, it is refreshing to find your letter of the eleventh.[1] I shall pass along to George Allen your comments about his Saturday Evening Post article; I know he will be gratified.[2]

As for the book that John McCallum wrote in cooperation with my brother Ed, I of course read it with interest. Ed sent me an advance copy some weeks ago—I think with some trepidation. But outside of a few points where my memory differs from my brother's, I thought it was a pretty good, readable account.[3]

With warm regard, *Sincerely*

[1] For background on the recent shooting down of a U.S. spy plane in Soviet territory see no. 1531; on the collapse of the Paris summit meeting see the following document. Heffelfinger (Yale 1920) was president of F. H. Peavey & Company in Minneapolis, Minnesota. He had served as vice-chairman of the Republican National Finance Committee from 1953 until 1955. His letter is in the same file as the document.

[2] Allen's article, "My Friend the President," had appeared in the April 9 issue (see

no. 1534). Heffelfinger said that the piece was "extra good" and that he had sent reprints to several people.

[3] The book to which Eisenhower was referring was John McCallum's *Six Roads from Abilene: Some Personal Reflections of Edgar Eisenhower* (Seattle, Washington, 1960). Heffelfinger said he had enjoyed the book and was trying to help McCallum, whom he had known for several years, promote it.

1538

EM, AWF,
International Series:
De Gaulle

To Charles André Joseph Marie de Gaulle

May 18, 1960

Dear Mr. President: I leave Paris with, of course, a measure of disappointment because our hopes for taking even a small step toward peace have been dashed by the intransigence and arrogance of one individual.[1] But in another respect I leave Paris with the warmth and strength of your friendship, so amply demonstrated and renewed under the stress of the last four days, an even more valued possession than ever before. You and I have shared great experiences in war and in peace, and from those experiences has come, for my part at least, a respect and admiration for you that I have for few men.

Certainly the word "ally" has for me now an even deeper meaning than ever before. I salute the staunch determination that you and your countrymen have shown.[2]

Permit me to thank you and your associates in the government, once again, for the many courtesies you extended to me and the party traveling with me.[3]

With assurances of my continuing high esteem, and my warm personal regard, *Sincerely*

[1] For background on the Summit Conference see no. 1523; see also State, *Foreign Relations, 1958–1960*, vol. IX, *Berlin Crisis 1959–1960; Germany; Austria*, pp. 340–43, 358–414. Soon after the Soviet Union had shot down an American U-2 reconnaissance plane (see no. 1531), Soviet Premier Khrushchev had announced that flights of this kind were "an open threat to peace" and that he had changed his estimate of President Eisenhower. He had not, however, revealed his intentions regarding the Summit Conference (State, *American Foreign Policy, Current Documents, 1960*, pp. 420–23). In a subsequent discussion of the U-2 and its effect on the summit, Eisenhower had told State Department officials that the best course was "to chuckle about it and turn the subject off." He planned to let Khrushchev talk as much as he wanted about the event and would then quietly suggest that he should speak privately to him about it (Goodpaster, Memorandums of Conference, May 10, 12, 16, 1960, AWF/D).

After arriving in Paris on May 15, Eisenhower had told Secretary Herter that he thought the U-2 was "a dead issue," and he would see Khrushchev alone if he raised the matter (Goodpaster, Memorandum of Conference, May 16, 1960, AWF/D). At this same time, however, Khrushchev was telling French President de Gaulle "that he could take no part in the conference unless Eisenhower made a public apology to the Soviet Union, condemned the aggression committed by the United States, announced what punishment would be meted out to those responsible, and [stated] that no American spy plane would ever fly over Soviet territory again" (de Gaulle, *Memoirs of Hope*, pp. 247–49; see also Khrushchev, *Khrushchev Remembers*, pp. 452–53; Macmillan, *Pointing the Way*, pp. 202–3; Walters, *Silent Missions*, pp. 340–41; Bohlen, *Witness to History*, p. 467; and State, *Foreign Relations, 1958–1960*, vol. IX, *Berlin Crisis 1959–1960; Germany; Austria*, pp. 416, 422–23).

At the first meeting of the four heads of government on May 16 Khrushchev had immediately attacked the "provocative act" of the U.S. government and had scorned the initial "ridiculous" explanation. Unless Eisenhower followed the course of action he had outlined to de Gaulle, Khrushchev stated, the conference should be postponed for six to eight months or until the United States reconsidered its policies. Khrushchev also withdrew his invitation to Eisenhower to visit the Soviet Union in June. Eisenhower responded by deploring "the distasteful necessity of espionage activities in a world where nations distrust each other's intentions." The overflights, however, had been suspended, he said, and would not be resumed. After subsequent statements by Macmillan, de Gaulle, and Khrushchev, the meeting ended. For the remainder of that day and the next the Western leaders and their advisers had discussed Khrushchev's statement and the future of the conference.

When the Soviet leader did not appear at a meeting arranged for 3:00 P.M. on May 17, the three allies issued a joint communiqué indicating regret that the conference could not take place and reiterating their belief that negotiation was the only way to settle international questions. In their final meeting on May 18 Eisenhower, Macmillan, de Gaulle, and their foreign ministers had discussed the need for an effective tripartite relationship, contingency planning in the event that communications in Berlin were disrupted, and disarmament issues. Eisenhower would leave Paris on the following day for a short visit to Portugal before returning to the United States (State, *Foreign Relations, 1958–1960*, vol. IX, *Berlin Crisis 1959–1960; Germany; Austria*, pp. 417–98; State, *American Foreign Policy; Current Documents, 1960*, pp. 426–31; Goodpaster, Memorandums of Conference, May 16, 27, 1960; Eisenhower, *Waging Peace*, pp. 553–57; Macmillan, *Pointing the Way*, pp. 204–14; de Gaulle, *Memoirs of Hope*, pp. 249–53; Khrushchev, *Khrushchev Remembers*, pp. 453–61; Bohlen, *Witness to History*, pp. 467–70; Walters, *Silent Missions*, pp. 342–48).

[2] After the Soviets had ended the conference, de Gaulle had told Eisenhower that no matter what Khrushchev did and no matter what happened, he was with him to the end (*ibid.*, p. 346; see also Goodpaster, Memorandum of Conference, May 16, 1960, AWF/D; and Eisenhower, *Waging Peace*, p. 556).

[3] De Gaulle would write that he was "sincerely touched" by Eisenhower's sentiments and that he shared the feelings the President had expressed. "At least these developments have enabled our countries to test the strength of the bonds uniting them" (de Gaulle to Eisenhower, May 20, 1960, AWF/I: de Gaulle; see also Herter to Eisenhower, May 28, 1960, *ibid.*). For developments see no. 1542.

1539

EM, AWF, Microfilm Series:
Geographic Series, Macmillan Corr.

To Harold Macmillan   *May 18, 1960*

That we did not succeed in our hopes to bring to the world a little greater assurance of the peace that must somehow be achieved is the unhappy fact that we must accept.[1] Certainly you did everything that you possibly could to bring about a degree of civilized behavior in the arrogant and intransigent man from Moscow; no one could have tried harder. I applaud your efforts; no one could have done more.

As we have said in our meetings, we shall have to make a reappraisal of the facts of today's world. I shall be in touch with you, I know, within the near future.[2]

Meantime, my thanks and warm personal regard.

[1] For background on the abortive Summit Conference see the preceding document.
[2] For developments see no. 1542.

1540   *EM, AWF, Administration Series*

To Lauris Norstad   *May 18, 1960*

Dear Larry:[1] Yesterday the Prime Minister and I had an opportunity to visit Marnes-la-Coquette.[2] By advice of our staffs, who felt that a visit to SHAPE would have too strong a military implication, we refrained from going over to the Headquarters.[3] We stopped briefly at the Villa St. Pierre and all your staff were more than cooperative and hospitable in showing us the grounds.[4] Please tell Isabelle that the steward was kind enough also to take us around the lower rooms of the house. Tell her I apologize for the intrusion, but wanted to indulge my nostalgic memories of the place.

After a visit there we called on Mayor Minaud to pay our respects. He was one big bundle of enthusiasm.[5] All in all it was by far the most pleasant hour I have had in Paris.

John McCone came to see me this morning, and his glowing report of your condition is most heartening and encouraging.[6] I am afraid I can't accept your invitation for fishing![7] However, all of us join in sending you our warmest good wishes for a speedy recovery and, of course, give my affectionate greetings to Isabelle. *As ever*

[1] General Norstad, Supreme Allied Commander, Europe, had apologized (May 15, 1960, AWF/A) for not meeting the President when he arrived in Paris. While vaca-

tioning in West Germany, he had suffered a mild heart attack and had remained there to recuperate. He planned to "get back to full and unrestricted duty" in about six weeks, he wrote.

[2] The President and British Prime Minister Macmillan had been in Paris to attend the summit meetings (see nos. 1538 and 1539). Marnes-la-Coquette, a picturesque village ten miles west of Paris, had been the Eisenhowers' home while the General served as Supreme Commander of the North Atlantic Treaty forces in Europe (for background see Galambos, *NATO and the Campaign of 1952*, no. 314).

[3] Supreme Headquarters, Allied Powers Europe, SHAPE, was located in Marly Forest, fifteen miles west of Paris and near Versailles (for background see Galambos, *NATO and the Campaign of 1952*, no. 45).

[4] In August 1951 the Eisenhowers moved into Villa St. Pierre, a country house with classic regency lines, in Marnes-la-Coquette (see Galambos, *NATO and the Campaign of 1952*, nos. 18, 298, and 314; and Alden Hatch, *Red Carpet for Mamie* [New York, 1954], pp. 230–34). Now it was the Norstads' residence.

[5] Jean Minaud was mayor of Marnes-la-Coquette. The President first had met Minaud in 1951 when he presented honorary citizenships to the Eisenhowers (see Galambos and van Ee, *The Middle Way*, no. 1258 and *New York Times*, Sept. 10, 1951).

[6] In April Atomic Energy Commission Chairman McCone had remained in Paris after participating in U.S.-French discussions on peaceful uses of atomic energy (*New York Times*, Apr. 10, 15, 1960).

[7] Norstad had mentioned in his letter that he had enjoyed "some really wonderful trout fishing" before his illness. "By helicopter," he wrote, "the stream can't be 15 minutes away from Munich."

1541   *EM, AWF,*
                                                    International Series: Colombia

To Alberto Lleras Camargo   *May 19, 1960*

Dear Mr. President:[1] In view of the happenings of the last few days, you may have some interest in my assessment of the trends regarding events—or rather the lack of them—at the Paris meeting and their significance to all of us.[2]

As you recall, I recently requested my ambassador to your country to outline to you in general terms the hopes I cherished for the relaxation of tensions as I prepared to come to Paris for the long-planned Summit Conference. These hopes were also expressed to me by the Presidents of the Latin American countries I was able to visit this last February and March.[3]

Unfortunately these hopes proved further away than I realized at the time. As a result of a chain of events within the Soviet Union which is not clear to me at this time, Mr. Khrushchev must have concluded before coming to Paris that progress at a Summit Meeting would be either undesirable or impossible. Accordingly, he embarked on a calculated campaign, even before it began, to insure the failure of the conference and to see to it that the onus for such failure would fall on the West, particularly the United States.

As a device, Mr. Khrushchev seized upon his successful downing of an unarmed United States civilian reconnaissance plane, which admittedly was flying over Soviet territory. I need not assure you that this activity was not intentionally provocative and certainly not aggressive; it constituted one phase of an intelligence system made necessary for defense against surprise attack on the part of a nation which boasts of its capability to "bury" us all[4]—and one which stubbornly maintains the most rigid secrecy in all its activities.

At the least this incident, while regrettable in the extreme, could not by any stretch of the imagination be of such magnitude as to justify the polemics and the abuse which Mr. Khrushchev saw fit to heap upon the United States. By so distorting and exaggerating this incident, he of course put an end, for the time being, to any hopes of progress.

My purpose in writing this letter, Mr. President, is primarily to assure you that my objectives, in spite of the occurrence at this meeting, remain completely unchanged. I am sure that this experience will serve to strengthen the ties that bind your country and mine, and that it will point up the long-term challenge to the Free World that requires the utmost in unity and cooperation.

I have every hope that as time goes by, the world will come to appreciate ever more strongly the urgent need for control of armaments, for mutual understanding, and for mutual respect among all men.

Please accept, Mr. President, the assurances of my continued respect and esteem.[5] *Sincerely*

[1] Dr. Lleras Camargo, president of Colombia since August 1958, had been ambassador to the United States during World War II. He had also served as Colombia's minister for foreign affairs, secretary-general of the Organization of the Americas, and president of the University of Los Andes. This message, drafted by State Department officials, was sent to the American embassy in Bogota for delivery. Similar messages were sent to the leaders of fifteen other Latin American countries and to the leaders of Greece, India, Iran, Italy, Morocco, Spain, Tunisia, and Turkey, countries Eisenhower had visited on his goodwill tour in December. The letters and the responses they generated are in AWF/I.

[2] On the collapse of the summit meeting see no. 1538.

[3] On Eisenhower's South American trip see no. 1403.

[4] See no. 1107 for Khrushchev's threat to bury the United States.

[5] President Lleras Camargo would tell Eisenhower that he had held "high hopes" for the reduction in international tension that might have resulted from a successful conference. "However," he wrote, "no careful observer of developments in Soviet policy could have failed to be somewhat skeptical of a total or partial agreement in the long-standing conflicts that characterize the period known as the Cold War" (Lleras Camargo to Eisenhower, May 28, 1960, AWF/I: Colombia; see also Calhoun to Goodpaster, June 8, 1960, *ibid.*).

To Harold Macmillan   *May 24, 1960*

Dear Harold:[1] I have just received your cable of May twentieth. I enthusiastically endorse your observation that you and I should remain as closely together as is humanly possible.[2]

When your message reached me, I was just dictating one to you concerning two newspaper stories, disturbing to me, that came out of London, one written by a man named Cook, the other by Middleton, both Americans. While the stories do not deal with the same phases of post-Paris events, both do refer to some fancied rift between you and me or between our respective associates and assistants.[3]

As you know, there is no slightest foundation for any such stories so far as Chris Herter and I are concerned. Moreover, in spite of the fact that one of the stories reports that some of the Americans who were left in Paris after the departure of Chris and myself voiced criticism of you and your efforts to bring about a Summit meeting, I cannot believe there is any foundation of fact for the story. All the people working around me and with me heard me time and again refer to the ideal association between you and myself and, indeed, between the both of us with General de Gaulle. Moreover, you and I agreed long ago that a Summit meeting was advisable, particularly after Mr. K. removed his alleged ultimatum on Berlin.[4]

Another item refers to a conclusion that your reception of Mr. K. on Sunday afternoon was ill-advised because by doing so you indicated or created a rift between our two delegations. Of course nothing could be more ridiculous. I was anxious for you to receive the man to see whether his afternoon story would be the same as the one he gave to General de Gaulle in the morning.[5]

Of course I know that you do not take such stories as these too seriously. I have respected your judgment and valued your friendship for more than seventeen years, and I want to assure you that my confidence in you is higher, if possible, than ever before.

After leaving Paris I spoke publicly both in Lisbon and in Washington and in both instances took occasion to point out that one good result of the failure of the conference was to bring the allies closer together. I referred especially to the splendid spirit that animated the three of us at all our meetings.[6]

With warm personal regard, *As ever*

[1] This message was sent by cable to the American embassy in London for delivery to Macmillan. At the request of Presidential Secretary Ann Whitman the cable was marked "personal." The State Department classified it "Confidential."

[2] Macmillan had written in response to an earlier letter from Eisenhower regarding

the abortive Paris summit (see no. 1539). "I cannot tell you how much I admired the magnanimity and restraint with which you acted throughout those trying few days," Macmillan told Eisenhower. "As for the future, no one can tell which way it will go. But certainly our experiences in Paris make it all the more important to strengthen our Western alliance" (AWF/I: Macmillan).

[3] Don Cook, chief of the London bureau of the *New York Herald Tribune*, had written that the "summit wreckage" had left Macmillan "the most weakened, diplomatically, of any of the Western Big Three leaders." He had played the middleman "past the point of diplomatic usefulness," Cook said, and consequently his advice was "unlikely to be sought or be very influential at Washington in these last months of the Eisenhower administration" (*New York Herald Tribune*, [May 23, 1960]).

Drew Middleton, chief London correspondent for the *New York Times*, had reported that some members of the U.S. delegation had said "that a conference of heads of government was always a bad idea, that Mr. Macmillan had talked President Eisenhower into it, that Mr. Macmillan's position with President Eisenhower had deteriorated as a consequence of the debacle at Paris and that the members of the British delegation differed among themselves on this and other points of the Macmillan policy" (*New York Times*, May 24, 1960; for background on Middleton's reporting see no. 88).

[4] On Secretary Herter's message to British Foreign Secretary Selwyn Lloyd regarding the stories see State, *Foreign Relations, 1958–1960*, vol. VII, pt. 2, *Western Europe*, pp. 868–69; on Khrushchev's withdrawal of the Berlin ultimatum see no. 1325.

[5] In his meeting with de Gaulle Khrushchev had harshly criticized Eisenhower and said that the "airplane incident" had made the summit impossible. Khrushchev had added that he was particularly disappointed because he had been prepared to present "many 'constructive' proposals" regarding disarmament (State, *Foreign Relations, 1958–1960*, vol. IX, *Berlin Crisis 1959–1960; Germany; Austria*, p. 486; see also de Gaulle, *Memoirs of Hope*, p. 253. With Macmillan Khrushchev had maintained his desire for peaceful coexistence and had chided the British leader for not putting more pressure on Eisenhower (Macmillan, *Pointing the Way*, p. 211).

[6] For the two speeches see *Public Papers of the Presidents: Eisenhower, 1960–61*, pp. 431–32, 435–37; see also *New York Times*, May 20, 1960.

"Of course I did not take the Cook-Middleton story seriously," Macmillan would answer. "It was very good of you to send me such a generous letter and to speak so warmly. You know how much I value your friendship and I think that our sort of close feeling for each other is the kind of thing which grows stronger with the years" (Macmillan to Eisenhower, June 2, 1960, PREM 11/2995). For developments see no. 1553.

1543   *EM, AWF, DDE Diaries Series*

To Edward Harold Litchfield   *May 24, 1960*

Dear Dr. Litchfield:[1] A transoceanic trip provided me with enough leisure time to study carefully your address of May second, which I had previously read only sketchily.[2] I think you said something that needed to be said, and did it splendidly.

In reading the text, it strikes me that there are two points that might have deserved passing mention. The first of these is that, while you use the word "knowledge" to imply, also, the concept of understanding, I think too many people use the word to mean only knowledge of a fact, a technique, a profession or possibly of many facts in many fields.[3]

Your talk does deal with one phase of understanding, particularly the understanding between the American corporation and its influence on relations between our country and others.[4] But to give one example of what I am getting at, I find medical scientists constantly talking about their new knowledge that has permitted them to prolong life expectancy. Although the major portion of this accomplishment came about because of the reduction in infant mortality, the fact is that our population is including a higher and higher proportion of older people. Certainly, then, there should be some understanding of the new problems thus created—and a whole host of questions suggest themselves. Two principal ones are: "Do we consider the arbitrary ages we set for retirement to be correct, and if they are correct now, will they be so in a few years when we have even a higher percentage of people beyond the age of 65?" I rather think that it might be a good thing if we put as much research into providing greater opportunity for useful lives for older people as we do into the effort merely to prolong their days.

The second question that suggests itself is determining to what extent should we insist that every individual make provision for his own support when he is no longer active and what are the true responsibilities of the several echelons of government in this regard. It is of course easy for the vote seeker to assure every individual that he can shift such responsibilities to government. But I often wonder whether any wholesale and practically complete transfer of the responsibility to government will not have a most unfortunate effect on the pride and sturdy self-dependence of the individual. Those are values as important as any other.

In any event, I think that we should make it clear that when we talk about knowledge, we are talking also of the relationship between one problem and another and of one type of knowledge to other types.

The second point that I think might have been treated a little bit more specifically is the responsibility of the combined management-labor leader group in any corporation to the people it serves. Indeed, I am not convinced that the leaders of our very greatest individual establishments are fully aware of the influence their actions can have on the economy.

Editors, commentators, and even some students of economics talk a great deal about the responsibility of government to see that our national economy remains healthy and expanding. Of course the government has a considerable influence in this regard, particularly through its financial and fiscal policies. It obviously affects the economy by its taxation and spending habits. Yet I believe that when we consider how great is the effect upon the economy of some of the decisions made by small groups of directors and labor leaders, at the bargaining table or elsewhere, we must conclude that in some instances the effects of these decisions can defeat, in a free competitive enterprise, anything that government itself might do in a contrary direction. Consequently, I think we need to use the term "management-labor statesmanship" more than we do.

I remember one group of business leaders, representing several important industries, who stated to me that not only were they losing foreign markets that they had formerly held, but insisted that they needed higher tariffs if we were going to avoid substantial unemployment in this country. They pled as the reason for their loss of markets rising labor costs.

When I, in turn, queried them as to the reasons for granting wage rises that would throw them out of foreign markets, they said that in the domestic scene they were not able to stand a strike because they would lose their competitive position at home.

I asked them if their level of profits had anything to do with this difficulty. When I remarked that their plan of raising tariffs would cause further loss in the foreign market, they were unimpressed— in fact, they more or less preached economic isolationism. To my mind this is the kind of thing that requires what I call a bit of business statesmanship.

This letter is far from being critical of your talk. On the contrary, I was so impressed by it that it occurred to me that you might want to consider emphasizing, in the future, these two points.

While this letter is written rather hastily and, so to speak, shooting from the hip, these matters have been on my mind for a long time and I really wish I knew how to get people, in general, to think about them more intensively.

With personal regard, and again thanks for your courtesy in sending me your speech, *Sincerely*

P.S. As you know, my schedule for May and June has been somewhat altered by the recent events in Paris.[5] If, therefore, you and Gwilym Price still want to see me, I suggest you call my appointment secretary, Mr. Stephens, who will set up a date.[6]

---

[1] University of Pittsburgh chancellor Litchfield was chairman of both the Smith-Corona Marchant Corporation and the Governmental Affairs Institute. A draft of this letter containing Eisenhower's handwritten emendations is in AWF/AWD.

[2] On the President's trip to Southeast Asia see no. 1530. Litchfield had delivered the address to the first general session of the forty-eighth annual meeting of the U.S. Chamber of Commerce. The speech, entitled "Voluntary Action and the Modern Corporation," is in AWF/AWD. Litchfield had focused on the corporation's participation in the definition and solution of local and national problems.

³ Litchfield had said that Americans did not "cherish knowledge as one of their greatest values. Material wealth, comfort, leisure (and not necessarily a constructive leisure) stand higher in our scale of values than does knowledge or the process of learning, or the self-discipline necessary to both."

⁴ Litchfield had told the corporate executives that they represent organizations that have "the most extensive pattern of relationships with other cultures" of any part of American society.

⁵ On the collapse of the Paris summit see no. 1538.

⁶ The President would decide not to send this letter. On August 16 he and Litchfield would discuss Litchfield's speech at the White House. Westinghouse president Gwilym Price would not attend the meeting (AWF/AWD).

1544   *EM, AWF, International Series: Japan*

To Nobusuke Kishi   *May 24, 1960*
*Cable*¹

Dear Mr. Prime Minister: I was heartened to learn that the Lower House of the Japanese Diet has given its approval to the new Treaty of Mutual Cooperation and Security between Japan and the United States.² This action was a welcome demonstration of Free World unity and is a great step forward to the consummation of that indestructible partnership which you and I have long held as our common goal.³ I feel it promises significant progress in our search for peace with justice.⁴

With warm personal regard, *Sincerely*

¹ This message was cabled to the American embassy in Tokyo to be delivered to Prime Minister Kishi. A draft of this letter containing Eisenhower's handwritten emendations and a May 20 cover letter to the President from Secretary Dillon are in AWF/I: Japan. See also Herter to Eisenhower and enclosed drafts containing Eisenhower's handwritten emendations, April 23, 1960, *ibid.*, and Memorandum of Conference with the President, May 23, 1960, AWF/D.

² On January 19 Eisenhower had witnessed Kishi and Secretary Herter signing the treaty (in Washington). On May 20 the lower house had approved the treaty. The pact provided that the United States would defend Japan in case of an attack; the United States also promised to consult with the Japanese if U.S. forces based in Japan were to be deployed to other areas. Japan would take action if either nation were attacked in the territories under Japanese administration. The Diet proceedings had been conducted in an atmosphere of mounting tension. Leftist demonstrators had condemned the treaty as one that would expose Japan to involvement in possible war between the United States and Communist China or the Soviet Union (see no. 1564). For background on the recent U-2 incident, which had heightened fears of Soviet retaliation, see no. 1531. Some American U-2 spy planes operated from Japanese airfields.

Adoption of the treaty was virtually assured because the Japanese government held a majority of nearly two-to-one in the upper chamber, or House of Councillors. The treaty would be automatically ratified on June 20. It would be ratified by a 90-2 vote in the United States Senate on June 22 and would become effective that same day

(*Congressional Quarterly Almanac*, vol. XVI, *1960*, pp. 228–29; State, *Foreign Relations, 1958–1960*, vol. XVIII, *Japan; Korea*, pp. 295–301; Eisenhower, *Waging Peace*, p. 561, and *New York Times*, May 20, 22, 24, 26, 27, June 19, 21–23, 1960).

[3] Eisenhower would repeat these sentiments in a radio and television address to the American people on June 27 (*Public Papers of the Presidents: Eisenhower, 1960–61*, pp. 529, 532–34).

[4] For developments on U.S.-Japanese relations see nos. 1571 and 1647.

1545   *EM, AWF, Name Series*

To WILLIAM EDWARD ROBINSON   *May 24, 1960*

Dear Bill: Thanks so much for your letter—and particularly for setting down for me your thoughts on the general tenor you think the
talk tomorrow night should take.[1] I agree wholeheartedly with you,
and I think most of the staff are coming around to your point of
view. I am shortly to have a lengthy session on the speech itself, and
I appreciate very much your crystallization of the general idea for
me.[2]

I trust you'll be among my unseen audience!

With warm regard, *As ever*

[1] Robinson had written regarding Eisenhower's speech to the nation on the collapse
of the Paris summit meeting (see no. 1538). The majority of the country supported
him, Robinson told the President, and were "not interested in who said what to whom
when the U-2 plane was caught in Russia." "And they bitterly resent the Khrushchev
attack on you." Robinson believed that "any semblance of an apology or even an 'explanation' would be a mistake" (Robinson to Eisenhower, May 23, 1960, AWF/N).
[2] Eisenhower would tell Secretary Herter that he wanted the message to be "positive
without being truculent and to give an explanation of events without being defensive." He wanted to keep the door open for negotiation but knew that any negotiation must be done "from strength rather than from weakness" (Goodpaster, Memorandum of Conference, May 26, 1960, AWF/D; see also Ann Whitman memorandum,
May 24–June 6, 1960, AWF/AWD). For the President's speech see *Public Papers of the
Presidents: Eisenhower, 1960–61*, pp. 437–45.

1546   *EM, AWF,*
                                    International Series: Canada

To JOHN GEORGE DIEFENBAKER   *May 25, 1960*

Dear John:[1] I am most grateful for the special statement you made
before the House of Commons on May eighteenth. Not only did it

accord with views which I share, but it was also a very generous as well as forceful gesture on the part of a close friend and ally.[2]

Unquestionably we must be firm in our unity and in support of our common ideals.[3] Negotiation remains the best way toward the solution of present problems and I think that the Free World will ultimately succeed, since surely the other side realizes the stakes involved.

I am looking forward to your coming here as my guest and will welcome your views of the world situation as it now exists.[4]

Again, my thanks for the strong support of your Government as expressed in your forthright speech.

With warm regard, *Sincerely*

[1] A State Department draft of this message, with Eisenhower's handwritten emendations, is in AWF/I: Canada. The message was sent by cable to the American embassy in Ottawa for delivery to Diefenbaker (see Herter to Eisenhower, May 23, 1960, *ibid.*).
[2] Diefenbaker had spoken regarding the collapse of the Summit Conference (see no. 1538). For unjustifiable reasons Khrushchev had refused to meet with Western leaders, Diefenbaker had said. Any cause for complaint had been removed by Eisenhower's guarantee that U-2 flights would end, and Khrushchev had given no such assurances regarding secret Soviet activities. Diefenbaker had assured the lawmakers that Khrushchev's effort to divide the West had strengthened Western determination to remain united (Herter to Eisenhower, May 23, 1960, AWF/I: Canada; see also NSC meeting minutes, June 1, 1960, AWF/NSC).
[3] At this point in the original draft Eisenhower had deleted language that expressed his belief that the two nations should be firm in their "resolve to weather this storm."
[4] In their meeting on June 3 the two leaders would discuss continental air defense, surplus wheat disposal, a reassessment of NATO's plans and purposes, seismic research on Canadian soil, Geneva nuclear test negotiations, aid to underdeveloped nations, and relations with Communist China (State, *Foreign Relations, 1958–1960,* vol. VII, pt. 1, *Western European Integration and Security; Canada,* pp. 801–7; see also Herter to Eisenhower, May 27, 1960, AWF/I: Canada).

Diefenbaker would write Eisenhower that their meetings had "re-emphasized the meaning of the term 'Good neighbors'—who share the same ideals and objectives—and whose mutual purpose is to view the problems of the other with reason based on a desire to resolve such differences as arise from time to time" (Diefenbaker to Eisenhower, June 7, 1960, *ibid.*).

1547   *EM, AWF, DDE Diaries Series*

To Lucille Dawson Eisenhower   *May 25, 1960*
Personal

Dear Lucy: Thank you very much for your nice note of May twenty-second. I think the best way I can explain my own attitude—and that of Nixon—is by saying that we are both basically conservatives.

By this I mean that we want to conserve all of the admirable traits of character in the American population, to avoid paternalism, and therefore, as we see it, to prevent a deterioration in the fibre of the average citizen.[1]

The difficulty comes in putting into practice the middle-of-the-road position that was so clearly defined by Abraham Lincoln more than one hundred years ago. The "spenders" can always develop a very great deal of popular support because the consequences of over-spending seem to be long-term and vague, whereas the advantages claimed are supposed to be immediate and discernible to all.[2] To have a philosophy is necessary; only those who are in a position of responsibility to apply that philosophy know the difficulties encountered when principle and selfish desire come into open conflict.

The Republican Party tries to follow Lincoln; too many in the other party like to depend on Walter Reuther.[3]

With warm regard,[4] *As ever*

[1] Mrs. Eisenhower's letter is in AWF/N. She had noted that the President, like herself, had difficulty explaining the difference between the political parties. In spite of Nixon's "liberalism," Mrs. Eisenhower said she would work for him. (For background on Mrs. Eisenhower's opinion of the Vice-President see no. 1528). Her cautiousness, she wrote, was matched by "many, many others." Some degree of paternalism was desirable, she admitted, but her "chief concern" was the "approach towards a desirable end."

[2] Americans needed to be encouraged to help themselves, the President's sister-in-law had written, and she wanted "everyone in the country working for a common cause, i.e., self-reliance and independence"—the traits upon which the United States had been built. She lamented that the "trend today" seemed to be "that more money will cure any ailment."

[3] Since 1955 Walter Philip Reuther had been president of the Congress of Industrial Organizations division of the combined organization of the American Federation of Labor and the Congress of Industrial Organizations (see also no. 583).

[4] See the following document.

1548   *EM, AWF, DDE Diaries Series*

To LUCILLE DAWSON EISENHOWER   *May 25, 1960*
Personal

Dear Lucy: I am sending your letter regarding Sergeant Hoiles' death to the Secretary of the Army and asking for an investigation to be made concerning the irregularities you indicate. I enclose a copy of my letter to the Secretary.[1]

There was a paragraph near the end of your letter which goes as follows:

"Sgt. Hoiles' tenure of service with the Army was a frustrating but dedicated one, as is that of so many of the troops. From what I have seen recently of their plight, I pledge them my utmost compassion!"

I lived in the Army over forty years and I am constantly in touch with some of its members from the grade of private to general. I can understand your "compassion" for their sometimes meager pay, but you must understand that the vast majority of them are serving because of a sense of dedication. Moreover, in the installations I have seen—and particularly at Benning—I find that morale is high and that individuals are proud of their work.[2]

Frankly, except for my age I would think it quite exciting and rewarding to be back in the Army! *As ever*

---

[1] Mrs. Edgar Eisenhower's brother-in-law, U.S. Army Sergeant Walter Hoiles, had been killed in an auto-train accident near Fort Benning, Georgia (Lucille Eisenhower to Eisenhower, May 22, 1960, AWF/N). At the time of the accident Hoiles was taken to the post hospital; following his death an autopsy was performed without Mrs. Hoiles's consent. Although Mrs. Hoiles, Lucille Eisenhower's sister, had been denied access to the Army's report of its investigation, the railroad company had received the report immediately after the accident.

Mrs. Eisenhower was disturbed by the Army's "favoritism and biased attitude toward the railroad company" and the apparent lack of concern regarding the soldiers' rights. She asked: "Would this same favoritism have been shown had the body been that of the commanding general or another officer?" Mrs. Eisenhower and her sister had visited the site of the accident and said that the rail signs at prominent crossings were weather-worn and unreadable. The area's residents, she reported, were concerned that a similar accident could happen to a soldier's wife with a carload of children. Any attention to this matter, she concluded, would be greatly appreciated.

On this same day the President would write to Secretary of the Army Wilbur M. Brucker. He asked Brucker to investigate the matter and to send an appropriate reply to Mrs. Hoiles's attorney. There is no further correspondence on this matter in EM.
[2] The President had attended a demonstration of Army equipment at Fort Benning on May 3 (see no. 1528, n. 12). In 1926 he had served as an inspector, assistant executive for training and mobilization, and athletic director at the Infantry School at Fort Benning. Major John Eisenhower had been stationed there from 1953–1954 (Galambos and van Ee, *The Middle Way*, no. 313).

1549 *EM, AWF, Miscellaneous Series: Correspondence*

To Albert Arby Lemieux *May 25, 1960*

Dear Reverend Lemieux: Thank you very much for your letter of May twentieth. I am complimented by your invitation to join the Board of Regents of Seattle University.[1]

With regard to the other reason you give, concerning the injection of religion into political campaigns, I consider the raising of such an issue as deplorable as do you, and have often stated so publicly.[2] However, I have steadfastly refused to make any commitments that involve my possible connection with any kind of institution before January twentieth of next year, and I do not feel that I can, in justice to other requests I have been obliged to refuse, do other than to decline, at this time, to do so.

With best wishes, *Sincerely*

[1] Lemieux (A.B. Gonzaga University 1931; Ph.D. University of Toronto 1945) had been dean at Gonzaga from 1944 to 1948, when he was appointed president of Seattle University. He had written Eisenhower on May 20, inviting him to become a member of Seattle University's board of regents ("Realizing that you have a brother in Tacoma and that, upon retirement, you may find many opportunities to visit him. . . .").

[2] Lemieux had explained that although Seattle was a Jesuit university, there were "many distinguished Protestants serving on our Board." He and his colleagues felt that Eisenhower's acceptance of their invitation to become a member of Seattle's Board of Regents would deal "a resounding death blow" to the religious issue that had been raised by the candidacy of Catholic Democratic Senator John F. Kennedy, "and would serve as inspiration and example throughout the country." Eisenhower had already stated that questioning Kennedy's fitness to serve on religious grounds during the campaign was "very, very bad for this country" (*Public Papers of the Presidents: Eisenhower, 1960–61*, p. 411; see also Theodore H. White, *The Making of the President 1960* [New York, 1967], pp. 105–8, 237–43; and Ambrose, *Nixon*, vol. I, *The Education of a Politician, 1913–1963*, pp. 545, 565–67).

1550   *EM, WHCF,*
President's Personal File 437

To William Randolph Hearst, Jr.   *May 27, 1960*
Personal

Dear Bill: I have just heard that you have been advanced to the position of Chairman of the Board of the Hearst Publications.[1] I send you my warm congratulations.

Writing this note gives me also an opportunity to express my satisfaction over the balanced and reasonable way the Hearst papers handled the recent U-2 incident and the "Summit" meeting. I thought that some of the pieces by Bob Considine[2] were excellent, and of course from my viewpoint they were highly complimentary.[3] I never forget the old saw—"He is a great man; he agrees with me."[4]

With all the best in your new and responsible position, and with warm personal regard, *Sincerely*

[1] Hearst had been director of the Hearst Corporation and Hearst Radio, Inc., and editor-in-chief of the Hearst newspapers (*New York Times,* May 23, 1960).

[2] Columnist and author Robert Bernard Considine had begun his career as a sports writer. During World War II he was a war correspondent with the International News Service. Among his many publications were the well-known *Thirty Seconds over Tokyo* (New York, 1943) and *MacArthur the Magnificent* (Philadelphia, 1942).

[3] On the downing of the American U-2 spy plane see no. 1531; on the collapse of the Paris summit meeting see no. 1538.

[4] Eisenhower may have been referring to the statement "My idea of an agreeable man . . . is a person who agrees with me." It appeared in chapter 25 of Benjamin Disraeli's *Lothair* (New York, 1870).

1551   *EM, AWF, Administration Series*

To Wilber Marion Brucker   *May 31, 1960*

Dear Wilber: Thank you so much for your courtesy in advising me in advance that John was to be promoted to Lieutenant Colonel today. His mother and I are, of course, delighted.[1]

Incidentally, your thoughtfulness permitted us to have a mild family celebration of the occasion in Gettysburg this weekend.[2]

With warm regard, *Sincerely*

[1] There is no correspondence on this subject from Secretary of the Army Brucker in AWF. On the President's interest in his son's military career see Galambos and van Ee, *The Middle Way,* nos. 313 and 371.

In March 1959 Major Eisenhower had been among some 1300 majors recommended for promotion as places became available. The list included many officers from his West Point class of 1944 (*New York Times,* June 1, 1960; see also his memoir, *Strictly Personal,* pp. 281, 304).

[2] The Eisenhowers had visited their Gettysburg farm for the Memorial Day weekend (May 26–30). Major Eisenhower and his family lived in a cottage on land adjacent to the Eisenhower farm (see no. 96). On Monday, May 30, the President had motored to his son's residence and shortly thereafter the President and his son drove to Fort Ritchie for a tour of the post.

1552   *EM, AWF, DDE Diaries Series*

To Henry Merritt Wriston   *June 3, 1960*
Personal

Dear Henry: I found in the June first issue of the *Wall Street Journal* an article that is said to be excerpts from a lecture you delivered at Bowdoin College.[1] I am sure that already you have had many congratulatory comments on your effort. But I was personally so struck not only by what you had to say but how well you said it that I simply had to send you a "fan letter."

Eleven or twelve years ago, in welcoming to Columbia University the college freshmen of that year, I took great issue with the pursuit of security as opposed to the seeking of opportunity.[2] I pointed out that if any person wanted to abandon all higher purposes in life merely to achieve security, he had only to commit some crime for which he could be sentenced for life to a comfortable penitentiary— food, medical attention, clothing and all the necessaries would of course be provided. This got a chuckle from the class and a great deal of bitter criticism from a few newspapers whose reporters picked up this homely example of "security."

Having been aware for some years of what you label the search for security through collectivism, you can imagine with what enthusiasm I applaud your statement.[3] Indeed, there is only one clause in the entire three columns that gives me a moment of unhappiness. You say "If we are to believe our thought leaders—the columnists—we are not happy." I shall not bother trying to give you my opinion of columnists, but I assure you I should never use the term "thought leaders."[4]

Otherwise, A-Plus!

With warm personal regard, *Sincerely*

[1] The article featured an excerpt from a lecture on "Leadership: Individualists vs. Security" that Wriston, former president of Brown University and chairman of the Committee on National Goals (for background see no. 1428), had delivered at Bowdoin College (*Wall Street Journal,* June 1, 1960).

[2] Eisenhower had spoken to incoming students at Columbia University's annual opening ceremony on September 29, 1949. He had encouraged them not to settle for "perfect security," but to embrace opportunities around them in life and at the university. He hoped they would "learn to love the fight that opportunity brings" (*New York Times,* Sept. 29, 1949).

[3] Wriston had noted that criticisms of the lack of leadership and national purpose in the country were cast in collective terms rather than in terms of the individual and his responsibility. Americans, he had suggested, denigrated the "rugged individualism" of the past, and had instead assumed a defensive character. This had led some people toward a "fetish of security," which in some ways resembled the Soviet policy of economic determinism. With security as the "opiate of the people," America did not get the "boldness" politicians called for, nor dedication to public service nor responsible citizenship. Wriston thought these developments were fatal to the concept of leadership (*Wall Street Journal,* June 1, 1960). For more on these themes see nos. 1462 and 1515.

[4] Wriston had stated: "It has been said times without number that the poor cannot be interested in freedom, that democracy can flourish only among the relatively well-to-do. . . . All the evidence, when fairly examined, is against that shallow view. Our forefathers who set our democratic pattern, were not leaders of a wealthy nation." "If wealth meant happiness," he reasoned, "we, incomparably the wealthiest people in the world, should correspondingly be the happiest. But the weight of the evidence

is to the contrary; if we are to believe our thought leaders—the columnists—we are not happy" (*ibid.*).

1553

EM, AWF, International Series:
Macmillan

To HAROLD MACMILLAN
Cable. Secret

June 4, 1960

Dear Harold:[1] I want to thank you for the thoughtful memorandum on improving tripartite consultation which you sent me with your letter of May 25. In accordance with your suggestion the three Foreign Ministers met here in Washington and had a profound and, I believe, useful discussion of ways and means to improve the consultative process.[2]

As you pointed out, we have had a series of tripartite meetings in recent years but these have not always been as efficiently organized as they might have been. This we hope to improve in the future. During the June first discussions here Chris Herter suggested that Livie Merchant, who has global responsibilities within the State Department, be charged with keeping in touch with his opposite numbers in the French and British Foreign Offices.[3] The three could prepare agenda and discussion papers for future meetings and could assure both system and continuity in our tripartite consultations without, however, creating an official secretariat or other apparatus which might lead sensitive members of the alliance such as Italy or Canada to believe that an "inner directorate" had been created.

This proposal sounds eminently sensible to me. It is essentially that which you proposed in your memorandum.

I believe that our consultations should concentrate on those areas where the Three Powers have special responsibilities and on global questions in which the Three have unique interests. I believe that we should also continue to develop consultation in NATO, paralleling progress toward more effective tripartite consultation.

I agree with you that we must be most circumspect about our tripartite meetings in order to avoid upsetting unnecessarily other Governments, both our allies and those newly-emergent countries, especially in Africa, who look with suspicion on consultation among the Western powers on African matters. We cannot, on the other hand, maintain such a tight secrecy that our motives and actions are suspected. This seems especially true in NATO. We have therefore suggested that a means be worked out to keep other NATO members generally informed of our conversations.

From our talks should emerge a means by which we can have more regular and better organized consultation among the three of us on political problems facing the Free World. We cannot, however, be sure that we have satisfied General de Gaulle's desires. This was hinted at by the French Foreign Minister when he said that the problem of military coordination is a matter for future discussion. The memorandum which General de Gaulle promised to send to us should give us a further insight into his thinking and I am sure we will want to consult about how to reply to it after it is received.[4]

In essence, I believe that we have moved somewhat along the path towards a greater harmonization of our policies. It seems to me essential to continue this effort.

With warm personal regard, *As ever*

[1] This message, drafted by State Department officials, was sent by cable to the American embassy in London for delivery to Prime Minister Macmillan (see Herter to Eisenhower, June 2, 1960, AWF/I: Macmillan).

[2] For background on tripartite consultations among U.S., British, and French officials see no. 1445. Macmillan had suggested that the three foreign ministers meet every two or three months and that the agenda should be approved in advance by the heads of government and include immediate and concrete problems as well as long-term questions. Furthermore, a member of each foreign office would both prepare the agenda and ensure that subsequent follow-up action was taken. Macmillan also advocated that the heads of government should be free to supplement their direct correspondence with each other by meeting informally at other times (AWF/I: Macmillan).

At their meeting on June 1 Secretary Herter, British Foreign Secretary Lloyd, and French Foreign Minister Couve de Murville had discussed preparation for future meetings, medium range ballistic missiles for NATO, the deployment of nuclear weapons in West Germany, and the French position regarding nuclear weapons on French territory (State, *Foreign Relations, 1958–1960*, vol. VII, pt. 2, *Western Europe*, pp. 372–79).

[3] Livingston T. Merchant was Under Secretary of State for Political Affairs. He would be working with Charles Lucet, minister of the French embassy, and Frederick Hoyer Millar, British Permanent Under Secretary of State for Foreign Affairs.

[4] For developments see no. 1565.

1554   *EM, AWF, Dulles-Herter Series*

To Christian Archibald Herter   *June 7, 1960*

Dear Chris: Enclosed is a copy of a letter from Sinclair Weeks. Will you get in touch with him if there is, as he puts it, another side to the coin of whether Argentina should be included in the conference he mentions?[1]

Offhand, and admittedly I know none of the intricacies of this particular subject, I should think that President Frondisi raises a pertinent point, particularly if it is true that Argentina is the only one of the countries to the South that would be interested in attending such a conference.

I'd like an informal report from you, too, just to satisfy my own curiosity.[2]

With warm regard, *As ever*

[1] For background on U.S.-Argentine relations see no. 658. Former Secretary of Commerce Weeks, who had just returned from leading the United States delegation at Argentina's celebration of one hundred fifty years of independence, had written describing President Frondizi's concern over Argentina's agricultural exports (Weeks to Eisenhower, June 2, 1960, AWF/D-H); see also a second letter from Weeks to Eisenhower, also dated June 2, 1960, in WHCF/OF 160). Frondizi, he said, wanted Argentina, a major meat and grain producer, to be included in upcoming discussions of agricultural commodities between the United States, Australia, New Zealand, Canada, and the European Economic Community (Common Market). Agricultural exports figured heavily in Argentina's economy and balance of payments, and Frondizi did not want any resulting agreements to harm Argentina. Weeks had advised that, while the United States had not pressed for Argentina's inclusion, the Administration should now support Frondizi's request because the United States had improved relations with Argentina over the past several years. Argentina also tended to support the United States in the United Nations and the Security Council and was the only Latin American nation interested in the conferences. Eisenhower told Weeks that the State Department would look into the matter and Secretary of State Herter would contact him (Eisenhower to Weeks, June 7, 1960, *ibid.*; see also State, *Foreign Relations, 1958–1960*, vol. V, *American Republics*, pp. 618–19).

[2] Under Secretary of State C. Douglas Dillon would tell the President that the Europeans did not want Argentina in the meetings (see also *New York Times*, May 25, 26, and June 26, 1960; and no. 1415), but that the United States could include Argentina in its talks with other exporting countries (Memorandum of Conference with the President, July 5, 1960, AWF/D). Frondizi would tour several European capitals during June on behalf of his nation's agricultural interests (*New York Times*, June 25 and 27, 1960). For developments see no. 1640.

1555   *EM, AWF, DDE Diaries Series*

To GERMAINE ALBERTINI   *June 7, 1960*

Dear Miss Albertini: Thank you very much for your letter and for your moving description of Liberation Day in Paris.[1]

I trust that you are not too badly disturbed by Mr. Khrushchev's tirades against me. My basic feeling during the period I was in Paris was how sad it was that the whole world was denied, because of his bad deportment, some small bit of realization of its great hope for progress toward peace with justice.[2] I make this statement because of the sincerity of President de Gaulle and Prime Minister Macmillan, and of my own, in exploring any avenue that might lead toward an arrangement with the Soviets on many of the questions that divide the world.

Your expressions of gratitude for one who has not only loved France and the French people, but had some little part in its Liberation sixteen years ago, so moved me that I wanted particularly to assure you of my appreciation of your heart-warming letter. I was additionally touched by the sensitivity you showed in resenting the bad manners of any guest in your great country.[3]

It would seem rather improbable that I shall return to Paris at any time during the months that remain to me in the position of President of the United States. Should some happier circumstance bring me back there, I shall have one of my associates invite you to the American Embassy residence so that I may express personally my thanks to you.

With best wishes, *Sincerely*

[1] Miss Albertini had written (May 17, AWF/D) that she had been in Paris on August 23, 1944, when the American troops arrived. On that day, she wrote, the Parisians had followed closely the radio reports on the approach of the allied armies. Defying the German machine guns firing from the roofs along the Place de la Concorde and the Champs Elysees, the Parisians were "screaming their joy." It was "an unforgettable and picturesque spectacle," she said. With the arrival of the Allies "everything was given back to us suddenly, the essence of our lives—freedom." For background on the Allies' liberation of France see Ambrose, *Citizen Soldiers*, 105–6; Chandler, *War Years*, nos. 1907, 1908, 1909, 1910; and Eisenhower, *Crusade in Europe*, pp. 257, 283, 296–98.

[2] For background on the summit meetings in Paris see no. 1397. The opening session of the conference (May 16) had ended abruptly when Soviet Premier Khrushchev issued an ultimatum requiring the President to denounce and terminate the U-2 flights. Eisenhower had not complied (see nos. 1531, 1538, 1539, and 1541); see also Eisenhower, *Waging Peace*, pp. 553–57; and *New York Times*, May 17, 18, 1960. For Khrushchev's account see his memoir, *Khrushchev Remembers*, pp. 449–55.

[3] Albertini had thought the President might be comforted to know that thousands of Frenchmen "personally feel the insult you have received in our country . . . from a guest whom you and we had entertained lavishly."

1556   *EM, WHCF, Official File 101-XD*

To Garrison Holt Davidson   *June 8, 1960*

Dear Gar: Again I must tell you how grateful I am for the many courtesies you showed to me and my party during our visit to West Point.[1] You and your staff made everything as pleasant as it could possibly be.

You remarked to me that you had received no reply from John to your letter to him of the sixteenth. The record shows that he mailed his reply on the twenty-fifth. However, I think he sent something of an indecisive answer, because of prior commitments I have made.[2] So far as my official papers are concerned, I am committed to giving them to the General Services Administration, where they will be under the custody of the Archivist. Their actual location will be in the Eisenhower Library at Abilene, Kansas.[3] I regret that the matter had gone so far before you made the suggestion of trying to concentrate at West Point all records of modern military operations.

Remember me warmly to Verone and of course all the best to yourself. And, needless to say, once again the very best of luck in your new assignment.[4]

With warm regard, *As ever*

[1] The President had spent the weekend of June 4–7 at West Point attending a reunion of the class of 1915 (see *New York Times,* June 7, 1960; on the members of the presidential party and the specific activities see the President's daily appointments, June 4–7, 1960).

[2] On Lieutenant Colonel John Eisenhower's role in preparing the President's papers for removal from Washington see John S. D. Eisenhower, *Strictly Personal,* pp. 282–84.

[3] For background on the disposition of Eisenhower's official papers see no. 1504. On the Eisenhower Library in Abilene see no. 899.

[4] Davidson, superintendent of the United States Military Academy since 1957 (see no. 431), had been appointed to command the United States Seventh Army in Europe (*New York Times,* May 14, 1960).

1557   *Gruenther Papers*

To Alfred Maximilian Gruenther   *June 10, 1960*

Dear Al:[1] This letter comes to you—and to a few of my other friends—because of some things I learned about a remarkable individual in the *Reader's Digest* for May. Later I met and talked with him at Notre Dame. His name is Tom Dooley.[2] The story of this man is high drama. Through some years of service in the United States Navy he met thousands of Asiatics who, in great areas, were not only starving, almost naked, and badly sheltered, but were in addition suffering from many diseases. The wholesale misery, suffering and privation made an indelible impression upon him—in fact it preyed continuously on his mind. He finally decided something had to be done about this—and started a one-man crusade of assistance. He found a couple of willing helpers, and with the most meager of equipment, set up a hospital in Laos.[3] (I hope you will read the account of this adventure in the enclosed reprint from the *Reader's Digest.*)[4]

He and his assistants get nothing—their need is solely for medicines and facilities. They are truly dedicated men.

Some years after starting this enterprise Dr. Dooley contracted cancer of the most malignant character. A few months ago he had an operation but has been clearly informed that there is no chance for him to live longer than a few additional months. Instead of allowing himself to be brokenhearted and defeated by this circumstance, he is devoting his remaining time on earth to establishing similar hospitals in a number of the backward countries.[5]

You will be interested to know that he refuses to take a cent of public money, even though the International Cooperation Administration has in some instances offered to support his efforts. Moreover, he charges something for the services he renders to every individual that comes under his care. He told me that at times the payment is nothing but a potato, at others a chicken, or even two or three bananas. But he is as determined to sustain the self-respect of the patient as he is to restore his bodily health.

His brother, who operates his supply service, gave up a $20,000 year job to help provide the required material assistance for the project.[6] As you will note in the copy of the attached letter this brother sent to me, the organization is qualified under Treasury regulations for gifts that are tax exempt.

Dr. Dooley, himself, is momentarily in this country making a whirlwind trip to major cities, seeking funds required for medicines, tentage, equipment, etc.[7] He is returning to Laos in two or three weeks where he lives in the most primitive of conditions.

If you should become sufficiently interested in the project to want to give anything to the enterprise, I assure you I would be more than pleased. Incidentally, Dr. Dooley told me that most of his contributions come in nickels, dimes, quarters and dollar bills. He prefers modest gifts. I also want to assure you I would be most embarrassed if you would conclude that I suggest any large gift. While of course money is necessary to any such work as is described in the enclosed reprint, what I am particularly concerned in is the assurance of broadened interest and concern in helping to further a cause which I think so well-conceived and well-executed.[8]

With warm regard, *As ever*

P.S. Attached is also a list of the people to whom I have sent identical letters.

---

[1] The lists of recipients are in Gruenther Papers and WHCF/OF 373.

[2] Eisenhower had met Dr. Thomas Anthony Dooley, III (M.D. St. Louis University 1953) at the University of Notre Dame on June 5, 1960, when the President deliv-

ered the commencement speech. Both men had been awarded honorary degrees (*New York Times,* June 6, 1960; for background see James T. Fisher, *Dr. America: The Lives of Thomas A. Dooley, 1927–1961* [Amherst, 1997], p. 239).

3 Admired for his medical philanthropy, Dooley had become a popular national figure who had strong ties to the Catholic community, Dooley had first gained recognition for his work with refugee evacuation camps in Vietnam, where he had been serving as a medical officer at the end of the Indochina War. In 1956 he had published a best-selling book based on his experiences. After completing a successful lecture tour, he resigned from the military. He used the proceeds from the book and tour to establish a hospital in Laos. After another successful book and lecture tour describing his work there, he had founded the Medical International Corporation (MEDICO), which provided medical teams and hospital facilities to underdeveloped nations, primarily in South Asia.

4 Eisenhower was referring to Dooley's book, *The Night They Burned the Mountain* (New York, 1960), excerpted in the May 1960 issue of *Reader's Digest.* The excerpt described Dooley's work in Laos and his battle with cancer.

5 Dooley would die on January 18, 1961, at the age of thirty-four (*New York Times,* Jan. 19, 24, 1960).

6 Eisenhower had met Tom Dooley's brother, Malcolm W. Dooley, at the Notre Dame ceremonies. Malcolm, a graduate of Notre Dame, had become executive director of MEDICO (Dooley to Eisenhower, June 8, 1960, WHCF/OF 373; see also *Report from MEDICO,* Sept. 1960, *ibid.*).

7 At the President's request, Dooley had written briefly describing the MEDICO organization and its tax exempt status (Malcolm Dooley to Eisenhower, June 8, 1960, *ibid.*).

8 Ann Whitman would send the President's $100.00 donation, and one of her own, to Malcolm Dooley, along with a copy of this letter. Several friends would send their contributions directly to the White House. Dooley would write that letters were "coming in from around the country in response to the President's request," and he would thank the President for his "warm feeling" and "friendly help and pen" (Whitman to Dooley, June 11 and 27, 1960; Dooley to Whitman, June 16, 1960; Dooley to Eisenhower, June 30, 1960, all in *ibid.*).

1558   *EM, AWF, International Series:*
                                                           Macmillan

To Harold Macmillan   *June 10, 1960*
Cable. Confidential

Dear Harold: I have learned that you may be considering a visit to some of the Latin American countries later on this year. I hope that you will decide to go.[1] To my mind such a trip should be of great value in demonstrating your interest in the countries of that continent, and it could very well help us in our dealings with them, too.[2]

With warm personal regard, *As ever*

1 Macmillan would not make the trip.
2 For background on U.S. relations with Latin America see nos. 1466 and 1532.

To CEMAL GURSEL   *June 11, 1960*

Dear Mr. President: My several visits to Turkey have given me a deep and abiding interest in the Turkish people and the problems that over the years have confronted them.[1] When you recently became head of state, I followed with particular interest the constructive public statements which you made to your countrymen and to the world at large.[2]

Your expressed determination to hold elections and to turn over the government administration to the newly-elected authorities has been welcome by all of Turkey's friends. It is the deep hope of all of us that these elections and the new constitution being prepared under your authority will mark another milestone in the development of democracy in Turkey.

The intention of your government to preserve Turkey's ties with NATO and CENTO was also a source of great satisfaction to me and to all those associated with Turkey in these collective security organizations dedicated to the defense of the free world. My government looks forward to continuing cordial relations with Turkey in the tradition of friendship and cooperation that has always marked the relations of the Turkish and American people.[3]

You have, Mr. President, my warmest wishes for success in realizing the high ideals to which you have dedicated your government, and in dealing with the problems now confronting it.[4] *Sincerely*

[1] Eisenhower had visited Turkey in December 1959 (see no. 1388), and early in 1952 (see Galambos and van Ee, *NATO and the Campaign of 1952*, pp. 1049–51).

[2] For background see no. 1524. On May 27 the Turkish army had overthrown the civilian government. The uprising was led by sixty-five-year-old Lieutenant General Gursel, who had recently resigned as commander of ground forces as a protest against the government's increasingly repressive actions toward political opponents. A 1929 graduate of the Turkish War College and a veteran of several wars, Gursel had a long and distinguished military career. The day after the coup, he had formed a provisional government, naming himself President and Premier. He had claimed that he would not establish a dictatorship and promised elections. He had also announced that the provisional government would revise the constitution and that after a transitional period, he would retire from the government and politics. The army had stated that Turkey would continue to be part of the Western Alliance and would remain committed to NATO and CENTO. A new constitution would be approved by referendum in July 1961 and the first elections would be held four months later (*New York Times*, May 28, 29, June 1, 5, 1960, and July 12, Oct. 27, 1961). Gursel would be elected to the presidency. For developments see no. 1578, and *Public Papers of the Presidents: Eisenhower, 1960–61*, pp. 901–2.

[3] Shortly after the coup, Herter had told Eisenhower that the new Turkish foreign minister had requested a declaration of United States support for Turkey. The minister had claimed that a show of support would be useful in dealing with Russian overtures to the new government and would strengthen the morale of the Turkish people as well as his position vis-a-vis the provisional government and military. Herter

had suggested that it was in the United States' interest to express confidence in the new government. This letter, drafted by the State Department, was sent with no changes (Herter to Eisenhower, June 10, 1960, AWF/I: Turkey).

[4] Gursel would thank Eisenhower for the message, replying that the main purpose for the government reorganization was to end a "dictatorship" that has been "steering along a path likely to endanger the supreme interests of the country." The new set of democratic rules being prepared by a committee of scholars, he said, would strengthen his country and make Turkey a better partner to its allies in their joint endeavor to preserve world peace (Gursel to Eisenhower, June 18, 1960, *ibid.*).

1560   *EM, AWF, Administration Series*

TO RICHARD MILHOUS NIXON   *June 11, 1960*

Dear Dick: This morning I had a telephone talk with Oveta Hobby. We discussed a number of things, but she wanted to pass along to you this one urgent recommendation.[1]

She believes that your forthcoming speech in North Dakota is going to be one of your most important. It will undoubtedly have national coverage and national significance, and cannot be interpreted as a mere effort to elect Governor Davis.[2] Her recommendation is that you say nothing to drive away from you the Independents and the switch-voting Democrats. Apparently she has Texas very much in mind when she makes this suggestion; personally I concur in it. Of course I don't know of anything you have ever said that could be considered calculated to drive these people away from you, but I suppose it comes about through some misapprehension that has been raised for a long time in certain quarters.[3]

In any event, if I do not get to talk to you on the phone, this note gives me a chance to say Adios.[4]

With warm regard, *As ever*

[1] For background see no. 1530. On that morning Eisenhower had called the former Secretary of Health, Education and Welfare (see Ann Whitman memorandum, June 11, 1960, AWF/AWD).

[2] On June 20 the Vice-President would deliver a speech supporting the creation of a United Nations surplus-food pool to feed the world's hungry. This would be part of a program to reduce domestic agricultural surpluses. John Edward Davis (B.S. University of North Dakota 1935), governor of North Dakota since 1957, was a senatorial candidate in a special election. On June 28 Davis would lose the election to his Democratic opponent.

[3] Nixon had alienated some Texas Republicans by supporting the Administration's civil rights bill (see Ambrose, *Nixon*, vol. I, *The Education of a Politician, 1913–1963*, pp. 536–37).

[4] The President would leave the following day for a two-week trip to the Philippines, Taiwan, Korea, and Japan (see no. 1529).

To Henry Robinson Luce   *June 11, 1960*
Personal

Dear Harry: I am truly grateful for your very fine letter of the tenth. You have not only cleared up a number of misapprehensions that I had begun to develop, but you also reassured me immeasurably.[1]

If time permitted I would write you a long letter because you have raised several subjects that are most important to me.[2] One of them, as you will guess, is my feeling that Nelson is being too much influenced by a man who has no capacity for giving sensible advice.[3] When I get back from this Far East trip, maybe we can have a personal meeting.[4] I should like it very much.

Again my thanks.

With warm personal regard, *As ever*

[1] Time-Life publisher Luce's June 10 letter (AWF/N) had been forwarded to *Time's* Washington bureau with instructions that it be delivered to the White House the following morning (see Mohr to Whitman, n.d., AWF/N, Luce Corr.).

[2] Luce had written about Eisenhower's trip to India (see no. 1389), a meeting at the National Presbyterian Center in Buffalo, and "the very involved subject of Emmet Hughes, his book, his Rockefelleritis, etc."

[3] Luce and Eisenhower were referring to Emmet John Hughes, former presidential assistant and speechwriter. In March Hughes had been appointed senior adviser on public policy and public relations to the Rockefeller family (*New York Times,* Mar. 11, 1960). *America the Vincible* (New York), Hughes's call for an American international policy based on "realism," had appeared in 1959. According to one critic, the book was a "consistent attack on the chief policies of the late John Foster Dulles" and suggested a "massive disagreement endemic in Administration circles almost from the Presidential inauguration of January, 1953" (*New York Times,* Nov. 8, 1959). Luce had told Eisenhower that *America the Vincible* had been written without his approval: "He asked for my criticism of the manuscript and I sent him quite a bag full. But to no effect."

[4] On Eisenhower's Far East trip see no. 1529. On this same day Eisenhower would write to *Life* publisher C. D. Jackson regarding his correspondence with Luce: "Frankly I had come to feel that the ways of *Life* and me had diverged quite markedly. His letter has got me back on the rails" (June 11, 1960, AWF/N). On June 28 Eisenhower and Luce would meet at the White House.

1562   *EM, AWF, International Series:*
                                                    Canada

To John George Diefenbaker   *June 12, 1960*

Dear John: On this first leg of my journey to the Far East, I am just entering the air space of your great country.[1] By this message I send warm greetings to your people and my thanks to your government for its courtesy in authorizing my direct passage to Alaska.[2]

Thinking of this peaceful and unobstructed passage, I cannot fail to observe that if this practice were, as a matter of routine, permitted throughout the world, all of us would achieve a greater serenity of mind and the feeling that we were truly progressing toward the just peace for which humanity yearns.

My warm greetings to Mrs. Diefenbaker and every good wish for you both.[3] *Sincerely*

[1] On this same day the President had left Washington, D.C., to undertake what he called "a journey of understanding" (see *Public Papers of the Presidents: Eisenhower, 1960–61,* pp. 470–72, and *New York Times,* June 13, 1960). For background on the trip see no. 1529. A copy of this handwritten document, containing Eisenhower's extensive emendations, is in AWF/I: Canada.

[2] On the President's visit to Alaska see the following document.

[3] Mrs. Diefenbaker was the former Olive Evangelie Freeman. The Prime Minister would thank Eisenhower for the message on June 13 (AWF/I: Canada).

1563   *EM, AWF, International Series:*
                                                          Far East Trip

To John Hersey Michaelis   *June 14, 1960*

Dear Mike: I can't tell you what a pleasure it was to find you and Mary on the spot when my plane arrived at Elmendorf yesterday (I still insist it was yesterday despite the confusion in dates!).[1] Particularly I was delighted to see how well you are looking: I pray that you are completely and for all time rid of the difficulty that put you out of commission for a short time.[2]

On the official side, I want to thank you for your part in the official program that was laid out for me; I was glad that I had the opportunity to visit Fort Richardson and to note at first hand the evident fitness and alertness of the men and officers under your command.[3]

With affectionate regard to Mary, and all the best to yourself, *As ever*

[1] Michaelis (USMA 1936) had been the commanding general of the U.S. Army in Alaska since 1959. He had served as a senior aide to General Eisenhower while he was Chief of Staff (1947–48), and in 1951 had joined Eisenhower's SHAPE (Supreme Headquarters Allied Powers, Europe) staff (for background see *Eisenhower Papers,* vols. VI–XIII). Mrs. Michaelis was the former Mary Wadsworth. The President had begun his journey to the Far East on June 12 (see the preceding document). Due to the changes in the time zones he had arrived at Elmendorf Air Force Base in An-

chorage, Alaska, on June 12. For his remarks upon his arrival see *Public Papers of the Presidents: Eisenhower, 1960–61*, pp. 472–73.

[2] General Michaelis recently had undergone radiation treatments at Walter Reed Army Hospital for a malignant growth in his throat (*New York Times,* Apr. 16, May 9, 1960).

[3] After inspecting the Elmendorf base, the President would go to the U.S. Army installations at nearby Fort Richardson and would attend a secret briefing on the role of the Alaskan Defense Command. He would also tour Anchorage (*New York Times,* June 13, 1960). For developments see the following document.

1564   *EM, AWF, International Series: Japan*

To Nobusuke Kishi   *June 16, 1960*
Cable. Secret

My dear Prime Minister: I have just received the news of your government's decision to request postponement of my projected visit to Japan. I hasten to assure you of my full and sympathetic understanding of the situation that developed in spite of your strenuous efforts to avert it.[1]

Further, I accept, without question, your conviction that the visit would now be untimely and could lead to even greater difficulty in your country. Of course I completely concur in your action in releasing your decision promptly.

I share your sadness that a violent minority could disrupt the proper and orderly processes of democratic government and compel the postponement of a visit that had no other purpose than to promote good will between the peoples of our two nations.[2] I send to you assurances of my continued admiration and esteem and request that you convey to his imperial majesty my expressions of regret in missing this opportunity to meet him as well as my best wishes for his continued health and well-being.[3] I should like, through you, to say to all those millions of Japanese who were ready to see in my planned visit a simple act of courtesy to a great people that the people of the United States will not allow a misguided fraction of the Japanese nation to lessen their friendship and admiration for the Japanese democracy.[4]

Finally I should like for you again to assure his Imperial Highness the Crown Prince that I shall be looking forward with keen anticipation to the visit that he and the crown princess are to make to the United States this fall.[5] *Sincerely*

[1] For background on the President's plans to visit Tokyo see no. 1381-A. Earlier this same day Premier Kishi had announced that the Japanese government had to post-

pone Eisenhower's visit. Demonstrations in opposition to the Kishi government had led to riots and bloodshed in Tokyo (State, *Foreign Relations, 1958–1960*, vol. XVIII, *Japan; Korea*, pp. 337–71; *New York Times*, June 17, 1960).

[2] The postponement was seen by many as a Communist victory in the Far East (*New York Times*, June 17, 1960; Eisenhower, *Waging Peace*, p. 563). In his statement to the media, White House Press Secretary Hagerty would condemn the Tokyo outbursts as the work of "a small organized minority, led by professional Communist agitators acting under external direction and control" (June 16, 1960, AWF/I: Japan, Far East Trip, Cancelled).

[3] Emperor Hirohito also would send a message to Eisenhower regretting postponement of the visit. He added that he "still" hoped that he could receive the President in the future (State, *Foreign Relations, 1958–1960*, vol. XVIII, *Japan; Korea*, p. 367).

[4] In his apology to the President (June 17, AWF/I: Japan, Far East Trip, Cancelled), Kishi said that the overwhelming majority of Japanese people "eagerly awaited" the visit. He claimed to have "exerted every possible effort to make the preparation which in every way would be fully consonant with the significance" of the visit. Kishi said he firmly believed that the "exceptional circumstances" currently existing would not "affect in the least" the relations of mutual friendship and trust between Japan and the United States. He looked forward to the time when Japanese people could welcome the President with their "traditional courtesy and hospitality." For developments on U.S.-Japanese relations see no. 1617.

[5] Crown Prince Akihito and Crown Princess Michiko would visit Washington, D.C., September 27–28 (State, *Foreign Relations, 1958–1960*, vol. XVIII, *Japan; Korea*, pp. 409–13; and *New York Times*, May 8, Aug. 6, Sept. 28–30, 1960).

1565

EM, AWF,
International Series:
De Gaulle

To Charles André Joseph Marie De Gaulle
Cable. Secret   *June 18, 1960*

Dear General de Gaulle: Your letter of June 10, with which you enclosed a copy of your reply to Prime Minister Macmillan's letter of May 25, was received just after my departure for the Far East. It has been sent on to me here in Manila.[1] I have read both letters carefully and am pleased to see that we are in general accord on the necessity and means of improving our political consultation.[2] I will give the matter of strategic cooperation the careful study it deserves after my return to Washington. My immediate personal reaction is to be somewhat doubtful of the practicability of using any part of the NATO mechanism, such as the standing group, for strategic consultations, because of the certainty that Allies would object. However, I am sure we can develop appropriate consultative processes.[3]

With warm personal regard,

[1] The President had left Washington on June 12 for a two-week trip to the Philippines, Formosa, and Korea (for background see nos. 1529, 1568, and 1571).
[2] De Gaulle had agreed to Macmillan's suggestions for handling tripartite consultations (see no. 1553). He believed that the procedures Macmillan had outlined would strengthen political coordination among the three countries but would not address cooperation in the field of military strategy. The groundwork for those matters, he suggested, could be laid by each country's military representatives in the NATO Standing Group in meetings separate from their regular deliberations. These negotiations could be supplemented by meetings of the chiefs of staff or ministers of defense, as well as by the three heads of government (State, *Foreign Relations, 1958–1960*, vol. VII, pt. 2, *Western Europe*, pp. 384–86).
[3] For developments see no. 1572.

1566   *EM, AWF, Name Series*

To Mamie Doud Eisenhower   *June 18, 1960*

Dear Mamie: We are presently in Taipei, leaving here tomorrow morning.[1] During my thirty hours on the ship I tried twice to telephone you with little success, but I did manage to get an indirect message to the effect that you knew of my efforts.[2]

Both John and Barbie, and so far as I know the entire party, is in good health.[3] The shortening of my trip because of the cancellation of my invitation to Japan, will bring me back to Hawaii 48 hours earlier than originally planned.[4] From here on my schedule includes the next twenty-four hours of ceremonies and conferences here in Taipei, several hours in Okinawa, 24 hours in Seoul, and of course the usual parade through Honolulu.[5] If nothing goes wrong, I shall have completed these chores by Monday evening, and then I shall try to get some rest in Hawaii for two or three days.[6] From the time I reach Honolulu I should be in easy telephone communication with you and be able to report regularly and personally.

I hope that you are improving steadily.[7]

Barbie and John join me in sending Love. *Devotedly*

[1] For background on Eisenhower's visit to the Far East see nos. 1529 and 1564. For the President's program and his remarks in Taipei see no. 1571; *Public Papers of the Presidents: Eisenhower, 1960–61*, pp. 503–7; and *New York Times*, June 18, 19, 1960.
[2] Eisenhower and his official party had boarded the U.S.S. *St. Paul* on the evening of June 16 (for background see no. 1529; for developments see no. 1569).
[3] Lieutenant Colonel John S. D. Eisenhower and his wife were among the thirty-five people who accompanied the President on the trip (see Eisenhower, *Waging Peace*, p. 562, and *New York Times*, June 13, 1960).
[4] On the cancellation of the trip to Japan see no. 1564.
[5] On Eisenhower's activities for the remainder of the trip see no. 1568; see also Eisenhower, *Waging Peace*, pp. 564–66; Smith, *A President's Odyssey*, pp. 228–39; *Public Pa-*

pers of the Presidents: Eisenhower, 1960–61, pp. 508–25; *New York Times*, June 18–25, 1960; and State, *Foreign Relations, 1958–1960*, vol. XVIII, *Japan; Korea*, pp. 371–74, 668–72.
[6] The President would receive a warm greeting in Honolulu on Monday, June 20. The following day he would sign letters and attend to administrative matters before playing a round of golf with members of his party. On June 25 he would return to Washington, D.C. (*New York Times*, June 23, 26, 27, 1960). He would deliver a radio and television report on the trip on June 27 (see no. 1571).

[7] The First Lady had been undergoing treatment for acute asthmatic bronchitis at Walter Reed Army Hospital since May 31. She would return to the White House on June 21 (*New York Times*, June 2–5, 9, 10, 18, 1960).

1567   *EM, AWF, International Series:*
                                                            Macmillan

To Harold Macmillan   *June 20, 1960*
Cable. Top secret

Dear Harold:[1] Thank you for your letter of June 15. I, too, am pleased that the talks between your Minister of Defense and Secretary Gates results in general understanding of the program for mutual cooperation in Skybolt. I feel confident that the details can be worked out to meet the requirements of both bomber command and our own strategic air command.[2]

I fully appreciate the political difficulties confronting you and your colleagues regarding provision of facilities for our Polaris submarines in the Clyde. Nevertheless, I do hope that you will find it possible to proceed this year with the arrangement upon which we reached agreement in principle at Camp David, and I will look forward to hearing from you on the outcome of your cabinet consideration.[3]

With warm personal regard, *As ever*

[1] This message, drafted by State Department officials and approved by the Defense Department, was sent by cable to the American embassy in London for delivery to Prime Minister Macmillan (see State, *Foreign Relations, 1958–1960*, vol. VII, pt. 2, *Western Europe*, p. 872).

[2] In 1958 the U.S. Air Force had begun to develop Skybolt, an air-launched ballistic missile, in part to increase the capability of its manned bombers. Skybolt was also designed to be compatible with British aircraft and was to serve as a possible substitute for their own surface-to-surface Blue Streak missile. During the course of the negotiations between British Defence Minister Harold Watkinson and Defense Secretary Thomas Gates, the Skybolt project had become linked to the British desire for U.S. Polaris missiles and submarines and to the U.S. request for Polaris bases in the Clyde River in Scotland. At the Camp David meetings in March (see no. 1459) Eisenhower had agreed to provide Skybolt missiles to Britain, and Macmillan had agreed "in principle" to the establishment of a submarine base in Scotland. A bilat-

eral decision regarding sale of Polaris missiles was to be considered after NATO plans to develop and deploy medium-range ballistic missiles (MRBMs) had been discussed. During meetings in Washington on June 1 and 6 Watkinson had told Gates that adverse public reaction in Britain could be reduced if the submarine berthing facilities were presented as a joint project and if the site could be moved to a less populated area (Watson, *Into the Missile Age*, pp. 373–74, 562–67; State, *Foreign Relations, 1958–1960*, vol. VII, pt. 2, *Western Europe*, pp. 860–65, 869–72; Kistiakowsky, *A Scientist at the White House*, pp. 206–7, 278, 396; and Macmillan, *Pointing the Way*, pp. 252–55). On June 15 Macmillan had written that he was pleased that the talks had worked out so well, and he had asked for "a more precise agreement, including detailed arrangements" for the development of the Skybolt missile (Macmillan to Eisenhower, June 15, 1960, AWF/I: Macmillan).

[3] Macmillan had reiterated his promise at Camp David to do his best regarding the use of Scottish ports. "You will realize that this is a pretty big decision for us to take," he wrote. "It will raise political difficulties for us in view of all the pressures and crosscurrents of public opinion here." He told Eisenhower that he would place the issue before the Cabinet when Parliament reassembled the following week (*ibid.*). For developments see no. 1573.

1568

EM, AWF, International Series: Japan, Far East Trip, Cancelled

To Douglas MacArthur II
Personal

June 22, 1960

Dear Doug: This is almost the first moment I have had to dictate since news of the cancellation of the visit to Japan reached me, the last evening we were in Manila.[1] I am sure you know that, from the press and official reports, the receptions in Taipei and Seoul were tremendous (and exhausting) and the schedules crowded.[2]

I simply want to augment my one sentence telegram to you.[3] I fully realize what you have gone through in the last few weeks; adding to the worry that I know you naturally felt during the period is, of course, the attack that some members of the press have felt called upon to make upon you. To their comments I hope you pay not the slightest attention; I have learned, perhaps the hard way, that an individual in public life must ignore such things.[4]

I assure you, as I also assured the Prime Minister, that I fully understand the necessity for cancelling the current arrangements for a visit to Japan.[5] That a small destructive minority could so embarrass the government is a cause for concern on the part of us all; nevertheless, I firmly believe, from everything I can gather from reading and my conversations with well informed individuals in all parts of the Far East, that the vast majority of the Japanese people are true friends of the United States and regret, as I do, that I could not visit them to bring them the greetings of the people of America.

I have been thinking much these last few days of you and Wahwee, and send to you both my warm personal regard.[6] *Sincerely*

[1] For background on Eisenhower's trip to the Far East see nos. 1529 and 1566. On June 16 the Japanese government had requested that the President postpone his visit due to Communist-led demonstrations which had made Tokyo the scene of riots and bloodshed (see no. 1564). On June 10 a mob of some 6,000 had surrounded MacArthur's car while en route to Tokyo. The demonstrators had shattered the windows and had attempted to slash the tires and overturn the car. Japanese police had cleared a path for a helicopter to rescue the party. No one suffered any "real injury," MacArthur reported, although the helicopter was damaged (MacArthur to Eisenhower, June 10, 1960, AWF/I: Japan, Far East Trip, Cancelled; see also State, *Foreign Relations, 1958–1960*, vol. XVIII, *Japan; Korea*, pp. 331–35, and *New York Times*, June 11, 1960).

[2] See nos. 1566, 1571, and *New York Times*, June 17–21, 1960.

[3] Upon learning that the Japanese government had asked him to cancel the trip (June 16), the President wired MacArthur: "I think I have some faint understanding of what you have just been through." In a wire sent the following day MacArthur had expressed his sorrow regarding the decision (June 17, 1960, both in AWF/I: Japan, Far East Trip, Cancelled).

[4] Most press reports had characterized the cancellation as a Communist victory that illustrated a deterioration of U.S.-Japanese relations (*New York Times*, June 17, 18, 1960). For developments in U.S. ties to Japan see no. 1647; see also nos. 1528 and 1571.

[5] The President's letter to Japanese Prime Minister Kishi is no. 1564.

[6] MacArthur's wife was the former Laura Louise Barkley.

1569

EM, AWF,
Administration Series:
USS St. Paul

To Herbert Gladstone Hopwood   *June 24, 1960*

Dear Admiral Hopwood: It was most kind and courteous of you to make your boat available to me and my party. I had the opportunity to take only one cruise which I enjoyed thoroughly.[1] I must report to you, however, that my daughter-in-law has made full use of the boat and had one of the most enjoyable holidays she ever had through its use.[2] I am deeply grateful to Chief Coley and his crew, not only for their work on the boat, but also for being so kind as to instruct Barbara in "skin diving."[3]

I also want to mention another "boat ride" I had with Admiral Griffin's wonderful Seventh Fleet.[4] This cruise was a Godsend to me after a rather strenuous visit in the heat and humidity of Manila. I was very impressed with the officers, men and ships of the Seventh Fleet, and I am fully confident of their ability to perform their important mission as roving linebacker in our Far Eastern defensive arc. Further, I would like to ask you to pass my thanks to all the vessels who covered my long overwater routes over the Pacific. This I know took a great effort on the part of the Pacific Fleet and it is largely an unheralded task, but appreciated nonetheless by me.

It was a pleasure to see you and Mrs. Hopwood again, and visit your Marines here at Kaneohe.[5]

With best wishes and warm regard, *Sincerely*

[1] In Hawaii the President had taken a two-hour cruise aboard a launch on June 24. Hopwood (USNA 1919) had been Commander in Chief of the U.S. Pacific Fleet since 1958. Advancing to the grade of rear admiral by the end of World War II, he had served as Director of Budget and Reports in the Navy Department (1946–1950), and as Deputy Comptroller of the Navy (1950–1952). He would retire in September (*New York Times*, Sept. 2, 1960).

Following their trip to the Far East, the President and his party had flown to Hawaii for a brief holiday (for background on the trip see no. 1529; on the holiday see no. 1566 and n. 5 below).

[2] Lieutenant Colonel John Eisenhower and his wife Barbara had accompanied the President on his Far East trip (see no. 1566).

[3] We have been unable to identify Chief Coley.

[4] Charles Donald Griffin (USNA 1927) commanded the Seventh Fleet, which included 125 warships and 500 aircraft (*New York Times*, Jan. 27, 1960). On June 16 the President had boarded the U.S.S. *St. Paul* to travel to Taiwan (see nos. 1529 and 1571). The cruiser had been escorted by 100 planes, two aircraft carriers and four destroyers. On June 18 the President would commend the officers and men of the Seventh Fleet for their skill, efforts, and devotion to duty (see *Public Papers of the Presidents: Eisenhower, 1960–61*, pp. 502–3).

[5] Hopwood's wife was the former Jean Fulton. Eisenhower was staying at the Kaneohe Marine Corps Air Station, located on the Kaneohe Bay on the east coast of Oahu (*New York Times*, June 21–26, 1960). For the President's remarks upon arriving in and leaving Honolulu see *Public Papers of the Presidents: Eisenhower, 1960–61*, pp. 524–26.

1570　　　　　　　　　　　　　　　　　*EM, WHCF, Official File 3-K*

To Frederic William Boye　　　　　　　　　*June 27, 1960*
Personal

Dear Fred: For a number of months I have been using all of the normal contacts available to me to get some Senate action to correct the Retirement Bill. Obviously if I had a Republican majority in the Senate, this would be an easy thing; as it is, every effort I have made has run into a dead end.[1]

Today I am making a final effort. In view of past experiences I am not hopeful, but at the very least I am putting the whole matter on a personal basis so far as I can, just to make sure that I have left no stone unturned.[2]

While I shall be seeing you at dinner tomorrow night, such affairs provide little opportunity for personal conversations—hence this note.[3]

With warm regard, *As ever*

[1] The Military Pay Bill (P.L. 422), as passed on May 20, 1958, had provided for lesser payments to those who retired prior to enactment (June 1, 1958) because they were not included in the dollar-pay readjustment made in the new law. Those who would retire subsequently would receive higher retirement pay (see nos. 564, 969, and 1230).

Brigadier General Boye, Eisenhower's West Point classmate, had retired in 1950 to become the executive vice-president of the U.S. Equestrian team in Warrenton, Virginia. He had written to the President asking him to take "direct action" to recommend that the Senate approve the Pay Equalization Bill. Boye had sent the letter through Presidential Secretary Ann Whitman with a cover letter stating that the bill meant much to Eisenhower's old companions in the service (both letters are dated July 25, 1960, and are in WHCF/OF 3-K). In an undated note to Ann Whitman, Bryce Harlow said that the legislation was held up by Mississippi Senator John C. Stennis, a Democrat whom Harlow termed "a one-man barricade." Harlow observed that the situation looked "very gloomy" (*ibid.*).

[2] For developments see no. 1617.

[3] Boye would attend a White House dinner honoring the King and Queen of Thailand (see no. 1585 and *New York Times*, June 28, 1960).

1571   *EM, WHCF, President's Personal File 275*

To Harry Amos Bullis   *June 29, 1960*

Dear Harry: This note brings you my appreciation both of your telegram concerning my Monday evening telecast, and of the letter of the twentieth that I found awaiting me on my return from the Far East.[1] As always, I am grateful for your support. I was interested, too, in your letter to Senator Cooper.[2]

I had never been to Taipei before, and of course I have no real basis for judging the progress that has been made there (such as you would have if you paid a return visit).[3] But I was struck particularly with the bustle, the vigor and the youth of the country. I was told that they have a larger percentage of people under twenty than any other nation—and all of them, it seemed to me, are Westernized in dress and in manner, and all extremely friendly to the United States. I found the entire experience there most heartening.[4]

With warm regard, *Sincerely*

[1] Bullis had congratulated Eisenhower for the "sterling informative address" he had delivered upon his return from the Far East (June 28, 1960). Bullis noted also the warm and enthusiastic welcome Eisenhower had received in the Philippines, Taiwan, and Korea (see also Bullis to Whitman, June 20, 1960, and King to Bullis, June 23, 1960). The journey, Bullis wrote, was "certain to produce more enlightened public opinion in the Free World without which statesmen can do very little to reduce world tensions." For background on the President's trip to the Far East see nos. 1529, 1564, and 1566.

In his remarks to the American people on June 27 Eisenhower had said that the trip had strengthened relations with the Philippines, Taiwan, Korea and Okinawa. In Manila, Taipei and Korea, he said, there was an "outpouring of friendship, gratitude and respect for America," even though the Communists had sought every method to stop the expressions of support. The President had characterized the disorders in Tokyo, which had led the Japanese government to request postponement of Eisenhower's visit, as Communist-inspired efforts to weaken U.S.-Japanese relations (see no. 1564). Ratification of the U.S.-Japanese security pact, he said, was a "signal defeat for International Communism" and far outweighed, in importance, the postponement of his visit. (On the treaty see no. 1544; for developments in U.S.-Japanese relations see no. 1647). In conclusion Eisenhower said that although he had no plans for another trip overseas during the final months of his Administration, if an unforeseen situation should arise that would convince him that another journey would strengthen the bonds of friendship between the United States and others, he would not hesitate to undertake the trip (*Public Papers of the Presidents: Eisenhower, 1960–61*, pp. 529–36, and *New York Times*, June 28, 1960).

[2] On June 20 Bullis had thanked Senator John Sherman Cooper (Rep., Ky.) for supporting appropriations requested by Eisenhower for the Mutual Security Program (for background on the program see no. 1536). Bullis added that current events supported his conviction that the Far East was the most vulnerable spot in the free world. The "aggressive-minded" Mao-tse Tung, Khrushchev's partner in the Communist world axis, would concentrate on Southeast Asia, the weakest point on Communist China's borders.

[3] Bullis had visited Taiwan in 1953 as a member of a government team investigating the mutual security program. As a result of his trip, he had developed "certain ideas regarding the next move of the Communists in that part of the world. . . ."

[4] On June 18 the President had received a rousing greeting from Chinese government officials and citizens at Sungshan Airport in Taipei. Later that same day he delivered an address to those attending a mass rally in Taipei, and in the evening he had proposed a toast to President Chiang Kai-shek at a dinner given in his honor. The following day Eisenhower and Chiang issued a joint statement reaffirming the two governments' dedication to the "untiring quest for peace with freedom and justice." Noting the continuing threat of Communist aggression against the free world, the two leaders expressed "full agreement on the vital necessity of achieving closer unity and strength among all free nations" (see State, *Foreign Relations, 1958–1960*, vol. XIX, *China*, pp. 675–87; *Public Papers of the Presidents: Eisenhower, 1960–61*, pp. 503–11, and *New York Times*, June 17–19, 1960).

To Harold Macmillan

June 30, 1960

Cable. Secret

Dear Harold:[1] The ideas set forth in your letter of June 27 about our future tripartite political consultations are quite satisfactory to us.[2] Your original suggestions and the discussion held here in Washington on June 1 appear to provide a means by which the tripartite meetings of our foreign ministers can be made more useful. I assume that their next meeting will take place this fall in New York in connection with the United Nations General Assembly. The arrangements for this meeting would, in accordance with the suggestion we have all approved, be made by Sir Frederick Hoyer Millar, Mr. Merchant and by whomever the French select for this task.[3]

While this arrangement should improve our tripartite political consultation, it does not meet General de Gaulle's desire to see such consultation paralleled by strategic discussions by military representatives along the lines he proposed in his original memorandum.[4] In his letter to you of June 10, of which he sent me a copy, General de Gaulle suggested that our military representatives in the Standing Group could hold talks outside the regular deliberations of that body. In my reply I expressed to him my doubts as to the practicability of using any part of the NATO mechanism for strategic consultations, believing that our Allies would object.[5] I am sure that this would be the case, as it would be difficult to keep secret such consultations and the very fact that our representatives to the Standing Group were meeting separately to discuss global strategic matters would lead other members of the alliance to believe that we had, in fact, established some sort of inner directorate. This impression we must avoid.

It does seem, however, that we must find some way to cope with this aspect of General de Gaulle's thinking. It might be possible, for instance, to have talks here in Washington by appropriate military representatives. You and the French might delegate this responsibility to a senior military officer assigned to Washington. The French might, in such case, select their representative to the Standing Group. We, on the other hand, could select an appropriate general officer who has no connection with the Standing Group itself. These talks, of course, would have to be conducted along previously-agreed guidelines, but I am sure that we could work this out.

In this connection, I would like to recall that a year ago we did hold tripartite talks on Africa under the chairmanship of Robert Murphy. At these talks military representatives were present. Both you and the French were represented by your members of the Standing Group. At those talks the French requested separate and continuing military talks. After a period of consideration we agreed to do this, selected an appropriate officer to head up our side, and informed the French we were ready. They have never responded to this offer.[6]

I think, nevertheless, that we could re-new this offer and I would propose so doing in my reply to General de Gaulle. This may not be the organized strategic planning on a global scale, including the question of the use of nuclear weapons anywhere, which he appears to want. It is, however, a definite move forward in the field of military consultation which may in the end strengthen our alliance. It will, of course, have to be carefully and discreetly conducted.

I will ask the State Department to discuss this matter more fully with your Embassy here with the hope that we can work out promptly a common position which we can communicate to General de Gaulle.[7]

With warm personal regard, *As ever*

[1] The State Department cabled this message to the American embassy in London for delivery to Prime Minister Macmillan.

[2] For background on consultations among U.S., British, and French officials see no. 1565. Expanding on the ideas he had set forth in his May 24 memorandum (see no. 1553), Macmillan had suggested that the foreign ministers take advantage of any meetings of international organizations in order "to have some unobtrusive discussions among themselves on tripartite subjects." He also believed that the heads of the three governments should meet from time to time on an *ad hoc* basis. He had asked Eisenhower for his reaction to de Gaulle's proposal for closer military cooperation (Macmillan to Eisenhower, June 27, 1960, State Department Files, Presidential Correspondence).

[3] On the June 1 foreign minister meetings see no. 1553. Charles Lucet, minister of the French embassy in Washington, would represent France. The three foreign ministers would next meet in New York on September 20–22, following the opening of the 15th Session of the U.N. General Assembly.

[4] For de Gaulle's September 1958 memorandum on the Atlantic Alliance see no. 901; see also State, *Foreign Relations, 1958–1960,* vol. VII, pt. 2, *Western Europe,* pp. 81–84, 88–107.

[5] See no. 1565.

[6] The talks on Africa had taken place in Washington on April 16–21, 1959. At the time, Robert Murphy was Deputy Under Secretary of State for Political Affairs. Ambassador Harold Caccia and Secretary General of the Foreign Ministry Louis Joxe headed the British and French delegations. The U.S. Joint Chiefs of Staff had subsequently designated Major General Douglas Valentine Johnson to take part in the exploratory military talks (see State, *Foreign Relations, 1958–1960,* vol. XIV, *Africa,* pp. 44–53).

[7] For developments see no. 1597.

To Harold Macmillan   *June 30, 1960*
Cable. Top secret

Dear Harold:[1] Thank you very much for your letter of June 24, 1960, wherein you offer to do all you can to assist us in our POLARIS submarine enterprise, but at the same time point out some serious political considerations which must necessarily be taken into account. Although I had not realized that there were such considerations when we discussed the matter at Camp David, I must of course recognize that they do exist for you. In any case, we now have a better understanding of the problems which could arise from our joint participation in a missile submarine program at this time, and much appreciate the consideration which you have given to our request.[2]

We readily agree with you that insofar as your given reasons are concerned, Loch Linnhe would be a better location for the POLARIS submarine tender and drydock than the Clyde. Other factors important to our ballistic missile submarine needs, however, compel us reluctantly to decline your offer of Loch Linnhe. These reasons would include the need for greater shore facilities for logistical support, more immediate access to open seas and international waters, and the need for comparative ease and safety of navigation. Furthermore, and quite aside from these operational considerations, the other points raised in your letter would present difficulties for us.

In line with considerations discussed between Mr. Watkinson and Mr. Gates on June 6, the U.S. Navy has now made plans to keep the drydock in the United States for another year, and to delay deployment of the tender until other arrangements can be made. This would include the possibility of basing them in the United States.[3]

I was glad that Mr. Watkinson and Mr. Gates had such a satisfactory discussion concerning SKYBOLT and POLARIS MRBM's. I hope that we can both continue to seek an effective solution to the NATO MRBM program which we consider of great importance.[4]

With warm personal regard, *As ever*

---

[1] This message was sent by cable to the American embassy in London for delivery to Prime Minister Macmillan.

[2] For background on the Polaris issue and the discussions at Camp David in March see no. 1567. Macmillan had told Eisenhower that his Cabinet colleagues had supported the plan to base Polaris submarines in Scotland to reinforce the West's deterrent capabilities. The proposed location, however, would cause great controversy. "Ours is a small and densely populated island," Macmillan said, "and we already provide facilities for a substantial share of the strategic striking force of the West." Public support could only be gained if the location of such a major nuclear facility were

somewhere other than the Clyde River, close to Glasgow, "the third largest and most overcrowded city in this country." Macmillan had suggested Loch Linnhe, which was farther to the north and in a more rural area. He also wanted the entire operation to be known as a joint enterprise, and he suggested that a British naval officer could share operational control of the submarines with an American commander. Finally, Macmillan asked Eisenhower to agree that submarines would not launch missiles within 100 miles of British territory without British consent (Macmillan to Eisenhower, June 20, 1960, PREM 11/2940; see also Macmillan, *Pointing the Way*, pp. 254–55).

Both State and Defense Department officials had disapproved of Macmillan's conditions (Watson, *Into the Missile Age*, p. 566).

[3] On the meetings between Defense Secretary Gates and British Minister of Defence Harold Watkinson see *ibid.*, pp. 565–66; see also no. 1567.

[4] Gates and Watkinson had agreed that the United States would make every effort to complete development of the air-launched Skybolt ballistic missile by 1965. The British could then purchase approximately 100 of the weapons. They also agreed that as part of its participation in the development of a medium-range ballistic missile program for NATO, Britain would purchase two Polaris submarines, each with sixteen warheads, subject to congressional approval (Watson, *Into the Missile Age*, p. 566). For developments see no. 1584.

1574   *EM, AWF, Ann Whitman Diary Series*

DIARY   *July 1, 1960*

44th wedding anniversary. Spent weekend at Gettysburg. Came back evening of 4th.[1]

[1] The Eisenhowers were married on July 1, 1916; see the President's memoir, *At Ease*, pp. 113–14, 117–18, and Susan Eisenhower, *Mrs. Ike*, pp. 36–43. They would spend July 1–4 at their farm in Gettysburg with their son John and his family and some close friends. The President would also play golf. See also *New York Times*, July 2–5, 1960.

1575   *EM, AWF, Ann Whitman Diary Series*

DIARY   *July 5, 1960*

A long day.[1] Breakfast with Chmn. of Nat. Com. And Len Hall and Clif Folger.[2] Talked finance of campaign of 1960. Decision to hold a "closed circuit" television dinner—to raise money.[3] Under Sec. State with Sec. Treas. and others here to discuss international situation—especially Cuba.[4]

[1] Eisenhower made this notation by hand on his July 1960 calendar.

[2] Thruston Morton had succeeded Leonard Hall as chairman of the Republican Na-

tional Committee in April 1959 (see *New York Times*, Apr. 12, 1959). John Clifford Folger had served as U.S. Ambassador to Belgium from 1957–1959; he currently was chairman of the Republican National Finance Committee.
³ "Victory Fund" dinners, broadcast by closed-circuit television, would be held on September 29 (see *New York Times*, Sept. 30, 1960).
⁴ C. Douglas Dillon was Under Secretary of State; Robert Anderson was Secretary of the Treasury. The "others" included Richard Nixon, Henry Cabot Lodge, Wilton Persons, and James Hagerty. On the situation in Cuba see no. 1370; for developments see nos. 1578 and 1582.

1576   *EM, AWF, Name Series*

To Henry Robinson Luce   *July 6, 1960*
Personal

Dear Harry: Thank you for the succinct report on your experience before the Jackson Senate Subcommittee.[1]

It seems to me that there is no doubt that you and I agree in basic positions.[2] Indeed so far as the shelter program is concerned, I have time and time again urged such a program upon the American people. I have, however, pointed out that in this field I believe that the Federal government should provide the knowledge, techniques, pilot models and so on, but that the bulk of the responsibility rests upon the locality and the private citizen. There are of course certain areas of specific Federal responsibility, (Federal buildings, establishments, etc.), but I think that my generalization as to responsibility has at least one realistic element in its favor. This is that *unless* the *private citizen does become interested and has a definite sense of responsibility for himself and family*, there is little that the government, by itself, can do.[3]

As to your favoring an additional expenditure for defense of up to two billion dollars, I have this much to say. Under the post-war policy of unilateral disarmament in the late 40's and early 50's, we had gotten down to something under 13 billion dollars annually in expenditures for our entire defense establishment. (This, incidentally, was certainly a contributory cause to the attack on South Korea). During the period of the Korean War expenditures naturally went up. After the armistice stopped the active fighting, it appeared that our expenditures would stabilize, under conditions then existing, at about 33 to 35 billion dollars.

However, as intelligence reports in 1953 and 1954 began to indicate a rapid growth in the Russian technical competence in the military field, and our own scientists concluded that ballistic missiles of great accuracy could be designed and built, these expenditures began gradually to rise. This year they reached the level of 41 billion dollars; a sizeable sum by any comparison.

In such matters no individual's conclusions and convictions are sacrosanct. All that I can do is make sure that I have honest conclusions of the finest body of technical experts in this field that can be mobilized, and then to make such personal decisions as accord with whatever experience and wisdom I may have, in the hope that they may reflect the path of reason. I have always tried to lean to the side of generosity in these decisions and have invariably allowed more money than is approved by the Budget Bureau studies and analyses. I cannot take my oath that an expenditure of an additional two billion dollars would not be justified; on the other hand I could easily make cuts of an equal amount that would not damage our defenses except as we make assumptions of a dark hue.[4]

Incidentally, the Congress has, in five instances, reduced my defense estimates—in three (all election years) it has increased them.

One political individual who has lately been urging a three billion dollar additional expenditure gives this as his cost estimate of the additional programs he recommends. Some of my people are estimating that his programming would cost ten rather than three billion dollars additional.[5]

Finally, no one could agree more than I do with your argument as to the need for equitable tax reform. I have made public speeches on this for years. Likewise, I agree with your contention that expenditures other than for defense should be held down.[6] If you know of any way to accomplish this, I would be glad to have your formula. (In the matter of the pay rise, the Congress certainly disagreed with my convictions in overwhelming fashion.)[7]

Quite naturally, I am gratified that LIFE finds it possible to put a stamp of approval on my eight years of effort. I shall read the editorial with great interest.[8]

With warm personal regard, *As ever*

[1] Luce, publisher of *Time, Life,* and *Fortune,* had testified on June 28, 1960, before the Senate Subcommittee on National Policy Machinery. The committee, chaired by Henry M. Jackson, was examining the nation's ability to plan and coordinate cold war strategy (for background see nos. 1211 and 1344; *Congressional Quarterly Almanac,* vol. XVI, *1960,* p. 725). Luce characterized his discussion with the committee members as "amicable and non-partisan." Luce had met with the President that same day and had discussed, among other things, "the inroads of public spending on the vitals of free government" (Luce to Eisenhower, June 29 and July 6, 1960, AWF/N).
[2] Luce had written that he thought that his overall position was basically in agreement with the President's, despite some differences on specific points (Luce to Eisenhower, July 2, 1960, AWF/N).
[3] Luce had testified, he said, that the nation must make victory in the cold war its primary aim even though this would increase the risk of "hot war." He had added that the United States needed a more effective civil defense system, including a fed-

eral fallout shelter program in spite of the public's lack of concern (*ibid.*; New *York Times*, June 29, 1960; see also no. 1472).

[4] Luce had "disclaimed his expertism" on military expenditures, he said, but had nevertheless testified for a substantial increase in defense spending (Luce to Eisenhower, July 6, 1960, AWF/N). See nos. 448, 472, and 1107.

[5] Eisenhower was probably referring to either Democratic Senator Stuart Symington, a former secretary of the Air Force (see nos. 884 and 1724), or New York Governor Nelson A. Rockefeller; both had asked for a three billion dollar increase in national security expenditures (*New York Times*, May 27, June 9, 29, 1960).

[6] Despite their differences, Luce could "square" with the President, he said, on the need for fiscal responsibility because both men thought that tax revenues should be raised through equitable reform and that expenditures, except for military and civil defense, should be held down (Luce to Eisenhower, July 6, 1960, AWF/N). On tax reform see, for example, Eisenhower's budget messages, *Public Papers of the Presidents: Eisenhower, 1959*, p. 41, and *1960–61*, pp. 43–44, 943–44).

[7] See nos. 1570 and 1216.

[8] Luce had told Eisenhower that the July 1960 issue of *Life* magazine would contain an editorial praising Eisenhower's contributions as President (*Life*, July 4, 1960, pp. 22–23).

1577   *EM, AWF, International Series: Nehru*

To Jawaharlal Nehru   *July 6, 1960*

Dear Prime Minister:[1] Being deeply aware of your devotion to the cause of peace and disarmament, I would like you to know my thoughts on disarmament in light of the break-up of the Geneva ten-nation talks.[2]

I will never permit temporary set-backs to interfere with man's progress towards a world of permanent peace. The folly of the arms race must, sooner or later, come to an end. I retain the belief that human reason will prevail—that the movement of events must be toward universal disarmament, not toward universal destruction.

Reason dictates that each country must do all it can to see that no opportunities for serious negotiations are lost or overlooked. The United States always has been, and I hope always will be, ready to negotiate on disarmament. We are ready to accept as large a cut in our military strength as any country in the world. We ask only that no other country gain a military advantage as the result of American disarmament, and that there be means of assuring ourselves that this is so. This consideration is at the root of our insistence on adequate controls. We are all aware of what resulted from unbalanced disarmament after World War II.

While our ultimate goal must be general and complete disarmament, my conviction is that progress in disarmament negotiations can best be made by the process of earnestly searching for those measures which are presently feasible, most urgently needed, and in the interest of all parties concerned. In the world as it is today, this patient approach is the one which strikes me as most likely to produce results. It is an approach seeking not propaganda victories but positive achievements in arms reductions.

The proposals which the United States and its friends in the Ten-Nation Disarmament Conference submitted last March were designed to serve the purpose of helping the negotiators find and focus on specific measures which could be the starting point for a disarmament program. The measures which we and our partners proposed were not intended to be the final answer to the problem of disarmament. I had hoped, however, that among these measures there might be some which would enable us to get started with disarmament without delay, recognizing that making a beginning is the most difficult part of disarmament. At the same time, we left no doubt that our goal was general and complete disarmament, including all militarily significant states without exception.

We were confronted, however, with a concept of how disarmament negotiations should be conducted that was totally different from our own. We found it impossible to discuss any specific disarmament measure because of the insistence of the Soviet Union that a treaty covering the full gamut of disarmament must be negotiated before any single measure of disarmament can be implemented or any inspection arrangement can be designed. Determined that the gap between the opposing views should not be unbridgeable, I felt the United States should modify its position where it could, in order that the two sides might move closer together. Our friends in the Conference also favored wholehearted attempts at accommodation.

Accordingly, the United States Government prepared a revised plan which it intended to place before the Ten-Nation Disarmament Committee after consultation with its allies. This fact was widely known. What happened thereafter is also well known. The revised United States plan, a copy of which I am asking my Ambassador to leave with you, was laid before the Committee, but the Soviet delegation did not wait to see it.

I am greatly concerned as to what meaning such an action may hold for the future of disarmament negotiations. The United States can do no less, however, than use every available diplomatic channel to open the way for an early resumption of negotiations. I feel sure we have your support in this. The United States delegation, and those of its allies, have remained in Geneva and are ready to go back to the conference table.[3] We have expressed to the Soviet Government our hope that it will reconsider its decision to terminate the disarmament conference. We expect, also, that at an appropriate time there will be a constructive discussion of this matter in the United Nations.

Our discussions in New Delhi were extremely useful to me. If you care to share with me your views on what might be done at this time to further the cause of disarmament, they would be most welcome.[4]

With warm regard, *Sincerely*

[1] State Department officials drafted this message, which was sent by cable to the American embassy in New Delhi for delivery to Prime Minister Nehru (see Dillon to Eisenhower, July 5, 1960, AWF/I: Nehru).

[2] For background on the Ten-Nation Committee on Disarmament, which had begun meeting in Geneva on March 15, see no. 1341; see also State, *Foreign Relations, 1958–1960*, vol. III, *National Security Policy; Arms Control and Disarmament*, pp. 836–46. On March 16 the representatives of the Western nations had presented "A Plan for General and Complete Disarmament in a Free and Peaceful World," a proposal designed to be implemented in three stages. After the Soviet Union had rejected the plan, insisting that an agreement on general principles was necessary at the outset, the foreign ministers of the five participating Western nations agreed to a counter proposal that would emphasize both general objectives as well as specific matters for immediate discussion. On June 27, however, before the plan had been presented to the conference, the Soviet and the Soviet bloc delegations had walked out. In a subsequent letter Soviet Premier Khrushchev had told Eisenhower that the Western plan was one of control without disarmament, a form of "legalized military espionage" designed "to gain one-sided military advantages for the NATO countries at the expense of the security of the Soviet Union" (*ibid.*, pp. 867–73, 879–88; State, *Documents on Disarmament, 1960*, pp. 68–71, 79–82, 100–111, 126–36; see also NSC meeting minutes, May 25, 1960, AWF/NSC).

Acting Secretary Douglas Dillon and U.S. Ambassador to India Ellsworth Bunker had suggested that Eisenhower explain the Western proposals to Nehru in order "to capitalize on Indian dismay at the Soviet walkout" (Dillon to Eisenhower, July 5, 1960, AWF/I: Nehru).

[3] Frederick McCurdy Eaton was the U.S. representative to the conference.

[4] On Eisenhower's meetings with Nehru during his eleven-nation goodwill trip the previous December see no. 1389. In his July 24 response Nehru would comment on the substance of the problem but would offer no suggestions (Calhoun to Goodpaster, Aug. 6, 1960, AWF/I: Nehru). For developments see no. 1627.

1578   *EM, AWF, Ann Whitman Diary Series*

DIARY   *July 6, 1960*

Gordon Gray to plan N.S.C. meetings for rest of summer.[1] Also to approve directive requiring all depts to study applicability of our policies in light of global unrest as evidenced in overthrow of Rhee in Korea—Menderes in Turkey—actions of Castro in Cuba—mob influence on Kishi in Japan.[2] (Indeed, it appears that our Congress is beginning to watch and obey pressure groups—postal workers—more than it does common sense and public intent.[3]

Approved emergency sugar act and after 2 long conferences today, issued applicable proclamation and accompanying statement.[4] Have warned all to be alert to Cuban reaction because when dealing with a "little Hitler" anything can happen. Have an appointment with Drummond and Krock this even—5:30.[5]

[1] Gray was Special Assistant to the President for National Security Affairs. For developments see no. 1667.

[2] On the situation in Korea see no. 1526; on developments in Turkey see no. 1559; for developments regarding Cuba see nos. 1582 and 1606; and for background on the cancellation of Eisenhower's trip to Japan see nos. 1564 and 1568.

[3] See no. 1448.

[4] For background see no. 1488. On this day Eisenhower had signed into law P.L. 86-592, which modified the 1956 Sugar Act and gave the President temporary authority to reduce the amount of sugar that Cuba could export to the United States. The law also established a fixed formula for redistributing among other countries any portion of Cuba's quota that might be cut. Eisenhower had immediately reduced Cuba's remaining 1960 quota by about ninety-five percent; he had also issued a proclamation stating that Castro's "deliberate policy of hostility" had raised doubts about Cuba's reliability as a source of sugar (*Public Papers of the Presidents: Eisenhower, 1960–61*, pp. 562–63, 877). Meeting with officials from the State, Agriculture, and Treasury Departments, as well as members of the White House staff, the President had characterized the quota reductions as "economic sanctions" (State, *Foreign Relations, 1958–1960*, vol. VI, *Cuba*, pp. 976–83; see also Kistiakowsky, *A Scientist at the White House*, p. 360). In retaliation the Cuban government, having already seized several oil refineries, authorized the expropriation of other U.S.-owned property (*New York Times*, July 7, 1960; Eisenhower, *Waging Peace*, p. 535).

[5] The meeting with Arthur Krock, *New York Times* columnist, and Roscoe Drummond, Washington Bureau chief for the *New York Herald Tribune*, is not listed in the President's daily appointments.

1579　　　　　　　　　　　　　　　　　　　　　　　　*EM, WHCF,*
　　　　　　　　　　　　　　　　　　　　　　　　　Official File 3-A-17

To William Childs Westmoreland　　　　　　　　　*July 7, 1960*

Dear General Westmoreland: When I was at West Point in the early part of June, I discussed with General Davidson and others the possibility of my sending there some object or objects that might be of interest to the West Point Museum. As I explained at that time, most of my memorabilia from the war have already been disposed of.[1]

It did occur to me, however, that you might like to have a set of the car flags that I have used since I have been in the White House. I am therefore taking the liberty of sending you a 48 star, 49 star, and 50 star flag, all of which have been flown from my automobiles during the past years. I hope that you will consider this set of flags an appropriate item for the Museum.[2]

With warm regard, *Sincerely*

P.S. As you already know, I gave the museum at West Point a sword used by Napoleon when he was First Consul. It was presented to me by General de Gaulle in 1945.[3]

[1] General Westmoreland (USMA 1936) had been Commanding General of the 101st Airborne Division and Fort Campbell, Kentucky, before he was appointed Superintendent of the United States Military Academy on May 13 (see no. 1457). He had served as a battery officer in the 8th Field Artillery at Schofield Barracks, Hawaii, from 1936–1941, and as Chief of Staff on the 9th Infantry Division in World War II. On the President's visit to West Point and his conversation with outgoing Superintendent Garrison Holt Davidson see no. 1556, and Streiff to Whitman, July 6, 1960, same file as document.

[2] The flags would arrive at the Military Academy on July 18, and Westmoreland would thank the President the following day (same file as document).

[3] On June 14, 1945, Eisenhower had attended ceremonies honoring the successful conclusion of World War II. Napoleon's sword, a token of the French people's esteem and friendship, was among the gifts he received (see Chandler and Galambos, *Occupation, 1945*, no. 121, and Butcher, *My Three Years*, pp. 864–66).

1580

EM, AWF,
International Series:
Brazil

To Juscelino Kubitschek de Oliveira

July 8, 1960

Dear Mr. President: On May 28, 1958 you were thoughtful enough to write me to express your own eloquent ideas for a dynamic joint effort in which all of the American Republics could devote themselves. I was happy then, as I am now to join you in this hemisphere-wide effort which has come to be known as "Operation Pan America".[1]

During the past two years much progress has been made. The Committee of 21 has met twice, first in Washington and last year in Buenos Aires. The steering group for that committee, known as the Committee of 9, has just finished a successful meeting here where the basis was laid for the next meeting of the Committee of 21, scheduled for Bogotá in early September.[2] I am sure that we can count on additional concrete accomplishments in Bogotá, especially in the fields of: (1) financing economic development; (2) the role of technical assistance to achieve increased industrial and agricultural productivity; and (3) further consideration of commodity problems.[3] I understand that the economic studies which were authorized at the Buenos Aires meeting, and which have now been re-quested by eleven countries, are under way and that they will contribute importantly to the knowledge which we need for sound economic and social advancement.[4]

Meanwhile, reports which have come to me regarding the progress being made in the structural organization of the Inter-American Development Bank are most encouraging. In less than two years, this Bank has been planned, its complex structure negotiated, and its charter agreed upon by 20 of our American Republics. Most of the first instalment on its capital has been paid in and it is hoped that the first loans will be made prior to the end of this year.[5]

Only three months ago it was a great pleasure to visit you personally in your marvelous new capital city of Brasilia, and later in your fabulous cities of Rio de Janeiro and São Paulo.[6] The discussions which I held with you were most inspiring and contributed to the further review which I have been conducting, during and since that trip, of the situation in this hemisphere. I have now concluded that, notwithstanding our past efforts, we all need to exert additional strength in our common program to meet the challenge of this new decade during which our peoples are determined to progress to a new high plane of dynamic living, socially, economically, politically and spiritually. I wanted you to know that I will be announcing within the next few days something of the plans of the United States toward participating more effectively toward our hemisphere objectives. I hope to request authority of the Congress which will be coming back into session early next month to move ahead with this program.[7]

Cordially and sincerely yours

[1] See nos. 729, 730, and 967 for background on the new program promoted by Brazil's President.

[2] In September 1958 the Council of the Organization of American States had formed the Committee of 21 to study new measures for economic cooperation among the American nations. The Committee had met in Washington in October and November of 1958, and in Buenos Aires, Argentina, in April and May 1959. It would meet again in Bogotá, Colombia, in September 1960 (Council of the Organization of American States, Special Committee to Study the Formulation of New Measures for Economic Cooperation, *Act of Bogotá, October 11, 1960* [Washington, D.C., 1961], pp. 3–4).

[3] For developments see nos. 1640 and 1644.

[4] The Committee had passed a resolution calling for country-by-country studies of the problems and possibilities of economic development (*New York Times*, Mar. 22, 27, and May 9, 1959).

[5] For background see nos. 1130 and 1170.

[6] On Eisenhower's trip see no. 1403.

[7] For background see no. 1532. A final sentence later added to the President's letter noted that he had asked John Moors Cabot, U.S. Ambassador to Brazil since July 1959, to take this letter to Kubitschek personally. On July 11 Eisenhower would of-

ficially announce plans for a new program of economic assistance to Latin America (*New York Times*, July 9, 12, 1960). Geared toward promoting economic growth and social change, the program would be designed to fund housing, education, public health, and similar projects as well as agricultural improvements. Eisenhower emphasized that the program would be a joint and hemispheric project, embodying the multilateralism embedded in Kubitschek's "Operation Pan America" (*Public Papers of the Presidents: Eisenhower, 1960–61*, pp. 568–75; *New York Times*, July 7, 12, 16, 1960; see also Robert J. Alexander, *Juscelino Kubitschek and the Development of Brazil* [Athens, Oh., 1991], pp. 279–305). On August 8 Eisenhower would request $500 million to start the program, an amount which Congress subsequently approved (*Congressional Quarterly Almanac*, vol. XVI, *1960*, pp. 216–17; see also Noble, *Christian A. Herter*, pp. 219–25, *New York Times*, Aug. 18, 1960).

In his reply President Kubitschek would thank Eisenhower for his initiative, but he would suggest that an even broader commitment was necessary (July 30, 1960, AWF/I: Brazil). Department of State officials would recommend that Eisenhower not answer, for continued correspondence might potentially cause "embarrassment" because of the "inability to accede fully to Brazil's desire for economic aid" (Calhoun to Goodpaster, July 30, 1960, *ibid.*; see also State, *Foreign Relations, 1958–1960*, vol. V, *American Republics*, pp. 777–81). For developments see nos. 1640 and 1644.

1581   *EM, AWF, International Series:*
                                                                  Macmillan

To Harold Macmillan   *July 9, 1960*
Cable. Secret

Dear Harold:[1] I have been giving considerable thought to the handling of the nuclear detonations in the seismic research program. This program is essential if we are to reach an agreement on the cessation of nuclear testing of the kind you and I proposed on March 29, and if the moratorium which we are prepared to agree to is to provide us answers on the underground detection problem.[2]

We have explored here, and with your people, various ways of dealing with the safeguards for these nuclear detonations. One possibility is a pool approach whereby devices of the U.K., the U.S., and the USSR would be used on a reciprocal basis. Another approach would be an offer by the United States to open its seismic research devices to inspection by representatives of the U.K. and the USSR. Either approach would, as you know, require Congressional authorization.[3]

With respect to the first proposal it is probable that the Soviets will reject it inasmuch as they have already stated that they have no intention of using nuclear explosions in seismic research. In spite of this I feel it is important that we put the pool idea forward as a proposal. It will be another evidence of our desire to find a cooperative solution. A further reason that I believe it is desirable to put this forward is the strong feeling expressed by certain members of the Congress that a safeguards arrangement should be reciprocal. Having made this proposal, we would then be in a better position to obtain Congressional support for the second course of action. I have concluded that we should not put forward this proposal accompanied by any sort of warning of possible unilateral action in the event of Soviet rejection.

If the Soviets reject the pool proposal in spite of our best persuasion, we plan to offer to open devices used in the United States seismic research program for examination by the United Kingdom and the USSR. This proposal would also be put forward without a warning of possible unilateral action in event of Soviet rejection. Implementation of this proposal would of course be subject to Congressional action which I could request in August if the Soviets show any likelihood of accepting.

However, should the Soviets reject this reasonable proposal or should they delay their response for an unreasonable period it would be our intention to announce that we are proceeding with the U.S. seismic research program and that we intend to invite United Nations or other international observation of these experiments. If this proposal does not satisfy the Soviets I doubt that there is anything we can devise which would, and under those circumstances I believe our action in going ahead would be widely understood and supported.

As for timing, it is our objective to put forward these proposals and be prepared in the event of Soviet rejection or undue delay to make the above mentioned announcement sometime during August.

To protect our negotiating position we are limiting knowledge of the second proposal and our future intentions to the smallest possible group.[4]

With warm personal regard, *As ever*

[1] State Department officials drafted this message and sent it by cable to the American embassy in London for delivery to Prime Minister Macmillan (see State, *Foreign Relations, 1958–1960*, vol. III, *National Security Policy; Arms Control and Disarmament,* p. 891).

[2] For background on the Geneva negotiations regarding nuclear testing and the seismic research program see no. 1445. On March 19 the Soviet Union had proposed a program of joint research and experiments with the West to identify more accurately seismic events below 4.75 on the Richter scale (see no. 1493). Eisenhower and Macmillan had discussed the need for nuclear detonations in any seismic research program in their meeting at Camp David on March 28. Eisenhower had said that the research program "must include actual nuclear testing if it is to be real and productive." On the following day the two men publicly stated that they believed a comprehensive test ban agreement was possible if the negotiators could work out an adequate quota of on-site inspections, the composition of the Control Commission, and

the arrangements for the detonations necessary for the research program (State, *Foreign Relations, 1958–1960*, vol. III, *National Security Policy; Arms Control and Disarmament*, pp. 848–54, 864–66; Goodpaster, Memorandum of Conference, Mar. 24, 1960, AWF/D; State, *Documents on Disarmament, 1960*, pp. 77–78; Kistiakowsky, *A Scientist at the White House*, pp. 281, 285–89; and Macmillan, *Pointing the Way*, pp. 190–91).

[3] For more on these discussions see State, *Foreign Relations, 1958–1960*, vol. III, *National Security Policy; Arms Control and Disarmament*, pp. 874–80. The meeting that prompted this message to Macmillan was on July 7 (see John S. D. Eisenhower memorandum, July 7, 1960, AWF/D; see also Kistiakowsky, *A Scientist at the White House*, pp. 348–49, 360, 362–63, 364–65).

[4] Macmillan, who would agree with Eisenhower's reasoning regarding the "pool approach," expressed satisfaction that the proposal would not include a warning of possible unilateral U.S. action. "Under your second proposal," Macmillan wrote, "the Russians should have ample assurance that any nuclear explosions in the research programme are not concealed tests and I think it would be very difficult for them to refuse such a proposal." He asked that Eisenhower consult with him before proceeding with unilateral action in the event that the Russians rejected the second proposal. "We cannot conceal from ourselves that this would be a most serious decision in the eyes of the world" (Macmillan to Eisenhower, July 13, 1960, FO 371/149336; see also Macmillan to Caccia, July 12, 1960, PREM 11/3584).

The U.S. representative to the Geneva negotiations would present the proposal for safeguards regarding the use of nuclear devices for seismic research on July 12 (State, *Documents on Disarmament, 1960*, pp. 142–52). For developments see no. 1627.

1582   *EM, AWF, International Series: Macmillan*

To Harold Macmillan   *July 11, 1960*
Cable. Secret

Dear Harold:[1] The expression in your last letter of sympathy and support with respect to the Cuban problem was especially heartwarming. It was a great comfort to know you were with us at a time when difficult decisions had to be made and we found ourselves forced, by the course Castro has elected to follow, to engage ourselves and our prestige more directly and publicly than heretofore to resolving this challenge to our security and vital interests.[2]

Because the Cuban problem so profoundly affects not only the security of the United States but is also related to the security of the Free World as a whole, it might be well to review the dimension of the problem as we see it and what we are trying to do about it, although I am sure you and Selwyn have followed the matter closely.

Since Castro took over Cuba a year and a half ago, our policy toward Cuba can be divided roughly in three phases. The first phase might be called the testing phase. Although the known radical and anti-American background of the Castro brothers, and especially their previous involvement in Communist-front causes, gave cause for deep skepticism, the evidence was not altogether conclusive and it could not be foretold how these youthful leaders would react under the sobering responsibilities and opportunities which were theirs. More importantly, at that time there were with Castro's Government Cubans of ability and moderation who had joined with Castro in pledging that Cuba would have a democratic, elected government, that it would respect Cuba's international obligations and that, within that framework, it would carry out certain reforms which, in principle, we could all agree were not only popular but needed in Cuba. There was thus some chance that this moderate, experienced and democratic element would check the extremists and this chance had to be tested not only for our own satisfaction but because the great popularity which Castro then enjoyed throughout the Hemisphere and the world gave us no alternative but to give him his chance.

Our first actions, therefore, were directed to give Castro every chance to establish a reasonable relationship with us. As a first gesture, we extended quick recognition and I immediately appointed a new Ambassador to Cuba who was singularly well regarded by Cubans and Latin Americans and who could have established a fruitful relationship with Castro if anyone could.[3] When Castro came to the United States under private auspices in April of last year, he was not only well received by the public and the press, but our own Governmental contacts with him then were calculated to make cooperation possible if he had any disposition for it.[4] We sharply curbed all inclination to retort and strike back at his early diatribes against us, leaving the way open to him to climb off of this line and get down to the serious business of running the affairs of his country responsibly.

Before the first six months had ended, it was clear Castro had failed this test and by Fall I was reluctantly forced to the conclusion, as a basis for our Government's actions, that there was no reasonable chance that Castro and his lieutenants would cooperate in finding a reasonable *modus vivendi* with us. The story of the cancellation of elections, of the ascendancy of the Communist-oriented group and purge of the moderates, of the executions and the hounding of all anti-Communists, of the abortive Cuban-supported efforts to overthrow various Caribbean governments, and of the shrill anti-American diatribes is too well known to require details. We were directly affected when Castro, choosing the Agrarian Reform Law version advanced by the extremists, authorized the expropriation of extensive American properties without acceptable provision for compensation. When this was implemented, it turned out that not even these unsatisfactory conditions were observed but our people's properties were seized without even a pretense of observing the Castro regime's own laws; so far as I know the promised bonds have not even been printed. This naturally aroused widespread disillusionment and indignation in this country but, in the longer view, it was perhaps not so serious and irrevocable as the increase of Communist influence in Cuba. With the moderates gone and the Prime Minister equating anti-Communism with treason to his revolution, our intelligence increasingly indicated that the Communists began permeating Cuba's life and government. The Communist Party was the only party allowed to operate, its members infiltrating every key government and military department. I imagine that Cuba today is the only country outside the Bloc whose security chief is a Communist.

Despite these developments, it was not feasible for us immediately to take a hard line towards Castro. The second phase of our policy towards him, which acquired the popular misnomer of "policy of restraint," has covered roughly the last year. Its primary objective and effect was to make clear to the Cuban people and to the world that the deteriorated situation was of Castro's making, not of ours. We are deeply committed, especially in this Hemisphere, to the policy of non-intervention, and our standing in the world is probably due more than to any other single factor to the instinctive realization of all people that, while we offer aid and leadership, we respect the rights of weaker nations and do not seek to impose our will upon them. We could simply not afford to appear the bully. In this, of course, we realized that our own sources of information as to what was actually happening in Cuba were vastly superior to those available to the public, especially in the Latin American Republics, and that Castro continued to enjoy an undeserved degree of popular hero-worship. It took time and effort on our part for the process of disillusionment in other countries to catch up with the process here.

The third, and more active phase, of our policy is the one on which we are now embarking. The critical element is the degree to which Cuba had been handed over to the Soviet Union as an instrument with which to undermine our position in Latin America and the world. The Soviets, at first, showed some measure of caution as to the degree of their commitment to Castro. The Latin American Communist Party leaders were instructed at the Soviet Party Congress in Moscow last year to give full support to Castro, but Khrushchev and the Soviet leadership did not commit themselves openly to Castro until Mikoyan's visit last January, a year after Castro came to power. The trade and credit agreements reached then exposed fully the intent of Castro, despite Cuba's formal commitments under the Rio Treaty and the Charter of the Organization of America States, to orient himself toward the Soviet Union.[5]

It is interesting to speculate about the degree to which the Communists are committed to Castro in the context of the current Soviet-Communist Chinese ideological struggle. We have noted that the Bloc leaders and the Communist theoretical publications have gone out of their way to endorse Castro while largely ignoring of late other positive neutralists. Khrushchev chose, perhaps significantly enough, the Indian Parliament this Spring to endorse Castro. He singled out the Cuban Revolution again at his press conference in Paris at the close of the Summit.[6] It would appear that the Communists see in Castro a reconciliation of Khrushchev's views on peaceful co-existence and the Chinese Communists more aggressive line. In distinction to other neutralist leaders, Castro fully incorporates the Communists in his regime, carries out a precipitant revolution against the existing social order, and is far more internationalist in his pretensions to spread his revolution to surrounding countries than the usual type of nationalist whom the Communists court. If the Communists could find other leaders who met Khrushchev's standards of "peaceful co-existence" and Mao's of a Communist revolutionary we would be in very serious trouble indeed. I have been told that Mikoyan on returning to Moscow from Cuba, was exuberantly rejuvenated, finding that what was going on in the youthful and disorganized Cuban Revolution brought him back to the early days of the Russian Revolution.

As it appears to us, the Castro Government is now fully committed to the Bloc. We cannot prudently follow policies looking to a reform of Castro's attitude and we must rely, frankly, on creating conditions in which democratically minded and Western-oriented Cubans can assert themselves and regain control of the island's policies and destinies. We fully recognize, of course, that the pre-Castro regimes of Cuba are discredited and have lost their appeal. Moreover, any solution to the Cuban problem must hold out to the Cuban people the promise of democratic government and reform without the extremism of the present government, which has mortgaged itself to the Soviets and to how far the Soviet leadership is willing to go to support it. It is encouraging, in this respect, that ever increasing numbers of the moderates who are committed to reform have left Castro and are organizing an embryonic resistance movement. Although it is still too early to hope that the Cubans themselves will set matters right, it would, of course, be preferable that they do so rather than force us and the other American Republics to take more drastic action.

As we enter this new phase, our primary objective is to establish conditions which will bring home to the Cuban people the cost of

Castro's policies and of his Soviet orientation and also to establish a climate in which those who recognize the necessity of eventually beneficial relations between Cuba and the United States can assert themselves. This objective underlays the action which I took this week in eliminating all but a fraction of the Cuban sugar quota for the balance of this year, although there are, of course, ample economic reasons why the United States should not rely heavily as a source of supply for an important commodity on a country whose government has made clear its intent to orient itself towards the Communist Bloc. Nor, in the fact of Castro's hostility, ties with communism, and treatment of our property and other rights could we justify in effect subsidizing his revolution with the premium price we pay for Cuban sugar. I anticipate that, as the situation unfolds, we shall be obliged to take further economic measures which will have the effect of impressing on the Cuban people the cost of this communist orientation. We hope, naturally, that these measures will not be so drastic or irreversible that they will permanently impair the basic mutuality of interests of Cuba and this country.

We also look to some form of action in the Organization of American States. This has been and remains a most difficult problem. By now, the Governments of most of the other Latin American Republics seem to be recognizing that Castro and the degree to which his movement has become an instrument of the Communists represents a very real threat to them. Yet they remain reluctant to step forward on the issue, in great part because of concern about provoking leftist and deluded elements in their countries but also because, unable to exact decisive pressure themselves and preoccupied with domestic problems, they have little eagerness to side with us against a sister Latin American country.[7] Nevertheless, especially if a solution can be found to the emotionally-charged problem of the Dominican Republic, whose regime is universally hated in Latin America, there is room for hope that we will get some support in facing up to the Castro dictatorship.[8]

In the immediate future there are a number of problems in which your help could be most useful. The most important of these, perhaps, concerns the United Nations. It is highly probable that Cuba, recognizing its lack of support among American Republics, will attempt to by-pass the Organization of American States and present to the Security Council or to this Fall's General Assembly some sort of charge against us and that they will receive Soviet support. We should be well prepared for this, and shall rely heavily on your cooperation. You will recall that when Guatemala made a complaint in 1954 (although the cases have more dissimilarities than similarities) there were some divergences between our two governments.[9] We have always held that, under the Charter, we were obligated in the first instance to seek bilateral settlement and go to the Organization of American States, before the United Nations considered the case.

Another and more immediate problem concerns tankers. As you know, Castro's insistence on displacing Free World petroleum with Soviet oil led to the taking over of British and American refineries, despite the fact that the companies concerned had in effect previously extended substantial credits to finance continued petroleum exports to Cuba. It appears that the Castro Government now has a commitment from the USSR to supply the oil, but that the latter is having substantial difficulties in finding tankers to move it on this long haul. We think that there is every reason discreetly to discourage the use of Free World tankers to bring Soviet oil to refineries which have been taken from our companies and yours and, more importantly, that a petroleum shortage in Cuba would not only raise questions there about Castro's capabilities but also crystallize doubts about the reliability of the USSR. Your help, not only with respect to British tankers, but in influencing other tanker-owning countries would be invaluable.

We are also reviewing our arms export and war materiel policies with a view to tightening them up. We have been deeply grateful for the cooperation of your government in the past in this field, all the more so because we realize fully the difficulties which a restrictive policy has caused. However, I am deeply concerned about the quantities of arms which the Castro Government has on hand as a result of the imports which have been made to add to what was taken over from the previous government. There is not only the threat that this increasing stockpile, which may include items being supplied by the Bloc, will be used in movements against other Latin American Governments but the danger that indiscriminate issue of arms and equipment when the Castro Government is threatened or falls will result in civil war or chaos. This would confront us with a most difficult problem. We shall notify your government very shortly of the details of our arms policy, and would be grateful if it were possible for you to take parallel action and help us to obtain the concurrence of NATO and other supplying companies.

Before signing this long—although I think necessary—exposition of our Cuban policy, I should like to reiterate my full endorsement of the trip I understand you are contemplating making to Latin America later this year.[10] In relation to the Cuban problem, I can scarcely think of anything more useful than the very fact of your presence and evident interest in Latin America to impress on the leaders there what is involved in Cuba is a challenge to the unity and security of the Free World, not just a quarrel on property or economic questions between us and Cuba.[11]

With warm regard, *As ever*

[1] State Department officials drafted this message, which was sent to the American embassy in London for delivery to Prime Minister Macmillan (see State, *Foreign Relations, 1958–1960*, vol. VI, *Cuba*, p. 1000).

[2] For background on the situation in Cuba see no. 1370. Deteriorating relations with the Castro government and the signing of a Cuban-Soviet trade and aid agreement in February had prompted Eisenhower to begin a propaganda campaign against the Castro regime and to initiate a plan of covert operations against Cuba that included the training of Cuban exiles. A USIA report in April had described a "grim" situation that was rapidly worsening. Communists were becoming increasingly prominent in government, and the state was taking control of the media. The refusal of U.S. oil companies to process Soviet crude oil in their Cuban refineries had prompted Castro to seize the Texaco refineries on June 29, and the Esso and Shell refineries on July 1. This action had led to Eisenhower's proclamation reducing Cuban sugar imports by 95 percent (see no. 1578; see also State, *Foreign Relations, 1958–1960*, vol. VI, *Cuba*, pp. 826–32, 848–54, 891–92, 904–6, 911–14, 947–49, 955–68, 979–80; Goodpaster, Memorandums of Conference, Jan. 25, 26, Mar. 18, 1960, AWF/D; *Public Papers of the Presidents: Eisenhower, 1960–61*, pp. 125–34; NSC meeting minutes, Feb. 18, Mar. 14, 17, Apr. 14, June 15, July 11, 1960, AWF/NSC; Eisenhower, *Waging Peace*, pp. 533–35; Rabe, *Eisenhower and Latin America*, pp. 127–33; and Bonsal, *Cuba, Castro, and the United States*, pp. 129–53).

Macmillan had asked Eisenhower what the British could do. "We will try to help you in any way we can over what might develop into a really serious Russian threat" (Macmillan to Eisenhower, July 2, 1960, AWF/I: Macmillan).

[3] Philip Wilson Bonsal (A.B. Yale 1924) had served as vice-consul in Havana in 1938 and was former director of the Office of Philippine and South East Asian Affairs in the State Department. He had been U.S. Ambassador to both Colombia and Bolivia before becoming U.S. Ambassador to Cuba in March 1959.

[4] See no. 1142.

[5] On the Cuban visit of Anastas I. Mikoyan, First Deputy Chairman of the Council of Ministries of the Soviet Union, and the subsequent trade agreement between the two countries see NSC meeting minutes, Feb. 18, 1960, AWF/NSC; on the Inter-American Treaty of Reciprocal Assistance of 1947 (Rio Treaty) see Galambos and van Ee, *The Middle Way*, no. 870.

[6] For Khrushchev's address to the Indian parliament on February 11 see *New York Times*, February 12, 1960; on his remarks at his May 18 news conference see *New York Times*, May 19, 1960. See also no. 1538.

[7] On Cuba and the Organization of American States see Herter to Eisenhower, June 30, 1960, AWF/D-H; see also no. 1516.

[8] For background on the situation in the Dominican Republic see no. 1516.

[9] On U.S. involvement in Guatemala see Galambos and van Ee, *The Middle Way*, no. 965. Great Britain had sympathized with a Guatemalan complaint to the U.N. Security Council that forces based in Nicaragua and Honduras had encroached upon Guatemalan territory, and the British had supported a proposal for a Security Council investigation (Rabe, *Eisenhower and Latin America*, pp. 53, 60).

[10] Macmillan would not visit Latin America in 1960. He would tell Eisenhower that he wanted to travel to Malaya, Singapore, and other Commonwealth countries that he had not "visited properly" until then (Macmillan to Eisenhower, July 22, 1960, AWF/I: Macmillan).

[11] For developments see no. 1606.

To Michael Joseph Mansfield   *July 13, 1960*

Dear Senator Mansfield:[1] Thank you for your telegram in which you suggest that the matter of the shooting down of the U. S. Air Force RB 47 airplane be brought before the Security Council of the United Nations.[2]

As you will have noted from this government's reply of July 12th to the Soviet note of July 11th, the United States has proposed to the Soviet government that a joint investigation be made.[3] This action was taken pursuant to the provisions of the United Nations Charter, which calls upon the parties to an international dispute to attempt to settle their differences by negotiation or similar means prior to any action within the United Nations itself.

Press reports just received indicate that instead of responding to our proposal, the Soviet government is requesting a meeting of the Security Council on this subject. While we had contemplated recourse to the Security Council only after trying bilateral remedies specified in the Charter, we welcome the Security Council consideration of this question.[4] We propose to make full use of this opportunity to focus world attention on the lawless actions and reckless threats of the Soviet government.[5] *Sincerely*

[1] State Department officials had drafted this message to Senator Mansfield for the President, then vacationing in Newport (Telephone conversations, Eisenhower and Herter, July 13, 1960, Herter Papers, Telephone Conversations).

[2] On July 1 the Soviet Union had shot down a U.S. Air Force RB-47 reconnaissance plane in the Barents Sea and had rescued two crew members. Ten days later the Soviet government had acknowledged the event in a note that had accused the United States of a "new gross violation" of Soviet air space. The surviving airmen were to be tried as spies. Notes protesting the incident were sent to Great Britain, where the flight had originated, and to Norway, over which the plane had flown. Eisenhower had told Secretary Herter that he understood that the plane was thirty miles from the Soviet border; however, if the downed airmen indicated that they may have been lost, "then we are in for it again." The United States had replied to the Soviet charges by claiming that they had "wantonly attacked" a plane that was over international waters. The plane was conducting electromagnetic research, the note said, an activity that had been carried on for more than ten years with the knowledge of the Soviet government.

The incident, Mansfield had said, was a "grave matter" and underscored "the very real danger of war erupting on the borders of Russia and enveloping the entire world." He had asked that the issue be placed before the United Nations as quickly as possible (Mansfield to Eisenhower, July 13, 1960, WHCF/OF 225-E-1; State, *Foreign Relations, 1958–1960*, vol. X, pt. 1, *Eastern Europe Region; Soviet Union; Cyprus*, pp. 540–44; Telephone conversations, Herter and Eisenhower, Goodpaster, Gates, and Hagerty, July 11, 12, 1960, Herter Papers, Telephone Conversations; and *U.S. Department of State Bulletin* 43, no. 1101 [August 1, 1960], 163–65; on the downing of a U-2 reconnaissance plane on May 1 see no. 1531).

[3] The United States had proposed that the Soviet Union and any other authority ac-

ceptable to both sides join in a thorough search for the downed plane and in an investigation of its remains.

[4] Eisenhower had suggested to Secretary Herter that a sentence similar to this one be added to the original draft (Telephone conversation, Eisenhower and Herter, July 13, 1960, Herter Papers, Telephone Conversations).

[5] A subsequent Soviet note delivered to the American embassy in Moscow on July 15 would denounce the U.S. statement as a "fabrication" and reiterate the allegations presented in their earlier note. During discussions with State Department officials regarding the preparation of the case to be presented to the U.N. Security Council, Eisenhower had stressed that the United States should not "be caught out in any story, as in the U-2 case," where the story had to be changed and an untruth acknowledged (Goodpaster, Memorandum of Conference, July 21, 1960, AWF/D). The council would begin consideration of the Soviet complaint on July 22. Four days later it would reject the Soviet resolution denouncing U.S. actions by a vote of nine to two (see *U.S. Department of State Bulletin* 43, no. 1102 [August 8, 1960], 210–11; and no. 1103 [August 15, 1960], 235–44; State, *Foreign Relations, 1958–1960*, vol. X, pt. 1, *Eastern Europe Region; Soviet Union; Cyprus*, pp. 543–44; Telephone conversation, Herter and Goodpaster, July 14, 1960, Herter Papers, Telephone Conversations; and *New York Times*, July 27, 1960). For developments see no. 1587.

1584   *EM, AWF, International Series:*
                                                            Macmillan

To Harold Macmillan   *July 15, 1960*
Top secret

Dear Harold:[1] Thank you for your prompt response to my message about facilities for our POLARIS submarines. Please be assured that there was no misunderstanding at Camp David on the question of location. I mentioned only Scottish ports; all of our technical problems concerning specific locations have been handled on other intergovernmental levels.[2]

Our Navy still insists that Loch Linnhe won't do from a technical standpoint and I therefore am happy to accept your offer to reconsider the question. Indeed, this has become a matter of some urgency, as we need a firm basis now for locating the submarine tender this fall either in the Gareloch or elsewhere. Although our Navy is keeping the drydock in the U.S. this year, we would expect to locate it in the Gareloch next spring if you find Gareloch can be used for the tender.

You were also kind enough to ask for a frank expression of my views on the other questions you have raised.[3] First, on the question of control, we agree that our POLARIS missiles would not be launched within your territorial waters without your consent. To extend any form of dual control beyond territorial waters would, however, present us with a number of problems, some of which I believe might be of concern to you as well. For example, the one hundred-mile proposal could form a most difficult precedent with respect to the utilization of weapons in other waters, such as the Mediterranean and the Caribbean. We are of course prepared to work out such coordinating measures as may be necessary.

As you know, we believe that a successful MRBM program is of importance to NATO.[4] A bilateral arrangement with the U.K. on POLARIS missiles outside the NATO framework could jeopardize favorable consideration of the NATO MRBM program. For this reason, I heartily support the initial discussions of our respective Defense Ministers along the lines that the acquisition of POLARIS submarine missile systems by the U.K. should constitute a British contribution to the NATO MRBM program. Such a procedure would avoid serious NATO repercussions and also meet your need for a cooperative POLARIS submarine undertaking. The prospect of such a British contribution to the NATO MRBM program it seems to me should be discussed in NATO before it is revealed publicly. I am sure that we can later reach agreement on the handling of this matter.[5]

I was glad to have your expression of support with regard to Cuba, and have written you separately on this most serious situation.[6]

We have followed with interest recent developments in the Cyprus negotiations and were gratified to learn of their successful conclusion. This seems to me a high tribute to the long and patient effort you have devoted to this difficult problem.[7]

With warm personal regard, *As ever*

[1] This message was sent by cable to the American embassy in London for delivery to Prime Minister Macmillan.

[2] For Eisenhower's letter to Macmillan and for background regarding the stationing of U.S. submarines in Scotland see no. 1573. Although Macmillan was disappointed that the Loch Linnhe site was unacceptable to the U.S. Navy, he agreed to have the question of the Clyde River site reexamined. "It would be very sad," he wrote, "if such a valuable strategic plan had to be abandoned." He also regretted any misunderstanding over locations that may have occurred during his talks with Eisenhower at Camp David in March (Macmillan to Eisenhower, July 2, 1960, AWF/I: Macmillan; see also Zulueta to Macmillan, [July 2, 1960], PREM 11/2940. On the Camp David talks see no. 1567).

[3] For Macmillan's previously expressed concerns see no. 1573.

[4] For background see no. 1567.

[5] For developments see no. 1600.

[6] See no. 1582.

[7] For background on the Cyprus situation see no. 1064. Representatives of Greece, Turkey, and Cyprus had initialed the draft text of a Cypriot constitution on April 4 and had presented it to the British government. On July 7, after British and Cypriot representatives had reached a settlement on the British base issue and Greek and Turkish Cypriots had agreed to a division of responsibilities in the new government, the text of a bill granting independence to Cyprus had been presented to the House

of Commons. Parliament would pass the measure on July 29, and the Republic of Cyprus would come into existence on August 16 (State, *Foreign Relations, 1958–1960,* vol. X, pt. 1, *Eastern Europe Region; Soviet Union; Cyprus,* pp. 833, 835).

1585   *EM, AWF, International Series:*
                                                                                    Macmillan

TO HAROLD MACMILLAN   *July 15, 1960*
Cable. Confidential

Dear Harold: The King and Queen of Thailand recently visited us.[1] They made a very charming couple and the Queen in particular is very shy and retiring. I had planned at a much earlier date than this to ask your help in allaying her fear that she might make unwitting mistakes in the capitals of Europe but I allowed the matter to slip my mind. I am sure that whatever you can do to make her feel easy, particularly regarding matters of protocol and official deportment, would add much to the visit.[2]

When you have the opportunity won't you please convey my warm greetings to Her Majesty the Queen and, of course, Prince Philip.

With all the best to yourself, *As ever*

[1] King Bhumibol Adulyadej (also cited as Phumiphon Adundet and Phumiphol Aduldet)and Queen Sirikit Kitiyakara had been touring the United States and had spent June 28 to July 2 in Washington, D.C. Upon his arrival the thirty-two-year old monarch said the United States was half his "mother-land" because he was born in Cambridge, Massachusetts, while his father attended Harvard Medical School (*New York Times,* June 29–July 8, 1960). On June 29 he addressed a joint session of Congress and met privately with the President, with whom he discussed Thailand's economy, with particular reference to agricultural surpluses (State, *Foreign Relations, 1958–1960,* vol. XV, *South and Southeast Asia,* pp. 1131–36). For developments see no. 1696.
[2] The royal couple would travel to New York City; Cambridge, Massachusetts; and Oak Ridge, Tennessee, before leaving the United States for London (*New York Times,* July 5, 6, 8, 10, 20, 31, 1960).

1586   *EM, AWF, Dulles-Herter Series*

TO CHRISTIAN ARCHIBALD HERTER   *July 18, 1960*

Memorandum for the Secretary of State: I note that Norland, in the Ivory Coast, reports a conversation with Houphouet concerning the possibility of organizing better African resistance to Communist penetration.[1] While I know that you are doing everything that is feasible and practicable to support this movement, I should like at your convenience some time in the next two or three weeks to talk about this matter with you.[2]

[1] Donald Richard Norland (B.A. University of Minnesota 1948) was U.S. Consul General in the Ivory Coast, an autonomous republic in the French Union. A member of the U.S. Foreign Service since 1952, he had previously served in Morocco and Washington before going to the Ivory Coast in 1958.

Félix Houphouët-Boigny, who had been a leader in his country's drive for independence from France, had become Prime Minister in 1959. Elected to the presidency after the Ivory Coast became independent in August 1960, he would hold that office until his death in 1993 and would pursue a pro-Western, free-enterprise policy, emphasizing agricultural development and exports at a time when other newly-independent African nations turned their efforts toward state-run industrialization. On July 15, 1960, Norland had met with Houphouët, who had emphasized the Communist threat to Africa and had asked for more aid from the United States (see State, *Foreign Relations, 1958–1960*, vol. XIV, *Africa*, p. 216).

[2] Herter would write the President on August 5 to explain developments in the Ivory Coast and the surrounding region undergoing the transition from colonial rule. The French were extremely reluctant to let the United States operate aid programs in the area, he said, even in countries scheduled to attain independence. The United States would, however, make surveys of the four countries comprising the former French West Africa with the intent of forming an International Cooperation Administration mission there. Herter would also recommend urging Houphouët to bring regional economic experts with him to the upcoming United Nations General Assembly. A show of U.S. support and sympathy would, he thought, reassure the Prime Minister, whose influence the United States hoped to strengthen (*ibid.*, pp. 216–17).

1587   *EM, AWF, International Series:*
                                                                    Macmillan

To HAROLD MACMILLAN   *July 19, 1960*
Cable. Top secret

Dear Harold:[1] I appreciated hearing from you regarding your remarks in the House of Commons about our use of bases in Great Britain. I thought you handled this matter very well indeed. I am particularly happy to have you say that the RB 47 incident has increased the sense of solidarity between us.[2]

I can understand, however, there may be some public concern in your country whether our arrangements for consultation are effective and that you felt it necessary to state you were taking up with me the question whether there should be any modification or improvement in our working arrangements. I am entirely in agreement that it is useful to review our existing working arrangements.

I trust you will agree, however, that in any public statements we should make it clear that these talks are not in any sense negotiations, nor is their purpose to consider major modifications of our present satisfactory operating procedures. It is clear that we are up against a ruthless Soviet campaign against our free world bases, which would be aided by any suggestion we are weakening in the face of Khrushchev's threats. I understand your Embassy and Chris Herter's people are presently considering arrangements to get the discussions under way in Washington in the near future.[3]

With warm regard, *As ever*

---

[1] This message, drafted by the State Department, was sent by cable to the American embassy in London for delivery to Prime Minister Macmillan.

[2] For background on the downing of a U.S. Air Force RB-47 reconnaissance aircraft by the Soviet Union see no. 1583. The flight had originated from a U.S. base in Great Britain. On this same day Macmillan had suggested to the Commons that people should "minimize and not magnify" such incidents and declared that the British were "not to be separated" from their allies "by threats or unduly worried by propaganda." He also said US-UK discussions regarding the use of American bases in Great Britain were making "good progress" (Macmillan, *Pointing the Way*, pp. 237–41; see also *New York Times*, July 20, 1960).

[3] For developments see no. 1589.

1588

EM, WHCF, Confidential File:
State Department

To Samdech Preah Norodom Sihanouk Upayvareach
July 19, 1960

Dear Prince Sihanouk: Ambassador Trimble's return to Cambodia gives me the opportunity personally to convey to you my regrets at being unable to accept the friendly invitation of your Government to visit Cambodia.[1] I should have been very happy to see you again and to learn more at first hand about the progress being achieved in Cambodia under your dedicated leadership.[2]

I am gratified that the United States has been able to contribute in some measure to the advances Ambassador Trimble has described.[3] I firmly hope that our two countries will continue to work together in this endeavor as well as in a broader sense toward the common goal of peace for all nations. While circumstances have required Cambodia and the United Sates each to determine its own particular course in world affairs, the United States understands and respects Cambodia's sovereign choice of a policy of neutrality as the means of protecting its national integrity and of furthering world peace. I and my Government welcome Cambodia's contribution to this end, and the United Sates remains steadfast in its intention to help support Cambodia's sovereignty and independence.

I congratulate you upon your re-entry into public life at the head of the Cambodian people, who again had impressively demonstrated their confidence in you. I am sure that as Chief of State of the Kingdom you will find continued expression of American friendship in the policies of my Government.[4]

I send my best wishes to you personally and my high hopes for the happiness and prosperity of the Cambodian people.[5] Please convey my respects also to your mother, Her Majesty the Queen.[6]

With warm regard, *Sincerely*

[1] Ambassador William C. Trimble had been in the United States on home leave and would return to Cambodia in late July.

[2] Eisenhower had traveled to the Far East in June (see no. 1529).

[3] For background see no. 1268. Earlier this day, at Secretary of State Herter's suggestion, Eisenhower had met with Trimble (Herter to Eisenhower, July 13, 1960, same file as document; President's daily appointments). The two men had discussed the possibility that newly installed Chief of State Prince Sihanouk would attempt to establish closer relations with the Sino-Soviet bloc. Sihanouk had recently requested an increase in U.S. military aid, and State Department officials thought this indicated Cambodia's decreased confidence that the United States would protect her from threats—"real or imagined"—by her two anti-Communist neighbors, Thailand and South Vietnam. Sihanouk wanted additional assurances of U.S. interest and support, Herter said, even though the United States had already indicated its willingness to consult with the Cambodian government and to moderate disputes. Herter had suggested that Sihanouk held the President in high esteem and a letter from Eisenhower would undoubtedly reassure the Prince and pave the way for constructive diplomatic consultations (Herter to Eisenhower, July 13, 1960, same file as document). Eisenhower's minor emendations to the letter appear on a draft in the same file as this document. For developments see no. 1775.

[4] After the death of his father, King Norodom Suramarit, Prince Sihanouk had assumed the newly created position of chief of state (June 1960); this followed a vote of confidence in a public referendum. (Sihanouk had previously been King of Cambodia from 1941 until 1955, when he had abdicated in favor of his father.) He had stated that he would continue to follow a policy of neutrality in the cold war (*New York Times*, Apr. 13, June 13, 24, 1960).

[5] Trimble was unable to deliver the President's letter and meet with Sihanouk until September 2, 1960 (State, *Foreign Relations, 1958–1960*, vol. XVI, *East Asia-Pacific Region; Cambodia; Laos*, pp. 379–82). Sihanouk would thank Eisenhower for his message and would indicate that he thought the two countries could continue to work together toward shared goals even while Cambodia remained neutral (Sihanouk to Eisenhower, Sept. 3, 1960, AWF/I: Cambodia).

[6] Queen Kossamak Nearireak.

To Harold Macmillan   July 23, 1960
Cable. Confidential

Dear Harold:[1] I was grateful to receive your letter of July 18 enclosing a copy of your note and your personal letter to Mr. Khrushchev about the RB 47 incident.[2]

I thought the tone of the note was fine and your letter was excellent. I feel you were entirely correct to make some sort of counterattack, particularly about the dangerous trend of Soviet policy since the Summit Meeting.[3]

With warm regard, As ever

[1] This message, drafted by State Department officials, was sent by cable to the American embassy in London for delivery to Prime Minister Macmillan (see Herter to Eisenhower, July 21, 1960, AWF/I: Macmillan).

[2] For background see no. 1583. "You will see," Macmillan had written, "that while the Note is a formal rejection of the Soviet protest, I have attempted in my letter to make some counter-attack on Mr. Khrushchev." Macmillan's personal letter to Khrushchev had criticized the Soviet leader for his actions in breaking up the May summit meeting (see no. 1538), in leaving the Geneva disarmament conference just as the United States was to present new proposals (see no. 1577), and in accusing Great Britain of a conspiracy to break up the newly independent state of Congo (see no. 1599). Macmillan referred to Khrushchev's past assurances that the Soviet Union wanted peaceful coexistence and detente in international relations. "I simply do not understand," he wrote, "what your purpose is today" (Macmillan to Eisenhower, Macmillan to Khrushchev, July 18, 1960, AWF/I: Macmillan and PREM 11/3122).

[3] Eisenhower had told Secretary Herter that he had been heartened by Macmillan's letter, and he had commented that "many people have been saying that the British are being soft these days." The President and Herter had discussed ways to handle the current Soviet "saber-rattling" and had agreed that a decision to bring U.S. defense forces into a greater state of readiness would have a "major psychological effect" (Goodpaster, Memorandum of Conference, July 21, 1960, AWF/D; and State, Foreign Relations, 1958–1960, vol. X, pt. 1, Eastern Europe Region; Soviet Union; Cyprus, p. 546). For developments see no. 1638.

1590   EM, WHCF, Official File 107-B

To Harry Amos Bullis   July 25, 1960

Dear Harry: Thanks for your note about the budget surplus.[1] I am gratified that such an achievement was possible; my regret is that so little attention has been paid to it by the press.

Incidently, you speak of golf in a temperature of 95 degrees. Here

in Newport we have almost ideal weather and always the temperature is at least 20 degrees less than is reported for Washington—for
that matter—the Midwest.[2] But we shall see what Chicago brings
forth tomorrow.[3]

With warm regard, *As ever*

[1] General Mills Corporation Director Bullis had written on July 21, 1960 (same file
as document) to commend the Administration for achieving a budget surplus for
the fiscal year 1960. (For background see no. 1474.) On July 20 the President had
announced a $1.1 billion budget surplus: "This demonstration of fiscal responsibil-
ity not only reinforces economic strength here at home, but reaffirms to the world
that the United States intends to run its financial affairs on a sound basis" (*Public
Papers of the Presidents: Eisenhower, 1960–61*, p. 583).

[2] Bullis had written that "even though the temperature was 95 degrees," he was en-
joying playing golf. "I hope that you will continue to get out on the golf course as
often as you can. You are entitled to as much recreation as possible while you are at
Newport." The President had arrived in Newport for his summer vacation on July 7.
Leaving Newport on July 26 to attend the Republican National Convention in
Chicago, he would return to Newport again on August 1.

[3] On Eisenhower's appearance at the convention see no. 1592.

1591   *EM, AWF, International Series: Korea*

To The Students of   *July 26, 1960*
The Republic of Korea[1]

Throughout my life I will cherish the memory of the warm and
gracious welcome recently accorded me by the people of Korea.[2]
For this I wish to express my heartfelt gratitude. Your welcome afforded convincing proof, if it were necessary, of the friendly and
strong bonds between our two peoples.

The world well knows the dedication of the youth and students
of Korea to the cause of freedom. You have proven your courage
and your willingness to defend man's most precious possession. You
and your country are now embarked upon the intricate, more difficult task of ensuring that the liberties you have won will find lasting expression in the Republic of Korea.

Youth has the priceless assets of vigor and enthusiasm. Yet, you
must also bring to your tasks a sense of infinite patience, broad vision, and deep humility if you are to meet the challenge which faces
Korea and the world. Courage alone will not suffice. You must
demonstrate that sense of individual responsibility and self-restraint
which will serve to guarantee both freedom and its inseparable twin,
justice. Free men face a difficult choice: whether they will dissipate
their liberty through license; or whether they will take up the bur-

dens which liberty imposes and go forward in the service of mankind. For freedom must be served as well as sought. It imposes duties and obligations, as well as bestowing rights and liberties. Your success in fulfilling these obligations will determine whether your generation will succeed in maintaining a balance between the extremes of license on the one hand and repression on the other.

There are those who would deny you your freedom to achieve their aims—indeed, they want to dominate the world. They exploit both anarchy and servitude. They seek to convince you that the free world poses a threat to peace and progress. In this they persist despite clear evidence that they, not we, have brought a third of the world's people into brutal subjugation; that they, not we, foment anarchy in troubled lands; that they, not we, refuse to disarm and, instead, threaten to rain down instruments of destruction upon the weak and the powerful alike. There is, indeed, existing a threat to peace and progress, to your right of self-determination and your liberties; it is posed by the ruthless colonial aggressions which characterize international communism.

Your generation, in Korea and elsewhere, faces as none before it the issue as to whether mankind is to progress united in freedom and justice or whether nations will fall victim one by one to a new and deadly colonialism. Upon your response depend the future of your nation and, in considerable measure, the future of the free world. I have deep confidence that you are equal to the task before you, and I wish you full and complete success in this great responsibility. *Sincerely*

---

[1] Daeyung Kim, a student at Changung University in Seoul, had asked Eisenhower to send a message to the students of Korea, who respected him "so much" and were "always ready to fight for freedom" (Kim to Eisenhower, June 28, 1960, AWF/I: Korea). Kim had been inspired, he said, by Eisenhower's "Open Letter to America's Students," and he wanted to publish the message in the student newspaper he edited, the *Changung Herald* (Eisenhower had published letters in the *Thirtieth Anniversary Reader's Digest Reader* in 1951 and in the October 1948 edition of the *Reader's Digest;* see Galambos, *Columbia University*, p. 351). Secretary of State Herter had recommended that Eisenhower respond. The students, he wrote, had played an instrumental role in the April "revolution" (see no. 1526) and had welcomed the President en masse during his visit (Herter to Eisenhower, July 23, 1960, AWF/I: Korea). A message, "counseling patience and responsibility" would serve to remind students before the upcoming Korean elections "that the ideal of freedom must be served as well as sought." He also thought it could have as much "broad potential utility" as Eisenhower's earlier letter to Chilean students (see no. 1490). Eisenhower's changes to the State Department's draft are in AWF/I: Korea; see also *Public Papers of the Presidents: Eisenhower, 1960–61*, pp. 609–10, and Eisenhower, *Waging Peace*, p. 566.

[2] On the President's June 19–20 visit to Korea see nos. 1529 and 1564 and *New York Times*, June 19 and 20, 1960. Along with his request, Kim had sent a picture of Eisenhower taken during his visit to Seoul. "The President of the United States looked like a generous grandfather," he wrote, and he and his fellow students called him

"Grandfather Ike—Ike Haraboji in Korean" (Kim to Eisenhower, June 29, 1960; see also Eisenhower to Kim, July 26, 1960, both in AWF/I: Korea).

1592   *EM, WHCF, Official File 107-B*

To G. Keith Funston   *July 26, 1960*

Dear Keith: Your letter of the twenty-second arrived here only an hour or so before I am due to take off for the Republican Convention in Chicago.[1] I simply wanted you to know how much I appreciate your comments about the surplus.[2] I shall never understand the philosophy of what I am calling tonight the "free spending clique"—in times like these.[3]

With warm regard, *Sincerely*

[1] Funston (B.A. Trinity College 1932) had been New York Stock Exchange president since 1951. During World War II he had taken leave from his position as purchasing director for the Sylvania Electric Products Corporation in order to serve as a special assistant to the Chairman of the War Production Board in Washington. He had also been President of Trinity College from 1944 until 1951. Funston had written on July 22 to thank Eisenhower for his autographed picture, which he said would "be an heirloom for my children" and would "gain luster as history adds to the fame of our 34th President" (same file as document). On Eisenhower's July 26 appearance before the Republican Convention on "Thank you, Ike" day, see *New York Times*, July 27, 1960.

[2] Funston had written that he knew how happy the President was to announce a large budget surplus (see no. 1590). "You, and you alone, are entitled to the credit for that. I think back to that day early in November, after the elections of 1958, when we talked about the budget at breakfast. The Democrats were hooraying about the money they were going to spend. Most of the Republicans were inclined to think that there was no way of stopping such expenditures, but you made up your mind you were going to do it and, by golly, you did." For background see no. 1474.

[3] In his address to the Republican Convention the President had said: "During all the years of this Administration, I've heard much from the opposition—especially from its free-spending clique—about increasing the rate of economic growth, by depending principally on governmental activity, with vastly increased Federal expenditures" (*Public Papers of the Presidents: Eisenhower, 1960–61*, p. 592).

1593   *EM, AWF,*
                                             Ann Whitman Diaries Series

To Richard Milhous Nixon   *July 27, 1960*
Telegram

My astonishment at your nomination on the first ballot is something less than complete.[1] Nevertheless I am delighted that you are at last free to speak freely and frankly in expressing your views on the present and future of our great country. To your hands I pray that I shall pass the responsibilities of the office of the Presidency and will be glad to do so.[2]

My old friend Aksel Nielsen is of the belief that Colorado Republicans want Lodge for your running mate with Anderson as their second choice for that post.[3]

May God Bless you, *As ever*

[1] A handwritten draft of this letter is in AWF/AWD. On the Republican convention and Nixon's nomination see *New York Times*, July 28, 1960, and White, *The Making of the President 1960*, pp. 180–208; for background see no. 1477. A note at the bottom of the typed version of this text indicates that the message was telephoned to Rose Mary Woods, Nixon's personal secretary, to keep it from leaking to the press. Herbert Klein, Nixon's press secretary, later released the document to the media. See *New York Times*, July 28, 1960.

[2] Eisenhower had originally written "I shall be glad and proud to commit the responsibilities of the office."

[3] On the selection of Henry Cabot Lodge as the Republican vice-presidential nominee see Eisenhower, *Waging Peace*, p. 597; see also White, *The Making of the President 1960*, pp. 206–7, and no. 1530.

On July 28 Eisenhower would send a congratulatory letter to Nixon and Lodge (AWF/D), calling the Republican ticket one with "real stature." Acknowledging that the campaign would not be easy, Eisenhower stated that he was "confident that you will attract to the cause of maintaining good government a large majority of the independent voters and even a great many discerning Democrats. These, together with the united efforts of all the members of our party, will insure victory at the polls."

1594

EM, AWF,
Dulles-Herter Series

To Andrew Jackson Goodpaster, Jr.   *July 27, 1960*

In Security Council we will make an announcement that no mention of such possibilities—(canal thru Mexico) will be mentioned or hinted at.[1] DE

[1] The Eisenhower Administration had for several years been studying the possibility of a new sea-level, trans-isthmus canal at various sites in Columbia and Nicaragua, as well as Panama and Mexico (Memorandum of Conference with the President, Mar. 21, 1960, AWF/AWD; Cabinet meeting minutes, Apr. 29, and May 22, 1960, and related material, AWF/Cabinet; see also Cutler to Adams, Nov. 19, 1957, AWF/A: AEC). The project was to be part of Plowshare, a federal program established in 1957 for finding peaceful uses for nuclear explosives (Memorandum of Conference with the President, Mar. 22, 1960, AWF/AWD; for background see Hewlett and Holl, *Atoms for Peace and War*, pp. 528–29; Ambrose, *Eisenhower*, vol. II, *The President*, pp. 565, 568,

and 591). Secretary of State Herter had advised the President (Herter to Eisenhower, July 27, 1960, AWF/D-H) not to announce publicly a promise to dig a canal across Mexico pending negotiations; Eisenhower had said he would like to make such a statement during a speech to the United Nations planned for September (Memorandum of Conference with the President, July 7, 1960, AWF/AWD; Kistiakowski, *Diary*, pp. 6, 364–65, 375–76).

Herter said his recommendation was based on both political and technical considerations: excavations using nuclear explosives had not yet proven successful in practice and the repercussions were unknown. The Mexicans were "notably skittish" about nuclear matters, and the project would involve the relocation of more than 100,000 people. He thought that premature public discussion could generate adverse reactions and jeopardize the test ban negotiations (Herter to Eisenhower, July 27, 1960, AWF/D-H; see also nos. 1445, 1454, 1493, and 1581). Herter pointed out that the impact on U.S. relations with Panama needed to be considered due to the current difficulties over control of the canal (see nos. 1355, esp. n. 1, and 1443). He recommended Panama, not Mexico, as the best site for a sea-level canal. Eisenhower wrote his note to Goodpaster by hand on Herter's July 27 memo.

At a National Security Council meeting on January 5, 1961, Eisenhower would decide that it might not then be politically possible to construct a canal across Mexico (NSC minutes, Jan. 5, 1961, AWF/AWD). No second canal would be built.

1595   *EM, AWF, DDE Diaries Series*

TO MAMIE EISENHOWER MOORE   *July 29, 1960*

Dearest Mamie: Whenever I am assured of the affection and approval of anyone close to me and who knows me well I experience a glow that cannot be conveyed by compliments from strangers.[1]

Our families and our real friends know our faults of disposition, mannerism and conduct as well as they know whatever virtues we may possess. We are fortunate when intimate associates find our virtues to outweigh our obvious defects. So your letter is gratifying not only as an expression of affection but also of your confidence that I have tried to do whatever has seemed to me to be the best for America and the free world.

I am deeply interested in your comments about what some of us older ones say about your generation. In my own case I plead "not guilty." In the first place, I have never heard the accusations of "wild language", "insecure generation" and "I don't care" as applied to Americans of your years. As for "beatnik" I am not even sure what the word is supposed to mean.[2]

So I cannot speak intelligently on these allegations. I know we have far too much juvenile delinquency, and that we must combat it ceaselessly and effectively. But I have met across the nation large numbers of our younger people, and I am convinced that the vast majority comprises fine, decent and attractive Americans. I think we should hear more about, and from, these.[3]

At least I can assure you on one point—deeply embedded in my dedication and devotion to America is a great faith in and affection for America's youth. They are our nation's hope—so far as I am concerned they are my pride. And among them all you are one of my favorites; I love you very much.[4] *Affectionately*

[1] Moore, the President's niece and goddaughter, would turn eighteen on August 5. She had written on July 27 (AWF/D) to thank her uncle for his efforts to bring about world peace, to balance the budget, and to keep "a foothold behind the Iron Curtain." She added that although she was not very good as a history student, she knew that even before his presidency, he had "stopped a war that had already begun."

[2] Moore had said that the older generation's perceptions of youth were wrong, and that young people understood more and cared more than people thought. She had also written that her generation had been called "beatniks," a derisive term used to characterize members of the so-called "Beat Generation," a social and literary, bohemian movement that had started in the 1950s. The *avant-garde* style of the movement had entered popular consciousness in part as a result of a beatnik character who appeared in "The Many Loves of Dobie Gillis," a weekly television program that appealed to young people (Alex McNeil, *Total Television: The Comprehensive Guide to Programming from 1948 to the Present*, 4th edition [New York, 1996], pp. 222–23).

[3] On the President's efforts to combat juvenile delinquency see nos. 1172 and 1654. On his efforts to reach out to young people see, for example, no. 1290, and his remarks to the graduates of the University of Notre Dame on June 5 (*Public Papers of the Presidents, Eisenhower: 1960–61*, pp. 461–67).

[4] It was difficult to express her deep opinions with family and friends, Ms. Moore wrote, but she wanted Eisenhower to know that she thought he was "the greatest man today. . . . You are the heart of the American people." For developments see no. 1663.

1596   *EM, AWF, Name Series*

To Aksel Nielsen   *July 30, 1960*

Dear Aksel: Usually it seems to me that I am so pressed to do the proper thing to strangers who may be helpful to me in one way or another that I ignore an expression of my gratitude to old and good friends. I know you understand always that I am lastingly indebted to you, but just this once I want to put it in writing.

I go back to the East fully conversant on Denver growth and real estate, up to date on a lot of national problems, confident of what I like to think is my fishing skill, relaxed by the Colorado sun and, more importantly, by the warmth of your friendship.[1]

So—thank you for everything!

With warm regard, *As ever*

¹ After the Republican National Convention in Chicago (see no. 1592), the Eisenhowers had gone to Denver to visit Elivera Doud, the First Lady's mother. Nielsen had been overseeing the President's real estate investments in Denver for many years (see, for example, nos. 309 and 1070, and Whitman to Schulz, July 30, 1960, AWF/ N). While in Denver Eisenhower went fishing with Nielsen and other friends (*New York Times*, July 28–31, Aug. 1, 1960).